Handbook of Multicultural Assessment

Lisa A. Suzuki, Joseph G. Ponterotto,
Paul J. Meller, Editors

· ·

Handbook of Multicultural Assessment

Clinical, Psychological, and Educational Applications

Second Edition

JOSSEY-BASS
A Wiley Company
San Francisco

Published by

JOSSEY-BASS
A Wiley Company
350 Sansome St.
San Francisco, CA 94104

www.josseybass.com

Jossey-Bass books and products are available through most bookstores. To contact Jossey-Bass directly, call (888) 378-2537, fax to (800) 605-2665, or visit our website at www.josseybass.com.

Substantial discounts on bulk quantities of Jossey-Bass books are available to corporations, professional associations, and other organizations. For details and discount information, contact the special sales department at Jossey-Bass.

We at Jossey-Bass strive to use the most environmentally sensitive paper stocks available to us. Our publications are printed on acid-free recycled stock whenever possible, and our paper always meets or exceeds minimum GPO and EPA requirements.

Library of Congress Cataloging-in-Publication Data

The handbook of multicultural assessment : clinical, psychological, and educational applications, second edition / Lisa A. Suzuki, Joseph G. Ponterotto, Paul J. Meller, editors.
    p. cm.
    Rev ed. of: Handbook of multicultural assessment. 1st ed. c1996.
    Includes bibliographical references and index.
    ISBN 0-7879-5177-3 (hardcover : alk. paper)
    1. Psychological test—Social aspects.   2. Psychometrics—Social aspects.
    3. Educational tests and measurements—Social aspects.   4. Multiculturalism.
    I. Suzuki, Lisa A., 1961. II. Ponterotto, Joseph G. III. Meller, Paul J. IV. Handbook of multicultural assessment.
BF176 .H36 2000
150´.28´7—dc21   00-059008

FIRST EDITION
HB Printing   10 9 8 7 6 5 4 3 2

Contents

· ·

Foreword to the First Edition

. . . .

Eric F. Gardner

The *Handbook of Multicultural Assessment* is an ambitious under-taking. It encompasses assessment in the conventional culture of the United States, plus assessment in the variety of new cultures introduced by the large numbers of new immigrants. It permits focusing on the number of prejudices already existing about what assessment is and how it should be undertaken as well as raising issues that will add to such questions.

There has been severe criticism of the use of personality and cognitive measures with diverse ethnic populations. Even the most widely used measures of achievement have been attacked because of claimed cultural and ethnic bias, while measure of aptitude have fared even worse. While much research has addressed these issues conducted by individuals and by publishing companies to refute the claims of bias in their publications, the information remains unin-tegrated, and much is scattered across various disciplines, especially in the fields of education and psychology.

The *Handbook of Multicultural Assessment* brings together con-tributions by scholars in the areas of psychometrics, assessment, and evaluation who have expertise in the application of testing and assessment in multicultural environments. Considering the changing demographics of the country and the need for valid and reliable measurement of psychological constructs, the *Handbook of*

Multicultural Assessment fills an important need. It not only provides a comprehensive view of various cultural issues but offers updated information pertaining to the usage of major psychological instruments. Special stress is placed on the fact that, in addition to the cultural differences incorporated in the construction of the items themselves, the normative data are primarily based on samples of U.S. participants rather than on those of the specific subculture to which the individual to be assessed belongs.

The tendency to ignore the variability existing among subcultures within a commonly accepted subculture is explored, and many illustrations such as the differences in Spanish vocabulary between Mexican and Puerto Rican children are given. For the relatively few U.S. tests for which a translation into a single language exists, warnings as to errors in interpretation by clinicians are prevalent.

The topics covered are extensive and range from a review and integration of the most current literature on multicultural assessment issues to information about the usage cross-culturally of the most popular psychological measures. For example, there are such interesting chapters as "Multicultural Usage of the MMPI-2" and "Language Assessment: Multicultural Considerations."

Every educational or social program is initiated, continues, or is discarded because of some form of evaluation that is buttressed by various types of assessment. One's major concerns should be to ascertain that the assessments are systematic and that the value implications are explicit. The authors of the *Handbook of Multicultural Assessment* have this objective in mind. The various topical chapters provide important information to assessment educators and students as well as to practitioners in the field. In view of its competitive focus, the book will have utility for most mental health professionals.

Syracuse University   Eric F. Gardner
November 1995

Preface

. . . .

The first edition of the *Handbook of Multicultural Assessment* (1996) was published to fill a great need in the fields of psychology and education, for a comprehensive text focusing on major assessment issues and popular assessment instruments and their application to diverse populations. Because of the growing number of racial and ethnic minorities in the United States and in recognition of the multitude of variables that affect performance on cognitive and personality tests, the second edition provides updated reviews and conceptual extensions of the topics covered in the 1996 text. Though many books have focused on multicultural issues related to assessment, the *Handbook* continues to serve as the most comprehensive resource in the area.

Once again, the authors of the various chapters represent experts in the field. Among them are academicians and clinicians working with particular assessment instruments and procedures. This edition also includes chapters written by the individuals actively involved in developing particular instruments (for example, UNIT, TEMAS and MBTI). The chapters are reviews of the most current literature on multicultural assessment issues and usage of the most popular psychological and educational measures with diverse populations. This book is appropriate for graduate courses in multicultural counseling, therapy, and assessment. Given the comprehensive scope of the *Handbook*, it will be of use to all mental health professionals.

It is beyond the scope of any text to cover all of the tests currently used in educational and clinical settings. The editors and chapter authors have attempted to review the most popular instruments in each area. Our hope is that readers can gain an understanding of the complexities of the assessment process and obtain general information that assists them in selecting, administering, and interpreting other instruments, with key information on multicultural considerations.

Certain topics such as acculturation, racial or ethnic identity, bilingualism, and ethics are repeatedly mentioned throughout the text in different assessment contexts. These are important key concepts that need to be understood within all testing settings.

This edition is divided into two major parts. The first pertains to general multicultural assessment issues, and the second to particular testing issues and instruments. Part One is divided into two sections, focusing on general assessment issues (critical issues, the clinical interview, cultural identity, and clinical diagnosis) and daily living assessment (family, vocational, and quality of living). Part Two is divided into sections on personality assessment (narrative assessments, Rorschach, objective personality assessment, the Myers-Briggs Type Indicator, MMPI-2/A, and Millon), and cognitive ability assessment (ability testing, IQ and aptitude, neuropsychological infant and preschool, geriatric, dynamic, and achievement).

The organization of this text represents a significant departure from the first edition of the *Handbook*. New areas have been added to broaden the coverage of the field (for instance, "normal" personality assessment, and quality of life) in addition to updated chapters on the most popular instruments. The text is designed to give the reader practical and in-depth reviews. Although there are other outstanding books in the area, this *Handbook* provides the greatest breadth of coverage in the assessment area.

We are pleased to offer this new edition to the growing field of multicultural assessment. It is, as always, our hope that this book continues to stimulate interest and ongoing debate regarding appropriate multicultural assessment practices. The complexities of the assessment process and the need for higher standards for clinical and educational practice make work in this area a growing imperative for all mental health professionals and educators.

Acknowledgments

We would like to sincerely thank Lyndon Aguiar for his assistance in reviewing and editing the various chapters in this book. Without his hard work and constructive feedback, the publication of this book would have been much slower and more difficult.

We would like to acknowledge the support and assistance of Alan Rinzler, Jossey-Bass executive editor. We are deeply grateful for his patience and support.

Completion of this book often took us away from our families and significant others for long periods of time. We will always be grateful for their support, love, and understanding.

New York University   Lisa A. Suzuki
Fordham University   Joseph G. Ponterotto
Hofstra University   Paul J. Meller
September 2000

The Editors

Lisa A. Suzuki is an assistant professor in the Department of Applied Psychology at New York University. Prior to this appointment, she taught at Fordham University and the University of Oregon. She received her B.A. degree in psychology from Whitman College (1983), her M.Ed. in counselor education from the University of Hawaii-Manoa (1985), and her Ph.D. degree in counseling psychology from the University of Nebraska-Lincoln (1992).

Her main research interests have been in the areas of multicultural assessment, training, and qualitative research methods. She is coeditor of the *Handbook of Multicultural Counseling* and *Using Qualitative Methods in Psychology*, and coauthor of *Intelligence Testing and Minority Students: Foundations, Performance Factors and Assessment Issues*. She is also coauthor of numerous publications focusing on multicultural assessment and intelligence testing. She currently serves on the editorial board of the *Journal of Multicultural Counseling and Development* and is editorial consultant of the *Asian Journal of Counselling*.

Joseph G. Ponterotto received his B.A. in psychology from Iona College and his M.A. in counseling and Ph.D. in counseling psychology from the University of California at Santa Barbara (1985). His first academic position was in the counseling psychology program at the University of Nebraska–Lincoln. In 1987, he moved to Fordham University, where he is currently professor of education in the counseling programs. His primary teaching interests are in multicultural counseling, career development, psychological measurement, and qualitative research methods.

Ponterotto has written extensively in the area of multicultural counseling and is the coeditor or coauthor of a number of books on the topic, including the *Handbook of Multicultural Counseling*, the *Handbook of Racial/Ethnic Minority Counseling Research*, *Preventing Prejudice*, and *Multicultural Counseling Competencies*. His empirical research program uses both quantitative and qualitative methods to investigate an array of topics in multicultural counseling. He has served on the editorial boards of various counseling journals and is currently international forum coeditor for the *Counseling Psychologist*.

Paul J. Meller is an associate professor in the school and community psychology program at Hofstra University. He earned a B.A. in psychology from the State University of New York at Stony Brook; an M.A. in developmental psychology from Teachers College, Columbia University; and a Ph.D. in school psychology from Syracuse University. He has worked as a psychologist or consulting psychologist in numerous school districts, Head Start programs, and community mental health centers.

His principal research activities have involved prevention of adjustment difficulties and promotion of social competence in young children who are at high risk. He has authored numerous papers, curricula, and treatment programs in the area of preventive mental health, authentic assessment, social validity of interventions, and cross-cultural consultation. His recent work has focused on prevention of adjustment difficulty of children going through divorce.

Meller has been active in numerous professional organizations, including the New York Association of School Psychologists, the National Association of School Psychologists, and the Division of School Psychology of the American Psychological Association.

The Contributors

Felito Aldarondo is an assistant professor in the Department of Educational Studies at Purdue University, where he is coordinator of the mental health counseling program and a faculty member in the counseling psychology program. He is licensed as a psychologist and mental health counselor in the state of Indiana. He earned his Ph.D. (1998) in counseling psychology from Indiana University—Bloomington. His primary research interests center around group work, psychological assessment, and health behavior. He holds memberships in the American Psychological Association and in the American Counseling Association.

Amanda L. Baden is an assistant professor of counseling and coordinator of the bilingual school counseling program at St. John's University. She earned her Ph.D. degree (1999) in counseling psychology at Michigan State University. Her main research activities have focused on identity issues related to transracial adoption and multicultural counseling and development issues. She has published articles on a model describing the identity experiences of transracial adoptees and on training issues for multicultural competence. She is a member of the APA's Section for the Advancement of Women of Division 17.

Mark A. Bolden is a doctoral student in the counseling psychology program in the Department of Professional Psychology and Family

Therapy, School of Education and Human Services, at Seton Hall University, where he earned his B.A. degree (1996) in psychology, minoring in African American studies. His research interests focus on time orientation, procrastination, Africentric theory and practice, and Kemetic conceptualizations of therapy. He has coauthored an article on the Africultural Coping Systems Inventory in the *Journal of Black Psychology*. He is the state coordinator for the Student Circle of the New Jersey State Association of Black Psychologists, and a member of the National Association of Black Psychologists and the APA.

Bruce A. Bracken is a school psychologist and professor at the College of William and Mary. He earned his M.A. and Ph.D. at the University of Georgia. He has published more than one hundred articles, reviews, and book chapters, as well as several tests and books. He authored the original and revised Bracken Basic Concept Scale, Multidimensional Self Concept Scale, and Assessment of Interpersonal Relations, and coauthored the Universal Nonverbal Intelligence Test. Bracken cofounded and coedits the *Journal of Psychoeducational Assessment* and sits on the editorial boards of several national and international journals. He chaired the APA's Committee on Psychological Testing and Assessment, served as APA's delegate to the International Test Commission, is a Fellow in the APA and a Diplomate in the American Board of Assessment Psychology, and is currently serving on a panel for the National Academies of Science.

Christa F. Brown is a first-year doctoral student in the counseling psychology program at Seton Hall University. She earned her M.A. (1996) in agency counseling at the University of Nebraska at Omaha. Prior to pursuing her doctoral degree she was a professional counselor for three years. Her research has entailed spirituality and how it relates to ethnicity and culture; her research interests are in promoting mental health within the African American community, specifically on issues and concerns of African American women. She is a member of the New Jersey Chapter of the Association of Black Psychologists and the APA.

Christine H. Carrington is chief psychologist, Department of Psychiatry, Howard University College of Medicine and Hospital. She received her Ph.D. degree from the University of Maryland, College Park in 1979 and postdoctoral training from the University of Pennsylvania's Center for Cognitive Therapy in 1981. She is a licensed psychologist in Maryland and the District of Columbia, board certified in clinical psychology from the American College of Forensic Examiners, listed in the National Register of Health Service Providers, and a member of the Board of Examiners of Psychologists in Maryland. She is adjunct associate professor of psychiatry at Georgetown University; a member of the American Psychological Association; Founding Fellow, Academy of Cognitive Therapy (a national and international accrediting body), Association for the Advancement of Science; and on the board of directors of the Association of Medical School Psychologists. Carrington has researched and written extensively on depression and its manifestations in African Americans. She is currently involved in research with anxiety, depression, and comorbidity in cancer patients. Her contributions to this book were in her capacity as a licensed psychologist with more than thirty-five years of experience in academia, medical centers, and the private sector in the practice of psychology.

Rita J. Casey is director of the Merrill-Palmer Institute for Child and Family Development and associate professor of psychology at Wayne State University. Her Ph.D. (1988) is in clinical and developmental psychology. Before becoming a psychologist she taught kindergarten and elementary school and served as a preschool teacher. She has also served on the faculty of the University of Iowa. She was nominated for an early career award given by the APA for her research in emotional development.

Mark H. Chae is a doctoral student in the counseling psychology program in the Department of Professional Psychology and Marriage and Family Therapy at Seton Hall University. He earned his M.A. (1997) in applied psychology and Ed.M. degree (1999) in counseling psychology from Teachers College, Columbia University. His research interests include multicultural counseling, ethnic identity development, and group dynamics. Recently, he coauthored an article with David W. Cheng in the *Journal for Specialists in Group Work*.

Rahul V. Chauhan is a doctoral student in the counseling psychology program at Fordham University. His M.S.Ed. (1996) is in social agency counseling at the University of Dayton. His current research activities include a qualitative approach to understanding the multicultural counseling process; his dissertation is on understanding the psychocultural identity formation process for Indian Americans. He is currently an adjunct counselor at Baruch College, City University of New York, and will be completing his APA internship requirement at the University of Pennsylvania in 2000–01.

Giuseppe Costantino is the clinical director of the Sunset Park Mental Health Center of Lutheran Medical Center; senior research associate at the Center for Hispanic Mental Health Research, Fordham University; adjunct professor at St. John's University's graduate school psychology program; and adjunct professor at Carlos Albizu University, San Juan, Puerto Rico. He earned his Ph.D. (1975) in clinical and community psychology at New York University. He developed the multicultural projective TEMAS (Tell-Me-A-Story) test. He is also collaborating with foreign psychologists in the standardization of the TEMAS test in Argentina, Puerto Rico, Spain, Italy, and Taiwan. He has published more than fifty articles and contributed several book chapters on cross-cultural and multicultural mental health research. He is the consulting editor for the *Journal of Personality Assessment* and the *Hispanic Journal of Behavioral Science* (the latter since 1990).

Richard H. Dana is a research professor (honorary) at the Regional Research Institute, Portland State University; a distinguished scholar in the Psy.D. program in clinical-community psychology at the University of La Verne; and program consultant for cultural competency at Tri-City Mental Health Center in Pomona, California. His M.S. (1951) and Ph.D. (1953) in psychology are from the University of Illinois. Before retirement from the University of Arkansas in 1988 as University Professor Emeritus, he served as professor, director of clinical training, departmental chair, and dean in various state and private universities. His research activities since retirement have focused on mental health services for multicultural populations, cultural competency training for psychologists, and multicultural assessment training. He has authored *Multicultural Assessment Perspectives for Professional Psychology*, and *Understanding Cultural Identity in Intervention and Assessment*; he has edited the *Handbook of Cross-Cultural and Multicultural Personality Assessment* as an introduction to the multicultural assessment intervention process model. The recipient of numerous awards, he was consulting editor of the *Journal of Personality Assessment* for twenty years and was on the editorial board of other journals.

Rosemary Flanagan is a school psychologist in Baldwin, New York, is an adjunct associate professor in the school psychology program at St. John's University, and maintains an independent practice in Hempstead, New York. She earned her Ph.D. degree (1986) in clinical and school psychology at Hofstra University, where she previously taught. Her main research activities have focused on child and adolescent personality assessment and cognitive-behavioral interventions. She has published articles on assessment and intervention. She is currently the president of the School Division of the New York State Psychological Association, and has served on the Association's Council of Representatives. She is also the president-elect of the American Academy of School Psychology and has recently been elected a member of the American Board of School Psychology.

Craig L. Frisby is an associate professor of school psychology at the University of Missouri, Columbia. He earned a Ph.D. degree (1987) from the University of California, Berkeley. He served as a school psychologist for two years in the Pittsburg, California, Unified School District and taught at the University of Florida for nine years. He is the former associate editor for *School Psychology Review*, the official journal of the National Association of School Psychologists. He is coeditor of *Test Interpretation and Diversity: Achieving Equity in Assessment*, published by the APA. His research interests include the influence of culture and cultural differences in psychoeducational testing and assessment.

Kathy A. Gainor is an assistant professor in the Department of Counseling, Human Development, and Educational Leadership at Montclair State University. She earned her Ph.D. degree (1997) in counseling psychology at Michigan State University. Prior to joining the faculty at Montclair State, she was a staff psychologist for four years at the Rutgers College Counseling Center at Rutgers, the State University of New Jersey. Her publications and research interests include social cognitive factors affecting academic and career development in black students, racial identity development, career development and counseling with black women, cross-cultural supervision, and integrating cultural diversity in training and practice. She is a member of the APA and the American Counseling Association. She is also involved in a number of educational reform initiatives at Montclair State.

Denise Gretchen is a doctoral student in the counseling psychology program at Fordham University. She earned her M.A. (1996) in organizational psychology and M.Ed. (1997) in counseling psychology at Columbia University. Her research interests include multicultural counseling theory and assessment, ethnic identity, supervision of psychologists, and mentoring women. She has been chair of the Counseling Psychology Action Committee, a doctoral student advocacy group, at Fordham University since 1998. She is also a member of Phi Beta Kappa and a student affiliate of the American Psychology Association Division 17 (counseling psychology).

Elena L. Grigorenko is a research scientist in the Department of Psychology and the Child Study Center at Yale University and Associate Professor at Moscow State University. She holds a Ph.D. in general and developmental psychology from Moscow State University (1990), and Ph.D.s in psychology and genetics from Yale University (1995). She is the author of approximately eighty publications in psychology and learning disabilities; she has won a number of fellowships in Russia and the United States. She is associate editor of *Contemporary Psychology* and guest editor of the *Educational Psychology Review*'s special issue on intelligence (to appear in 2000). She is a member of the APA, American Educational Research Association, Behavior Genetics Association, International Society for the Study of Individual Differences, Russian Psychological Society, and Society for Research in Child Development.

Gordon C. Nagayama Hall is professor of psychology at the Pennsylvania State University. He received his M.A. in theology and his Ph.D. in clinical psychology, in 1982, from the Graduate School of Psychology at Fuller Theological Seminary. He worked as a psychologist at Western State Hospital in Washington state and was professor of psychology at Kent State University before coming to Penn State. He is a Fellow of the APA and has served as president of the APA's Society for the Psychological Study of Ethnic Minority Issues. He has authored *Theory-Based Assessment,*

Treatment, and Prevention of Sexual Aggression and is coeditor of *Sexual Aggression: Issues in Etiology, Assessment, and Treatment*. His research interests are in cultural risk and protective factors associated with psychopathology, particularly sexual aggression.

Carrie L. Hill is a doctoral candidate in the counseling psychology program at Indiana University. She received her M.A. in community counseling and applied gerontology from Ball State University. Her research and scholarly interests include multicultural assessment and competence, clinical judgment, and mental health issues affecting nursing home residents and employees.

Arthur MacNeill Horton Jr., received his Ed.D. degree in counselor education from the University of Virginia in 1976. He also holds Diplomates in clinical psychology and behavioral psychology from the American Board of Professional Psychology and the American Board of Professional Neuropsychology. He is the author or editor of ten books, more than two dozen book chapters, and more than one hundred journal articles. He is a past president of the American Board of Professional Neuropsychology. In addition, he is a current member of the State of Maryland Board of Examiners of Psychologists.

John Kugler is a licensed psychologist and director of a learning disabilities program at Bay Ridge Prep in Brooklyn, New York. He received his M.S. in educational psychology and Ph.D. (1993) in school psychology from Fordham University. He formerly directed the Learning Center at Manhattan Eye, Ear, and Throat Hospital and the Rosa Hagin School Consultation Center at Fordham University. He specializes in the assessment of learning and reading disorders.

Kwong-Liem Karl Kwan is an assistant professor in the Department of Educational Studies at Purdue University. He earned his Ph.D. degree (1996) from the counseling psychology program at the

University of Nebraska-Lincoln. While pursuing his doctorate, he was a research assistant at the Buros Institute of Mental Measurements. Prior to coming to the United States, he was employed as a research interviewer by the Psychiatric Epidemiology Research Unit in the Department of Psychiatry at the Chinese University of Hong Kong. He has written articles on the applicability of the MMPI-2 with Chinese and Koreans in the United States, ethnic identity of Asian Americans, psychological assessment of Asian Americans, and effects of racial salience on cross-cultural relations. He is a member of the APA, the American Counseling Association, and the Asian American Psychological Association. He serves on the editorial boards of *The Counseling Psychologist* and *Asian Journal of Counselling*.

Ometha Lewis-Jack has been an assistant professor in the department of psychology at Howard University since 1996. She teaches both undergraduate and graduate classes in the department. Currently, she is director of the Clinical Psychology Program and a licensed clinical psychologist in the District of Columbia. She earned her doctorate in clinical psychology from Howard University in 1993. Her specialty includes assessment of neurological disorders and diagnosis and treatment of substance use disorders. Lewis-Jack has had ten years of experience working with substance abusers and people who have sustained severe brain injury. She has published in the area of clinical neuropsychology; her interests currently lie in the neuropsychological assessment and treatment of persons with alcohol and drug dependency.

Carol S. Lidz is director of the school psychology program at Touro College in New York. She obtained a Psy.D. degree in school psychology from the Graduate School of Applied and Professional Psychology at Rutgers University. She has worked for more than thirty years as a school psychologist and was the coordinator of the early childhood specialization in the school psychology program at

Temple University. She has published a number of books, chapters, and articles on topics relating to preschool assessment and parent-child interaction. She is currently continuing work on applications of dynamic assessment, cognitive consequences of adult-child interactions, and development of the Application of Cognitive Functions Scale and "Let's Think About It" parent education program.

Robert G. Malgady is professor of quantitative studies at New York University and director of doctoral studies in the Department of Teaching and Learning. He served as director of evaluation for HIV/AIDS training for health care professionals in New York City. He earned his Ph.D. degree in experimental psychology and statistics at the University of Tennessee (1975). He has authored and coauthored several books and more than eighty articles on such topics as cognitive psychology, psycholinguistics, mental retardation, and culturally sensitive mental health assessment and intervention. He has served on the editorial boards of *Psychological Assessment*, *Journal of Educational Psychology*, and *Education Quarterly*. He is a fellow of the APA and the American Orthopsychiatric Association. He is a reviewer for the National Institute of Mental Health, the National Institute of Drug Abuse, and the Substance Abuse and Mental Health Services Association.

Rebecca A. Marcus is a certified school psychologist. She is currently a doctoral student in the combined clinical and school psychology program at Hofstra University. She received her B. A. degree (1994) from Hofstra University. Her research interest is in high-conflict divorce.

R. Steve McCallum is professor and the chair of the Department of Educational Psychology at the University of Tennessee, Knoxville (UTK). He earned the Ph.D. in educational psychology (major in school psychology) at the University of Georgia in 1979. He worked as a school psychologist in the public schools for four years and has been a trainer of school psychologists for seventeen years. He teaches courses related to diagnosis and treatment of childhood psychopathology. He is the author or coauthor of more than one hundred scholarly works, is the cofounder and coeditor of the *Journal of Psychoeducational Assessment,* and recently coauthored *Essentials of Nonverbal Assessment of Intelligence* (Wiley). He was elected a Fellow of the APA in 1992.

Mary H. McCaulley is president of the Center for Applications of Psychological Type (CAPT) in Gainesville, Florida. She and Isabel Briggs Myers founded CAPT in 1975 as a nonprofit organization for research, training, and practical applications of the Myers-Briggs Type Indicator. She earned her Ph.D. degree (1964) in clinical psychology at Temple University in Philadelphia. From 1964 to 1985 she served on the graduate faculty of the Department of Clinical Psychology at the University of Florida. After meeting Isabel Myers in 1969, she focused her energies on the Myers-Briggs Type Indicator. McCaulley created the first MBTI newsletter, the first MBTI computer scoring, and the first MBTI professional training. She followed up Isabel Myers's longitudinal medical sample, and wrote a state-of-the-art monograph on the MBTI in the health professions. After Isabel Myers's death in 1980, she revised the MBTI Manual. She was a founding member of the Association for Psychological Type in 1979. She is also a member of the APA, the American Counseling Association, and the American Educational Research Association.

Raymond A. Moody is an associate professor of Spanish and Portuguese in the Department of Languages and Literatures of Europe and the Americas at the University of Hawaii. He received his Ph.D. degree (1967) in Hispanic languages and literatures from the University of California, Los Angeles. He has taught at Indiana University, the University of Wisconsin, Universidad Iberomerica in Mexico City, and the Universidad de Guadalajara. His research focuses on the application of personality theory to language teaching and learning. He is the principal organizer of the International Conference on Psychological Type and Culture: East and West in Honolulu (1993, 1996, 1998, 2001). He has served as president of the Hawaii Association of Language Teachers and as an advisor for the high school language programs. He is a member of the Association for Psychological Type, and a founding member of the Hawaiian chapter of APT.

Phyllis S. Ohr is an associate professor of clinical and school psychology in the psychology department at Hofstra University. She received her professional diploma (1983) in school psychology and her Ph.D. degree in clinical child psychology from St. John's University. Her expertise is in early childhood development and parenting. She has numerous publications and presentations based upon her research on infant temperament and parenting. She is also a clinical supervisor and directs all early intervention cases at the Psychological Evaluation, Research, and Counseling Center at Hofstra University. She has served as consultant for early intervention programs, school districts, and child care centers.

Amado M. Padilla is professor of psychological studies in education at Stanford University. Before joining the faculty at Stanford, he was professor of psychology at UCLA where he also directed the Spanish Speaking Mental Health Research Center and the Center for Language Education and Research. He earned his Ph.D. (1969) in experimental psychology from the University of New Mexico. He has authored or edited seven books and published extensively on a variety of topics ranging from acculturation to resiliency among Latino students. He received a Lifetime Achievement Award, for significant and distinguished contributions to psychology for increased understanding of ethnic minority populations, from Division 45 of the APA.

Amber H. Phung is a doctoral student at the Pennsylvania State University adult clinical program. She earned her M.S. degree (1997) in human development at the University of Rochester. Her research interests include ethnic minority issues, forensics psychology, and normal and abnormal personality characteristics. She served as a student editor for the journal of *Cultural Diversity and Ethnic Minority Psychology*.

Alex Pieterse is a doctoral student in counseling psychology at Teachers College, Columbia University. He earned his M.A. degree in counseling at New York University (1997) and his bachelor's degree in health sciences at the Australian Catholic University in Sydney. His research interests include cultural influences in personal identity development and cultural factors related to the experience of trauma and loss. He is a registered professional nurse and has worked in the area of cancer and related illnesses.

Charles R. Ridley is a professor in the counseling psychology program and associate dean in research and the University Graduate School at Indiana University. He received his Ph.D. in counseling psychology from the University of Minnesota. He is a licensed psychologist and consultant. His research and scholarly interests include multicultural issues in applied psychology, organizational consultation, therapeutic change, and the integration of psychology and theology.

Barry A. Ritzler is a professor of psychology at Long Island University. In addition, he is a member of the faculty of Rorschach Workshops, Inc. (directed by John Exner, Jr.) and an adjunct instructor at New York University, Yeshiva University, and Columbia University. He is a graduate of the Wayne State University Ph.D. program in clinical psychology and served as president of the Society for Personality Assessment from 1995 to 1997. He also is an associate editor of the *Journal of Personality Assessment* and an editorial consultant for several other psychology journals.

Daniel T. Sciarra is assistant professor of counselor education at Hofstra University. He earned his Ph.D. degree (1994) in counseling psychology from Fordham University. Before joining the faculty at Hofstra, he taught at the University of Tennessee, Chattanooga. Prior to a career in academia, he was a school counselor in the South Bronx section of New York City. His main research interests have focused on Latino family development and academic achievement. He has published articles on bilingual family therapy, separation in the immigrant family, and multicultural school counseling, is the author of *Multiculturalism in Counseling,* and is currently writing a book on school counseling. He is an active member of the APA, the American Counseling Association, and the American School Counselor Association.

Ellen L. Short is a doctoral student in counseling psychology at New York University. She received her M.A. degree (1997) in counseling psychology at Northwestern University. She also works as a research associate and therapist for the Center for HIV/AIDS Educational Studies and Training (CHEST) at New Jersey City University. Her research interests include the study of group and organizational dynamics as they are related to variables of race, ethnicity, gender, and sexual preference; research-based therapeutic intervention for HIV/AIDS substance-using men and women to promote safer sex practices; and, multicultural assessment of intelligence and IQ tests. She has received an honorable mention for the APA Minority Fellowship.

Robert J. Sternberg is IBM Professor of Psychology and Education in the Department of Psychology at Yale University. Sternberg received the B.A. from Yale in 1972, summa cum laude and Phi Beta Kappa, and the Ph.D. from Stanford University in 1975.

He holds an honorary doctorate from the Computense University of Madrid. He is a fellow of eleven divisions of the APA and a fellow of the American Academy of Arts and Sciences, the American Association for the Advancement of Science, and the American Psychological Society. He has received a number of prestigious awards and is president-elect of APA Division 24 (theoretical and philosophical psychology), president of Division 10 (psychology and the arts), and former president of Division 1 (general psychology) and Division 15 (educational psychology), as well as past editor of the *Psychological Bulletin* and editor of *Contemporary Psychology*. He has authored more than eight hundred articles, books, and book chapters.

Ruby Takushi is a research scientist in the Addictive Behaviors Research Center at the University of Washington's Department of Psychology. She received her M.A. (1989) in theology from Fuller Theological Seminary, School of Theology, and her Ph.D. (1990) in clinical psychology from the School of Psychology at Fuller. Her clinical and research interest in addictive behavior includes substance use and gambling disorders. In addition, she has a special interest in group work and completed two years of postdoctoral training in group psychotherapy at St. Elizabeths Hospital in Washington, D.C. While in Washington, she served on the faculty of the clinical psychology program at Howard University. She has a private practice in Seattle.

Jay M. Uomoto is the director of research for the School of Psychology, Family, and Community at Seattle Pacific University. He is also an associate professor of clinical psychology in the Department of Graduate Psychology. He received his M.A. (1983) in theology from Fuller Theological Seminary, School of Theology, and his Ph.D. (1985) in clinical psychology from the School of Psychology at Fuller. He is a practicing clinical neuropsychologist and rehabilitation psychologist whose clinical work occurs in a private-practice setting, and with the Swedish Medical Center Rehabilitation Units in Seattle, Washington. He is certified in health care ethics and is currently conducting research on the determinants of long-term care in older Japanese Americans and examining the risk factors for dementia in this population with grants from the National Institute on Aging.

Shawn O. Utsey is an assistant professor in the Department of Professional Psychology and Family Therapy at Seton Hall University. He is also the director of the M.A. program in counseling in the same department. He received his B.A. in psychology from North Carolina A & T State University and his Ph.D. in counseling psychology from Fordham University. His primary areas of research are the psychological and physical impact of racism on African Americans, white racism and white Americans, and African and black psychology. He is the author of the widely used Index of Race-Related Stress and the Africultural Coping Systems Inventory. He currently serves on the editorial board of the *Journal of Multicultural Counseling and Development*. He is a member of the Association of Black Psychologists, the APA, and the American Counseling Association.

Deborah L. Wiese is a doctoral student in the counseling psychology program at the University of Wisconsin-Madison. She received her M.S. in counseling and counselor education from Indiana University. Her research and scholarly interests include the relationship of culture and psychological health, sexual harassment issues, and sexual trauma.

Grace Wong is currently a psychologist at South Beach Psychiatric Center in Staten Island, New York. She earned her Ph.D. from Fuller Graduate School of Psychology, where she also earned an M.A. in theology. Her main areas of clinical interest are cross-cultural issues, gerontology, and religious issues. She has presented at numerous conferences on cross-cultural and geriatric issues both as separate topics and in combination. She is the author of two articles on cross-cultural issues. Besides being on staff at South Beach, she is in private practice and consultation with organizations and currently is on the panel for cultural competence with the New York Psychological Association.

Part I

General Assessment Issues

Section One

· ·

General Multicultural Assessment Issues

Part One of the *Handbook of Multicultural Assessment: Clinical, Educational, and Psychological Applications (Second Edition)* is concerned with general issues in assessing people from diverse backgrounds, and gathering appropriate clinical data. Topics in this first section of Part One include general issues; ethics; and interviewing people from diverse ethnic, racial, and cultural groups.

Chapter One is an update to the material written by Amado Padilla and Antonio Medina for the first edition of the *Handbook*. The chapter addresses appropriate selection of testing assessment instruments and strategies to be used with diverse populations. It defines culturally sensitive assessment and raises key issues regarding criteria for instrument selection, use of translations, and testing practices. The chapter also addresses the issue of high-stakes testing with people from ethnic and racial minority groups.

Chapter Two is written by Charles Ridley, Carrie Hill, and Deborah Wiese. The authors lay out a comprehensive yet practical model for maintaining high ethical standards in multicultural assessment. The chapter includes a detailed guideline for applying the model to clinical practice.

In Chapter Three, Ruby Takushi and Jay Uomoto discuss critical issues in generating an interview and interpreting the results. Topics discussed are emic and etic distinctions; analyzing both verbal and nonverbal communication data; and attending to affect, language, and thought processes.

In Chapter Four, Joseph Ponterotto, Denise Gretchen, and Rahul Chauhan address the issues associated with assessing cultural identity and acculturation. The chapter begins with a "meta-review" of the current literature, and the authors then discuss nomothetic and idiographic models for assessing cultural self-perceptions.

Chapter Five, written by Richard Dana, is concerned with clinical diagnosis of people from diverse cultures. Dana discusses the importance of understanding "symptomatology" in a cultural context. He points out that although there have been great strides in bringing a cross-cultural context to nosological systems (such as the DSM-IV), significant bias still exists. Dana outlines a six-stage model of clinical diagnosis, specifically designed to reduce bias in clinical classification.

1

Issues in Culturally
Appropriate Assessment

Amado M. Padilla

There is a longstanding debate regarding appropriate testing and assessment strategies for use with minority populations that include women, ethnic minorities, limited English speakers, and the physically challenged. According to Samuda (1998), psycho-educational assessment is an area of professional practice that has been particularly criticized because of differential treatment of racial and ethnic minorities. Mensh and Mensh (1991) have noted that it is possible for standardized testing to contribute to perpetuation of social, economic, and political barriers confronting racial and ethnic minorities. Gregory and Lee (1986) note that standardized tests are used primarily for selecting and screening; consequently, if tests or their users are discriminatory toward particular groups, such groups may be unfairly denied access to educational and career opportunities.

Researchers, educators, and scholars have long argued that instruments normed on majority group populations or developed using Eurocentric approaches cannot be indiscriminately used with individuals who differ from the normative population. Anyone intent on using tests with ethnic minorities needs to understand

---

This chapter is an update of the text written for the first edition of the *Handbook of Multicultural Assessment* by Amado M. Padilla and Antonio Medina, titled "Cross-Cultural Sensitivity in Assessment: Using Tests in Culturally Appropriate Ways."

and appreciate the heterogeneity within the specific ethnic group. The reason is simply this: the reliability and validity of a test used with individuals of different cultural or linguistic groups who were not included in the standardization group are questionable. Thus, it is important to recognize that diversity may exist between test examiners and examinees even if the differences are not readily apparent. An example is a Latino adolescent who appears acculturated to the test examiner but who nonetheless is more adept in Spanish than English (Padilla, 1992). Such an adolescent may have more difficulty on a timed test if it is administered in English. Also, the experiential background of culturally diverse individuals may differ from that of the group on whom the tests were standardized, resulting in questions about the validity of the test instrument (Sue, 1998).

This chapter is similar to that which appeared in the first edition of this book. It has been updated by incorporating more recent materials, but the arguments are the same, since issues of culturally appropriate assessment have not changed since the original chapter was written. Perhaps what has evolved since the first edition is the increased importance of high-stakes testing and concerns about accountability. Together these conditions make the challenges of culturally appropriate testing more relevant than ever. Thus, we summarize the major issues and offer recommendations for using assessment instruments and procedures in ways that hopefully are culturally sensitive.

What Is Culturally Sensitive Assessment?

We take the position in this chapter that psychological assessment is made culturally sensitive through a continuing and open-ended series of substantive and methodological insertions and adaptations designed to mesh the process of assessment and evaluation with the cultural characteristics of the group being studied. The insertions and adaptations span the entire assessment and evaluation process, from development or adaptation of instruments—including translation—to administration of the measure, and to analysis or scoring and interpretation of the scores. Thus, assessment is made culturally sensitive through an incessant, basic, and active pre-occupation with the culture of the group or individual being assessed.

Cultural sensitivity in assessment is complex because test users need to be conscious of culturally specific behaviors or areas of development, such as ethnic identity or acculturation, that have not been viewed as significant concerns in test theory or development. Issues having to do with formal education, English language proficiency, length of residence in the United States, and level of acculturation are particularly important for Latinos and Asian Americans (Sue, 1998).

There are three major ways in which tests may be biased. First, the very content or construction of test items may be biased in the sense that they give unfair advantage to one group over another. Second, there may be incidental features, such as formatting, mode of test administration, or even examiner personality factors, that favor one group of examinees over another. Third, bias may occur through inappropriate application, which results in identifying one set of applicants over others. In the first type of bias, the content of a test can be easily manipulated to favor one cultural or social group over another. Speed tests are a good example of the second bias, should an administrative procedure serve to penalize test takers who are not proficient in English. Finally, tests have sometimes been used to select individuals for a particular job even though the test really has little bearing on the tasks to be carried out in performing the job.

The search for culturally fair strategies or selection rules has long been hampered by the lack of consensus on what constitutes "cultural fairness" (Samuda, 1998). This is an important problem because it demonstrates some of the relevant activities of the measurement community in attempting to find solutions to bias selection. Bias in the selection process may result in unfair treatment and unequal opportunity or access for some groups. Williams (1983) also notes that consideration of selection rules is important because such rules are tools for determining which applicants are potentially successful or unsuccessful for purposes of admission or employment.

Bracken and Barona (1991) note that practitioners' need for appropriate instrumentation to use in assessing children from varying cultural and linguistic backgrounds has long been a pervasive problem in education and psychology. This situation has become a major concern in education today because approximately 14 percent of all school age children nationally come from non-English-language homes (National Center for Educational Statistics, 1994). This problem is even more critical in certain states; for example, in California about one-third of all students in K–12 enter school as limited English proficient, or LEP (California State Department of Education, 1994). A similar situation occurs in other states with large school-age immigrant populations, notably New York, Texas, Arizona, New Mexico, Illinois, Florida, Massachusetts, and New Jersey (National Center for Educational Statistics, 1994).

Research results have shown that because of varying cultural backgrounds, approximately five million students are inappropriately tested each year by standardized assessment instruments—including standardized achievement tests (Torres, 1991). As a result of mandated testing, it has been estimated that, on the average, each student in the U.S. public school system takes between three and eight district- or state-mandated standardized tests each year (Haney, Madaus, and Lyons, 1993).

There is also a debate as to whether psychometricians and consumers of tests should use one that is considered "biased," or culturally bound in some way, with someone who is not middle class. Tests may be considered biased if they project only predominant values and knowledge and do not consider the full range of linguistic and cultural experiences of people in the United States. Such testing procedures definitely affect the assessment, interpretation, or placement outcomes of a large segment of the U.S. population today. The implication here is that test performance of an individual who comes from a nondominant cultural background or is lower in social status may be affected in ways not intended by the test maker. Thus, even though normative test information is very helpful, we need to know what the instrument assesses when used with social groups for which it was not standardized (Sommers, 1989).

Johnson, Vickers, and Williams (1987) note that federal Public Law 94-142 in part provided impetus for using techniques for nonbiased assessment: "Among other guidelines for evaluation, it requires the establishment of procedures for the selection and use of a variety of tests that are not racially or culturally discriminatory" (p. 334). There are arguments to be made for a purely technical definition of bias and validity, but there are also strong arguments for including politics, values, and culture in considering the full context of test interpretation and test use in which issues of test bias arise (Messick, 1989).

Low-Stakes Versus High-Stakes Testing

The major concern that arises when culturally sensitive testing procedures are not followed has to do with how the test outcomes are used. In today's test-conscious environment, where tests have acquired so much prominence for diagnosis, selection, certification, and accountability, it is vitally important to contextualize this discussion in the language of low-stakes and high-stakes decision making. An example of low-stakes testing is weekly classroom tests to determine what the student knows and then to use such information to aid instructional practice. The intent here is to use tests for improving learning environments for students. One of the difficulties of such testing is that it may result in classifications and labels between students that are not followed by effective educational support for students identified as at-risk, in need of remedial help, or not ready for grade promotion.

By contrast, high-stakes testing results in decision making that has an important and long-term consequence for academic placement, scholarship awards, certification, or professional and graduate school entry. Once test scores become numbers in a file, they are basis for high-stakes decisions concerning selection, placement, and promotion that are made without consideration of inequities imposed by the original testing situation (Lam, 1993). Examples of high-stakes testing are use of a test outcome to determine whether a teacher is eligible for certification to teach in a state with a teacher competency requirement. Another example is using end-of-year achievement test scores to determine whether schools or teachers should be rewarded or penalized by receiving or being denied incentive monies.

It is commonplace in education, industry, and mental health services to make important decisions based on information provided by test results. Latinos and Asian Americans are becoming more prominent in the workforce because of their increasing numbers and youthfulness relative to the aging majority population (Hayes-Bautista, Schink, and Chapa, 1988). These facts attest to the need to consider seriously issues inherent in the psychological testing of Latinos and Asian Americans in order to ensure their educational and occupational opportunity and success. In so doing, the social well-being of all Americans is fostered. Furthermore, because so many crucial life decisions are in one way or another based on high-stakes testing, it is important to recognize the heterogeneity within the U.S. population and the difficulties that it poses for test developers and consumers alike.

In spite of the fact that standardized achievement tests have long been criticized for their potential bias against minority students (Lam, 1993), it is still a common practice in education to use assessment procedures to track students into vocationally or academically oriented classes (Oakes, 1985). Educators driven by the need to be accountable to school boards and state-level educational agencies feel they are helping select and place students according to their intellectual capacity, personal skills, and interests. Some proponents of testing argue that achievement tests are necessary for determining which students have the relevant knowledge and to what degree, and thus which ones are adequately prepared to complete college-oriented, high-track classes (Oakes, 2000).

In sum, testing procedures and outcomes can be placed within a framework of low-stakes and high stakes testing. Low-stakes testing is used for such things as implementation of curriculum to increase a student's knowledge or to diagnose and determine what students need to know. High-stakes testing results in decision making that has important and long-term consequences, ranging from placement in special-education classes to high-ability classes, scholarships, professional and graduate school admission, and job promotion. Clearly, the concern for appropriate assessment is critical because students who do poorly on a low-stakes test are not prepared to do well in a high-stakes test the result of which may be "vocational tracking" or "gatekeeping" from higher education. The concern for such consequences is even more important today with increased discussion of national testing standards and educational accountability. Student progress in academic subject matter at selected grade levels is now a reality in many states as a means of determining school accountability. As this move takes hold, the need for fair assessment measures and practices is more critical than ever.

Raising Questions About Assessment Instruments

Questions about the reliability and validity of aptitude and achievement tests were discussed by a Latino psychologist nearly seventy years ago (Sanchez, 1932a, 1932b). Little attention was given to Sanchez's critique at that time, despite his intimate knowledge of Latino culture and the fact that he published his critiques in reputable journals of the day. We might ask: If Sanchez raised questions about the lack of cultural sensitivity of tests some seventy years ago and such concerns have continued to the present day, why has so little attention been given to these problems? The answer to this rhetorical question is that people of color have probably not had the political clout, either in society generally or in the field of psychological assessment specifically, to insist that their concerns be taken seriously (Padilla, 1992).

Over the years, numerous other investigators have criticized the administration of tests in English to linguistic minority children. The argument has long been that such testing is not valid, and numerous recommendations have been offered to assist in appropriate assessment of limited English speakers or otherwise unacculturated individuals. For example, six decades ago Mitchell (1937) suggested that a corrective factor be added to the mental test score of a Spanish-language-dominant child if tested in English, a correction that would more accurately reflect the child's level of intellectual functioning. Mitchell arrived at this recommendation after noting that children perform better in Spanish than in English on the Otis Group Intelligence Scale. This innovative idea was not implemented at the time since it was considered too radical. However, the recommendation was implemented in a procedure developed four decades later in the work of Jane Mercer (1979). She offered a System of Multicultural Pluralistic Assessment (SOMPA) that includes four sociocultural scales (urban acculturation, SES status, family structure, and family size) combined with the WISC-R (Wechsler Intelligence Scale for Children, Revised) to determine an IQ score for children from minority backgrounds.

Although Mitchell's recommendation for a corrective scoring procedure did eventually become reality with Mercer's SOMPA procedure, the Civil Rights Act of 1991 has made the practice illegal. The ban on group-adjusted scoring procedures came about because of the controversy surrounding the federal Department of Labor's General Aptitude Test Battery (GATB), used by the U.S. Employment Service (USES) for referring job applicants to employers. The GATB has been in widespread use for years but was shown to have an adverse impact on African Americans and Hispanics. Thus, to reduce the negative impact of the GATB on certain ethnic minority groups, the USES decided to use within-group scoring; however, the practice was challenged by the Justice Department in 1986. The argument was that within-group scoring was unfair to white candidates (Sackett and Wilk, 1994). The debate about within-group scoring became so heated that a National Academy of Sciences panel was commissioned to study and provide guidance for the Department of Labor in using the GATB. The report of the NAS panel supported the concept of within-group norming (Hartigan and Wigdor, 1989).

As public attention continued to focus on the practice of within-group norming, the debate escalated to the point where the Congress added a provision to the Civil Rights Act of 1991 prohibiting any form of group-adjusted scoring. Specifically, Public Law 102-166 stated that it is unlawful practice for any employer "in connection with the selection or referral of applicants or candidates for employment or promotion to adjust the scores of, use different cutoffs for, or otherwise alter the results of employment related tests on the basis of race, color, religion, sex, or national origin" (Section 106).

Because Section 106 of Public Law 102-166 is not specific with respect to the type of test that is implied, the ban on "adjusted scoring" applies equally to personality tests, interest inventories, cognitive ability tests, and physical ability tests. This is an important consideration since it means that test developers and consumers cannot adjust scores in any way because of their possible adverse impact on the majority group. At the same time, the possible adverse impact of tests on minority-group individuals is confined to an examination of potential test bias, without recourse to strategies for correcting for bias and adverse impact (Sackett and Wilk, 1994).

Concerns in Culturally Sensitive Testing

Gopaul-McNicol and Brice-Baker (1998) note that there is evidence to suggest that children from varying cultural backgrounds interpret test items differently, bring to the test situation differing sets of expectations and knowledge, and generally do not score as high as members of the mainstream culture on standardized tests. Although adequately translated tests can greatly enhance the accuracy of test results, examiners should not ignore the important influence of the examinee's cultural experience and history on the assessment process: "The specific individual experience of non-majority culture individuals will greatly influence their educational, emotional and language development" (Bracken and Barona, 1991, p. 129). Thus, it is important to consider the test taker's cultural and individual differences, in addition to language, in the assessment process. Also, when trying to fully understand minority test takers, it is important to consider information related to their immigration and educational status (Bracken and Barona, 1991). This information is important because it provides critical data about the linguistic and cultural proficiency of the person about to be assessed. For instance, from this information the examiner has a better idea of whether the assessment instrument is appropriate for the individual to be tested.

Gregory and Lee (1986) hold that consumers of psychoeducational assessments such as psychotherapists, school administrators, and social workers need to include the synthesizing of complex information to judge the validity of test data whenever concerns of bias exist. Decisions about the validity of test results can be particularly complex if test data are used to make high-stakes decisions.

The *Ethical Principles of Psychologists and Code of Conduct* (American Psychological Association [APA], 1992) direct professionals to offer thorough discussion of the limitations of tests for the individual or group being assessed. This is especially important if test outcomes touch on social policy or might be construed to the detriment of persons in specific age, sex, ethnic, or socioeconomic groups. Gregory and Lee (1986) add that the *Standards for Educational and Psychological Testing* (American Psychological Association, 1985) make it clear that test users must avoid bias in test selection, administration, and interpretation; they should avoid even the appearance of discriminatory practice. It is the appearance of discriminatory practices, however, that has led to the familiar controversy over the issue of test bias.

Aside from postulating a normal distribution of the population, standardization procedures have also assumed that Euro-white, middle-class standards, values, attitudes, beliefs, experience, and knowledge are the only correct ones, thereby denying minority groups and poor whites recognition of their cultural distinctiveness (Samuda, 1998). In other words, minority individuals are often forced to compete on unequal terms with Euro-white, middle-class persons, giving the latter a marked advantage. It is not surprising, then, that scores on tests of all types are consistently lower for individuals who differ from the normative population. Thus if a test designed for one cultural group is administered to another cultural group, the test automatically favors the group for whom the test was designed. Williams (1983) also noted that the match or mismatch between a student's cultural experiences and those of the school environment calls into question the validity of both predictor and criterion variables.

Standardized achievement testing procedures that are insensitive to the linguistic and cultural needs of minority students can deflate students' test performances, and the resulting scores in turn result in inappropriate academic labeling and placement, such as retention in grade or low-expectation education tracks (Oakes, 1985). Thus, high-stakes educational decisions based on invalid tests reduce self-esteem and academic interest and can ultimately cause students to achieve at lower levels because they feel helpless about their low status in school.

According to Sommers (1989), the pragmatic element of language mitigates against both measures of reliability and validity, since an individual's language is influenced by factors other than those found in the formal testing atmosphere of normative studies. Sommers also notes that since individual children are more or less influenced by these pragmatic factors, standardized samples fail to reflect the diversity of their language understanding and use, and measures to standardize language in testing may consequently lack validity. It also has been suggested that age equivalent scores should be considered less reliable than others, such as standard scores or percentile ranks.

Sommers (1989) further mentions that a related problem is use of norm-referenced language tests with students from minority populations. Sommers argues that it is rare to complete efforts to adapt some norm-referenced tests to make them fairer and more accurate representations of some aspects of students' linguistic abilities by modifying their content and form of administration, particularly prior to publication of the test.

Language screening tests designed for younger students are often ineffective in accurately identifying need for special language assistance because such instruments are not designed for learners who have differing first-language exposure (Sommers, 1989). From a theoretical standpoint, the model used to assess language performance and competence is typically based on a monolingual view of language acquisition and functioning. Its underlying assumption is that individuals must attain and demonstrate certain competencies in English deemed essential for a person to function effectively as a member of society. However, as was noted earlier, there is a large population of students for whom English is not the first *and* only language they must learn. Thus, another part of culturally appropriate assessment must be to incorporate features that credit individuals for bilingual competency skills.

Bernal (1990) stated that something about the test(s) or testing situations affects how minority subjects perform and suggested that English language proficiency, socioeconomic status, test sophistication, motivation, and degree of acculturation all have an impact on an examinee's performance. In a review of issues in assessing English language learners, Olmedo (1981) argued that acculturative, linguistic, psychological, and sociocultural factors must all be considered in order to understand how a person fits both within his or her own culture as well as the host culture. Understanding an individual's acculturation level and biculturalism helps to explain how culture differentially influences academic and test-taking performance (Barona and Pfeiffer, 1992).

In many instances, behaviors that characterize individuals in the process of learning English or becoming acculturated into American society may be interpreted as indicators of learning disabilities (Gopaul-McNicol and Brice-Baker, 1998). When such tests are used with individuals coming from a cultural or language background different from that of the normative population, opportunities increase for inaccurate interpretation of test results (Santos de Barona and Barona, 1991). Thus such scales may lack usefulness for interpreting the performance of individuals from diverse backgrounds. Such an assessment requires a skilled individual who is fluent in the examinee's language and who can separate problems "related to issues of language competence and those that are associated with deficits in learning" (Barona and Santos de Barona, 1987, p. 192).

The latter is important in that individuals who speak the same language but originate from varying geographic regions may use different expressions to describe the same object, situation, or phenomenon (Santos de Barona and Barona, 1991). There are numerous examples of how the English spoken by Americans deviates from that spoken in Great Britain or Australia. Psychologists who are bilingual have noted that failure to account for such differences can inappropriately penalize individuals for using words, expressions, or concepts that are acceptable within their particular cultural framework but not when examined from another cultural perspective.

In sum, children or adolescents with limited or no English language skills must be assessed carefully within the context of their cultural environment if appropriate educational or psychological services are to be offered (Gopaul-McNicol and Brice-Baker, 1998). Such modifications, however, should not merely be static adjustments but rather consider, individually, the unique circumstances of each person. It's a well-known fact that lower socioeconomic class and minority status are associated with lower level of performance on assessment measures of all types. With the demographic shifts that are taking place in our society today and projected to continue into the future, the time has come to acknowledge that assessment measures and practices need to reflect the richer cultural fabric that now constitutes the U.S. population.

Outcomes of Poor Testing Practices

In essence, identical treatment—the definition most consonant with accurate prediction—presupposes access to the same experiences; this is especially true of cognitive type testing. According to Williams (1983), this supposition is not met in our educational system because bias is often inherent in educational expectations on lower academic tracks. A substantial amount of research documents that minority and white children are indeed exposed to differing curricula through the practice of ability tracking (Oakes, 2000). Poor learning environments therefore lead directly to poor performance on achievement tests and account for the accurate "predictive validity" cited by researchers.

Gregory and Lee (1986) note that standardized tests are used to select and screen. They further add that if these tests or their users discriminate particular groups negatively, the groups are unfairly denied access to educational and career opportunities. According to Padilla (1988), the result of inappropriate assessment procedures has been overrepresentation of Mexican American children in special-education classes. Padilla (1988) further explains that studies at that time showed that this practice continues, but in modified form. For example, a study of special-education referral practices in large urban school settings found that more than 60 percent of the Mexican American students referred were diagnosed as learning-disabled or language-impaired, categories that were almost nonexistent before 1980.

Overrepresentation of Mexican Americans in special-education classes has resulted in numerous legal suits brought against the educational establishment. In one of the early legal cases, *Diana v. California State Board of Education* (1970), the suit questioned the practice of testing children in English when it was not their first or dominant language. Padilla (1988) notes that although this case was settled out of court and in favor of the plaintiff, it has had little impact on professional practice and overrepresentation of students in special classes.

Most culturally diverse children of preschool age have not interacted extensively in structured group situations. It has been estimated that fewer than one out of four minority children aged four years or younger have attended preschool programs (Fradd, 1987). For these children, most learning has occurred through the family, which itself may be isolated experientially from the mainstream culture (Santos de Barona and Barona, 1991).

Extrapolating to success in higher education, Samuda (1998) holds that scores on a test of scholastic aptitude, or developed ability to reason with words and numbers posing collegelike problems, inform the user about how much trouble a student may expect to have in moving immediately into college work. However, these instruments and their outcomes say nothing about the odds against which the student has had to struggle in developing the particular abilities or about the energy and determination the individual will put into college work (Samuda, 1998). A student's ability to solve problems posed in another language or cultural context may or may not be reflected in the scores, depending on how widely divergent the two cultures at issue are.

Importantly for a student whose schooling has been of lower quality or whose home and perhaps predominant community language is other than English, a mediocre score on a test may represent a triumph of ability, devotion to study, and persistence. The test scores by themselves are not designed to reflect these characteristics, not because the qualities themselves are unimportant but because testing has not yet produced ways to measure them. In educational assessment and selection practices, the student's biographical record, demonstrated interest, and long-term perseverance as reflected in school grades, especially as further illuminated by the comments of those who know his or her history, are the indispensable bases for understanding the meaning of the scores resulting from the test.

Translation and Adaptation of Tests

Sperber, Devellis, and Boehlecke (1994) have shown that the practice of translating tests from a "source" language into a second, "target" language has not generally been an acceptable solution to the pervasive problem of inappropriate assessment. Translation of tests is complex for many reasons. Here are some important considerations:

- Test directions are frequently too psychotechnical, difficult, stilted, or "foreign" to allow easy translation.

- Practitioner-produced translations are rarely translated back and forth to ensure equivalent meanings across languages (Brislin, 1980).

- The underlying psychological constructs assessed by translated tests are sometimes not universal across cultures (van de Vijver and Poortinga, 1982).

- Content assessed on achievement tests can differ in many important ways across cultures or languages.

- Examinee test-taking behaviors and orientations toward test directions and procedures can vary from one culture to another (Samuda, 1998).

- There has been a general failure to develop workable translation procedures or standards against which to systematically judge the equivalence of translations and constructs across languages or cultures (Brislin, 1970).

Each of these potential threats to translation validity highlights the need for special care and attention in the procedures for producing translations of tests for multicultural-multilingual assessment (Bracken and Barona, 1991). However, because of the great cost involved in translating and adapting a test (when it is well done), in reality few tests are ever translated for use with limited English speakers.

Werner and Campbell (1970) offer five basic recommendations to facilitate producing quality test translation:

1. Test items should consist of simple sentences.
2. Pronouns should be avoided in test directions and items; rather, nouns should be repeated.
3. Test items should not contain metaphors or colloquialisms.
4. Avoid the passive voice in test directions and items.
5. Hypothetical phrasing and subjective mood in test directions and items should be avoided.

Bracken and Barona (1991) point out that a back-translated version of an instrument should be contrasted with the original version of the test for grammatical structure; comparability of concepts; level of word complexity; and overall similarity in meaning, wording, and format. Like the original translator, the back-translator should be well educated, fully bilingual, and familiar with the psychotechnical concepts and language employed in the source test's materials (Bracken and Barona, p. 123).

Because translating tests can be difficult, time consuming, very expensive to complete, and inherently error-prone, an instrument being considered for translation should be maximally useful, practical, and error-free in its translated version. A comprehensive, multistep translation and validation process is essential ultimately for normative interpretation of assessment instruments (Geisinger, 1994).

Recommendations for Nonbiased Assessment Practices

Culturally biased assessment has been described as constant error in decisions, predictions, and inferences about members of particular ethnic or cultural groups. Historically, strategies employed to eliminate these discriminatory aspects included attempts to minimize the cultural and verbal components of testing—so-called culture-fair testing. One of the most publicized approaches to nonbiased assessment has been the use of pluralistic norms, such as the SOMPA (Mercer, 1979). However, civil rights legislation has made it unlawful to use group-adjusted norm scores.

Even if techniques for group adjustment of scores were lawful, the fact would remain that few school psychologists are trained in nonbiased assessment and therefore know little about procedures for evaluating students from diverse backgrounds. Some educators who have suggested that psychologists seldom use techniques that could reduce bias during assessment of students from minority groups generally support the finding. Complex judgments concerning appropriate and equitable test use can best be made by users such as school psychologists, familiar with the students and the environment in which the test is administered (Lam, 1993).

Eurocentric approaches to studying ethnic minority populations in education is based on the fact that these approaches have frequently resulted in erroneous interpretations because of specific biases inherent in the paradigms themselves. Research emphasis is also usually placed on a comparative approach that uses similar measures to compare groups of people who differ in culture, language, or social class. We must keep in mind the importance of understanding how the cultural background that the ethnic respondent brings to the task of completing interviews, surveys, and question-naires of various types determines the response patterns that emerge. An appropriate or bias-free sample may be a more likely outcome if the ethnic community is involved in the psychological assessment enterprise. All consumers of assessment measures need to address the relevance of mainstream paradigms that test developers use to define their approach.

As the authors of the various chapters in this book show, users of tests (regardless of the assessment instruments involved or the context of the assessment) must ensure that the tests and procedures for their implementation are appropriate for diverse populations. Attaining the competence necessary for becoming culturally sensitive in assessment procedures is not an easy task. Psychologists who employ tests as part of their professional responsibility may be unaware of how their ethnic and cultural experiences and position in mainstream society influence knowledge construction, selection of particular tests, and the interpretations they derive from psychological instruments. Standard norms in assessment usually reflect the middle class, and any deviations from it are interpreted as deficits or differences that might require intervention.

A paradigm shift is required, wherein the study of a specific ethnic group is valued for its own sake and need not be compared to another group, especially if the comparison is likely to be biased. Instruments that are biased and favor a particular group should not be used to evaluate differences between culturally distinct groups of people. Educational research involving ethnic populations should not examine students from the perspective of their failures in the educational system; rather, it should concentrate on how to achieve success regardless of the task or level involved. Further, instruments must also be appropriate for properly assessing changes in learning or behavior that are due to a treatment or educational program. However, if assessment devices are inappropriate in a pretest context, they will also be poor measures of postintervention learning or behavior changes.

Test makers and users need to be aware of how test performance is influenced by inequality in educational opportunity, parents' educational attainment, cultural orientation, language spoken at home, proficiency in English, socialization experiences, family structure and dynamics, family income, and level of motivation to do well. If sufficient information is given beforehand about possible confounding variables in deciding to test a particular individual or group, an informed decision can be made about the suitability of the test to be used.

To increase the cross-cultural assessment competency of test examiners, such individuals must be knowledgeable and comfortable with the traditional customs and communicative styles of many individuals who do not represent the prototypical middle-class person on whom most assessment instruments are based. We recommend that test users involve minority community members in selecting instruments to be used in a school, employment venue, placement center, and so forth. This practice increases the minority community's trust and rapport regarding testing practices and results in more appropriate assessment measures, practices, and decision making.

In conclusion, it is important to sensitize professionals to discriminatory practices while broadening assessment methods. In advocating for a systems approach that is culturally sensitive, we believe it is crucial to redouble our efforts to increase the pool of qualified minority psychologists who are trained in psychometric theory and test construction. Further, we need to train individuals who are expert in psychological assessment of all types to assume leadership positions in the field. There are too few psychologists with the expertise necessary to advance our discussion of culturally sensitive assessment beyond what has prevailed for the past three decades. In the new millennium, we look forward to assessment practices that better reflect the multicultural face of America.

References

American Psychological Association. (1985). *Standards for educational and psychological testing*. Washington, DC: Author.

American Psychological Association. (1992). *Ethical principles of psychologists and code of conduct*. Washington, DC: Author.

Barona, A., & Pfeiffer, I. S. (1992). Effects of test administration and acculturation level on achievement scores. *Journal of Psychological Assessment, 10*, 1224–1232.

Barona, A., & Santos de Barona, M. (1987). A model for the assessment of limited English proficient students referred for special education services. In S. H. Fradd & W. J. Tikunoff (Eds.), *Bilingual education and bilingual special education: A guide for administrators* (pp. 183–210). Boston: College Hill Press.

Bernal, E. M. (1990). Increasing the interpretative validity and diagnostic utility of Hispanic children's scores on tests of achievement and intelligence. In F. C. Serafica, A. Schwebel, R. K. Russell, P. D. Isaac, & L. B. Myers (Eds.), *Mental health of ethnic minorities* (pp. 108–138). New York: Praeger.

Bracken, B. A., & Barona, A. (1991). State of the art procedures for translating, validating and using psychoeducational tests in cross-cultural assessment. *School Psychology International, 12*, 119–132.

Brislin, R. W. (1970). Back translation for cross-cultural research. *Journal of Cross-Cultural Psychology, 1*, 185–216.

Brislin, R. W. (1980). Translation and content analysis of oral and written material. In H. C. Triandis & J. W. Berry (Eds.), *Handbook of cross-cultural psychology* (Vol. 2). New York: Allyn & Bacon.

California State Department of Education. (1994). *Fall language survey results for school year 1993–1994*. Sacramento: Office of Bilingual Education.

Civil Rights Act of 1991, Pub. L. No. 102-166, 105 Stat. 1071 (Nov. 21, 1991).

Diana v. California State Board of Education, Civ. No. C-70–37 RFP (N.D. Cal., 1970).

Fradd, H. S. (1987). *Bilingual education and bilingual special education: A guide for administrators*. Boston: Little, Brown.

Geisinger, K. F. (1994). Cross-cultural normative assessment: Translation and adaptation issues influencing the normative interpretation of assessment instruments. *Psychological Assessment, 6*, 304–312.

Gopaul-McNicol, S., & Brice-Baker, J. (1998). *Cross-cultural practice: Assessment, treatment, and training*. New York: Wiley.

Gregory, S., & Lee, S. (1986). Psychoeducational assessment of racial and ethnic minority groups: Professional implications. *Journal of Counseling Psychology and Development, 14*, 635–637.

Haney, W. M., Madaus, G. F., & Lyons, R. (1993). *The fractured marketplace for standardized testing.* Boston: Kluwer.

Hartigan, J. A., & Wigdor, A. K. (Eds.). (1989). *Fairness in employment testing: Validity generalization, minority issues, and the General Aptitude Test Battery.* Washington, DC: National Academy Press.

Hayes-Bautista, D. E., Schink, W. O., & Chapa, J. (1988). *The burden of support: Young Latinos in an aging society.* Stanford, CA: Stanford University Press.

Johnson, B. A., Vickers, L., & Williams, C. (1987). School psychologists' use of techniques for nonbiased assessment. *College Student Journal, 21*, 334–339.

Lam, T.C.M. (1993). Testability: A critical issue in testing language minority students with standardized achievement tests. *Measurement and Evaluation in Counseling and Development, 26*, 179–191.

Mensh, E., & Mensh, H. (1991). *The IQ mythology: Class, race, gender, and inequality.* Carbondale, IL: Southern University Press.

Mercer, J. R. (1979). *Technical manual: System of Multicultural Pluralistic Assessment (SOMPA).* New York: Psychological Corporation.

Messick, S. (1989). Validity. In R. Linn (Ed.), *Educational measurement* (pp. 447–474). New York: ACE/Macmillan.

Mitchell, A. J. (1937). The effect of bilingualism in the measurement of intelligence. *Elementary School Journal, 38*, 29–37.

National Center for Educational Statistics. (1994). *The condition of education 1994.* Washington, DC: U.S. Department of Education.

Oakes, J. (1985). *Keeping track: How schools structure inequality.* New Haven, CT: Yale University Press.

Oakes, J. (2000). Grouping and tracking. In A. E. Kazdin (Ed.), *Encyclopedia of psychology.* Washington, DC: American Psychological Association.

Olmedo, E. L. (1981). Testing linguistic minorities. *American Psychologist, 36*, 1078–1085.

Padilla, A. M. (1988). Early psychological assessment of Mexican-American children. *Journal of the History of the Behavioral Sciences, 24*, 113–115.

Padilla, A. M. (1992). Reflections on testing: Emerging trends and new possibilities. In K. F. Geisinger (Ed.), *Psychological testing of Hispanics* (pp. 271–284). Washington, DC: American Psychological Association.

Sackett, P. R., & Wilk, S. L. (1994). Within-group norming and other forms of score adjustment in preemployment testing. *American Psychologist, 49*, 929–954.

Samuda, R. J. (Ed). (1998). *Psychological testing of American minorities: Issues and consequences* (2nd ed.). Thousand Oaks, CA: Sage Publications.

Sanchez, G. I. (1932a). Group differences in Spanish-speaking children: A critical review. *Journal of Applied Psychology, 40,* 223–231.

Sanchez, G. I. (1932b). Scores of Spanish-speaking children on repeated tests. *Journal of Genetic Psychology, 40,* 223–231.

Santos de Barona, S. M., & Barona, A. (1991). The assessment of culturally and linguistically different preschoolers. *Early Childhood Quarterly, 6,* 363–376.

Sommers, R. K. (1989). Language assessment: Issues in the use and interpretation of tests and measures. *School Psychology Review, 18,* 452–462.

Sperber, A. D., Devellis, R. F., & Boehlecke, B. (1994). Cross-cultural translation: Methodology and validation. *Journal of Cross-Cultural Psychology, 25,* 505–524.

Sue, S. (1998). Measurement, testing, and ethnic bias: Can solutions be found? In G. R. Sodowsky & J. C. Impara (Eds.), *Multicultural assessment in counseling and clinical psychology* (pp. 7–36). Lincoln, NB: Buros Institute of Mental Measurement.

Torres, J. (1991). Equity in education and the language minority student. *Forum, 14*(4), 1–3.

van de Vijver, F.J.R., & Poortinga, Y. H. (1982). Cross-cultural generalization and universality. *Journal of Cross-Cultural Psychology, 13,* 387–408.

Werner, O., & Campbell, D. (1970). Translating, working through interpreters, and the problem of decentering. In R. Naroll and R. Cohen (Eds.), *A handbook of method in cultural anthropology* (pp. 398–420). New York: Natural History Press.

Williams, T. S. (1983). Some issues in the standardized testing of minority students. *Journal of Education, 165,* 192–208.

2

Ethics in Multicultural Assessment

A Model of Reasoned Application

Charles R. Ridley, Carrie L. Hill, and
Deborah L. Wiese

Meldon (1967) stated that "the theoretical interest in the subject matter of ethics, whatever the conditions of its origin may be, must not be confused with the practical interest of moral beings. The theoretical interest is concerned with knowing; the practical interest is concerned with doing" (p. 3).

The implication of this quote is simple yet profound: knowing about ethics does not guarantee that one will behave in an ethically appropriate manner. There are two reasons someone who is knowledgeable about ethics might engage in behavior that is ethically inappropriate. The first is if the person has a theoretical interest in ethics but does not have a practical interest in acting in an ethically appropriate fashion. The second reason is if the person has a practical interest in ethics but does not know how to translate his or her knowledge of ethics into ethically appropriate conduct. In either case, the result is ethically inappropriate action that usually causes some degree of harm to others.

This chapter is concerned with ethics in multicultural assessment. Drawing from the quote, we conclude that clinicians who are knowledgeable about ethical issues pertaining to multicultural assessment do not necessarily choose to engage in ethically appropriate behavior when conducting multicultural assessments. Their ethically inappropriate conduct might originate from lack of interest in the practical application of ethics, or from simply not understanding how to translate what they know into actual professional practice. In either case, the result is ethically inappropriate multicultural assessment activities and conclusions. Moreover, flawed assessment conclusions foil the effectiveness of treatment interventions. The ultimate price is a poor treatment outcome, which is contrary to the goal of ethically appropriate practice.

The purpose of this chapter is to give clinicians a model for translating ethical knowledge into ethically appropriate multicultural assessment practice. The chapter rests on several assumptions. First, both theoretical and practical considerations in ethics are necessary for conducting ethically appropriate multicultural assessment. Second, the majority of clinicians are interested in theoretical as well as practical aspects of ethics as they pertain to multicultural assessment. The third assumption naturally ensues from the second: if most clinicians are interested in putting their ethical knowledge into practice, then the occurrence of ethically inappropriate multicultural assessment is due to clinicians' not understanding how to translate their ethical knowledge into ethically appropriate behavior.

To explain our model, we divide the chapter into four sections. First, competence is discussed as the superordinate ethical principle of multicultural assessment. Second, four ethical standards are highlighted as the basic units of ethical knowledge to be applied to multicultural assessment practice. Third, three fundamental activities of multicultural assessment are described. Fourth, a set of guidelines is offered to help clinicians conduct reasoned application of the ethical standards to the activities of multicultural assessment.

Competence: The Superordinate Ethical Principle

As an ethical principle, the purpose of competence is to hold clinicians accountable for their professional behavior (Cottone and Tarvydas, 1998). In regard to multicultural assessment, clinicians are accountable for making accurate, comprehensive, and impartial case conceptualizations (Ridley, Li, and Hill, 1998). In the *Ethical*

Principles of Psychologists and Code of Conduct (APA Ethics Code; American Psychological Association, 1992), competence (Principle A) is categorized as a general ethical principle; we regard it as superordinate in multicultural assessment. By *superordinate* we mean that competence is the most crucial and relevant principle for achieving ethically appropriate multicultural assessments. We acknowledge that other principles also are important to this activity (for example, integrity, respect for people's rights and dignity), but we believe that competence is the polestar—a central, guiding principle for the practice of ethically sound multicultural assessment. Certainly, incompetence typically leads to inaccurate, incomplete, and partial case conceptualizations.

The designation of competence as the first general principle in the APA Ethics Code implies its perceived importance to the profession of psychology. However, we are dissatisfied with the lack of attention devoted to clearly defining *competence*. For example, the first sentence describing competence in the APA Ethics Code states that "Psychologists strive to maintain high standards of competence in their work" (American Psychological Association, 1992, p. 1599). Obviously, using a word to define itself does not elucidate the meaning of the word. Instead, it renders an ambiguous definition.

Additionally, the second sentence describing competence states that psychologists "recognize the boundaries of their particular competencies and the limitations of their expertise" (American Psychological Association, 1992, p. 1599). In this sentence, a new word is introduced: *competencies*. But it is never defined, nor is it distinguished from the word *competence*. Therefore, we raise the question: Do the words *competence* and *competencies* have the same meaning? If so, how are these words defined? If not, how do they differ in meaning? Unfortunately, more confusion than clarity is created when similar but undefined words are used to describe the same phenomenon.

The APA Ethics Code describes its general principles as aspirational but not enforceable (American Psychological Association,

1992). Perhaps, enforcement is impossible because one cannot enforce a principle that is not operationalized. Defining indicators are conspicuously absent from the current description of the principle of competence. Failing to adequately define *competence* lets psychologists off the hook and actually deflates its aspirational quality. How can psychologists aspire to something they do not understand? Obviously, they cannot.

Consequently, if competence is inadequately defined in a document as influential as the APA Ethics Code, how can psychologists conceptualize competence in a more specific domain such as multicultural assessment? Unfortunately, not much help is found in the multicultural literature. Despite the proliferation of scholarship on multicultural competence, inconsistencies and conceptual difficulties remain (Ridley, Baker, and Hill, in review). Fortunately, there has been some progress in the specific area of multicultural assessment. A host of suggestions about how to assess clients across cultures have been critiqued and systematized into a Multicultural Assessment Procedure, or MAP (see Ridley, Li, and Hill, 1998).

Based on recent efforts to conceptualize competence-based professional practice (Ridley, Baker, and Hill, in review) and on the tenets and facets of the MAP (Ridley, Li, and Hill, 1998), we offer our own definition of competence in multicultural assessment. We define multicultural assessment competence as the ability and committed intention to consider cultural data in order to formulate accurate, comprehensive, and impartial case conceptualizations. Both *ability* and *committed intention* are included in the definition because we believe that each is necessary but not sufficient for competence. To "consider cultural data" means to collect as well as interpret the data. Finally, case conceptualizations must be accurate, comprehensive, *and* impartial in order for multicultural assessment to be successful.

Multicultural assessment competence encompasses several competencies. Competencies are smaller components of overall competence, but each competency by itself does not equal competence (Ridley, Baker, and Hill, in review). The ability to apply the ethical standards of the APA Ethics Code to multicultural assessment practice is a competency of overall multicultural assessment competence. Examples of other competencies are collecting cultural data, interpreting cultural data, and formulating a sound case conceptualization. All of the competencies together constitute multicultural assessment competence. Therefore, it is evident that the general ethical principle of competence is superordinate in multicultural assessment. It subsumes the ability to apply ethical standards to multicultural assessment practice as one of several multicultural assessment competencies.

The ability to apply ethical standards to multicultural assessment requires a sound reasoning process. However, the APA Ethics Code does not provide a reasoning process. A sound reasoning process is the missing link between knowledge of ethics and ethically appropriate practice. Our model is an attempt to present this missing link. Guidelines for reasoned application of ethical standards follow discussion of relevant ethical standards and the activities entailed in multicultural assessment.

Ethical Standards: Subordinate to Competence

Several standards in the APA Ethics Code pertain to multicultural assessment. In order to give clinicians a cogent model for translating standards into ethically appropriate practice, we chose four that we believe are most relevant to multicultural assessment. Theoretically, the guidelines we suggest for reasoned application of ethical standards could be used for any standard—but these four are considered especially germane.

The APA Ethics Code does not discuss the relationship between its ethical principles and standards. However, we suggest that these four standards serve a subordinate function to the superordinate principle of competence. This follows from our previous discussion of competence and competencies. The ethical standards pertain to a specific competency of overall multicultural assessment competence.

Accordingly, the principle of competence is superordinate to the ethical standards.

1. *Reliance on scientific and professional knowledge (Standard 1.06)*. Clinicians are expected to rely on scientific and professional knowledge derived from research, training, course work, clinical experience, supervision, and continuing education when making clinical judgments and engaging in clinical practice. In the realm of multicultural assessment, clinicians are expected to use scientific and professional knowledge about theories and models of the assessment process, about procedures and norms for psychological testing, about incorporating cultural variables during assessment, about systems of diagnosis and their limitations, and about clinical judgment strategies.

2. *Development of competence to service human differences (Standard 1.08)*. Clinicians are expected to seek and achieve competence when they encounter human differences that significantly affect their work. The variety of human differences include age, gender, race, ethnicity, national origin, religion, sexual orientation, disability, language, and socioeconomic status. If they cannot obtain the necessary training, experience, consultation, or supervision, clinicians need to make a referral. It is easy to see the relevance of this standard to multicultural assessment. If clinicians do not develop competence to service human differences, they will not know how to consider cultural data during their assessments, which leads to unsound case conceptualizations.

3. *Prevention of unfair discrimination (Standard 1.10)*. Clinicians should not participate in unfair discrimination based on human differences such as those listed in the previous standard (age, race, religion, and so on). Earlier in this chapter, we stated our assumptions. One was that the majority of clinicians are interested in conducting ethically appropriate practice in addition to simply knowing about ethics. Unfortunately, ethically inappropriate practice still occurs. It follows that most clinicians want to participate in fair treatment of their clients, although unfair discrimination still

occurs. This unfair discrimination is most likely unintentional, as in the case of unintentional racism (Ridley, 1995). Unintentional discrimination is still ethically inappropriate, and there is an ethical imperative for clinicians to overcome it.

4. *Appropriate use of assessment techniques (Standard 2.04)*. There are three parts to this standard. First, clinicians are expected to be familiar with the assessment procedures and instruments they use, including the reliability, validity, and outcome effectiveness of various approaches and tests. Second, clinicians are expected to understand the inherent degree of uncertainty they face when making clinical decisions. Third, clinicians are expected to identify situations in which particular assessment techniques may be inappropriate or may need adjustment in administration or interpretation owing to factors of human difference. Perhaps this standard speaks most directly to ethical issues during multicultural assessment.

Despite the relevance of these ethical standards to multicultural assessment, the standards are not clearly operationalized and function mainly as heuristics for practice (Keitel, Kopala, and Adamson, 1996). For example, we chose to include Standard 1.08 among the four most relevant to multicultural assessment even though its use of the word *competence* is problematic. In addition, despite their vagueness, it is difficult to extrapolate the standards to account for the complexity inherent in clinical practice—especially the complexity intrinsic to multicultural assessment (Ridley, Liddle, Hill, and Li, in press). We hope that our guidelines for reasoned application of ethical standards to the fundamental activities of multicultural assessment compensate for the weaknesses of the standards themselves.

Fundamental Activities of Multicultural Assessment

As previously mentioned, competence is the superordinate unit of ethical knowledge to be applied to multicultural assessment practice. In addition, the four ethical standards are the subordinate units. But what makes up the broad-based practice of multicultural assessment? To make the application of standards more manageable, we have divided the process into three fundamental activities. The first is collecting clinical data, which includes cultural data. The second is interpreting clinical data, including cultural data. The third is formulating a sound case conceptualization. Each activity is briefly described.

Collecting clinical data, including cultural data, refers to the process of identifying and gathering information about the client for the purpose of formulating a case conceptualization. Clinicians use a variety of methods to collect clinical data, among them structured and unstructured clinical interviewing; using standardized instruments, nonstandardized methods, and culture-specific instruments; and conducting behavioral observations and analyses (Ridley, Li, and Hill, 1998). In particular, collecting cultural data entails asking about culture and observing culture (Ridley, Li, Hill, and Levy, in preparation). These are interdependent strategies that rely on cultural sensitivity (Ridley and others, 1994) and cultural empathy (Ridley and Lingle, 1996).

Interpreting clinical data, including cultural data, refers to the process of generating and testing multiple clinical hypotheses about the client based on the data collected. Generating multiple hypotheses requires clinicians to actively attend to all clinical and cultural data (Ridley, Li, and Hill, 1998) and to use a divergent hypothesis strategy (Wantz and Morran, 1994). Testing multiple hypotheses entails ruling out medical explanations for psychological presentations, using psychological instruments to examine the validity of hypotheses, and comparing clinical and cultural data with criteria from the *Diagnostic and Statistical Manual of Mental Disorders—Fourth Edition* (DSM-IV, American Psychiatric Association, 1994).

Formulating a sound case conceptualization involves organizing the interpretations of clinical and cultural data into a written product. A sound product has clinical utility—that is, the product guides the clinician toward effective treatment interventions. Case conceptualizations having clinical utility are accurate, comprehensive, and impartial.

Each of these words deserves a brief explanation. In using the word *accurate*, we are not implying that there is only one clinical truth for each client. Instead, we assume that some clinical decisions are clearly more reasoned and precise than others and that decisions can be improved dramatically if a thoughtful, systematic assessment procedure is used (Spengler, Strohmer, Dixon, and Shivy, 1995). With the word *comprehensive*, we mean that in addition to one or more diagnoses, case conceptualizations should include discussion of the client's prognosis, severity, strengths and resources, social supports, and recommended treatment interventions. By using the word *impartial*, we suggest that case conceptualizations should be fair and free from bias. Formulating a sound case conceptualization is the culmination of all other assessment activities, and its soundness depends, to a significant extent, on how well the other activities were executed.

It is evident that the fundamental activities of collecting data, interpreting data, and formulating a sound case conceptualization comprise several subactivities. In this way, they represent categories of activity indicative of multicultural assessment. They are interdependent categories that interact nonlinearly during multicultural assessment. For example, a clinician may begin an assessment by collecting clinical or cultural data through a semistructured interview. The clinician proceeds to interpret the data by formulating a number of hypotheses about the client. Returning to the collection of clinical and cultural data, the clinician gathers psychological test results in order to evaluate the multiple hypotheses. Arriving at a sound conclusion, following hypothesis testing, is the culmination of the aforementioned activities. Admittedly, clinicians could benefit from more clarity about the vast activities of multicultural assessment. We hope that our guidelines for reasoned application of ethical standards to these fundamental activities brings some clarity to the multicultural assessment process.

Guidelines for Reasoned Application

Immanuel Kant stated that reason is required for the derivation of action from laws or standards (Beck, 1949). We agree, which is why we conceptualize the transition from ethical knowledge to ethically appropriate practice as the "reasoned application" of the four ethical standards to the three fundamental activities of multicultural assessment. A reasoned application is logical, rational, sound, consistent, articulate, and lucid. It is an exercise of critical and creative thinking.

Our conceptualization of reasoned application is based on the assumption that each of the four ethical standards is relevant to each fundamental activity of multicultural assessment (see Figure 2.1). Competence is placed at the top as the superordinate ethical principle for multicultural assessment. Below it, the four ethical standards and three fundamental activities are depicted. Arrows point from each ethical standard to each fundamental activity. The arrows represent the necessity for clinicians to make a reasoned application of each ethical standard to each fundamental activity.

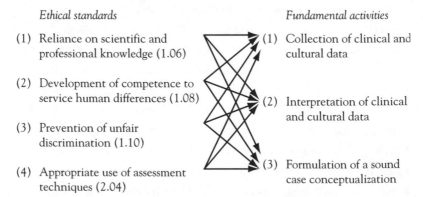

Competence
(superordinate ethical principle)

Ethical standards

(1) Reliance on scientific and professional knowledge (1.06)

(2) Development of competence to service human differences (1.08)

(3) Prevention of unfair discrimination (1.10)

(4) Appropriate use of assessment techniques (2.04)

Fundamental activities

(1) Collection of clinical and cultural data

(2) Interpretation of clinical and cultural data

(3) Formulation of a sound case conceptualization

Figure 2.1. Model of the reasoned application of ethical standards to the fundamental activities of multicultural assessment.

This process might seem daunting to clinicians. However, we argue that dissecting the area of ethics in multicultural assessment into these smaller units helps clinicians form linkages between ethical knowledge and ethical practice. Additionally, we believe this approach makes it easier for clinicians to navigate through the task of ethically appropriate multicultural assessment while still accounting for its complexity. When clinicians make reasoned applications of ethical standards to multicultural assessment activities, they should not ask themselves, "*Is* this ethical standard relevant?" Instead, they should inquire, "*How* is this ethical standard relevant?"

Welfel (1998) called for specific guidelines for reasoned ethical thinking in counseling and psychotherapy. We propose five guidelines to help clinicians make reasoned applications of ethical standards to the fundamental activities of multicultural assessment:

1. *Determine whether all ethically relevant information has been obtained, and if not, collect the necessary data.* Gathering ethically relevant information is crucial to applying an ethical principle (Myser, Kerridge, and Mitchell, 1995). For example, a clinician is applying the ethical standard "development of competence to service human differences" to interpretation of clinical and cultural data. Before the clinician can ascertain whether any gaps in competence exist in relation to human differences, the clinician must know the client's age, gender, race, ethnicity, national origin, religion, sexual orientation, disability, language, and socioeconomic status. This is ethically relevant information that has an impact on the application of the standard. Not having this data reduces the probability that the clinician develops competence in needed areas. The result is misinterpretation of clinical and cultural data.

2. *Determine how personal factors might affect application of the standard to the activity.* Examples of personal factors are the clinician's values and theoretical assumptions (Spengler, Strohmer, Dixon, and Shivy, 1995), cultural biases (Garb, 1998), countertransference issues (Ridley, 1995), and motivation to act in an

ethically appropriate manner. For example, a straight male clinician is applying the ethical standard "prevention of unfair discrimination" to the collection of clinical and cultural data for a gay male client. The client reminds the clinician of a gay man the clinician was acquainted with several years ago who made sexual advances toward the clinician. The sexual advances made the clinician very uncomfortable, and he stopped associating with the acquaintance. The clinician now must consider how countertransference issues might affect his ability to prevent unfair discrimination against the client. The clinician may be at risk of dismissing or distorting pertinent clinical and cultural data about the client's sexual orientation.

3. *Determine how client factors might affect application of the standard to the activity.* Examples of client factors are mental status, strengths and resources (Garb, 1998), and the client's wishes (Myser, Kerridge, and Mitchell, 1995). For example, a clinician is applying the ethical standard "appropriate use of assessment techniques" to collection of clinical and cultural data with a Puerto Rican client. The clinician would like to use a standardized instrument (say, the MMPI-2) to gather data, but the client refuses. The client states that other Puerto Rican clients at the mental health center who have taken the MMPI-2 felt that they were misdiagnosed. The clinician must take the client's wishes into account when deciding the most appropriate use of assessment techniques for the collection of clinical and cultural data.

4. *Determine how contextual factors might affect application of the standard to the activity.* Wicker (1985) noted that the consideration of context places problems in a larger domain and helps clarify the practical implications of behavior. By considering contextual factors, our attention is directed to the extended social world in which multicultural assessment occurs. Examples of contextual factors are the procedures and expectations of the mental health service delivery system; the impact of managed care on multicultural

assessment; the availability of training resources for professional development; and the client's access to health insurance, transportation, employment services, and child care. For example, a white clinician is applying the ethical standard "reliance on scientific and professional knowledge" to formulating a sound case conceptualization for an Asian American client. The clinician works at a mental health center in a rural, predominantly white community. The mental health center houses few professional resources regarding effective treatment interventions with the Asian American population. The clinician needs to consider the context of professional development opportunities within her mental health service network in order to determine how she can formulate a sound case conceptualization that includes culturally appropriate treatment recommendations.

5. *Determine the cognitive and behavioral indicators of ethically appropriate application of the standard to the fundamental activity.* Professional competence has cognitive as well as behavioral requirements (Ridley, Baker, and Hill, in review). Clinicians must articulate the specific cognitions and behaviors that indicate an ethically appropriate application of the ethical standard to the multicultural assessment activity. Otherwise, it is difficult for the clinician to successfully actualize the application. This is a highly individualized process because of the unique set of clinical and cultural data and the particular personal, client, and contextual factors affecting each multicultural assessment. Clinicians must consider what they have determined from the first four guidelines and formulate a cognitive and behavioral plan. For example, an African American clinician is applying the ethical standard "prevention of unfair discrimination" to interpretation of clinical and cultural data for a Mexican American client. The clinician collects all ethically relevant information and considers personal, client, and contextual factors that might affect application of the standard. The clinician identifies a number of cognitive and behavioral indicators of her

attempting to prevent unfair discrimination while interpreting the client's clinical and cultural data:

• The clinician has worked with a small number of Mexican Americans in the past and has had problems with them dropping out of treatment before she can finish the assessment. The clinician is aware that she holds a bias that Mexican American clients are unmotivated in counseling, leaving her unmotivated to attend to all clinical and cultural data or to spend energy generating and testing multiple hypotheses. However, she realizes that failing to thoroughly interpret the client's data is unfairly discriminating against the client. The clinician makes a cognitive commitment to herself to assess the client idiographically (Ridley, 1995). This means that she makes a conscious effort to see the client as a unique individual who might very well be motivated to participate in assessment and therapy.

• In relation to the first indicator, the clinician makes a behavioral commitment to identify the client's strengths and resources by asking about perceived strengths and resources and observing them during sessions. By identifying the client's strengths and resources, the clinician is less likely to unfairly label the client as unmotivated to participate in the assessment. She is also able to generate a greater number of viable hypotheses.

• The client has shared that he is Catholic and that Catholicism is an important source of strength for him and his family. The clinician identifies herself as a Baptist and acknowledges her personal discomfort with some aspects of Catholicism. She knows that she may unfairly discriminate against the client if she fails to attend to data about the client's religious beliefs and identity. She makes a commitment to avoid imposing her religious values on the client by remaining cognitively vigilant about her reactions to religious subject matter as they surface during the assessment.

• The mental health agency at which the clinician works has a limited number of psychological tests available. The clinician is unsure whether any of the instruments have appropriate cultural norms for use with her client. She is worried that the data she acquires from using these tests might unfairly discriminate against the client when she uses the results to test her clinical hypotheses. She may be pointed toward an inaccurate diagnostic conclusion. The clinician decides to research the norms of each test and only use those instruments that are culturally appropriate for her client.

Conclusion

Clinicians who are competent in multicultural assessment make reasoned applications of relevant ethical standards to the activities of multicultural assessment. A significant problem in the area of multicultural assessment, we believe, is lack of guidance about how to translate ethical knowledge into ethically appropriate practice. In response to this problem, we have offered a model that places competence as a superordinate and guiding principle for ethically appropriate multicultural assessment. The model also includes four ethical standards deemed especially relevant to multicultural assessment and three fundamental activities of multicultural assessment.

Finally, we offer five guidelines for making meaningful linkages between the ethical standards and the fundamental activities in the model. By following these guidelines, clinicians can make reasoned applications of relevant ethical standards to the fundamental activities of multicultural assessment. The applications are reasoned because they are logical, careful, and sound. They also give clinicians details for thinking and behaving in an ethically appropriate manner. There is a greater chance that clinicians fulfill the intentions of the ethical principles and standards while uniquely applying them to each multicultural assessment.

We encourage professionals to experiment with this model during their clinical, training, and research endeavors. We also encourage them to offer us constructive feedback. In so doing, we can continue to work toward the goal of achieving ethically appropriate practice in multicultural assessment.

References

American Psychiatric Association. (1994). *Diagnostic and statistical manual of mental disorders* (4th ed.). Washington, DC: Author.

American Psychological Association. (1992). Ethical principles of psychologists and code of conduct. *American Psychologist, 47,* 1597–1611.

Beck, L. W. (1949). *Critique of practical reason and other writings in moral philosophy by Immanuel Kant.* Chicago: University of Chicago Press.

Cottone, R. R., & Tarvydas, V. M. (1998). *Ethical and professional issues in counseling.* Upper Saddle River, NJ: Prentice Hall.

Garb, H. N. (1998). *Studying the clinician: Judgment research and psychological assessment.* Washington, DC: American Psychological Association.

Keitel, M. A., Kopala, M., & Adamson, W. S. (1996). Ethical issues in multicultural assessment. In L. A. Suzuki, P. J. Meller, & J. G. Ponterotto (Eds.), *Handbook of multicultural assessment: Clinical, psychological, and educational applications* (pp. 29–48). San Francisco: Jossey-Bass.

Meldon, A. I. (1967). On the nature and problem of ethics. In A. I. Meldon (Ed.), *Ethical theories: A book of readings* (pp. 1–19). Englewood Cliffs, NJ: Prentice Hall.

Myser, C., Kerridge, I. H., & Mitchell, K. R. (1995). Ethical reasoning and decision-making in the clinical setting: Assessing the process. *Medical Education, 29,* 29–33.

Ridley, C. R. (1995). *Overcoming unintentional racism in counseling and therapy: A practitioner's guide to intentional intervention.* Thousand Oaks, CA: Sage.

Ridley, C. R., Baker, D. M., & Hill, C. L. *Multicultural counseling competence: Reexamination, reconceptualization, and practical application.* Manuscript in review.

Ridley, C. R., Li, L. C., & Hill, C. L. (1998). Multicultural assessment: Reexamination, reconceptualization, and practical application. *The Counseling Psychologist, 26,* 827–910.

Ridley, C. R., Li, L. C., Hill, C. L., & Levy, J. J. *Incorporating cultural data: A core competency in multicultural assessment.* Manuscript in preparation.

Ridley, C. R., Liddle, M. C., Hill, C. L., & Li, L. C. (in press). Ethical decision making in multicultural counseling. In J. G. Ponterotto, J. M. Casas, L. A. Suzuki, & C. M. Alexander (Eds.), *Handbook of multicultural counseling* (2nd ed.). Thousand Oaks, CA: Sage.

Ridley, C. R., & Lingle, D. W. (1996). Cultural empathy in multicultural counseling: A multidimensional process. In P. B. Pedersen, J. G. Draguns, W. J. Lonner, & J. E. Trimble (Eds.), *Counseling across cultures* (4th ed., pp. 266–292). Thousand Oaks, CA: Sage.

Ridley, C. R., Mendoza, D. W., Kanitz, B. E., Angermeier, L., & Zenk, R. (1994). Cultural sensitivity in multicultural counseling: A perceptual schema model. *Journal of Counseling Psychology, 41*, 125–136.

Spengler, P. M., Strohmer, D. C., Dixon, D. N., & Shivy, V. A. (1995). A scientist-practitioner model of psychological assessment: Implications for training, practice, and research. *Counseling Psychologist, 23*, 506–534.

Wantz, D. W., & Morran, D. K. (1994). Teaching counselor trainees a divergent versus a convergent hypothesis-formation strategy. *Journal of Counseling and Development, 73*, 69–74.

Welfel, E. R. (1998). *Ethics in counseling and psychotherapy: Standards, research, and emerging issues.* Pacific Grove, CA: Brooks/Cole.

Wicker, A. W. (1985). Getting out of our conceptual ruts: Strategies for expanding conceptual frameworks. *American Psychologist, 40*, 1094–1103.

3

The Clinical Interview from a Multicultural Perspective

Ruby Takushi and Jay M. Uomoto

In an initial meeting, the clinician is faced with the difficult task of establishing a comfortable and sustainable relationship while gathering valid information. Because the beliefs, values, and attitudes of an individual are directly related to psychological functioning, the multicultural perspective of the client must be considered. Only when the clinician is willing to explore broad worldviews held by a cultural group, as well as the individual expression of those views, can a foundation be laid for comprehensive understanding of the client and conceptualization of effective treatment interventions. Here, *multicultural* refers to the interaction of ethnic, socioeconomic, regional, and spiritual variables in conceptualizing the psychosocial status of the client.

All of these variables cannot be fully covered in this chapter; however, some of the salient multicultural characteristics and common themes that are likely to have an impact on the interview are highlighted. Because it is common to conduct a mental status examination in the initial phases of assessment, we also discuss cultural variations that may occur during this standard procedure.

Client-Therapist Communication and the Gathering of Valid Data

In his description of the basic concepts involved in the psychiatric interview, Sullivan (1954) suggests that during interviews the clinicians ask themselves the clarifying question, "Now, could this mean something that would not immediately occur to me? Do I know what [the client] means by that?" (p. 19). Sullivan understood the interview as an interpersonal phenomenon that yields valid information only if the clinician is aware that the principle instrument of collecting the data is the interviewer. Because the data emerge through participant observation, and such observation is subject to the biases and prejudices of the therapist, professional ethics underscores the importance of being aware of such biases and prejudices (Corey, Corey, and Callanan, 1993).

In practice, these biases increase the likelihood the clinician will misidentify salient issues to which interventions can be directed. A clinician may conceptualize client behaviors or verbalizations (poor eye contact, or deferential attitude) as specific to an ethnic group (for example, Southeast Asian), whereas such behavior may be reflective of a commonly shared disorder (say, dysphoria). Corey, Corey, and Callanan (1993; and Berg-Cross and Takushi-Chinen, 1995) recommend that clinicians involve themselves in activities that raise to awareness one's own biases, thus identifying "cultural and ethnic blind spots" (p. 263). Gathering valid data thus requires sensitivity to the perspectives of both interviewer and client.

Emic-Etic Distinctions in Clinical Conceptualization

When considering the perspective of the client, the clinician must make a distinction between what may be universal characteristics of human functioning and what behaviors, attitudes, and beliefs may be specific to a particular culture. *Emic* characteristics refer to those behaviors and views that are common to an ethnic or minority group. For example, it is thought that Asian families tend toward a strong hierarchical structure, which represents an emic aspect of the case conceptualization. *Etic* dimensions are those aspects of human functioning that are more universal to peoples across cultures. Physiological dimensions such as increased heart rate, vasoconstriction, and increased breathing rate are etic manifestations of anxiety, likely to be found in a similar pattern across cultures.

However, the meaning of anxiety may differ significantly from culture to culture, and such a difference in meaning represents an emic conceptualization. Certain concepts such as self-efficacy, for instance, are conceptualized similarly across cultures (Earley and Randel, 1995), thus making self-efficacy an etic dimension of human functioning. To understand client communications from either an emic or an etic perspective, the clinician is encouraged to review the research and clinical literature related to specific multicultural groups (see among others Dana, 1992; McGoldrick, Giordano, and Pearce, 1996; Sue and Sue, 1999). Using common literature search engines such as MEDLINE and PsycInfo via Internet access allows the clinician to readily and easily access the most current literature on a particular multicultural topic and be better prepared to be sensitive to the cultural nuances of the clinical interview.

Verbal and Nonverbal Behavior

Communication that is culturally congruent is an important aspect of developing and maintaining an alliance with all clients, especially with the multicultural client. When working with monolingual clients or with those for whom English is a second language, the assistance of a translator in conveying the meaning of questions and responses is invaluable. Not only must the clinician be aware of the potential meaning of the client's communication, it is essential to remember that clients are simultaneously interpreting our behavior as well. As a brief guide, a few elements of verbal and nonverbal communication style are considered here.

Conversational *turn exchange* refers to the style of alternating dialogue that is typical of casual discussion. Individuals from some cultures (Asian, Hispanic) may be initially uncomfortable with the cadence of verbal conversation exchange with a majority-culture therapist. The therapist may be seen as the professional to be respected; thus the client remains silent or terse in his remarks, expecting the professional to provide advice and direction. Open-ended questioning may tip the balance of the turn exchange toward more verbal disclosure than the client is accustomed to and may produce significant discomfort. In these cases, responsibility for balancing this turn exchange may be better placed on the therapist.

Similarly, elicitation of clinical data during the first session often takes a question-and-answer format. In some cultures, the client may expect the therapist to take a directive role: asking questions rather than encouraging the client to structure her own communications, and being more nondirective. Client discomfort with a nondirective therapist may be misinterpreted as an anxiety problem, or as evidence of oversensitivity to the intentions of others.

The amount and depth of *disclosure* can also have cultural variations. Many newly immigrated individuals, who may also have difficulty with majority-culture language, can be unaccustomed to making personal and intimate disclosures during the initial clinical interview. The culturally sensitive clinician may then choose to pace the depth and breadth of taking a psychosocial history, and take longer to collect data usually obtained in one or two sessions.

Nonverbal behaviors are thought to communicate more interpersonal data and meaning than verbal behaviors. During the clinical interview, a host of nonverbal behaviors are interpreted by clients of varying multicultural backgrounds in different ways. Some variables to take into consideration include *personal space*, the boundaries of which differ among cultures. The meaning of maintaining *eye contact* can normatively vary between cultures, and the unknowing clinician may violate social comfort zones by keeping too much eye contact with the client. Similarly, lack of eye contact may not necessarily connote social introversion or dysphoric affect.

In family therapy, some therapists may wish to allow the family to seat themselves within the room in order to assess *structural aspects* of family dynamics. In some cultures, family members may look to the therapist for direction in something as seemingly benign as the seating arrangement. However, rapport may be challenged if the therapist proceeds nondirectively with regard to seating the family during the initial interview.

These nonverbal behaviors are a few that may require a "cultural check" to best understand to what extent they represent emic aspects of normal functioning within the client's culture.

In addition to sensitivity to emic versus etic communication and nonverbal behaviors, the clinician must also be aware of several other interview assessment goals relevant to all clients, but in particular to the multicultural client.

Interview Assessment Goals

Broad goals for the interview assessment include:

- Establishing a therapeutic alliance

- Clearly defining the clinical question

- Assessing the client's strengths (personal, family, community resources)

- Gathering background information

- Developing a tentative diagnosis (Langs, 1989; Shea, 1988)

In their overview of the issues associated with appraising and assessing the multicultural client, Lonner and Ibrahim (1996) describe quantitative and qualitative methods of obtaining data. Quantitative data are typically gathered using standardized instruments; such methods are addressed elsewhere in this volume. Qualitative dimensions can be accessed informally in the interview and include assessing the client's worldview, cultural identity, and acculturation level.

Worldview is understood as how one "sees the world from a moral, social, ethical, and philosophical perspective" (Lonner and Ibrahim, 1996, p. 295). Both the clinician and client come to the interview with beliefs and assumptions rooted in their worldview. The specific way in which these beliefs and assumptions are expressed is related to the individual's cultural and ethnic identity. *Cultural and ethnic identity* refers to the degree to which the individual is committed to cultural views and practices, and the outcome of integrating these views into the overall sense of self (Aponte and Barnes, 1995).

Sue and Sue (1999) revised a model of minority identity development that was originally formulated by Atkinson, Morten, and Sue (1989). The newer conceptualization was termed the Racial/Cultural Identity Development Model (R/CID). It proposes five stages in the process of integrating into the larger majority culture. A thorough discussion of the assessment of cultural identity occurs elsewhere in this volume, but briefly the stages reflect the possible orientations (positive, negative, or ambivalent) the individual may have toward both the culture of origin and the host culture.

In stage one, the client assumes a stance of conformity toward the majority culture, with a deprecating attitude toward the self and cultural group. Stage-two clients experience ambivalence toward their own culture and the majority culture. In stage three, the client appreciates the minority group culture while deprecating the majority culture. Stage-four clients are able to sustain positive views of the minority culture while reconsidering the basis for devaluing the majority culture. In stage five, the client is able to fully appreciate minority status while valuing selected aspects of the majority culture.

Ideally, the clinician assesses the client's cultural identity throughout the course of treatment. But during the initial interview in particular, establishing a reference point of cultural identity is essential to accurate conceptualization of the client's presenting problems and appropriate treatment intervention planning.

Although cultural and ethnic identity refers to the outcome of integrating the cultural values of both the group of origin and the majority culture, *acculturation* focuses on the process of psychological change in values, beliefs, and behaviors when adapting to a new culture. Aponte and Barnes (1995) summarize the acculturation process and offer a model for how ethnic and majority-group variables affect psychological functioning and symptom presentation. The psychological functioning of the multicultural client is influenced by the unique characteristics of the individual, the degree of acculturation, cultural variables of the group of origin, and the experience of the cultural group in the host country.

Cultural variables related to the group of origin include the type of acculturating group (to be discussed later in this chapter), socioeconomic status, and family and community structure. The reader is referred to Grieger and Ponterotto (1995), who provide case examples that synthesize the concepts of worldview and acculturation. They suggest several components that can be examined in the clinical setting. Briefly, they are:

- *The client's level of psychological mindedness* which refers to the degree to which the client understands their problem as psychological or emotional in nature.
- *The family's level of psychological mindedness and attitude toward counseling* are related concepts that influence the level of support the client receives and consequent degree of comfort she has in speaking with mental health professionals.
- *The client and family's level of acculturation* are often not identical and influence the degree of comfort each feels in the therapeutic situation, and the freedom the client feels to make choices consistent with mainstream American values.
- *The family's attitude toward acculturation* is also an important element to assess; it refers to how supportive the family is of the client's efforts to become acculturated. Parents may prefer a low

level of acculturation for themselves while supporting the efforts of their children to adopt the values of the new culture.

Defining the Clinical Question and Assessing Client Strengths

The clinician's primary task during the initial interview is to clarify the clinical question. In addition, elicit circumstances surrounding the symptom (anxiety, insomnia) in an effort to discern what typically precedes the onset of the problem and what consequences the client experiences as a result of the problem. Throughout this process, be aware that the client's understanding of the presenting problem can yield insight into the strengths and resources the client brings to the situation. For example, when making standard inquiries focused on the onset, frequency, and severity of the problem, consider including questions aimed at defining the developmental stage of the individual in her group of origin. Such questions may be phrased as, "What does your community expect from someone your age?" "What do you think of those expectations?" "How does your community support (or not support) members experiencing difficulties similar to yours?" "How have you tried to cope with your current situation in the past?"

Clarifying the client's understanding of what behaviors are valued and expected from someone in her social and cognitive developmental stage and what support the group of origin offers in return can yield invaluable insight into the presenting problem.

Because the way in which any individual expresses a need or concern is culturally derived, Berg-Cross and Takushi-Chinen (1995) suggest that culturally relevant issues emerge if the interviewer poses questions related to how the individual meets basic human needs. They recommend including items from the Person-in-Culture Interview (PICI), which is based on the four major motivational theories of our time: psychodynamic psychology, humanistic psychology, family (systems) psychology, and existential psychology. Further, when defining the clinical question, Tanaka-Matsumi and Higginbotham (1996) advise using four criteria that are relevant to all clients but of special use when assessing the multicultural client. The four criteria and items from the PICI (Berg-Cross and Takushi-Chinen, 1995, pp. 333–356) that might be used to address them are to:

1. Know the client's culture-specific definition of deviancy. Include questions such as:

   What would be the best (most pleasurable) part about getting rid of your problem?

   In what way do your current problems create pain for you? For your family?

   Describe your most embarrassing experience in the past year and in your life, or describe what might be an embarrassing situation.

   What kinds of things make you angry, and how would someone know you were angry?

   How can your life be more meaningful?

2. Know what accepted norms of behavior are.

   How do all the members of your family express anger?

   What types of things make you feel important?

   How do the people in your family get that feeling of importance and self-esteem?

   If you fit in at home and in your community, tell what a normal day would be like. What type of normal day are you striving for?

   Each little community has certain images of a successful person. In what ways would your community judge you to be successful or unsuccessful?

3. Be familiar with culturally acceptable methods of social influence (for instance, advice from an elder, or healing rituals).

Draw a totem pole of the important people in your life. Put the weakest person on the bottom, and the most powerful person on the top. Be sure to include yourself and anyone in the community or elsewhere who is very important in your life.

On a day-to-day basis, how do you learn new things?

Who gives you new information?

How do you go about learning new information?

4. Know what community resources are available to the client and which ones are likely to be used.

What types of things make you feel that you are living life to the fullest?

Who are the people closest to you?

Who are the people most distant from you?

What types of things do you feel you are responsible for on a day-to-day basis as a human being?

What types of things do you feel your family is responsible for?

What types of things do you think your society or community is responsible for?

Obtaining Background Information and Developing a Tentative Diagnosis

In addition to the usual questions regarding psychosocial (childhood, adolescence, education, work, interpersonal), family, medical, and psychological history, assessing the type of acculturating group to which a client belongs is essential to the interview process (Aponte and Barnes, 1995). Immigrant groups may voluntarily arrive in this country in search of educational or economic opportunities, they may be involuntary refugees, or they may be an indigenous or ethnic group that has unique values with regard to adapting to the dominant culture. Or the client may be an international student who only plans to be in the host country temporarily. Thus, when obtaining background information and formulating a diagnosis, additional issues to address are recency of immigration, the circumstances surrounding the immigration (was it forced, or voluntary?), the generation of the client, trauma and loss experienced, experiences of discrimination in the host country, and the influence of the move on family structure.

Bemak, Chung, and Bornemann (1996) describe the complex mental health concerns of refugees to this country. Many who have immigrated to the United States have done so secondarily to fleeing adverse sociopolitical conflicts; they may have endured marked oppression in their homeland and consequently present with symptoms of posttraumatic stress after leaving these situations. This type of immigration history then plays into the larger clinical conceptualization of the etiology of psychological stress and disorder found in immigrant clientele. Adjustment for such clients often involves the need to initially secure a sense of physical and psychological safety, and acquiring skills relevant in the new culture (such as language and employment). Ambivalence toward the majority culture is not uncommon. The client may feel gratitude toward the majority culture but resentful that he cannot assume the same socioeconomic status he knew in his home country.

Further, these changes often wreak havoc with traditional family relationships, as younger members of the community develop language and employment skills ahead of older members of the group. Leong and Chou (1996) reviewed the literature and discuss guidelines for counseling international students, who may experience a host of adjustment problems but who do not necessarily intend to remain in the new culture permanently. The counseling needs of such sojourners focus on problems experienced by all students as well as those specific to the international student. Some unique concerns of the international student that can be explored in the initial interview include the anxiety and depression associated with *culture shock*, which refers to the potentially disorienting

experience of entering a new culture; adjustment to a new academic system; language difficulties; reduced socioeconomic security;
experiences of discrimination; and the need to interact with other
students who come from the same country of origin but from
markedly different political, social, or religious backgrounds.

Assessing Mental Status in a Cultural Context

It is common to conduct a mental status examination when completing a clinical interview. The mental status examination can take
the form of making specific behavioral observations of the client. It
can be achieved by asking a structured set of questions to elicit mental status variables. There are also a number of mental status testing procedures designed to obtain psychometric data on the client.
Many of these procedures have been developed and validated on
majority-culture clientele. Therefore, there exists a need to highlight cultural variations on standard mental status examination procedures. The mental status examination has many components; its
broad categories are addressed here. For more detailed descriptions
of the mental status examination, see Trzepacz and Baker (1993)
and Strub and Black (1993).

Behavioral Presentation

Much can be gleaned from the initial presentation of the multicultural client. The *attire of the client* can reveal to what extent that
person may approve of, or adhere to, the culture within which he
or she lives. Clothes that are contemporary (for example, an adolescent from another cultural background who dresses as peers in
high school do) may connote movement toward or acceptance of
the majority culture. Comparing garb between generations in a
multicultural family may also ascertain differences in acceptance
within the family of the majority culture.

As noted earlier, the level of maintaining eye contact may have
cultural significance and can easily be overinterpreted as indicative

of affective disturbance or having import with regard to personality traits.

The *apparent age* of the client may be misleading in terms of psychosocial significance. For example, those who hail from Asian countries or who come from Asian ancestry tend to appear younger than their stated age. By implication, a clinician may see this as lack of evidence for psychosocial stress in the client's life, compared to a similarly aged client who appears much older than the client's actual age. On the other hand, those clients whose immigration or migration history was traumatic may indeed appear older than their actual age because of the physical and emotional deprivation they may have experienced.

The *attitude* of the clients during the intake session can vary depending upon the extent to which they have been oriented to what they might expect during the interview. Many clients from diverse cultural backgrounds (including majority-culture clients) may misperceive the goals of the first session. Some may expect advice, medications, or other interventions that are meant to "heal" or "cure" the problem, and this runs counter to the typical goal of a clinical interview to ascertain information to conceptualize the problem. An initial presentation of cooperativeness may lead to a tenor of uncertainty, even hostility. Others may not return for a follow-up appointment, a phenomenon that is well documented in the multicultural mental health literature regarding rates of early termination among multicultural clients (see Evans, Acosta, Yamamoto, and Skilbeck, 1984).

Affect and Mood

Affect refers to the behavioral presentation of the client from which the clinician infers the underlying experience of mood. There are several dimensions of affect from which a client can be described, among them the range, reactivity, intensity, and degree to which a client's affect is consistent with experienced mood. Depending upon the cultural heritage of the client, there is also wide variance in the normative presentation of affect, especially in the context of an initial interview. A restricted range of affect in an Asian American client, or wide and reactive range of affect in an African American or Italian American client, may have emic significance.

Gathering background data, especially on the socialization patterns of the client, can be helpful to understand if cultural modeling and modulation of affect is significant, and therefore relevant to the affective presentation of the client. If affect restriction is common in the client's family and is consistent with what may be commonly found within traditional cultural social practices, then the clinician may deemphasize its significance regarding the client's underlying mood.

Mood refers to the experience of the client with regard to certain states: dysphoria, anxiety, anger, and so on. Many words can be used to describe each of these moods in the United States, though equivalent words may not be available in other cultures. For example, the term mood itself does not have an equivalent form in Spanish; it may be better to ask about behaviors such as the frequency of crying, or feeling sad, or having a sense of loss. Having appropriate bilingual-bicultural translation available can be of significant benefit in ascertaining mood variables.

The amount of self-disclosure of mood states during the initial interview can vary among cultures. Therefore mood assessment may need to be conducted across several sessions rather than relying on impressions gained in the initial clinical interview. Using standardized mood assessment instruments can also be problematic thanks to norming insufficiencies across cultures (for example, see Wohi, Lesser, and Smith, 1997).

Speech and Language

Assessing verbal output variables and language usage is a standard part of the mental status examination. In the monolingual client who has limited English language ability, this can be extremely difficult. Here again, having a bilingual-bicultural translator can be invaluable in understanding the verbal output ability of the client.

The usual rules of *prosody* (the rate and rhythm of speech output) may not fully apply to the bicultural client. In many Asian cultures, inflection of the pronunciation of a word or phrase can significantly distinguish meanings. Here, prosody is specific to the particular usage of a phrase. Discrepancies between tonal inflection and the meaning of a phrase within the content of the client's conversation may be indicative of cognitive impairment. This can best be ascertained with a culturally knowledgeable bilingual examiner.

Speech *fluency* refers to the flow of speech. The bilingual client who uses English during the clinical interview may not possess the skill to speak fluidly, and the examiner may interpret this as word-finding (oral word fluency deficits) or motor-speech (dyspraxic verbal output) difficulties.

Reading comprehension and *writing* ability should also be assessed in the bilingual client to ensure adequate understanding of written materials such as consent forms, background data forms, and insurance claim forms. Additional time may be necessary prior to starting the clinical interview to review and explain consenting procedures, and to informally quiz patients to ascertain their understanding of the overall meaning of giving informed and written consent.

Thought Processes and Content

The mental status examination often requires review of the patient's thought processes to ascertain the presence of perceptual or delusional disturbances. Thought processes may be tracked throughout the interview in terms of loose associations or tangential tracking of topics. In some cultures, unfamiliarity with the language may account for some rambling content presentation; it is over the course of the clinical interview and following sessions that one can clarify the extent to which this may be a manifestation of thought disorder.

Perceptual disturbances may also have cultural significance, as a client relates visions of seeing deceased relatives or ancestors. A check on the cultural significance of these perceptions, be they auditory or visual, can put into context the degree to which a thought disorder may be present. This is not to say one cannot have both. On the contrary, manifestations of thought disorder can have cultural content. The persistence of these perceptions and the extent to which they interfere with everyday functioning determine the level of intervention that is necessary for a bicultural client.

There are many spiritual practices and rituals that may be endemic to a particular culture. The culturally sensitive clinician may require consultation with non-Western or indigenous practitioners to better conceptualize the problem. Culture-bound syndromes remain poorly studied, but they are significant to many clients whose beliefs may include these conceptualizations (Sue, Sue, and Sue, 1997). Such culture-bound syndromes may present in the mental status examination in terms of pervasive ruminations about death or deceased loved ones, superstitions, or preoccupation with specific rituals for example.

At the same time, the clinician should assess the degree to which these preoccupations may evidence a disabling obsessive or compulsive disorder. Input from other family members, other bicultural professionals, or significant others in the client's community can bring valuable input to assessing such presentations. It can be helpful to consult texts that have an international perspective on psychiatric diagnosis and on psychopathology (for example, Mezzich, Kleinman, Fabrega, and Parron, 1996) to check a particular client's thought content, to determine the external validity of particular thoughts or ideas.

Cognitive Functioning

There are several methods of assessing cognition, notably the commonly applied Mini-Mental State Examination (Folstein, Folstein, and McHugh, 1975), structured interview and testing bedside examinations (Strub and Black, 1993), and comprehensive neuropsychological testing procedures (for example, see Stringer, 1996). Many questions that are addressed in this type of examination are appropriate across cultures where cognitive impairment may be inferred.

Orientation assesses a patient's mental awareness and accuracy by way of name, current year, season, month, day of the week, date, and place of interview. Few modifications are usually necessary for the monolingual or bicultural client as long as appropriate language translation is provided.

Registration of information—by asking the client to repeat the names of three objects and recall them after five to ten minutes— can be employed, also without modification so long as objects that are common across cultures are chosen (tree, chair, ball).

The appropriateness of conducting serial subtraction of numbers depends upon educational attainment, which can vary widely, particularly in immigrant clients. The clinician may opt to ask the client to repeat digit strings of increasing length and then recite them backwards, rather than having the client spell a particular word backwards.

Rote recall of information to assess *recent memory* can be obtained formally by asking for recall of the objects repeated earlier. Informal testing might also include asking the client to recollect information provided earlier in the interview. Asking the patient to copy an object (cf. the MMSE) and asking for the client to reproduce the geometric design usually requires little modification.

Remote memory should be assessed, using information that a person of a particular culture may have better committed to long-term recall (for example, birthplace, where the client was raised, leader of the country of origin if the client is an immigrant) rather than using information markers from the United States (name of current president, governor of the state; current event on television).

Calculation abilities may require modification, again depending upon the educational attainment level of the client. If the client is able, using alternative modalities such as paper and pencil, or a calculator (to assess everyday reasoning skill), can broaden the scope of the examination. The clinician then has the opportunity to examine the client's problem-solving ability, while not unduly penalizing a client because of limited mental or written calculation ability.

Reasoning and problem-solving questions ("What would you do to find your way out of a forest in which you were lost in the daytime?") should be framed with details with which a client from another culture would have some reasonable familiarity. For example, rather than asking "What would you do if, while in a theater, you were the first to see smoke and fire?" it may be more appropriate to ask, "What would you do if you came home to find your place on fire?"

Questions aimed at assessment of *abstracting* skill may also need to be modified for the multicultural client. Some questions may be universally answerable ("In what way are an orange and a banana alike?" or "In what way are a table and a chair alike?"), but others may not be readily applicable ("In what way are a boat and an automobile alike?" or "In what way are a corkscrew and a hammer alike?").

Proverb interpretation has been used to assess abstracting skill. Many expressions familiar to people in the United States have significant roots in Western society (ask the client to explain the saying, "Strike while the iron is hot.").

Mental status examination procedures can be useful to ascertain enough information to raise hypotheses about neurocognitive functioning, but they should also be carefully interpreted in light of cultural variables. As is usually the case, concerns raised by the mental status examination during the clinical interview require detailed evaluation by a neurologist, neuropsychologist, or other qualified health care professional.

Summary

This chapter has touched on issues pertinent to conducting a multiculturally sensitive initial interview and mental status examination. Central to the process of gathering valid information is awareness that as with all clients, the data obtained are subject to both the biases of the interviewer and the unique cultural experience of the interviewee. While attending to the broad goals of the interview, the clinician must also be mindful of the client's worldview, cultural identity, and level of acculturation. How the individual expresses a psychological need is deeply rooted in the person's cultural history, so clarifying how culture may be influencing the presenting problem is essential in providing appropriate care.

References

Aponte, J. F., & Barnes, J. M. (1995). Impact of acculturation and moderator variables on the intervention and treatment of ethnic groups. In J. F. Aponte, R. Y. Rivers, & J. Wohl (Eds.), *Psychological interventions and Cultural Diversity* (pp. 19–39). Needham Heights, MA: Allyn & Bacon.

Atkinson, D. R., Morten, G., & Sue, D. W. (1989). A minority identity development model. In D. R. Atkinson, G. Morten, & D. W. Sue (Eds.), *Counseling American minorities* (pp. 35–52). Dubuque, IA: W. C. Brown.

Bemak, F., Chung, R. C., & Bornemann, T. H. (1996). Counseling and psychotherapy with refugees. In P. B, Pedersen, J. G. Draguns, W. J. Lonner, & J. E. Trimble (Eds.), *Counseling across cultures* (4th ed., pp. 243–265). Thousand Oaks, CA: Sage.

Berg-Cross, L., & Takushi-Chinen, R. (1995). Multicultural training models and the Person-in-Culture Interview. In J. G. Ponterotto, J. M. Casas, L. A. Suzuki, & C. M. Alexander (Eds.)., *Handbook of multicultural counseling* (pp. 333–356). Thousand Oaks, CA: Sage.

Corey, G., Corey, M. S., & Callanan, P. (1993). *Issues and ethics in the helping professions*. Pacific Grove, CA: Brooks/Cole.

Dana, R. H. (1992). *Multicultural assessment perspectives for professional psychology*. New York: Allyn & Bacon.

Earley, P. C., & Randel, A. (1995). Cognitive causal mechanisms in human agency: Etic and emic considerations. *Journal of Behaviour Therapy and Experimental Psychiatry, 26*, 221–227.

Evans, L. A., Acosta, F. X., Yamamoto, J., & Skilbeck, W. M. (1984). Orienting psychotherapists to better serve low income and minority patients. *Journal of Clinical Psychology, 40*, 90–96.

Folstein, M. F., Folstein, S. E., & McHugh, P. R. (1975). Mini-Mental State: A practical method for grading the cognitive state of patients for the clinician. *Journal of Psychiatric Research, 12*, 189–198.

Grieger, I., & Ponterotto, J. G. (1995). A framework for assessment in multicultural counseling. In J. G. Ponterotto, J. M. Casas, L. A. Suzuki, &

C. M. Alexander (Eds.)., *Handbook of multicultural mounseling* (pp. 357–374). Thousand Oaks, CA: Sage.

Langs, R. (1989). *The technique of psychoanalytic psychotherapy* (Vol. 1). Northvale, NJ: Jason Aronson.

Leong, F.T.L., & Chou, E. L. (1996). Counseling international students. In P. B. Pedersen, J. G. Draguns, W. J. Lonner, & J. E. Trimble (Eds.), *Counseling across cultures.* (4th ed., pp. 210–242). Thousand Oaks, CA: Sage.

Lonner, W. J., & Ibrahim, F. A. (1996). Appraisal and assessment in cross-cultural counseling. In P. B. Pedersen, J. G. Draguns, W. J. Lonner, & J. E. Trimble (Eds.), *Counseling across cultures* (4th ed., pp. 293–322). Thousand Oaks, CA: Sage.

McGoldrick, M., Giordano, J., & Pearce, J. K. (Eds.). (1996). *Ethnicity and family therapy* (2nd ed.). New York: Guilford Press.

Mezzich, J. E., Kleinman, A., Fabrega, H., & Parron, D. L. (Eds.). (1996). *Culture and psychiatric diagnosis: A DSM-IV perspective.* Washington, DC: American Psychiatric Association Press.

Shea, S. C. (1988). *Psychiatric interviewing: The art of understanding.* Philadelphia: Saunders.

Stringer, A. Y. (1996). *A guide to adult neuropsychological diagnosis.* Philadelphia: F. A. Davis.

Strub, R., & Black, F. W. (1993). *The mental status examination in neurology.* Philadelphia: F. A. Davis.

Sue, D. W., & Sue, D. (1999). *Counseling the culturally different: Theory and practice* (3rd ed.). New York: Wiley.

Sue, D., Sue, D. W., & Sue, S. (1997). *Understanding abnormal behavior* (4th ed.). Boston: Houghton-Mifflin.

Sullivan, H. S. (1954). *The psychiatric interview.* New York: Norton.

Tanaka-Matsumi, J., & Higginbotham, H. N. (1996). Behavioral approaches to counseling across cultures. In P. B. Pedersen, J. G. Draguns, W. J. Lonner, & J. E. Trimble (Eds.), *Counseling across cultures* (4th ed., pp. 266–292). Thousand Oaks, CA: Sage.

Trzepacz, P. T., & Baker, R. W. (1993). *The psychiatric mental status examination.* New York: Oxford University Press.

Wohi, M., Lesser, I., & Smith, M. (1997). Clinical presentations of depression in African American and white outpatients. *Culture, Diversity and Mental Health, 3,* 279–284.

4

. . . .

Cultural Identity and Multicultural Assessment

Quantitative and Qualitative Tools for the Clinician

Joseph G. Ponterotto, Denise Gretchen, and Rahul V. Chauhan

In a way, multicultural assessment and cultural identity assessment are synonymous, in that one cannot conduct a comprehensive clinical assessment without accounting for issues of cultural identity, including racial, ethnic, spiritual, sexual-orientation, and gender components of that identity. This chapter focuses on assessing cultural identity as an integral component of the assessment process. Our particular emphasis is on issues of racial identity, ethnic identity, and acculturation, though we acknowledge the importance of assessing one's spiritual identity, sexual-orientation identity, gender identity, and social-class identity (Bowman and others, in press; Fouad and Brown, 2000; Fukuyama and Sevig, 2000; Lowe and Mascher, in press; Pope-Davis and Coleman, in press).

This chapter addresses both nomothetic (quantitative) and idiographic (qualitative) measures of cultural identity. Our use of the

---

This chapter is dedicated to the memory of Leo Goldman (1920–1999), who was a pioneer in promoting qualitative tools for the assessment process. Leo was also very courageous, speaking his mind even if the "voice" was a dissenting or unpopular one.

terms *nomothetic* and *idiographic* parallels that of Hood and Johnson (1997), who were writing from a counseling perspective.

Nomothetic, originating in the Latin *nomos*, refers to law and focuses on assessments that are standardized and that allow comparison of the individual client with larger normative data sets. Multiple-choice and Likert-type acculturation and identity assessments used primarily for large-sample research would fall in the nomothetic category of assessment.

By contrast, the term *idiographic*, with its semantic origins in the Latin *idios*, or "personal," focuses on garnering a descriptive and comprehensive understanding of an individual client without regard to comparative normative data.

Our discussion opens with a brief review of the status of nomothetic assessment in cultural identity and directs the reader to recent major integrative reviews of these instruments. The second and more substantive part of this chapter reviews and integrates semistructured assessment protocols that consider identity in an individualized or idiographic manner. Our bias is that both quantitative and qualitative assessment measures are of value, and that the astute clinician will be familiar with assessments across the testing spectrum. The chapter includes a detailed Appendix, which presents an integrated idiographic multicultural assessment protocol that can serve as a helpful road map for the clinician working in a culturally diverse society.

Nomothetic Identity Assessment Instruments

The last decade has witnessed extensive attention to developing and testing nomothetic measures of acculturation, ethnic identity, and racial identity. Incorporating these measures is now common practice in multicultural studies, as researchers acknowledge and attempt to assess the great heterogeneity existing within racial and ethnic groups residing in the United States.

In the past decade, there have been a number of integrative reviews of the roughly one hundred self-report instruments that assess some component of cultural identity. Rather than replicate these recent reviews by critiquing individual assessment instruments, we instead provide a brief meta-review of the extant reviews. Our meta-review incorporates the reviews of Kohatsu and Richardson (1996), Burlew, Bellow, and Lovett (2000), Cuellar (2000), Roysircar-Sodowsky and Maestas (2000), Kim and Abreu (in press), and Fischer and Moradi (in press).

In the inaugural edition of this *Handbook*, Kohatsu and Richardson (1996) classified cultural identity instruments along three tiers or levels. Tier one included a critique of instruments based on Nigrescence (Cross, 1995) and racial identity (Helms, 1995) theory that were widely used in psychological research. Among the instruments critiqued were Helms's racial identity scales and the Developmental Inventory of Black Consciousness (Milliones, 1980).

Second-tier measures included more recently developed scales that Kohatsu and Richardson (1996) perceived as psychometrically promising on the basis of initial data reports. Included in this category were the Visible Racial/Ethnic Group Identity Attitude Scale (Helms and Carter, 1990), the African Self-Consciousness Scale (Baldwin and Bell, 1985), and the Oklahoma Racial Attitudes Scale (Choney and Behrens, 1996).

Finally, third-tier measures reviewed by Kohatsu and Richardson (1996) included newer identity measures and some unpublished instruments that the authors thought held psychometric promise. The most notable instrument reviewed in this section was the Multigroup Ethnic Identity Measure (Phinney, 1992).

In the concluding section of the review, Kohatsu and Richardson (1996) highlighted recent progress in construct operationalization but also called for more sophisticated identity measures that tap multiple components of identity development, and that use qualitative methodology to gain greater insight into the complexity of the constructs.

Recently, Burlew, Bellow, and Lovett (2000) critiqued nineteen racial identity measures organized into four broad categories. The first category, labeled "identity formation," included instruments conceptualized from stage models and from broader developmental bases (clusters of behavioral tendencies). Examples of instruments included in this category were the Black Personality Questionnaire (Williams, 1981), and the Racial Identity Attitude Scale (Parham and Helms, 1981).

The second category, "cultural connectedness," focused on affiliation with one's racial group and commitment to traditions and values associated with that racial heritage. Instruments reviewed under this rubric included the Multidimensional Racial Identification Scale (Sanders-Thompson, 1992), the African Self-Consciousness Scale (Baldwin and Bell, 1985), and the African American Acculturation Scale (Landrine and Klonoff, 1994).

Burlew, Bellow, and Lovett's third classification of racial identity measures (2000) was labeled "multicultural experiences/racial attitudes." This broad grouping of instruments assessed racial attitudes and perceptions of experiences and interactions with other racial groups. Instruments included in this section (Cultural Mistrust Inventory, Terrell and Terrell, 1981; Acculturation Stress Scale, Williams-Flourney and Anderson, 1996; and Perceived Racism Scale, McNeilly and others, 1996) are not usually associated with racial identity per se but were included in this category given Burlew, Bellow, and Lovett's belief that to "the extent that individuals develop perceptions about and interactions with other groups, it is important to have measures that facilitate research in this area" (2000, p. 176).

The fourth category of instruments reviewed in Burlew, Bellow, and Lovett (2000) was labeled "multidimensional measures" because the content of the chosen instruments transcended two or more of the other categories and included multidimensional components. Examples of such instruments were the Multidimensional Inventory of Black Identity (Sellers and others, 1997) and the Multigroup Ethnic Identity Measure (Phinney, 1992).

A strength of the Burlew, Bellow, and Lovett (2000) review was the logical classification of instruments into rationally selected labels: identity formation, cultural connectedness, multicultural experiences and racial attitudes, and multidimensional instruments. By examining specific item content, the authors were able to logically locate and identify the emphasis underlying each instrument. A limitation of the Burlew, Bellow, and Lovett review was that it failed to identify specific psychometric limitations of the instruments. The many validity and reliability concerns repeatedly expressed with regard to the whole set of instruments were glossed over (see Sabnani and Ponterotto, 1992).

In an interesting contribution to the literature, Cucllar (2000) traces the history of acculturation measurement, identifying, in chronological sequence, thirty-one acculturation measures. Importantly, Cuellar discusses the complexity of acculturation in terms of unidirectional and orthogonal models. The unidirectional model implies that as a person acculturates to the host U.S. mainstream culture, there is a corresponding weakening of ties to the home culture (culture of origin). This unidirectional approach is now seen by most researchers to underestimate the complexity of acculturation, a construct that is now viewed as orthogonal and bidimensional. The orthogonal view (see Kim and Abreu, in press) holds that an immigrant to the United States can be simultaneously committed (or uncommitted) to both the culture of origin and the U.S. mainstream culture.

Cuellar's review (2000) further notes that clinical scales (such as the MMPI) are more sensitive to the influence of acculturation than to normal personality traits. He also concludes that less acculturated persons who are also less educated and of lower socioeconomic means tend to score higher (more severe) on psychopathology measures. However, we believe these conclusions should be interpreted cautiously since the particular studies Cuellar (2000) reviewed to arrive at these conclusions were not specified, nor was the particular acculturation measure or model (unidimensional versus orthogonal) used, nor was cultural validity of the pathology measures assessed.

A major strength of the Cuellar review (2000) is that he links acculturation measurement to personality assessment and clinical assessment practices. The instruments traced by Cuellar were not critiqued psychometrically, as that was not the purpose of his chapter.

In another recent contribution to cultural identity, Roysircar-Sodowsky and Maestas (2000) also trace historic developments in acculturation research from the late 1970s to the present. These authors clarify the distinction between acculturation and ethnic identity, claiming that acculturation is a useful construct for first-generation immigrant groups that engage in a continuous process of adapting to U.S. mainstream culture. By comparison, ethnic identity is perceived as befitting U.S.-born children of immigrants who grapple with what aspects of their original ethnic cultures are most important to retain and fit into their evolving worldview. Incorporating a thorough review of the literature, Roysircar-Sodowsky and Maestas conclude that ethnic identity and acculturation alike are mediated—both at the individual and group level—by acculturative stress and intercultural competence.

As part of their review, Roysircar-Sodowsky and Maestas (2000) summarize psychometric data on eleven acculturation instruments, two acculturative stress instruments, and three ethnic identity instruments. A major contribution of this review is the depth and care taken by the authors to distinguish between acculturation and ethnic identity, and the acknowledgement of acculturative stress in mediating these processes.

Recently, Kim and Abreu (in press) reviewed thirty-three instruments, the majority of which focused on Hispanic Americans. Each instrument was reviewed along three categories: measurement model (unilinear, bilinear), dimensions (values, behaviors, knowledge, and cultural identity), and psychometrics. With regard to the measure-ment model, unilinear instruments were further classified as either monocultural or dual cultural. A monocultural unilinear instrument (for instance, Na Mea Hawai'I, a Native Hawaiian acculturation scale; Rezentes, 1993) yielded one continuous scale where the end-points indicated low and high involvement in one's culture.

Dual-cultural unilinear instrumentation (such as the African American Acculturation Scale; Landrine and Klonoff, 1994) also used one continuous scale, but one endpoint indicated high involve-ment in one's culture of origin while the opposite endpoint indicated high involvement with the host U.S. culture (and consequently low involvement with the culture of origin). A midscore on dual-cultural unilinear measures is considered bicultural. Bilinear scales reviewed by Kim and Abreu (for example, the Acculturation Rating Scale for Mexican Americans II; Cuellar, Arnold, and Maldonado, 1995) were those that yielded two independent scores representing both the cul-ture of origin and the host culture. Thus, in this measurement model, one can be high (or low) in both cultures simultaneously.

Each instrument was examined for its representative dimen-sional emphasis, which could fall under values (beliefs about cul-tural customs), behavior (friendship choices), knowledge (culture-specific information), and cultural identity (cultural iden-tification). Finally, reliability and validity evidence for each instru-ment is presented and evaluated. The Kim and Abreu review represents a state-of-the-art contribution in acculturation theory and measurement because the authors successfully disentangle the confusion regarding the complexity and dimensions of the accul-turation construct. It has been very difficult to integrate the results of past acculturation studies because so many instruments based on differing definitions and dimensions have been used. Guidelines pre-sented in Kim and Abreu allow researchers to work systematically in examining psychological correlates of acculturation.

Whereas the Kim and Abreu review (in press) focused on accul-turation, the recent Fischer and Moradi (in press) review focused on instruments assessing racial and ethnic identity. These authors critiqued twelve instruments selected for their focus on "the meaning and importance of race or ethnicity to an individual at a given time" (p. 3). The instruments were generally rooted in social identity theory, with an emphasis on a sense of belonging to one's racial or ethnic group; and in identity formation theory, with an emphasis on developmental aspects of making meaning and decisions about the role of ethnicity in one's life (see Phinney, 1992).

The Fischer and Moradi review (in press) examines the theoretical base, psychometric development, and reliability and validity status of the selected instruments. Particular strengths of this review include the care the authors took to define their concepts and find their focus, the depth and sophistication of the psychometric critiques, the purposeful coverage of varied instruments across many groups (such as Jewish identity and various multigroup measures), and the specific directions and guidelines for future research on racial and ethnic identity development.

Collectively, the set of reviews we have covered in this section have brought the field of cultural identity assessment to a higher plateau of sophistication. These reviewers have clarified the multiple dimensions of identity and acculturation and have posited important directions for theoretical work. After years of often scattered and fragmented research, we are now at the point where systematic research can proceed using sophisticated quantitative instrumentation. We now turn to some guidelines for using quantitative measures in research.

Guidelines for Selecting and Using Quantitative Identity Measures for Research

As the multicultural emphasis in applied psychology continues to grow (Heppner, Casas, Carter, and Stone, 2000; Fouad and Brown, 2000; Ponterotto, Fuertes, and Chen, 2000), so too does reliance on cultural identity measures in research programs. Given the large selection of instruments available, we offer the following general guidelines for selecting and using these research instruments.

Construct Clarity and Definition

Researchers should attend carefully to the construct they are attempting to measure. Is it acculturation, racial identity, or ethnic identity? Careful definition of the construct should be presented and linked rationally to the particular research instrument chosen. As highlighted in the reviews discussed in the previous section, some identity measures focus heavily on behavior (preferred language and foods, friendship choices), while others focus more on a sense of pride and affiliation with one's racial or ethnic group of origin. Researchers should consider which content emphasis most closely matches their construct definition and research plan.

Construct Dimensionality

Closely related to construct clarity is the instrument's proposed and documented dimensionality. Investigators should match their definition of the identity construct with distinct dimensions measured by a particular instrument. If an instrument is designed to be multidimensional (that is, with independent or interrelated subscales), researchers should take care that a sufficient number of scale items be included within each dimension or subscale.

Psychometric Properties

A reading of the reviews discussed previously, along with our own assessment of these measures (see Ponterotto, Baluch, and Carielli, 1998; Sabnani and Ponterotto, 1992), leads us to conclude that a majority of identity instruments have minimal to moderate levels of validity and reliability. This raises concern as the collective group of measures is witnessing increasing use in research without adequate attention to psychometric concerns. Notwithstanding this caveat, some instruments are more conceptually robust and psychometrically sound than others (see particularly Fischer and Moradi, in press; and Kim and Abreu, in press, for selecting particular measures). Therefore, we offer researchers a number of psychometric guidelines in selecting particular measures.

Construct Validity

The construct validity of the instrument should be established through both convergent and discriminant tests (Ponterotto, 1996). Hopefully, the instrument has factor analysis support using both exploratory (see Merenda, 1997; Thompson and Daniel, 1996) and structural equation modeling (specifically, confirmatory factor analysis) procedures (Quintana and Maxwell, 1999). This is essential in supporting the proposed dimensionality of the instrument.

Criterion-Related Validity

Criterion-related validity, whether through concurrent or predictive means (Ponterotto, 1996), should be available on each of the instrument's dimensions or subscales. It is not helpful to report criterion-related validity for an instrument's total score only, if in fact the instrument's structure is bidimensional or multidimensional. In these cases, criterion validity coefficients should be calculated for each dimension or subscale; in doing so, criterion measures often need to be differentially selected for each dimension, dependent on theoretical predictions and subscale interdependence.

Reliability

Both internal-consistency (coefficient alpha) and test-retest stability measures of reliability should be available on the instrument and its respective subscales. For large-sample research, where participants are anonymous and group mean comparison or correlational tests are incorporated, we recommend a minimum coefficient alpha of .70 (see Ponterotto, 1996).

Test Validity and Reliability

Importantly, dependent on the extent of available psychometric data on an instrument, we suggest researchers use their studies to further test the validity and reliability of selected measures. Accordingly, we advocate conducting factor analyses and internal consistency tests for each new sample, rather than simply using the identity measure as an independent or dependent variable. Furthermore, means and standard deviations for subscale scores can be compared to extant samples and normative data to assess response patterns in the new sample. Given the relative youth (in psychometric terms) of identity measures, such added procedures in all ongoing research contribute to collective assessment of instrument strengths and limitations.

Idiographic Tools

The quantitative self-report measures we have discussed are frequently used in research on cultural identity, racial identity, and acculturation. The instruments are user-friendly, relatively brief, and easily incorporated into research packets completed by clients and students. In our experience, however, we find that clinicians, in their day-to-day therapy work, rarely incorporate content from these instruments. The measures are not readily adaptable to flowing clinical conversation, though various authors have attempted to adapt the research-based instruments for such use (see Garrett and Pichette, 2000; Ponterotto, 1987; Ponterotto, Baluch, and Carielli, 1998).

Over the years, practitioner-oriented scholars have developed more idiographic, semistructured interview protocols that help the clinician and client explore issues of cultural identity, acculturation, racial and ethnic identity, and so forth. We have come across a number of these interview protocols in the literature and have used them in our multicultural training and practice over the past decade or so. In this section, we briefly review six semistructured interview protocols or clinical frameworks for multicultural assessment generally, and cultural identity assessment specifically.

After reviewing the separate protocols, we integrate their content and emphases to form a holistic and comprehensive clinical interview guide. The six frameworks for practice (Table 4.1) are the DSM Fourth Edition's Outline for Cultural Formulation (American Psychiatric Association, 1994), Dana's Cultural

Table 4.1. Cultural identity assessment models.

Stage	DSM IV (1994)	Washington (1994)	Grieger and Ponterotto (1995)	Dana (1998)	Jacobsen (1988)	Berg-Cross and Takushi-Chinen (1995)
1	Cultural identity of individual	Cultural inventory	Client's level of psychological mindedness	Relationship based on client-provider match	Obtaining client's ethnocultural heritage	Psychodynamic questions: how does client deal with feelings of shame and anger?
2	Cultural explanations of the individual's illness	Cultural literacy	Family's level of psychological mindedness	Acculturation evaluation	Client's ethnocultural translocation	Humanistic questions: what needs are being met and what needs are not, as based on Maslow's hierarchy (1968)?
3	Cultural factors related to psychosocial environment and levels of functioning	Cultural history	Client's and family's attitudes toward helping and counseling	Problem specification	Client's perception of family's ethnocultural adjustment	Family systems questions: distribution of power and family cohesiveness

4	Cultural elements of the relationship between individual and clinician	Client's level of acculturation	Formal assessment	Client's view of his or her individual ethnocultural adjustment	Existential questions: how does client confront the most basic philosophical issues of his or her existence?
5	Overall cultural assessment for diagnosis and care	Family's level of acculturation	Cultural interventions	Consideration of therapist's ethnocultural background	
6		Family's attitude toward acculturation	Evaluation of assessment		

Assessment Model (1998), Jacobsen's Ethnocultural Assessment Model (1988), Washington's Wittgensteinian Model (1994), Grieger and Ponterotto's Applied Assessment Framework (1995), and Berg-Cross and Takushi-Chinen's Person-in-Culture Interview (1995). This section of the chapter can serve as a supplement to the previous chapter in this volume, which also focuses on idiographic assessment.

DSM-IV Outline for Cultural Formulation

DSM-IV's Outline for Cultural Formulation is a supplement to the DSM's multiaxial diagnostic assessment and attempts to address the difficulties that occur in applying DSM-IV criteria within a multicultural environment (DSM-IV; American Psychiatric Association, 1994). The outline allows the clinician to assess and evaluate the client's symptoms within a cultural context.

The outline details five areas that allow the clinician to create a narrative of the client's cultural formulation. The first area, *cultural identity of the client*, involves noting the individual's cultural identity, which includes culture of origin, host culture, and language abilities. The second, the *cultural explanation of the individual's illness*, involves identifying how the individual communicates distress to the clinician. Here, the clinician notes the perceived severity of the individual's symptoms in relation to the norms of the client's cultural group. Also, the clinician notes any past treatment of distress and illness within the client's cultural group practices.

The third area in the cultural formulation, *cultural factors related to psychosocial environment and levels of functioning*, involves the clinician noting the client's cultural interpretations of social stressors, available social supports, and levels of functioning and disability. The fourth area, *cultural elements of the relationship between the individual and the clinician*, instructs the clinician to explore any differences in culture and social status between the clinician and the individual that influence diagnosis and treatment. This includes any language barriers and difficulties building intimacy in the relationship for proper assessment and diagnosis. The fifth and final area, *overall cultural assessment for diagnosis and care*, involves a discussion of how cultural issues influence diagnosis and care.

Dana's Cultural Assessment Model

Dana's Six-Step Cultural Assessment Model (1998) begins with an assessment of a client-provider match with regard to race, ethnicity, language, service delivery style, service setting décor, and client perception of the provider's personality and competence. The second step requires an acculturation assessment, which leads to client disclosure and discussion of his or her cultural identity formulation. This step allows the client to disclose his or her issues within the context of culture and leads the counseling process to the third step, which is specification of the client's problem.

The fourth step in Dana's model involves selecting and administering psychological assessment tools and providing feedback regarding assessment results to the client, family, and significant others. The fifth step includes deciding upon culture-general or culture-specific interventions. Culture-general interventions are more mainstream, those commonly taught in most counseling and clinical psychology programs. These interventions are likely to be effective with assimilated or highly acculturated clients who are fully fluent in the English language.

Culture-specific interventions use cultural formulations for diagnosis, referral to indigenous healers, and selection of interventions that incorporate cultural elements. These interventions are typically emphasized with non-English speakers or those clients with rudimentary English fluency who have a traditional worldview, health and illness beliefs, culture-specific symptomology, or culture-bound disorders. For bicultural clients, for whom English is a second language, Dana recommends a combined interactive approach using both culture-general and culture-specific interventions. The final step in Dana's model includes evaluation of the assessment procedures used by the counselor, the client, and others involved in the treatment process.

Jacobsen's Ethnocultural Assessment Model

Jacobsen's Five-Stage Ethnocultural Assessment Model (1988) considers the various transitions and determinants of ethnocultural identity. Jacobsen discusses ethnocultural identity as an important aspect of one's whole identity that is influenced by transitional circumstances, such as migration and changes in group sociopolitical, economic, or health status. One's transitions at various points in the life cycle are tied to the sociocultural character and saliency of ethnocultural transitions occurring frequently in the United States.

The ethnocultural assessment model allows the practitioner to assess and explore the client's intellectual and emotional understanding of his or her ethnocultural identity. It stems from a perspective that the client's ethnocultural identity has evolved through a history of circumstances. The model's five stages of assessment are designed to assist clinicians working with ethnoculturally translocated clients. It can be used to explore the cultural determinants of identity in a psychotherapeutic or diagnostic setting.

Jacobsen's first stage of assessment involves gathering accurate information on the client's ethnocultural heritage by asking specific questions related to the individual's maternal and paternal lines of cultural origin. Jacobsen (1988) sees this as an intensive process that includes information beyond questions regarding geographical origin, so that the practitioner can avoid stereotyping and develop greater understanding of complex multicultural backgrounds. The second stage focuses on the circumstances of the client's ethnocultural translocation by asking questions that relate to the sociopolitical issues occurring in the country of origin. Other questions relate to the thoughts and feelings of the client's translocation. Jacobsen points out that the historical account of the client is invaluable in the assessment process.

The third stage focuses on the client's cognitive and emotional perceptions with regard to the family's developing a "niche" in their new home host country. Questions of whether the family has stayed together in the new country or whether they are dispersed through-out the country are relevant here. Often the client's perception of current family identity varies from that described as having existed back in the culture(s) of origin.

The fourth stage examines the client's own personal cultural experience and challenges transitioning into the new country as separate from the family's adjustment. The fifth and final stage of the assessment focuses on the practitioner's ethnocultural back-ground. The practitioner reflects on her or his own ethnocultural identity and assesses any overlap with the patient. This step includes self-exploration of transference, countertransference, and identifi-cation issues. Jacobsen asserts that the therapist's self-examination is essential if he or she is to understand feelings concerning the dif-ferences between the therapist's background and that of the client.

Washington's Three-Step Wittgensteinian Model

Washington's Three-Step Wittgensteinian Model (1994) outlines a process that instructs counselors to become aware of their own culture and their client's culture. Washington discusses the theoretical framework for his study as being based on Ludwig Wittgenstein's view of culture. The Wittgensteinian approach incorporates the assumption that Western culture consists of numer-ous cultural institutions and that activities in institutions are char-acterized by certain language games and activities. Washington points out that assessment of culture requires understanding "how" the language games or customs play a role in the individual's life. Washington asserts that a major responsibility of counselors involves helping clients unravel emotional language games, char-acterized by distinctive sets of rules, beliefs, symbols, meanings, and role models, from their other cultural acts.

The first step in Washington's model requires the counselor to identity his or her own culture through a cultural inventory. The inventory asks questions about family, language, community, reli-gion, peers, education, and aesthetics. Through this procedure, the individual learns to identify the different institutions, beliefs, and rituals in her or his life. The second step focuses on understanding the client's culture from both etic and emic perspectives. Counselors learn about the culture of the clients they work with. Counselors should be aware of the places in which new knowledge about a client's race, ethnicity, and culture coincide or conflict with preexisting knowledge and beliefs.

Finally, the third step involves taking the client's cultural history. Washington suggests that this is where the counseling process should begin. In this step, the counselor learns the client's cultural history through the Critical Life Events Survey. The survey asks questions about the client's cultural history within the context of the individual's various cultural institutions: education, work, legal issues, health, neighborhood, religion, peer relations, boyfriend or girlfriend or spouse relationships, family, and children. One of the major contributions of counselors may be the teasing out of interpretations of the rules, beliefs, and symbols of the critical skills that are problematic in their lives.

Grieger and Ponterotto's Six-Step Applied Assessment Framework

Grieger and Ponterotto's Six-Step Applied Assessment Framework (1995) considers the importance of assessing clients both as unique individuals and as members of a specific family and cultural group. The framework allows the counselor to obtain an understanding of the "client's orientation to and experience of the counseling process" (p. 358). Central in the assessment framework is the necessity for the practitioner to understand the client's worldview and level of acculturation. Both constructs relate to the client's psychosocial identity process, influenced by cultural variables.

Applying the framework for assessment is done by way of six steps, which assess identified aspects of the client's worldview and level of acculturation that are integral to the counseling process. The first step, *the client's level of psychological mindedness*, examines the client's framework for understanding and interpreting the presenting problems. This step assesses whether the client conceptualizes the concern from a Western psychological perspective or from a more culturally indigenous framework.

The second step, *the family's level of psychological mindedness*, involves understanding the family's interpretation of psychological concerns and the helping process. It is important to note that the family and individual may have differing interpretations of psychological problems. The family's perspective of the client's distress is valuable for the counselor to understand and acknowledge to the client.

In the third step, *the client's and family's attitudes toward helping and counseling*, the counselor attends to both the client's and family's issues around attitudes toward receiving help from outside the family. In this step, it is important to assure the client of confidentiality and appreciate the level of conflict the client may be experiencing in sharing "family secrets" with an outsider.

The fourth step of the model involves assessing the *client's level of acculturation*. Grieger and Ponterotto (1995) indicate that the more acculturated the client is in terms of middle-class American values, the more the client may feel comfortable with the counseling process; conversely, the less acculturated client who is less familiar with Western psychological practices may feel greater distrust of the counseling process.

The fifth step, the *family's level of acculturation*, cautions the counselor not to assume that the client's level of acculturation is similar to the family's level of acculturation. The counselor appreciates and assesses the differences in acculturation level of clients and the clients' families. The differences in acculturation level may create conflict within the client during the counseling process. For example, it is important for counselors to consider what the impact of giving the client "permission" to make choices about assimilation and follow mainstream American culture might be in terms of exacerbating tensions in the family.

The final step in the framework, the *family's attitude toward acculturation*, involves assessing the family's attitude toward both the larger family's and the individual's acculturation attitudes. Sometimes, low-acculturated parents expect the children to also maintain low levels of acculturation; at other times, however, low-acculturation parents may want their children to reach higher levels of acculturation into mainstream Anglo society. The astute counselor appreciates this complexity with regard to negotiating among and between the multiple acculturation levels and attitudes present in the same nuclear and extended family.

Berg-Cross and Takushi-Chinen's Person-in-Culture Interview

Berg-Cross and Takushi-Chinen's Person-in-Culture Interview (PICI; 1995) is a twenty-five-item interview that allows counselors to engage in an interpersonally close encounter with their clients to cultivate cross-cultural understanding. The interview process fosters a therapeutic alliance with culturally different clients and helps the counselor understand the client's cultural worldviews, values, and experiences. It can be used during intakes with culturally different clients, for training therapists working with a diverse clientele, and for other nonclinical purposes (such as personnel or human resource training) to foster tolerance and understanding of cultural differences.

Berg-Cross and Takushi-Chinen assert that the PICI can help counselors avoid errors of stereotyping. They highlight that cultural knowledge devoid of personal knowledge inevitably leads to stereotyping and inability to relate empathically to clients. The PICI provides a cross-cultural assessment experience that is sensitive to cultural issues without stereotyping any particular individual.

The PICI is a one-on-one, open-ended, twenty-five-item interview that incorporates questions formulated from psychodynamic, humanistic, family (systems), and existential psychology. The first seven questions are psychodynamic in nature and relate to the client's unconscious pains and emotions of shame and anger.

The next ten questions are humanistic in orientation and ask about the client's satisfaction of needs based on Maslow's hierarchy of needs (1968). The next two questions are the family systems questions that relate to the power structure and cohesiveness of the client's family. Finally, the last five questions are existential in nature and relate to basic human philosophical issues around existence. Thus, the PICI is designed to help participants explore both the broad worldviews a cultural group may hold and individual expression of these views.

Integration of Idiographic Models

The goal of this section is to integrate the six idiographic assessment models presented in the previous section of this chapter. Here we follow the Gestalt principle that the whole is greater than the sum of its parts. Thus, while each model makes its own unique contribution to assessment of cultural identity, a deeper understanding emerges if the six form a system that incorporates the strengths of its individual contributors.

We begin this brief section with a discussion of provider responsibilities that transcend the various assessment models; we then close with a review of the contextual framework for assessment and with a presentation of a comprehensive protocol.

Provider Responsibilities

Important provider responsibilities focus on understanding power in the therapeutic relationship, and on the necessity of provider self-exploration and self-awareness.

Understanding the Power Differential

Before any provider conducts an assessment of a client's cultural identity, he or she must understand the unique ingredients in such a relationship. Too often, providers of assessment services become engrossed in the activity of assessment and do not reflect on the nature and meaning of assessment itself. Clients come to the assessment process with a belief that the provider has the knowledge and skills to understand their life experiences and meet their expectations, and it is up to the provider not to abuse this trust.

Dana (1998) encourages providers to recognize and understand the power differential that exists between providers and their clients and reminds providers to use the general ethical principles of justice, autonomy, nonmaleficence, and beneficence in conducting assessments. The power and lack of power inherent in the roles of provider and client and in their cultural group status can affect the assessment process and outcome.

Thus, Dana (1998) charges providers with several ethical responsibilities. They should recognize that the meanings conveyed by their own communications are always culture-specific. They are obligated not to misuse their power by demeaning, exploiting, manipulating, sexualizing, stereotyping, or pathologizing their clients. Clinicians must provide services using complete and timely knowledge of information and technical skills, and continuously update this knowledge for the benefit of their clients. Finally, they have an ethical responsibility to protect the provider-client relationship from extraneous influences that impinge on the provider's sense of competency in delivering necessary services (Dana, 1998).

Thus, providers must understand, not deny, the situations in which power exists and has existed for them. They also need to understand how power is used and how they use it. Recognizing the many situations in which power or lack of power may be experienced helps providers clarify the needs, expectations, and tendencies they bring to the cross-cultural assessment situation. We explain the importance of this clarification in greater detail in discussing the importance of provider self-awareness, in the next section.

Provider Self-Exploration and Self-Scrutiny

Related to understanding and awareness of the power differential that exists between providers and their clients are understanding and awareness of the provider's own cultural history and identity.

Washington (1994) and Dana (1998) both mention this element in their models, but neither explains *why* this is important in any great detail. Dana believes providers have an obligation to self-scrutinize their own motives, needs, and behaviors. This, he says, is needed because our society lacks the public scrutiny and community monitoring of the provider's entire life experience that once accompanied the traditional healer. Group practice, peer review, credentialing processes, continuing education, and personal counseling or psychotherapy are poor substitutes for the community protection once provided by living under the constant public scrutiny of the traditional healer in a small village (Dana, 1998). Thus, it is up to the provider to replace the lost social control of his or her behavior with self-control and personal ethics.

Washington (1994) includes a procedure in his three-step model for identifying and discovering one's cultural background as a first step in developing cultural awareness. Through this procedure, the individual learns to identify the different institutions, beliefs, and rituals in his or her life. Although this may intuitively make sense to providers of assessment services to culturally diverse clients, the reason this is important is not readily apparent. Many models of assessment overlook the fact that the provider is a cultural being who brings a network of personal and social identities to the assessment process that can serve as barriers or resources in developing effective provider-client relationships.

Awareness of one's own values, assumptions, and behaviors is necessary for developing the skills that facilitate empathic interaction with clients and appreciation of culturally different others. Such awareness means identifying distortions learned from cultural indoctrination as well as psychological need, and it requires in-depth understanding of one's own cultural background and its meaning (Pinderhughes, 1989). The freedom to assess accurately the many factors that affect a client's life depends on practitioners' clarity and understanding of themselves and their own cultural identity, including the societal position of their own cultural group (Pinderhughes, 1989). It is not possible to assist clients in examining issues concerning cultural identity if providers have not done this work for themselves.

Contextual Framework for Assessment

After the provider has understood the role of power and his or her own cultural identity in the assessment process, the actual assessment can begin. The model presented in the Appendix to this chapter is qualitative or idiographic in nature, and explains what should be assessed when meeting a client in a face-to-face interaction. Assessment is a highly complex process that gathers what can appear to be an overwhelming amount of information about a client. In cross-cultural counseling, it is necessary to assess the client as a cultural entity before any intervention can be implemented (Lonner and Ibrahim, 1996).

We divide the knowledge gained from assessment into four categories. The first three move from micro to macro levels of understanding, while the fourth category creates an interactive context for the helping relationship: (1) the client's worldview and understanding of his or her problem; (2) the client's family background; (3) cultural explanations of the individual's illness; and (4) cultural elements of the provider-client relationship, which highlights the importance of the provider's understanding of the impact his or her own culture has on the assessment process.

The framework we propose here mirrors that presented in the DSM-IV, but it goes beyond the DSM's model and incorporates recommendations from all six models. It should be noted that although we discuss these elements in a particular sequence with what appears to be clear boundaries between levels, actual face-to-face assessment is not such a linear process. A provider must be aware that information from all four levels appears more or less simultaneously. It is the provider's responsibility to ensure all relevant information is obtained from the assessment, as well as to consciously monitor cultural elements that affect the provider-client relationship. The clinical framework presented in the Appendix is meant to be an outline providers can follow when consulting with clients about their presenting problems. The data collected using such an idiographic assessment process is expected to take more than one session and is viewed as a continuous part of the therapeutic interaction. Clinicians can modify and adapt this model to meet the specific demands of their service delivery setting.

References

American Psychiatric Association. (1994). *Diagnostic and statistical manual of mental disorders* (4th ed.). Washington, DC: Author.

Baldwin, J. A., & Bell, Y. (1985). The African Self-Consciousness Scale: An Africentric personality questionnaire. *Western Journal of Black Studies, 9*, 61–68.

Berg-Cross., L., & Takushi-Chinen, R. (1995). Multicultural training models and the Person-in-Culture Interview. In J. G. Ponterotto, J. M. Casas, L. A. Suzuki, & C. M. Alexander (Eds.), *Handbook of multicultural counseling* (pp. 333–356). Thousand Oaks, CA: Sage.

Bowman, S. L., Rasheed, S., Ferris, J., Thompson, D., McRae, M., & Weitzman, L. (in press). Interface of feminism and multiculturalism: Where are the women of color? In J. G. Ponterotto, J. M. Casas, L. A. Suzuki, & C. M. Alexander (Eds.), *Handbook of multicultural counseling* (2nd ed.). Thousand Oaks, CA: Sage.

Burlew, A. K., Bellow, S., & Lovett, M. (2000). Racial identity measures: A review and classification system. In R. H. Dana (Ed.), *Handbook of cross-cultural and multicultural personality assessment* (pp. 173–196). Hillsdale, NJ: Erlbaum.

Choney, S. K., & Behrens, J. T. (1996). Development of the Oklahoma Racial Attitudes Scale preliminary form (ORAS-P). In G. Roysircar Sodowsky & J. C. Impara (Eds.), *Multicultural assessment in counseling and clinical psychology* (pp. 225–240). Lincoln, NB: Buros Institute of Mental Measurements.

Cross, W. E., Jr. (1995). The psychology of nigrescence: Revising the Cross model. In J. G. Ponterotto, J. M. Casas, L. A. Suzuki, & C. M. Alexander (Eds.), *Handbook of multicultural counseling* (pp. 93–122). Thousand Oaks, CA: Sage.

Cuellar, I. (2000). Acculturation as a moderator of personality and psychological assessment. In R. H. Dana (Ed.), *Handbook of cross-cultural and multicultural personality assessment* (pp. 113–129). Hillsdale, NJ: Erlbaum.

Cuellar, I., Arnold, B., & Maldonado, R. (1995). The Acculturation Rating Scale for Mexican Americans–II (ARSMA-II): A revision of the original ARSMA scale. *Hispanic Journal of Behavioral Sciences, 17,* 275–304.

Dana, R. H. (1998). *Understanding cultural identity in intervention and assessment.* Thousand Oaks, CA: Sage.

Fischer, A. R., & Moradi, B. (in press). Racial and ethnic identity: Recent developments and needed directions. In J. G. Ponterotto, J. M. Casas, L. A. Suzuki, & C. M. Alexander (Eds.), *Handbook of multicultural counseling* (2nd ed.). Thousand Oaks, CA: Sage.

Fouad, N. A., & Brown, M. T. (2000). Role of race and social class in development: Implications for counseling psychology. In S. D. Brown & R. W. Lent (Eds.), *Handbook of counseling psychology* (3rd ed., pp. 379–408). New York: Wiley.

Fukuyama, M. A., & Sevig, T. D. (2000). *Integrating spirituality into multicultural counseling.* Thousand Oaks, CA: Sage.

Garrett, M. T., & Pichette, E. F. (2000). Red as an apple: Native American acculturation and counseling with or without reservation. *Journal of Counseling and Development, 78,* 3–13.

Grieger, I., & Ponterotto, J. G. (1995). A framework for assessment in multicultural counseling. In J. G. Ponterotto, J. M. Casas, L. A. Suzuki, & C. M. Alexander (Eds.), *Handbook of multicultural counseling* (pp. 357–374). Thousand Oaks, CA: Sage.

Helms, J. E. (1995). An update of Helms's white and people of color racial identity models. In J. G. Ponterotto, J. M. Casas, L. A. Suzuki, & C. M. Alexander (Eds.), *Handbook of multicultural counseling* (pp. 181–198). Thousand Oaks, CA: Sage.

Helms, J. E., & Carter, R. T. (1990). *A preliminary overview of the Cultural Identity Attitude Scale.* Unpublished manuscript. Department of Psychology, University of Maryland, College Park.

Heppner, P. P., Casas, J. M., Carter, J., & Stone, G. L. (2000). The maturation of counseling psychology: Multifaceted perspectives, 1978–1998. In S. D. Brown & R. W. Lent (Eds.), *Handbook of counseling psychology* (3rd ed., pp. 3–49). New York. Wiley.

Hood, A. B., & Johnson, R. W. (1997). *Assessment in counseling: A guide to the use of psychological assessment procedures* (2nd ed.). Alexandria, VA: American Counseling Association.

Jacobsen, F. M. (1988). Ethnocultural assessment. In L. Comas-Diaz & E.E.H. Griffith (Eds.), *Clinical guidelines in cross-cultural mental health* (pp. 135–147). New York: Wiley.

Kim, B.S.K., & Abreu, J. (in press). Acculturation measurement: Theory, current instruments, and future directions. In J. G. Ponterotto, J. M. Casas, L. A. Suzuki, & C. M. Alexander (Eds.), *Handbook of multicultural counseling* (2nd ed.). Thousand Oaks, CA: Sage.

Kohatsu, E. L., & Richardson, T. Q. (1996). Racial and ethnic identity assessment. In L. A. Suzuki, P. J. Meller, & J. G. Ponterotto (Eds.), *Handbook of multicultural assessment: Clinical, psychological, and educational applications* (pp. 611–650). San Francisco: Jossey-Bass.

Landrine, H., & Klonoff, E. (1994). The African American Acculturation Scale: Development, reliability, and validity. *Journal of Black Psychology, 20,* 104–127.

Lonner, W. J., & Ibrahim, F. A. (1996). Appraisal and assessment in cross-cultural counseling. In P. B. Pedersen, J. G. Draguns, W. J. Lonner, & J. E. Trimble (Eds.), *Counseling across cultures* (4th ed., pp. 293–322). Thousand Oaks, CA: Sage.

Lowe, S. M., & Mascher, J. (in press). The role of sexual orientation in multicultural counseling: Integrating bodies of knowledge. In J. G. Ponterotto, J. M. Casas, L. A. Suzuki, & C. M. Alexander (Eds.), *Handbook of multicultural counseling* (2nd ed.). Thousand Oaks, CA: Sage.

Maslow, A. (1968). *Toward a psychology of being.* New York: Van Nostrand Reinhold.

McNeilly, M., Anderson, N., Robinson, E., McManus, C., Armsteas, C., Clark, R., Pieper, C., Simons, P., & Saulter, T. (1996). Convergent, discriminant, and concurrent validity of the Perceived Racism Scale: A multidimensional assessment of the experience of racism among African Americans. In R. Jones (Ed.), *Handbook of tests and measurements for black populations* (Vol. 2, pp. 359–374). Hampton, VA: Cobb and Henry.

Merenda, P. F. (1997). A guide to the proper use of factor analysis in the conduct and reporting of research: Pitfalls to avoid. *Measurement and Evaluation in Counseling and Development, 30,* 156–164.

Milliones, J. (1980). Construction of a black consciousness measure: Psychotherapeutic implications. *Psychotherapy: Theory, Research and Practice, 17,* 175–182.

Parham, T. A., & Helms, J. E. (1981). The influence of black students' racial identity attitudes on preferences for counselor's race. *Journal of Counseling Psychology, 28,* 250–257.

Phinney, J. S. (1992). The Multigroup Ethnic Identity Measure: A new scale for use with diverse groups. *Journal of Adolescent Research, 7,* 156–176.

Pinderhughes, E. (1989). *Understanding race, ethnicity, and power: The key to efficacy in clinical practice*. New York: Free Press.

Ponterotto, J. G. (1987). Counseling Mexican Americans: A multimodal approach. *Journal of Counseling and Development, 65*, 308–312.

Ponterotto, J. G. (1996). Evaluating and selecting research instruments. In F.T.L. Leong & J. T. Austin (Eds.), *The psychology research handbook: A guide for graduate students and research assistants* (pp. 73–84). Thousand Oaks, CA: Sage.

Ponterotto, J. G., Baluch, S., & Carielli, D. (1998). The Suinn-Lew Asian Self-Identity Acculturation Scale (SL-ASIA): Critique and research recommendations. *Measurement and Evaluation in Counseling and Development, 31*, 109–124.

Ponterotto, J. G., Fuertes, J. N., & Chen, E. C. (2000). Models of multicultural counseling. In S. D. Brown & R. W. Lent (Eds.), *Handbook of counseling psychology* (3rd ed., pp. 639–669). New York: Wiley.

Pope-Davis, D. B., & Coleman, H.L.K. (Eds.). (in press). *The intersection of race, class, and gender: Implications for multicultural counseling*. Thousand Oaks, CA: Sage.

Quintana, S. M., & Maxwell, S. E. (1999). Implications of recent developments in structural equation modeling for counseling psychology. *Counseling Psychologist, 27*, 485–527.

Rezentes, W. C. (1993). Na Mea Hawai'I: A Hawaiian acculturation scale. *Psychological Reports, 73*, 383–393.

Roysircar-Sodowsky, G., & Maestas, M. V. (2000). Acculturation, ethnic identity, and acculturative stress: Evidence and measurement. In R. H. Dana (Ed.), *Handbook of cross-cultural and multicultural personality assessment* (pp. 131–172). Hillsdale, NJ: Erlbaum.

Sabnani, H. B., & Ponterotto, J. G. (1992). Racial/ethnic minority-specific instrumentation in counseling research: A review, critique, and recommendations. *Measurement and Evaluation in Counseling and Development, 24*, 161–187.

Sanders-Thompson, V. (1992). A multifaceted approach to the conceptualization of African American identification. *Journal of Black Studies, 23*, 75–85.

Sellers, R., Rowley, S., Chavous, T., Shelton, J. N., & Smith, M. (1997). Multidimensional Inventory of Black Identity: A preliminary investigation of reliability and construct validity. *Journal of Personality and Social Psychology, 73*, 805–815.

Terrell, F., & Terrell, S. (1981). An inventory to measure cultural mistrust among blacks. *Western Journal of Black Studies, 5*, 180–185.

Thompson, B., & Daniel, L. G. (1996). Factor analytic evidence for the
    construct validity of scores: A historical overview and some guidelines.
    Educational and Psychological Measurement, 56, 197–208.

Washington, E. D. (1994). Three steps to cultural awareness: A Wittgensteinian
    approach. In P. Pedersen & J. C. Carey (Eds.), *Multicultural counseling in
    schools: A practical handbook* (pp. 81–102). Needham Heights, MA: Allyn
    & Bacon.

Williams, R. L. (1981). *The collective black mind: An Africentric theory of black
    personality.* St Louis: Williams and Associates.

Williams-Flourney, D., & Anderson, L. (1996). The Acculturative Stress Scale:
    Preliminary findings. In R. Jones (Ed.), *Handbook of tests and measurements
    for black populations* (Vol. 2, pp. 351–358). Hampton, VA: Cobb and Henry.

Appendix

Holistic Idiographic Framework for Practice

This framework represents the many areas of information clinicians
can gather about their clients to better appreciate and understand
the client's presenting issues and concerns. Based on the six semistructured interview protocols or clinical frameworks for multicultural assessment reviewed in this chapter, this framework outlines
a broad data-gathering approach that is meant to be employed
throughout the counseling process, not just during intake procedures. Included in each section are examples of the kinds of information that clinicians can inquire about. This outline is not meant
to be exhaustive; rather, it is meant to augment clinicians' own
data-gathering techniques.

I. Client's Worldview and Perception of the Problem
    A. Demographics
        Sample questions to ask: Work history, education,
        language(s), health problems/illnesses, current
        medications, marital status, children, SES, religion
    B. Client's explanation of the problem(s)
        Sample questions to ask: What brought the client to seek
        assessment at this time? What factors are contributing to

the problem(s), as the client understands them? What has the client done thus far to deal with the problem(s)? What has worked? What has not worked?

C. Client's level of psychological mindedness

Sample questions to ask: Are basic Western psychological constructs within the client's frame of reference? Does the client conceptualize problems from a psychological point of view? Does the client have the construct of emotional disturbance as part of his or her interpretative lens?

D. Client's attitudes toward helping and counseling

Sample questions to ask: How does the client feel about getting help for emotional problems? What are the current preference for and past experience with professional and popular sources of care? What are the client's attitudes about discussing "problems" outside of his or her family?

E. Cultural identity of the client

Sample questions to ask: Cultural and ethnic reference groups? Culture of origin for maternal and paternal lines? The client's view of his or her cultural adjustment as an individual? The client's view of his or her cultural adjustment as compared to the family's level of cultural adjustment? Language abilities, use and preference, including bilingualism or multilingualism? Feelings and emotions associated with speaking the native language? Are there instances in which the native language is preferred? What are they?

F. Religion

Sample questions to ask: What is the client's religion? How important is religion to the client? What are the rules for being a religious person for someone from the client's religion? What religious beliefs does the client

value most? Have the client describe a significant
religious experience he or she has had.

G. Education and Work

Sample questions to ask: Which experiences in school
does the client remember and value the most? What are
the client's beliefs about work? How will the client
obtain the job he or she wants? What benefits will a
good job bring the client?

H. Peers

Sample questions to ask: What is the age and gender
makeup of the client's peer group? What are or were the
"critical" peer activities the client considered most
important during early childhood, elementary school
years, and adolescent years? What activities does the
client enjoy doing with friends? What are the areas of
conflict or trouble experienced between the client and
friends? What is the cultural and ethnic makeup of the
client's neighborhood?

I. Leisure activities

Sample questions to ask: What are the client's favorite
music and musicians, dancers, artists, authors, maga-
zines, etc.? What are the client's hobbies? What does he
or she do with free time? What types of activities,
interactions, and thoughts are most and least rewarding
to the client?

II. Client's Family Background

A. Family roles

Sample questions to ask: What is a "typical" day in the
client's family like? What is the role of kin networks in
providing support to the client? What are the rules that
characterize a good mother? a good father? What are the
rules for being a good son or daughter? What are the rules
for a good marriage? Who are the role models for family
life that have meant the most to the client, and why?

    B. Family values and norms

        Sample questions to ask: How do the members of the client's
family express anger? How do members of the client's family feel important and increase their self-esteem? What types of things make family members feel safe?

    C. Family's view of client's problem

        Sample questions to ask: Why would the client's family
want the client to get rid of the problem? In what way do the client's problems create pain in the client's family? Does the family conceptualize the problems as psychological in nature? How does the family seek help for "emotional" problems? How do they view help from an "outsider" to the family?

    D. Family acculturation status

        Sample questions to ask: Where do family members live?
When did family members immigrate? Did the family stay together, or are they dispersed? What are the family's relations with similar others like? What are family members' attitudes toward acculturation for themselves, and for the children?

III. Cultural Explanations of the Individual's Presenting Illness

    A. Appraisal of acculturative stress

        Sample questions to ask: What are the cultural definitions
of behavioral options, beliefs about operating in mainstream system, group efficacy, availability of family, community and social networks? Cultural idioms of distress? Meaning and perceived severity of the client's symptoms in relation to norms of the cultural reference group? What is the local illness category used to identify the condition? What are the perceived causes or explanatory models used to explain the illness?

IV. Cultural Elements of the Provider-Client Relationship

    A final thought to providers of mental health services.
Differences in culture and status between provider and

client may cause difficulty in communicating in the client's first language, eliciting symptoms or understanding their cultural significance, negotiating an appropriate relationship and level of intimacy, and determining if a behavior is normative or pathological (American Psychiatric Association, 1994). Clinicians should consider the client-provider match on ethnicity, race, language, service delivery style, service setting decor, the client's perception of the provider's personality, and client perception of general professional competence. This match must be sufficiently acceptable to sustain the client during the initial session and result in willingness to return for additional meetings (Dana, 1998).

5

Clinical Diagnosis of Multicultural Populations in the United States

Richard H. Dana

Clinical diagnosis has become increasingly aligned with the *Diagnostic and Statistical Manuals* (DSM), published by the APA beginning with DSM-I (American Psychiatric Association, 1952) and currently with DSM-IV (American Psychiatric Association, 1994). These manuals have changed over time from a biopsychosocial approach to a disease-centered model (Castillo, 1996), although a majority of standard objective tests have not been revised or restandardized to reflect changes in these diagnostic models and classification criteria. Unfortunately for diagnosticians and patients, DSM criteria and all tests have histories of Euro-American culture-specific, or emic, bias in construction and usage, with potentially adverse consequences for multicultural patient populations. Nonetheless, as Malgady (2000) has emphasized, DSM-IV not only displays "an unprecedented recognition of the cultural diversity of clients" but also "improves cultural boundaries on many psychiatric disorders which were previously conceived of as biologically invariant" (p. 58).

The objective of clinical diagnosis is to reduce emotional distress and suffering by reliable classification of disorders leading toward optimal designation of effective intervention as a consequence of diagnostic procedures. However, cultural and racial differences in symptoms, syndromes, and dysfunctional conditions can lead to erroneous diagnoses of individual patients as well as to overpathologization or minimization of pathology (López, 1989). Neglect of these differences in this rapidly growing population has been a major source of bias, particularly affecting persons who have retained traditional cultural values or who remain only partially acculturated to mainstream American society. This history of bias has been reflected in both the diagnostic tools and in the criterion DSM classification systems as a consequence of minimizing differences among persons and assuming the universality of Euro-American emics. These issues will assume increased importance over time because the non-White mental health population in the United States is approximately 40 percent in the year 2000 (Issacs-Shockley, Cross, Bazron, Dennis, and Benjamin, 1996).

Short-term remediation for bias is described in this chapter. However, interim exercises in cultural sensitivity, though now mandatory for ethical reasons (Dana, 1994), cannot adequately address the inherent problem of using an emic or culture-specific diagnostic system as a cultural universal or etic. More persuasive and definitive resolutions for bias are required, which can only occur by way of major modifications in diagnostic practices or by development of comprehensive and potentially universal theories of personality and psychopathology that are compatible with culture-specific diagnostic criteria. Only as a consequence of placing culture at the heart of training, research, and practice can bias be responsibly addressed and the goal of cultural competence among diagnosticians eventually realized.

Cultural Differences in Expression of Psychological Distress

As understood in DSM-IV, psychological distress is a Euro-American encoding of mind-body dualism to describe psychopathology in modern, secular, Western societies. The DSM-IV accepts without question the Euro-American "acquired consciousness that interferes with total absorption in lived experiences" (Kleinman, 1988, p. 50).

This acquired consciousness is not universal; many people—particularly African Americans, American Indians, and Alaska Natives—have what has been described as an altered consciousness (Dana, 1998c, 2000b; McGee and Clark, 1974). Alteration of consciousness permits highly focused attention similar to a trance state, unreflective responsivity to crisis, and increased potential for accessing spiritual contents (Bell, 1982). These characteristics were once survival techniques for human beings.

An alteration of consciousness also favors a self with weak or permeable boundaries and contents that potentially can admit and include family members, other persons, community or tribe, natural phenomena, and spiritual forces (Dana, 1998c). The relative importance, strength, and magnitude of these components of the self vary within as well as between racial and cultural groups. All DSM versions fail to recognize a self that contains more than the individual; they pathologize a self that does not have rigid boundaries to restrict the entrée of new and diverse contents into the self.

What is included in DSM-IV is primarily applicable to Euro-Americans, but what is excluded has special relevance for non-Euro-Americans. One area of exclusion—the effects of oppression, discrimination, and racism—has been addressed by African American psychologists who have proposed categorizations of major mental disorders that neither overlap nor are related to any DSM contents (Akbar, 1991; Azibo, 1989).

The Africentric nosology (Azibo, 1989) is a comprehensive system of eighteen African American personality disorders developed from an African view of human nature embodied in Africentric personality theory. In this system, psychological health is defined as congruence of genetic and psychological blackness; psychological distress occurs in the absence of congruity. Akbar (1991) believes that racism experienced in a pathological society provides the genesis for alien-self, antiself, self-destructive, and organic disorders.

An alien-self disorder occurs when societal standards of the larger society are adopted and subsequent behaviors become inimical to the individual's own welfare and wellbeing. This disorder is associated with Nigrescence, or racial identity theory, and provides a formal label for stage one, in which middle-class persons adopt a Eurocentric worldview with denigration of blackness, political naïveté, subservience, repressed rage, and alienation (Dana, 1993). Identification with white oppressors is the hallmark of the antiself disorder. In both of these disorders, however, behaviors that may be optimal for Euro-Americans become destructive for African Americans because internalized hostility becomes self-directed.

Self-destructive disorders include the range of survival behaviors typically used by marginal persons to jeopardize life and compromise the well-being of their communities. Drugs, alcohol, prostitution, suicide, within-group homicide, crime, and gangs are examples. Akbar believes that organic disorders, including severe mental deficiency, organic brain disorders, and most schizophrenia, also result from social conditions.

At least five kinds of distress occur with high frequency among multicultural populations:

1. Culture-general conditions, or the conventional DSM psychopathologies

2. Culture-bound syndromes exemplified by the contents of DSM-IV, Glossary I

3. Problems-in-living that vary in prevalence and severity according to group and acculturation status

4. Oppression-induced conditions

5. Acculturative stress-related symptomatology

These categories have considerable overlap; precise delineation has been infeasible for multicultural populations. Separation into these categories suggests their importance and the desirability of differential intervention strategies by group and by category (Dana, 1998f). Because the various DSM versions are Euro-American emics, the categories have not been adequately represented for multicultural populations.

Culture-General Disorders

Culture-general disorders are characterized in DSM-IV as schizophrenia, depression, somatoform disorders, and anxiety reactions (including phobia), among others. These disorders are ostensibly universal because they are found in all groups. However, their forms of expression in symptomatology and syndromes differ markedly across racial and ethnic groups. Moral, religious, political, or social crises may be responsible for symptomatology (Fabrega, 1991). Descriptions of schizophrenia, depression, and anxiety overlap with other DSM-IV disorders and with culture-bound syndromes. The impact of cultural variance on prevalence rates and group differences in symptomatology increases the likelihood of misdiagnosis due to bias or ignorance.

Culture-Bound Syndromes

The culture-bound syndromes are briefly described in the DSM-IV Glossary, without any stated inclusion-omission criteria. They represent only a small fraction of all known culture-specific conditions (see Simons and Hughes, 1985), although some syndromes frequently encountered in the United States were included. Simons and Hughes offered more complete descriptions of symptomatology, locales, and afflicted populations, and they included major references. Syndromes were classified as either culture-general, with wide distribution and possible biological contribution to etiologies, or culture-specific syndromes, folk explanations of diagnosis rather than actual disorder. These culture-based syndromes have puzzled Western psychiatrists and anthropologists and have been described as "exotic" or "unclassifiable" (Hughes and Wintrob, 1995).

Phenomenological reality and cultural validity of culture-based syndromes stems from different conceptions of the self and an absence of mind-body dualism in their cultures of origin. I believe that these conditions occur most frequently among those who maintain a traditional culture and lifestyle or actively resist acculturation. Immigrants, refugees, and students or other sojourners are prone to experience culture-bound syndromes because they are traditional persons who ordinarily do not speak English as a first language. American Indians and Alaska Natives often maintain a traditional worldview and resist acculturation in order to survive as conquered nations.

Problems-in-Living

Problems-in-living, or social disorders (Albee and Ryan-Finn, 1993), may be group-specific as well as culture-general. These problems are omnipresent and destructive in all cultural groups, but there has never been any consensus on a classification system. A proposed DSM addition for relational problems would include severe dysfunction, particularly family violence with physical or sexual abuse (Committee of the Family Group for the Advancement of Psychiatry, 1995). Non-DSM systems include a Psychological Health Classification System to define behavior conditions and dysfunctions within a professional psychology perspective (Teicher, 1995), and a social-work diagnostic system—Person in Environment—is also available (Williams, Karls, and Wandrei, 1991). Problems-in-living are considered here to be group-specific because of group differences in prevalence and differential effectiveness of intervention by group (Dana, 1998f).

Visible racial and ethnic groups all experience problems-in-living that may be either coextensive with problems in the Euro-American population or culturally distinctive. Problems such as alcohol and substance abuse are included among DSM disorders, or overlap with the criteria for these disorders, and receive special treatment as a result. For example, the very high substance-abuse rates among African Americans (Eaton and Kessler, 1985) may be responsible for the high-prevalence rate of cognitive disorders (Griffith and Baker, 1993). The personality disorders included in

DSM have high prevalence rates for visible racial and ethnic groups but are blatantly culturally biased because these disorders are based on white American middle-class cultural standards for personal conduct and interpersonal behaviors. Any marked deviation from these emic cultural expectations, or "normalcy," is deemed pathological and requires a specific diagnosis (Alarcon and Foulks, 1993). Post-traumatic stress disorder (PTSD) can be included under this rubric because it describes the effects of repeated assaults or traumas in the daily experience of many people. PTSD may be manifested across generations, particularly among American Indians and Alaska Natives (Manson and others, 1996), African Americans (Allen, 1996), and Japanese American descendents of those interned during World War II (Nagata, 1990).

Oppression Effects and Disorders

Historically, Fanon (1967) recognized that oppression of blacks in the Caribbean Antilles exacerbated problems-in-living and led to various forms of disorganizing alienation. Alienation from oneself; from one's personal identity; from family and group; from the general other by violent and paranoid behavior; and from culture, language, and history were described by Bulhan (1985) in an examination of psychopathology relevant for African Americans in the United States.

Oppression effects and disorders may be considered problems-in-living, although specific adverse effects of oppression have been overlooked, ignored, or minimized by Euro-American diagnosticians as a bona fide source of distress requiring intervention. For example, Puerto Rican idioms of distress include anger dimensions of aggression, assertiveness, and vindictiveness presented with increased depression, anxiety, and somatization (Malgady, Rogler, and Cortes, 1996). Asian Americans do not frequently express experiences with oppression because their cultural norms inhibit overt expression of feelings while supporting avoidance of confrontation and feelings of shame and inferiority as a consequence of victimization. As a consequence, somatization with culture-specific symptomatology often occurs to medicalize psychological problems.

Acculturative Stress

Acculturative stress is included because emotional distress that may or may not be incapacitating or necessarily result in psychopathology frequently accompanies the acculturation process. Culturally relevant events for each element in the Lazarus-Folkman model (Lazarus and Folkman, 1984) were incorporated and evaluated from studies of Cambodian refugees and African Americans (Slavin, Rainer, McCreary, and Gowda, 1991). This research demonstrated increased complexity of life for multicultural persons. Acculturative stress is magnified for refugees who have experienced war, imprisonment, and torture.

History of Bias

Three major sources of bias—cultural, individual, and institutional—have effects on research and practice using tests and the DSM (Griffin, 1991). Cultural bias occurs through stereotyping groups as inferior, invidious and denigrating group comparisons with Euro-American standards, and continued use of the conventional null hypothesis (Malgady, 1996). Individual bias in the form of social stereotypy occurs in survey findings, hospital admissions, and diagnostic decision making during encoding of data and distortions that accompany information retrieval (Adibimpe, 1994; Lawson, Hepler, Holladay, and Cuffel, 1994). For example, using identical patient data except for race, psychiatrists and residents judged a low-IQ black patient as less able to benefit from psychotherapy than a white patient with the same IQ because the black patient was "less articulate, competent, introspective, self-critical, sophisticated about mental health centers, and psychologically minded" (Geller, 1988, p. 124). Bias in policy can also fail to recognize cultural and racial differences and serves to discourage, restrict, or deny services to those in multicultural populations (Dana, Conner, and Allen, 1996; Dana, 1998d).

Test bias occurs whenever a standard test used for clinical diagnosis has not been demonstrated to have conceptual, linguistic, and metric equivalence for cultural or racial populations not represented adequately in the normative data. Conceptual equivalence, or equivalence in psychological meaning, is rarely established for standard tests developed in the United States because these tests are erroneously assumed to be genuine etics. Construct validity is extremely difficult to demonstrate using the preferred method, the multitrait-multimethod matrix, to examine convergent-discriminant reliability and validity correlation matrices. Factor analysis has been easier to apply for construct validation purposes, although it probably should be limited to confirming factor analyses or cross-validating the factor structure across groups, as one of several preliminary investigative tools including regression analysis and item response modeling (Allen and Walsh, 2000).

Tests are frequently translated using recognized procedures to reduce linguistic bias for people whose first language is not English. Since a significant proportion of those requiring clinical diagnosis for mental health services are refugees or second-language English speakers of Asian or Latin American origin, translations are often required. Unfortunately, acceptable translation procedures may not be used at all or applied incompletely, as in the case of the MMPI/MMPI-2 (Nichols, Padilla, and Gomez-Maqueo, 2000). Metric bias describes dissimilar psychometric properties, including distributions and ranges of scores, and is reflected by unequal item endorsement in different cultural and racial groups. The item bias literature includes a number of special MMPI scales constructed for black populations. Metric bias has been used to delineate distinctive cultural/racial personality characteristics in the MMPI-2 MEX scale (Gomez-Maqueo and Reyes-Lagunes, 1994). Item bias has also been demonstrated by using moderator variables such as the Racial Identity Attitude Scale (RIAS; Helms, 1990), a measure of cognitive-emotional aspects of racial identity development and outcome. However, the RIAS has been criticized for psychometric deficiencies (see Whatley, Allen, and Dana, 1999; Dana, 1993; and Ponterotto and Wise, 1987).

Test bias can pathologize multicultural individuals who are diagnosed using standard tests. In the absence of definitive research on equivalence of psychopathology constructs in these tests, extreme caution should be exercised in applying diagnostic labels to test data or to test scores that appear significantly elevated in comparison with available norms. The norms for standard tests are frequently not applicable because too few individuals in a particular cultural or racial group have been included or the individuals have not been matched on relevant variables with the mainstream Euro-American sample (social class, ethnicity, acculturation status, and so on).

Developing new acculturation status norms is now a necessary ethical consideration because a significant culture-psychopathology confound has been documented for all major cultural and racial groups on the MMPI/MMPI-2 (Dana, 1993). Norms for standard tests may also fail to include social class, especially differences in social class designation by ethnic and racial group and percentages of persons within each class. Norms may thus be responsive to a social class–psychopathology confound in addition to racial and ethnic bias.

Remediation for Bias

Remediation for bias in clinical diagnosis is feasible at several levels. First, there can be "tinkering" with the DSM and diagnostic tests or structured interviews. This can be informal and personal on the part of diagnosticians or part and parcel of an informed critique of tests and the DSM. Second, acceptance among some diagnosticians of a null hypothesis reversal (Malgady, 2000) is embodied in use of an assessment-intervention model. Cultural and racial differences are then accepted until ruled out by the information subsequently made available in response to a series of questions throughout the process. A quest for relevant information can render diagnostic tests more valid, provide substance for cultural formulations, and help to match clients with effective treatments incorporating cultural elements when required. Knowing when to ask relevant questions and how to locate information sources can result in effective utilization of all available treatments and a high rate of beneficial outcomes. Third, at the most macro level, cross-cultural research on etic-emic theory, or universal diagnostic categories and culture-specific diagnostic criteria, ultimately can offer more satisfactory resolution than interim, piecemeal corrections for instruments and the DSM-IV.

Tinkering with Tests

Some diagnosticians now accomplish tinkering informally by deliberately violating the rules for administration, scoring, or interpretation of standardized tests in a search for increased reliability of diagnostic outcome for their multicultural clients. Such tinkering is an individualized and personalized interim phenomenon, although it has been justified as an attempt to be fair and to reduce bias. However, greatly increased knowledge of what diagnosticians actually do in practice is necessary. This information should be formalized and available as an incentive for research to suggest the parameters of tinkering as well as to create an empirical basis for accepting or rejecting specific practices.

Tinkering with established tests can also be accomplished by formalizing options to improve the reliability of interpretation and the validity of diagnosis, although some members of the assessment establishment do not believe these options are necessary and have disparaged their utility. For example, strong disapproval of my published suggestions that the MMPI/MMPI-2 should be "corrected" for culture appeared in an unpublished commentary (Velásquez, Butcher, Garrido, and Cayiba, 1996). These recommended adjustments include using moderator variables, special norms, special scales, and translations, as well as guidelines for interpretation (Dana, 1995, 1996b). They are described here in sufficient detail to permit readers to decide for themselves the extent to which correction for culture may be used on an interim basis to increase the reliability of MMPI/MMPI-2 diagnosis with multicultural populations.

Moderator variables, such as the Acculturation Rating Scale for Mexican Americans (ARSMA/ARSMA-II; Cuéllar, Harris, and Jasso, 1980; Cuéllar, Arnold, and Maldonado, 1995), have demonstrated that a traditional cultural orientation significantly elevates many MMPI clinical scales for Asian Americans, American Indians and Alaska Natives, and Hispanic Americans (Dana, 1993). Blacks who are developing an Africentric racial identity, as evidenced by racial identity measures, also obtained significantly elevated scores on selected MMPI scales (Whatley, Allen, and Dana, 1999). The use of moderator variables simply yields information concerning the likelihood that a standard test is grossly invalid for traditional individuals. "Invalid" in this context refers to pathologization, caricature, or dehumanization as a result of using Euro-American emics to describe personality or psychopathology constructs.

The majority of multicultural people in the United States are marginal, bicultural, or assimilated. For many of these persons, standard tests are appropriate for clinical diagnosis, although it may be necessary to give bicultural people a choice of standard, modified, or culture-specific measures and interventions. Marginal individuals may require cultural formulation to increase the accuracy of their DSM-IV diagnoses. Nonetheless, it has been estimated that at least 20 percent of all multicultural individuals are traditional in their cultural orientation (Dana, 1998f), with much higher percentages among less acculturated immigrants, sojourners, and foreign students.

For all traditional persons, information from moderators should be used to develop cultural formulation for DSM-IV. Nonetheless, diagnosticians have been reluctant to incorporate moderator variables into their assessment batteries. It is unlikely that moderators will be used routinely unless their advantages and utility can be documented by research, or until significant items from existing instruments can be incorporated into standard interviews. Research is beginning to identify some of the items that may be incorporated eventually into interviews (Tanaka-Matsumi, Hsia, and Fyffe, 1998; Zane, 1998). However, diagnosticians have not taken the next step by augmenting current interview content with selected acculturation items.

A longstanding argument holds that norms for particular cultural groups are neither relevant nor useful because of extreme within-group heterogeneity. This argument has merit, except for a few isolated, homogeneous Indian tribes for which it has been documented that all MMPI clinical scales are elevated sufficiently to produce a 50 percent misclassification rate (see, for example, Charles, 1988). Still, the argument has been made repeatedly that the norms for new standard tests used with multicultural populations should reflect acculturation status in order to increase their cross-cultural construct validity (Dana, 1998a, 1998f). Traditional and acculturated people thus would have separate norms. A demonstration for Hispanics on selected Halstead-Reitan neuropsychological tests strongly endorsed development of acculturation status norms (Arnold, Montgomery, Castanada, and Longoria, 1994).

This suggested modification of standard tests by developing cultural orientation status norms is perhaps the most important consideration for improving DSM-IV reliability. It would still be necessary to use moderator items in interviews or as formal tests administered at the onset of the diagnostic process to describe acculturation status in cultural formulation, but dual norms markedly alter test profiles and can potentially resolve the confound between culture and psychopathology. Caldwell (1997) suggested that profiles based upon MMPI and MMPI-2 norms be inspected simultaneously to minimize interpretive shortcomings. The MMPI-2 lacks the fifty-year research history of the MMPI, and neither sample is census representative, particularly in omitting a majority of those with less than a high school education and including almost three times as many college graduates. As this example indicates, socio-economic and educational status may also be confounded with psychopathology, especially for multicultural persons. Although this confound is beyond the scope of this chapter, a detailed examination is available elsewhere (Dana, 2000c).

Special scales for the MMPI-2 can identify cultural and racial characteristics to make available descriptive information. These scales can be readily developed whenever matching of groups has not included a sufficient number of relevant variables. However, it should be recognized that as the groups to be matched become more similar in middle-class lifestyle, education, socioeconomic status, and occupation, the number of differences decreases as more traditional and marginal individuals are expunged from the samples (Dahlstrom, Lachar, and Dahlstrom, 1986). The content of special scales constructed on the basis of group difference generates information on the magnitude of difference between a cultural and racial group and the mainstream Euro-American normative population. A recent example, the MEX scale of the MMPI-2 (Gomez-Maqueo and Reyes-Lagunes, 1994), identified items with a large difference in endorsement rate between the United States restandardization sample and a Mexican college sample. Correlations between the MEX scale and clinical scales suggest appreciable metric and linguistic nonequivalence for a Mexican translation, although the conventional standards for translation were followed.

Translations are necessary for those whose first language is not English. Even in Western Indo-European languages such as Spanish and English, separate translations are required for each Latin American country and for Spain because "standard" Spanish is not identical among those countries. This creates a problem in the United States where, in addition to Mexican, Puerto Rican, and Cuban cultural origins, there are many individuals from seventeen other Spanish-speaking countries. The differences between Indo-European languages and other language families are infinitely greater.

In fact, they are sometimes so great that satisfactory translation cannot be accomplished at all in spite of standard translation procedures (for instance, English to Hopi). Translations of the MMPI/MMPI-2, using Butcher's strategy (1996), generally approximate linguistic equivalence, although there has been no field testing to establish discrepancies between the linguistic habits of the monolingual target group and the bilingual translators (Nichols, Padilla, and Gomez-Maqueo, 2000).

Modified interpretation procedures are available as an aid to interpretation in published guidelines for using standard tests and in the recommendations for cultural formulation used in DSM-IV. For example, guidelines for assessment of Latinos with projective methods include:

- Recognition of the diversity of this population

- Preferences for Spanish language

- A service delivery style perceived as *simpatico*

- A formal evaluation of acculturation status for selection of tests and for information applicable to DSM-IV cultural formulation

- The availability of personality theory relevant to country of origin and major subgroup in the United States (Dana, 1998e)

Following all of these suggested guidelines should increase the likelihood that cultural formulation improves the reliability of DSM-IV clinical diagnoses, although this presumption has not been documented by research.

Remediation for Bias: DSM-IV

Approximately 15 of the 849 pages of the DSM-IV contain caveats regarding culture, age, and gender. Although these caveats do constitute unprecedented recognition of culture, they offer no substance for diagnosticians. However, diagnosticians can find descriptive summaries of major cultural and racial group perspectives, as well as how culture is manifested in specific psychopathologies, and commentary on culture-bound syndromes in a separate volume from DSM-IV (Mezzich, Kleinman, Fabrega, and Parron, 1996), which is a mandatory reference for diagnosticians using the DSM-IV with multicultural populations.

Cultural formulation is now required for multicultural patients who are traditional in cultural orientation status, and it may be necessary for marginal and bicultural patients as well. The outline for cultural formulation is the most important addition to DSM-IV. It was designed for systematic review of a patient's cultural history, including cultural identity, cultural explanations for illness, cultural factors in the social environment, levels of functioning or disability, and cultural factors in the relationship with the diagnostician. An overall assessment for diagnosis and care concludes the formulation. In DSM-IV, this outline precedes the glossary and is presented without examples of how to use it with patients or information on where to obtain the necessary cultural knowledge.

It is not surprising that Euro-American diagnosticians have been reluctant to use cultural formulation because they have received no formal training concerning cultural influences on personality, psychopathology, and social functioning. In workshops, seminars, and assessment courses, I have noted little enthusiasm for the immense investment in time and effort required for learning about culture as an ethical requirement for diagnosticians. Indeed, in the absence of sustained living experience in other cultural settings, familiarity with languages in addition to English, and assessment training that is multicultural in focus, diagnosticians have little opportunity to gain sufficient knowledge to prepare a cultural formulation.

I recommend that students and clinicians prepare assessment reports on their multicultural clients using several sources of information. First, there are general cultural information resources (such as Comas-Díaz and Greene, 1994; Dana, 1998c; Lipson, Dibble, and

Minarik, 1996; McGoldrick, Giordano, and Pierce, 1996). Second, specific readings on how to prepare a cultural formulation are now available (Cuéllar and Gonzalez, 2000; Dinges, Atlis, and Ragan, 2000; Lu, Lim, and Mezzich, 1995; Mezzich, 1995; Novins and others, 1997). Third, the case examples published in *Culture, Medicine and Psychiatry* since 1996 constitute models of cultural formulations that indicate how cultural knowledge can be used to understand psychopathology within a psychiatric frame of reference.

The cultural issues that complicate cross-cultural clinical diagnosis cannot be readily absorbed as add-ons to clinical training in particular courses, limited supervised experience, or workshops. This assertion was documented by a majority of professional psychologists in a national survey, who readily admitted feeling incompetent to offer adequate services for their multicultural clients despite their having experience with multicultural faculty, diverse training cases, and their own multicultural clients (Allison and others, 1994).

Long-Term Remediation for Bias

Long-term approaches to reduce bias in clinical diagnosis can only occur as a result of training, professional practice, and research that place cultural issues at the focus of attention in psychology and other mental health professions. There have been conspicuous beginnings, but any transformation of professions has a political context in the larger society that may be more salient by 2050, when more than half the population will be multicultural in composition. Adequate academic training settings must have culturally competent staff members representing major cultural and racial groups who function within programs that integument cultural issues in all courses, practicum experiences, and internships. Selection of students should emphasize life experiences in a variety of cultural settings and skill in at least one language other than English, in addition to the historic academic criteria.

Training students to assess psychopathology can incorporate scientific method for critical thinking about research on cultural issues and preparation of cultural formulations that routinely employs appropriate diagnostic case materials (López, 2000). A learning process that encourages use of multiple frames of reference, or etic and emic lenses, for integrating data from tests and observation is necessary for culturally informed assessment and cultural competence. Training should also include exposure to and immersion in varying cultural perspectives, an ingredient that is at present recognized only in cultural psychology programs. Research design, statistics, and research process have to be reconceptualized following careful examination of bias in the historic use of Euro-American emic methodology.

Malgady (1996, 2000) has suggested revising the null hypothesis to place culture centrally in research considerations; other authors have presented methods to reduce bias that demonstrate serious attention to culture and cultural variables (for example, Allen and Walsh, 2000; van de Vijver, 2000; and Cuéllar, 2000). Making better use of available quantitative methods can be coupled with qualitative methods, particularly within the same projects (Billson, 1995; Mohatt, 1999). The next two sections describe examples of "conspicuous beginnings" for feasible long-term remedies for clinical diagnostic bias at the practitioner and theoretical levels.

An Assessment-Intervention Model

A model to place culture at the center of the diagnostic process has been described as a means for increasing the reliability of clinical diagnosis and the efficacy of recommended intervention with individuals from multicultural populations (Dana, 1997, 1998b, 2000b). This model is presented as a flow chart (Figure 5.1) requiring the clinician to ask seven culture-relevant questions at appropriate steps in the diagnostic process. This model is still incomplete; it can be modified or augmented by developing additional questions and resources for information as competent research accumulates.

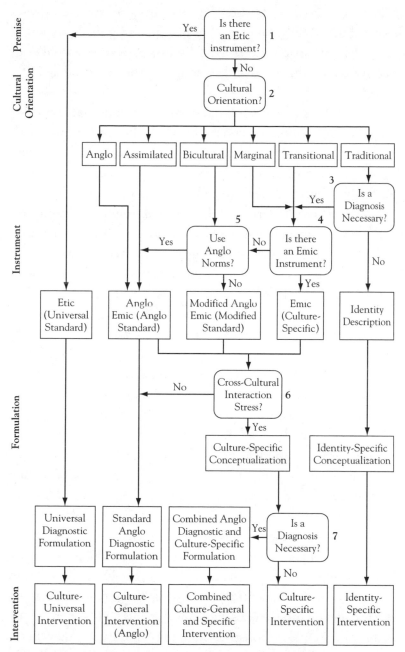

Figure 5.1. Multicultural assessment intervention process model.
Source: Dana (2000a). Reprinted with permission.

A first question—Is there an etic instrument?—is always answered negatively at present, but incorporating this question in the model anticipates subsequent discussion of an eventual etic-emic avenue for increased understanding of the clinical diagnostic process.

The answer to the second question—Cultural orientation?—indicates the appropriateness of a DSM-IV diagnosis per se, with or without a cultural formulation, and subsequently whether using a standard intervention, a combined intervention, or a culture-specific intervention is likely to be helpful. Cultural orientation status in one of six categories can be inferred from performance on acculturation measures as well as by judicious use of interview content. This cultural information suggests whether or not standard interview content and assessment instruments should be used with a particular client. If the first language is not English, any test in English is suspect and should not be used without independent confirmation of the client's language facility. This signals that the subsequent diagnostic process must be conducted in the client's first language, including any tests, and that a cultural formulation is a mandatory step in developing any clinical diagnosis.

A negative answer to a third question—Clinical diagnosis necessary?—for traditional, transitional, and marginal persons can lead away from a cultural formulation. Nonetheless, cultural information, particularly on personality and problems-in-living of cultural origin, is still required for an identity conceptualization that leads to appropriate intervention by a provider from the same culture.

If a diagnosis is required, however, question four—Is there an emic instrument?—requests information on available tests for a particular non-Euro-American client. Although many African American emic instruments are now available (Jones, 1996), there are few emics for other groups. Emic instruments for other groups are needed and should be constructed because if only standard Euro-American tests are available, corrections may need to be applied, as described earlier in this chapter.

Question five—Anglo norms?—raises the issue of the general inapplicability of Euro-American norms for culturally diverse patients. Since these available norms are skewed for social class and education and often underrepresent particular cultural or racial groups, they should be applied only within an enlarged context of cultural information concerning behavior in current life situations. Because pathologization is an artifact of inappropriate norms, the diagnostician must have in-depth knowledge of a patient's culture as well as cultural orientation status to interpret accurately any information on concurrent patient behavior in other settings. If Anglo norms can be used, then no cultural formulation is necessary for a DSM-IV diagnosis.

Question six—Cross-cultural interaction stress?—requires information concerning the presence or absence of cultural issues. Whenever cultural issues are present in an individual whose cultural orientation status is bicultural, marginal, transitional, or traditional, then a cultural formulation is required before a formal clinical diagnosis can be made. Knowledge of the individual's culture and the particular cultural issues presented is important, and can be developed during an interview, but at this point instruments are needed that yield more relevant information than simply cultural orientation status. Acculturation instruments for Hispanics, particularly Mexican Americans, are available for this purpose (see Dana, 1996a). As noted earlier, there are instruments to examine many facets of life and personality for African Americans in addition to racial identity (see Jones, 1996). Because few instruments now exist for other multicultural groups, the clinician is responsible for acquiring sufficient relevant cultural information to develop a cultural formulation.

Question seven—Is a diagnosis necessary?—reiterates the necessity for a clinical diagnosis after a competent cultural formulation becomes available. It is possible, although not an everyday occurrence, that the cultural formulation will document absence of diagnosable psychopathology, particularly in traditional individuals from cultures relatively infrequent and less well known in the

United States (such as Ethiopians), although the presenting problem may still benefit from a culture-specific intervention. If the cultural formulation describes DSM-IV psychopathology, then a combined intervention that incorporates relevant cultural elements is preferable to a standard intervention.

Etic-Emic Theory

The assessment-intervention model began with the premise that eventually there will be universal or etic instruments to measure psychopathology. A search for universals or etics has occurred in anthropology, biology, language and linguistics, and psychology (Lonner, 1980). Cross-cultural psychologists have examined emic operationalization of etic models (for instance, Davidson and others, 1976), and most psychologists are familiar with the semantic differential demonstration of the pancultural generality of affective meaning systems (Osgood, May, and Miron, 1975). In these examples, the construct is identified, measured, and subjected to cross-cultural comparisons; the methodology for this process is well established (Hui and Triandis, 1985). These methods have often been overlooked, omitted, or applied ineptly by professional psychologists (see Allen and Walsh, 2000; Cuéllar, 2000; and van de Vijver, 2000).

In spite of consensus that some psychopathology constructs may be universal, the DSM-IV assumes universality by fiat rather than as a result of empirical demonstrations. Nonetheless, there is compelling evidence from application of the Rorschach Comprehensive System in Iberoamerica, for example, that the consistencies across emic normative data from many of these countries contrasts markedly with norms developed in the United States (Vinet, 2000). These findings are important because some major Rorschach constructs (notably experience balance or *Erlebnistypus*) have compelling demonstrations of cross-cultural equivalence using a variety of objective and projective measures (see Dana, 1993).

One reason for the worldwide acceptance of DSM-IV as a genuine etic may be that research demonstrations of an etic-emic approach to cross-cultural validation of psychopathology constructs have not been available. However, there is research documenting clear emic manifestation of particular psychopathology constructs. For example, emotional words for *depression* could be clustered in Indonesia, Japan, and Sri Lanka but not in Australia, Korea, Puerto Rico, and Malaysia, although these groups did have a sadness concept that included depression (Brandt and Boucher, 1986). These depression clusters also differed in complexity. Sadness was the primary ingredient in the United States, with alienation, shame-guilt, and anxiety only marginally related. In Japan, however, anxiety, pain, misery, sad-lonely, regret-repent, and bored-lacking were primary, with doubtful, anger, dislike-unpleasant, jealousy-hatred, fear, tense, busy, shame-guilt, unbearable, restraint-excess, and pity marginally related.

This study (Brandt and Boucher, 1986) suggested how the experience of depression is conceptualized differently by using a variety of languages with specific vocabularies to structure the cultural meanings of the experience. Although the DSM-IV depression syndrome contains specific affective, cognitive, behavioral, and somatic symptoms, the distribution of these symptoms varies for multicultural groups in the United States, and some symptoms are omitted for particular groups in standard depression instruments.

A second reason for the international success of DSM-IV is the absence of a competing universal schema to translate affective, organismic, perceptual-cognitive, and social-behavior domains into pathological extremes representing depression or manic states, neurosis, schizophrenia, and personality disturbance respectively, as Draguns has suggested (personal communication in Lonner, 1980). Although there may be oversimplification in these dimensions, delineation of psychopathology constructs within these domains offers a beginning that is analogous to reconceptualizing Murray's need-press personality theory into an etic-emic paradigm (Ephraim, 2000).

Peroration

This chapter has been critical of the DSM, including DSM-IV, and some major standard tests used for clinical diagnosis of psychopathology. It is no longer acceptable to export as universal the psychopathologies constructed by Euro-American emic diagnostic standards and assessment instruments, or to maintain this psychiatric oligarchy with burgeoning multicultural populations in the United States.

Fortunately, the mental health professions are now attracting recruits from multicultural populations in the United States. These new professionals offer energy and dedication, but what is of even greater importance is that they are determined to generate constructions of the cultural reality of their own lives—including their psychopathologies—instead of accepting these constructions from Euro-Americans. These contrasting interpretations and expositions of differing cultural realities will be grounded in research, and their proponents will be teaching and practicing diagnostic assessment. I believe that these new emics can complement current Euro-American emic standards and instruments and lead to increased utilization of mental health services, including assessment, with remarkably better outcomes for multicultural individuals than they have hitherto experienced.

An adaptation of the assessment-intervention model for African Americans constitutes a cogent example of this process (Morris, 2000). By the same token, developing applications of an academic cultural psychology into applied professional areas of assessment and intervention signals a transformation within psychology in which culture becomes central to our research process rather than peripheral. Finally, the continuing interface between the academic-research area of cross-cultural psychology and the applied areas of counseling, clinical, and community psychology is a union that can foster development of etic-emic psychopathology theory.

References

Adibimpe, V. R. (1994). Race, racism, and epidemiological surveys. *Hospital and Community Psychiatry, 45*, 27–31.

Akbar, N. (1991). Mental disorders among African Americans. In R. L. Jones (Ed.), *Black psychology* (3rd ed.). Berkeley, CA: Cobb and Henry.

Alarcon, R. D., & Foulks, E. F. (1993, January). Cultural factors and personality disorders: A review of the literature. In NIMH-sponsored Group on Culture and Diagnosis, *Cultural proposals and supporting papers for DSM-IV* (3rd rev., pp. 250–254). Pittsburgh, PA: University of Pittsburgh.

Albee, G. W., & Ryan-Finn, K. D. (1993). An overview of primary prevention. *Journal of Counseling and Development, 72*, 115–123.

Allen, I. M. (1996). PTSD among African Americans. In A. J. Marsalla, M. J. Friedman, E. T. Gerrity, & R. M. Scurfield (Eds.), *Ethnocultural aspects of post-traumatic stress disorder: Issues, research, and clinical applications*. Washington, DC: American Psychological Association.

Allen, J., & Walsh, J. A. (2000). A construct-based approach to equivalence methodologies for cross-cultural/multicultural personality assessment research. In R. H. Dana (Ed.), *Handbook of cross-cultural and multicultural personality assessment* (pp. 63–85). Hillsdale, NJ: Erlbaum.

Allison, K. W., Crawford, I., Echemendia, R., Robinson, L., & Knepp, D. (1994). Human diversity and professional competence: Training in clinical and counseling psychology. *American Psychologist, 49*, 792–796.

American Psychiatric Association (1952). *Diagnostic and statistical manual of mental disorders*. Washington, DC: Author.

American Psychiatric Association (1994). *Diagnostic and statistical manual of mental disorders* (4th ed.). Washington, DC: Author.

Arnold, B. R., Montgomery, G. T., Castanada, I., & Longoria, R. (1994). Acculturation and performance of Hispanics on selected Halstead-Reitan neuropsychological tests. *Assessment, 1*, 239–248.

Azibo, D. Y. (1989). African-centered theses on mental health and a nosology of Black/African personality disorder. *Journal of Black Psychology, 15*(2), 173–214.

Bell, C. C. (1982). Black intrapsychic survival skills: Alteration of states of consciousness. *Journal of the National Medical Association, 74*(10), 1017–1020.

Billson, J. M. (1995). *Keepers of the culture: The power of tradition in women's lives.* New York: Lexington.

Brandt, M. E., & Boucher, J. D., (1986). Concepts of depression in emotion lexicons of eight cultures. *International Journal of Intercultural Relations*, 10, 321–346.

Bulhan, H. A. (1985). *Frank Fanon and the psychology of oppression*. New York: Plenum.

Butcher, J. N., (1996). Translation of the MMPI-2 for international use. In J. N. Butcher (Ed.)., *International adaptations of the MMPI-2* (pp. 3–46). Minneapolis: University of Minnesota Press.

Caldwell, A. B. (1997). Whither goes our redoubtable mentor, the MMPI/MMPI-2? In J. A. Schinka & R. L. Greene (Eds.), *Emerging issues and methods in personality assessment* (pp. 47–68). Hillsdale, NJ: Erlbaum.

Castillo, R. J. (1996). *Culture and mental illness: A client-centered approach*. Pacific Grove, CA: Brooks/Cole.

Charles, K. (1988). *Culture-specific MMPI norms for a sample of Northern Ontario Indians*. Unpublished M. A. thesis, Lakehead University, Thunder Bay, Ontario, Canada.

Comas-Díaz, L., & Greene, B. (1994). *Women of color: Integrating ethnic and gender identity in psychotherapy*. New York: Guilford Press.

Committee of the Family Group for the Advancement of Psychiatry (1995). A model for the classification and diagnosis of relational disorders. *Psychiatric Services*, 46, 926–931.

Cuéllar, I. (2000). Acculturation as a moderator of personality and psychological assessment. In R. H. Dana (Ed.), *Handbook of cross-cultural and multicultural personality assessment* (pp. 113–129). Hillsdale, NJ: Erlbaum.

Cuéllar, I., Arnold, B., & Maldonado, R. (1995). Acculturation rating scale for Mexican Americans-II: A revision of the original ARSMA scale. *Hispanic Journal of Behavioral Sciences*, 17, 275–304.

Cuéllar, I., & Gonzalez, G. (2000). Cultural identity description and cultural formulation for Hispanics. In R. H. Dana (Ed.), *Cross-cultural and multicultural personality assessment* (pp. 605–621). Hillsdale, NJ: Erlbaum.

Cuéllar, I., Harris, L. C., & Jasso, R. (1980). An acculturation scale for Mexican American normal and clinical populations. *Hispanic Journal of Behavioral Sciences*, 2, 199–217.

Dahlstrom, W. G., Lachar, D., & Dahlstrom, L. E. (1986). *MMPI patterns of American minorities*. Minneapolis: University of Minnesota Press.

Dana, R. H. (1993). *Multicultural assessment perspectives for professional psychology*. Needham Heights, MA: Allyn & Bacon.

Dana, R. H. (1994). Testing and assessment ethics for all persons: Beginning and agenda. *Professional Psychology: Research and Practice*, 25, 349–354.

Dana, R. H. (1995). Culturally competent MMPI assessment of Hispanic populations. *Hispanic Journal of Behavioral Sciences, 17*, 305–319.

Dana, R. H. (1996a). Assessment of acculturation in Hispanic populations. *Hispanic Journal of Behavioral Sciences, 18*, 317–328.

Dana, R. H. (1996b). *Silk purse or sow's ear: An MMPI commonground.* Unpublished manuscript.

Dana, R. H. (1997). Multicultural assessment and cultural identity: An assessment-intervention model. *World Psychology, 3*(1–2), 121–142.

Dana, R. H. (1998a). Cultural identity assessment of culturally diverse groups: 1997. *Journal of Personality Assessment, 70*, 1–16.

Dana, R. H. (1998b). Multicultural assessment of personality and psychopathology in the United States: Still art, not yet science, and controversial. *European Journal of Psychological Assessment, 14*, 62–70.

Dana, R. H. (1998c). Personality and the cultural self: Emic and etic contexts as learning resources. In L. Handler & M. Hilsenroth (Eds.), *Teaching and learning personality assessment* (pp. 325–345). Hillsdale, NJ: Erlbaum.

Dana, R. H. (1998d). Problems with managed care for multicultural populations. *Psychological Reports, 83*, 283–294.

Dana, R. H. (1998e). Projective assessment of Latinos in the United States: Current realities, problems, and prospects. *Cultural Diversity and Mental Health, 4*, 165–184.

Dana, R. H. (1998f). *Understanding cultural identity in intervention and assessment.* Thousand Oaks, CA: Sage.

Dana, R. H. (2000a). An assessment-intervention model for research and practice with multicultural populations. In R. H. Dana (Ed.), *Handbook of cross-cultural and multicultural personality assessment* (pp. 5–16). Hillsdale, NJ: Erlbaum.

Dana, R. H. (2000b). The cultural self as locus for assessment and intervention with American Indians/Alaska Natives. *Journal of Multicultural Counseling and Development, 28*, 66–82.

Dana, R. H. (2000c). Culture and methodology in personality assessment. In I. Cuéllar & F. Paniagua (Eds.), *Handbook of multicultural mental health: Assessment and treatment of diverse populations* (pp. 97–120). San Diego: Academic Press.

Dana, R. H. (in press). Mental health for African Americans: A cultural/racial perspective. *Cultural Diversity and Ethnic Minority Psychology.*

Dana, R. H., Conner, M. G., & Allen, J. (1996). Cost-containment and quality in managed mental health care: Policy, education, research, advocacy. *Psychological Reports, 79*, 1395–1422.

Davidson, A. R., Jaccard, J. J., Triandis, H. C., Morales, M. L., & Diaz-Guerrero, R. (1976). Cross-cultural model testing of the etic-emic dilemma. *International Journal of Psychology, 11*(1), 1–13.

Dinges, N. G., Atlis, M. M., & Ragan, S. L. (2000). Assessment of depression among American Indians and Alaska Natives. In R. H. Dana (Ed.), *Handbook of cross-cultural and multicultural personality assessment* (pp. 623–646). Hillsdale, NJ: Erlbaum.

Eaton, W. W., & Kessler, L. G. (Eds.) (1985). *Epidemiologic field methods in psychiatry*. New York: Academic Press.

Ephraim, D. (2000). A psychocultural approach to TAT scoring and interpretation. In R. H. Dana (Ed.), *Handbook of cross-cultural and multicultural personality assessment* (pp. 427–445). Hillsdale, NJ: Erlbaum.

Fabrega, H., Jr. (1991). Somatization in cultural and historical perspective. In L. J. Kimayer & J. M. Bobbins (Eds.), *Current concepts of somatization: Research and clinical perspectives* (pp. 181–189). Washington, DC: American Psychiatric Press.

Fanon, F. (1967). *Black skins, white masks*. (C. L. Markmann, Trans.). New York: Grove Atlantic.

Geller, J. D. (1988). Racial bias in the evaluation of patients for psychotherapy. In L. D. Comas-Diaz & E.E.H. Griffith (Eds.), *Clinical guidelines in cross-cultural mental health* (pp. 112–134). New York: Wiley.

Gomez-Maqueo, E. L., & Reyes-Lagunes, I. (1994). New version of the Minnesota Multiphasic Personality Inventory for Mexican college students. *Revista Mexicana de Psicologia, 11*, 45–54.

Griffin, J. T. (1991). Racism and humiliation in the African American community. *Journal of Primary Prevention, 12*, 149–167.

Griffith, E.E.H., & Baker, F. M. (1993). Psychiatric care of African Americans. In A. C. Gaw (Ed.), *Culture, ethnicity, and mental illness* (pp. 147–173). Washington, DC: American Psychiatric Press.

Helms, J. E. (Ed.). (1990). *Black and white racial identity: Theory, research, and practice*. Westport, CT: Greenwood Press.

Hughes, C. C., & Wintrob, R. M. (1995). Culture-bound syndromes and the cultural context of clinical psychiatry. In J. M. Oldham & M. B. Riba (Eds.), *Review of psychiatry* (Vol. 14, pp. 565–597). Washington, DC: American Psychiatric Press.

Hui, C. H., & Triandis, H. C. (1985). Measurement in cross-cultural psychology. *Journal of Cross-Cultural Psychology, 16*, 131–152.

Issacs-Shockley, M., Cross, T., Bazron, B. J., Dennis, K., & Benjamin, M. B. (1996). Framework for a culturally competent system of care. In B. A.

Stroul (Ed.), *Children's mental health. Creating systems of care in a changing society* (pp. 23–39). Baltimore: Paul Brookes.

Jones, R. L. (1996). *Handbook of tests and measurements for Black populations* (Vols. 1 and 2). Hampton, VA: Cobb and Henry.

Kleinman, A. (1988). *Rethinking psychiatry: From clinical category to personal experience*. New York: Free Press.

Lawson, W. B., Hepler, N., Holladay, J., & Cuffel, B. (1994). Race as a factor in inpatient and outpatient admissions and diagnosis. *Hospital and community Psychiatry, 45*, 72–74.

Lazarus, R. S., & Folkman, S. (1984). *Stress, appraisal, and coping*. New York: Springer-Verlag.

Lipson, J. G., Dibble, S. L., & Minarik, P. A. (1996) (Eds.), *Culture and nursing care: A pocket guide*. San Francisco: UCSF Nursing Press.

Lonner, W. J. (1980). The search for psychological universals. In H. C. Triandis & W. W. Lambert (Eds.), *Handbook of cross-cultural psychology: Perspectives* (Vol. 1). Needham Heights, MA: Allyn & Bacon.

López, S. R. (1989). Patient variable biases in clinical judgment: Conceptual overview and methodological considerations. *Psychological Bulletin, 108*, 1–20.

López, S. R. (2000). Teaching culturally informed psychological assessment. In R. H. Dana (Ed.), *Handbook of cross-cultural and multicultural personality assessment* (pp. 669–687). Hillsdale, NJ: Erlbaum.

Lu, F. G., Lim, R. F., & Mezzich, J. E. (1995). Issues in the assessment and diagnosis of culturally diverse individuals. In J. M. Oldham & M. B. Riba (Eds.), *Review of Psychiatry* (Vol. 14). Washington, DC: American Psychiatric Press.

Malgady, R. G. (1996). The question of cultural bias in assessment and diagnosis of ethnic minority clients: Let's reject the null hypothesis. *Professional Psychology: Research and Practice, 27*, 73–77.

Malgady, R. G. (2000). Myths about the null hypothesis and the path to reform. In R. H. Dana (Ed.), *Handbook of cross-cultural and multicultural personality assessment* (pp. 49–62). Hillsdale, NJ: Erlbaum.

Malgady, R. G., Rogler, L. H., & Cortes, D. E. (1996). Cultural expression of psychiatric symptoms: Idioms of anger among Puerto Ricans. *Psychological Assessment, 8*, 265–268.

Manson, S., Beals, J., O'Nell, T., Piasecki, J., Bechtold, D., Keane, E., & Jones, M. (1996). Wounded spirits, ailing heart: PTSD and related disorders among American Indians. In A. J. Marsella, M. J. Friedman, E. T. Gerrity, & R. M. Scurfield (Eds.), *Ethnocultural aspects of posttraumatic stress disorder: Issues, research, and clinical applications* (pp. 255–283). Washington, DC: American Psychiatric Association.

McGee, D. P., & Clark, C. X. (1974, August–September). Critical elements of Black mental health. *Journal of Black Health Perspectives*, 52–58.

McGoldrick, M., Giordano, J., & Pierce, J. K. (1996). *Ethnicity and family therapy* (2nd ed.). New York: Guilford Press.

Mezzich, J. E. (1995). Cultural formulation and comprehensive diagnosis: Clinical and research perspectives. *Psychiatric Clinics of North America*, *18*, 649–657.

Mezzich, J. E., Kleinman, A., Fabrega, H., Jr., & Parron, D. L. (Eds.). (1996). *Culture and psychiatric diagnosis: A DSM-IV perspective*. Washington, DC: American Psychiatric Press.

Mohatt, G. (1999). People Awakening Project: Alaska Native pathways to sobriety. NIH grant in progress.

Morris, E. F. (2000). Assessment practices with African Americans: Combining standard assessment measures within an Africentric orientation. In R. H. Dana (Ed.), *Handbook of cross-cultural and multicultural personality assessment* (pp. 573–603). Hillsdale, NJ: Erlbaum.

Nagata, D. K. (1990). The Japanese American internment: Exploring the transgenerational consequences of traumatic stress. *Journal of Traumatic Stress*, *3*, 47–69.

Nichols, D. S., Padilla, J., & Gomez-Maqueo, E. L. (2000). Issues in the cross-cultural adaptation and use of the MMPI-2. In R. H. Dana (Ed.), *Handbook of cross-cultural and multicultural personality assessment*. (pp. 247–266). Hillsdale, NJ: Erlbaum.

Novins, D. K., Bechtold, D. W., Sack, W. H., Thompson, J., Carter, D. R., & Manson, S. M. (1997). The DSM-IV outline for cultural formulations: A critical demonstration with American Indian children. *Journal of the American Academy of Child and Adolescent Psychiatry*, *36*, 1244–1251.

Osgood, C. E., May, W. H., & Miron, M. S. (1975). *Cross-cultural universals of affective meaning*. Urbana: University of Illinois Press.

Ponterotto, J. G., & Wise, S. L. (1987). Construct validity study of the Racial Identity Attitude Scale. *Journal of Counseling Psychology*, *34*, 218–223.

Simons, R. C., & Hughes, C. C. (1985). *The culture-bound syndromes: Folk illnesses of psychiatric and anthropological interest*. Boston: Reidel.

Slavin, L. A., Rainer, K. L., McCreary, M. L., & Gowda, K. K. (1991). Toward a multicultural model of the stress process. *Journal of Counseling and Development*, *70*, 156–163.

Tanaka-Matsumi, J., Hsia, C., & Fyffe, D. (1998, August). *Measurement of acculturation: An examination of psychometric properties.* Paper presented at the International Association for Cross-Cultural Psychology Fourteenth International and Silver Jubilee Congress, Bellingham, WA.

Teicher, A. (1995). Proposal for a psychological classification system. *Independent Practitioner, 15*(2), 82–84.

van de Vijver, F. (2000). The nature of bias. In R. H. Dana (Ed.), *Handbook of cross-cultural and multicultural personality assessment* (pp. 87–106). Hillsdale, NJ: Erlbaum.

Velásquez, R. J., Butcher, J. N., Garrido, M., & Cayiba, J. J. (1996). *Dana's culturally competent MMPI assessment of Hispanics: A case of "rounding up the usual suspects."* Unpublished manuscript.

Vinet, E. V. (2000). The Rorschach Comprehensive System in Iberoamerica. In R. H. Dana (Ed.), *Handbook of cross-cultural and multicultural personality assessment* (pp. 345–365). Hillsdale, N.J.: Erlbaum.

Whatley, P. R., Allen, J., & Dana, R. H. (1999). Racial identity and psychopathology: African-American Racial Identity Attitude Scale and MMPI scale score differences. Manuscript submitted for publication.

Williams, J., Karls, J., & Wandrei, K. (1991). The person in environment system for describing problems in social functioning. *Hospital and Community Psychiatry, 40,* 1125–1127.

Zane, N. (1998, December). *Major approaches to the measurement of acculturation: A conceptual analysis and empirical validation.* Paper presented at the International Conference on Acculturation: Advances in Theory, Measurement, and Applied Research, University of San Francisco.

Section Two

· ·

Daily Living Assessment

In this second section of Part One, three chapters focus on components of daily living: assessment of family systems, vocational issues, and quality of life.

Assessing diverse families is addressed by Daniel Sciarra. Chapter Six stresses the structural components of family systems from a multicultural perspective. A range of assessment techniques, including self-report scales, diagrammatic approaches, and observations, are critically reviewed. Sciarra demonstrates an integrated approach of obtaining and interpreting data on diverse family systems.

Chapter Seven addresses issues related to vocational assessment of culturally diverse populations. In this chapter, Kathy Gainor discusses the benefits of vocational assessment for ethnic and racial minority clients in terms of helping to increase their awareness of educational possibilities, as well as the pitfalls of perpetuating the status quo. Gainor offers a detailed review of common instruments used in the field, as well as suggestions for how cultural diversity should be integrated into existing assessment approaches.

In Chapter Eight, Shawn Utsey, Mark Bolden, Christa Brown, and Mark Chae discuss assessing the quality of life within a cultural context. The authors stress that the construct "quality of life" is in and of itself a by-product of Western thinking and philosophy, therefore making it difficult to assess across other cultures. The chapter identifies a number of quality-of-life constructs that are more meaningful in non-Western cultures, and mechanisms to assess them.

6

Assessment of Diverse Family Systems

Daniel T. Sciarra

A ssessment has been part of marriage and family counseling since the 1930s, and an evolution of measurement techniques has followed. Early measures were dedicated to evaluating and predicting success and happiness in both marriage and family according to an individual's background and personality. However, with the advent of the family systems movement, assessment began to examine the family's level of cohesiveness and adaptability, moving from an individual to a within-system perspective of behavior (Bray, 1995).

For a complete treatment of issues related to multicultural assessment of families, it is necessary to begin with an understanding of the family as a system. Following a section dedicated to systemic thinking, the chapter continues with assessment issues particular to families. The second half of the chapter deals with families from diverse cultural backgrounds and multiculturally sensitive methods available for assessing such families.

Family as a System

In order to understand the family as a system, one must first understand how a systemic focus differs from the focus of traditional psychotherapy.

Systems Thinking Versus Traditional Psychotherapy

A colleague of mine once described the difference between in-depth individual psychotherapy and family counseling as that between an onion and an orange. With an onion, one peels away the layers to arrive at the core (as might be the case in psychodynamic psychotherapy); by contrast, with an orange one separates pieces that fit together side by side (George Simon, personal communication, April 1994). This visual example helps to define the nature and purposes of systemic thinking: how the pieces (members) of this particular system (family) can function cohesively and harmoniously. A second way that family systems work deviates from traditional individual psychotherapy is the requirement that the people with whom an individual is having problems be in the same room. Whereas traditional thinkers such as Freud reasoned if family (that is, mother and father) is the cause of an individual's problems, then the individual should be treated in isolation (Ackerman, 1958), family therapy reasons the exact opposite: if family is part of the problem, the only way to treat individuals is in conjunction with their family members (Gladding, 1998).

A further distinction between traditional psychotherapy and family systems work involves understanding behavior in terms of one's past, known as the evolutionary perspective (Freud's metaphor of the analyst as archeologist of the mind; Gay, 1988), as opposed to understanding behavior in terms of its here-and-now function within a system, known as the functionalist perspective. Functionalism believes that any behavior should be seen for its adaptive value in the wider context of its environment (Nichols and Schwartz, 1998). For family therapists, this wider context is the family.

However, the family as a whole is also interacting in a wider context—the environment—and in this sense there is an open system in which a constant exchange exists between the two. Because a family feels the continuous impact of environmental events, its response to such changes can stimulate further development

(see Carter and McGoldrick, 1988, 1999 for a widely accepted trea-
tise on family development). But families may become "stuck,"
unable to adapt functionally to changes in the family or the larger
environment. This stagnation often results in designating an identified patient (IP), a member of the family who is seen as having an
individual problem but who is really reflecting a systemic problem.
Systemic family therapists are committed to understanding how any
behavior, regardless of its pathological severity, is serving some function for the entire system. A simple but common example is a child
who develops symptoms in response to the parents' fighting. As a
result, the parents cease fighting while they focus on their sick or
troubled child.

Fundamental Concepts in Family Systems

From understanding the family as a system, a number of fundamental concepts have developed. Some of these may have
emanated from a particular theory of family therapy, but they are
used by most eclectic therapists and also are important for issues of
assessment.

Homeostasis

Homeostasis is "the tendency of a system to regulate itself so as to
maintain a constant internal environment in response to changes
in external environment" (Nichols and Schwartz, 1998, p. 90). All
systems seek homeostasis. A heating and cooling system is a good
example. When a room becomes too hot or too cold, the system
kicks in to restore the room to a predetermined, agreeable temper-
ature. All systems seek to balance themselves and seek homeostasis, and families are no expectation.

An obvious and fundamental way a family maintains homeostasis is through rules and regulations. Parents may say to a child,
"You can go out as long as you are home by 11:00 P.M." Here, the
parents recognize the child's need for a certain amount of freedom
and their own need for having the child return at an agreed-upon

time. Over time, rules and regulations have to be amended, or even dispensed with, in order to meet the changing needs of the system and the environment. This is known as second-order change. Families with a limited capacity for adaptation have difficulty effecting second-order change and often become stuck, resulting in children's acting-out behavior.

Though overly mechanistic in its purely conceptual form, when applied to families homeostasis means that at times behaviors can be understood as regulating the family system and protecting it from a perceived external threat. A typical example is a child who develops school phobia after his or her mother returns from an operation in the hospital. The threat of illness is counteracted by the child's constant vigilance over the mother. The concept of homeostasis has been much criticized by contemporary family counselors as fostering an overly mechanistic view of families. This criticism is valid, because no family system is so mechanical. Nevertheless, the concept of homeostasis gives family practitioners a useful tool in assessing the effects and purposes of symptomatic behavior upon the family system.

Circularity

In opposition to a linear understanding of behavior that searches in the past to explain problematic behavior in the present, the concept of circularity examines behavior within a system as reverberating, circling, or looping around, thus creating patterns of interaction and communication among its members. The linear perception of A → B is replaced by A → B → A. Take the example of a punitive father and his acting-out son. The son's acting out causes the father to be punitive, which in turn causes further acting out on the son's part. A good family counselor becomes skilled at tracking the interaction and communication patterns of a family through enactment in a family counseling session. By using the concept of circularity, the counselor can intervene effectively to interrupt such patterns.

Family Structure

Concern with family structure resulted from the work of two great pioneers in the field of family counseling: J. Haley (1963, 1976) and Salvador Minuchin (Minuchin and Fishman, 1981; Minuchin and others, 1967). Haley became concerned with issues of power and control in families and viewed behavior as a function of these two ends. This, in turn, led to the concepts of hierarchy, subsystems, boundaries, and coalitions. A healthy family has a parental subsystem functioning as the hierarchy, with clear boundaries around the subsystems. However, to illustrate structural dysfunction, a mother who is having difficulties in the relationship with her husband can enter into a coalition with one or more of the children against the father in order to lessen his authority and influence.

Minuchin capitalized on Haley's work and classified family boundaries as rigid, clear, or diffuse, leading to interpersonal relationships that are disengaged, normal, or enmeshed. Structural family counselors are known for their creative and strategic techniques aimed at restructuring a family to create a functional hierarchy with a clear boundary around itself and the sibling subsystem.

Triangulation

Murray Bowen (1976) introduced the concept of triangles into family counseling to illustrate lack of differentiation among family members. Bowen believed fusion among family members to be a chief cause of symptomatic behavior. When two undifferentiated people in a relationship face anxiety, there is a tendency to draw in a third party as a way of reducing the couple's anxiety. In families, this usually takes the form of children being triangulated into conflicts between their parents. A triangulated person is not allowed to differentiate, which in turn can lead to symptomatic behavior. Thus family counselors recognize that a daughter's behavior depends on her relationship with her mother, which depends on the mother's relationship with the father. Bowen believed all behavior is basically triadic rather than dyadic.

Contemporary Criticisms of Family Counseling

These are some of the basic concepts of family systems assessment that are still very much used today. An understanding of these basic ideas facilitates multicultural application to family counseling. However, the concepts have also given birth to an understanding of families that contemporary perspectives criticize severely.

Contemporary criticisms of the family therapy movement have come from a number of fronts, namely constructivism, feminism, psychoeducation, and multiculturalism (Nichols and Schwartz, 1998).

Constructivism

Constructivism is an epistemology maintaining that what is known as real is merely a construction of the observer. Since individuals are constructed of their own biases, assumptions, and cultural determinants, there is no one truth about reality. Rather, there is construction of reality, whose meaning can vary from person to person, group to group, and culture to culture. The task of the family counselor is therefore to collaborate with a family in the search for meaning in present behaviors and alternative meanings for the same behaviors. The constructivist critique undermines traditional family counseling because of its tendency to impose upon families a universally accepted truth about how families ought to function and to focus on actions rather than meanings.

Feminism

Similar to constructivism, the feminist critique accused traditional family counseling of treating families out of context. Family counseling by and large ignored the historical and societal context of women, which encouraged them to desire positions of economic dependency and domesticity over responsibility. Family counselors—themselves steeped in patriarchy—tended to view such roles as pathological; the solution was to have the man (father) of the family come to the rescue by assuming a more involved role in the family. Feminists reacted strongly to this pathologizing of women and the power-assuming position of the counselor, which only replicates society's inequality between men and women.

Psychoeducation

Psychoeducation is antithetical to traditional family counseling in its approach to families with a disturbed member, in that it viewed the family system as suffering the consequences rather than causing the symptomatic behavior. For example, in working with families of schizophrenia, the best form of counseling is to educate the family about the disease and give them better resources in how to deal with it. Psychoeducational counseling believed that if there is dysfunction in the family system it is caused primarily by not knowing how to deal with a disturbed member. Thus the illness causes the family system to dysfunction—not vice versa, as traditional family counseling would have us believe.

Multiculturalism

The family counseling movement encountered still another challenge in the eighties from multicultural counseling, which accused it of being Eurocentric. The map of the healthy family was based upon a particular culture, that of the white, Eurocentric middle class. There was little regard for how family systems could vary across cultures and how family structure, considered dysfunctional in one culture, would not be in another. The 1980s saw a dramatic rise in different family structures, among them the single-parent family, grandmother as primary caretaker, and homosexual couples raising children. This, together with the steady increase of nonwhite immigrants to the United States, created a challenge for traditional family counseling, which tended to impose universally upon families what was culture-specific.

This discussion between the multiculturalists and the structuralists continues into the 1990s and shows no signs of abating. The structuralists have reworked their position to say, for example, that issues of disengagement and enmeshment exist in all families regardless of culture; what is culture-specific is the degree to which such relationships are tolerable. For example, one would not impose the same standard of enmeshment upon an Iowa farm family and a Latino family.

All of these critiques have in common the belief that traditional family counseling is too myopic in its vision of families. The family therapy movement began by trying to understand individuals in their wider context, that of the family system. How ironic, then, that beginning in the late eighties and continuing into the nineties, family therapy has been accused of being too narrow, of not considering the wider contexts of race, gender, ethnicity, and culture.

Szapocznik and Kurtines (1993) suggested seeing the relationship among the individual, family, and culture as concentric circles. The individual continues to be understood within the context of family, and family is understood within the context of culture. Issues of hierarchy, communication, family values, family roles, and intergenerational perspective still dominate the work of family counselors who are multiculturally sensitive. Although family process may be the same across cultures, the content varies considerably, and sensitivity to these variations defines the competent multicultural family counselor.

Issues in Family Assessment

Assessment has played a major role in family systems work; however, the kinds of assessment technique differ sharply from those used in traditional individual psychology. Boughner, Hayes, Bubenzer, and West (1994) found that of 598 family and marital workers, only 20 percent used at least one standardized assessment instrument. Assessment methods in family systems fall into three principal categories: self-report, observational, and diagrammatic methods. The constructs most commonly measured in family systems work are communication, conflict, problem solving, bonding and cohesion (structure), affect and emotion, intimacy, differentiation and individuation, triangulation, stress, and roles (Bray, 1995).

Self-Report Methods

The three most frequently used standardized self-report measures in family systems are the Family Adaptability and Cohesion Evaluation Scales III (FACES III; Olson, 1986); the Family Environmental Scale (FES; Moos and Moos, 1974), and the Family Assessment Device (FAD; Epstein, Baldwin, and Bishop, 1983).

FACES III

FACES III is a twenty-item Likert scale measuring family cohesion and adaptability. It can be administered to individuals, couples, and families. Each item asks the frequency of a particular behavior using a 5–point response format ranging from *almost never* to *almost always*. Sample items are "Family members like to spend free time with each other" and "Rules change in our family." Scores tend to vary significantly among family members, with the authors reporting correlations in the .30 to .40 range. The authors also report Cronbach's alpha to be .77 for cohesion, .62 for adaptability, and .68 for the total scale (Buehler, 1990).

FES

FES is a ninety-item true-false measure scored on ten subscales (cohesion, expressiveness, conflict, independence, achievement orientation, intellectual-cultural orientation, active-recreational orientation, moral-religious emphasis, organization, and control). Three forms exist: the "real form," measuring a member's perception of the current environment; the "ideal form," measuring conception of ideal environments; and the "expectations form," measuring expectation about new family settings. The FES has been widely used in research. The authors report internal consistency for the ten subscales ranging from .61 to .78, while test-retest correlation are reported to range from .68 to .86 (Buehler, 1990).

FAD

FAD is a 4–point, sixty-item Likert-type questionnaire based on the McMaster Model of Family Functioning, which delineates family functioning on six dimensions: problem solving, communication, roles, affective responsiveness, affective involvement, and behavior control. These dimensions are the six subscales of the FAD. Cronbach's alpha is reported to range from .72 to .83 for the six subscales, with test-retest reliability from .66 to .76 (Buehler, 1990).

All three instruments reportedly have good psychometric properties (see Grotevant and Carlson, 1989; and Touliatos, Perlmutter, and Strauss, 1990, for a thorough review of these and other family assessment devices), but their appropriateness for use with culturally diverse families is questionable. For example, Morris (1990) found that among a sample of Hawaiian American and Japanese American families the FAD misinterpreted cultural differences regarding healthy family functioning. More recently, Fine (1993) cautioned against using measures developed on one ethnic group to assess families from diverse backgrounds. As stated previously, the multicultural movement critiqued traditional family models based on a single ethnic group. Unfortunately, most of the standardized assessment devices used in the field today are a result of these very same models.

Observational Methods

Observational methods are the most common form of assessment in family systems work. Structural family therapy's concept of enactment is the result of believing that within a very short period after entering the therapy room a family will enact its typical way of behaving. The therapist observes carefully who sits next to whom, who speaks to whom, what others are doing (verbally or nonverbally) while one member is speaking, and numerous other variables that assume more or less importance according to the therapist's theoretical orientation.

Some observational and interviewing methods have even been standardized (Floyd, Weinand, and Cimmarusti, 1989). An example is to have the family perform a certain task (which can be almost anything, from problem solving to planning a trip) in a certain place (home, office, clinic). Trained observers, using global coding systems, then make ratings or judgments about the family interaction after viewing all or part of the session (Bray, 1995). Coding systems can be geared toward identifying patterns of interaction (Gottman, 1993), or use standardized cards to rate the family interactions and processes (Wampler, Halverson, Moore, and Walters, 1989). However, these standardized observations were developed from a monocultural perspective and suffer the same cross-cultural validity concerns as other methods of standardized assessment for families.

Diagrammatic Methods

Two diagrammatic methods of assessment have been widely used in the field of family systems treatment since its beginning: the genogram (Guerin and Pendergast, 1976; McGoldrick and Gerson, 1985) and the eco-map (Hartman, 1978). Both of these methods are multiculturally useful.

The Genogram

The genogram pictures a family through time, at least three generations, for the purpose of understanding how each individual is part of an historical saga that has dictated commands, roles, expectations, and patterns of living and relating (Hartman, 1995). The genogram depicts factual information (births, deaths, illness, marriage, divorce, and other significant events) along with physical, psychological, and social changes (McPhatter, 1991). Furthermore, the genogram depicts the quality of important relationships (signifying them as enmeshed or diffuse, close or distant) along with coalitions that may divide family members. The overall purpose of the genogram is to depict patterns across generations, to help both the practitioner and the family understand how certain issues may be part of a larger historical context. Figure 6.1 illustrates a sample genogram. For an instructional guide to composing genograms, the reader is referred to McGoldrick and Gerson (1985).

The genogram is culturally sensitive in that it helps the practitioner discover patterns across generations that can lead to further understanding about and insight into the client's culture. The genogram is particularly useful with the elderly, who oftentimes are fountains of historical information, can reminisce and organize memories, and see themselves as a link between the past and the future (Hartman, 1995).

The Eco-Map

If the purpose of the genogram is to depict a family in time, the eco-map seeks to depict a family in its present space. At the beginning of this chapter, the point was made that the family system interacts with other, complex systems in the environment. The eco-map can help both the practitioner and the family assess the impact and importance of these larger systems by characterizing nurturing and adverse connections between the family and the external environment (McPhatter, 1991). Figure 6.2 illustrates a completed form of the eco-map. For more detailed information on how to administer and use the eco-map, the reader is referred to Hartman (1978, 1995).

The eco-map helps to assess the strengths and resources the family system possesses outside of itself. The ecological perspective helps to focus on the client's wider cultural milieu and assess good or bad fit among the individual, the family system, and the larger environment (McPhatter, 1991). In this sense, the eco-map is particularly useful with families from nondominant cultural backgrounds who often have to contend with societal racism, sexism, ethnocentricity, and other environmental stressors and difficulties.

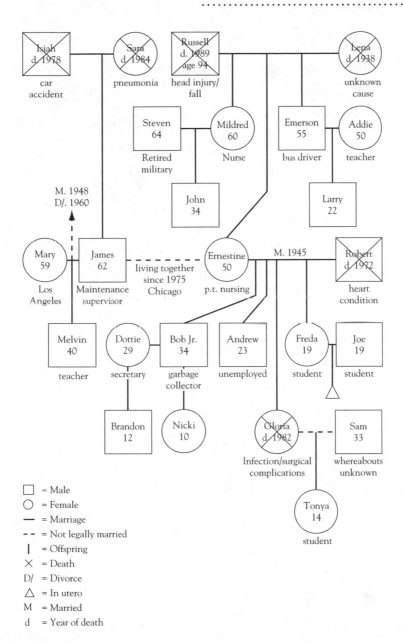

Figure 6.1. Example of a family genogram.

Source: McPhatter, A. R. "Assessment Revisited: A Comprehensive Approach to Understanding Family Dynamics." *Families in Society*, 1991, 72, 11–22. Reprinted with permission.

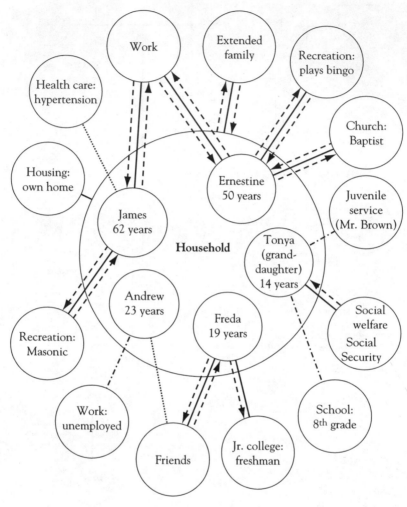

— = Indicates strong connections

⋯⋯ = Tenuous

–·– = Stressful

➤ = Flow of energy, resources

Figure 6.2. Completed form of the eco-map.

Source: McPhatter, A. R. "Assessment Revisited: A Comprehensive Approach to Understanding Family Dynamics." *Families in Society,* 1991, *72,* 11–22. Reprinted with permission.

Multicultural Assessment of Families

More recently, assessment tools specifically designed for working with families around issues of diversity have begun to emerge. Two of them, the culturagram (Congress, 1994) and the gendergram (White and Tyson-Rawson, 1995), are extensions of and supplements to both genogram and the eco-map.

The Culturagram

The culturagram (see Figure 6.3) elicits information about an immigrant family important to understanding its current functioning and planning for its treatment. Issues such as reasons for immigration, age of the family members at the time of immigration, length of

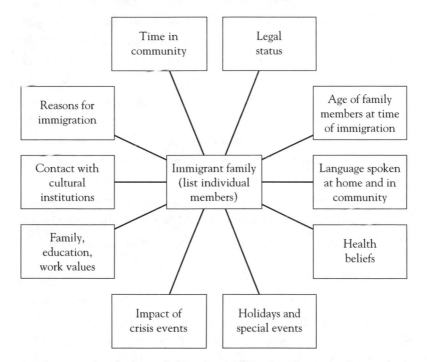

Figure 6.3. The culturagram.

Source: Congress, E. P. "The Use of Culturagrams to Assess and Empower Culturally Diverse Families." *Families in Society*, 1994, 75, 531–540. Reprinted with permission.

time in the host country, and legal versus nonlegal status can deepen the practitioner's understanding of the family's dynamics. Information about contact with cultural institutions; family, education, and work values; languages spoken; health beliefs; and holidays and special events can reveal the forms and levels of second-culture acquisition of the family as a whole and of the individual members. Assessment of second-culture acquisition is extremely important and receives separate treatment later.

The Gendergram

Like the genogram, the gendergram (see Table 6.1) attempts to access multigenerational beliefs and traditions, but specifically in relationship to gender and gender roles. Assessment sensitive to diversity should pay careful attention to gender issues as possible causes of conflict within a family system. As pointed out earlier in this chapter, the feminist critique of family therapy attacked its stereotypical approach to gender roles and lack of attention to changes in these roles.

The gendergram is administered in the form of a semistructured interview (for a complete description on how to administer the gendergram, see White and Tyson-Rawson, 1995). The two main purposes of the gendergram are to assess how gendered beliefs underlie the problems that the family presents and to assess how these beliefs of the various members blend with each other (White and Tyson-Rawson, 1995). The gendergram should be used if the clinician suspects that gender issues may be the cause of family dysfunction.

The Family Assessment Wheel

The family assessment wheel (Mallick and Vigilante, 1997), shown in Figure 6.4, emanates from a social constructionist perspective. Social constructionism is a derivative of constructivism in that both share the notion that the meaning one attaches to events is what makes reality. Social constructionism emphasizes more the mutually agreed-upon meanings of a particular group and their role in shaping individual constructions (Berger and Luckmann, 1966; Gergen and Gergen, 1991; Guba and Lincoln, 1989; Schwandt, 1994).

Table 6.1. Suggested questions for creating the gendergram.

Questions pertaining to each of the significant individuals identified by the client	1. What are your significant memories of this person? 2. Try to remember how you experienced life at this age. How did this person influence how you felt about yourself as a female (or male)? What did you learn about being a woman (man) from this person? 3. What did you learn from this person about how women (men) interacted with other women (men)? What did you learn from this person about how women (men) interacted with men (women)? 4. As an adult looking back on these relationships, in what ways has this person had a lasting influence on how you view yourself as a woman (man)?
Questions pertaining to aspects of individual development	1. How did changes in your physical appearance, whether from maturation, accidents, or illness, influence how you felt about yourself as a woman (man)? 2. What did you learn about your sexuality during this time period? How did you learn it? 3. How did what you learned impact your definition of yourself as a woman (man)? 4. What spiritual or religious influences were important to you at this time and how do you think they have informed your feelings about yourself as a woman (man)?

(Continued)

Table 6.1. Suggested questions for creating the gendergram. (*Continued*)

Questions pertaining to the environment of the family of origin	1. Describe the emotional climate of your home during this time. 2. How was affection expressed between women? between men? between women and men? between parents or adults and children? 3. How was conflict handled? 4. Did men and women express the same emotions differently? 5. How secure did you feel when you were at home? 6. How was conformity to your family's gender norms rewarded? How was nonconformity punished? 7. What did men and women do in your family (in the family, at work, in the community, for recreation, as caregivers, as disciplinarians, and generally in relationships with others)? 8. What were your family's criteria for a successful man? a successful woman?
Questions pertaining to the larger society	1. What were your peer group's gender norms or rules at this time, and how was conformity to them rewarded? How was nonconformity punished? 2. Were there any conflicts between the gender norms or rules of your family and those of your peer group? If so, how did you handle them? 3. What did you learn at school or work during this time about the roles of men and women?

Table 6.1. (*Concluded*)

	4. At this time, how would you have described the ideal female? The ideal male?
	5. Do you remember anything from television or other media that influenced your ideas about being a woman (man)?
Summary questions linking the past with the present	1. What gender-related roles do you notice yourself playing at this stage of your life?
	2. What patterns do you see in gender issues at this stage of your life?
	3. Are there repetitive themes in your relationships?
	4. Which of these roles, patterns, and themes do you want to enhance and continue?
	5. Which of these roles, patterns, and themes do you want to work to change?

Source: White, M. B., and Tyson-Rawson, K. J. "Assessing the Dynamics of Gender in Couples and Families: The Gendergram." *Family Relations*, 1995, 44, p. 256. Copyrighted ©1995 by the National Council on Family Relations, 3989 Central Ave. NE, Suite 550, Minneapolis, MN 55421. Reprinted by permission.

Social constructionism is an approach to working with diversity in which the primary task becomes accessing and understanding the meaning clients give to their experiences. Often, clients from diverse cultures attach meanings to events and experiences that are quite different from the counselor's own meanings and interpretations of the very same event. Thus, assessment is a process, between the practitioner and the client, of sharing and understanding meanings of events (Mallick and Vigilante, 1997). Rather than fit the client into the clinician's preconceived categories, there occurs a mutual exchange of stories to broaden the understanding of reality.

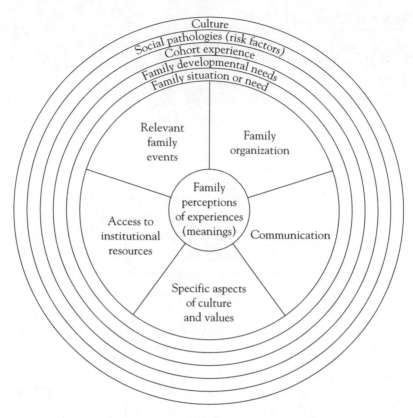

Figure 6.4. The family assessment wheel.
Source: Mallick, M. D., and Vigilante, F. W. "The Family Assessment Wheel: A Social Constructionist Perspective." *Families in Society,* 1997, *78,* 361–369. Reprinted with permission.

The family assessment wheel encourages family members to express their views (perceptions) of experience. Within the hub of the wheel are recorded the meanings of the family's situation and needs as they play a central role in the assessment process. The clinician continues to access views on the other elements represented by the four concentric circles. The spokes of the wheel are domains individualizing the family's experience (Mallick and Vigilante, 1997).

Although the family assessment wheel is a recently developed assessment instrument, it promises to be useful for those who are working cross-culturally and who believe that assessment is a collaborative effort between practitioner and client to deconstruct meanings (along with their narratives) that are debilitating and construct new ones that are less problematic. For those who reject a categorical diagnostic approach to assessment and treatment, the family assessment wheel should prove very appealing.

Assessment of Second Culture Acquisition

Multicultural family counseling demands awareness that family members acculturate differently. Because of their facility in learning language and their more frequent contacts with the new culture through school and friends, in general children more easily assume characteristics of the dominant culture than their parents do. Parents, on the other hand, are often more closely allied with the culture of the country of origin. As time goes on, these differences may be minimized as parents slowly acquire aspects of the dominant culture. Still, a rift between parents and children may develop if parents withdraw from the dominant culture and children continue to ally with it, causing conflict between the subsystems. It is at this point that many immigrant families may present for counseling.

The first task of the multicultural family counselor is to assess the second-culture acquisition process of the various family members. One of the easiest ways to do this is through language (Sciarra and Ponterotto, 1993). What language does the family speak? Do the children prefer to speak in English? Do the parents speak or try to speak in English, or insist on using their native language? If spoken to by their parents in their native language, do the children answer in the same language, or switch to English?

If counselors are bilingual, even more possibilities exist for assessment since they can switch from one language to another in addressing family members and observing which language they use to respond. As a bilingual (Spanish) family counselor, my experience was that when speaking to client children in Spanish they answered in English in spite of knowing Spanish. Whether they do this also with their parents is very important to assess.

A vignette illustrates some of the dynamics around language and second-culture acquisition. Mr. M. attempts, though poorly, to speak in English to his two sons, who speak better English than Spanish. Mrs. M., on the other hand, is a monolingual Spanish speaker. From a systems point of view, one could hypothesize that Mr. M. is in a coalition with his sons against his wife. From an acculturative point of view, one could assess the children as more identified with the dominant culture, Mrs. M. as not identified or withdrawn from the dominant culture, and Mr. M. with willingness to become more identified with the dominant culture. Surely, the counselor will investigate further to define issues of acculturation; nevertheless, acute observation of the use of language in an initial session can give the counselor a map of the family system to be used for further exploration.

Another way to assess the form of second culture acquisition in families is to gather information about celebration of holidays and food. Does the family continue to eat ethnic food? Do the children complain about having to eat such food? Are holidays of either or both the dominant and nondominant cultures celebrated? Are special days of the week reserved to maintain traditions of the non-dominant culture?

Frank is a good example of issues of this kind.

> Frank is a recent Italian immigrant and father of four. He works long hours six days a week in a grocery store. Sunday is the only day he can spend with his family, and as in his native country he feels the Sunday meal is very important. He wants his children present for the big noontime Sunday meal, which continues for several hours, relaxing and talking with extended family members.

Through their contacts at school, two of Frank's children have become involved in a soccer league; many of the games are on Sunday. Though Frank likes the idea of his children playing soccer, he resents their refusal to be present at the Sunday meal. Frank cannot understand why Americans schedule games at times that interfere with family. The children, on the other hand, can't understand why they have to be home on Sunday for so many hours when no one else in their peer group does. Frank feels his children are disrespectful.

In this scenario, levels of acculturation are revealed through adherence to the customs of the native country or lack thereof. This kind of information gathering and observation of interactional patterns among family members is a form of enactment, a strategy of great importance to traditional family counseling. Multicultural skilled counselors also employ enactment, but they filter the information through the lens of acculturation. They are asking themselves, *How is what I am seeing and hearing revealing the second-culture acquisition process of the family system, along with different forms of acculturation among its members?*

Measures of Acculturation

Over the years, numerous measures of acculturation have been developed for various groups. Some of these are designed for general use with racial or ethnic groups, while others are for specific groups within a particular racial category. Examples of the former are the African American Acculturation Scale (Landrine and Klonoff, 1994, 1995), the Suinn-Lew Asian Self-Identity Acculturation Scale (Suinn, Rickard-Figueroa, Lew, and Vigil, 1987), and the Acculturation Scale for Hispanics (Marin, Sabogal, Marin, and Otero-Sabogal, 1987). Examples of intragroup measures of acculturation are the Acculturation Rating Scale for Mexican Americans (Cuellar, Harris, and Jasso, 1980; Cuellar, Arnold, and Maldonado,

1995), the Greek American Acculturation Scale (Harris and Verven, 1996), the Taiwan Aboriginal Acculturation Scale (Cheng and Hsu, 1995), the Hawaiian Acculturation Scale (Rezentes, 1993), and the Acculturation Scale for Southeast Asians (Anderson, Moeschberger, Chen, and Kunn, 1993).

Measures of acculturation tend to adopt a standard Likert-scale format of behaviors indicative of the subject's native culture and the dominant culture. These behaviors may include food preferences, celebration of holidays, socialization experiences, relationship with family, contacts with the native country, and dominant-language facility. The goal of these measures is to quantify placement along a continuum bounded by two polarities, the native culture and the dominant culture, and thus assess the level of acculturation.

Use of Acculturation Measures

A measure of acculturation can be given to individual members of a family system to determine if levels and forms of second-culture acquisition are conflicting and are the basis of the family's problems. Measures of acculturation are typically the result of a unidirectional conceptualization of second-culture acquisition. Most acculturation measures attempt to quantify movement from the culture of origin toward the dominant culture. In view of more recent studies on second-culture acquisition that suggest it being bidirectional and multidirectional, these measures of acculturation ought to be used circumspectly. In addition to the problem of unilinear measurement, Marin (1992) has criticized acculturation measures for Hispanics as lacking in psychometric properties; relying too heavily on language use and proficiency; and failing to consider important variables such as cognitive style, personality, and attitudes.

Szapocznik, Kurtines, and Fernandez (1980) developed the Bicultural Involvement Questionnaire, which yields two separate and independent scores for a client's involvement in Hispanic and European American cultures (Atkinson, Morton, and Sue, 1998). The ARSMA-II (Cuellar, Arnold, and Maldonado, 1995) has attempted to move beyond unidirectional measures of acculturation by having a Scale 1 divided into the Anglo orientation subscale (AOS) and Mexican orientation subscale (MOS). The two subscales can be used independently as measures of biculturalism and dependently by subtracting one score from the other to yield a single linear acculturation score (Atkinson, Morton, and Sue, 1998).

Although measures of acculturation may serve the purpose of initial assessment, they tend to oversimplify the process of second-culture acquisition. However, recent developments in this field prove promising as the process of cultural adaptation is increasingly understood as more multidimensional and multidirectional than previously thought.

Racial and Cultural Identity

Unlike most models of second-culture acquisition, racial and cultural identity theory does not endeavor to locate an individual's beliefs, values, and behaviors on a continuum between the dominant and nondominant cultures. Rather, the central focus of this paradigm is to describe an individual's psychological orientation to membership in both the dominant and nondominant cultures in the United States (Gushue and Sciarra, 1995). Racial and cultural identity theory suggests that an individual's attitudes toward both of these groups (dominant and nondominant) are linked, and that specific clusters of attitudes toward both groups define the particular racial and cultural identity "status" (Helms, 1995) that predominates at a given point in a person's development.

Models of racial and cultural identity development have been created for members of both nondominant and dominant cultures in the United States. Tables 6.2 and 6.3 represent two models in which individuals move from a naïve position on race and culture to an appreciation of their own and other cultures. Individuals can move in and out of the statuses; development is not necessarily linear. Relationships between the client and counselor are defined as progressive, regressive, or parallel, depending on whether the counselor enjoys a higher-, lower-, or same-status relationship with the client. For example, a counselor from the dominant culture at the

Table 6.2. A nondominant-culture identity development model.

Stage	Description
Conformity	Naïve acceptance of dominant culture's values. Tendency to denigrate one's own culture and idealize the dominant culture.
Dissonance/ introspection	Beginning to question uncritical assimilation to dominant culture in self and others. Growing interest in one's own cultural heritage.
Resistance	Exclusive interest and pride in one's own culture. Outright rejection of the dominant culture's values. Awareness of and resistance to cultural and political hegemony of the dominant group.
Awareness	Critical interest and pride in one's own culture. Critical acceptance of certain aspects of the dominant culture, combined with continued efforts to resist political margination and cultural assimilation to "the mainstream."

Source: Based on Helms and Carter (1984, cited in Carter, Fretz, and Mahalik, 1986). Gushue, G. V. "Cultural Identity Development and Family Assessment: An Interaction Model." *Counseling Psychologist*, 1993, *21*, p. 497. Copyright © 1993 by Sage Publications. Reprinted with permission of Sage Publications.

Disintegration status with a client from the nondominant culture who has Awareness status would be in a regressive relationship. In terms of cultural identity, the client is at a higher level of development than the counselor, and the prognosis for successful counseling is not good.

In a seminal article, Gushue (1993) was the first to apply the cultural identity development model to families. He suggests a tripolar mapping of families to include the counselor, the parental subsystem, and the sibling subsystem. However, the counselor is not limited to these three polarities. For example, a member or members of the extended family may form a fourth polarity. Unlike the dyad in individual counseling, family counseling presents several polarities from which to assess parallel, regressive, or progressive relationships.

Table 6.3. A dominant-culture identity development model.

Stage	Description
Contact	Monocultural perspective. Assumes universality and validity of dominant group's values, attitudes, etc. Complete unawareness of other cultural points of view.
Disintegration	Initial intercultural contacts spark curiosity as person "discovers" other cultures. Naïve enthusiasm for the "exotic" combined with initial consciousness of membership in dominant (oppressive) culture. Possible attempts to reconcile these two perspectives via paternalism or overidentification.
Reintegration	Retreat into and idealization of dominant culture. Denigration of and hostility (overt or covert) toward nondominant cultures.
Pseudoindependence	Intellectual awareness of the validity of differing cultural perspectives. Intellectual acceptance of membership in dominant group (and the consequences for self and for members of nondominant cultures) as starting point for intercultural contacts.
Immersion/emersion	Introspective time of cognitive and emotional restructuring. Attempt to work out a nonoppressive dominant-culture identity. Search for dominant-culture role models who have achieved a multicultural perspective.
Autonomy	Multicultural perspective. Beyond acceptance to affective appreciation of difference. Valuing rather than tolerating diversity. Commitment to work for a society that reflects this perspective.

Source: Based on Helms (1984, 1990). Gushue, G. V. "Cultural Identity Development and Family Assessment: An Interaction Model." *Counseling Psychologist,* 1993, *21*, p. 498. Copyright ©1993 by Sage Publications. Reprinted with permission of Sage Publications.

Progressive relationships in general offer better prognosis for treatment than regressive or parallel relationships. Family counseling is no exception, but assessment issues are more complicated. For example, suppose an autonomy-stage counselor from a dominant cultural group enjoys a progressive relationship with parents and siblings from a nondominant cultural group who are at the conformity and resistance stages respectively (see Figure 6.5).

The prognosis for treatment is good. However, since the counselor's level of cultural identity is closer to that of the siblings (the parents being at the first stage of development), he or she must be careful about entering into a coalition with the children against the parents. In actuality, this could be a non-White family whose executive subsystem accepts the ways of the dominant culture. The sibling subsystem is taking a good deal of pride in its own culture and rejecting the ways of the dominant culture.

Like the paradigm of second-culture acquisition, cultural identity development can assess this conflict of the family from a non-

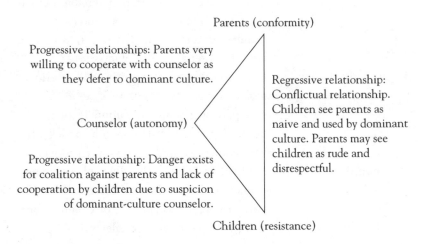

Figure 6.5. Relationship of dominant-culture counselor and nondominant-culture family.

Source: Gushue, G. V. "Cultural Identity Development and Family Assessment: An Interaction Model." *Counseling Psychologist,* 1993, *21,* p. 500. Copyright ©1993 by Sage Publications. Reprinted with permission of Sage Publications.

dominant culture in terms of differing attitudes toward the dominant and nondominant cultures. For instance, Black parents in this scenario who complain about the opposition of their children can be told something on the order of, "I don't think your children dislike you. I believe that they're asking for your help in how to relate in a world that they feel doesn't like Black people." The counselor, using the cultural identity development model, is able to assess the conflict in terms of attitude toward the dominant culture.

If, in this same scenario, a nondominant counselor at the conformity stage is substituted, the prognosis for treatment is not good (see Figure 6.6). The counselor has a parallel relationship with the parents and a regressive relationship with the children. A real danger exists for a coalition between counselor and parents against the children. Furthermore, the counselor does not enjoy a level of cultural identity development to handle the suspicion and hostility characterized by the children's resistance stage. On the other hand,

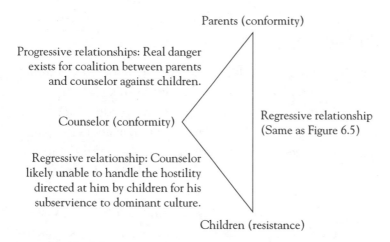

Figure 6.6. Relationship of nondominant-culture counselor and non-dominant-culture family.

Source: Adapted from Gushue, G. V. "Cultural Identity Development and Family Assessment: An Interaction Model." *Counseling Psychologist,* 1993, *21,* p. 503. Copyright ©1993 by Sage Publications. Reprinted with permission of Sage Publications.

counselors from a nondominant culture at the awareness stage would be able to handle such hostility toward themselves and also be able to reframe such hostility toward the parents from a cultural identity development perspective.

Even though standardized measures of racial and cultural identity development do exist (see Sciarra, 1999, for a review of instrumentation), cultural identity attitudes can be assessed qualitatively by the family practitioner. The counselor listens carefully for the cues for cultural identity development in the speech of particular family members. When discovered, the counselor should be quick to follow up and elicit the reactions of other family members to what is being said. The goal of the assessment is to determine to what degree individual levels of cultural identity development among family members may be responsible for the conflict. Cultural identity development is a rich and exciting paradigm; its application to family systems can generate considerable important assessment information.

Conclusion

The goal of this chapter has been orientation on assessing families from diverse cultural backgrounds. To arrive at this goal, the chapter began with an overview of family systems therapy, included a critical review of the better-known assessment devices used in family therapy, and ended with application to family systems of recent constructs (second-culture acquisition and cultural identity development) in multicultural psychology.

Standardized assessment has played a limited role in the history of family therapy, which has relied more on qualitative assessment for observing patterns of interactions among family members. In addition, with the few standardized instruments that do exist the validity for families of diverse cultural backgrounds is questionable. As a result, the thrust of this chapter has been to apply more qualitative forms of assessment (the genogram, the culturagram, the gendergram, the eco-map, and the family assessment wheel) for assessing families from nondominant cultural backgrounds. Finally, this chapter has urged readers to pay particular attention to differences among family members in terms of second-culture acquisition and cultural identity development. The forms of second-culture acquisition as well as the statuses of cultural identity development may very well be the cause of conflict among family members who come from nondominant cultural backgrounds. Multicultural assessment should pay careful attention to such issues. Hopefully, this chapter heightens that attention and also gives clinicians some basic tools for performing such an assessment.

References

Ackerman, N. (1958). *The psychodynamics of family life*. New York: Basic Books.

Anderson, J., Moeschberger, M., Chen, M. S., & Kunn, P. (1993). An acculturation scale for Southeast Asians. *Social Psychiatry and Psychiatric Epidemiology, 28*, 134–141.

Atkinson, D. R., Morton, G., & Sue, D. W. (1998). *Counseling American minorities*. New York: McGraw-Hill.

Berger, P., & Luckmann, T. (1966). *The social construct of reality*. New York: Anchor Books.

Boughner, S. R., Hayes, S. F., Bubenzer, D. L., & West, J. D. (1994). Use of standardized assessment instruments by marital and family therapists. A survey. *Journal of Marital and Family Therapy, 20*, 69–75.

Bowen, M. (1976). Theory in the practice of psychotherapy. In P. J. Guerin (Ed.), *Family therapy: Theory and practice*. New York: Gardner.

Bray, J. H. (1995). Family assessment: Current issues in evaluating families. *Family Relations, 44*, 469–477.

Buehler, C. L. (1990). Adjustment. In J. Touliatos, B. F. Perlmutter, & M. A. Strauss (Eds.), *Handbook of family measurement techniques* (pp. 493–574). Thousand Oaks, CA: Sage.

Carter, B., & McGoldrick, M. (1988). *The changing family life cycle*. New York: Gardner.

Carter, B., & McGoldrick, M. (1999). *The expanded family life cycle* (3rd ed.). Needham Heights, MA: Allyn & Bacon.

Cheng, A. T., & Hsu, M. (1995). Development of a new scale for measuring acculturation: The Taiwan Aboriginal Acculturation Scale (TAAS). *Psychological Medicine, 25*, 1281–1287.

Congress, E. P. (1994). The use of culturagrams to assess and empower culturally diverse families. *Families in Society, 75*, 531–540.

Cuellar, I., Arnold, B., & Maldonado, R. (1995). Acculturation Rating Scale for Mexican Americans II: A revision of the original ARSMA Scale. *Hispanic Journal of Behavioral Sciences, 17*, 275–304.

Cuellar, I., Harris, L. C., & Jasso, R. (1980). An acculturation scale for Mexican American normal and clinical populations. *Hispanic Journal of Behavioral Sciences, 2*, 199–217.

Epstein, N. B., Baldwin, L. M., & Bishop, D. S. (1983). The McMaster family assessment device. *Journal of Marital and Family Therapy, 9*, 171–180.

Fine, M. A. (1993). Current approaches to understanding family diversity: An overview of the special issue. *Family Relations, 42*, 235–237.

Floyd, F. J., Weinand, J. W., & Cimmarusti, R. A. (1989). Clinical family assessment: Applying structured measurement procedures in treatment settings. *Journal of Marital and Family Therapy, 51*, 115–124.

Gay, P. (1988). *Freud: A life for our time*. New York: Norton.

Gergen, K. J., & Gergen, M. M. (1991). Toward reflexive methodologies. In F. Steier (Ed.), *Research and reflexivity* (pp. 76–95). Thousand Oaks, CA: Sage.

Gladding, S. T. (1998). *Family therapy: History, theory, and practice* (2nd ed.). Upper Saddle River, NJ: Prentice Hall.

Gottman, J. M. (1993). A theory of marital dissolution and stability. *Journal of Family Psychology, 7*, 57–75.

Grotevant, H. D., & Carlson, C. I. (1989). *Family assessment. A guide to methods and measures*. New York: Guilford Press.

Guba, E. G., & Lincoln, Y. S. (1989). *Fourth generation evaluation*. Thousand Oaks, CA: Sage.

Guerin, P. J., & Pendagast, E. G. (1976). Evaluation of family system and genogram. In P. J. Guerin (Ed.), *Family therapy: Theory and practice* (pp. 450–464). New York: Gardner.

Gushue, G. V. (1993). Cultural identity development and family assessment. An interaction model. *Counseling Psychologist, 21*, 487–513.

Gushue, G. V., & Sciarra, D. T. (1995). Culture and families. In J. G. Ponterotto, J. M. Casas, L. A. Suzuki, & C. M. Alexander (Eds.), *Handbook of multicultural counseling* (pp. 506–606). Thousand Oaks, CA: Sage.

Haley, J. (1963). *Strategies of psychotherapy*. Philadelphia: Grune and Stratton.

Haley, J. (1976). *Problem-solving therapy*. San Francisco: Jossey Bass.

Harris, A. C., & Verven, R. (1996). The Greek-American Acculturation Scale: Development and validity. *Psychological Reports, 78*, 599–610.

Hartman, A. (1978). Diagrammatic assessment of family relationships. *Social Casework*, 59, 465–476.

Hartman, A. (1995). Diagrammatic assessment of family relationships. *Families in Society*, 76, 111–122.

Helms, J. E. (1984). Toward a theoretical explanation of the effects of race on counseling: A Black and White model. *The Counseling Psychologist*, 13, 695–710.

Helms, J. E. (1990). Toward a model of White racial identity development. In J. E. Helms (Ed.), *Black and White racial identity: Theory, research, and practice* (pp. 245–247). Westport, CT: Greenwood Press.

Helms, J. E. (1995). An update of Helms' White and people of color racial identity models. In J. G. Ponterotto, J. M. Casas, L. A. Suzuki, & C. M. Alexander (Eds.), *Handbook of multicultural counseling* (pp. 181–198). Thousand Oaks, CA: Sage.

Landrine, H., & Klonoff, E. A. (1994). The African American Acculturation Scale: Development, reliability, and validity. *Journal of Black Psychology*, 20, 104–127.

Landrine, H., & Klonoff, E. A. (1995). The African-American Acculturation Scale II: Cross validation and short form. *Journal of Black Psychology*, 21, 124–152.

Mallick, M. D., & Vigilante, F. W. (1997). The family assessment wheel: A social constructionist perspective. *Families in Society*, 78, 361–369.

Marin, G. (1992). Issues in the measurement of acculturation among Hispanics. In K. F. Geisinger (Ed.), *Psychological testing of Hispanics* (pp. 235–251). Washington, DC: American Psychological Association.

Marin, G., Sabogal, F., Marin, B. V., & Otero-Sabogal, R. (1987). Development of a short acculturation scale of Hispanics. *Hispanic Journal of Behavioral Sciences*, 9, 183–205.

McGoldrick, M., & Gerson, R. (1985). *Genograms in family assessment*. New York: Guilford Press.

McPhatter, A. R. (1991). Assessment revisited: A comprehensive approach to understanding family dynamics. *Families in Society*, 72, 11–22.

Minuchin, S., & Fishman, H. C. (1981). *Family therapy techniques*. Cambridge, MA: Harvard University Press.

Minuchin, S., Montalvo, B., Guerney, B. G., Rosman, B., & Schumer, F. (1967). *Families of the slums: An exploration of their structure and treatment*. New York: Basic Books.

Moos, R., & Moos, B. (1974). *The Family Environmental Scale*. Palo Alto, CA: Consulting Psychologists Press.

Morris, T. M. (1990). Culturally sensitive family assessment: An evaluation of the family assessment device used with Hawaiian-American and Japanese American families. *Family Process, 29*, 105–116.

Nichols, M. P., & Schwartz, R. C. (1998). *Family therapy: Concepts and methods* (4th ed.). Needham Heights, MA: Allyn & Bacon.

Olson, D. H. (1986). Circumplex model VII: Validation studies and FACES III. *Family Process, 25*, 337–351.

Rezentes, W. C. (1993). Na Mea Hawai'I: A Hawaiian acculturation scale. *Psychological Reports, 73*, 383–393.

Schwandt, T. A. (1994). Constructivist, interpretivist approaches to human inquiry. In N. K. Denzin & Y. S. Lincoln (Eds.), *Handbook of qualitative research* (pp. 118–137). Thousand Oaks, CA: Sage.

Sciarra, D. T. (1999). *Multiculturalism in counseling.* Itasca, IL: Peacock.

Sciarra, D. T., & Ponterotto, J. G. (1993). Counseling the Hispanic bilingual family: Challenges to the therapeutic process. *Psychotherapy, 28*, 473–479.

Suinn, R. M., Rickard-Figueroa, K., Lew, S., and Vigil, P. (1987). The Suinn-Lew Asian Self-Identity Acculturation Scale: An initial report. *Educational and Psychological Measurement, 47*, 401–407.

Szapocznik, J., & Kurtines, W. M. (1993). Family psychology and cultural diversity. *American Psychologist, 48*, 400–407.

Szapocznik, J., Kurtines, W., & Fernandez, T. (1980). Bicultural involvement and adjustment in Hispanic-American youths. *International Journal of Intercultural Relations, 4*, 401–407.

Touliatos, J., Perlmutter, B. F., & Strauss, M. A. (1990). *Handbook of family measurement techniques.* Thousand Oaks, CA: Sage.

Wampler, K. S., Halverson, C. F., Moore, J. J., & Walters, L. H. (1989). The Georgia family q-sort: An observational measure of family functioning. *Family Process, 28*, 223–238.

White, M. B., & Tyson-Rawson, K. J. (1995). Assessing the dynamics of gender in couples and families. *Family Relations, 44*, 253–260.

7

Vocational Assessment with Culturally Diverse Populations

Kathy A. Gainor

A ssessment has been an integral part of vocational guidance and career counseling. In fact, the birth of counseling and counseling psychology occurred at the crossroads of the vocational guidance and (intelligence) testing movements. Perhaps more than any other form of assessment and evaluation, vocational assessment affects nearly every person at an extremely crucial juncture in the individual's development, that is, vocational or career choice.

Assessment has been synonymous with career counseling. Given that career and vocational choice has been one major way in which people of color and other members of diverse populations have had limited access to a full range of opportunities, using vocational assessment in facilitating such choices is of critical concern to counselors and psychologists (Smith, 1983).

According to Fouad (1993), vocational assessment is a "means to appraise all the vocationally relevant variables that may influence an individual's vocational decisions" (p. 4). The purpose of assessment in vocational and career counseling is to help clients gather and interpret information relevant to career decision making (Forrest and Brooks, 1993). Such information and variables include, but are not limited to, vocational and personal interests,

The author would like to thank Beverly Greene of St. John's University for her invaluable assistance in preparing this chapter.

needs, values, aptitude and abilities, maturity, self-efficacy, decision-making skills, and perceptions of career barriers. It is presumed that these and other data arm clients with information for making appropriate and successful decisions regarding occupations or careers. Further, contrary to using extended career intake interviews as the primary assessment tool, vocational assessments allow counselors to gather a great deal of vocationally related data in a short period of time. Information gathered from vocational assessments can then be used to better focus and direct an interview.

Vocational assessment in its most ethical and democratic form should broaden the career options available to people and increase their chances of satisfaction and success. Therefore, each counseling professional engaged in vocational assessment with any client has a choice: either use it to perpetuate an oppressive system that denies equal access to occupational opportunities to all, or use it to increase access for those who have been previously denied access. The former happens more easily than one might think. Even the well-meaning, culturally aware counseling profession can unintentionally behave in ways that maintain the status quo (Ridley, 1995).

The purpose of this chapter is to address the role of vocational and career assessment with culturally diverse populations. First, the prevailing theoretical and methodological criticisms are reviewed. Prevailing justifications for each criticism are evaluated. Second, challenges to inclusiveness of vocational assessment with culturally diverse populations are discussed. Suggestions are made for how to manage such challenges to maximize empowerment and inclusion for culturally diverse clients. Third, suggested future directions for research and practice in the field of multicultural vocational assessment are offered. Some attention is given to vocational assessment in rehabilitation counseling with culturally diverse populations, but the predominant focus is on career and vocational assessment as typically used in college and community career centers with adolescents, college students, and adults.

Criticisms of Vocational Assessment with Culturally Diverse Populations

A major criticism of using vocational assessment inventories has consisted of accusations of racial, gender, and even class bias in both the inventories and the theories underlying the respective assessments. Theories underlying the development of most vocational instruments originate in White, Western, English-speaking, middle-class, linguistic, heterosexual, male perspectives that are not applicable to many people with differing racial, cultural, class, affectional and sexual, and gender identities (Fitzgerald and Betz, 1994; Leong and Gim-Chung, 1995). These theories of career choice and development idealize traditional Western values such as individualism over collectivism, competition over cooperation, materialism over spirituality, and control of nature over life in harmony with nature (Sue and Sue, 1999). These values often conflict with the traditional values of non-Western cultural groups. Therefore, the relevance of these traditional theories to culturally diverse populations continues to be debated (Brooks, 1990; Hackett and Lent, 1992; June and Pringle, 1977; Leong and Gim-Chung, 1995; Smith, 1983).

Most inventories and assessments were not designed to reflect the experiences of people of color; gay men, lesbians, bisexuals, and transgendered people; women; the poor; or people with disabilities. Therefore, unintentional bias can pervade the development and use of inventories. Without a clear understanding of the historical and cultural factors affecting people of diverse cultural groups, counselors and psychologists continue to interpret assessment results without a clear cultural context for their understanding. For example, research has shown that many African Americans score high in social interests and are hence counseled into primarily social occupations with little to no consideration for the social and historical reasons for those interests or the possible social benefits of other occupations (that is, investigative or realistic careers). One can not divorce the social and historical imperatives that affect people's lives from the career interests that they express. For example, as Gainor and Forrest (1991) have pointed out, a person's identity or self-concept (as related to race, gender, and/or unique self) can influence a Black woman's career decisions. Therefore, one's particular view of interests or expression of interests (for instance, social) should not necessarily lock one into a narrow range of occupational possibilities.

Related to the biases underlying the theories from which vocational assessment has derived is the legacy of assumptions brought from such early developers of intelligence tests as L. M. Terman and H. H. Goddard. These assessment pioneers presumed the inferior intelligence of the new immigrants during the first half of the century and developed assessment procedures to prove their assumptions. Despite the fact that the bias of these early test developers has been revealed (Guthrie, 1996), such assumptions prevail in the modern thinking of professionals who use assessment instruments with individuals viewed by society as being inferior in intelligence, motivation, skills, and values.

Even if practitioners do not assume inferiority in their culturally diverse clients, they may still erroneously conclude that assessments developed from a Eurocentric, middle-class perspective with primarily European American, middle-class, male, heterosexual, and able-bodied individuals are readily applicable to racial or ethnic minority clients; poor and working class; women; gay men, lesbians, bisexuals, and transgendered people; and people with disabilities.

Further, most inventories have been initially developed by, with, and for individuals whose primary language is English. Such instruments may not be valid and reliable when used with individuals for whom English is a second (or even a third) language. "Clearly, a test written in English is inadequate to measure the performance of a person who does not understand English well or at all" (Rodriguez, 1992, p. 13). Fouad (1993) suggests that assessments used cross-culturally should be validly translated, have conceptual and linguistic equivalence, and be free from bias.

In addressing conceptual and linguistic equivalence, Lonner (1985) has articulated four levels of equivalence that are essential in comparing individuals across cultures. First, assessments used with culturally diverse populations must possess functional equivalence; that is, the role a behavior plays needs to be equivalent across cultures. For example, the function of work varies in different cultures.

The second equivalence important in cross-cultural assessment is conceptual equivalence. This refers to the similarities in meaning assigned to a behavior or concept. For example, a "church worker" in Mexico is an elderly widow who no longer fully occupies the home; this contrasts with a church volunteer in the United States (Fouad, 1993).

Third is metric equivalence, which refers to whether the scale measures the same constructs in different cultures. The fourth equivalence, linguistic, is "perhaps the most single stumbling block to effective cross-cultural assessment (Lonner, 1985, p. 603). Linguistic equivalence refers to language comfortability for the person being assessed. Fouad (1993, 1994) outlines four steps for valid translation, and therefore linguistic equivalence, of vocational assessment. These steps are literal translation, back-translation (to check for conceptual equivalence between initial and second English forms), committee consensus (to reconcile differences), and bilingual field test (to correlate between the English and translated versions). The 1984 Strong-Campbell Interest Inventory and the Career Decision-Making System (Harrington and O'Shea, 1992) have undergone rigorous translation processes (Fouad, 1994).

A third criticism of using vocational assessment instruments with diverse populations concerns insufficient representation of minority groups in the normative samples for the various instruments. Lack of adequate representation threatens the validity of the instruments and therefore violates the principle of generalizability. Therefore, using these instruments with people who are not representative in the normative sample does not give statistical support to any conclusions made. For example, although the 1994 General

Reference Sample (GRS) for the Strong Interest Inventory (SII; Harmon, Hansen, Borgen, and Hammer, 1994) consists of 1,167 people who readily identify as African Americans, Asian Americans, Hispanic Americans, or Native Americans, they make up only 10 percent of the total GRS. In the normative sample of the Self-Directed Search (SDS; Holland, Fritzsche, and Powell, 1994), people of color and members of other ethnic groups constitute only 25 percent of the total sample. Further, no data are given on the socioeconomic status of the SDS normative group. One must speculate about this factor from other demographic data (for instance, community and educational settings).

Commenting on recently accumulated evidence of considerable and remarkable invariance in the structure of interests, Swanson and Gore (2000) conclude that although mean differences continue to be seen among racial and ethnic groups (see Kaufman, Ford-Richards, and McLean, 1998), there is strong evidence to support that "the theoretical models underlying interests seem to provide equally adequate representation for a variety of individuals" (p. 253). Studies conducted by Day and Rounds (1998) and Day, Rounds, and Swaney (1998) are said to offer strong evidence for universality of interest structure.

I believe that some caution is warranted with regard to recent declarations of universality. Fouad and Dancer (1992, as cited in Fouad, 1995) questioned whether Holland's theory, for example, is universal or whether it "ethnocentrically define[s] the structure of interests by a White standard against which all deviations are abnormal" (p. 224). Without careful consideration of the role and influence of such factors as acculturation, assimilation, and racial and ethnic identity, we cannot fully understand the similarities and differences in interests (or values, needs, and so on) found across cultures. Further, "more study is needed . . . to determine whether similarity is modified by SES, geographic region, acculturation . . ., or number of generations in the United states, among other variables" (Fouad, 1995, p. 170).

Despite prevailing criticisms and concerns clouding the use of vocational assessment with people from culturally diverse groups, there seem to be a number of ways that vocational assessment interviews and inventories can be used to broaden the options available to everyone. With proper preparation and an appropriate amount of caution, counselors can find effective and culturally relevant use for vocational assessment instruments with culturally diverse populations.

Challenges to and Suggestions for Inclusion and Empowerment

As Subich (1996) points out, calls to revise or reform career assessment for all clients are not new. However, instrument developers, researchers, and practitioners need clear guidelines for how to use vocational assessments cross-culturally.

First and foremost, the counselor aiming to use vocational assessment with culturally diverse populations needs to ensure at least minimum competence in the multicultural counseling standards (Arrendondo and others, 1996; Sue and others, 1998) recently adopted by the American Counseling Association and the American Psychological Association. Essentially, counselors must demonstrate the three dimensions of multicultural counseling competence:

1. Awareness of own values, biases, preconceived notions, and assumptions about human behavior
2. Understanding of the worldviews of culturally different clients
3. Development and practice of appropriate, relevant, sensitive, and ethical intervention strategies and skills for working with culturally different clients (Arrendondo and others, 1996; Sue and others, 1998)

Effective use of these inventories varies with the multicultural competence of the counselor.

Fundamentally, the counselor would possess attitudes, knowledge, and skills concerning awareness of his or her own assumptions, values, and biases about human behavior and people from culturally diverse groups. Biases can operate in the attitudes and expectations of counselors who are trained in primarily Western models of counseling. For example, Leong and Gim-Chung (1995) point out that leaving home during one's twenties is considered quite normative in American experience, "whereas many Asian cultures encourage extended families living together or living at home until marriage" (p. 203).

Counselors should assess their own perceptions that certain people, by virtue of their membership in particular cultural groups, are suited for (meaning, are intelligent enough, or motivated for) particular occupations. Such perceptions can negatively affect the interpretation of data gleaned from vocational assessment instruments.

For example, a counselor can demonstrate bias in his or her interpretation and use of the Learning Environment (LE; formerly Academic Comfort) special scale of the SII. The LE scale measures the client's level of formal education (Harmon, Hansen, Borgen, and Hammer, 1994). High scores characterize people with college and graduate degrees, while low scores indicate people with high school or technical training.

If bias and discrimination is part of the counselor's countertransference (conscious or unconscious), he or she can prematurely interpret a low score to mean that the client is unable to engage in formal educational pursuits. This could lead even the well-intentioned counselor to conclude that such a client should avoid institutions of higher education altogether. A culturally diverse client, whose educational experiences have been fraught with discriminatory and oppressive experiences related to the student's race, gender, class, sexual orientation, and so on, would not necessarily express or have a high level of comfort with a formal educational environment despite a personal interest or motivation toward higher education. Such a client would be better served with an opportunity to use the counseling sessions to explore and work through emotional scars left from previous, discriminatory, school-related traumas and to develop effective coping strategies for dealing with any further prejudice and discrimination. The client could then pursue the higher levels of education necessary for broadening the range of occupational opportunities.

In another example, students of color scoring high in science interests (that is, investigative) are too often steered away from those occupations altogether or into lower-status investigative occupations (X-ray technician or science teacher) with no consideration for higher-status investigative careers (doctor, scientist, engineer). Even in a college of engineering, a Black student could be counseled into pursuing mechanical engineering while White students are encouraged to pursue a higher-status branch of engineering (say, chemical engineering).

The purpose of career theories and models like Holland's is to assist clients in finding work environments that fit or match their personality. This is too often translated into narrowing the range of occupations individuals should consider rather than examining ways to broaden their options yet find work environments that allow people "to exercise their skills and abilities, express their attitudes and values, and take on agreeable problems and roles" (Holland, 1992, p. 4). Therefore, failure to assess and work through one's own biases and prejudices makes one vulnerable to even unintentional discrimination in using vocational assessment with a culturally diverse population.

Every counselor using vocational assessment with culturally diverse clients must also have a clear understanding of the clients' cultural worldviews. Cultural identity development is another important variable that presents a challenge to using assessment results in an inclusive and empowering manner. The role and impact of cultural identities, for example, on the development of the client's interests, abilities, values, and so on as they affect work and career choice is an important factor to consider during vocational assessment. The meaning or interpretation of the results should be evaluated within an appropriate sociocultural context.

With regard to people of color, the concepts of racial identity and acculturation seem to have critical relevance to career choice and development, and therefore vocational assessment. The impact of racial identity on vocational behavior (Tinsley, 1994) and career assessment (Walsh, 1994) has received special attention in the professional literature.

Racial identity (Helms, 1990) or *racial salience* (Helms, 1994; Helms and Piper, 1994) refers to a person's perception that he or she shares a common heritage with a particular racial group, and to the extent to which the person perceives his or her race as a significant definer of work options. Recent studies have indicated that racial identity may play at least a small role in academic and career choice for African American college students (Evans and Herr, 1994; Gainor and Lent, 1998; Woods, 1991).

It is argued that racial identity potentially explains at least some aspects of vocational development and career counseling for people of color. It is possible, for example, that racial identity helps to explain the process of vocational decision making (Helms and Piper, 1994) or may be particularly relevant to perceptions of opportunities, supports, and barriers (Parham and Austin, 1994). Bowman (1993, 1995) has suggested that racial identity may also affect approaches to career counseling with racial and ethnic minority-group members. Level of racial salience has been shown to influence preference for the race of the counselor (Helms, 1986; Helms and Carter, 1991; Parham and Helms, 1981). For example, clients in the immersion stage who may not trust counselors of any racial group other than their own (Bowman, 1995). Further, the interaction between client racial identity and counselor racial identity (Helms, 1986) might influence how career assessment is presented by the counselor and perceived by the client, how the client approaches completing the inventories (incomplete items or response bias), how the counselor presents the results, and how both the counselor and client understand and interpret the results.

Others have explored how identity development may affect career choice and development for women (Hackett and Lonborg, 1993) and gay men and lesbians (Mobley and Slaney, 1996). For these populations, issues concern gender role analysis and sexual orientation identity development. A formal or informal assessment of cultural identity may offer important information for understanding the context in which people of diverse cultural backgrounds make career decisions. Hartung and others (1998) suggest including an assessment of the client's cultural identity development as part of the initial interview in which the client shares his or her life's narrative.

Dana (1996) argues that it is ethically mandatory for clinicians to have knowledge of the client as a "cultural being," or cultural orientation information. Such information is required prior to assessment so as to know whether the assessment technology and service delivery style developed within the Anglo American society is applicable to a particular client from a visible racial or ethnic group. To assist in this end, Dana describes four categories of acculturation or cultural orientation: traditional, marginal, bicultural, and assimilated.

Related to the level of acculturation are issues concerning consideration of language and linguistic equivalence, conceptual equivalence, and experience with test taking (that is, being test-wise; Fouad, 1994). According to Dana (1996), knowledge of the client's cultural orientation affords clues regarding selection of credible tests (standard or culture-specific), methods of the subsequent assessment process, how to present the results, and where and to whom (student, client, parents) feedback should be given .

Fouad, Harmon, and Hansen (1994) remind us of the importance of not assuming that the clients are familiar with interest (and other) inventories. In addition, as a result of individual and collective negative experiences with testing and assessment, some culturally diverse clients (say, African Americans) may not trust and therefore may be suspicious of the assessment process. Asian American clients, as a result of living within authoritarian family and social structures, may be unlikely to directly question or challenge the counselor, but may choose to terminate prematurely unless the counselor offers a sufficient explanation of the nature and purpose of the test. In addition, maintaining face and avoiding loss of face are very important interpersonal dimensions that can greatly influence Asian American client responses on an assessment inventory (Leong and Gim-Chung, 1995).

Cultural diversity can be integrated into existing assessment batteries or protocols. For example, Hartung and others (1998) have expanded the Career-Development Assessment and Counseling (C-DAC; Super and others, 1992) model to consider cultural identity as a significant variable in career development and vocational behavior. The C-DAC model incorporates a comprehensive battery of five career assessment measures designed to assess the "career stage and concerns and level of career maturity or career adaptability" (Hartung and others, 1998, p. 278). The core C-DAC battery consists of the Salience Inventory (SI), the Adult Career Concerns Inventory (ACCI), the Career Development Inventory (CDI), the Values Scale (VS), and the SII. Hartung and others (1998) propose that making the C-DAC model culturally relevant entails (1) making cultural identity a core component of the model, (2) encouraging cultural relevance in implementing each of the four steps of the model, and (3) specifying culturally sensitive assessments and counseling interventions as part of the core C-DAC assessment battery and counseling process.

Additional suggestions include taking into account discriminatory attitudes and practices in the current job market and world of work; recognizing how acculturation is a significant moderator of racial and ethnic minority-group career development and vocational behavior; understanding cultural value orientations (for instance, individualism-collectivism) as another dimension of cultural group differences that can affect career development and vocational behavior; and identifying how stereotypes, prejudice, and discrimination can affect career development, vocational behavior, and career counseling itself (Hartung and others, 1998).

The salience of cultural variables (race, gender, sexual orientation) and the influence of such variables on the individual's career development and vocational behavior should be clearly understood by the counselor. Hartung and others (1998) acknowledge the potential problems of using traditional career-related measures and instruments with culturally diverse populations. Hence, they recommend using the measures in alternative ways (that is, qualitatively, to explore the meaning and significance of the responses to the client; or using C-DAC items in the initial interview, framing them in a cultural context). In addition, Hartung and colleagues support using two culture-specific assessments, the Multicultural Career Counseling Checklist (MCCC) and the Career Counseling Checklist (CCC; Ward and Bingham, 1993).

Originally developed by Ward and Bingham (1993) for career counseling with ethnic minority women, the MCCC (for counselors) and the CCC (for clients) facilitate accurate assessment with people of color. The MCCC helps to remind counselors of the issues and concerns that may be significant for the ethnic minority female client, while the CCC was designed to help the client and counselor understand and think more thoroughly about her career concerns.

Swanson and Bowman (1994) have proposed addressing a number of areas with African American clients that can be appropriately applied to people from various other racial and cultural groups. During the initial interview, the counselor can explore a number of important areas: the client's perceptions of occupations considered "open" or "closed" to members of the client's cultural group, the extent of the client's exposure to the wide range of occupations within the world of work, the client's perception of barriers in education and work and planned strategies for overcoming potential barriers, the client's access to available role models in one's cultural group across a range of occupational fields, messages the client holds about work, messages the client perceives society to hold about workers from his or her cultural group, and the role of cultural and familial factors in the client's career choice (Swanson and Bowman, 1994).

The suggestions outlined by Hartung and others (1998) and Swanson and Bowman (1994) point to the critical importance of the assessment or intake interview in working with people from culturally diverse groups. As mentioned earlier, using inventories enables counselors and clients to gather much information in a short period of time. However, a properly conducted interview helps create a context from which to select, administer, and interpret the more formal assessment instruments.

Equally important to the intake interview are the sessions devoted to communicating and interpreting the assessment results to the client. Careful consideration of relevant cultural variables for the individual client can shed additional light on the assessment findings and therefore broaden the range of career options considered by the client. For example, if African American students score stereotypically (high social interests), the postassessment can yield valuable information on the role of racial salience in the scores.

In my professional experience, providing career counseling to college students, it is not unusual for Black and Hispanic students with high altruistic and social values to score high in social interests. Those with high abilities in math and science may forgo technological career choices in favor of careers perceived to have more potential to directly affect the students' communities. Such students can be encouraged to consider potentially social or altruistic value in traditionally technological careers (for example, an engineer who designs or builds toys for children with physical disabilities).

Counselors should also make use of inventories that include culturally sensitive variables. For example, the Life Values Inventory (LVI; Crace and Brown, 1996), derived from Brown's (1996) values-based, holistic model of career and life-role choice and satisfaction, includes values that vary with culture and subculture. Traditionally Western and non-Western values (such as independence for the former, loyalty to family or group among the latter) are included in the LVI. In addition, the level of importance of several variables (concern for the environment, concern for others, spirituality) can vary with the level of cultural orientation. The LVI also has an open-ended response section, which permits qualitative examination of the role of cultural diversity in the development of the values influencing the client's career choice and life satisfaction.

In addition to integrating cultural diversity into commonly used measures of career choice and development, career counselors need to thoroughly assess and incorporate other broad aspects of career development (say, environmental and contextual factors). Feminist and multicultural counselors and therapists emphasize empowering clients by attending to sociocultural conditions that contribute to the client's concerns (Forrest and Brooks, 1993; Sue and Sue, 1999).

One model that holds much promise in addressing environmental and contextual variables is Lent, Brown, and Hackett's (1994) social cognitive career theory. SCCT addresses the interplay between the person and the environment as well as the person's perceptions of his or her environment (as in perception of support and barriers). In this model, Lent and colleagues emphasize three social-cognitive mechanisms relevant to academic and career development: self-efficacy beliefs, outcome expectations, and goal mechanisms. They also attempt to explain how these mechanisms influence career development in combination with other important person, contextual, and experiential factors (race, gender, socio-economic status, social supports and barriers).

Quantitative and qualitative assessments of contextual and environmental factors (supports, resources, institutional and cultural barriers) must be part of the vocational and career counseling with culturally diverse clients. Measures such as the Career Barriers Inventory (CBI; Swanson and Daniels, 1991; Swanson, Daniels, and Tokar, 1996), which includes perceptions of racial and gender discrimination, can be particularly useful. At least one attempt has been made to develop culturally relevant versions of the CBI in a Chinese culture (Tien, 1998).

Last, but certainly not least, career and vocational counselors should use standards and guidelines for evaluating assessment instruments judiciously. The *Standards for Educational and Psychological Testing* (American Educational Research Association, American Psychological Association, and National Council on Measurement in Education, 1999) and the *Multicultural Assessment Standards* (Prediger, 1993) provide essential information for evaluating and administering assessment instruments. For example, according to these standards, each counselor should conduct a thorough evaluation of the test manual prior to using the particular instrument.

Counselors should also adhere to the administration standards outlined in these two documents. This does not, however, preclude any qualitative analysis of the quantitative data gleaned from the instruments. For example, when discussing the results (the objective scores), the client and counselor can work collaboratively to construct an interpretation grounded in a sociocultural context that is appropriate and relevant to the individual client.

Future Directions for Practice and Research

Vocational assessment with diverse populations should be conducted in the context of good, sound, multicultural competence. Therefore, courses in career counseling, vocational development, and measurement and testing should fully integrate cultural diversity throughout the curriculum rather than relegate it to one or two sessions on the syllabus (Gainor, 2000). Counselor educators must themselves demonstrate competencies in both multicultural counseling (Arrendondo and others, 1996; Sue and others, 1998) and career counseling (NCDA, 1997) and receive proper training in dealing with resistance to multicultural training (Kilesca, 1999; Mio and Awakuni, 2000).

Theorists, instrument developers, researchers, and clinicians need to critically evaluate the meaning of universality or "no difference." Are we seeing no bias in our instruments, or manifestations of cultural dominance in our culturally diverse clients?

Summary and Conclusions

It is clear that with continued empirical examination and modern technological advances in administration, validation, and interpretation of vocational and career instruments, vocational assessment remains an important component of career counseling and development. Vocational and career counselors must be multiculturally competent professionals. Further, using vocational assessments with culturally diverse clients has to be grounded in a cultural context.

References

American Educational Research Association, American Psychological Association, & National Council on Measurement in Education. (1999). *Standards for educational and psychological testing* (2nd ed.). Washington, DC: American Educational Research Association.

Arrendondo, P., Toporek, R., Brown, S., Jones, J., Locke, D. C., Sanchez, J., & Stadler, H. (1996). Operationalization of the multicultural counseling competencies. *Journal of Multicultural Counseling and Development, 24*, 42–78.

Bowman, S. L. (1993). Career intervention strategies for ethnic minorities. *Career Development Quarterly, 42*, 14–25.

Bowman, S. L. (1995). Career intervention strategies and assessment issues for African Americans. In F.T.L. Leong (Ed.), *Career development and vocational behavior of racial and ethnic minorities* (pp. 137–164). Hillsdale, NJ: Erlbaum.

Brooks, L. (1990). Recent developments in theory building. In D. Brown, L. Brooks, & Associates, *Career choice and development* (2nd ed., pp. 338–363). San Francisco: Jossey-Bass.

Brown, D. (1996). Brown's values-based, holistic model of career and life-role choices and satisfaction. In D. Brown, L. Brooks, & Associates, *Career choice and development* (3rd ed., pp. 337–372). San Francisco: Jossey-Bass.

Cheatham, H. E. (1990). Africentricity and career development of African Americans. *Career Development Quarterly, 38*, 334–346.

Crace, R. K., & Brown, D. (1996). *Life Values Inventory.* Chapel Hill, NC: Life Values Resources.

Dana, R. H. (1996). Culturally competent assessment practice in the United States. *Journal of Personality Assessment, 66*, 472–487.

Day, S. X., & Rounds, J. B. (1998). Universality of vocational interest structure among racial and ethnic minorities. *American Psychologist, 53*, 728–736.

Day, S. X., Rounds, J. B., & Swaney, K. (1998). The structure of vocational interests for diverse racial-ethnic groups. *Psychological Science, 9*, 40–44.

Evans, K. M., & Herr, E. L. (1994). The influence of racial identity and the perception of discrimination in the career aspirations of African American men and women. *Journal of Vocational Behavior, 44*, 173–184.

Fitzgerald, L. F., & Betz, N. E. (1994). Career development in cultural context: The role of gender, race, class, and sexual orientation. In M. L. Savickas & R. W. Lent (Eds.), *Convergence in career development theories: Implications for science and practice* (pp. 103–117). Palo Alto, CA: Consulting Psychologists Press.

Forrest, L., & Brooks, N. (1993). Feminism and career assessment. *Journal of Career Assessment, 1*, 233–245.

Fouad, N. A. (1993). Cross-cultural vocational assessment. *Career Development Quarterly, 42*, 4–13.

Fouad, N. A. (1994). Career assessment with Latinos/Hispanics. *Journal of Career Assessment, 3*, 226–239.

Fouad, N. A. (1995). Career behavior of Hispanics: Assessment and career intervention. In F.T.L. Leong (Ed.), *Career development and vocational behavior of racial and ethnic minorities* (pp. 165–191). Hillsdale, NJ: Erlbaum.

Fouad, N. A., Harmon, L. W., & Hansen, J. C. (1994). Cross-cultural use of the Strong. In L. W. Harmon, J. C., Hansen, F. H. Borgen, & A. L. Hammer, *Strong Interest Inventory: Applications and technical guide* (pp. 255–280). Palo Alto, CA: Consulting Psychologists Press.

Gainor, K. A. (2000, June). Integrating cultural diversity into career development and career counseling courses. Workshop presented at the 9th Global Conference of the National Career Development Association, Pittsburgh, Pennsylvania.

Gainor, K. A., & Forrest, L. (1991). African American women's self-concept: Implications for career decisions and career counseling. *Career Development Quarterly, 39*, 261–272.

Gainor, K. A., & Lent, R. W. (1998). Social cognitive expectations and racial identity attitudes as predictors of math choice intentions in Black college students. *Journal of Counseling Psychology, 45,* 403–413.

Guthrie, R. V. (1996). *Even the rat was white: A historical view of psychology* (2nd ed.). Needham Heights, MA: Allyn & Bacon.

Hackett, G., & Byars, A. M. (1996). Social cognitive theory and the career development of African American women. *Career Development Quarterly, 44,* 322–340.

Hackett, G., & Lent, R. W. (1992). Theoretical advances and current inquiry in career psychology. In S. D. Brown & R. W. Lent (Eds.), *Handbook of counseling psychology* (pp. 419–415). New York: Wiley.

Hackett, G., & Lonborg, S. D. (1993). Career assessment for women: Trends and issues. *Journal of Career Assessment, 1,* 197–216.

Harmon, L. W., Hansen, J. C., Borgen, F. H., & Hammer, A. L. (1994). *Strong Interest Inventory: Applications and technical guide.* Palo Alto, CA: Consulting Psychologists Press.

Harrington, T. F., & O'Shea, A. J. (1992). *The Harrington, O'Shea Career Decision-Making System.* Circle Pines, MN: American Guidance Service.

Hartung, P. J., Vandiver, B. J., Leong, F.T.L., Pope, M., Niles, S. G., & Farrow, B. (1998). Appraising cultural identity in career-development assessment and counseling. *Career Development Quarterly, 46,* 276–293.

Helms, J. E. (1986). Expanding racial identity to cover counseling process. *Journal of Counseling Psychology, 33,* 62–64.

Helms, J. E. (Ed.). (1990). *Black and White racial identity.* Westport, CT: Greenwood Press.

Helms, J. E. (1994). Racial identity and career assessment. *Journal of Career Assessment, 2,* 199–209.

Helms, J. E., & Carter, R. T. (1991). Relationships of White and Black racial identity attitudes and demographic similarity to counselor preferences. *Journal of Counseling Psychology, 38,* 446–457.

Helms, J. E., & Piper, R. E. (1994). Implications of racial identity theory for vocational psychology. *Journal of Vocational Behavior, 44,* 124–138.

Holland, J. L. (1992). *Making vocational choices: A theory of vocational personalities and work environments* (2nd ed.). Odessa, FL: Psychological Assessment Resources.

Holland, J. L., Fritzsche, B. A., & Powell, A. B. (1994). *The Self-Directed Search technical manual.* Odessa, FL: Psychological Assessment Resources.

June, L. N., & Pringle, G. N. (1977). The concept of race in the career development theories of Roe, Super, and Holland. *Journal of Non-White Concerns in Personnel and Guidance, 6,* 17–24.

Kaufman, A. S., Ford-Richards, J. M., & McLean, J. E. (1998). Black-White differences on the Strong Interest Inventory General Occupational Themes and Basic Interest scales at ages 16 to 65. *Journal of Clinical Psychology, 54,* 19–33.

Kiscelica, M. S. (Ed.). (1999). *Confronting prejudice and racism during multicultural training.* Alexandria, VA: American Counseling Association.

Lent, R. W., Brown, S. D., & Hackett, G. (1994). Toward a unified social cognitive theory of career/academic interest, choice, and performance. [Monograph.] *Journal of Vocational Behavior, 45,* 79–122.

Leong, F.T.L., & Gim-Chung, R. H. (1995). Career assessment and intervention with Asian Americans. In F.T.L. Leong (Ed.), *Career development and vocational behavior of racial and ethnic minorities* (pp. 193–226). Hillsdale, NJ: Erlbaum.

Lonner, W. J. (1985). Issues in testing and assessment in cross-cultural counseling. *Counseling Psychologist, 13,* 599–614.

Mio, J. S., & Awakuni, G. I. (2000). *Resistance to multiculturalism: Issues and interventions.* Philadelphia: Brunner/Mazel.

Mobley, M., & Slaney, R. B. (1996). Holland's theory: Its relevance for lesbian women and gay men. *Journal of Vocational Behavior, 48,* 125–135.

National Career Development Association. (1997). *Career counseling competencies.* Columbus, OH: Author.

Parham, T. A., & Austin, N. L. (1994). Career development and African Americans: A contextual reappraisal using the nigrescence construct. *Journal of Vocational Behavior, 44,* 139–154.

Parham, T. A., & Helms, J. E. (1981). Influence of a Black student's racial identity attitudes on preference for counselor race. *Journal of Counseling Psychology, 28,* 250–257.

Prediger, D. J. (Ed.). (1993). Multicultural assessment standards: A compilation. Alexandria, VA: Association for Assessment in Counseling.

Ridley, C. R. (1995). *Overcoming unintentional racism in counseling and therapy.* Thousand Oaks, CA: Sage.

Rodriguez, O. (1992). Introduction to technical and societal issues in the psychological testing of Hispanics. In K. F. Geisinger (Ed.), *Psychological testing of Hispanics* (pp. 11–16). Washington, DC: American Psychological Association.

Smith, E. J. (1983). Issues in racial minorities' career behavior. In W. B. Walsh
& S. H. Osipow (Eds.), *Handbook of vocational psychology: Vol. 1—
Foundations* (pp. 161–222). Hillsdale, NJ: Erlbaum.

Subich, L. M. (1996). Addressing diversity in the process of career assessment.
In M. L. Savickas & W. B. Walsh (Eds.), *Handbook of Career Counseling
Theory and Practice* (pp. 277–289). Palo Alto, CA: Davies-Black.

Sue, D. W., Carter, R. T., Casas, J. M., Fouad, N. A., Ivey, A. E., Jensen, M.,
LaFromboise, T., Manese, J. E., Ponterotto, J. G., & Vazquez-Nutall, E.
(1998). *Multicultural counseling competencies: Individual and organizational
development.* Thousand Oaks, CA: Sage.

Sue, D. W., & Sue, D. (1999). *Counseling the culturally different: Theory and
practice.* (3rd ed.). New York: Wiley.

Super, D. E., Osborne, W. L., Walsh, D. J., Brown, S. D., & Niles, S. G. (1992).
Developmental career assessment and counseling: The C-DAC model.
Journal of Counseling and Development, 71, 74–83.

Swanson, J. L., & Bowman, S. L. (1994). Career assessment with African-
American clients. *Journal of Career Assessment, 3,* 210–227.

Swanson, J. L., & Daniels, K. K. (1991). Development and initial validation of
the Career Barriers Inventory. *Journal of Vocational Behavior, 39,* 344–361.

Swanson, J. L., Daniels, K. K., & Tokar, D. M. (1996). Assessing perceptions of
career-related barriers: The career barriers inventory. *Journal of Career
Assessment, 4,* 219–244.

Swanson, J. L., & Gore, P. A., Jr. (2000). Advances in vocational psychology
theory and practice. In S. D. Brown & R. W. Lent (Eds.), *Handbook of
counseling psychology* (3rd ed., pp. 233–269). New York: Wiley.

Tien, H. S. (1998, August). *Development and initial validation of a Chinese career
barriers inventory.* Paper presented at the 106th Annual Conference of the
American Psychological Association, San Francisco.

Tinsley, H.E.A. (Ed.). (1994). Racial identity and vocational behavior [Special
issue]. *Journal of Vocational Behavior, 44*(3).

Walsh, W. B. (Ed.). (1994). Special feature: Career assessment with racial and
ethnic minorities. *Journal of Career Assessment, 2*(3).

Ward, C. M., & Bingham, R. P. (1993). Career assessment for ethnic minority
women. *Journal of Career Assessment, 1,* 246–257.

Woods, P. A. (1991). *Racial identity and vocational orientation of Black college
students as related to traditionality of academic major choice and expressed
occupational preference.* Unpublished doctoral dissertation. University of
Maryland, College Park.

8

Assessing Quality of Life in the Context of Culture

Shawn O. Utsey, Mark A. Bolden, Christa F. Brown, and Mark H. Chae

Quality of life (QOL) and subjective well-being (SWB) are two interrelated and interdependent constructs that have received increased attention in the psychological and health-related literature during the past decade. Historically, QOL and SWB have been concerned with describing individuals' level of satisfaction with their life-as-a-whole or in general (Anderson and Robinson, 1991). Chambers and Kong (1996) describe the concept of QOL as being based on subjective perceptions of well-being as well as the ability to function in daily life. Others have suggested that QOL is determined by satisfaction with one's role at home, work, and in the community (Croog, Levine, and Testa, 1986). QOL is defined by the World Health Organization as "an individual's perception of their position in life in the context of the culture and value system in which they live and in relation to their goals, expectations, standards, and concerns" (WHOQOL Group, 1994, p. 28). Moreover, WHO views QOL as a broad concept influenced by people's physical health, psychological well-being, personal beliefs, social relationships, and relationship with their environment.

In this chapter, we discuss the theoretical ambiguity inherent in cross-cultural applications of QOL concepts as well as technical considerations in assessing of QOL across cultures, and we review several QOL measures. In the first section, we compare QOL concepts in collectivistic versus individualistic cultures. Concepts such as spirit, harmony, and time orientation are presented as important aspects of QOL in many collective cultures. The second section addresses technical issues related to QOL assessment across cultures, such as conceptual equivalence, semantic equivalence, item equivalence, and scalar equivalence. Finally, several QOL measures, including phenomenological approaches, are reviewed in light of the relevant factors associated with assessing QOL across cultures.

Although QOL and SWB have received increased attention in the psychological and health-related literature, some ambiguity still exists with regard to the components that make up the construct and the applicability of these components across cultures. For example, Chambers and Kong (1996) posit that SWB is a psychological summary of an individual's quality of life, and that psychological concepts such as depression, self-esteem, anxiety, and alienation indirectly tap aspects of QOL.

According to King and Napa (1998), QOL and SWB are determined by an individual's perceived happiness, sense of purpose in life, and financial security. They note, however, that concern for internal states such as happiness and personal fulfillment are Western notions of SWB and QOL. In contrast, Kagawa-Singer (1988) proposed a conceptual framework of QOL that is transcultural and heuristic in its focus and application. This framework is inclusive of the basic need for safety and security (food, shelter, clothing, physical comfort), a sense of integrity and purpose (contributing to the well-being and support of one's group), and a sense of connectedness and belonging. Another component not included in Western conceptualizations of QOL and SWB, but necessary for cross-cultural applications of these constructs, is the dimension of existential and spiritual well-being (Nobles, 1990).

Understanding QOL and SWB in the context of culture and worldview is especially important given that cultural beliefs and behaviors play a considerable role in determining how quality of life is defined for individuals across cultures (Padilla and Kagawa-Singer, 1998). Moreover, it should be noted that questions remain as to whether the concept of QOL can be accommodated in cross-cultural translation given that some cultures have no equivalent concept (for instance, the Japanese culture; see Kuyken, Orley, Hudelson, and Sartorius, 1994) or where QOL has a different meaning (as with African cultures; see Nobles, 1990). Other researchers not only concur that it is inappropriate to assume cultural universality with regard to the concept of QOL but go further in questioning whether the research methods currently being used are capable of detecting a universal dimension of QOL should one exist (Greenfield, 1997; O'Boyle, 1994).

A major issue in conceptualizing and measuring QOL is that both the construct and the existing instrumentation are steeped in a Western cultural epistemological framework and worldview. For example, in accordance with Western worldviews, most definitions of QOL (see Chambers and Kong, 1996; King and Napa, 1998; WHOQOL Group, 1994) focus on individualism and personal happiness. In the Western worldview, personhood is synonymous with autonomy, individual rights, self-determination, and privacy (O'Boyle, 1994). In contrast, traditional societies (African, Asian, Aboriginal) view personhood as intricately linked to family, ethnic group, village, or social group membership; the individual perceives himself or herself as an extension of the group (family, tribe, and so on) as well as an intermediary between ancestors and future generations. Here the emphasis is not on the self but the "familial self," which is characterized by a close emotional bond between family members, a sense of interdependence among members of the closely knit family unit, and a sense of togetherness among all members of the clan or village (O'Boyle, 1994).

Inherent in most definitions of QOL, including those intended for international and cross-cultural application (as with the WHO-QOL Group), is a focus on the individual and his or her perceived well-being and adaptive functioning. Concepts such as life satisfaction, self-esteem, and happiness, all of which have been linked to QOL in research with Western cultures (Chambers and Kong, 1996; Diener and Diener, 1995), are manifestations of individualist cultures (such as the United States and Western Europe). In individualist cultures, people are motivated to feel good about themselves, strive for attainment of personal goals, and become independent of others by developing personal qualities that serve to distinguish them from others (Suh, Diener, Oishi, and Triandis, 1998).

In contrast, persons from collectivist cultures view QOL (and related concepts) as ultimately and inextricably linked to family, community, or ethnic or racial group (Arrindell and others, 1997). In collectivist cultures, individuals seek fulfillment through cultivating and maintaining harmony within the group (family, community, nation) as well as in interpersonal relationships (Kwan, Bond, and Singelis, 1997). Oftentimes, enhancing group harmony and interpersonal relationships is done at the expense of personal goals and aspirations (Arrindell and others, 1997). Note that the primary focus of the concept of relationship harmony is the relationship itself, not the satisfaction or support the individual derives from the relationship. Given the fundamental differences between collectivist and individualist cultures, it may be necessary to arrive at both emic and etic definitions of QOL for conceptual clarity.

Conceptual Issues Related to Assessing QOL Across Cultures

Numerous authors have suggested that QOL concepts have an inherent cultural context (Keith, Heal, and Schalock, 1996; Kuyken, Orley, Hudelson, and Sartorius, 1994; Kwan, Bond, and Singelis, 1997; Padilla and Kagawa-Singer, 1998; Saxena, 1994). Moreover, each culture along with its related QOL concepts evolves from a specific philosophic origin. Consequently, efforts aimed at providing a cultural context to QOL concepts must include the philosophical branches of cosmology, ontology, axiology, and epistemology (Kwan, Bond, and Singelis, 1997; Saxena, 1994). Understanding the philosophical underpinnings of QOL concepts is all the more important given that concepts have names that, when written or spoken, assume the language context of the culture of origin (see Table 8.1).

Table 8.1. Cultural group, worldview, quality of life concepts, and instrumentation for assessing quality of life across cultures.

Cultural Group	Worldview	Quality of Life Concepts	Assessment	Evaluator
African	Collective, universal order, flexible time orientation, relationship with ancestors, spirit-centered	Group/relationship harmony, harmony with nature ancestor alignment, *Ntu, Njia Moyo*	Phenomenological, divination, oracular, spiritual technology	Babalawa, diviners, minister santeros, *Okfunto Nganga Ngoma*
Asian	Mind and body indivisible, group/collective consciousness, familism, hierarchical relationship structure	Ki, harmony with nature, balance among mind-body-spirit, tao	Phenomenological	Monk, mudang or mansin
Indian	Collective, mind and body indivisible, all living things possess spirit	Familial, social, cosmic harmony, balance between mind and body, liberation of the spirit, dharma	Phenomenological	Shaman Yogi
Native American	Wellness = harmony among spirit-mind-body, plants, animals, humans are all part of spirit world	Harmony with nature and spirit world, reciprocity	Phenomenological, ceremonial	Medicine man, angakok
European	Individualism, action orientation, linear time, quantifying human experiences, quantifiable ontology	Self-esteem, individual happiness, material wealth, satisfaction with life	Paper-and-pencil measures, structured interview	Psychologist

Naming is an act of empowerment when the context is culturally and linguistically congruent with the philosophic framework of the population being studied (Nobles, 1990). Conversely, when externally imposed by an alien culture, naming is oppressive if not authenticated by the indigenous population for whom the concept is intended (Freire, 1994). Therefore, the phrase *quality of life*—how people subjectively place value (quality) on their views of existence (life)—contains inherent assumptions that may pose a conceptual dilemma if culturally appropriate contexts are ignored. This is especially problematic since both values and views of existence are influenced by culture (Hall, 1966).

According to Kroeber and Kluckhohn (1952), culture consists of "patterns, explicit and implicit of and for behavior acquired and transmitted by symbols. Constituting the distinctive achievement of human groups . . . the essential core of culture consists of traditional . . . ideas and . . . attached values; culture systems may, on the one hand, be considered as products of action, on the other as conditioning elements of further action" (p. 127).

Within the context of QOL, culture shapes ethical behavior for individuals within a communal context (Padilla and Kagawa-Singer, 1998). Along with shaping behavior, culture affords a group a shared notion of historic reality that explains past behavior and conditions for "elements of further action." It is within this context that a proper cultural analysis of QOL conceptualization must occur.

As applied to cross-cultural assessment of QOL, Western psychology's interpretation of Greek philosophy (Nobles, 1986) and the English Renaissance (Ani, 1994; Christopher, 1999) is inadequate and potentially offensive and oppressive (Freire, 1994). Western cosmology separates the material basis of the world from its spirit basis by dichotomizing God, man, and nature through science (specifically physics), which denies the presence of a pervasive universal spirit acknowledged by the metaphysical systems of all collective cultures (Ani, 1994). The axiologic perspectives of Western cultures determine one's worth by quantifying the person's material acquisitions (Ani, 1990, 1994; Hall, 1966; Jackson, 1982).

Moreover, in a Western cultural context the nature of knowing (epistemology) occurs through an individual's "rational" and "logical" thought. This is in stark contrast to Eastern and African cultures, where approaches to knowledge combine "logic" with intuition affect, spiritual wisdom, and insight. In Western cultures, truth is "proven" through probability and measurement via the five physical senses that account for the tangible quality and quantity of a phenomenon (Meyers, 1991). Descartes' premise that "I think, therefore, I am" is, for example, incompatible with an African ontological perspective (Mbiti, 1969) that posits "I am because we are, therefore I am; we are because I am." Thus, to assess QOL in collective cultures, the indigenous philosophy must be understood in order to have an authentic, culturally congruent perspective of how cultures define, conceptualize, and assess QOL.

QOL Concepts in Collective Cultures

Assessing QOL in most collective cultures includes conceptualizing spirit, harmony, and cyclical time orientations (Saxena, 1994). The spirit, which according to Nobles (1998) differs from spirituality, is "the energy, force or power that is both the inner essence and the outer envelope of human beingness. . . . Human beings experience their 'Spiritness' simultaneously as a metaphysical state and an ethereal extension or connection into and between the supra world of Deities, the inter world of other beings, and the inner world of the self" (p. 193).

Spirit

Quality of life assessments need to include methods of assessing an individual's internal energy (spirit, soul, vitality). Internal energy, known by various names across cultures, is the ethereal source endowed by the creative force that allows one to exist. The concept of internal energy is known as *Ki* (pronounced "chee") in Buddhist cultures (Furuya, 1996) and *Ashé* in the African religious system of

Yoruba (Gonzalez-Wippler, 1992). In the Bantu tradition, the concept of vitality is known as *Moyo* (Fu-Kiau, 1991), while the Yogis of India call it *prana* or *kundalini* (Ornstein, 1972). Given its fundamental importance among many collective cultures and worldviews, the concept of spirit should be included in the conceptualization of QOL. Its absence in Western QOL assessment stems from the absence of spirit and related concepts in the study of human behavior (Ani, 1994; Saxena, 1994).

Harmony

Collective cultures that conceptualize the universe as a pervasive spirit require "total harmony . . . with the global unit of the social body of the community . . . also with the wholeness of the universe because the human being is only a *kengele* ('tiny element, electron') in the *bungila kia makengele* ('body of tiny elements or electronic body')" (Fu-Kiau, 1991, p. 39). Thus harmony is a key component of QOL (Kwan, Bond, and Singelis, 1997). In collective cultures, harmony is a core component of group identity. Individual self-esteem is secondary to the healthy functioning of group relationships (Saxena, 1994). Interpersonal relationships are therefore the most important factor in collectivist cultures. In fact, communal living "requires a certain ability to subordinate private needs and wants to the good of the collective" (Finch, 1991, p. 72).

The notion of harmony is essential to conceptualizations of quality of life across cultures (Kwan, Bond, and Singelis, 1997). Harmony is the maintenance of balance in a relationship between interdependent entities. Harmony imparts rhythm to a society and manifests in the relationships that human beings have with nature, which consists of human beings, invisible spirits, ancestors, land, plants, animals, and the metaphysical higher force (Jahn, 1961). This cosmology is present in certain metaphysical systems:

- Japan's Shintoism and China's Taoism (Axelson, 1999)

- Mali's Dogon (Ani, 1994)

- Congo's Bantu (Fu-Kiau, 1991)

- Ghana's Akan (Ephirim-Donkor, 1997)

- India's Buddhism and Hinduism (Saxena, 1994)

- Native American Sioux and Cherokee (Axelson, 1999)

Thus, relationship harmony requires polymetric syncopation with all of the elements of nature. Polymetric syncopation is the essence of rhythm in collective societies (Nobles, 1990). In this sense, rhythm relates to behavioral movement according to the natural environment. Hence, harmony maintains a natural rhythm that necessitates a time orientation congruent with nature's harmony.

Time Orientations

Conceptualization of time is an essential aspect of cross-cultural assessment (Pennington, 1990). Many collective cultures have a circular time orientation that stems from a cosmological perspective in which spirit is the essence of life (Ani, 1994; Kuyken, Orley, Hudelson, and Sartorius, 1994). The notion of a pervasive universal spirit allows collective societies to function according to a natural, universal order and provides a cultural time orientation that focuses on the spirit's cultivation and infinitude within phenomenological time (Pennington, 1990). Hence, time consciousness focuses on being "in time" and is marked by fluidity (Ornstein, 1972; Jackson, 1982). The notion of an in-time perspective allows one to affectively engage in the interaction of the present moment. The in-time orientation necessitates not only harmony with nature but oneness, which typifies the connectedness of collective cultures (Ani, 1990).

Time orientations in Western psychological constructs of QOL are linear, with a definite beginning and a finite end (Hall; 1969; Jackson, 1982). European or Western culture focuses on maximizing efficiency, which is the notion of producing a higher volume of product in a shorter amount of time with less effort and cost.

Progress occurs and QOL is enhanced when mechanical technology, the tool of efficiency, achieves the desired result (Ani, 1994). This is a future time orientation, which is unidimensional, linear, and limited. Moreover, the North American (Western) time orientation has a present-centered aspect that manifests in a need for immediate gratification (Hall, 1966).

In collective cultures with a cyclical time orientation, the life span is dependent upon the spirit and soul of a person; therefore, attention must be given to the quality of a person's spirit. Hence, in the context of collectivistic cultures QOL is viewed as a developmental process in which one returns to one's ethereal source. This return is manifest in the symbolic cosmological concept of *Sankofa* in the Akan metaphysical system (Ephirim-Donkor, 1997). Similarly, other cultures have metaphysical explanations about what occurs after physical death, by way of their cosmology. For example, Indian philosophies posit that one's *dharma,* or reincarnation, is influenced by one's *karma,* the consequence of one's actions (S. Kheper, personal communication, Sept. 8, 1999). In African cultures, the physically deceased continue to exist in the form of the living dead and their ancestors (Mbiti, 1969). The concept of an afterlife focuses on continuity of spirit, which requires balance, rhythm, and harmony while in the manifestation of a human being. Spirit continuity is part and parcel of a cyclical time orientation.

Technical Issues in Assessing QOL Across Cultures

The current technology available for assessing QOL in a cultural context consists primarily of paper-and-pencil measures. For the most part, these instruments ask respondents to indicate, on a Likert scale, whether they strongly agree, agree, disagree, or strongly disagree with a given statement regarding their QOL. Several researchers have noted the inherent difficulty with this simplified approach to developing measures suitable for use across cultures (Keith, Heal, and Schalock, 1996; Kuyken, Orley, Hudelson, and Sartorius, 1994). Specifically, successfully transporting psychological measures across cultures depends in large part on the researcher's ability to establish conceptual, semantic, item, and scalar equivalence between the host culture and the target culture (Kuyken, Orley, Hudelson, and Sartorius, 1994).

Conceptual Equivalence

Conceptual equivalence relates to the existence of a given concept in both the host culture and the target culture. For conceptual equivalence to be achieved, not only must the concept exist in both cultures but its expression must also be identical across cultures. Establishing conceptual equivalence is of considerable importance in determining whether a measure is valid for use in both host and target cultures. With regard to QOL assessment, conceptual equivalence is particularly relevant where a measure has been developed for use in an individualistic culture and attempts are made to transport that measure to a collectivistic culture.

Semantic Equivalence

Semantic equivalence in cross-cultural assessment is determined by the denotative and connotative uniformity of words (Kuyken, Orley, Hudelson, and Sartorius, 1994). The denotative meaning of a word refers to its symbolic representation and is primarily determined by its dictionary meaning. The primary mode of evaluating the denotative meaning of a word is through linguistic analysis. Connotative equivalence, on the other hand, is the meaning implied by a word. For example, words associated with happiness (*satisfied, gratified, fulfilled,* and others) in Western culture may evoke different associations in Asian or African cultures (words equivalent to *harmony, balance, spiritness*). For cross-cultural assessment to be effectively carried out, both denotative and connotative equivalence must exist.

Item Equivalence

Cross-cultural assessment requires the contextual equivalence of the items belonging to the measure being used to evaluate the construct of interest (Kuyken, Orley, Hudelson, and Sartorius, 1994). Without contextual equivalence, the validity of the evaluative process is compromised. For example, if researchers want to measure the effects of depression on QOL across cultures, they must first establish that depression occurs in the same context across cultures and then that the items intended to measure depression have the same ability to do so in each culture.

Scalar Equivalence

Scalar equivalence assess whether the measurement scale of a given instrument intended for cross-cultural assessment has equivalent value in both cultures for where it is intended for use (Kuyken, Orley, Hudelson, and Sartorius, 1994). For example, a QOL measure that employs a Likert scale with a range of 1 to 7, with 1 = very happy and 7 = very unhappy, assumes that happiness can be quantified in a linear fashion in both the host and target culture. But Likert scales have been found to be ineffective in cultures where adhering to the social norm is desirable (Mertens, 1998). In such cases, respondents are likely to choose a response typifying the tendency to select a value close to the middle of the scale so as not to appear different from the group.

Review of Instruments and Techniques for Assessing QOL in a Cultural Context

A number of scholars have noted the paucity of research focused on culturally sensitive QOL measures (Kuyken, Orley, Hudelson, and Sartorius, 1994; Padilla and Kagawa-Singer, 1998). The majority of QOL assessment tools operate on the premise that instruments normalized on European society are applicable and relevant to all populations (Keith, Heal, and Schalock, 1996). However, most models are grounded in Western society cultural values and consequently may be inappropriate for use in cross-cultural assessment. Three assessment instruments have emerged in the psychological literature that employ culturally sensitive approaches to assessing QOL with "minority" populations (see Table 8.2).

Table 8.2. Reliability and validity coefficients for quality-of-life measures.

	Authors	Validity Coefficients	Reliability
SEIQoL	Broadhead et al., 1998;	.70	Cronbach's alpha = 74
	Coen et al., 1993;	.70	None reported
	O'Boyle, 1994	.49–.74*	None reported
WHOQOL-100	De Vries &	.60–.70*	Cronbach's alpha = 96
	Van Heck, 1997;		
	Pazaki and Nakane, 1998;	.58–.72*	None reported
	The WHO Group, 1998	.89	None reported
CCAQLCQ	Keith et al., 1996	.64	None reported

* Validity coefficients are reported in ranges.

Schedule for the Evaluation of Individual Quality of Life (SEIQoL)

The SEIQoL, a phenomenological approach to measuring QOL, may be an ideal method for obtaining subjective QOL data in cross-cultural situations (Broadhead, Robinson, and Atkinson, 1998; Coen, O'Mahony, O'Boyle, and Joyce, 1993; O'Boyle, 1994). The subjective nature of the scale is favorable because it does not impose a standard format. Rather, the participant selects important life domains that reflect his or her own needs and goals. Quality of life is then constructed from the description of each cue as appropriated by the client. Each cue is identified and then further described in order that the practitioner may assess the specific meaning and degree of life satisfaction it affords the client.

When the instrument is administered, the participant is asked to divide a pie diagram into five parts, each differing in size depending on the significance attached to the part. Measuring the size of each part of the pie diagram results in scores on the QOL life dimensions. This approach yields five independent and continuous scores, ranging from 0 to 100. Whereas traditional quality-of-life scales may assess concerns such as self-esteem and job satisfaction, the SEIQoL allows participants to identify salient life-satisfaction domains unique to the individual. For example, an economically disadvantaged first-generation Asian couple may be less interested in personal status and income, and more interested in their children's education. If their children are excelling in school, they may report a relatively high quality of life, despite what most people from majority society would regard as poor quality of life.

Although this measure welcomes a diverse span of content domains in regard to life satisfaction, clients from some cultural backgrounds may be hesitant to nominate certain domains because of fear of how they appear to the researcher. Therefore, they may alter their choices to appear "socially appropriate" (Kazdin, 1982). For instance, the domain of sexuality may be embarrassing for an Asian participant who may want to avoid the possibility of bringing shame upon herself or himself. She or he may choose another socially acceptable domain such as job satisfaction instead. In order to reduce the chance of this type of error, it may be helpful to include a qualitative method of inquiry to add clarity. Information regarding the validity and reliability of the SEIQoL can be found in Table 8.2.

World Health Organization Quality of Life— 100 (WHOQOL-100)

The WHOQOL-100 is a QOL measure that purports to evaluate a person's overall quality of life (De Vries and Van Heck, 1997; WHOQOL Group, 1998). It focuses upon an individual's objective state, behaviors, and capacity, as well as evaluations of those aspects. The WHOQOL-100 was developed by quality-of-life experts from around the world to ensure that the measure embodied and reflected the worldviews of an international population. Unlike traditional quality-of-life instruments, there are no standard questions addressing the client's personal health and life satisfaction. The instrument is considered a generic measure that assesses both positive and negative components of QOL.

Following a rigorous process of development and construct clarification (Kuyken, 1994), WHO produced the instrument for measuring individuals' perceptions of the quality of their life. The measure consists of one hundred questions that assess six domains of quality of life, within which twenty-four facets are considered. The six domains covered are physical health; psychological functioning; level of independence; social relationships; environment; and spirituality, religion, and personal beliefs. Items are rated on a 5–point scale. The WHOQOL-100 has been shown to have adequate internal consistency and validity (see Table 8.2).

WHO's purpose in developing the WHOQOL-100 addressed the scant availability of genuinely cross-culturally sensitive instruments. Because this scale was developed within a number of field centers in pluralistic cultures, it transcends the values and worldviews of any one culture. The instrument is available in more than twenty languages and appears to reflect the organization's commitment to a holistic perspective on health. The WHOQOL-100 can be used in a medical context or for psychological evaluation, research, and policy development.

Cross-Cultural Assessment of Quality of Life Concepts Questionnaire (CCAQLCQ)

This CCAQLCQ (Keith, Heal, and Schalock, 1996) assesses ten domains of quality of life for persons with disabilities. Quality-of-life experts from Australia, England, Finland, Germany, Taiwan, the Republic of China, the United States, and Japan were consulted to translate the scale into their respective languages. The questionnaire was then translated back into English to ensure that the meaning and intent of words were not lost in the conversion. Each representative was then responsible for distributing the scale to at least ten post-B.A. persons. The ten domains of quality of life were determined by reviewing salient themes in the quality-of-life literature. Each domain was assessed using a 7–point Likert scale.

Concepts were rated based on three bipolar adjective pairs: value (for example, good-bad), potency (strong-weak), and activity (active-inactive). Among six of the seven national samples that participated in a study using the scale, concepts such as relationships, health, inclusion and growth were especially valued (Keith, Heal, and Schalock, 1996). However, economic security (financial status) and personal control were found to have less value. Although this scale has considerable international consistency, Keith, Heal, and Schalock (1996) contend that it may not be appropriate for those who hold a collectivistic value system. Validity and reliability coefficients are reported in Table 8.2.

Qualitative Inquiry and QOL Assessment

Qualitative inquiry as an approach to cross-cultural assessment may be the most appropriate method for providing a detailed account of how persons in different cultures view their QOL. Given that many paper-and-pencil measures have been developed on specific cultural groups, and therefore that they may lack cross-cultural relevance, the flexibility inherent in qualitative assessment is a desirable alternative for assessing QOL across cultures. Moreover, qualitative inquiry seeks to capture the context of the person's experience through methods of exploration, discovery, and inductive logic (Mertens, 1998).

Phenomenological

The phenomenological approach to assessing QOL focuses on understanding the meaning events have for the person being evaluated. In this framework, the emphasis is on what people say and do as a reflection of how they interpret the world (Mertens 1998; Taylor and Bogdan, 1998). Those using the phenomenological approach in assessing QOL should base their interpretations of events on the indigenous cultural perspectives of the target population (Taylor and Bogdan, 1998). Thus, in assessing QOL across cultures, it is essential for the evaluator to step outside the comfort zone of his or her own worldview so that the individuals being evaluated may be viewed in the context of their unique reality. Feminist research, symbolic interactionism, grounded theory, and naturalistic observation are related methods of phenomenological inquiry that can be applied to QOL assessment (Mertens, 1998).

Interpretive and Constructivist

According to the interpretive and constructivist perspective, the type of inquiry used to understand a given phenomenon should not impose its structure upon the person's worldview; rather, the individual's worldview should inform the type of assessment to be used. The interpretive and constructivist view posits that "multiple realities exist that are time and content dependent" (Mertens, 1998, p. 11). In QOL assessment, it is important for researchers to explore and understand the indigenous culture's worldview in order to develop appropriate instrumentation and techniques. If QOL can be assessed only by way of cultural emergence, then the ethnographic approach is the most appropriate course of study.

Ethnography

Ethnography has been described as the most frequently used qualitative method in educational and psychological research (Mertens, 1998). This method of inquiry can be used to describe and analyze QOL across cultures and communities. Ethnographic research is informed by anthropological, psychological, or educational theory (Mertens, 1998). This approach to qualitative inquiry can be used to understand concepts related to QOL from both within the culture (emic) and from the outside (etic). Traditionally, researchers who use the ethnographic approach to study QOL make a decision as to what and who will be studied, and how the data will be analyzed and interpreted. In this light, it is important that researchers using this approach avoid imposing their reality on the participants whom they are studying.

In assessing QOL cross-culturally, the ethnographic approach requires experience and first-hand knowledge of the culture being studied (Taylor and Bogdan, 1998). The general ethnographic approach to studying QOL cross-culturally occurs through observing participants and then conducting open-ended discussions and interviews (Greenfield, 1997). Ethnographic observation helps to determine learning styles and cognitive abilities specific to that culture, which facilitates knowledge of the axiology, epistemology, and communication present in that culture. Ethnography also permits detection, correction, and prevention of errors in cross-cultural assessment by grounding researchers (Greenfield, 1997).

Conclusion

Assessing QOL across cultures is a complex and multifaceted task that requires both conceptual flexibility and appropriate instrumentation. Currently, QOL is conceptually trapped in a Western worldview and epistemological framework. This is also true of the instrumentation available for assessing QOL across cultures. There is a clear need to move beyond simply translating traditional paper-and-pencil QOL measures into the language of the target culture and proceeding with the business of assessment as if this procedure alone were adequate. As we continue to move toward a global community, the need is greater than ever for researchers to recognize the limitations of transporting so-called etic conceptualizations of QOL across cultures. Instead, efforts should be directed at employing qualitative methods of inquiry that allow indigenous ontological, axiological, and epistemological influences to determine conceptualizations of QOL.

In reviewing QOL concepts across cultures, we found that one salient theme is the focus on metaphysical concepts (spirit, internal energy, Chi) as important factors influencing the quality of one's life. Given the focus on spirituality and other metaphysical phenomena by people living in collectivistic cultures, researchers are encouraged to update their technology (theory, instrumentation, and methodology) in an effort to provide more appropriate cross-cultural assessment.

Another theme to emerge from reviewing the literature on quality of life as experienced across cultures is a focus on harmony. Harmony with the environment, harmony with nature, and harmony with others are important factors in almost all of the collectivistic cultures sampled in this chapter. It is important for future research to place more emphasis on examining the nontangibles when assessing QOL across cultures.

References

Anderson, M., & Robinson, J. (1991). Measures of subjective well-being. In J. P. Robinson, P. S. Shaver, & L. S. Wrightsman (Eds.), *Measures of personality and social psychological attitudes: Volume 1 in measures of social psychological attitudes series* (pp. 61–114). New York: Academic Press.

Ani, M. (1990). *Let the circle be unbroken: The implications of African spirituality in the diaspora.* New York: Nkonimfo.

Ani, M. (1994). *Yurugu: An African-centered critique of European cultural thought and behavior.* Trenton, NJ: African World Press.

Arrindell, W. A., Hatzichristou, C., Wensink, J., Rosenberg, E., Twillert, B., Stedema, J., & Meijer, D. (1997). Dimensions of national culture as predictors of cross-national differences in subjective well-being. *Personality and Individual Differences, 23,* 37–53.

Axelson, J. A. (1999). *Counseling and development in a multicultural society* (3rd ed.). Boston: Brooks/Cole.

Broadhead, J. K., Robinson, J. W., & Atkinson, M. J. (1998). A new quality of life measure for oncology: The SEIQOL. *Journal of Psychosocial Oncology, 16,* 21–35.

Chambers, J. W., & Kong, B. W. (1996). Assessing quality of life: Construction and validation of a scale. In Reginald L. Jones (Ed.), *Handbook of tests and measurements for Black populations.* Hampton, VA: Cobb & Henry.

Christopher, J. C. (1999). Situating psychological well-being: Exploring the cultural roots of its therapy and research, *Journal of Counseling and Development, 77,* 141–152.

Coen, R., O'Mahony, D., O'Boyle, C., & Joyce, C. (1993). Measuring the quality of life of dementia patients using the schedule for the evaluation of individual quality of life. *Irish Journal of Psychology, 14,* 154–163.

Croog, S. H., Levine, S., & Testa, M. A. (1986). The effects of antihypertensive therapy on the quality of life. *New England Journal of Medicine, 314,* 1657–1664.

De Vries, J., & Van Heck, G. (1997). The world health organization quality of life assessment instrument (WHOQOL-100): Validation study with the Dutch version. *European Journal of Psychological Assessment, 13,* 164–178.

Diener, E., & Diener, M. (1995). Cross-cultural correlates of life satisfaction and self-esteem. *Journal of Personality and Social Psychology, 68,* 653–663.

Ephirim-Donkor, A. (1997). *African spirituality: On becoming ancestors.* Trenton, NJ: African World Press.

Finch, C. S., III. (1991). *Echoes of the old Darkland: Themes from the African Eden.* Decatur, GA: Khenti.

Freire, P. (1994). *Pedagogy of the oppressed* (New rev. 20th anniv. ed.). New York: Continuum.

Fu-Kiau, K.K.B. (1991). *Self healing power and therapy: Old teachings from Africa.* New York: Vantage Press.

Furuya, K. (1996). *Kodo ancient ways: Lessons in the spiritual life of the warrior/martial artist.* Santa Clarita, CA: Ohara.

Gonzalez-Wippler, M. (1992). *The power of the orishas: Santeria and the worship of saints.* Plainview, NY: Original Publications.

Greenfield, P. M. (1997). You can't take it with you: Why ability assessments don't cross cultures. *American Psychologist, 52,* 1115–1124.

Hall, E. T. (1966). *The dance of life: The other dimension of time.* New York: Doubleday.

Hall, E. T. (1969). *The hidden dimension.* New York: Doubleday.

Jackson, G. G. (1982). Black psychology: An avenue to the study of Afro-Americans. *Journal of Black Studies, 12*(3), 241–260.

Jahn, J. (1961). *Muntu: An outline of the new African culture.* New York: Grove Press.

Kagawa-Singer, M. (1988). *Bamboo and oak: A comparative study of adaptation to cancer by Japanese-American and Anglo-American patients.* Unpublished doctoral dissertation, University of California at Los Angeles.

Kazdin, A. (1982). Observer effects: Reactivity of direct observation. In D. P. Hartmann (Ed.), New directions for methodology of social and behavioral science (no. 14): *Using observers to study behavior* (pp. 5–19). San Francisco: Jossey-Bass.

Keith, K., Heal, L., & Schalock, R. (1996). Cross-cultural measurement of critical quality of life concepts. *Journal of Intellectual and Developmental Disability, 21*(4), 273–293.

King, L. A., & Napa, C. K. (1998). What makes a life good? *American Psychologist, 75,* 156–165.

Kroeber, A. L., & Kluckhohn, C. (1952). *Culture: A critical review of concepts and definitions.* New York: Random House.

Kuyken, W. (1994). Development of the WHOQOL: Rationale and current status. *International Journal of Mental Health, 23*(3), 24–56.

Kuyken, W., Orley, J., Hudelson, P., & Sartorius, N. (1994). Quality of life assessment across cultures. *International Journal of Mental Health, 23,* 5–27.

Kwan, V.S.Y., Bond, M. H., & Singelis, T. M. (1997). Pancultural explanations for life satisfaction: Adding relationship harmony to self-esteem. *Journal of Personality and Social Psychology, 73,* 1038–1051.

Mbiti, J. S. (1969). *African religions and philosophies* (2nd ed.). Portsmouth, NH: Heinemann.

Mertens, D. M. (1998). *Research methods in education and psychology: Integrating diversity with quantitative and qualitative approaches.* Thousand Oaks, CA: Sage.

Meyers, L. J. (1991). Expanding the psychology of knowledge optimally: The importance of worldview revisited. In R. E. Jones (Ed.), *Black psychology* (pp. 15–28). Berkeley, CA: Cobb and Henry.

Nobles, W. (1986). *African psychology: Towards its reclamation, reascension and revitalization.* Oakland, CA: Institute for the Advanced Study of Black Family Life and Culture.

Nobles, W. (1990). African philosophy: Foundation of Black psychology. In R. E. Jones (Ed.), *Black psychology* (pp. 47–63). Berkeley, CA: Cobb and Henry.

Nobles, W. (1998). To be African or not to be: The question of identity or authenticity—some preliminary thoughts. In R. E. Jones (Ed.), *African American identity development* (pp. 185–206). Berkeley, CA: Cobb and Henry.

O'Boyle, G. A. (1994). The Schedule for Evaluation of Individual Quality of Life (SEIQoL). *International Journal of Mental Health, 23,* 3–23.

Ornstein, R. O. (1972). *The psychology of consciousness.* San Francisco: Freeman.

Padilla, G., & Kagawa-Singer, M. (1998). Quality of life and culture. In C. King & P. Hinds (Eds.), *Quality of life from nursing and patient perspectives: Theory, research and practice.* Sudbury, MA: Jones and Bartlett.

Pazaki, M., & Nakane, Y. (1998). WHOQOL instruments as a valid health-related QOL measure. *Japanese Journal of Behaviormetrics, 25*(2), 76–80.

Pennington, D. (1990). Time in African culture. In M. K. Asante & K. Welsh-Asante (Eds.), *African culture: The rhythms of unity* (pp. 123–140). Trenton, NJ: Africa World Press.

Saxena, S. (1994). Quality of life assessments in cancer patients in India: Cross-cultural issues. In J. Orley & W. Kuyken (Eds.), *Quality of life assessment: International perspectives*. Heidelberg, Germany: Springer-Verlag.

Suh, E., Diener, E., Oishi, S., & Triandis, H. C. (1998). The shifting basis of life satisfaction judgments across cultures: Emotions versus norms. *Journal of Personality and Social Psychology, 74,* 482–493.

Taylor, S. J., & Bogdan, R. (1998). *Introduction to qualitative research methods: The search for meaning* (3rd ed.). New York: Wiley.

WHOQOL Group. (1994). Development of the WHOQOL: Rationale and current status. *International Journal of Mental Health, 23,* 24–56.

WHOQOL Group. (1998). Group development of the world health organization WHOQOL-BREF quality of life assessment. *Psychological Medicine, 28*(3), 551–558.

Part II

Testing Issues

Section One

Personality Assessment

Part Two of the *Handbook of Multicultural Assessment* focuses on testing issues, specifically personality assessment (Section One) and assessment of cognitive abilities (Section Two). The chapters in Part Two address the use of major instruments and assessment procedures with members of different racial and ethnic groups.

Section One of Part Two comprises chapters related to personality assessment. In Chapter Nine, Giuseppe Costantino, Rosemary Flanagan, and Robert Malgady highlight the use of narrative assessments, namely, the Thematic Apperception Test (TAT), the Children's Apperception Test (CAT), and the Tell-Me-A-Story test (TEMAS). They discuss the historical development of these instruments and give overviews of the TAT and CAT with regard to multicultural applications. The authors focus on the development of the TEMAS. Their chapter concludes with case examples to illustrate the use of this multicultural instrument.

Chapter Ten, by Barry Ritzler, examines multicultural use of the Rorschach Comprehensive System. Ritzler begins with a description of the test as a "culture free" method and describes the development and standardization of the Rorschach. Comparative data from Exner norms and international studies are provided. The author also cites research conducted in the United States with Israeli natives and Latin Americans.

Chapter Eleven represents a new addition to the second edition of the *Handbook*. Karl Kwan and Felito Aldarondo focus on multicultural use of the Sixteen Personality Factor Questionnaire (16PF) and the California Personality Inventory (CPI) with U.S. racial and ethnic minorities. The 16PF and CPI are two of the most popular instruments designed to assess "normal" personality functioning. Kwan and Aldarondo describe numerous studies conducted to address cross-cultural applicability of these measures related to issues of equivalence in the testing process.

Also new is inclusion of the Myers-Briggs Type Indicator (MBTI) in a chapter by Mary McCaulley and Raymond Moody. Chapter Twelve is written from the Jungian perspective; the authors provide historical information regarding the theoretical roots and evolution of the MBTI from research to actual publication. Issues of reliability and validity are also noted, and case examples are interwoven throughout the text.

Chapter Thirteen, by Gordon Nagayama Hall and Amber Phung, highlights the use of the current versions of the Minnesota Multiphasic Personality Inventory (MMPI) and the Millon Clinical Multiaxial Inventory (MCMI) with diverse populations. Specific studies are cited with regard to racial and ethnic group performance with these two measures. Limitations in the research are noted along with implications for clinical practice.

9

Narrative Assessments
TAT, CAT, and TEMAS

Giuseppe Costantino, Rosemary Flanagan,
and Robert G. Malgady

For millennia, storytelling, the oldest form communication, was the sole method of educating and fostering personality development in young children (McClelland and Friedman, 1952). Several cognitive psychologists—among them Bruner (1986), Mair (1989) and, in particular, Howard (1991)—affirm that the development of human cognition and personality occurs as a result of life-story construction. Furthermore, Howard (1991) describes the technique of storytelling as the most appropriate process in understanding culturally diverse individuals and consequently in conducting culturally competent psychotherapy. Hence narrative assessment, also known in the literature as projective assessment and thematic apperception testing, has been described as an innovative technique. It was first pioneered by Murray (1943) and subsequently methodologically validated by McClelland (McClelland and Friedman, 1952; McClelland, Atkinson, Clark, and Lowell, 1953) as "the most important and virtually untapped resource we have for developing our understanding of the behavior of an animal distinguished by its unique competence in language and use of symbols" (Atkinson, 1981, p. 127).

This chapter offers information regarding use of the Thematic Apperception Test, the Children's Apperception Test, and Tell-Me-A-Story with diverse populations. Specific attention goes to Tell-Me-A-Story, given its multicultural applicability. Two case studies are offered that use Tell-Me-A-Story as part of an integrative test battery.

Overview of Thematic Apperception Test (TAT)

The Thematic Apperception Test (TAT; Murray, 1943) is one of the instruments most frequently used in the United States (Piotrowski, Sherry, and Keller, 1985; Watkins, Campbell, Nieberding, and Hallmark, 1995) and in foreign countries (Dana, 1999). Morgan and Murray (1981, as cited in Gieser and Stein, 1999) developed the TAT on the assumption that storytelling was an important technique in understanding the underlying dynamics and behavior of an examinee. Originally the TAT was developed as a technique to facilitate the process of self-revelation by the client during the early stage of therapy. In storytelling in response to the cards, the client would be forced to reveal the dominant drives, emotions, sentiments, complexes, and conflicts (Murray, 1938) fairly early in treatment, thus accelerating a process that would otherwise take several months of analysis. Subsequently, the test has became a classic assessment instrument (Stein and Gieser, 1999).

Stimulus Cards

The test consists of thirty cards, with a set of twenty cards designed for adult men and women and two other sets for boys and girls. Although Murray (1943) indicated the instrument may be used with children aged four and older, there are actually six cards (1, 7GF, 8BM, 12BG, 13B, and 13G) depicting child characters or events familiar to children; and the examiner is forced to select other cards in order to administer a complete set of nine, which seems to be the standard number of cards administered. Groth-Marnat (1997) indicated the pull for the following cards: aggression (3BM, 8BM, 12M, 14, and 17BM), relationship with parents with respect to love, rejection, and punishment (7GF and 13), to pull in addition to the cards used for aggression, and achievement motivation (1, 3BM, 7GF, and 13).

Administration

Administration is conducted with examinee and examiner seated face to face. Murray originally instructed having the examinee sitting with back turned to the examiner in order to facilitate spontaneous storytelling.

Scoring

Notwithstanding its widespread use, the TAT does not have an objective scoring system. Murstein (1963) spent an entire sabbatical year in Iceland in an attempt to develop such a system but was able to develop objective scoring only for moderately ambiguous cards (such as card number 1). Dana (1959) proposed an early objective system and spent approximately ten years "amassing TAT data on five needs and providing feedback from reports based on those needs and conventional high inferences interpretation. These five needs proved to be insufficient data for low inference interpretation and I subsequently abandoned the use of objective systems for the TAT" (Dana, 1998, p. 3). Nonetheless, several scoring systems, including Murray's, are taught in graduate schools. However, those systems are not objective and require clinical experience and a systematic approach (Dana, 1982).

Cross-Cultural Multicultural Application

Modified pictures of the TAT have been used in research with culturally diverse groups (Henry, 1947), but there is not a set with both emic and etic validity to be used clinically with the culturally and linguistically diverse groups in the United States today. The original Murray TAT (1943) continues to be used in a biased manner with minority groups; this indiscriminate use has been deplored by Rossini and Moretti (1997) and Dana (1993, 1999). Among others, Dana (1999) urges that the future of the TAT as a valid assessment instrument rest on developing "culturally recognizable pictures, scoring variables germane to the culture, availability of normative data, and culturally specific interpretation procedures for these TAT applications." Furthermore, Dana clarifies that a valid etic-emic approach uses those TAT card stimuli recognized as familiar by culturally diverse groups, and an etic scoring system that has been validly used in culturally diverse settings; for an emic approach, he suggests that new TAT card stimuli be redrawn to reflect multicultural characters, settings, and possibly themes, with a correlate scoring system.

Overview of the Children's Apperception Test (CAT)

The CAT was originally developed by Bellak and Bellak (1949) as a derivative instrument of the TAT to assess sibling rivalry, relationship with significant other, aggression, and other functions related to conflicts associated with the anal and oedipal stages of child development. There are three parallel versions of this test, all having a series of ten picture cards. The original CAT was designed with cards depicting animal figures; the CAT-Supplement (Bellak and Bellak, 1952), also with animal pictures, was designed to pull for stories of physical fitness, injuries, competition, body image, and school situations; the third version, CAT-H, contains human pictures in lieu of animals.

Although the animal pictures were originally developed to facilitate young children's identification with the animal characters, later research indicated that the human pictures seemed to appeal to children aged seven to ten with normal-to-bright IQ (Bellak and Abrams, 1997). Administration of the CAT is less formal than with the TAT and more playlike. In fact, the author suggests that the examiner tell the child that they are going to play a game in which the child will tell a story describing what the characters are doing now, what happened before, and what will happen next. Once the story is ended, the examiner should go over the story and ask for elaboration and clarification as necessary.

Scoring is accomplished by doing content analysis of the CAT stories; the interpretation should take into consideration ten variables:

1. The main theme
2. The main hero
3. Main needs and drives of the hero
4. The environment
5. Perception of the figures
6. Main conflicts
7. Nature of anxieties
8. Main defenses
9. Function of the superego
10. Integration of the ego

Because of the etic content validity of the animal picture, the original CAT has been widely used in various foreign countries, especially in the practice of psychology in emerging countries (in Latin America, for example, Argentina and Brazil). However, its clinical utility has been diminished by the limited psychodynamic theoretical framework, lack of an objective scoring system, and absence of psychometric properties (Hatt, 1985). Obrzut and Cummings (1983) indicate that the lack of psychometric properties is counterbalanced by the rich imaginative personal data inherent in the CAT stories. However, Kerlinger (1973, as cited in Hatt, 1985, p. 315) pointed out that "all methods of observation and measurement must satisfy the same scientific criteria" and since projective tests are used as assessment instruments they "must be subjected to the same type of reliability testing and empirical validation as any other psychometric techniques."

Overview of the Tell-Me-A-Story (TEMAS) Thematic Apperception Test

The TEMAS (Costantino, 1987; Costantino, Malgady, and Rogler, 1988), as the multicultural offspring of the TAT (Costantino and Malgady, 1999), is a perceptual-cognitive projective instrument that assesses child and adolescent personality cognitive functioning. It is available in parallel majority and ethnic-minority versions. It is the only omnibus personality measure that offers nonminority and minority norms for four groups (African American, Puerto Rican, other Hispanic, and White). The TEMAS stimuli present the youngster with a conflict to be resolved through a storytelling task; the components of the story and its resolution are scored according to personality, affective, and cognitive functions.

The stimulus cards were designed to pull for specific personality functions (interpersonal relations, aggression, anxiety and depression, achievement motivation, delay of gratification, self-concept, sexual identity, moral judgment, and reality testing). Affective functions represent the affect(s) present in the story told, such as happy or sad. Cognitive functions (for instance, reaction time, total time, fluency, omissions, transformations) reflect the formal characteristics of the story. Aggregated data are compared to norms; raw scores are converted to normalized T scores ($X = 50$; $SD = 10$) and clinical cut-off points set at the 90th percentile. The results of the objective scorings do not preclude interpretation according to the clinical judgment and theoretical orientation of the examiner as well.

The TEMAS was designed within an interpersonal-cognitive framework, which is operationalized as meaning that personality development occurs within a sociocultural system. In addition to being designed with consideration for cultural sensitivity, it may be useful within cognitive-behavioral and social learning frameworks because the respondent must address a conflict or solve a problem appropriately to score in the nonclinical range. Such information may be desirable for treatment planning such as development of an individual education plan (IEP) for schoolchildren, an individual treatment plan (ITP) for clinical children, or behavior modification plan, or setting therapeutic goals because information about an individual's thoughts and coping mechanisms is supplied.

Using the TEMAS in a Psychological Evaluation

A strength of the TEMAS is the information that it uniquely contributes to a psychological evaluation. Test data yield information about coping and the extent to which the child complied with task expectations. A clear advantage of the TEMAS is that such information is normed. This offers some level of control for examiner error or inexperience as well as limitations in clinical judgment. Problems related to limitations in clinical judgment are of concern in any situation and are exacerbated when using a projective measure (Vane and Guarnaccia, 1989).

TEMAS is the only measure that directly assesses the effectiveness of problem solving. The personality functions serve this role. The terms used in the TEMAS manual refer to this aspect of the instrument as the adaptiveness of the resolution of the conflict. Personality functions are scored on a 4-point scale, with higher scores indicative of more adaptive functioning. This choice of words may be misleading to some test users; a more accurate operationalization of this notion is that test data are intended to serve as a measure of coping when the examinee is faced with particular emotions or scenarios.

The aspect of the TEMAS that assesses task compliance is the cognitive functions. These functions are important because they indicate the usefulness, richness, or productiveness of the data. The functions are scored in the direction that generally reflects the examinee's failure to do something. Examples of such functions are the examinee failing to note the presence of the intended conflict in a story; failing to respond to an examiner's structured inquiry; or failing to tell a story with a beginning, a middle, and an end. The absence of such information limits the clinical utility of the data.

The special utility of the TEMAS lies in the constructs assessed as well as the relationship of these same constructs with other assessment data. In a preliminary study (Flanagan, 1999), it was found that some TEMAS personality function scores bore an inverse relation to some of the constructs assessed by the Self-Report of Personality of the Behavior Assessment System for Children (BASC; Reynolds and Kamphaus, 1992). This was interpreted as the constructs being complementary, which means that information is then available about one's level of a construct (for instance, aggression) as well as one's ability to cope with situations that prompt the emotion. This combination is powerful because levels of problem as well as healthy behavior are obtained, along with information about one's repertoire of personal resources. This becomes particularly useful for developing cognitive-behavioral interventions.

Some clinical case material is helpful in illustrating these points.

Case One: "Joe"

"Joe" (the name of the youngster has been changed) was an eleven-year-old sixth-grade student. His parents referred him for evaluation because there was a history of school problems that were currently escalating. These were secondary to his diagnosis of attention deficit hyperactivity disorder (ADHD). There had been numerous parent-teacher meetings, including contact with the principal. The classroom teacher, however, had considerable difficulty managing this youngster, who also happened to be bright and highly verbal. Joe frequently displayed problems in regard to impulse control and low frustration tolerance, such that the most frequent complaints were calling out in class, missing assignments, and interpersonal difficulties such as arguing, which were more pronounced in unstructured situations. He was prescribed medication during the school day at the time of the referral.

Test data indicated that he was functioning at the high-average level of cognitive ability. This may have been a minimal estimate of his ability in that he performed at the superior level on a group-administered test, and his behavior during the evaluation may have compromised the results. He was out of his seat often, was complaining about his teacher, had several snacks during testing, at times behaving like a younger child, and was often distractible.

Achievement testing indicated superior skills in reading and mathematics, and average written language skills. Grades and school work were merely good and generally not commensurate with his ability. This was primarily attributed to inattentiveness, poor organizational habits, and missing assignments.

Personality assessment data included use of the BASC and the TEMAS. The BASC is an omnibus assessment measure, available in parent, teacher, and self-report forms. The scales are generally organized into composites that yield information about externalizing and internalizing, and school problems as well as social-adaptive skills. Data are reported as T scores. Constructs are operationalized identically across forms and age levels; the norming samples contained the same individuals for the different BASC forms. This makes data from different raters directly comparable.

This combination of measures resulted in multiple ratings and projective test data. According to McClelland, Koestner, and Weinberger (1989), this approach would be expected to yield information about different aspects of personality, consequently affording a thorough assessment. Joe's overall psychoeducational assessment was conceptually similar to procedures recommended by McConaughy and Achenbach (1989). That model advocates use of multiple raters and multiple methods, and assessment of multiple aspects of functioning.

Personality assessment data indicated that Joe was seen differently by various raters, which is common and expected (Edelbrock and others, 1986). His mother saw him as exhibiting clinical levels of conduct problems and attentional difficulties. Near-clinical levels of depressive behavior and affect were noted. His teacher placed him in the clinical range for all areas rated. Interestingly, his teacher rated the internalizing problems a greater concern than the externalizing problems. This could be interpreted as suggesting that the acting-out behavior was his method of coping with negative affect.

Self-report data indicated absence of clinical concerns. This is not unusual. Data obtained form the TEMAS, however, revealed somewhat different results. Test data indicated that Joe encountered considerable difficulty coping with negative emotions, such as anxiety, depression, and aggressive emotion. The coping skills included weak problem solving (low T scores on Personality Functions) and choosing not to address, or perhaps avoiding, the task at hand (illustrated by the occurrence of cognitive functions or N scores (function not pulled) for personality functions).

The numerical data in Tables 9.1 and 9.2 illustrate these notions more clearly.

The disposition of this case was to provide support services within the school setting, continue medication, and obtain psychotherapy in the private sector to address deficiencies in social problem solving, manage negative affect, and increase frustration tolerance.

Case Two: "Mike"

"Mike" (the name of the youngster has been changed), a thirteen-year-old seventh grader, was referred by his parents because they were concerned that he might have a learning disability. Data indicated average intellectual ability and generally commensurate achievement. Math computation skills were weak, but not sufficiently so (low-average level) to constitute a possible learning disability. His parents also presented Mike's attentional difficulties as a concern. Although he was placed within the clinical range on the Conners Parent Rating Scales (Conners, 1989), test data also noted concomitant conduct problems and learning problems, which reinforced his parents' reluctance to seek a consultation for possible medication. In addition, both parents expressed considerable frustration with this youngster (which may have tainted the ratings to an unknown degree).

Table 9.1. "Joe's" ratings on the Behavior Assessment System for Children (BASC).

Scale	Parent Rating Scales	Teacher Rating Scale	Self-Report of Personality
Hyperactivity	52	49	
Aggression	53	50	
Conduct problems	71	51	
Anxiety	53	83	42
Depression	62	54	43
Somaticization	56	66	
Atypicality	59	92	46
Learning problems		94	
Withdrawal	35	81	
Attention problems	63	99	
Adaptability	59	26	
Social skills	40	56	
Leadership	48	24	
Study skills		36	
Attitude toward school			49
Attitude toward teacher			49
Locus of control			39
Social stress			42
Depression			43
Sense of inadequacy			51
Relations with parents			45
Interpersonal relations			49
Self-esteem			57
Self-reliance			51

Notes: T−Scores ($X = 50, S.D. = 10$)
Each rater does not rate all scales.

The TEMAS was administered to provide some personality assessment data and resolve questions posed by the data that were already collected. Data indicated that Mike was generally making an appropriate adjustment and demonstrated numerous coping skills within normal limits. For the Personality Functions for which he demonstrated weaknesses in coping (Aggression, Moral

Table 9.2. "Joe's" TEMAS scores.

Cognitive Functions		Cognitive Functions	
Reaction time	53	Conflict	Significant
Total time	57		
Fluency	42		
Total omissions	0		
Personality Functions		Personality Function "N" Scores	
Interpersonal relations	26		
Aggression	30		
Anxiety/depression	28	Significant	
Achievement motivation	47		
Delay of gratification	37	Present, not significant	
Self-concept	29		
Sexual identity	52		
Moral judgment	29	Present, not significant	
Reality testing	52		
Affective Functions		Affective Functions	
Happy	30	Neutral	Significant
Sad	36		
Angry	54		
Fearful	66		

Notes: Quantitative scale *T*-scores ($X = 50$, $S.D. = 10$); qualitative scales are significant at the 90th percentile.

Judgment, and Reality Testing), the data must be considered within the context of other variables. He did not address the aggression in two of three stories and obtained a significant score for not pulled. In the instance that he provided a story that addressed the aggression, his response was mildly maladaptive, which in his case was to become ineffectual because the main character was frightened.

A similar pattern repeated for Moral Judgment, with one story providing a slightly maladaptive response and in the other the function was scored as not pulled. The slightly maladaptive response involved recognition of wrongdoing, but no consequences, and the other situation depicted the main character as hoping that he would not get in trouble for mild misbehavior. The weak score on Reality Testing was probably a reflection of immaturity, as he depicted the main character as dreaming, but the outcome of the story might not be known until the next dream. Other test data indicated clinically significant failure to note the conflict depicted in the stimulus card and tendencies to avoid affect, by giving responses that would score as neutral for an affective function.

Within the context of this case, the data seemed consistent with a youngster who had social skills deficits, particularly in the area of problem solving. Evidence suggested that he preferred not to deal with a situation that might be challenging or emotionally provocative. Other weaknesses with social problem solving seemed to be associated with his mother's poor parenting skills. His mother was clearly weak in applying structure and limits, and this may also have accounted for the ratings that indicated conduct problems. Noteworthy is that his test data did not display many Cognitive Indicators. Aside from the two instances in which the conflict was not addressed in the story, in all there were only three omissions of character, setting, or event, which is within normal limits. This is interesting, as research (Costantino, Malgady, Colon-Malgady, and Perez, 1991) indicates that children diagnosed with ADHD evidenced considerably more cognitive indicators (for example, failure to comply with the task requirements) than normal public school children. Thus, there are some data provided by the TEMAS that substantiate the notion of possible ADHD for this youngster. The disposition of this case was family psychotherapy, with emphasis upon effective parenting skills.

Case Three: "Deana"

"Deana" (the name of the youngster has been changed), a nine-year-old fourth-grade student, was referred by her parents because they were considering a change of school and wanted an opinion as to whether their daughter was in need of special-education services. The intellectual evaluation indicated that she has average ability. Achievement testing was within expected limits, based on her measured IQ score. Deana had some attentional and organizational problems, and she was believed to have ADHD, for which she was prescribed medication. However, she did not take the medication on test days. She was currently engaged in a course of psychotherapy with a private practitioner for social skills issues and relationships with authority figures. Self-ratings using the BASC did not reveal any clinical concerns. Social-adaptive skills were rated within normal limits. Parent and teacher ratings, however, revealed a somewhat different picture.

Teacher ratings on the BASC indicated above-average to near-clinical levels ($T = 70$) of internalizing problems, such as the tendency to somaticize. Mild learning problems were noted, with a particular weakness in study skills ($T = 40$). Ratings on the Conners Teacher Rating Scales-Revised (Conners, 1997) indicated a number of symptoms consistent with the inattentive type of ADHD. Parent ratings on the BASC indicated mild depressive affect and attending problems, placing Deana in an at-risk range as opposed to the clinical range. Social-adaptive skills were rated slightly below normal limits. The Conners Parent Rating Scales-Revised also indicated symptoms consistent with the inattentive type of ADHD, as well as tendencies to variable moods and mild oppositional behavior.

In view of the findings thus far, Deana was administered the Children's Depression Inventory (CDI; Kovacs, 1992) and the TEMAS. The CDI indicated that the tendency to overall depressive affect was within normal limits. Examination of factors indicated that her dissatisfaction with interpersonal relationships was bordering on the clinical range ($T = 65$). Data obtained from the TEMAS suggested difficulty managing negative affective states, such as anxiety and depression. T scores that supported these interpretations were 24 for Anxiety and Depression, 32 for Interpersonal Relations, and 24 for Aggression. Self-Concept was low, with a T score of 30, and Moral Judgment was similarly low, with a T score of 30.

The Self-Concept score must be interpreted with caution, as it is based on one stimulus card that clearly pulls for academic self-concept. The weak Moral Judgment reflected the hope that one would not be punished for wrongdoing, which might be viewed as a notion held by immature individuals. Integration of the data suggested that the Aggression score on the TEMAS merited further discussion. It was possible that Deana's weak ability to cope with situations that produce aggressive affect was related to the variable moods and oppositional tendencies reported by her mother. In other words, her coping in such situations was ineffectual, as it appeared as negative behavior and affect. The TEMAS score for Anxiety and Depression also merits further discussion. Noteworthy in her protocol is that she addressed the emotion in only two of the four opportunities presented by the stimulus cards, as she had received a score of not pulled ("N") in two situations. Of further interest is that she failed to detect the conflict in the stimulus card in those same two situations.

Thus data tell us that she chose not to deal with some stressful situations, and when she did she was not particularly successful. These data also raise an important point about the TEMAS scoring system: that is, if a Personality Function is scored as not pulled (N), a corresponding score is entered in the Omission of Event subscale of the Qualitative Cognitive Functions. Hence, the notion that those functions assess a failure on the part of the examinee to do something.

The disposition of this case was that the change of school was made, and she continued out-of-school psychotherapy.

Conclusions

Psychologists have numerous tests to choose from when selecting a battery. In recent years, there has been an explosion of materials from which to select. Youngsters are generally administered a psychoeducational battery, which addresses functioning in a variety of domains. In addition to determining whether there are academic problems in evidence, the social-emotional functioning of youngsters is an important area to evaluate. Too often this area is addressed in a cursory manner. Especially when testing multicultural groups, there are legitimate problems with the assessment enterprise and the instruments themselves. Considerable caution must be used, as it is too easy to evaluate a child from another culture and determine there is pathology, when there is not.

Traditional psychological tests have been criticized for their bias and poor emic-etic content and predictive validity with respect to culturally and linguistically diverse groups (Costantino, 1992; Costantino and Malgady, 1996; Dana, 1993). Assessment practices with multicultural groups in the United States require culturally competent instruments (Dana, 1998). Ritzler writes that "besides being the most cleverly named psychological test, the TEMAS (in English [it] is an acronym for 'Tell-Me-A-Story' and in Spanish and Italian means 'themes') represents a milestone in personality assessment. . . . It also represents the first time a thematic apperception assessment technique has been published in the United States with [the] initial, expressed purpose of providing valid personality assessment of minority (as well as non-minority) subjects" (1993, p. 381). Furthermore, the TEMAS test has been reviewed as a ". . . landmark event for multicultural assessment because it provides a picture-story test that has psychometric credibility" Dana (1996, p. 280).

In the same vein, Ritzler (1996) emphasizes that the TEMAS and the Rorschach Comprehensive System are the two most appropriate instruments to assess culturally diverse individuals because of their adequate multicultural construct validity. In addition, the TEMAS test has shown good validity when used in foreign countries (Costantino, Malgady, Casullo, and Castillo, 1991; Sardi and Summo, 2000; Walton, Nuttall, and Vazquez-Nuttall, 1997, 1998).

When applied in clinical or school settings, TEMAS reduces and limits the obstacles faced by the examiner in evaluating culturally diverse children and adolescents. Both the test materials and the psychometric properties make the TEMAS a markedly better choice than its competitors. The TEMAS, however, is not just for culturally diverse youngsters. The majority version does an admirable job in assessing Euro-American youngsters. The strength of the TEMAS lies in the constructs it assesses: social problem solving. For multicultural assessment, combining the TEMAS with an omnibus objective measure can provide a thorough narrative assessment. In general, the TEMAS should not be used alone, but as part of a complete battery designed to assess multiple aspects of a child's functioning.

References

Atkinson, J. W. (1981). Studying personality in the context of an advanced motivational psychology. *American Psychologist, 36,* 117–128.

Bellak, L., & Abrams, D. (1997). *The T.A.T, C.A.T., and S.A.T in clinical use* (6th ed.). Needham Heights, MA: Allyn & Bacon.

Bellak, L., & Bellak, C. P. (1949). *The Children's Apperception Test (C.A.T.).* Larchmont, NY: Authors.

Bellak, L., & Bellak, C. P. (1952). *The Children's Apperception Test, Human (C.A.T.-H.).* Larchmont, NY: Authors.

Bruner, J. (1986). *Actual minds, possible worlds.* Cambridge, MA: Harvard University Press.

Conners, C. K. (1989). *Conners Parent Rating Scales.* North Tonawanda, NY: Multi-Health Systems.

Conners, C. K. (1997). *Conners Rating Scales-revised.* North Tonawanda, NY: Multi-Health Systems.

Costantino, G. (1987). *Picture cards: The TEMAS (Tell-Me-A-Story) Test.* Los Angeles: Western Psychological Services.

Costantino, G. (1992). Overcoming bias in educational assessment of Hispanic students. In C. F. Geisenger (Ed.), *Psychological testing of Hispanics* (pp. 89–98). Washington, DC: American Psychological Association.

Costantino, G., & Malgady, R. G. (1996). Development of TEMAS, a Multicultural Thematic Apperception Test: Psychometric properties and cultural utility. In G. R. Sodowsky & J. C. Impara (Eds.), *Multicultural assessment in counseling and clinical psychology* (pp. 86–136). Lincoln, NB: Buros Institute of Mental Measurement.

Costantino, G., & Malgady, R. G. (1999). The Tell-Me-A-Story Test: A multicultural offspring of the Thematic Apperception Test. In L. Gieser

& M. I. Stein (Eds.), *Evocative images: The Thematic Apperception Test and the art of projection* (pp. 191–206). Washington, DC: American Psychological Association.

Costantino, G., Malgady, R., Casullo, M. M., & Castillo, A. (1991). Cross-cultural standardization of TEMAS in three Hispanic subcultures. *Hispanic Journal of Behavioral Sciences, 13,* 48–62.

Costantino, G., Malgady, R. G., Colon-Malgady, G., & Perez, A. (1991). Assessment of attention deficit disorder using a thematic apperception technique. *Journal of Personality Assessment, 57,* 87–95.

Costantino, G., Malgady, R. G., & Rogler, L. H. (1988). *TEMAS (Tell-Me-A-Story) manual* (chapters 1–7). Los Angeles: Western Psychological Services.

Dana, R. H. (1959). Proposal for objective scoring of the TAT. *Perceptual and Motor Skills, 11*(Suppl. 1), 27–43.

Dana, R. H. (1982). *Picture-story cards for Sioux/Plains Indians.* Fayetteville: University of Arkansas.

Dana, R. H. (1993). *Multicultural assessment perspectives for professional psychology.* Needham Heights, MA: Allyn & Bacon.

Dana, R. H. (1996). Culturally competent assessment practice in the United States. *Journal of Personality Assessment, 66,* 472–487.

Dana, R. H. (1998, August). Achievement motivation evidenced in TAT stories in four cultural groups. In G. Costantino (Chair), *Multicultural-cross-cultural motivation as measured by the TAT and TEMAS.* Symposium presented at the 106th Convention of the American Psychological Association, San Francisco.

Dana, R. H. (1999). Cross-cultural-multicultural use of the Thematic Apperception Test. In L. Gieser & M. I. Stein (Eds.), *Evocative images: The Thematic Apperception Test and the art of projection* (pp. 177–190). Washington, DC: American Psychological Association.

Edelbrock, C. Costello, A. J., Dulcan, M. K., Conover, N. C., & Kalas, R. (1986). Parent-child agreement on child psychiatric symptoms assessed via structured interview. *Journal of Child Psychology and Psychiatry, 27,* 181–190.

Flanagan, R. (1999). Objective and projective personality assessment: The TEMAS and the Behavior Assessment System for Children, self-report of personality. *Psychological Reports, 48,* 865–867.

Gieser, L., & Stein, M. I. (1999). *Evocative images: The Thematic Apperception Test and the art of projection.* Washington, DC: American Psychological Association.

Groth-Marnat, G. G. (1997). *Handbook of personality assessment* (3rd ed.). New York: Wiley.

Hatt, C. V. (1985). Review of Children's Apperception Test. *Ninth Mental Measurements Yearbook, I,* 315–316.

Henry, W. E. (1947). The thematic apperception in the study of culture-personality relations. *Genetic Psychology Monographs, 35,* 3–135.

Howard, G. S. (1991). Culture tales: a narrative approach to thinking, cross-cultural psychology and psychotherapy. *American Psychologist, 46,* 187–197.

Kovacs, M. (1992). *The Children's Depression Inventory.* North Tonawanda, NY: Multi-Health Systems.

Mair, M. (1989). *Between psychology and psychotherapy.* London: Routledge.

McClelland, D. C., Atkinson, J. W., Clark, R. A., & Lowell, E. L. (1953). *The achievement motive.* New York: Appleton-Century-Crofts.

McClelland, D. C., & Friedman, G. A. (1952). Child-rearing and the achievement motivation appearing in folktales. In G. E. Swanson, T. M. Newcomb, & E. L. Hartley (Eds.), *Readings in social psychology* (2nd ed., pp. 243–249). New York: Holt, Rinehart & Winston.

McClelland, D., Koestner, R., & Weinberger, J. (1989). How do self-attributed and implicit motives differ? *Psychological Review, 96,* 690–702.

McConaughy, S. H., & Achenbach, T. M. (1989). Empirically based assessment of serious emotional disturbance. *Journal of School Psychology, 27,* 91–117.

Morgan, C. D., & Murray, H. A. (1981). A method for investigation of fantasies: The Thematic Apperception Test. In E. S. Shneidman (Ed.), *Endeavors in psychology: Selections from the personology of Henry A. Murray.* New York: Harper & Row.

Murray, H. A. (1938). *Explorations in personality.* New York: Oxford University Press.

Murray, H. A. (1943). *The Thematic Apperception Test (T.A.T.).* Cambridge, MA: Harvard University Press.

Murstein, B. I. (1963). *Theory and research in projective techniques.* New York: Wiley.

Obrzut, J. E., & Cummings, J. A. (1983). The projective approach to personality assessment: An analysis of thematic picture techniques. *School Psychology Review, 12,* 414–420.

Piotrowski, C., Sherry, D., & Keller, J. W. (1985). Psychodiagnostic test usage: A survey of the Society for Personality Assessment. *Journal of Personality Assessment, 49,* 115–119.

Reynolds, C. R., & Kamphaus, R. W. (1992). *Technical manual: Behavior Assessment System for Children.* Circle Pines, MN: American Guidance Service.

Ritzler, B. A. (1993). Test review: TEMAS (Tell-Me-A-Story). *Journal of Psychoeducational Assessment, 11*, 381–389.

Ritzler, B. A. (1996). Projective methods for multicultural personality assessment: Rorschach, TEMAS, and the Early Memory Procedures. In L. A. Suzuki, P. J. Meller, & J. G. Ponterotto (Eds.), *Handbook of multicultural assessment: Clinical, psychological and educational applications* (pp. 115–136). San Francisco: Jossey-Bass.

Rossini, E. D., & Moretti, R. J. (1997). Thematic Apperception Test (TAT) interpretations: Practice recommendations from a survey of clinical psychology doctoral programs accredited by the American Psychological Association. *Professional Psychology: Research and Practice, 28*, 393–398.

Sardi, G. M., & Summo, B. (2000). Aggression in Italian school-age children as measured by TEMAS. Unpublished dissertation. Roma, Italia: Università di Roma "La Sapienza."

Stein, M. I., & Gieser, L. (1999). The Zeitgeists and events surrounding the birth of the Thematic Apperception Test. In L. Gieser & M. I. Stein (Eds.), *Evocative images: The Thematic Apperception Test and the art of projection* (pp. 15–22). Washington, DC: American Psychological Association.

Vane, J. R., & Guarnaccia, V. (1989). Personality theory and personality assessment measures: How useful to the clinician? *Journal of Clinical Psychology, 45*, 519.

Walton, J. R., Nuttall, R. L., & Vazquez-Nuttall, E. (1997). The impact of war on the mental health of children: A Salvadoran study. *Child Abuse and Neglect, 21*, 737–749.

Walton, J. R., Nuttall, R. L., & Vazquez-Nuttall, E. (1998, August). Effects of war on Salvadoran children's motivation reflected in TEMAS stories. In G. Costantino (Chair), *Multicultural-cross-cultural motivation as measured by the TAT and TEMAS.* Symposium presented at the 106th Convention of the American Psychological Association, San Francisco.

Watkins, C. E., Campbell, V. L., Nieberding, R., & Hallmark, R. (1995). Contemporary practice of psychological assessment by clinical psychologists. *Professional Psychology: Research and Practice, 26*, 54–60.

10

Multicultural Usage of the Rorschach

Barry A. Ritzler

For a personality assessment method to be appropriate to multicultural use, it must have one of two general features: it must have alternate forms that have been specifically standardized and validated for the culture of the subject being assessed, or it must be "culture-free." In Chapter Nine, a personality assessment method with culture-specific alternate forms is presented (the TEMAS, Costantino, Malgady, and Rogler, 1986). In this chapter, the Rorschach Comprehensive System (Exner, 1993) is presented as a culture-free method.

The Rorschach Comprehensive System (Exner, 1993) is a method that presents ten standard inkblots (Rorschach, 1921) to the subject with the simple instruction, "What might this be?" After responses to the ten blots have been obtained and transcribed verbatim, the examiner takes the subject through the ten blots again, conducting a nonleading inquiry to obtain adequate information and code each response according to an elaborate scoring system. Several standard coding systems existed for fifty years or more before the Comprehensive System, most notably Rorschach's original system (1921) and comparable systems by Klopfer (Klopfer and Kelley, 1942), Beck (1944), Rapaport (Rapaport, Gill, and Schafer, 1946), and Piotrowski (1957).

In the early 1970s, Exner (1974) systematically surveyed the previously mentioned systems and selected coding variables that passed stringent requirements for reliability and validity. He used the resulting data to develop a composite coding and interpretation system that became known as the Comprehensive System, which has become the most frequently used coding and interpretive method of Rorschach assessment. The Beck and Klopfer systems continue to be used by a substantial minority of assessment psychologists, with the Rapaport and Piotrowski systems having smaller, but loyal followings. Many of the variables from these earlier systems and the original system developed by Rorschach (1921) were incorporated in the Comprehensive System.

Stimulus Ambiguity

The Rorschach Comprehensive System is proposed as a culture-free assessment method for several reasons. First, the test stimuli (the inkblots) are sufficiently ambiguous to eliminate most cultural bias. It may be that members of some cultures have more familiarity with the concept of using inkblots for personality assessment, but it is unlikely that any culture provides more than occasional experience with the actual Rorschach method that uses ten specifically designed blots.

Taking a Rorschach is a novel experience for nearly everyone, regardless of culture. Also, the Rorschach inkblots are sufficiently ambiguous to avoid having any stimulus properties that may be biased for or against any culture. That is, it is unlikely that any of the blot configurations look very much like any culture-specific object. Each blot has so-called popular responses, reported by at least 26 percent of an American normative sample (Exner, 1993); however, none of the contents of these populars has clear cultural specificity. They are:

- I: bat or butterfly

- II: bear, dog, elephant, lamb

- III: human figure

- IV: human or humanlike figure

- V: bat or butterfly

- VI: animal skin, hide, pelt, or rug

- VII: human head or face

- VIII: animal

- IX: human or humanlike figure

- X: spider crab

It appears that the blots allow subjects to project their own content onto the various configurations. Cultural bias may appear in the response content, but this is much more likely to be the bias of the subjects themselves and not the product of the stimulus properties of the blots.

Standardization

The second characteristic of the Rorschach Comprehensive System that qualifies it as a culture-free method is its standard procedures for administration, coding (scoring), and interpretation. Proper application of the Rorschach Comprehensive System requires a standard administration followed by a complete coding of all responses and subsequent interpretation using a systematic procedure ensuring that all who use it cover all variables in the system (approximately 175) in an invariable step-by-step fashion tailored for each individual protocol. In other words, all subjects are assessed with exactly the same procedures regardless of their cultural identity. The psychologist carrying out these procedures is not permitted to deviate from the standard format; this minimizes the potential cultural bias of the psychologist, who may come from a culture other than that of the client.

Culture-Free Evidence

Recent evidence exists to support the notion that the stimulus properties of the Rorschach inkblots and the standardized procedures result in culture-free data. At the International Rorschach Society meeting in Amsterdam in July 1999, Comprehensive System data on nonpatient adults were presented from twelve countries (International Rorschach Society, 1999). Table 10.1 summarizes the results for selected variables from eight of these countries (results from the other four countries are not presented because the subjects were children or complete data were not available). Space restrictions prevent reporting more variables, but the ones selected are reasonably representative of the various personality dimensions assessed by the Rorschach Comprehensive System.

Inspection of the table reveals that there is remarkable consistency across countries on all variables in that very few of the means in each category are separated by more than one standard deviation. The rare exceptions are significant differences between Japan and Portugal (Pires, 2000) on M and X-%, with Japan higher in both cases (also higher than Finland on X-%). Clearly, the results are highly similar across countries with very different cultures for this set of variables, which is representative of the entire range of Comprehensive System variables in these studies.

Interpretation and the Normative Problem

Despite a culture-free stimulus and standardized procedures, the Rorschach Comprehensive System would still not be an appropriate multicultural assessment method if the interpretation process were culturally biased (Ephraim, 2000). The greatest risk for cultural bias in Comprehensive System interpretation is with the nonpatient norms (Exner, 1993), which are used to determine the significance of variables in a single subject's record.

Table 10.1. Comparison of means and standard deviations for selected Rorschach Comprehensive System variables across countries, from the International Rorschach Society nonpatient studies.

| | Country | | | | | | | |
Variable	Argentina (n = 54)	Belgium (n = 300)	Finland (n = 343)	Japan (n = 240)	Peru (n = 164)	Portugal (n = 309)	Spain (n = 520)	USA (n = 123)
M	4.26	3.37	3.22	5.63	3.77	2.84	4.21	3.64
	(2.69)	(2.71)	(2.66)	(3.14)	(2.87)	(2.60)	(2.69)	(2.65)
SumC	3.02	2.78	3.59	3.36	2.43	2.81	2.78	2.62
	(2.91)	(2.02)	(2.49)	(2.47)	(1.82)	(2.45)	(2.20)	(1.98)
Lambda	1.04	1.12	0.78	0.86	0.80	1.21	1.03	1.22
	(0.72)	(1.38)	(0.92)	(0.84)	(0.69)	(1.71)	(0.84)	(1.72)
X-%	17	21	15*	25*	18	12*	21	21
	(9)	(10)	(9)	(11)	(12)	(7)	(10)	(11)
Ego	0.43	0.36	0.39	0.33	0.40	0.39	0.40	0.37
	(0.13)	(0.15)	(0.13)	(0.11)	(0.18)	(0.18)	(0.15)	(0.14)
Isolation	0.24	0.18	0.26	0.17	0.19	0.22	0.19	0.19
	(0.17)	(0.12)	(0.18)	(0.12)	(0.16)	(0.17)	(0.13)	(0.15)
EA	7.28	6.15	6.87	8.98	6.20	5.65	6.99	6.26
	(3.70)	(3.74)	(4.27)	(4.21)	(3.38)	(4.20)	(3.77)	(3.71)
es	8.76	10.09	10.19	9.11	9.19	8.74	9.08	6.82
	(5.08)	(5.63)	(5.62)	(4.51)	(4.72)	(5.42)	(5.21)	(4.75)

Notes: Standard deviations given in parentheses.

Variable labels and brief description: M (human movement), cognitive resources; SumC (weighted sum of chromatic color), emotional resources; Lambda (proportion of pure form responses), psychological complexity; X-% (percentage of poor form responses), poor judgment and reality testing; Ego (Egocentricity Index), self-esteem; Isolation (Isolation Index), sense of isolation; EA (Experience Actual), total available resources; es (Experience Stimulation), total subjective stress.   * Denotes significantly different means.

Proper interpretation of Rorschach Comprehensive System data is based primarily on the established validity of the variables in the coding system (Exner, 1996). Direct content analysis is an important part of the interpretation technique, but it is not acceptably valid without integration with interpretations derived from the summary variables obtained from the coding method. Norms established in the United States delineate the range of scores typical of adequately functioning individuals free from serious psychological problems (Exner, 1996).

Using these norms, certain psychological problems and deficiencies can be detected, but the primary use of the Rorschach Comprehensive System is to describe the unique personality style of the subject. This is accomplished by describing how the subject's performance differs from the normative pattern of scores. The many variables in the coding system enable the assessment psychologist to obtain information about many components of personality functioning, such as cognition emotional expression, behavior control, self-image, and the perception of interpersonal relations. Effective multicultural assessment, of course, depends on the norms being relatively free of cultural bias.

With the addition of new, nonpatient data from the Amsterdam conference and the existence of previous normative data, the Rorschach—and in particular the Comprehensive System—might seem to have meaningful information for application across several cultural conditions; however, there is a fundamental problem with simply using a nonpatient normative sample. Individuals may be "nonpatients" because they lack the motivation, sophistication, or financial resources to consider treatment for psychological problems. Therefore, a substantial number of nonpatients may have poor or marginal overall adjustment.

This speculation is supported by previous studies that have shown that samples of culturally or economically disadvantaged individuals score in a less adaptive direction on the Comprehensive System variables (with rural Zairians, see Meernhout and Mukendi,

1980; inner-city children, Krall, 1983; and incarcerated Alaskan natives, Glass, Bieber, and Tkachuk, 1996). A better normative comparison sample might be individuals who qualify as "well-adjusted" according to criteria of psychological competence rather than simply having nonpatient status. The interpretation norms for the Comprehensive System were established by Exner (1993) through soliciting the participation of individuals who showed average to above-average coping ability. When compared with the nonpatient data from Amsterdam, Exner's norms are notably different. Table 10.2 summarizes a comparison of Exner's norms and the combined means from the Amsterdam studies.

Inspection of the table shows that for most variables (except Ego and Isolation), the Amsterdam results are in the less adaptive direction. This would suggest that the Amsterdam data might not represent average levels of adaptability. Discussion continues in assessment research circles as to what best constitutes a normative sample. Until more definitive conclusions are drawn, it might be advisable to rely on the original U.S. norms of the Comprehensive

Table 10.2. Comparison for selected variables between the Comprehensive System norms and the composite results from the Amsterdam nonpatient studies.

Variables	Mean Scores	
	Comprehensive System Norms (n = 700)	Amsterdam Data (n = 2,053)
M	4.30	3.81
SumC	4.52	2.95
Lambda	0.58	1.00
X-percent	7.00	18.80
Ego	0.39	0.38
Isolation	0.20	0.20
EA	8.82	6.79
es	8.21	9.23

System rather than the data from specific countries in the Amsterdam studies.

That tactic, however, increases the likelihood that Comprehensive System interpretations have a U.S. cultural bias. It is encouraging, though, that some evidence exists to suggest that when level of adaptability and cultural sophistication are controlled, culturally unique nonpatient samples yield data quite similar to the U.S. normative results (for example, with Japanese American children, Takeuchi and Scott, 1986; Latin American adults, Hernandez-Guzman, Rey-Clericus, San Martin-Petersen, and Vinet-Reichhardt, 1989; and Swedish children, Spigelman, Spigelman, and Englesson, 1991). Nevertheless, more work needs to be done on identifying appropriate norms for multicultural interpretation using the Rorschach Comprehensive System.

Some Multicultural Assessment Issues

Recent studies conducted with the Rorschach Comprehensive System at Long Island University have addressed some important issues in multicultural personality assessment. These are the effects of acculturation, language differences, and validation with other multicultural methods as criteria.

The Effects of Acculturation and Language Differences

Individuals who move across cultures show different levels of adaptation. Some accommodate well to the new culture. Their behavior style and even their attitudes become consistent with those of the new culture, and the ways and sensibilities of the old culture are much less apparent in their behavior. Such extensive acculturation is rare, however. Many individuals continue to show some personality characteristics more consistent with the old culture than the new one, even though considerable acculturation is apparent.

Others adapt with a blend of the old and new such that the result is nearly equal representation of both cultures. Still others keep the ways and attitudes of the old culture while accommodating to the new culture just enough to avoid major conflicts and misunderstandings. Finally, it is not rare to find individuals who resist, avoid, or fail to form even the most superficial accommodations and continue to be identified as true adherents to the old ways (Cross, 1991).

Because acculturation covers such a wide spectrum, an assessment psychologist must be able to determine the extent of acculturation in an individual client. (For more extensive discussion of this issue, see Choney, Berryhill-Parke, and Robbins, 1995; and Lu, Lim, and Mezzich, 1995.) Several reasonably adequate methods for assessing acculturation exist, depending on the subject's culture of origin (such as Cuellar, Harris, and Jasso, 1980; Franco, 1983; Marin and others, 1987; Mendoza, 1989; Olmedo, Martinez, and Martinez, 1978; and Suinn, Rickard-Figueroa, Lew, and Vigil, 1987). By using such methods, the assessment psychologist can arrive at a useful estimate of the extent to which the client is culturally different. If acculturation is minimal, much caution must be exercised in projective personality assessment, or at the very least the assessment psychologist must take the low degree of acculturation into account when administering the assessment methods and interpreting their results. Unfortunately, methods for assessing acculturation do not exist for many of the major cultures of origin of individuals in the United States.

Although knowing the client's level of acculturation is essential, it usually is not enough to assure valid assessment. It is apparent that even the most acculturated clients respond to projective methods differently in their native language than in English (Dana, 1993; Tiemann and Ritzler, 1999). Even when English is the native language, dialects can result in differing test performances if the dialect is unlike the one used in the test administration. If acculturation is minimal, the language factor looms larger, even when the client speaks fluent English (Hoffman, Dana, and Bolton, 1985; Malgady, Rogler, and Costantino, 1987).

In a study originating at Long Island University and conducted in the United States and Israel (Rosenberg and Ritzler, 1999), Rorschach Comprehensive System results were compared across three samples:

1. Israeli natives living in the United States and highly accultur-ated to U.S. culture

2. Israeli natives living in the United States who were not highly acculturated

3. Israeli natives living in Israel who never lived in the United States

All subjects spoke English fluently. The Rorschach was admin-istered twice for each subject, once in English and once in Hebrew. The results showed wholesale inconsistencies on most Compre-hensive System variables between the English and Hebrew protocols for all three samples. In contrast, however, the low-acculturation sample and the sample of Israeli natives who never lived in the United States consistently showed more psychological complexity and higher levels of adaptive functioning on their Hebrew proto-cols compared to the English. The high-acculturation groups, how-ever, showed no differences between their English and Hebrew protocols in terms of complexity and adaptive functioning even though there were very few consistencies on other variables between the two types of protocol.

The authors assumed that greater complexity and adaptive func-tioning in these nonpatients was indicative of more valid results. If this assumption holds, then it appears important to give the Rorschach to poorly acculturated individuals in their native lan-guage for valid results. The high-acculturation sample, however, presented a bit of a paradox. Even though the complexity and adap-tive quality of their protocols were the same, most of these subjects gave very different results in Hebrew compared to English.

As an extension of the Rosenberg and Ritzler (1999) study, Tiemann and Ritzler (1999) gave Rorschachs to highly acculturated

English-speaking Latin Americans and found results similar to those of Rosenberg and Ritzler, that is, equality in complexity and adaptability but inconsistencies across language protocols on many other variables. In this study, however, subjects were interviewed about their self-images while speaking English or Spanish. Most subjects reported that they experienced themselves as having personality characteristics that varied with the language.

Curiously, these reported differences in self-descriptions often matched those in the English and Spanish Rorschachs. For example, a subject who reported that she felt much more emotional in Spanish scored extratensive (that is, emotional) on her Spanish protocol and introversive (more cognitive, less emotional) on her English protocol. Such a major difference in personality style is almost never seen in the test-retest Rorschachs of adult U.S. natives speaking only English (Exner, 1993). The authors concluded that when acculturation is high, Rorschachs administered in the native language and in English yield assessment of personality contrasts that are due to language factors.

In conclusion, because of the frequently significant acculturation factor in multicultural projective assessment, it usually is advisable to administer the methods in the client's native language (Chafe, 1962; Lopez, 1988; Moon and Cundick, 1983; and Ervin, 1964). This tactic is less important if the client is highly acculturated. An exception to this general rule may be when the assessment psychologist is interested in learning about the psychological orientation of the client in the nonnative language (Tiemann and Ritzler, 1999).

Cross-Method Validation of the Multicultural Rorschach

Knowing the level of acculturation and administering the methods in the native language do not suffice if the assessment methods are not sensitive to personality characteristics indigenous to the client's culture (Costantino, Flanagan, and Malgady, 1995; Hui and Triandis, 1985; Paunonen and others, 1996; Allen, 1998; Okazaki, 1998; and

Cuellar, 1998). Personality characteristics that develop from cultural experiences may be misidentified or missed altogether by assessment methods that have emerged from cultures much different from that of the client (Low, 1985). Consequently, it would be informative as an additional check on the multicultural validity of the Comprehensive System to determine if the Rorschach results are consistent with the results of other methods independently validated for multicultural assessment.

Such a comparison was made in another study originating at Long Island University. Elliott and Ritzler (1998) compared the results of the Rorschach Comprehensive System and the TEMAS (Costantino, Malgady, and Rogler, 1986, presented in Chapter Nine). The subjects were Hispanic, African American, and Caucasian children who were administered the minority and non-minority forms of the TEMAS and the Rorschach. Rorschach variables were significantly correlated with conceptually similar TEMAS variables when the TEMAS form was appropriate to the ethnic identity of the subject. For instance, the correlations with the Rorschach were significant for the minority version of the TEMAS administered to Hispanic children, but not for the non-minority version. The same general finding applied to the African American and Caucasian children. The authors concluded that the results were evidence of the multicultural validity of the Comprehensive System.

Conclusions

The Rorschach Comprehensive System seems well suited for multicultural assessment. Its relatively ambiguous stimulus properties and its standard procedures protect the system from cultural bias. Although much more work needs to be done in providing appropriate culture-specific norms, the current data suggest that normative differences are not great across cultures, so norms developed in the United States probably can be used to assess results from other cultures. Care must be taken, however, to ensure that the normative issues are resolved in an appropriate fashion (see, for instance, the cautions of Howes and DeBlassie, 1989; and Shaffer, Erdberg, and Haroain, 1999). Nevertheless, studies involving differences in acculturation, language, and culture have supported the multicultural rigor of the Comprehensive System so far.

References

Allen, J. (1998). Personality assessment with American Indians and Alaska natives: Instrument considerations and service delivery style. *Journal of Personality Assessment, 70*, 17–42.

Beck, S. (1944). *Rorschach's test I: Basic processes*. Philadelphia: Grune and Stratton.

Chafe, W. (1962). Estimates regarding the present speakers of North American Indian languages. *International Journal of American Linguistics, 28*, 161–171.

Choney, S., Berryhill-Parke, E., & Robbins, R. (1995). The acculturation of American Indians: Developing frameworks for research and practice. In J. Ponterotto, J. Casas, L. Suzuki, & C. Alexander (Eds.), *Handbook of multicultural counseling* (pp. 73–92). Thousand Oaks, CA: Sage.

Costantino, G., Flanagan, R., & Malgady, R. (1995). The history of the Rorschach: Overcoming bias in multicultural projective assessment. *Rorschachiana: Yearbook of the International Rorschach Society, 20*, 148–171.

Costantino, G., Malgady, R., & Rogler, L. (1986). *Standardization and validation of TEMAS, a pluralistic thematic apperception test*. New York: Fordham University, Hispanic Research Center.

Cross, W. (1991). *Shades of black: Diversity in African-American identity*. Philadelphia: Temple University Press.

Cuellar, I. (1998). Cross-cultural clinical psychological assessment of Hispanic Americans. *Journal of Personality Assessment, 70*, 71–86.

Cuellar, I., Harris, L., & Jasso, R. (1980). An acculturation scale for Mexican-American normal and clinical populations. *Hispanic Journal of Behavioral Science, 2*, 199–217.

Dana, R. (1993). *Multicultural assessment perspectives for professional psychology*. Needham Heights, MA: Allyn & Bacon.

Dana, R. (1998). Cultural identity assessment of culturally diverse groups: 1997. *Journal of Personality Assessment, 70*, 1–16.

Elliott, T., & Ritzler, B. (1998). Comparisons between the TEMAS and the Rorschach Comprehensive System: A multicultural validation. Unpublished doctoral dissertation, Long Island University.

Ephraim, D. (2000). Culturally relevant research and practice with the Rorschach Comprehensive System. In R. H. Dana (Ed.), *Handbook of cross-cultural and multi-cultural personality assessment* (pp. 303–328). Hillsdale, N.J.: Erlbaum.

Ervin, S. (1964). Language and TAT content in bilinguals. *Journal of Abnormal Social Psychology, 86,* 500–507.

Exner, J. (1974). *The Rorschach: A comprehensive system* (Vol. 1). New York: Wiley.

Exner, J. (1993). *The Rorschach: A comprehensive system* (Vol. 1, 3rd ed.). New York: Wiley.

Exner, J. (1996). *A Rorschach workbook for the Comprehensive System* (3rd ed.). Asheville, NC: Rorschach Workshops.

Franco, J. (1983). An acculturation scale for Mexican-American children. *Journal of General Psychology, 108,* 175–181.

Glass, M., Bieber, S., & Tkachuk, M. (1996). Personality styles and dynamics of Alaska native and normative incarcerated men. *Journal of Personality Assessment, 66,* 583–603.

Hernandez-Guzman, P., Rey-Clericus, R., San Martin-Petersen, C., & Vinet-Reichhardt, E. (1989). Differences between Anglo-American and Latin-American cultures in responses given to the Rorschach Psychodiagnostic Test [translated title]. *Terapia Psicologica, 8,* 62–66.

Hoffman, T., Dana, R., & Bolton, B. (1985). Measured acculturation and MMPI-168 performance of Native American adults. *Journal of Cross-Cultural Psychology, 16,* 243–256.

Howes, R., & DeBlassie, R. (1989). Model errors in the cross cultural use of the Rorschach. *Journal of Multicultural Counseling and Development, 17,* 79–84.

Hui, C., & Triandis, H. (1985). Measurement in cross-cultural psychology: A review and comparison of strategies. *Journal of Cross-Cultural Psychology, 16,* 131–152.

International Rorschach Society. (1999). Tables for the international symposium on Rorschach nonpatient data: Findings from around the world I, II, III. Proceedings, triennial meeting, Amsterdam.

Klopfer, B., & Kelley, D. (1942). *The Rorschach technique.* Yonkers, NY: World Book.

Krall, V. (1983). Rorschach norms for inner city children. *Journal of Personality Assessment, 47,* 155–157.

Lopez, S. (1988). The empirical basis of ethnocultural and linguistic bias in mental health evaluations of Hispanics. *American Psychologist, 43,* 1095–1097.

Low, S. (1985). Culturally interpreted symptoms or culture-bound syndromes: A cross-cultural review of nerves. *Social Science and Medicine, 21,* 187–196.

Lu, F., Lim, R., & Mezzich, J. E. (1995). Issues in the assessment and diagnosis of culturally diverse individuals. In G. Marin, F. Sabogal, B. VanOss-Marin, R. Otero-Sabogal, & E. Perez-Sable (Eds.), Development of a short acculturation scale for Hispanics. *Hispanic Journal of Behavioral Sciences, 9,* 183–205.

Malgady, R., Rogler, L., & Costantino, G. (1987). Ethnocultural and linguistic bias in mental health evaluation of Hispanics. *American Psychologist, 42,* 228–234.

Marin, G., Sabogal, F., VanOss-Marin, B., Otero-Sabogal, R., & Perez-Sable, E. (1987). Development of a short acculturation scale for Hispanics. *Hispanic Journal of Behavioral Science, 9,* 183–205.

Meernhout, M., & Mukendi, N. (1980). Rorschach responses from another culture: A sample of rural Zairians [translated title]. *Bulletin de Psychologie Scolaire et d'Orientation, 29,* 61–70.

Mendoza, R. (1989). An empirical scale to measure type and degree of acculturation in Mexican-American adolescents and adults. *Journal of Cross-Cultural Psychology, 20,* 372–385.

Moon, T., & Cundick, B. (1983). Shifts and constancies in Rorschach responses as a function of culture and language. *Journal of Personality Assessment, 47,* 345–349.

Okazaki, S. (1998). Psychological assessment of Asian Americans: Research agenda for cultural competency. *Journal of Personality Assessment, 70,* 54–70.

Olmedo, E., Martinez, J., & Martinez, S. (1978). Measure of acculturation for Chicano adolescents. *Psychological Reports,* 159–170.

Paunonen, S., Keinonen, M., Trzebinski, J., Forsterling, F., Grisheno-Roze, N., Kouznetsova, L., and Chan, D. (1996). The structure of personality in six cultures. *Journal of Cross-Cultural Psychology, 27,* 339–353.

Pires, A. A. (2000). National norms for the Rorschach normative study in Portugal. In R. H. Dana (Ed.), *Handbook of cross-cultural and multi-cultural personality assessment* (pp. 303–328). Hillsdale, NJ: Erlbaum.

Piotrowski, Z. (1957). *Perceptanalysis.* New York: Macmillan.

Rapaport, D., Gill, M., & Schafer, R. (1946). *Diagnostic psychological testing* (Vols. 1 and 2). Chicago: Yearbook Publishers.

Rorschach, H. (1921). *Psychodiagnostik*. Bern, Switzerland: Bircher. Transl. Hans Huber Verlag, 1942.

Rosenberg, D., & Ritzler, B. (1999). Acculturation as a factor in the validity of Cross-cultural Rorschach Comprehensive System assessment. Unpublished manuscript.

Shaffer, T., Erdberg, P., & Haroain, J. (1999). Current nonpatient data for the Rorschach, WAIS-R, and MMPI-2. *Journal of Personality Assessment, 73*, 305–318.

Spigelman, A., Spigelman, G., & Englesson, I. (1991). Cross-cultural differences between American and Swedish children regarding their egocentricity index. *Tidsskrift for Norsk Psykolog., 28*, 316–319.

Suinn, R., Rickard-Figueroa, K., Lew, S., & Vigil, P. (1987). The Suinn-Lew Asian Self-Identity Acculturation Scale: An initial report. *Educational and Psychological Measurement, 47*, 401–407.

Takeuchi, M., & Scott, R. (1986). Educational productivity and Rorschach location responses of preschool Japanese and American children. *Psychology in the Schools, 23*, 368–373.

Tiemann, J., & Ritzler, B. (1999). Analysis of language-based differences on Rorschach Comprehensive System and TAT protocols of fluent bilinguals. Unpublished doctoral dissertation, Long Island University.

Use of 16PF and CPI with U.S. Racial and Ethnic Minorities

Issues of Cultural Application and Validity

Kwong-Liem Karl Kwan and Felito Aldarondo

The Sixteen Personality Factor Questionnaire (16PF) and the California Psychological Inventory (CPI) are two of the most widely used psychological instruments for "normal" personality assessment (Conoley and Impara, 1995; Kaplan and Saccuzzo, 1997). Cross-cultural studies have been conducted for both instruments; however, most have focused on international samples using translated versions of the previous editions. Few studies with U.S. racial and ethnic minorities have been conducted.

In this chapter, we review studies on application of the 16PF and CPI to U.S. racial and ethnic minorities. We evaluate the cultural validity of both instruments, and finally we delineate implications for practice and research.

Overview of the Sixteen Personality Factor Questionnaire

The 16PF was developed as an objective measure of normal personality (Cattell, 1946) and ongoing personality traits (Meyer and Deitsch, 1996). Since its initial publication, the questionnaire has undergone four revisions, evolving into the 16PF Fifth Edition (herein referred to as 16PF-5), published in 1994 (Conn and Rieke,

1994; Russell and Karol, 1994). The 16PF-5 yields scores on sixteen primary factors:

1. Warmth
2. Reasoning
3. Emotional Stability
4. Dominance
5. Liveliness
6. Rule-Consciousness
7. Social Boldness
8. Sensitivity
9. Vigilance
10. Abstractedness
11. Privateness
12. Apprehension
13. Openness to Change
14. Self-Reliance
15. Perfectionism
16. Tension

Five global, "secondary-order" factors (Extraversion, Anxiety, Tough-Mindedness, Independence, and Control) have also been identified.

The 16PF has engendered a number of related instruments, such as the Children's Personality Questionnaire, High School Personality Questionnaire, and the Clinical Analysis Questionnaire, and has been applied to a variety of populations in clinical, occupational, and school settings.

16PF Performance of U.S. Racial and Ethnic Populations

Although the 16PF has been translated into more than forty languages and adapted in other countries, very few studies using U.S. racial and ethnic populations have been conducted. Two studies using earlier versions of the 16PF were conducted with Hispanic Americans. DeBlassie and Franco (1983) compared direct assessment and indirect assessment of personality by asking fifty-one undergraduate Hispanic American college students to complete the Cattell, Eber, and Tatsuoka (1970) version of the 16PF (that is, indirect assessment) and to rate themselves (direct assessment) on the bipolar dimensions of the sixteen factors (Reserved versus Outgoing, Self-Assured versus Apprehensive, Relaxed versus Tensed). Results indicated that students were able to predict how they would score on eight of the 16PF scales: Intelligence, Emotional Stability, Assertiveness, Shyness, Conventionalism, Pretentiousness, Self-Confidence, and Carelessness of Protocol.

Whitworth and Perry (1990) administered the English 16PF (1968 version) to Anglo American and Mexican American undergraduate students, and a Spanish 16PF (1966 version) to another group of Mexican American students. Significant differences were found among the three groups. The largest number of scale differences were found between the Anglo American and Mexican students who were tested in Spanish, followed by that between the two Mexican American groups. The smallest number of differences was found between Anglo American and Mexican American students who were tested in English.

The 16PF was included as one of the instruments in two studies that compared African American and White American participants. Clark (1986) attempted to identify personality (for example, sex role) and sociocultural factors (such as socioeconomic class) that distinguished science (for example, chemistry) and nonscience (for instance, education) college majors. Among African American students, science majors were found to be more tough-minded and practical than the nonscience majors. Racial differences were found on intelligence, sober versus happy-go-lucky, and undisciplined versus self-control on the 16PF (Cattell, Eber, and Tatsuoka, 1970).

Knight and McCallum (1998) compared cardiovascular reactivity to induced stress, self-reported depression and anxiety, as well as positive stress appraisals of African American and White dementia caregivers. The Motivational Distortion (MD) scale from the 16PF (Cattell, Eber, and Tatsuoka, 1988) was used as one of the indicators of positive stress appraisal. Positive reappraisals and self-reported depression were found to be positively related to heart rate reactivity for Whites in two stress conditions (doing a mental arithmetic task and relating to a stressful caregiving problem that occurred in the previous month) but inversely related to heart rate reactivity for African Americans only in the caregiving problem condition. African American caregivers were found to use positive reappraisals more than White caregivers.

Wallbrown, Reuter, and Barnett (1989) examined the extent to which corrections for factor scores given in the 16PF test manual can be generalized to male felons, a group that might reasonably be expected to distort their scores to the maximum degree. The felon sample consisted of 244 White, 83 Black, and four Asian or Native Americans between seventeen and seventy-one years of age. Findings indicated a relatively strong significant relationship between the Motivational Distortion (MD) sten score and the sten scores for the several 16PF primary scales. Results of the respective racial and ethnic groups were not provided.

Johnson and others (1985) investigated the age versus cohort effects on the 16PF (Cattell, Eber, and Tatsuoka, 1970) and the Comrey Personality Scale (CPS; Comrey, 1970) among Americans from Chinese (27 females and 30 males), European (96 females and 105 males), and Japanese (71 females and 73 males) ancestries living in Hawaii. Results indicated a high degree of similarity in both magnitude and pattern of the correlation of personality scale scores with age across sex and ethnic groups, which suggested that age, not cohort, was the major influence on test scores.

16PF-5

A number of analyses were conducted with the racial and ethnic groups in the restandardization sample of the 16PF-5 (Conn and Rieke, 1994). The potential effect of race on the sixteen primary scales was examined. Analysis of variance using race as the independent variable showed a moderate relationship between race and Reasoning (Scale B) scores. Asian and Caucasian Americans were found to score highest, followed by Native, Hispanic, and African Americans.

Differential item functioning (DIF) analyses of the fifteen items in the Reasoning scale were conducted to examine if item bias contributed to score differences among racial groups. Because of the limited number of Asian and Native Americans, only random samples of African, Caucasian, and Hispanic Americans were included in the DIF analysis. None of the items in the Reasoning scale were found to possess bias when African and Caucasian American samples were compared. One item—number 172: "Tadpole is to frog as larva is to: (a) spider, (b) worm, (c) insect"— was found to be biased when Caucasian and Hispanic Americans were compared. Results indicated that a significantly higher proportion of Caucasians answered the item correctly compared to Hispanics. At the scale level, however, no significant differences among the three groups were found. Thus the item was retained. Except for the analyses reported in the *Technical Manual* (Conn and Rieke, 1994), no other studies of the 16PF-5 performance of African, Asian, and Hispanic Americans and American Indians can be identified.

Overview of the California Psychological Inventory (CPI)

The CPI was developed to assess "normal" personality traits for such purposes as inquiry into individual differences, career exploration, and personnel selection. Since its initial publication, the inventory has undergone several revisions (Gough, 1957, 1987, 1996). The third edition of the CPI (Form 434; Gough, 1996, hereafter referred to as the CPI-3) consists of 434 items that form twenty Folk scales and three Vector scales. Folk scales are purported to measure everyday personality constructs (Gough, 1987):

1. Dominance
2. Capacity for Status
3. Sociability
4. Social Presence
5. Self-Acceptance
6. Independence
7. Empathy
8. Responsibility
9. Socialization
10. Self-Control
11. Good Impression
12. Communality
13. Well-Being
14. Tolerance
15. Achievement via Conformance
16. Achievement via Independence
17. Intellectual Efficiency
18. Psychological-Mindedness

19. Flexibility

20. Femininity/Masculinity

Gough (1996) summarizes the twenty Folk scales in four categories: (1) "measures of poise, self-assurance, and interpersonal proclivities" (p. 12); (2) "measures of normative orientation and values" (p. 12); (3) "measures of cognitive and intellectual functioning" (p. 13); and (4) "measures of role and interpersonal style" (p. 13). Additionally, three Vector scales assessing the dimensions of Externality/Internality, Norm Questioning/Norm-Favoring, and Self-Realization are used for structural scale interpretation. McAllister (1996) succinctly describes how Vectors 1 and 2 are combined to determine one of four personality types: Alpha, Beta, Gamma, or Delta. Vector 3 produces a score along seven levels, which indicates a person's self-realization specific to his or her personality type.

The CPI has been translated into twenty-nine languages and adapted for numerous international samples (Gough, 1987, 1996). Gough (1996) noted that ninety-three studies of cross-cultural applicability of the CPI were conducted. However, the majority of these studies used cross-national samples. A small number of these studies were not published or cannot be located in common databases, such as PsycInfo and ERIC, and all of these studies used older versions of the CPI. For the identified studies, psychometric data (for instance, mean scale scores) of cross-national samples were not always provided. Studies of U.S. racial and ethnic populations remain sparse and present mixed findings.

CPI Performance of U.S. Racial and Ethnic Populations: Early Versions

In an early study, Mason (1969) compared the CPI scores among White, Mexican, and Native American students in a junior high school. Whenever group differences were found, White students tended to score the highest and Native American students the lowest. For males, White students scored significantly different than

Native American or Mexican American students on ten scales, including Capacity for Status, Responsibility, Socialization, Tolerance, Good Impression, Achievement via Conformance, and Intellectual Efficiency. White students scored significantly higher on nine of the ten scales. One exception was found on the Flexibility scale, on which Native American males scored significantly higher than both White and Mexican American males. For female students, significant group differences were found on six scales, with White students scoring significantly higher on all scales. Overall, Mexican and Native American women were found to obtain the lowest scores on a majority of the scales.

Cross, Barclay, and Burger (1978) compared the CPI performance of White and African American college freshmen and sophomores ($N = 772$). Significant differences were found on the basis of (1) race and (2) interaction of race and gender. Sample sizes of the respective racial and gender groups, however, were not reported. Differences were found on these scales:

- Capacity for Status

- Social Presence

- Well-Being

- Responsibility

- Socialization

- Tolerance

- Good Impression

- Communality

- Achievement via Conformance

- Achievement via Independence

- Intellectual Efficiency

Overall, African American students were found to score in the direction that suggested negative personality characteristics. Separate factor analyses were conducted, and different factor structures emerged for the two samples. The authors cautioned that results may lead an "unwary" test interpreter to attribute maladaptive and inferior personality to African Americans; they suggested that social factors (for example, racism, job discrimination) be considered when interpreting African Americans' test results.

In a subsequent study, Cross and Burger (1982) compared CPI (Gough, 1957) responses of African American (136 men and 218 women) and White American (181 men and 213 women) college undergraduates. Approximately 34 percent of items from each of eighteen scales were found to be significantly different, depending on the respondent group. Similar to the Cross, Barclay, and Burger (1978) study just discussed, the authors urged developers of personality tests to consider sociocultural factors that might contribute to differential responses to test items.

Davis, Hoffman, and Nelson (1990) compared the CPI performance of seventy Native Americans and one hundred White Americans applying for employment in a gaming casino. No significant differences in age, occupation, and education were found between the two groups. Native Americans, especially women, were found to score significantly lower on nine scales. According to norm-referenced interpretation, results suggested that (1) Native American men may show less conventionality, lower sensitivity to norm violation, and less adherence to rules and order, and (2) Native American women may demonstrate increased passivity, less dominance verbally, greater preference for inconspicuousness in social situations, and more likelihood of seeking assistance in decision making than their White counterparts. The role of culture in contributing to such scale differences, however, was not discussed or explored. Given that several of the scales in which racial differences were found are often used for personnel selection, Native Americans, especially women, may be at a disadvantage if these scales are used as selection criteria and results of this study are indiscriminately applied.

Ying (1990) examined CPI vector scores of 215 Taiwanese students before they embarked upon graduate studies in the United States. The Taiwan sample was administered the Chinese version of the CPI, and their scores were compared to CPI scores from the American college sample (Gough, 1987). Using two-tailed t-tests, significant differences were found for both Vector 2 and Vector 3, suggesting that those in the Taiwan sample were more norm-abiding and less actualized compared to the American college sample. Ying suggested that because the concepts for the CPI were developed in a Western society and because the notion of self-actualization is likely to be one of the most culture-bound among the Vector scales, the usefulness of the scale is probably greater with increased identification with Western culture. Thus, acculturation appears to be a factor in an individual's responses to items on the CPI, especially from scales (for example, Vector 3) representative of constructs that are largely Western in origin.

In another study, Ying (1994) administered the CPI and other assessment instruments to assess Taiwanese international students' level of adjustment following recent arrival to the United States. Results indicated that self-perceived language ability significantly related to psychological adjustment. Lower self-assessed language ability positively correlated with lower overall estimation of psychological adjustment. A significant implication of this study is that perceived language proficiency may influence test responses.

CPI Scales

Several studies of the cross-cultural applicability of individual CPI scales were conducted. One of the scales from previous versions of the CPI that has received frequent attention in cross-cultural study is the Femininity (Fe) scale (precursor to the current Femininity/Masculinity, or F/M, scale), whose primary function is to categorize individuals along a continuum of femininity and masculinity. Most of these studies were conducted with international samples using translated versions of the CPI (Ahmad, Anis-ul-Haque, and Anila, 1994; Gough, 1966; Gough, Chun, and Chung, 1968; Nishiyama, 1975; Pitariu, 1981; Torki, 1988; Ying, 1991), with the notion that these Folk concepts represent "culturally universal perceptions" (Williams and Best, 1982, as cited in Gough, 1996).

The scale was applied to U.S. racial and ethnic populations in two studies. Baldwin (1987) administered the F/M scale with 554 White and 664 African American college students in the Midwest over a fourteen-year period. The scales were found capable of significantly distinguishing between men and women for both racial groups. No significant differences between White and African American men or White and African American women were found. Moreover, sample means were found to be similar to that of the normative sample. Results provided support for the applicability of the scale to African Americans.

Blane and Yamamoto (1970) administered both the CPI and the Franck Drawing Completion Test to Japanese American, White American, and Japanese students in Hawaii. Japanese students were found to be more feminine on both measures. Within the American sample, Japanese Americans were found to be more feminine than White Americans on the CPI scales. However, results of the scale's ability to distinguish between male and female students were not reported.

CPI has also been frequently applied in predicting school achievement. Despite international studies using translated versions in Italy (Gough, 1964) and Greece (Repapi, Gough, Lanning, and Stefanis, 1983) that supported cross-national applicability, little research in this area has been conducted with U.S. racial and ethnic groups. Wood and Clay (1996) examined the role of structural barriers in predicting academic performance among 1,010 White and 352 Native Americans. The Socialization scale was found to be a significant predictor for both groups. In addition, White Americans were found to produce a significantly higher mean than Native Americans did, although a lenient significance level ($p < 0.10$) was used. Moreover, an inverse relation between academic achievement and blood quantum (or amount of Native American blood) was found. Wood and Clay hypothesized that those with higher blood quantum have more stereotypically Native American features and are likely to have heightened awareness of the influence of "race-specific structural constraints to their mobility within the Anglo opportunity structure" (p. 55).

The Socialization scale has also been used successfully to differentiate delinquent youths from nondelinquents in U.S. samples, with similar results in India and several other countries (Gough and Sanhu, 1964; Gough, 1965). The overall samples for the studies include eight languages and ten countries, with a total participant pool of more than twenty thousand individuals. Again, information regarding this scale's use with ethnic and racial minority groups in the United States is somewhat limited.

CPI-3

Three thousand men and three thousand women were included in the normative sample, which comprised multiple demographic groups such as subsets of high school students, college cohorts of various majors, graduate students from a variety of fields, numerous occupational titles, different populations of interest to helping professionals (for example, juvenile delinquents, prison inmates, psychiatric patients), and monozygotic and dizygotic twins. However, there is no breakdown of the samples by racial and ethnic categories, and no descriptive statistics for racial and ethnic group memberships were offered in the manual.

Gough (1996) reported in the CPI-3 manual that a minibibliography of studies of minority groups (nine reports on American Indians, eighteen on Blacks, thirteen on Chinese, twelve on Hispanics, six on Japanese, and thirty-five on other cross groups) was prepared several years ago. In addition, the manual refers to the preparation of a comprehensive bibliography that includes all known studies of CPI use with minority groups. The bibliography was not available at the time this chapter was being prepared. Literature searches of the PsycInfo and ERIC databases failed to yield CPI-3 studies on ethnic and racial minorities.

Applicability of 16PF and CPI: Cultural Validity Issues

When a psychological test developed and normed for one culture is applied to individuals who are different from those in the normative group, it is imperative to determine the cross-cultural equivalence of the instrument. Lonner (1985) contends that without establishing an instrument's cross-cultural equivalence, measurement errors and chance statistical occurrences may confound with actual cultural differences. Conceptual, linguistic, and metric equivalence have often been considered essential in evaluating the cultural validity of an assessment instrument (Brislin, 1986; Sue, 1996).

Conceptual Equivalence

Conceptual equivalence is concerned with whether the measured constructs convey the same meaning and serve the same assessment function across cultures (Brislin, 1986). It is related to the etic-emic nature of the instrument, namely, whether the instrument captures a construct that is culture-free and universal (etic) or culture-specific and indigenous (emic). Berry (1969, 1989) noted that most cross-cultural personality and psychological research typically starts with an "imposed etic" approach, in which concepts and notions rooted in and influenced by researchers' backgrounds are transported to members who come from another culture. Subsequent adaptation and empirical analysis of the original instruments progressively lead to formulating "derived etics" that are cross-culturally valid.

It appears that both the 16PF and CPI are shifting from an imposed etic origin toward a derived etic future in their journey of cultural application. The restandardization that culminated in the 16PF-5 and the CPI-3 took into consideration several issues in enhancing their cross-cultural applicability.

Normative Sample

For the 16PF-5, African, Asian, Hispanic, and Native American groups were included in the normative sample (Table 11.1). The proportional representation of various racial and ethnic groups in the 16PF-5 normative samples closely approximated that in the 1990 Census (U.S. Bureau of the Census), although both Asian and Hispanic Americans will be underrepresented, according to the projected census statistics for the year 2000.

Item Readability

For the 16PF-5, attempts were made to increase overall item readability by rewriting and simplifying items that were considered ambiguous. In addition, items that suggested race, gender, and disability bias were eliminated or revised. African and Hispanic consultants were included to review all items for content that might indicate racial bias. Given the heterogeneity among Native Americans and the increasing diversity among Asian Americans, consultants from these groups should also be included to determine the potential cultural bias of items against these two groups. Overall, the readability of the 16PF-5 is estimated at the fifth-grade level. For the CPI-3, psychological and other experts evaluated items against ADA (Americans with Disabilities Act) and EEOC (Equal Employment Opportunity Commission) stipulations; no further information related to adaptation for U.S. racial and ethnic populations was reported. An eighth-grade reading level is required for the CPI-3.

Despite these efforts, several conceptual equivalence issues need to be considered. In the development of both instruments, the personality constructs measured were rooted in the English language and the culture as expressed by the language. In the 16PF, for

Table 11.1. Representations of U.S. racial and ethnic minorities in the normative samples of the 16PF-5 and the CPI-3: a comparison with U.S. census data.

	African Americans				Asian Americans				Hispanic Americans				American Indians			
	Normative Sample		U.S. Census (in percent)[a]		Normative Sample		U.S. Census (in percent)[a]		Normative Sample		U.S. Census (in percent)[a]		Normative Sample		U.S. Census (in percent)[a]	
	N	Percent	1990	2000	N	Percent	1990	2000	N	Percent	1990	2000	N	Percent	1990	2000
16PF-5 (1994)	321	12.8	12.1	13	76	3.0	2.9	4.0	22.4[b]	9.0[b]	9.0	11	58	2.3	1.0	<1.0
CPI-3 (1996)[c]	—	—	12.1	13	—	—	2.9	4.0	—	—	9.0	11	—	—	1.0	<1.0

Sources: 16PF Fifth Edition (Russell and Karol, 1994); CPI Third Edition (Gough, 1996); and census data (U.S. Census Bureau, 1997a).
Notes: [a] By 2050, the projected populations for the four racial and ethnic groups are 15 percent African American, 9 percent Asian American, 24 percent Hispanic American, and 1 percent Native American.

[b] These participants from "Hispanic origin" also endorsed other racial categories (Russell and Karol, 1994, p. 63).

[c] Data not provided in the CPI manual.

example, factor scales that measure personality were originally derived through a factor analysis of a huge list of personality trait descriptors present in the English language. In the fifth edition, "best items" that showed substantial loadings on the respective factors based on five studies were retained. On the CPI, Gough (1987) contended that "folk concepts" emerge from the "processes of interpersonal life, and that [they] are to be found everywhere that humans congregate into groups and establish societal functions" (p. 1). Gough (1996) considered these constructs appealing "because of their hypothesized universality, their relevance to the daily demands of the social nexus, and their emergence and survival over long periods of time in the natural language" (p. 1).

By far, the cross-cultural validity of the 16PF-5 (Conn and Rieke, 1994) and CPI (Gough, 1996) is largely indicated by international studies in which the respective instrument was translated and adapted for a given local culture. There is an implicit assumption that the instrument was found to be cross-culturally valid whenever similar factor structures were replicated (see Levin and Karni, 1970; Sampo and Ashton, 1998). Inherent in the cross-cultural application of both instruments, therefore, is an etic assumption that these personality traits or folk constructs as expressed by the English language and reflecting the U.S. culture could capture the universality of human experience.

Reynolds and Kaiser (1990) have commented that all tests are culturally loaded toward the norms and values of the culture from which the test was created. Therefore, when 16PF and CPI psychological constructs developed for the majority group are applied to the increasingly diverse racial and ethnic populations in the United States, three questions suggested by Dana (1993, p. 101) need to be considered: (1) Does the construct exist in the language/culture of application? (2) Are components of the same construct between the compared cultural groups identical or different? (3) To what extent are the subjective experiences of the construct similar between two cultural groups?

Linguistic Equivalence

Linguistic equivalence is another criterion against which the cross-cultural applicability of an assessment instrument is evaluated. Test bias may be introduced when a minority person's response style and, subsequently, test scores are related to issues of language proficiency and familiarity of item content. This is especially an issue for the increasing foreign-born characteristics of the Asian and Hispanic American populations. If individuals do not understand the item content, then their endorsement may not reflect the intended assessment function of the item. The item endorsement of racial and ethnic minorities who are immigrants may therefore be related to their level of acculturation.

Whereas adaptations to local cultures enable imposed etics to be progressively discarded (Draguns, 1996), it should not be concluded that test scores of racial and ethnic people in the United States can then be compared against the U.S. norm. In other words, the fact that the cross-cultural validity of an instrument is indicated by an adapted version in Vietnam or Spain does not imply that the U.S. norm can be applied to Vietnamese or Hispanic Americans. Specifically, Kwan (1999) noted that

> the compatibility of the translated version is predicated on adaptations (e.g., culture-loaded items were modified in the translation and back translation process) in which cultural biases were reduced or controlled in an attempt to enhance the applicability of the test to subjects within a given . . . country. When the English version is administered to [U.S. racial and ethnic people,] the counseling professional is still confronted by questions regarding the extent to which the client is similar to and different from his or her ethnic group as well as the Euro-American majority, and how these issues affect the administration and interpretation of the client's test data [p. 237].

Metric Equivalence

Another question counseling professionals often raise concerns the extent to which test scores of racial and ethnic group members can be evaluated against the instrument's normative sample, especially if racial and ethnic groups are insufficiently represented in the normative sample. Kwan (1999) reviewed the test manuals of eleven major clinical assessment instruments in the United States; included were five that were most frequently cited in empirical studies (Impara and Plake, 1998, p. xi). Whereas Asian American and Hispanic American samples were either underrepresented or not represented in the majority of the tests reviewed, the proportional representation of the respective racial and ethnic samples in the 16PF-5 reflected that in the 1990 Census (U.S. Bureau of the Census).

In practice, the statistical representativeness of the respective racial and ethnic samples needs to be applied with caution, especially in light of the norm-referenced basis for test interpretation. Beyond the African, Asian, Hispanic, and Native American classification categories, important demographic information of the respective samples were not provided in both the *Administrative Manual* (Russell and Karol, 1994) and the *Technical Manual* (Conn and Rieke, 1994) for the 16PF-5. First, subgroups of Asian (Chinese, Japanese, Korean, Vietnamese), Hispanic (Cuban, Mexican, Puerto Rican), and Native (with tribal affiliation) Americans were not delineated. In the *Technical Manual* (Conn and Rieke), the authors also noted that the "totals [of racial groups] exceed 100 percent since Hispanics also endorsed one of the five race categories" (p. 37). There was also 1.5 percent in an "other" racial category that was not described.

Numerous multicultural psychologists have alerted counseling professionals to the differences (for example, personality styles and cultural adjustment experience) within the respective racial and ethnic groups (Sue, 1996; Helms and Cook, 1999; Sue and Sue, 1999). More important, the generic racial taxonomic label obscures the heterogeneity within each group, whose members are differentiated by various sociocultural demographics, such as generation status, command of the English language, and level of education (Helms and Cook, 1999; Kwan, 1999; Sue and Sue, 1999), as well as associated psychocultural characteristics, such as level of acculturation, status of racial and ethnic identity, and perception of prejudice (Paniagua, 1998; Sandhu, 1997; Sodowsky, Lai, and Plake, 1991). A Mexican American who grew up in a predominantly White environment in the rural Midwest, for example, may have modes of acculturation and experience of perceived prejudice that are different from those of others who grew up in a dense in-group community in Southern California. Sodowsky, Lai, and Plake (1991) have found that Vietnamese Americans were significantly less acculturated into the majority society than were Japanese Americans and Korean Americans.

These sociocultural and psychocultural characteristics, in turn, may be related to test performance and affect test scores. Sue, Keefe, Enomoto, Durvasula, and Chao (1996), for example, found that levels of acculturation significantly differentiated the MMPI-2 profiles of Asian Americans. Specifically, less acculturated Asian Americans obtained significantly more discrepant scores than more acculturated Asian Americans when compared to their White counterparts. If these sociocultural data are not provided, hypotheses about the moderating effects of psychocultural experiences on test performance cannot be generated and used to interpret test scores. Moreover, it is not clear how test scores of non-White test takers can be compared to those derived from their respective racial groups in the normative sample.

Some have contended that Western-based assessment instruments are indicators of level of acculturation of the non-White members. As Sodowsky and Kuo-Jackson (in press) noted, "when individuals are selected based on simplistic categorization . . ., it disregards the complex interplay of culturally relevant psychological dimensions . . . and of sociocultural variables . . . that may interact with the constructs of interest" (p. 19).

Implications for Practice and Research

Given that both the 16PF and CPI were derived from psychological constructs developed and standardized in the United States, clinicians need to determine the extent to which these constructs can be applied to U.S. racial and ethnic populations. A more important issue pertains to *how* the personality construct, as indicated by the test score, is interpreted by the clinician. The question is imperative since both the 16PF and CPI are norm-referenced instruments in which Caucasians constituted the majority in the normative samples.

Clinicians should therefore be familiar with the racial and ethnic compositions and characteristics of the normative samples. When racial and ethnic groups are underrepresented or not represented in the normative sample, interpretation of a minority individual's test score is essentially a process in which the White culture is being used as a "standard" against which a racial and ethnic minority is being compared or evaluated. Even statistical approximation of the proportion of racial categories in the census may still obscure the heterogeneity within the respective groups. Clinicians therefore need to be especially cautious if test scores of racial and ethnic minorities significantly deviate from the norm.

Clinicians should gather sociocultural and psychocultural information to assist test interpretation. If test scores significantly deviate from the norm and toward the "pathological" direction, clinicians should always assess the extent to which the scores are related to the interplay between sociocultural factors (for instance, being a racial minority in a predominantly White neighborhood) and psychocultural factors (stress experience provoked by racism and discrimination) instead of attributing them to deficiencies or deficits within the racial person. For example, a Native American who was raised on a reservation and who adheres to the tribal elder's teaching to live in interpersonal harmony may obtain a significantly lower score on the CPI's Dominance and Capacity for Status scales. Understanding relevant sociocultural data (that is, the cultural environment in which the person was raised) and psychocultural information (strong cultural identity to maintain interpersonal harmony) therefore helps put the low score in a cultural and contextual perspective.

Before administering the test materials to non-White test takers, especially recent immigrants or those for whom English is not their first language, clinicians should determine whether testing is appropriate and whether the individual understands the item content. In the restandardization that culminated in the 16PF-5 and CPI-3, attempts were made to revise items to increase readability and reduce biases against racial groups. Such efforts help minimize testing bias that results from lack of English proficiency, which is especially important in light of the increasingly foreign-born characteristics of Asian and Hispanic Americans and the generally lower educational level of some racial and ethnic groups. Test takers should be encouraged to ask for clarification or explanation of item content during the testing process so as to minimize random response from lack of item comprehensibility.

We emphasize that most 16PF and CPI cultural validity studies were conducted with translated versions linguistically and conceptually adapted for the local populations. Kwan (1999) discusses several concerns when positive results from translated versions of a test adapted in another country are used to support the test's applicability to U.S. racial and ethnic minorities. Several questions, such as whether or not to use translated versions with racial and ethnic minorities in the United States, which norms are most appropriate (those from another country or the U.S. normative sample), and how interpretations are to be modified, need to be addressed. When working with acculturating clients, the clinician may consider using both U.S. norm and the respective international norm for reference, especially with recent immigrants from a country in which the CPI or 16PF has been standardized using local samples.

Thus it is important for clinicians and researchers to also know the literature on international adaptation of instruments. At the same time, when referencing international norms, clinicians should not assume that the racial and ethnic minority individual can be compared to international norms from her or his country of origin because acculturation may have occurred to the point that the U.S. normative sample may be more appropriate. The clinician therefore has the somewhat ambiguous task of determining how different norms can facilitate test interpretations.

It is apparent that more studies of the 16PF-5 and CPI-3 performance of U.S. racial and ethnic minorities need to be conducted. In particular, studies using the current editions of the 16PF and CPI are needed since earlier versions were used in most existing studies. Acculturation has been conceptually discussed (Dana, 1993; Sue, 1996) and empirically found to be a significant variable that moderates test performances of racial and ethnic minorities (Asian Americans' MMPI-2; Sue, Keefe, Enomoto, Durvasula, & Chao, 1996). Both clinicians and researchers need to be aware of the interplay of sociocultural variables (for example, length of stay in the United States, level of education) and psychocultural variables (such as level of acculturation and experience of perceived prejudice), and their impact on the 16PF and CPI test patterns of the increasingly diverse racial and ethnic populations in the United States.

References

Ahmad, I., Anis-ul-Haque, M., & Anila, Y. (1994). Validation of Femininity/ Masculinity scale of California Psychological Inventory in Pakistan. *Pakistan Journal of Psychological Research, 9,* 27–35.

Baldwin, R. O. (1987). Femininity-masculinity of Blacks and Whites over a fourteen-year period. *Psychological Reports, 60,* 455–458.

Berry, J. W. (1969). On cross-cultural comparability. *International Journal of Psychology, 4,* 119–128.

Berry, J. W. (1989). Imposed etics-emics-derived etics: The operationalization of a compelling idea. *International Journal of Psychology, 24,* 721–735.

Blane, H. T., & Yamamoto, K. (1970). Sexual role identity among Japanese and Japanese-American high school students. *Journal of Cross-Cultural Psychology, 1,* 345–354.

Brislin, R. W. (1986). The wording and translation of research instruments. In W. J. Lonner & J. W. Berry (Eds.), *Field methods in cross-cultural research* (pp. 137–164). Thousand Oaks, CA: Sage.

Cattell, R. B. (1946). *The description and measurement of personality*. Orlando: Harcourt Brace.

Cattell, R. B., Eber, H. W., & Tatsuoka, M. M. (1970). *Handbook for the 16PF*. Champaign, IL: Institute for Personality and Ability Testing.

Cattell, R. B., Eber, H. W., & Tatsuoka, M. M. (1988). *Handbook for the 16PF*. Champaign, IL: Institute for Personality and Ability Testing.

Clark, M. L. (1986). Predictors of scientific majors for Black and White college students. *Adolescence, XXI*, 205–213.

Comrey, A. L. (1970). *Manual for the Comrey Personality Scales*. San Diego: Educational and Industrial Testing Services.

Conn, S. R., & Rieke, M. L. (1994). *16PF Fifth edition technical manual*. Champaign, IL: Institute for Personality and Ability Testing.

Conoley, J. C., & Impara, J. C. (Eds.) (1995). *The twelfth mental measurements yearbook*. Lincoln: University of Nebraska Press.

Cross, D. T., Barclay, A., & Burger, G. K. (1978). Differential effects of ethnic membership, sex, and occupation on the California Psychological Inventory. *Journal of Personality Assessment, 42*, 597–603.

Cross, D. T., & Burger, G. K. (1982). Ethnicity as a variable in responses to California Psychological Inventory items. *Journal of Personality Assessment, 46*, 153–158.

Dana, R. H. (1993). *Multicultural assessment perspectives for professional psychology*. Needham Heights, MA: Allyn & Bacon.

Davis, G. L., Hoffman, R. G., & Nelson, K. S. (1990). Differences between Native Americans and Whites on the California Psychological Inventory. *Psychological Assessment, 2*, 238–242.

DeBlassie, R. R., & Franco, J. N. (1983). The difference between personality inventory scores and self-ratings in a sample of Hispanic subjects. *Journal of Non-White Concerns, 11*, 43–46.

Draguns, J. G. (1996). Multicultural and cross-cultural assessment: Dilemmas and decisions. In G. R. Sodowsky & J. C. Impara (Eds.), *Multicultural assessment in counseling and clinical psychology* (pp. 37–84). University of Nebraska-Lincoln: Buros Institute of Mental Measurements.

Gough, H. G. (1957). *Manual for the California Psychological Inventory*. Palo Alto, CA: Consulting Psychologists Press.

Gough, H. G. (1964). A cross-cultural study of achievement motivation. *Journal of Applied Psychology, 48*, 191–196.

Gough, H. G. (1965). Cross-cultural validation of a measure of asocial behavior. *Psychological Reports, 17,* 379–387.

Gough, H. G. (1966). A cross-cultural analysis of the CPI Femininity scale. *Journal of Consulting Psychology, 30,* 136–141.

Gough, H. G. (1987). *The California Psychological Inventory administrator's guide.* Palo Alto, CA: Consulting Psychologists Press.

Gough, H. G. (1996). *California Psychological Inventory manual* (3rd ed.). Palo Alto, CA: Consulting Psychologists Press.

Gough, H. G., Chun, K., & Chung, Y. (1968). Validation of the CPI Femininity scale in Korea. *Psychological Reports, 22,* 155–160.

Gough, H. G., & Sanhu, H. S. (1964). Validation of the CPI Socialization scale in India. *Journal of Abnormal and Social Psychology, 68,* 544–547.

Helms, J., & Cook, D. (1999). *Using race and culture in counseling and psychotherapy: Theory and practice.* Needham Heights, MA: Allyn & Bacon.

Impara, J. C., & Plake, B. S. (Eds.). (1998). *The thirteenth mental measurements yearbook.* Lincoln: University of Nebraska Press.

Johnson, R. C., Ahern, F. M., Nagoshi, C. T., McClearn, G. E., & Vandenberg, S. G. (1985). Age and group-specific cohort effects on personality test scores: A study of three Hawaiian populations. *Journal of Cross-Cultural Psychology, 16,* 467–481.

Kaplan, R. M., & Saccuzzo, D. P. (1997). *Psychological testing* (4th ed.). Pacific Grove, CA: Brooks/Cole.

Knight, B. G., & McCallum, T. J. (1998). Heart rate reactivity and depression in African-American and white dementia caregivers: Reporting bias or positive coping? *Aging and Mental Health, 2,* 212–221.

Kwan, K.-L. K. (1999). Assessment of Asian Americans in counseling: Evolving issues and concerns. In D. S. Sandhu (Ed.), *Asian and Pacific Islander Americans: Issues and concerns for counseling and psychotherapy* (pp. 229–249). Commack, NY: Nova Science Publishers.

Levin, J., & Karni, E. (1970). Demonstration of cross-cultural invariance of the California Psychological Inventory in America and Israel by the Guttman-Lingoes smallest space analysis. *Journal of Cross-Cultural Psychology, 3,* 253–260.

Lonner, W. J. (1985). Issues in testing and assessment in cross-cultural counseling. *Counseling Psychologist, 13,* 599–614.

Mason, E. P. (1969). Cross-validation study of personality characteristics of junior high students from American Indian, Mexican, and Caucasian ethnic backgrounds. *Journal of Social Psychology, 77,* 15–24.

McAllister, L. W. (1996). *A practical guide to CPI interpretation* (3rd ed.). Palo Alto, CA: Consulting Psychologists Press.

Meyer, R. G., & Deitsch, S. E. (1996). *The clinician's handbook: Integrated diagnostics, assessment, and intervention in adult and adolescent psychopathology* (4th ed.). Needham Heights, MA: Allyn & Bacon.

Nishiyama, T. (1975). Validation of the CPI Femininity scale in Japan. *Journal of Cross-Cultural Psychology, 6,* 482–489.

Paniagua, F. A. (1998). *Assessing and treating culturally diverse clients: A practical guide* (2nd ed.). Thousand Oaks, CA: Sage.

Pitariu, H. (1981). Validation of the CPI Femininity scale in Romania. *Journal of Cross-Cultural Psychology, 12,* 111–117.

Repapi, M., Gough, H. G., Lanning, K., Stefanis, C. (1983). Predicting academic achievement of Greek secondary school students from family background and California Psychological Inventory scores. *Contemporary Educational Psychology, 8,* 181–188.

Reynolds, C. R., & Kaiser, S. M. (1990). Test bias in psychological assessment. In C. R. Reynolds & T. B. Gutkin (Eds.), *The handbook of school psychology* (2nd ed., pp. 178–208). New York: Wiley.

Russell, M., & Karol, D. (1994). *16PF fifth edition administration manual.* Champaign, IL: Institute for Personality and Ability Testing.

Sampo, P., & Ashton, M. C. (1998). The structured assessment of personality across cultures. *Journal of Cross-Cultural Psychology, 29,* 150–171.

Sandhu, D. S. (1997). Psychocultural profiles of Asian and Pacific Islander Americans: Implications for counseling and psychotherapy. *Journal of Multicultural Counseling and Development, 25,* 7–22.

Sodowsky, G. R., & Kuo-Jackson, P. Y. (in press). Determining cultural and racial validity of personality assessment: psychometrics, procedures, and popular measures. In D. Pope-Davis and H. Coleman (Eds.), *Interactions of race, class, and gender in multicultural counseling.* Thousand Oaks, CA: Sage.

Sodowsky, G. R., Lai, E.W.M., & Plake, B. S. (1991). Moderating effects of sociocultural variables on acculturation variables of Hispanics and Asian Americans. *Journal of Counseling and Development, 70,* 194–204.

Sue, D. W., & Sue, D. (1999). *Counseling the culturally different: Theory and practice* (3rd ed.). New York: Wiley.

Sue, S. (1996). Measurement, testing, and ethnic bias: Can solutions be found? In G. R. Sodowsky & J. C. Impara (Eds.), *Multicultural assessment in counseling and clinical psychology* (pp. 7–36). Lincoln: University of Nebraska Press.

Sue, S., Keefe, K., Enomoto, K, Durvasula, R. S., & Chao, R. (1996). Asian American and white college students' performance on the MMPI-2. In J. B. Butcher (Ed.), *International adaptations of the MMPI-2* (pp. 206–218). Minneapolis: University of Minnesota.

Torki, M. A. (1988). The CPI Femininity scale in Kuwait and Egypt. *Journal of Personality Assessment, 52,* 247–253.

U.S. Department of Commerce. (1997). *Population profile of the United States, Current Population Report, Special Studies P23-194.* Washington, DC: Author.

Wallbrown, F. H., Reuter, E. K., Barnett, R. W. (1989). Motivational distortion on 16PF primaries by male felons. *Measurement and Evaluation in Counseling and Development, 22,* 7–14.

Whitworth, R. H., & Perry, S. M. (1990). Comparison of Anglo- and Mexican-Americans on the 16PF administered in Spanish or English. *Journal of Clinical Psychology, 46,* 857–862.

Williams, J. E., & Best, D. L. (1982). *Measuring sex stereotypes: A thirty-nation study.* Thousand Oaks, CA: Sage.

Wood, P. B., & Clay, W. C. (1996). Perceived structural barriers and academic performance among American Indian high school students. *Youth and Society, 28,* 20–40.

Ying, Y. (1990). Use of the CPI structural scales in Taiwan college graduates. *International Journal of Social Psychiatry, 36,* 49–57.

Ying, Y. (1991). Validation of the California Psychological Inventory Femininity scale in Taiwan college graduates. *Journal of Multicultural Counseling and Development, 19,* 166–173.

Ying, Y. (1994). Initial adjustment of Taiwanese students to the United States. *Journal of Cross-Cultural Psychology, 25,* 466–478.

· ·

12

Multicultural Applications of the Myers-Briggs Type Indicator

Mary H. McCaulley and Raymond A. Moody

The Myers-Briggs Type Indicator, or MBTI, is a self-report questionnaire in the category of cognitive personality tests. It is concerned with individual differences in perception and judgment. Its history is unique among personality measures in that it was created in the 1940s and 1950s by two brilliant women who were not psychologists, had no graduate degrees, and were not in academia. Their purpose was to make it possible to validate and make practical use of that part of C. G. Jung's theory described in his *Psychological Types* (Jung, 1971), a theory that was not respected at the time and is still debated and misunderstood. The MBTI uses nonstandard psychometrics developed to fit the needs of the theory.

Because this book is written for clinicians, we begin with Jung's assumptions about the development of his types from infancy to maturity, and the influence of families and cultures in fostering or interfering with normal development. We follow that with a brief description of how Isabel Briggs Myers constructed the MBTI to be faithful to Jung's theory of psychological type, followed by sections covering reliability, validity, and applications of the MBTI in education, careers, and organizations. The chapter ends with comments on issues in translating the MBTI and its use in different cultures.

Jung's Theory of Psychological Types

Jung made it clear that his typology was not an armchair theory but had been validated in his clinical work hundreds of times. Jung's reasons for developing this part of his larger body of work included reducing the chaotic multiplicity of points of view into some kind of order; trying to understand his differences with Freud and Adler; describing the various aspects of consciousness; and finally, helping the practicing psychologist who, armed with an exact knowledge of his own differentiated and inferior functions, can avoid many serious blunders in dealing with his patients.

Jung's theory challenges two assumptions of much of personality theory today. First, Jung assumes type preferences are inborn, not learned. Second, traits are not basic in themselves but develop from the exercise of dichotomous inborn preferences.

The dichotomies in Jung's typology are between the extraverted and introverted *attitudes* toward the environment; the "irrational" sensing or intuitive *perceiving functions* for taking in information; and the "rational" thinking or feeling *judging functions* for drawing conclusions about what has been perceived.

The assumption of *type dynamics* is the key for understanding the characteristics of each of Jung's types. An infant is born with four basic mental powers, or *functions*: sensing, intuition, thinking, and feeling. One will become the most conscious, the favorite or *dominant function*. A second will be the *auxiliary* to balance the dominant. The third or *tertiary*, and the fourth or *inferior*, functions will lag behind in development. Jung describes the dominant function in strong words: "possesses the energy with which it is endowed by nature," "the most favored and most developed function," "vital to provide the conscious process of adaptation with clear and unambiguous aims," "absolutely reliable," and "under control of the will" (pp. 405–407).

Jung described eight types, pairing the attitude and the dominant function: extraverted sensing type, extraverted intuitive type, extraverted feeling type, and extraverted thinking type, and the comparable four types preferring introversion. Isabel Myers described sixteen types in the MBTI by including both the dominant and the auxiliary functions. For example, Jung's extraverted sensing type became the extraverted sensing type with thinking as auxiliary, and the extraverted sensing type with feeling as auxiliary.

In *Psychological Types* Jung acknowledged the importance of culture in strong words:

> Individuation . . . is a process of differentiation, having as its goal the development of the individual personality. . . . Individuation is a natural necessity inasmuch as its prevention by a leveling down to collective standards is injurious to the vital activity of the individual. Any serious check to individuality is an artificial stunting. . . . A social group consisting of stunted individuals cannot be a healthy and viable institution; only a society that can preserve the internal cohesion and collective values, while at the same time granting the individual the greatest freedom, has any prospect of enduring vitality. . . . If a plant is to unfold its specific nature to the full, it must first be able to grow in the soil in which it is planted. . . . I do not think it is improbable . . . that a reversal of type often proves exceedingly harmful to the physiological well-being of the organism, usually causing acute exhaustion [pp. 448–450].

We have seen examples of falsification, often stemming from families that devalue the dominant function of their child. For example, an adult client with a preference for intuition remembers being told, "Stop those crazy thoughts. You don't have any common sense. We worry how you will make it in the world. What will become of you?" In counseling, the client discovered that her intuitions were on target, and she began to trust them. At termination, she told the counselor, "I feel as if I have a gift I have been afraid of all these years. I feel so much more integrated with myself."

Common phrases in cultures may reflect pressure for conformity, as in the Australian "Don't be a tall poppy," or the Japanese "A nail that sticks up gets hammered down."

Given Jung's strong words on falsification of type, counselors reporting MBTI results to clients are careful to take time to discover if the MBTI type is indeed the best-fit type for the client.

Information about cultural differences is growing as the MBTI is translated all over the globe. Data so far show that all sixteen types appear in all cultures, but not in equal numbers. As cultural psychologists move away from their position that all of personality is taught by the culture, and as personality psychologists take into account that inborn type preferences may be supported or falsified by the culture, our understanding of human behavior is greatly enriched.

The Development of the Myers-Briggs Type Indicator

Katharine Cook Briggs had created her own typology before Jung's *Psychological Types* was translated into English in 1923 (Myers and Myers, 1980). She found her typology was consistent with Jung's, though his was more complete, and she began studying his book intensively. She shared her excitement with her daughter Isabel, and the two became "type watchers" for twenty years. During World War II, Isabel Briggs Myers saw many people taking jobs to be patriotic, but hating their work. She believed that Jung's typology could be a valuable tool for choosing a career. If the work called on a person's preferred perception and judgment, it would stay interesting and motivating. A major application of the MBTI today is in career counseling.

In retrospect, it was madness to think anyone could identify conscious and unconscious type preferences—and the dominant, auxiliary, tertiary, and inferior functions—with self-report questions about everyday life. Undaunted, Isabel Myers embarked on a journey that lasted to the end of her life. Steeped in Jung's theory, she knew her questions could not ask directly about Jung's theoretical constructs. Her items posed choices between ordinary behaviors that are "straws in the wind" for the underlying conscious and unconscious mental processes of Jung's typology. Her questions are in forced-choice format because the choices had to be between equally valuable preferences. Myers knew her straws in the wind would not be the same in all cultures. A challenge for translators today is to rewrite and test new questions whenever the original items are not suitable in that culture. She tested hundreds of questions on family and friends, and her children, Peter and Ann, tested them on friends at school.

She gave each preference a name and a letter:

- The attitudes Extraversion (E) or Introversion (I)

- The perceiving functions, Sensing (S) or Intuition (N)

- The judging functions Thinking (T) or Feeling (F)

- Two preferences implied but not described by Jung, Judging (J) or Perceiving (P)

The J-P scale was an important contribution by Isabel Myers. It describes whether a person favors a perceiving process (S or N) or a judging process (T or F) in the extraverted attitude. The J-P scale describes behaviors of interest in their own right, but more importantly, J-P is used to identify the dominant, auxiliary, tertiary, and inferior functions in each of the sixteen types. (For further explanation, see Myers, McCaulley, Quenk, and Hammer, 1998, pp. 27–31.)

When she created the Indicator, Isabel Myers sought precision at the midpoint of dichotomous scales. For example, for an S-N item, she asked herself, "How consistently does this person prefer sensing over intuition?" The assumption was that the development of sensing or intuition follows a *qualitatively* separate path in each case. Energy toward developing sensing leads to traits and behaviors such as practicality, realism, and enjoyment of the here and now. Energy toward developing intuition leads to traits and behaviors such as imagination, intellectuality, and future vision. (Note that dichotomous MBTI scales are different from many scales in psychology where one trait is measured on a normal curve, with a more positive aspect of a trait having a higher score and the more negative aspects having a lower score.)

Type Descriptions

An important last step in constructing the MBTI was the "type description." Isabel Myers wrote theory-based descriptions for each of the sixteen types. Each description shows the type at its best, with good development of the dominant and auxiliary functions. The description ends with brief comments about blind spots, or problems if the auxiliary is not well developed. The positive type descriptions (likened to horoscopes by those who do not understand the complexity and richness of Jung's theory), are a major source of the popularity of the MBTI. The many popular books about the MBTI contain descriptions also based on type dynamics.

The MBTI Becomes Known to the World

Throughout the 1940s, working alone in her living room, with financial help from her husband and her father, Isabel Myers continued to test and revise the MBTI. In the 1950s, with the endorsement of the Association of American Medical Colleges, she collected and analyzed data on a sample of 5,355 medical students from forty-five medical schools. She found predicted type differences in Medical College Aptitude Test scores and later in medical specialty choices. Consistent with Jung's theory, sensing types who prefer hands-on tasks with the immediate situation chose orthopedic surgery, obstetrics, and anesthesiology. Intuitive types who enjoy working with abstract ideas, theory, and symbols chose psychiatry, neurology, and internal medicine.

In 1956 Harold Wiggers, dean of the Albany (New York) Medical College, told Henry Chauncey, president of Educational Testing Service (ETS), about the "Briggs-Myers Type Indicator."

After an agreement in 1957 between Isabel Myers and ETS, she created Form E and the new standard MBTI Form F and wrote a manual. In 1962 ETS published the new forms and the new manual. The MBTI was in the ETS Office of Special Tests, sold only for research, and not listed in any ETS catalog (Saunders, 1991). A few visitors to ETS heard about the MBTI and began to use it. In 1968, Takeshi Ohsawa translated the MBTI into Japanese under an agreement with Isabel Myers.

In 1969, as a clinical psychologist at the University of Florida, I (McCaulley, co-author of this chapter, then a clinical psychologist at the University of Florida) discovered the MBTI by chance and began working with Isabel Myers. They created an unofficial Typology Laboratory at the university and with student help completed the first MBTI computer-scoring program in 1971. The head of the Division of Housing arranged for the University of Florida class of entering students in 1972 to take the Indicator. Work-study students keypunched and verified 2,514 Form F answer sheets. With the help of data supplied by the student affairs office, the Typology Lab prepared a report on type differences in academic aptitude scores and initial choice of fields of study. Word about the MBTI spread on the campus. Faculty and graduate students began other MBTI research.

In 1975, the MBTI took three major steps forward. First, an MBTI conference was held at the University of Florida. More than two hundred people came from all parts of the United States and Canada. Second, Myers and McCaulley closed the Typology Laboratory and founded the Center for Applications of Psychological Type (CAPT)[1] to continue and advance Isabel Myers's work. Initially CAPT was a field office of the American Medical Student Foundation. In 1979 it became an independent nonprofit organization. CAPT is still active in Gainesville, Florida. Third, Consulting Psychologists Press (CPP) became the publisher of the MBTI. When

CPP listed the MBTI in its 1976 catalog, the MBTI was no longer restricted to research and was at last available for practical use.

Under the watchful eye of Isabel Myers, CAPT created Form G in 1977, instituted MBTI training for psychologists, and followed up on the specialty choices of the medical students Isabel Myers had tested in the 1950s. Nineteen percent had changed their primary specialty. A significant number, particularly I-P types, had moved to a field that was a better fit for the type they reported as freshmen. In 1979, CAPT created the Association for Psychological Type, a membership organization for persons interested in the MBTI. APT still is active and has affiliates in other countries.

Isabel Briggs Myers died on May 5, 1980, but the MBTI continued to develop through the next two decades. Shortly after his mother's death, Peter Briggs Myers asked David Saunders, a psychologist who had worked with his mother at ETS, to create an MBTI form with every item she had ever used in any form of the Indicator. After extensive research, Saunders developed two new forms. In 1987 CPP published his 290-item Form J and a scoring report called the Type Differentiation Indicator, and in 1989 a shorter Form K, with 131 items, which generated an Expanded Analysis Report. In 1985 McCaulley completed the revision of the MBTI manual (Myers and McCaulley, 1985). Ten years later, CPP published *MBTI Applications: A Decade of Research on the Myers-Briggs Type Indicator* (Hammer, 1996).

In the mid-1990s, a research team at Consulting Psychologists Press conducted a major revision of the MBTI. Their research effort led to publication of Form M (the new standard version of the MBTI) and a new manual (Myers, McCaulley, Quenk, and Hammer, 1998). The Form M manual compares research from Form F and Form G to Form M. Earlier MBTI manuals had many tables analyzing MBTI data for E-I, S-N, T-F, and J-P. The Form M manual took seriously the fact that "type is the unit of measurement for the MBTI" and added many tables showing characteristics of the sixteen types. Its chapters cover MBTI applications in counseling and psychotherapy, education, career counseling, organizations, and multicultural settings. Chapter Fourteen of that manual, on multicultural settings, is of special interest to readers of this book. The authors, Linda K. Kirby and Nancy J. Barger, describe practical and technical issues of using the MBTI and provide extensive data on MBTI type distributions in other cultures.

The MBTI was almost unknown in 1976. It is now appreciated and used on every continent. An increasing body of MBTI research outside the United States is confirming forty years of research by Isabel Briggs Myers and more than thirty years of research by others.

MBTI Construction and Psychometrics

Jung believed the mental processes that are the foundation of his typology are inherent in all members of the human race. Two bodies of knowledge support Jung's assumption. The first is that around the globe, people of all cultures recognize differences between extraverts and introverts, sensing and intuitive types, thinking and feeling types, and judging and perceiving types.

The second is that Costa and McCrae (1992), seeking to develop a comprehensive description of personality using a totally different methodology based on decades of research in factor analysis, "discovered" Jung's type preferences. Their NEO-PI Extraversion identifies the E pole of MBTI E-I; Openness to Experience identifies the intuitive pole of the MBTI S-N; Agreeableness identifies the Feeling pole of MBTI T-F; and Conscientiousness identifies the Judging pole of MBTI J-P.

The fifth NEO-PI factor, Neuroticism, has no similar scale in the MBTI because Isabel Myers focused her research on the "constructive use of differences" and described each type at its best. However, from the beginning she was concerned with type development and included unscored research questions to study it. (To her, good type development meant perceiving the world accurately and making good decisions.) In his factor analyses of MBTI Form J, Saunders found seven factors that include Myers's research questions. He called them "Comfort Scales." These scales, along with subscales for E-I, S-N, T-F, and J-P, are part of the Type Differentiation

Indicator, available from Consulting Psychologists Press Scoring Service to professionals qualified to purchase Level C tests.

Psychometric Properties

The Myers-Briggs Type Indicator has unique psychometric properties. Statistics reported for reliability and validity reflect the intent of the instrument to measure a theory of dichotomies rather than one of continuous traits.

Reliability

From the beginning of her work, Isabel Myers clustered items in E-I, S-N, T-F, and J-P into subscales. As part of her analysis of reliability of the scales, she created an X half and a Y half for each preference. For example, on the E-I scale, instead of assigning E-I items to X or Y as they occurred on the answer sheet, she assigned equal numbers of items in each cluster to the X and Y halves. Reliability coefficients were computed by correlating these "logical split-half scales." The 1985 and 1998 manuals report high internal consistency reliabilities of Form G and Form M over a variety of samples for split-half correlations of X and Y scores. The 1998 manual also reports reliabilities for "consecutive split half scales." Internal consistency reliabilities for sample sizes from 37 to 2,859 are over .90, whether the analysis uses logical split-half, consecutive split-half, or coefficient alpha.

In her 1962 manual, Myers raised a question that persists today: "How much of any given result is the reliability of the Indicator and how much is the reliability of the person taking it? The potent but as yet unmeasurable variable of type development—i.e., the extent to which the person actually has developed the functions and the attitude he prefers—enters every equation as an unknown quantity" (Myers, 1962, p. 19).

Internal consistency of answering the Indicator is predicted to be higher for persons at higher levels of type development, on the assumption that people who know themselves better answer more consistently. Data for the 1985 manual confirmed the early work in the 1962 manual. Reliabilities were lower for grade school students and those in programs for low achievers. Reliabilities were higher for older students and adults and for samples having college education.

Myers also found that reliabilities are sometimes lower for the T-F scale. Her explanation was that good judgment, whether by thinking or feeling, is the most difficult part of type development. Others have suggested that in a period of changing values and social behaviors, the cultural guidelines for T-F decisions are less clear and T-F items may be answered less consistently. Most samples in the 1985 manual have T-F reliabilities about the same as the other scales, but if any scale shows lower reliability, it is most likely to be T-F.

The 1998 manual reports internal consistency data for Form M based on both split-half and coefficient alpha analyses. Samples include student groups, occupations, and age groups. Most coefficients are in the low nineties; a few on the T-F scale are in the high eighties. Form M coefficients for two "ethnic group" adult samples and four college student samples range from .80 to .96 (table 8.3 of the 1998 manual).

Test-Retest Reliability

MBTI test-retest reliabilities for E-I, S-N, T-F, and J-P continuous scores are higher over shorter periods of time and when the initial preferences are clear. The more interesting question is, How many people come out the same type on retest? Levels of agreement are well over 50 percent, much greater than the chance expectation of 6.25 percent. Those who report a change in type are most likely to agree on three of the four preferences of their original type. Changes occur more often on scales where the original choice was less clear. Reliabilities for Form M reported in the 1998 manual tend to be somewhat higher than earlier reliabilities for Form G.

Validity

The MBTI was designed specifically to make it possible to use Jung's insights about psychological types. Construct validity determines whether research results are consistent with predictions from type theory. Correlations of E-I, S-N, T-F, and J-P with other measures should be significant when the measure reflects a type preference and nonsignificant when it does not. The most significant validity correlations are between MBTI E-I and scales of extraversion or introversion on other instruments. Extraversion-introversion scales of other instruments do not, and should not, correlate with MBTI S-N, T-F, and J-P.

The 1985 and 1998 manuals have tables of correlations of the four MBTI preferences with other psychological tests, some of which have scales similar to those of the MBTI (for instance, the Millon Index of Personality Styles, the NEO-PI, and the Jungian Type Survey) and some of which are more general (the Adjective Check List, the Strong Interest Inventory, and the California Psychological Inventory).

The tables in the manual show the MBTI letter for significant correlations in a separate column, enabling the reader to scan the table for construct validity.

Recent research goes beyond the four preferences to report evidence for construct validity of type dynamics by analysis of whole type. The 1998 manual presents evidence of construct validity for the sixteen types using data from type distributions, self-reports, independent observer ratings, and new work on topographic mapping of brain activity.

Applications of Type

There are many application areas for the Myers-Briggs Type Indicator. In this section we focus on three of them: education, career counseling, and organizations.

Applications of the MBTI in Education

Although many school counselors use the MBTI with students to increase self-understanding and plan for careers, the main value of the MBTI for education comes from insights into the learning styles of different types of students. Teacher training affords rich understanding of curriculum and instruction—the content to be taught and tools for teaching. The MBTI helps the teacher focus on how students use their minds. Consider first the four dimensions. Extraverts need opportunities to talk about what they are learning, and Introverts need time for quiet reflection. Sensing types want practical reasons for learning the material. They look for concrete examples up front, prefer to learn by rote, and are happy with repetitive practice that consolidates learning. Intuitive types want the big picture, and where today's assignment fits in. They want to understand relationships among the specific parts. Once intuitives "see" the big picture, they quickly get bored with the details.

Thinking types (natural skeptics) look for logical connections between cause and effect. Feeling types want to know how the topic being studied is relevant to people and their world. Thinking types are in the majority among males, and Feeling types among females.

Judging types are usually eager to get the task done and may declare victory before they have collected all the information they need. Perceiving types are more curious. They aim to miss nothing and may seek out more information until the last-minute flurry is not enough to make the deadline.

Aptitude and Achievement

Considerable research has established that type plays a role in academic aptitude and achievement. Most aptitude measures are written tests. Academic learning tends to emphasize working with concepts and ideas, using words, symbols, and abstractions. The MBTI tools for this work are introversion and intuition. Data on type preferences and academic aptitude scores show a slight advantage for introverts and a clear advantage for intuitive types.

When types are compared for aptitude and grades, the perceiving types have an edge in aptitude, perhaps because their openness and curiosity bring more information across their path. Judging types have an edge in grades, perhaps because their goal-directed, orderly lives include meeting academic commitments. The differences, though, are not large. All sixteen types fall within a range of less than one standard deviation above and below the mean (see the 1998 manual, pp. 266–274.)

In the general population, extraverts and introverts are about equally divided. Introverts are somewhat more likely to seek higher education. The percentage of sensing types is estimated at 65–75 percent of the population. Higher education is more attractive to intuitive types where they are found in greater numbers, especially in the humanities and arts. This does not mean that intuitives are more intelligent than sensing types. Myers and Meyers (1980) observed that "Intuitives tend to define intelligence as 'quickness of understanding' and sensing types tend to define intelligence as 'soundness of understanding'" (p. 59). Clearly, both kinds of understanding are important.

Sensing types are more likely to prefer the closure of J, and intuitive types are more likely to prefer the openness of P. In most population samples, therefore, the solid and dependable S-J types outnumber the N-P independent spirits.

There are other trends to watch for in viewing the education system through the lens of type. In the lower grades, S-J types are the majority among students and teachers. S-P types, who want to learn by doing and with many hands-on activities, find classroom structure confining. They are more likely to be underestimated by teachers. S-P students are more likely to drop out of school and less likely to seek higher education. S-P students rarely have a kindred-spirit S-P teacher.

N-P students are the independent spirits. They are found in classes for gifted and in independent study programs. Teachers in these programs are frequently intuitives also.

The quiet I-N types rank high in academics and look forward to college and graduate school, where they find more kindred spirits among the students and the faculty. Of 2,514 incoming University of Florida Freshman in 1972, 25 percent were I-N types. Of the 75 later elected to Phi Beta Kappa, 48 percent were I-N types.

With knowledge of type, a teacher can identify student needs and select materials and activities appropriate to produce learning. As awareness of type differences has spread, new resources are becoming available for teaching writing (Jensen and DiTiberio, 1989; DiTiberio and Jensen, 1994; Thompson, 1997) and for learning a second language (Ehrman, 1996). Excellent guidance is also available to help teachers understand learning styles and their own teaching styles (Bargar, Bargar, and Cano, 1994; DiTiberio, 1998; Fairhurst and Fairhurst, 1995; Lawrence, 1993, 1997; Mamchur, 1996; VanSant and Payne, 1995).

An interesting cultural difference in academic aptitude scores recently appeared in an ongoing large-scale study of the SAT and MBTI in the multicultural schools of Worcester, Massachusetts. The two best predictors of high SAT scores were taking advanced courses and preferring intuition on the MBTI. There were clear differences in the type distributions of ethnic groups among the Worcester students. However, the "academic" I-N students in all ethnic groups were the most likely to take advanced placement courses (Keith McCormick, personal communication, 1999).

As the MBTI is becoming known internationally, users are beginning to observe schools in various countries to see what we can learn from schools with very different teaching strategies. Chapman (1994) provides a fascinating account of the part played by the MBTI in changing the Aleknagik school, an Eskimo school in rural Alaska.

The school was called "the political nightmare of the district"; all the teachers had resigned. A new principal came in and arranged to have an MBTI workshop for all the new staff and the entire student body. The results showed the students to be 90 percent introverts, 50 percent sensing types (all of whom were S-P), 70 percent thinking types, and 90 percent perceiving types. Type terminology became a standard component of student-student as well as student-teacher interactions. The new staff created a collegial, cooperative culture. A new program was developed, attuned to S-P learners and traditional Eskimo values and traditions. The curriculum favored action-oriented doing. Through using the MBTI, the entire school became a family of learners, including teachers, students, parents and grandparents. From the "nightmare of the district," it became a school with one of the highest test scores in the district, almost no absenteeism and tardiness, and high student and parent enthusiasm.

In the second year, the roof of the school collapsed. The next day, teachers and parents taught school in their living rooms. Students learned bandaging, splinting, and other emergency techniques. Students read about heroes and wrote about village heroes. In mathematics, they took measurements of the building. In social studies, they talked about the legislature and school funding, and students wrote letters to their representatives. A year of teaching in their living rooms made the village itself a classroom. Students interviewed elders and started a village history, making people as well as books their resources. In the words of Chapman (1994), "The walls between curricular areas and age and grade groups fell along with the school roof." After just four years, the Aleknagik Project was spreading to other schools.

The extraordinary success that teachers, students, and community achieved by incorporating type into teaching and native culture into the school's curriculum attests to the merit of practical application of a positive and comprehensive approach in responding to natural learning styles and cultural values.

Applications of the MBTI in Career Counseling

Career counseling was one of the first areas of applied research on type. The MBTI, often combined with career interest inventories, is widely used in schools, colleges, and business organizations. The MBTI is a framework of self-understanding from which to look at the world of work: "What are the gifts of my type?" "What will hold my interest?" "What kind of work setting will be satisfying?" "What strategies would work for me to modify the work environment to suit my type?" Kummerow discusses these issues in the chapter on career counseling in the 1998 manual. She contends that type can predict the kind of work environment that is most likely to support an individual and allow the person to do his or her best work.

A career survey of a national sample ($n = 3,036$) supports her position. Recall that there are sixteen types, eight of which are sensing types and eight of which are intuitive types. In this study, seven of the eight intuitive types put "variety of tasks" at the top of their list of work situations they liked. Only two of the eight sensing types (ESTP and ESFP) made this choice. Eighty percent or more of the eight extraverted types rated "working in a team" as something they liked. None of the eight introverted groups rated teamwork so high.

Once a counselor and client know both the kinds of participation a job entails and the client's type preferences, the client then has a much better picture of what may or may not appeal and can make an informed choice.

Many clients seek career counseling to find the "one specific job" that is "right" for them. This concept is limiting. Much more than type is involved in job selection. Other factors include family circumstances; geographic location; job market conditions; education; skills; cultural, ethnic, and gender identification; and personal interests and values (Kummerow, 1998). The *Atlas of Type Tables* (Macdaid, McCaulley, and Kainz, 1986) shows type distributions for more than two hundred occupations and is a basic resource for career counselors. A revision now in process will add information about the level of satisfaction of types in specific occupations.

All types are found in all occupations, but not in equal numbers. Type tables for occupations support the construct validity of the MBTI. Counseling careers, for example, attract enthusiastic and insightful N-F types and have relatively few practical and matter-of-fact S-T types. Accounting attracts many S-T types but few N-F types. Obviously, certain jobs are easier or more interesting for some types than for others. Occasionally, however, clients consciously choose a job atypical for their type in order to stretch their talents and develop new skills.

Kummerow (1998) points out that people in the same occupation do not develop a particular personality as a result of their work. It is more likely that people are attracted to and stay interested in an occupation because the choice lets them use their gifts, their natural preferences. "It's not that you're an ISTJ because you've been an accountant for twenty years," a counselor might say. "It's more likely that you chose accounting twenty years ago because accounting appeals to ISTJs."

Data also show niche groups within some occupations. For example, Scherdin (1994) found the type distribution of sixteen hundred librarians to favor I, N, and T; Kummerow (1998) collected qualitative job descriptions from librarians and found type differences in specialties within library work. These niches were consistent with type theory.

In summary, the MBTI offers five tools for career assessment and counseling:

1. Understanding one's type enhances appreciation of one's gifts and suggests a pathway to lifelong development.

2. Type tables offer the content for match or mismatch of one's interests and careers.

3. The decision-making model is a strategy to trust one's strengths and watch out for blind spots.

4. Counselors use an understanding of type differences to plan the best way for each type to cover the steps necessary for good career planning.

5. Finally, counselors learn to "talk the language" of the client's type and develop the strategies to improve the client-counselor process itself (McCaulley and Martin, 1995).

Applications of the MBTI in Organizations

In the last decade, consultants for business and governmental organizations have discovered and rapidly expanded applications of the MBTI in working with individuals, teams, and leaders. The aims of these programs include developing self-understanding; increasing appreciation for colleagues; improving communication; dealing with conflicts; enhancing teamwork; problem solving and decision making; planning, implementing, and managing organizational change; recognizing and managing stress; and executive coaching.

The MBTI and type concepts are useful in counseling in organizations. Psychologists who work with organizations as consultants, counselors, or coaches find that the MBTI is a powerful tool and transplants very well to other countries. For example, Barger and Kirby (1995) show how to help employees thrive in a world of change. Organizations themselves—whether large corporations, divisions within them, small workteams, volunteer and church groups, or even families—have a composite type (witness the "corporate culture") that influences how they operate (Bridges, 1992). Understanding this composite, along with its type dynamics and developmental aspects, helps identify core values and motivations that impinge upon and interact with those of its individual participants. For members of the culture, type concepts can enhance "clarity and comfort with their own work styles while constructively identifying possible blind spots and areas of vulnerability" (Kirby, Barger, and Pearman, 1998, p. 326).

A major type pattern that occurs in managers in all levels, and in all countries, is that over half of samples of these leaders fall into the four "tough-minded" T-J types (Fleenor, 1997; Kirby and Barger, 1998; Kirby, Barger, and Pearman, 1998).

Worldwide, the consensus seems to be that business leadership requires objective, analytical thinking (T) and organizational ability and decisiveness (J). The focus of the T-J leader is primarily on logical, objective rationale and cost-benefit analysis (T) within carefully structured plans and time frames (J). Effective leaders, however, must be able to call on *all* the preferences and use them as the situation may require (Pearman, 1998). Thus leaders must also be able to tap into the mission and values of the organization (F); adapt flexibly and incorporate midcourse changes as new information arrives and organizational needs change (P); give weight to situational pressures of the environment (E); provide a clear conceptual understanding of the problem (I); take into account the specifics of who, what, when, how, and how much (S); and include a future vision to enhance the organization's effectiveness (N). When leaders and other members of organizations are aware of the "specialties" of different types, they come to recognize conflicts as coming out of valid and valuable but different perspectives that each type contributes to solving problems. T-J types in leadership coaching are learning to take more seriously the "soft stuff."

Type Across Cultures

Type cuts across ethnicity and culture. However, there may be important differences in how types are distributed within various ethnic and cultural groups.

Applications of the MBTI extend broadly within the United States and around the world. Internationally, the major interest has been in business consulting. No truly stratified random sample exists for any group, so it is not yet possible to make definitive comparisons of type distributions in ethnic or national cultures. Nonetheless, tentative conclusions can be advanced, along with some of their consequences. (For a comprehensive review, see the chapter in the 1998 MBTI Manual by Kirby and Barger.)

In all cultures examined so far, all types exist, though with varying distribution. People in most cultures find the items of the MBTI easy to understand and the results "sensible and useful" (Kirby and Barger, 1998, p. 370). For example, Whites in South Africa (Zietsmann, 1996) and Blacks in South Africa (de Beer, 1997) accept the MBTI. It has been surprising to find people worldwide confirming that the descriptions of type, originally written by Isabel Myers and arising from middle-class America, fit them quite accurately (Kirby and Barger, 1998).

Translations of the MBTI

Translating the MBTI is more complex than translating text in a newspaper or a novel. The translator must understand Jung's theory of psychological types. When Isabel Myers wrote questions for the Indicator, she started with twenty years of study of Jung and had a deep understanding of his typology. MBTI questions are pointers to underlying unconscious processes.

Translators of the MBTI face two major challenges. The first is to choose words with the correct nuance of meaning. The second is to modify or substitute questions when the Myers question does not fit the culture (Saturday is not the same kind of day in all cultures). In the 1970s, a few unofficial translations were done—into Spanish by a college student, and into Arabic by an army corporal. It was only in the 1990s that quality translations in any number have been approved by the publisher, Consulting Psychologists Press. These include translations into Bahasa Malay, Chinese, Danish, Dutch, French (European), French (Canadian), German, Italian, Korean, Norwegian, Portuguese, Spanish (Castellano), Spanish (United States), and Swedish. Translations available only for research include Afrikaans, Arabic, Czechoslovakian, Finnish, Flemish, Greek, Hungarian, Icelandic, Indonesian, Russian, Thai, Vietnamese, and Zulu.

In 1994, after the Dayton Accords ended the fighting in Central Europe, a group of psychologists saw the MBTI as an instrument that could promote peace and understanding in their war-torn countries. Under license from CPP, the Central and Eastern European Center for Applied Psychology (CEECAP) was founded in October 1994. With the help of their students, psychologists began translations that now include Albanian, Bosnian, Bulgarian, Croatian, Hungarian, Latvian, Macedonian, Polish, Romanian, Serbian, Slovenian, and Turkish. CEECAP members, at great personal and financial sacrifice, have completed and validated translations and are writing support materials.

Charles Ginn, a psychologist at the University of Cincinnati, has been the CEECAP liaison in the United States and has arranged through his university for CEECAP faculty and students to have Internet access to the libraries of the Ohio Universities. Students in CEECAP countries are communicating by e-mail with students in the United states, comparing notes about their types and how similar and different they are in their cultures. CEECAP's efforts with the MBTI have already begun to create understanding among former enemies.

Although most translators find the MBTI questions understandable for citizens in their countries, cautions have arisen about administering the MBTI in collectivist cultures where the emphasis is on the group, not the individual. John Bathurst (1996) in New Zealand reported that the Maori have great difficulty with MBTI questions. They live in individualistic New Zealand but remain in their collectivist culture. They are more comfortable answering MBTI items according to their Maori lives rather than their individual preferences. Horikoshi (1998) asked Japanese Americans to complete the MBTI twice, once as the type their culture expected them to be and again as the type they thought they really were. Of the 113 participants, 99 (88 percent) answered S-J for the culture, but only 45 (40 percent) reported S-J for themselves.

The United States has many citizens from other countries whose lives bridge two cultures. Labarta (1983) noticed that in counseling sessions with clients whose native language was Spanish, the clients discussed more substantive issues when she conducted the session in Spanish rather than in English. In her dissertation, her bilingual subjects were asked to answer the MBTI twice—once in their Spanish environment, and once in their American environment.

They chose extraversion significantly more often in the Spanish frame of reference.

Conclusions

With more than two million administrations per year around the world, the MBTI has provided extensive and compelling evidence that Jung's theory of personality type is indeed universal. Despite its middle-class American origin, people of diverse cultures have found its results meaningful and useful in education, counseling, career development, and organizations.

Kirby and Barger (1998) conclude their discussion of multicultural issues and the MBTI in the fourteenth chapter of the MBTI manual in these words:

> This chapter has emphasized differences when the MBTI is used in multicultural settings and cautions about its use with people culturally different from those with whom it was developed. It is also important to recognize the positive experience of practitioners using the MBTI outside the United States:
>
> 1. Both psychological type and the MBTI have been used effectively in dozens of cultures, some very different from the U.S. middle-class culture.
> 2. Research and practitioner experience in using the MBTI multiculturally is overwhelmingly positive—clients recognize the patterns identified by psychological type, give examples of their use of preferences from their own experience, and find type's identification of normal differences very helpful in increasing their understanding of themselves and others.
> 3. The perspective and ethics associated with psychological type and the MBTI, summarized by

Myers as "the constructive use of differences," make type and the MBTI particularly useful in cross-cultural work and multicultural settings, where respect for human diversity is of paramount importance" [Kirby and Barger, 1998, p. 384].

Endnote

1. The MBTI bibliography and library are maintained by the Center for Applications of Psychological Type (CAPT) at 2815 N.W. 13th St., Suite 401, Gainesville, FL 32609. For bibliographic information or keyword searches, call CAPT's research librarian at (352) 375-0160 or e-mail requests to library@capt.org. As of May 2000, the MBTI bibliography contained 7,112 references. Visitors are welcome to use the library during normal CAPT business hours.

References

Bargar, J. R., Bargar, R. R., & Cano, J. M. (1994). *Discovering learning performance and learning differences in the classroom*. Columbus: Ohio Agricultural Education Curriculum Materials Service, Ohio State University.

Barger, N. J., & Kirby, L. K. (1995). *The challenge of change in organizations: Helping employees thrive in the new frontier*. Palo Alto, CA: Davies-Black.

Bathurst, J. (1996). Expressions of type in multicultural New Zealand. In R. A. Moody (Ed.), *Proceedings of the Second Multicultural Research Symposium of the Center for Applications of Psychological Type* (pp. 71–75), University of Hawaii, January 1996. Gainesville, FL: Center for Applications of Psychological Type.

Bridges, W. (1992). *The character of organizations: Using Jungian type in organizational development*. Palo Alto, CA: Consulting Psychologists Press.

Chapman, M. (1994). The Aleknagik Project: A success story of cooperative school restructuring based on traditional Eskimo learning patterns and Myers-Briggs type theory (an overview). In *Proceedings of the First Biennial International Conference on Education of the Center for Applications of Psychological Type* (pp. 1–10). Gainesville, FL: Center for Applications of Psychological Type.

Costa, P. T., & McCrae, R. R. (1992). *Revised NEO Personality Inventory (NEO-PI-R) and NEO Five-Factor Inventory (NEO-FFI) professional manual*. Odessa, FL: Psychological Assessment Resources.

de Beer, J. (1997). *South African Myers-Briggs type distribution: A comparative study*. Unpublished doctoral dissertation, Rand Afrikaans University, South Africa, 1997.

DiTiberio, J. K. (1998). Uses of type in education. In I. B. Myers, M. H. McCaulley, N. L. Quenk, & A. L. Hammer (Eds.), *MBTI Manual: A guide to the development and use of the Myers-Briggs Type Indicator* (3rd ed., pp. 253–284). Palo Alto, CA: Consulting Psychologists Press.

DiTiberio, J. K., & Jensen, G. H. (1994). *Writing and personality: Finding your voice, your style, your way*. Palo Alto, CA: Davies-Black.

Ehrman, M. E. (1996). *Understanding second language learning difficulties*. Thousand Oaks, CA: Sage.

Fairhurst, A. M., & Fairhurst, L. L. (1995). *Effective teaching, effective learning: Making the personality connection in your classroom*. Palo Alto, CA: Davies-Black.

Fleenor, J. W. (1997). The relationship between the MBTI and measures of personality and performance in management groups. In L. K. Kirby & C. Fitzgerald (Eds.), *Developing leaders: Research and applications in psychological type and leadership development* (pp. 115–138). Palo Alto, CA: Davies-Black.

Hammer, A. L. (Ed.). (1996). *MBTI Applications: A decade of research on the Myers-Briggs Type Indicator*. Palo Alto, CA: Consulting Psychologists Press.

Horikoshi, W. C. (1998). Cross-cultural conflict of Asians in the U.S.: Applications of MBTI in a multicultural environment. In R. A. Moody (Ed.), *Proceedings of the Second Multicultural Research Symposium of the Center for Applications of Psychological Type* (pp. 29–43), University of Hawaii, January 1996. Gainesville, FL: Center for Applications of Psychological Type.

Jensen, G. H., & DiTiberio, J. K. (1989). *Personality and the teaching of composition*. Norwood, NJ: Ablex.

Jung, C. G. (1971). Psychological types (H. G. Baynes, Trans., revised by R.F.C. Hull). *Collected works*, Vol. 6. Princeton, NJ: Princeton University. (Original work published in 1921)

Kirby, L. K., & Barger, N. J. (1998). Uses of type in multicultural settings. In I. B. Myers, M. H. McCaulley, N. L. Quenk, & A. L. Hammer (Eds.), *Manual: A guide to the development and use of the Myers-Briggs Type Indicator* (3rd ed., pp. 367–384). Palo Alto: Consulting Psychologists Press.

Kirby, L. K., Barger, N. J., & Pearman, R. R. (1998). Uses of type in organizations. In I. B. Myers, M. H. McCaulley, N. L. Quenk, & A. L. Hammer (Eds.), *Manual: A guide to the development and use of the*

Myers-Briggs Type Indicator (3rd ed., pp. 325–365). Palo Alto: Consulting Psychologists Press.

Kummerow, J. M. (1998). Using type in careers. In I. B. Myers, M. H. McCaulley, N. L. Quenk, & A. L. Hammer (Eds.), *MBTI Manual. A guide to the development and use of the Myers-Briggs Type Indicator* (3rd ed., pp. 285–324). Palo Alto, CA: Consulting Psychologists Press.

Labarta, M. M. (1983). The effects of cultural referent and acculturation on the four dimensions of psychological type (doctoral dissertation, University of Maryland—College Park, 1982). *Dissertation Abstracts International,* 44(06), 1965B. University Microfilms No. AAC83–23556.

Lawrence, G. D. (1993). *People types and tiger stripes* (3rd ed.). Gainesville, FL: Center for Applications of Psychological Type.

Lawrence, G. D. (1997). *Looking at type and learning styles.* Gainesville, FL: Center for Applications of Psychological Type.

Macdaid, G. P., McCaulley, M. H., & Kainz, R. I. (1986). *Atlas of type tables.* Gainesville, FL: Center for Applications of Psychological Type.

Mamchur, C. M. (1996). *A teacher's guide to cognitive type theory and learning style.* Alexandria, VA: Association for Supervision and Curriculum Development.

McCaulley, M. H., & Martin, C. R. (1995). Career assessment and the Myers-Briggs Type Indicator. *Journal of Career Assessment,* 3(2), 219–239.

Myers, I. B. (1962). *Manual: The Myers-Briggs Type Indicator.* Princeton, NJ: Educational Testing Service.

Myers, I. B., & McCaulley, M. H. (1985). *Manual: A guide to the development and use of the Myers-Briggs Type Indicator.* Palo Alto, CA: Consulting Psychologists Press.

Myers, I. B., McCaulley, M. H., Quenk, N. L., & Hammer, A. L. (1998). *Manual: A guide to the development and use of the Myers-Briggs Type Indicator* (3rd ed.). Palo Alto: Consulting Psychologists Press.

Myers, I. B., & Myers, P. B. (1980). *Gifts differing.* Palo Alto, CA: Consulting Psychologists Press.

Pearman, R. R. (1998). *Hardwired leadership: Unleashing the power of personality to become a new millennium leader.* Palo Alto, CA: Davies Black.

Saunders, D. R. (1987). *Type Differentiation Indicator manual: A scoring system for Form J of the Myers-Briggs Type Indicator.* Palo Alto, CA: Consulting Psychologists Press.

Saunders, D. R. (1989). *MBTI expanded analysis report manual: A scoring system for Form K of the Myers-Briggs Type Indicator.* Palo Alto, CA: Consulting Psychologists Press.

Saunders, F. W. (1991). *Katharine and Isabel: Mother's light, daughter's journey*. Palo Alto, CA: Consulting Psychologists Press.

Scherdin, M. J. (1994). Vive la difference: Exploring librarian personality types using the MBTI. In M. J. Scherdin (Ed.), *Discovering librarians: Profiles of a profession*. Chicago: Association of College and Research Libraries, American Library Association.

Thompson, T. C. (Ed.). (1997). *Most excellent differences: Essays on using type theory in the composition classroom*. Gainesville, FL: Center for Applications of Psychological Type.

VanSant, S., & Payne, D. (1995). *Psychological type in schools: Applications for educators*. Gainesville, FL: Center for Applications of Psychological Type.

Zietsmann, G. (1996, September). The validation of the MBTI on a South African sample: A summary of the results. *Proceedings of the fourth conference of the International Type User's Organization* (pp. 186–190), Sandton, South Africa.

13

Minnesota Multiphasic Personality
Inventory and Millon Clinical
Multiaxial Inventory

Gordon C. Nagayama Hall and Amber H. Phung

The Minnesota Multiphasic Personality Inventory (MMPI) and Millon Clinical Multiaxial Inventory (MCMI) are the most widely used measures of personality and psychopathology. There is empirical support that psychopathological groups differ from non-pathological ones on the MMPI (Parker, Hanson, and Hunsley, 1988; Zalewski and Gottesman, 1991). Both measures correspond reasonably well to the disorders that they are designed to measure (Blais, Benedict, and Norman, 1994; Libb, Murray, Thurstin, and Alarcon, 1992; McCann, 1991).

Although these instruments were not designed to be sensitive to ethnic differences, research on ethnic differences has been conducted with these measures, and they are commonly used to assess ethnic minority individuals. Thus, it is critical to examine the validity of these measures in assessing ethnic minorities.

In this chapter, we review the rationale and implications of the use of these measures with ethnic minorities. The focus is on ethnic groups within the United States. Although international research may be of some relevance to persons in the United States who have emigrated from particular nations, issues of coexistence with multiple cultural groups and of ethnic minority status are not critical in other nations that are primarily monocultural. We also review the primary conclusions of the research on ethnic differences on the MMPI and MCMI. We then discuss the limitations of this research and offer possible directions for future research and clinical applications.

Throughout this chapter, we refer to groups of color as ethnic minority groups and to issues of ethnicity rather than of race. Race is a biological concept, and there is much disagreement on its definition. For example, physical anthropologists have described from three to thirty-seven distinct racial groups (Yee, Fairchild, Weizmann, and Wyatt, 1993). Ethnicity has been defined as a social psychological sense of "peoplehood" in which members of a group share a unique social and cultural heritage that is transmitted from one generation to another (Phinney, 1996; Sue, 1991). Individuals in a particular ethnic group may share common behaviors, attitudes, and values. Persons of color in the United States constitute ethnic minority groups because they are minorities in terms of numbers and power relative to European Americans. Ethnicity is a construct that is more germane to behavioral science research and to clinical practice than is race.

The MMPI and MCMI are both etic measures (Dana, 1993). Etic measures may be oriented toward identifying universal behaviors and may be less sensitive to unique behaviors in cultural groups. The MMPI and MCMI were developed from a European American perspective. However, the developers of the measures contend that the test is not biased against ethnic minority persons because the most recent versions of both measures have included culturally diverse participants in their standardization samples. Nevertheless, a diverse standardization sample does not insure against potential conceptual or content bias (Zalewski and Greene, 1996).

A basic issue in assessing ethnic minorities is whether there are ethnic differences in personality and psychopathology. Cultural differences and ethnic minority status distinguish Americans of non-European backgrounds from European Americans (Hall, Bansal, and Lopez, 1999). Yet, epidemiological data suggest few ethnic differences in psychopathology (Huertin-Roberts, Snowden, and Miller, 1997; Kessler and others, 1994; Roberts and Sobhan, 1992).

However, even when particular behaviors are consistently identified across cultural groups, these behaviors may have varying meanings and importance as a function of specific cultural context (Gray-Little, 1995; Hall, Bansal, and Lopez, 1999). One potential reason for this apparent lack of ethnic differences in psychopathology is that participants in most studies are grouped into ethnic categories that are broad and heterogeneous. There is much variability within such broad ethnic groupings as European American, African American, Asian American, Latino American, and American Indian. Important issues of language fluency, acculturation, ethnic identification, perceived minority status, discrimination experiences, and social class are usually not examined. Thus, within-group ethnic heterogeneity may obscure differences between ethnic groups.

Ethnic-Comparative Research with the MMPI and MCMI

There appear to be two primary reasons for MMPI and MCMI research on ethnic differences. The first involves investigating test bias. Proponents of these measures want to demonstrate that the MMPI and MCMI are not biased against ethnic minority people. Such proponents contend that lack of difference between ethnic groups is evidence that the measures are culture-fair. Presumably, substantive ethnic differences on these measures could qualify as evidence of test bias. However, ethnic differences on the MMPI and MCMI are not necessarily evidence of test bias if, based on other external criteria (other tests, clinicians' diagnoses), it can be demonstrated that one group is more pathological than the other. In such cases, it is contended that, rather than being biased, the measures are simply assessing differing levels of between-group psychopathology that actually exist (Butcher, Braswell, and Raney, 1983; McNulty, Graham, Ben-Porath, and Stein, 1997).

Ethnic group similarities or differences on the MMPI and MCMI do not necessarily address whether the measures are biased or valid across cultures. Test bias is difficult to demonstrate. Equal scores on measures of personality and psychopathology do not necessarily rule out the possibility of test bias. For example, if one group is facing stressors (such as discrimination) that the other group does not, perhaps an unbiased measure should reflect these additional stressors for one group versus the other. Measures that result in equal scores for qualitatively different groups may be biased insofar as they are insensitive to group differences. Using external criteria does not automatically resolve the issue either. Consistency between a test and an external criterion, such as clinicians' diagnoses, could simply mean that the test and the criterion are both biased in the same direction (see Garb, 1997; Snowden and Cheung, 1990).

A second major reason for studying MMPI and MCMI ethnic differences involves investigating the cross-cultural utility of the measures. Proponents of these measures attempt to demonstrate that similar personality and psychopathology constructs exist across cultures. This approach is similar to the test bias approach insofar as the purpose is to demonstrate the validity of the tests. However, in the cross-cultural approach, there is more emphasis on the construct validity of the measures, as opposed to content validity in the test bias approach. Thus, in the cross-cultural approach, differences between ethnic groups are not as critical as whether ethnic groups display the same overall patterns of personality and psychopathology.

A major limitation of the cross-cultural approach is that even if ethnic similarities are detected by etic measures, there may be critical ethnic-specific characteristics that are not detected by such measures (Lewis-Fernandez and Kleinman, 1994). The cross-cultural approach also tends to categorize into broad groupings on the assumption that one group (say, European Americans) has more within-group similarities than another (perhaps African Americans). However, as discussed previously, within-group heterogeneity is likely to obscure between-group differences, and the apparent cultural universality of characteristics and behaviors that is created by the between-group approach may be somewhat illusory.

Another issue in cross-cultural research with non-English-speaking people is the cultural equivalence of translated measures. Rogler (1999) contended that current procedural norms for translations are culturally insensitive because the procedures require that standardized instruments be maintained in their exact original-language versions throughout the translation process. Although the aim of translation is to achieve equivalent meaning, many instruments used in mental health research are written using colloquial American phrases, which then makes them difficult to translate to another language and cultural context.

A suggested solution to overcome this particular difficulty with translation is to decenter the instrument, where both versions are subjected to possible revisions and alterations. Even if a foreign-born American speaks English, the person's level of language proficiency should be assessed in determining the language for administration of the test (Kwan, 1999). Translation involves not only language but also any other dimensions along which individuals may differ from the European Americans who developed the MMPI and MCMI, and who make up the majority of the standardization sample (Dana, 1993).

A broader issue in the study of ethnicity as it relates to personality and psychopathology is the sociopolitical ramifications of ethnic similarities and differences (Hall, Bansal, and Lopez, 1999). Ethnic similarities in personality and psychopathology may absolve some researchers and clinicians from the sense of any responsibility for cultural sensitivity. If European American models of personality and psychopathology are universally valid, then such models do not need to be modified (or discarded) for various ethnic groups. A business-as-usual approach to personality and psychopathology may appear to be effective across ethnic groups, but it is at best only partially effective if there are important differences between ethnic groups.

The consequences of ethnic-group differences in personality and psychopathology are also not benign. Differences from European American male norms have been associated with disadvantage, and psychological testing has a long history in the United States of being misused against ethnic minority persons (Jones, 1997; Suzuki and Valencia, 1997). Ethnic differences in personality and psychopathology are likely to be interpreted by some as evidence of cultural deficits in the ethnic minority groups rather than a response to current and historical life circumstances that differ from those of European Americans.

Moreover, the potentially adaptive aspects of ethnic differences are likely to be overlooked. For example, European American mainstream society generally values independence. Assertive and even many aggressive behaviors are generally viewed as acceptable. However, this high value on independence has resulted in the United States being the most violent society in the world (Hall and Barongan, 1997). Nevertheless, the high value placed on interdependence and interpersonal harmony in many American ethnic minority groups is unlikely to be viewed as a desirable standard of behavior for most European Americans. Human tendency is to overlook negative aspects of one's in-group and attribute negative characteristics to out-groups (Pettigrew and others, 1998). Thus, it is unlikely that European Americans will adopt the standards of out-group ethnic minorities, even if these standards are adaptive.

Unfortunately, most ethnic difference research on the MMPI and MCMI has been conducted in something of a conceptual and sociopolitical vacuum. Ethnic groups have been compared on these measures without a conceptual rationale for why one might expect between-group differences. Personality assessment researchers rarely discuss the sociopolitical implications of their findings, which are primarily left to those who interpret (and often misinterpret) the findings (Gray-Little, 1995; Velasquez, 1995). Thus, it is necessary to examine the possible reasons for substantive ethnic differences on the MMPI and MCMI, as well as the implications of ethnic similarities and differences. We review the ethnic difference research on the MMPI and follow that with a similar review of the research on MCMI ethnic differences.

The MMPI and MMPI-2

The MMPI is one of the most widely researched and used assessment measures. It was first published in 1943 and restandardized as the MMPI-2 in 1989 (Butcher and others, 1989). The restandardization sample was representative of the 1980 U.S. census, which is less culturally diverse than the 2000 census. Three Validity scales (L, F, K) and ten Clinical scales are most commonly used in research and practice. The MMPI-2 uses T scores, in which a difference of 5 points or more is considered clinically significant, and elevation of 65 or above is considered indicative of psychopathology.

Although proponents of the MMPI/MMPI-2 claim that it is atheoretical, the ten Clinical scales of the original MMPI correspond to the psychiatric nosology of the 1940s, and the majority of the content of the MMPI and MMPI-2 Clinical scales is identical (Helmes and Reddon, 1993). The names of the Clinical scales (1, Hypochondriasis; 2, Depression; 3, Hysteria; 4, Psychopathic Deviate; 5, Masculinity-Femininity; 6, Paranoia; 7, Psychasthenia; 8, Schizophrenia; 9, Hypomania; and 0, Social Introversion) are not necessarily indicative of what the scales measure, but a carryover from the original version of the MMPI.

Scales are currently referred to by number, and profile configurations (for example, 2–7–8 or 4–8) are usually more informative than interpretations based on individual scales (Graham, 1993). There is very limited ethnic difference research on MMPI/MMPI-2 profile configuration, that is, the manner in which the measure is interpreted in most clinical settings. Content scales were developed for the MMPI-2 to assess specific psychological problem areas, based on experts' judgments and statistical methods (Graham, 1993). However, there are too few ethnic difference studies on the MMPI-2 Content scales to make any conclusions.

Most of the comparative MMPI/MMPI-2 research on ethnic minorities has compared European Americans with African Americans or Latino Americans. There is a paucity of comparative research involving Latina Americans, Asian Americans, and American Indians. MMPI or MMPI-2 studies that compared African Americans and European Americans, and Latino Americans and European Americans, were recently reviewed in a meta-analysis (Hall, Bansal, and Lopez, 1999). No substantive between-group differences were found for any of the MMPI/MMPI-2 Validity or Clinical scales. There were also no substantive differences as a function of sociodemographic variables (such as education), research setting, or use of the MMPI as opposed to the MMPI-2. This lack of ethnic differences as a function of these potential moderator variables may be interpreted as evidence that the MMPI/MMPI-2 is not biased against ethnic minority persons.

One exception to the findings on moderator variables was that African American men had lower scores than European American men on MMPI Scale 4 in forensic settings (Hall, Bansal, and Lopez, 1999). Scale 4 assesses rebellion, including antisocial and criminal behavior at high elevation (Graham, 1993). Similarly, African American men had lower scores than European American men on MMPI Scale 7 in substance abuse settings (Hall, Bansal, and Lopez, 1999). Scale 7 deals with obsessive thoughts, feelings of fear and anxiety, and doubts about one's own ability (Graham, 1993). These lower scores for African Americans as opposed to European Americans in clinical settings may suggest lower criterion levels for psychopathology to qualify for involvement in these clinical settings (Hall, Bansal, and Lopez, 1999). In other words, it is possible that some communities may be biased toward a lower tolerance for psychopathology in African Americans than in European Americans. Nevertheless, all the effect sizes in the study were small, which renders speculation about the source of African American and European American differences moot.

Although it was a small effect size, the largest and most robust between-group difference in the Hall, Bansal, and Lopez (1999) meta-analysis was between Latino Americans and European Americans on MMPI/MMPI-2 Scale 5, with the mean score for

Latino Americans being lower. Lower Scale 5 scores may suggest stereotypically masculine preferences in work, hobbies, and other activities (Graham, 1993). Such characteristics are often considered to be patriarchal and sexist. However, there may be certain positive aspects of patriarchal cultures, including men's sense of responsibility to nurture their family (Sorenson and Siegel, 1992).

Moreover, patriarchal characteristics are not unique to Latino cultures (Casas, Wagenheim, Banchero, and Mendoza-Romero, 1995). Conservative European American political and religious groups also often share and may value these characteristics, although they may be expressed somewhat differently as a function of cultural context. It should be reemphasized that the effect size of the Latino American and European American difference on Scale 5 across studies is small and not substantive.

In contrast to the findings with Latino Americans, there is evidence that Latina Americans exhibit higher scores on Scale 5 than do European American women (Greene, 1987; Nelson, Novy, Averill, and Berry, 1996). High scores on Scale 5 for women suggest rejection of traditional female roles (Graham, 1993). Varying gender roles as a function of culture may help explain score differences on scale 5. It is possible that Latinos may accentuate their masculine role, while Latinas may feel dissatisfied with traditional feminine roles that have been passed onto them (Lucio and Reyes-Lagunes, 1996).

Many Asian Americans are immigrants to the United States, and acculturation has been demonstrated to influence MMPI scores. Asian Americans tend to express more somatic complaints, depression, anxiety, and feelings of isolation than European Americans do, and to exhibit greater elevation on scales L, F, 2, 6, 7, 8, and 0 (Kwan, 1999; Stevens, Kwan, and Graybill, 1993; Sue and Sue, 1974; Tran, 1996; Tsai and Pike, 2000). However, Asian Americans who are more acculturated to U.S. culture produce MMPI and MMPI-2 profiles that are more similar to those of European Americans than do Asian Americans who are less acculturated

(Sue and others, 1996; Stevens, Kwan, and Graybill, 1993; Tran, 1996; Tsai and Pike, 2000). Because the less acculturated Asian Americans generally exhibited MMPI and MMPI-2 profiles that were somewhat more elevated than the other groups, proponents of acculturation could contend that acculturation to Western society is the most adaptive alternative for Asian Americans. However, it is unclear whether the difference between less acculturated Asian Americans and the other groups is a function of psychopathology (for instance, acculturative stress) or reflects what may be acceptable in Asian American cultural contexts (Okazaki and Sue, 1995).

MMPI and MMPI-2 elevations may suggest cultural differences associated with accepted societal norms for Asians, not necessarily higher rates of psychopathology (Shiota, Krauss, and Clark, 1996). The presence of elevation on Scale 2 among Asians may represent cultural norms that emphasize modesty, restraint, and imperturbability, rather than being reflective of depressive qualities. Many Asians may also perceive overt displays of self-confidence and self-praise to be undesirable, preferring to focus on displays of humility and ready acknowledgment of their shortcomings rather than their advantages. However, there are many Asian American subgroups that differ vastly from one another. Thus, findings from one Asian American subgroup are not necessarily applicable to another (Sue and others, 1996).

Despite the scarcity of research on American Indian performance on the MMPI and MMPI-2, the reported differences suggest that American Indians tend to score higher than European Americans on most of the scales. American Indian women tend to have higher scores on Scales F, 1, 4, 5, 7, and 8, and American Indian men tend to have higher scores on Scales F and 4 (Butcher and others, 1989; Greene, 1987; LaDue, 1983).

Understanding American Indian culture may help to elucidate current findings on scale score elevation. These elevations alone do not necessarily equate to a presence of psychopathology; instead, one should consider the meaning of these scores within the

American Indian context. Highwater (1981) described American Indians as people who value close relationships between the individual and the tribe and tribal religion. Unlike the dominant culture, there appeared to be less ego orientation and social narcissism among American Indians. The prevalent sense of interrelatedness and interconnectedness, to both tribal members and all living things, is often associated with openness to alternative identity and willingness to tolerate aberrant behavior. The tolerance for deviant action, for example, is useful in understanding elevation on Scale 4 on the MMPI.

The overall conclusion in examining the literature of MMPI and MMPI-2 ethnic difference is that there are not substantive ethnic differences on these measures. Although some cultural explanations have been offered for the differences that have been found, the MMPI and MMPI-2 generally do not appear sensitive to behaviors that are culturally based. Conclusions about Latina Americans, Asian Americans, and American Indians are not possible, given the paucity of MMPI and MMPI-2 studies on these groups. However, it appears unlikely that the MMPI and MMPI-2 are any more sensitive to ethnic differences in these groups than they are among African Americans and Latino Americans.

MCMI

One of the goals involved in developing the Millon Clinical Multiaxial Inventory (MCMI) is to bridge the intersection between personality and psychopathology, while at the same time integrating facets from a number of disciplines to create an explicitly clinical inventory (Millon, 1981). The MCMI, MCMI-II, and MCMI-III are relatively consistent with the nosological system based on the DSM (American Psychiatric Association, 1994). The MCMI-III, the most recent version of the MCMI, contains eight subscales that examine moderate personality styles (schizoid, avoidant, dependent, histrionic, narcissistic, antisocial, compulsive, and passive-aggressive), three that examine pathological personality styles (schizotypal, borderline, and paranoid), and ten that examine clinical syndromes (anxiety, somatoform, bipolar manic, alcohol dependence, drug dependence, dysthymia, posttraumatic stress disorder, thought disorder, major depression, and delusional disorder). Personality styles correspond with DSM Axis II disorders, and clinical syndromes correspond with Axis I disorders.

Developing the MCMI with separate norms for various ethnic minority groups in the United States represents acknowledgment that race and ethnicity are potentially influential in ethnic minority performance on paper-and-pencil instruments of psychopathology (Davis, Greenblatt, and Pochyly, 1990). Millon (1994) contended that normality varies as a function of a particular cultural context. Therefore, norms for various ethnic minority groups were established as a way of recognizing that normality is based upon an optimum degree of congruence between an individual and his or her culture.

To date, there are only a handful of studies examining ethnic differences on the MCMI, with comparisons being made only between African Americans and European Americans. Many of these studies used either psychiatric inpatients or substance abusers as their samples, and participants were usually not matched for sociodemographic characteristics (Choca, Shanley, Peterson, and Van Denburg, 1990; Davis and Greenblatt, 1990; Donat, Walters, and Hume, 1992; Greenblatt and Davis, 1992).

Unlike a T score or percentile rank, MCMI profiles are given in terms of base rate scores (BRS), where an individual raw score is put on a common metric that is based upon the prevalence, or base rate, of a particular disorder in the normative sample. According to the score profiles on the MCMI, African Americans tend to produce higher scores than European Americans on fifteen of the subscales. Using a standard cutoff of BRS 75, some consistent and significant differences that emerged in these studies suggest that African Americans score higher than European Americans on psychotic delusion, avoidant, asocial, narcissistic, and drug abuse subscales

(Choca, Shanley, Peterson, and Van Denburg, 1990; Davis and Greenblatt, 1990; Donat, Walters, and Hume, 1992). There were no consistent gender differences. Item, scale, and structural analysis that Choca and his colleagues (1990) performed on their data revealed that 45 out of the 175 items in the MCMI were answered significantly differently by African Americans and European Americans. This number is considerably higher than one might expect to occur by chance. Choca and his colleagues (1990) contend that this differential endorsement frequency is evidence of test bias.

Although the dearth of studies on ethnic minorities and the MCMI render these findings inconclusive, how might one explain the presence of performance differences between African Americans and European Americans on this personality inventory? As Gynther (1981) argues, the elevated scores of African Americans on the MCMI may reflect an adaptive manner of having to live in a society that is historically oppressive and prejudicial for African Americans. Therefore, variations in social conditioning that may be the product of social and cultural opportunities could potentially be illustrated in differences between African Americans and European Americans in test scores on a personality inventory (Cross and Burger, 1982). In addition to experiences with oppression and prejudice, there also may be difference in cultural worldview among European Americans and African Americans. For example, African American worldviews may differ on attitudes toward time, rhythm, or recurring patterning of behavior within a given time frame; improvisation or combination of expressiveness and creativity occurring under time pressure; oral expression; and spirituality (Jones, 1986). It is possible that such variation in worldview may be reflected to some degree on measures such as the MCMI.

Conceptual and Methodological Issues

More than thirty years of comparative research with the MMPI and MMPI-2 has resulted in a general failure to reject the null hypothesis regarding possible differences between European Americans and either African Americans or Latino Americans (Hall, Bansal, and Lopez, 1999). It is unlikely that substantive ethnic differences will be detected with other ethnic groups or with the MCMI. As in any research context in which there is a failure to reject the null hypothesis, the meaning of this finding is unknown. Absence of between-group differences does not necessarily mean that the measures are not biased against ethnic minority groups. Thus, further research using the standard method of comparing two ostensibly divergent ethnic groups (say, African Americans and European Americans) with the MMPI or MCMI as the dependent measure seems rather pointless.

If research in ethnic differences with the MMPI and MCMI is to be informative, there must be a theoretical rationale. Without a conceptual rationale for why ethnic groups should differ on these measures, it is unclear why differences should be expected. Consider research in which ethnic identity is the dependent measure and psychopathological (for instance, depressed) and nonpsychopathological (nondepressed) groups are compared on levels of ethnic identity. In the absence of hypothesized differences, the relationship between psychopathology and ethnic identity is unknown. Ethnic identity could conceivably be health enhancing (say, promotes higher self-esteem; Phinney, 1989) or pathology inducing (creates a sense of alienation in a European American society; see Steele, 1997) for ethnic minority people. Such research is unlikely to be published because of it lacks conceptualization and an empirically driven nature.

Yet much of the MMPI and MCMI research on ethnic differences has been empirically driven and conducted in such a conceptual vacuum. This criticism is not specific to MMPI and MCMI ethnic difference research. Much research with these measures is on group differences, but without specifying how the groups differ.

Although the MMPI research suggests a general absence of ethnic differences in personality and psychopathology, many ethnic minority people in the United States experience stressors that European Americans do not, including discrimination in social, educational, and work settings. It is likely that these stressors have some influence on personality and psychopathology. Thus, equal scores on measures of personality and psychopathology may imply unequal levels of coping for the groups that experience greater stress (Hall and Barongan, 1997). Important contextual considerations in personality and psychopathology research on ethnic minority persons are the level of perceived discrimination and other stressors, and the level of coping with these stressors. Such stressors and coping efforts may mediate the relationship between ethnicity and personality or psychopathology.

In addition to the need for a conceptual basis for research in MMPI and MCMI ethnic differences, there is a need for a definition of ethnicity in this research. Ethnicity has been treated as a categorical variable in most of the ethnic difference research on the MMPI and MCMI. However, such ethnic categories (European Americans, African Americans) are heterogeneous. Moreover, the mechanisms of the potential difference between ethnic groups are usually not conceptualized or measured. It has been recommended that ethnicity be examined as a continuous construct; measures have been developed for assessing ethnic identity for individual ethnic groups, including European Americans, and across multiple ethnic groups (Dana, 1993; Kohatsu and Richardson, 1996; Phinney, 1992; Sabnani and Ponterotto, 1992; Zalewski and Greene, 1996). Investigating ethnic identity as a continuous construct may also stimulate investigating difference within the ethnic group, which is as interesting and important as between-group difference (Hall, Bansal, and Lopez, 1999; Zalewski and Greene, 1996).

Missing from most of the ethnic difference research on the MMPI and MCMI is consideration of the contextual meaning of the findings. This emphasis on individuals out of context may be because the MMPI and MCMI, as well as most conceptualizations of personality and psychopathology, have been developed in the tradition of individual psychology. The importance of contextual influences, such as family and culture, on behavior is increasingly being recognized in both ethnic minority and nonminority populations (Szapocznik and Kurtines, 1993). Contextual influences may be particularly important in ethnic minority contexts in which there is often greater emphasis on interdependence than in European American contexts (Greenfield, 1994; Hill, Soriano, Chen, and LaFromboise 1994; Sue and Sue, 1999).

Relatively few ethnic-comparative studies have employed extratest correlates to consider the impact of the behavior measured by the instruments. Nevertheless, this neglect of extratest measures could be justified because there is evidence, particularly with the MMPI, to suggest that the tests are correlated with extratest measures and have convergent validity (for example, Ben-Porath, Butcher, and Graham, 1991). However, etic extratest measures that are not culturally sensitive are no more likely to be informative for ethnic minority populations than the MMPI and MCMI have been.

Culturally sensitive emic assessment methods are needed to supplement etic measures of personality and psychopathology (Dana, 1993). Such methods may include (1) ratings by members of the individual's ethnic community, (2) ratings by mental health professionals in the individual's ethnic community, and (3) culturally sensitive measures of personality and psychopathology developed by ethnic minority experts (Hall, Bansal, and Lopez, 1999). Unfortunately, such methods have yet to be developed and evaluated.

Nevertheless, the demand for culturally appropriate assessment research on members of ethnic minorities is increasing, and the MMPI and MCMI will continue to be widely used in clinical practice with ethnic minorities. We now turn to consideration of the culturally sensitive use of the MMPI and MCMI in clinical settings.

Implications for Clinical Practice

Difficulties with evaluating cultural factors that may contribute to an individual's personality are exacerbated by the diversity and heterogeneity within a particular ethnic or racial group (Okazaki and Sue, 1995). Appropriate and effective psychological assessment of ethnic minorities in the United States should lead the health care provider to make competent and well-informed decisions that are rooted in the client's culture, experience, and personal worldview. Failure to extend adequate treatment to ethnic minorities may result from errors and incorrect assumptions by health care providers in assessing and evaluating these groups (Velasquez, 1995).

Individual experiences (such as gender roles, prejudice and discrimination, stress of acculturation, and processes of socialization) may produce variation in ethnic expression of symptoms of psychological distress (Velasquez, 1995). One might consider the possibility that expression of emotion is culturally influenced and that distinct ways of expressing distress that may be culturally acceptable within one context could lead to misdiagnosis of psychopathology within another (Mesquita and Frijda, 1992; Costantino, Malgady, and Rogler, 1988). Acculturative stress, for example, may be more evident among students who are recent immigrants. For these students, the desire to strive for high academic achievement may come at certain psychological and academic costs (Sue and Zane, 1985). In their efforts to survive in competitive university settings, recent immigrants may face such hardships as studying longer hours and restrictive career options, which in turn may contribute to manifesting psychological distress.

Sue and Sue (1987) stressed the importance of understanding the difference between personality and cultural features that may explain the exhibited behavior. For example, it would be difficult to discern whether items that assess nonassertiveness are endorsed as a result of personality features, such as lack of confidence, or if endorsing these items is the result of a cultural emphasis that may value maintaining interpersonal harmony. According to a survey conducted on service providers for ethnic minority groups, the four most frequently agreed-upon definitions of culture-sensitive treatment are

1. Awareness that there are differences
2. Working knowledge about the cultural background of the client

3. Distinguishing the difference between culture and pathology in assessment

4. Consideration of the client's culture (Zayas, Torres, Malcolm, and DesRosiers, 1996)

The first three definitions are easily applicable within the realm of psychological assessment.

Ridley, Li, and Hill (1998) have developed a comprehensive Multicultural Assessment Procedure (MAP) and have recommended first that standardized instruments be interpreted in a cultural context and second that cultural data and interpretations supplement standardized assessments. The clinician gains information on the clients' view of their concerns and problems.

Included among the cultural data and interpretations is an assessment of psychocultural adjustment. Psychocultural adjustment includes acculturation to the mainstream culture, identification with one's ethnic group, and bicultural competence. The clinician's task is to determine what it is about the client that may be idiosyncratic as well as what may be influenced by the client's culture. The MAP requires a high level of cultural knowledge and expertise on the part of the clinician. Although this approach involves many nonstandardized methods, there is also questionable validity in using standardized assessment methods with populations for whom the methods were not specifically designed.

Clinical assessment of ethnic minorities with the MMPI and MCMI is much more complex than administering the measures and using standard interpretations. Expertise in psychological assessment and in ethnic minority psychology would appear to be requirements before even considering using these measures with ethnic minority clients. Moreover, there is much diversity between and within ethnic minority groups, and it is unlikely that any single clinician has adequate skills to conduct culturally sensitive assessments with all ethnic groups. Nevertheless, a general approach that is culturally sensitive, such as the MAP, is likely to result in more useful psychological assessments of ethnic minority individuals than those "standard" assessments that are most commonly conducted.

Conclusions

The MMPI and MCMI are among the assessment measures most widely used with ethnic minority individuals. Evidence largely suggests limited differences on these measures between European Americans and ethnic minority groups. This lack of ethnic differences does not necessarily mean that the measures are unbiased or that cultural and minority status variables are irrelevant. Unfortunately, the cultural meaning of the behaviors assessed by these measures has not been examined. Between-group comparison of broadly defined ethnic groups is unlikely to yield much useful information. A conceptual basis for research on MMPI and MCMI ethnic difference is necessary, as is a conceptualization of ethnicity and the impact on the ethnic community of the behaviors assessed by these measures. For clinicians who use these measures, including ethnic minorities in the standardization samples of the MCMI and MMPI-2 is a far cry from assurance of cultural sensitivity. Clinicians and researchers who use these measures without consideration of clients' cultural contexts commit what has been referred to as "cultural malpractice" (Hall, 1997). Although the MMPI and MCMI are among the most widely researched and used tests, much more research, and research sophistication, is necessary in using these measures with ethnic minority populations. There is also a great need for culturally sensitive emic measures as standards by which the validity of the MMPI and MCMI with ethnic minority populations can be evaluated.

References

American Psychiatric Association. (1994). *Diagnostic and statistical manual of mental disorders*, (4th ed.). Washington, DC: American Psychiatric Association.

Ben-Porath, Y. S., Butcher, J. N., & Graham, J. R. (1991). Contribution of the MMPI-2 content scales to the differential diagnosis of schizophrenia and major depression. *Psychological Assessment, 3,* 634–640.

Blais, M. A., Benedict, K. B., & Norman, D. K. (1994). Associations among the MCMI-II clinical syndrome scales and the MMPI-2 clinical scales. *Assessment, 1,* 407–413.

Butcher, J. N., Braswell, L., & Raney, D. (1983). A cross-cultural comparison of American Indian, Black, and White inpatients on the MMPI and presenting symptoms. *Journal of Consulting and Clinical Psychology, 51,* 587–594.

Butcher, J. N., Dahlstrom, W. G., Graham, J. R., Tellegen, A., & Kaemmer, B. (1989). *MMPI-2: Manual for administration and scoring.* Minneapolis: University of Minnesota Press.

Casas, J. M., Wagenheim, B. R., Banchero, R., & Mendoza-Romero, J. (1995). Hispanic masculinity: Myth or psychological schema meriting consideration. In A. M. Padilla (Ed.), *Hispanic psychology: Critical issues in theory and research* (pp. 231–244). Thousand Oaks, CA: Sage.

Choca, J., Shanley, L., Peterson, C., Van Denburg, E. (1990). Racial bias and the MCMI. *Journal of Personality Assessment, 54,* 479–490.

Costantino, G., Malgady, R. G., & Rogler, L. H. (1988). *TEMAS (Tell-Me-A-Story) manual.* Los Angeles, CA: Western Psychological Services.

Cross, D. T., & Burger, G. (1982). Ethnicity as a variable in responses to California Psychological Inventory items. *Journal of Personality Assessment, 46,* 153–158.

Dana, R. H. (1993). *Multicultural assessment perspectives for professional psychology.* Needham Heights, MA: Allyn & Bacon.

Davis, W. E., & Greenblatt, R. L. (1990). Age differences among psychiatric inpatients on the MCMI. *Journal of Clinical Psychology, 46,* 770–774.

Davis, W., Greenblatt, R., & Pochyly, J. (1990). Test of MCMI Black norms for five scales. *Journal of Clinical Psychology, 46,* 175–178.

Donat, D., Walters, J., & Hume, A. (1992). MCMI differences between alcoholics and cocaine abusers: Effect of age, sex, and race. *Journal of Personality Assessment, 58,* 96–104.

Garb, H. N. (1997). Race bias, social class bias, and gender bias in clinical judgment. *Clinical Psychology: Science and Practice, 4,* 99–120.

Graham, J. R. (1993). *MMPI-2: Assessing personality and psychopathology* (2nd ed.). New York: Oxford University Press.

Gray-Little, B. (1995). The assessment of psychopathology in racial and ethnic minorities. In J. N. Butcher (Ed.), *Clinical personality assessment: Practical approaches* (pp. 140–157). New York: Oxford University Press.

Greenblatt, R., & Davis, W. (1992). Accuracy of MCMI classification of angry and psychotic Black and White patients. *Journal of Clinical Psychology, 48,* 59–63.

Greene, R. L. (1987). Ethnicity and MMPI performance: A review. *Journal of Consulting and Clinical Psychology, 55,* 497–512.

Greenfield, P. M. (1994). Independence and interdependence as developmental scripts: Implications for theory, research, and practice. In P. M. Greenfield & R. R. Cocking (Eds.), *Cross-cultural roots of minority child development* (pp. 1–37). Hillsdale, NJ: Erlbaum.

Gynther, M. D. (1981). Is the MMPI an appropriate assessment device for Blacks? *Journal of Black Psychology, 7,* 67–75.

Hall, C.C.I. (1997). Cultural malpractice: The growing obsolescence of psychology with the changing U.S. population. *American Psychologist, 52,* 642–651.

Hall, G.C.N., Bansal, A., & Lopez, I. R. (1999). Ethnicity and psychopathology: A meta-analytic review of 31 years of comparative MMPI/MMPI-2 research. *Psychological Assessment, 11,* 186–197.

Hall, G.C.N., & Barongan, C. (1997). Prevention of sexual aggression: Sociocultural risk and protective factors. *American Psychologist, 52,* 5–14.

Helmes, E., & Reddon, J. R. (1993). A perspective on developments in assessing psychopathology: A critical review of the MMPI and MMPI-2. *Psychological Bulletin, 113,* 453–471.

Highwater, J. (1981). *The primal mind: Vision and reality in Indian America.* New York: New American Library.

Hill, H. M., Soriano, F. I., Chen, S. A., & LaFromboise, T. D. (1994). Sociocultural factors in the etiology and prevention of violence among ethnic minority youth. In L. D. Eron, J. H. Gentry, & P. Schegel (Eds.), *Reason to hope: A psychosocial perspective on violence and youth* (pp. 59–97). Washington, DC: American Psychological Association.

Huertin-Roberts, S., Snowden, L., & Miller, L. (1997). Expressions of anxiety in African Americans: Ethnography and the Epidemiological Catchment Area studies. *Culture, Medicine and Psychiatry, 21,* 337–363.

Jones, J. M. (1986). Racism: A cultural analysis of the problem. In J. F. Dovidio & J. L. Gaertner (Eds.), *Prejudice, discrimination, and racism* (pp. 279–314). Orlando: Academic Press.

Jones, J. M. (1997). *Prejudice and racism* (2nd ed.). New York: McGraw-Hill.

Kessler, R. C., McGonagle, K. A., Zhao, S., Nelson, C. B., Hughes, M., Eshleman, S., Wittchen, H., & Kendler, K. S. (1994). Lifetime and 12-month prevalence of DSM-III-R psychiatric disorders in the United States. *Archives of General Psychiatry, 51,* 8–19.

Kohatsu, E. L., & Richardson, T. Q. (1996). Racial and ethnic identity assessment. In L. A. Suzuki, P. J. Meller, & J. G. Ponterotto (Eds.), *Handbook of multicultural assessment: Clinical, psychological, and educational applications* (pp. 611–650). San Francisco: Jossey-Bass.

Kwan, K. (1999). MMPI and MMPI-2 performance of the Chinese: Cross-cultural applicability. *Professional Psychology: Research and Practice, 30,* 260–268.

LaDue, R. A. (1983). Standardization of the Minnesota Multiphasic Personality Inventory for the Colville Indian reservation. *Dissertation Abstracts International, 43,* 3033.

Lewis-Fernandez, R., & Kleinman, A. (1994). Culture, personality, and psychopathology. *Journal of Abnormal Psychology, 103,* 67–71.

Libb, J. W., Murray, J., Thurstin, H., & Alarcon, R. D. (1992). Concordance of the MCMI-II, the MMPI, and Axis I discharge diagnosis in psychiatric inpatients. *Journal of Personality Assessment, 58,* 580–590.

Lucio, G., & Reyes-Lagunes, I. (1996). The Mexican version of the MMPI-2 in Mexico and Nicaragua: Translation, adaptation, and demonstrated equivalency. In J. Butcher (Ed.), *International adaptations of the MMPI-2* (pp. 265–283). Minneapolis: University of Minnesota Press.

McCann, J. T. (1991). Convergent and discriminant validity of the MCMI-II and MMPI personality disorder scales. *Psychological Assessment, 3,* 9–18.

McNulty, J. L., Graham, J. R., Ben-Porath, Y. S., & Stein, L.A.R. (1997). Comparative validity of MMPI-2 scores of African American and Caucasian mental health center clients. *Psychological Assessment, 9,* 464–470.

Mesquita, B., & Frijda, N. H. (1992). Clinical variations in emotions: A review. *Psychological Bulletin, 112,* 179–204.

Millon, T. (1981). *Disorders of personality.* New York: Wiley.

Millon, T. (1994). *Millon Clinical Multiaxial Inventory-III: Manual.* Minneapolis: National Computer Systems.

Nelson, D. V., Novy, D. M., Averill, P. M., & Berry, L. A. (1996). Ethnic comparability of the MMPI in pain patients. *Journal of Clinical Psychology, 52,* 485–497.

Okazaki, S. & Sue, S. (1995). Cultural considerations in psychological assessment of Asian-Americans. In J. N . Butcher (Ed.), *Clinical personality assessment: Practical approaches* (pp. 107–119). New York: Oxford University Press.

Parker, K.C.H., Hanson, R. K., & Hunsley, J. (1988). MMPI, Rorschach, and WAIS: A meta-analytic comparison of reliability, stability, and validity. *Psychological Bulletin, 103,* 367–373.

Pettigrew, T. F., Jackson, J. S., Brika, J. B., Lemaine, G., Meertens, R. W., Wagner, U., & Zick, A. (1998). Out-group prejudice in western Europe. In W. Stroebe & M. Hewstone (Eds.), *European Review of Social Psychology*, Vol. 8. (pp. 241–273). Chichester, England: Wiley.

Phinney, J. (1989). Stages of ethnic identity development in minority group adolescents. *Journal of Early Adolescence, 9*, 34–49.

Phinney, J. (1992). The Multigroup Ethnic Identity Measure: A new scale for use with diverse groups. *Journal of Adolescent Research, 7*, 156–176.

Phinney, J. S. (1996). When we talk about American ethnic groups, what do we mean? *American Psychologist, 51*, 918–927.

Ridley, C. R., Li, L. C., & Hill, C. L. (1998). Multicultural assessment: Reexamination, reconceptualization, and practical application. *Counseling Psychologist, 26*, 827–910.

Roberts, R. E., & Sobhan, M. (1992). Symptoms of depression in adolescence: A comparison of Anglo, African, and Hispanic Americans. *Journal of Youth and Adolescence, 21*, 639–651.

Rogler, L. H. (1999). Methodological sources of cultural insensitivity in mental health research. *American Psychologist, 54*, 424–433.

Sabnani, H. B., & Ponterotto, J. G. (1992). Racial/ethnic minority-specific instrumentation in counseling research: A review, critique, and recommendations. *Measurement and Evaluation in Counseling and Development, 24*, 161–187.

Shiota, N., Krauss, S., & Clark, L. (1996). Adaptation and validation of the Japanese MMPI-2. In J. Butcher (Ed.), *International adaptations of the MMPI-2* (pp. 67–87). Minneapolis: University of Minnesota Press.

Snowden, L. R., & Cheung, F. K. (1990). Use of inpatient mental health services by members of ethnic minority groups. *American Psychologist, 45*, 347–355.

Sorenson, S. B., & Siegel, J. M. (1992). Gender, ethnicity, and sexual assault: Findings from a Los Angeles study. *Journal of Social Issues, 48*, 93–104.

Steele, C. M. (1997). A threat in the air: How stereotypes shape intellectual identity and performance. *American Psychologist, 52*, 613–629.

Stevens, M. J., Kwan, K., & Graybill, D. (1993). Comparison of MMPI-2 scores of foreign Chinese and Caucasian-American students. *Journal of Clinical Psychology, 49*, 23–27.

Sue, D., & Sue, S. (1987). Cultural factors in the clinical assessment of Asian Americans. *Journal of Consulting and Clinical Psychology, 55*, 479–487.

Sue, D. W., & Sue, D. (1999). *Counseling the culturally different: Theory and practice* (3rd ed.). New York: Wiley.

Sue, S. (1991). Ethnicity and culture in psychological research and practice. In J. D. Goodchilds (Ed.), *Psychological perspectives on human diversity in*

America (pp. 51–85). Washington, DC: American Psychological Association.

Sue, S., Keefe, K., Enomoto, K., Durvasula, R. S., & Chao, R. (1996). Asian American and White college students' performance on the MMPI-2. In J. N. Butcher (Ed.), *International adaptations of the MMPI: Research and clinical applications* (pp. 206–220). Minneapolis: University of Minnesota Press.

Sue, S., & Sue, D. (1974). MMPI comparisons between Asian American and non-Asian students utilizing a student health psychiatric clinic. *Journal of Counseling Psychology, 21,* 423–427.

Sue, S., & Zane, N.W.S. (1985). Academic achievement and socioemotional adjustment among Chinese university students. *Journal of Counseling Psychology, 32,* 570–579.

Suzuki, L. A., & Valencia, R. R. (1997). Race-ethnicity and measured intelligence: Educational implications. *American Psychologist, 52,* 1103–1114.

Szapocznik, J., & Kurtines, W. M. (1993). Family psychology and cultural diversity: Opportunities for theory, research, and application. *American Psychologist, 48,* 400–407.

Tran, B. (1996). Vietnamese translation and adaptation of the MMPI-2. In J. Butcher (Ed.), *International adaptations of the MMPI-2* (pp. 175–193). Minneapolis: University of Minnesota Press.

Tsai, D. C., & Pike, P. L. (2000). Effects of acculturation on the MMPI-2 scores of Asian American students. *Journal of Personality Assessment, 74,* 216–230.

Velasquez, R. (1995). Personality assessment of Hispanic clients. In J. N. Butcher (Ed.), *Clinical personality assessment: Practical approaches* (pp. 120–139). Minneapolis: University of Minnesota Press.

Yee, A. H., Fairchild, H. H., Weizmann, F., & Wyatt, G. E. (1993). Addressing psychology's problems with race. *American Psychologist, 48,* 1132–1140.

Zalewski, C., & Gottesman, I. I. (1991). (Hu)man versus mean revisited: MMPI group data and psychiatric diagnosis. *Journal of Abnormal Psychology, 100,* 562–568.

Zalewski, C., & Greene, R. L. (1996). Multicultural usage of the MMPI-2. In L. A. Suzuki, P. J. Meller, & J. G. Ponterotto (Eds.), *Handbook of multicultural assessment: Clinical, psychological, and educational applications* (pp. 77–114). San Francisco: Jossey-Bass.

Zayas, L. H., Torres, L. R., Malcolm, J., & DesRosiers, F. S. (1996). Clinicians' definitions of ethnically sensitive therapy. *Professional Psychology: Research and Practice, 27,* 78–82.

Section Two

· ·

Assessment of Cognitive Abilities

Part Two, Section Two of the *Handbook* comprises chapters focusing on assessing cognitive abilities. The eight chapters in this final section examine use of particular instruments and procedures related to the cognitive area.

In Chapter Fourteen, Robert Sternberg and Elena Grigorenko present an interesting discussion of conceptual issues necessary for understanding ability testing in a multicultural context. They begin by discussing the "transportability" of ability tests and highlight how ability tests reflect values within a particular society. Various conceptions of ability across cultural groups are identified.

Lisa Suzuki, Ellen Short, Alex Pieterse, and John Kugler examine multicultural issues as they pertain to assessing aptitudes in Chapter Fifteen. Specific attention is paid to using the Scholastic Aptitude Test (SAT) and Wechsler scales of intelligence. Alternative testing practices and assessment competencies are also highlighted, along with a case example to illustrate various concepts.

Chapter Sixteen, by Rita Casey, discusses some of the central issues to be considered in conducting culturally sensitive assessments within the social-emotional domain. Strategies for approaching social-emotional assessment are noted and applied to illustrative case examples. The chapter has practical recommendations for taking social and emotional functioning into account during the assessment process.

In Chapter Seventeen, Bruce Bracken and R. Steve McCallum review nonverbal measures of ability. They give a historical overview of the integration of nonverbal subtests in many traditional measures of ability. They also note the diversity of language spoken in schools throughout the United States and the important needs addressed by nonverbal measures. The chapter includes a review of many popular nonverbal measures currently available.

In Chapter Eighteen, Arthur Horton, Christine Carrington, and Ometha Lewis-Jack present neuropsychological assessment in a multicultural context. Their review includes highlights of the history of neuropsychological assessment methods, major neuropsychological approaches, and specific information about various instruments and batteries. The authors acknowledge the impact of acculturation, ethnocentrism, linguistic issues, socioeconomic status, and other factors on this area. The results of studies including a number of racial and ethnic groups are reported.

In Chapter Nineteen, Paul Meller, Phyllis Ohr, and Rebecca Marcus describe the importance of family-oriented, culturally sensitive (FOCUS) assessment of young children. They discuss training issues and models of family-centered assessment. In addition, they provide information on how to best assess young children's developmental competencies within a cultural framework. Specific attention is given to particular methods and instruments in assessing infants and toddlers, including developmental inventories and behavioral observation measures.

In Chapter Twenty, Grace Wong and Amanda Baden explore multicultural assessment practices with older adults. They note special testing issues that must be taken into consideration in assessing the abilities of elderly minority group members. They highlight limitations of many commonly used psychological instruments when applied to an older population. The authors stress the importance of obtaining information on personal and medical history.

Specific attention is given to the use of the Mini-Mental Status Examination and intelligence tests with minority populations. In addition, testing issues related to depression and pseudodementia are described.

Carol Lidz presents information on multicultural issues and dynamic assessment in Chapter Twenty-One. She begins with a discussion of the need for alternative assessment procedures in view of criticisms of traditional, standardized test procedures. The use of dynamic assessment with minority populations is described. Specific studies are cited applying dynamic assessment to groups from diverse backgrounds. Implications of dynamic assessment for clinicians and educators are noted.

Chapter Twenty-Two, written by Craig Frisby, provides information about how academic achievement can be assessed: informal classroom assessment, curriculum-based assessment, individual standardized testing, group standardized testing, and performance or authentic assessment. Racial and ethnic group differences in academic achievement are discussed, with attention to mediating factors that may have an impact on performance.

In Chapter Twenty-Three, the editors (Lisa Suzuki, Joseph Ponterotto, and Paul Meller) look at the evolution of multicultural assessment practices. In particular, they examine the recommendations made in the final chapter of the first edition of the *Handbook of Multicultural Assessment* and take a retrospective look at changes in the field. Though many of the same issues are still evident, the editors note greater attention being paid in the literature to current assessment practices in relation to racial and ethnic minority groups.

14

Ability Testing Across Cultures

Robert J. Sternberg and Elena L. Grigorenko

Many investigators of human abilities take for granted Western views of what human abilities are. They may disagree as to which Western view they accept, but they nevertheless accept one such view. Still, many people in the world have views of abilities that do not correspond well to conventional Western views (Berry, 1974; Das, 1994).

The Transportability of Ability Tests

To what extent can ability tests be transported from one culture to another?

The Standard Positions

The importance of studying indigenous concepts of abilities from around the world has been recognized both by those who believe that cognitive ability tests are transportable from one culture to

Preparation of this article was supported under the Javits Act Program (grant no. R206R950001) as administered by the Office of Educational Research and Improvement, U.S. Department of Education. Grantees undertaking such projects are encouraged to express freely their professional judgment. This article therefore does not necessarily represent the position or policies of the Office of Educational Research and Improvement or the U.S. Department of Education, and no official endorsement should be inferred.

Requests for reprints should be sent to Robert J. Sternberg, Department of Psychology, Yale University, P.O. Box 208205, New Haven, CT 06520–8205.

another and by those who do not. Those researchers who support the first position argue for universalism (Lonner and Adamopoulos, 1997) and, usually, cross-cultural quantification. Because they are interested in discovering both what is universal and what is variable across cultures (Berry, Poortinga, Segall, and Dasen, 1992; van de Vijver and Leung, 1997), these scientists view conventional Western tests as anchors with known psychometric properties that, when translated as necessary, can produce basic data for cross-cultural comparative purposes (Poortinga, 1989).

The underlying assumption here is that universal sets of the "best" ability tests can work anywhere, as long as they are adequately translated and administered by a "native" tester. In this tradition, studying indigenous folk conceptions of abilities means understanding how a particular culture differs from the gold standard of universal abilities captured by the most respected ability tests. The assumption underlying this research, then, is of the universality of abilities despite some degree of cultural specificity in folk conceptions of intelligence.

Adherents to the second position—that ability tests are not transportable from one culture to another—have argued that the concept of intelligence and hence tests of intelligence and cognitive abilities are in large part cultural inventions (for example, Berry, 1974; Sternberg, 1996b; Stigler, Shweder, and Herdt, 1990). When unfolded, this argument implies that conventional ability tests:

1. Presuppose a particular cultural framework, which is not universally shared (Greenfield, 1997)

2. Potentially create closed educational systems that select children and then reward them for abilities tested by conventional tests at the same time that they largely ignore other abilities (Sternberg, 1997)

3. Produce information on developed skills rather than on the ability to develop such skills (Grigorenko and Sternberg, 1998; Sternberg, 1998)

4. Are not easily or at all transportable among cultures (Cole, 1996; Cole, Gay, Glick, and Sharp, 1971; Greenfield, 1997; Laboratory of Comparative Human Cognition, 1982)

Indeed, the abilities needed to adapt to the demands of one culture may be different from those needed to adapt to another (Biesheuvel, 1943; Biesheuvel and Milcenzon, 1953; Gladwin, 1970; Kearins, 1981; Sternberg and others, 2000). According to investigators in this tradition, studying indigenous concepts of abilities is an attempt to recognize and appreciate the natural variability of cultural folk conceptions of abilities. The assumption underlying the research here, then, is the specificity of both intelligence and folk concepts of it.

Regardless of which tradition we are speaking of, the richness of approaches used by psychologists and anthropologists to describe the complexity of indigenous ideas about intelligence is quite remarkable (Sternberg and Kaufman, 1998). These approaches have been developed by cultural outsiders (for example, Berry and Bennett, 1992) and insiders (for example, Mukamurama, 1985).

Approaches to assessment include interviewing parents (for example, Dasen, 1984) and analyzing Piagetian conservation (Greenfield, 1966). Cultural and cross-cultural researchers use methodologies of participatory observation (for example, Fortes, 1938) and firsthand experience of the settings in which abilities are shown (for example, Colby, Jessor, and Shweder, 1996); they use linguistic (for example, Kagame, 1976) and cognitive (for example, Cole, Gay, Glick, and Sharp, 1971) approaches; and they analyze their data with traditional (for example, Super, 1983) and original, specially developed (for example, Wober, 1974) statistical techniques.

Many of the conventional models of human abilities posit a relatively fixed set of entities that are the same from one culture to another. According to these models, abilities are more or less stable entities of individual differences that have a fixed structure and set of relationships in the mind. Ability tests measure some kind of qualities of this structure and set of relationships.

Abilities as Developing Expertise: A Third View on Transportability

An alternative view—the one advanced here—is that of abilities as developing expertise (Sternberg, 1998, 1999). According to this view, conventional mental-ability tests measure only a limited aspect of the range of human ability because they measure only a limited aspect of developing expertise at a particular fixed point in time.

Developing expertise is defined here as the ongoing process of acquiring and consolidating a set of skills needed for a high level of mastery in one or more domains of life performance. All skilled performances go through a process of acquisition by which expertise develops over time, with one or more rates of learning, to an asymptote (which represents a stable, although not necessarily maximal, level of expertise).

The performances that are valued in one culture may differ from those valued in another culture. Hence the kinds of expertise viewed as worthy of being tested may vary as well. Gladwin (1970) has documented the case of the Puluwat, who are able to navigate ships from one island to another without any obvious cues. If most of the readers of this chapter were to take a test relevant for performance in Puluwat society, chances are they would do quite poorly.

The difference in what is important, and where, is not limited to the Puluwat culture. Nuñes (1994) has reported related findings from a series of studies she conducted in Brazil (Ceci and Roazzi, 1994). Street children's adaptive intelligence is tested to the limit by their ability to form and successfully run a street business. If they fail to do so successfully, they risk starvation or, should they resort to stealing, murder at the hands of death squads. Nuñes and her collaborators have found that the same children who are doing the mathematics needed for running a successful street business cannot do well with the same type of mathematics problem presented in an abstract, paper-and-pencil format.

From the standpoint of conventional abilities, this result is puzzling. From the standpoint of developing expertise, it is not. Street children grow up in an environment that fosters development of practical skills, but not academic mathematical ones. We know that even the conventional academic kind of expertise often fails to show transfer (for example, Gick and Holyoak, 1980). It is scarcely surprising, then, that there would be little transfer here. The street children have developed the kind of practical arithmetical expertise they need for survival and even success, but they will get no credit for these skills if they take a conventional ability test.

It also seems likely that if the scales were reversed, and privileged children who do well on conventional ability tests or in school were forced out onto the street, many of them would not survive long. Indeed, in the ghettoes of urban America, many children and adults who, for one reason or another end up on the street, barely survive—or do not make it at all.

Differences in cultural adaptation apply not only in developing cultures. The skills required to survive in war-torn Kosovo might leave many high-IQ people dead. Even in modern-day Russia, many of the high-IQ people who made it into once prestigious jobs such as that of college professor are now poor and in some cases having trouble surviving, whereas people who have entrepreneurial skills but not necessarily the highest IQ have risen to the top. Indeed, Grigorenko and Sternberg (in press) have found that tests of practical ability measure skills that are more important to adaptation in modern-day Russia than do tests of conventional fluid and crystallized abilities. In particular, the tests of practical ability were better predictors of reduced levels of anxiety and depression and of higher levels of physical health than were the academic-ability tests.

Good performance on ability tests, then, requires certain kinds of expertise. To the extent these kinds of expertise overlap with those required by schooling or the place, there is a correlation between the tests and performance in school or the workplace. But such correlations represent no intrinsic relation between abilities and other kinds of performance; rather, they show overlaps in the kinds of expertise needed to perform well under various circumstances. Thus, abilities represent a form of attainment, as do other forms of attainment. A culture might value forms of attainment quite different from those relevant to conventional tests of ability.

In a collaborative study among children near Kisumu, Kenya (see Sternberg and Grigorenko, 1997; Sternberg and others, in press), we devised a test of practical ability that measures informal knowledge for an important aspect of adaptation to the environment in rural Kenya, namely, knowledge of the identity and use of natural herbal medicines that can be used to combat illness. The children use this informal knowledge on average once a week in treating themselves or suggesting treatments to other children, so this knowledge is a routine part of their everyday existence. By *informal knowledge*, we are referring to kinds of knowledge not taught in school and not assessed on tests given in school.

The idea of our research was that children who knew what these medicines were, what they were used for, and how they should be dosed would be in a better position to adapt to their environment than children without this informal knowledge.

We found substantial individual differences in tacit knowledge of these natural herbal medicines among like-aged and schooled children. More important, however, was the correlation between scores on this test and scores on an English-language vocabulary test (the Mill Hill), a Dholuo equivalent (Dholuo is the community and home language), and the Raven Coloured Progressive Matrices. We found significantly *negative* correlations between our test and the English-language vocabulary test, as well as with tests of school-based English-language achievement. Correlations of our test with the other tests were also negative. The better the children did on the test of indigenous tacit knowledge, the worse they did on the tests of conventional abilities and achievement, and vice versa. Why might we have obtained such a finding?

From our ethnographic observation, we believe a possible reason is that parents in the village may emphasize either a more indigenous or a more Western education. Some parents (and their children) see little value to school. They do not see how success in school connects with the future of children who will spend their whole lives in a village, where the parents do not believe the young people need the expertise the school teaches. Other parents and children seem to see Western schooling as having value in itself, or potentially as a ticket out of the confines of the village. The parents thus tend to emphasize one type of education or the other for their children, with corresponding results. The kinds of developing expertise the families value differ, and so therefore do scores on the tests. From this point of view, the intercorrelational structure of tests tells us nothing intrinsic about the structure of intelligence per se, but rather something about how abilities as developing forms of expertise structure themselves in interaction with the demands of the environment. Although we cannot now prove it, we doubt this kind of finding is limited to rural Kenya or to Africa, or to developing countries.

There is nothing privileged about conventional ability tests. Although they are used as predictors, they can be and sometimes are used as criteria. One could as easily use, say, academic achievement to predict ability-related scores as ability-related scores to predict academic achievement.

According to this view, although ability tests may have temporal priority relative to various criteria in their administration (that is, ability tests are administered first; later, criterion indices of performance, such as grade point average or achievement test scores, are collected), the constructs measured by the ability tests have no psychological priority. All of the various kinds of assessment are of the same kind psychologically. What distinguishes ability tests from other kinds of assessment is how the ability tests are used (usually predictively) rather than what they measure. There is no qualitative distinction among the various kinds of assessment. All tests measure various kinds of developing expertise.

Conventional tests of abilities measure achievement that individuals presumably should have accomplished several years back (see also Anastasi and Urbina, 1997). Of course, this presumption assumes Western schooling and thus is very limited. Tests such as vocabulary, reading comprehension, verbal analogies, arithmetic problem solving, and the like are all, in part, tests of achievement. Even abstract-reasoning tests measure achievement in dealing with geometric symbols—skills taught in Western schools (Laboratory of Comparative Human Cognition, 1982). One might as well use academic performance to predict ability test scores.

The problem regarding the traditional model is not in its statement of a correlation between ability tests and other forms of achievement but in its proposal of a causal relation whereby the tests reflect a construct that is somehow causal of, rather than merely temporally antecedent to, later success. The fine distinction between ability and achievement tests is shown in dynamic testing, which combines elements of each (see Brown and Ferrara, 1985; Budoff, 1987a, 1987b; Campione, 1989; Carlson and Wiedl, 1980; Feuerstein, Rand, and Hoffman, 1979; Grigorenko and Sternberg, 1998; Guthke, 1992; Lidz, 1987, 1995; Vygotsky, 1978).

In a collaborative study in Bagamoyo, Tanzania (Sternberg and others, 1999), we have been investigating dynamic tests administered to children. Although dynamic tests have been developed for a number of purposes (see Grigorenko and Sternberg, 1998), one of our particular purposes was to look at how dynamic testing affects score patterns. In particular, we developed more or less conventional ability tests but administered them in a dynamic format. The tests were of sorting geometric figures, linear syllogisms, and twenty questions. First, students took a pretest. Then they received a short period of instruction (generally no more than ten to fifteen minutes per subtest) on how to improve their performance in the expertise measured by each test. Then the children took a posttest.

A first finding was that scores increased significantly from pretest to posttest. Such an effect could be due, of course, to practice effects. But the finding suggests that the scores are not stable and that one probably should not draw strong conclusions about the level of abilities of people in developing cultures on the basis of scores on a single administration of a static test (as did, for example, Herrnstein and Murray, 1994).

A second finding was that the correlation between pretest and posttest scores, although statistically significant, was weak (about .3). In other words, even a short period of instruction fairly drastically changed the rank order of the students on the test. Thus, identifying "bright" students on the basis of a static test appeared to be a questionable enterprise.

The third finding pertained to correlating test scores with other kinds of performance. The critical question, of course, is not whether there is a change, but what it means. In particular, which predicts other kinds of cognitive performance better: pretest scores or learning? We found that posttest scores predicted other kinds of cognitive performance better than did pretest scores. We examined the pretest data for floor effects, as the lower correlation for the pretest might have been due to those effects. There were no such effects.

We again interpret these results in terms of the model of developing expertise. The Tanzanian students had developed very little expertise in the skills required to take American-style intelligence tests. Thus even a short intervention could have a fairly substantial effect on their scores. Once the students developed somewhat more of this test-taking expertise through a short intervention, their scores changed and became more reflective of their true capabilities for cognitive work.

The developing-expertise view in no way rules out the contribution of genetic factors as a source of individual difference in who is able to develop a given amount of expertise. People may differ genetically in their ability to acquire expertise. But how genes play themselves out inevitably is affected by the environment. Phenotypes always represent covariation and interaction between genotypes and the environment. The contribution of genes to an individual's intelligence cannot be directly measured, or even directly estimated. Rather, what is measured is a portion of what is expressed, namely, manifestations of developing expertise.

What Abilities Should Be Measured?

Intelligence is a term that is sometimes used to refer to those abilities deemed most important by a society and thus worthy of measurement. What is intelligence? It turns out that the answer depends on whom you ask, and it differs widely across disciplines, time, and place. Ability tests need to reflect these differences.

Western Psychological Views

How have Western psychologists conceived of the abilities constituting intelligence? Almost none of these views are adequately expressed by Boring's operationistic view of intelligence (1923): what intelligence tests test. Thus, whatever ability tests measure is what should be measured. This definition is about as circular as one can get.

Not all definitions have been circular, however. In a symposium on experts' definitions of intelligence ("Intelligence and its measurement . . . ," 1921), researchers emphasized the importance of the ability to learn and the ability to adapt to the environment. Sixty-five years later, Sternberg and Detterman (1986) conducted a similar symposium, again asking experts their views on intelligence. Learning and adaptive abilities retained their importance, and a new emphasis crept in: metacognition, or the ability to understand and control oneself. Of course, the name is new but the idea is not, because long before Aristotle emphasized the importance for intelligence of knowing oneself.

Views from Cultures Around the World

It is not simply that, in some cases, Western notions about intelligence are not shared by other cultures. Consider, for example, at the mental level, the Western emphasis on speed of mental processing (Sternberg, Conway, Ketron, and Bernstein, 1981; see also Berry, 1984). Other cultures may even be suspicious of the quality of work that is done very quickly. Indeed, some of them emphasize depth rather than speed of processing. They are not alone: some prominent Western theorists have pointed out the importance of depth of processing for full command of material (for example, Craik and Lockhart, 1972).

Yang and Sternberg (1997a) have reviewed Chinese philosophical conceptions of intelligence. The Confucian perspective emphasizes the characteristic of benevolence and of doing what is right. As in the Western notion, the intelligent person spends a great deal of effort in learning, enjoys learning, and persists in lifelong learning with a great deal of enthusiasm. The Taoist tradition, in contrast, emphasizes the importance of humility, freedom from conventional standards of judgment, and full knowledge of oneself as well as of external conditions.

The difference between Eastern and Western conceptions of intelligence may persist even in the present day. Yang and Sternberg (1997b) studied contemporary Taiwanese Chinese conceptions of intelligence and found five underlying factors:

1. A general cognitive factor, much like the g factor in conventional Western tests

2. Interpersonal intelligence

3. Intrapersonal intelligence

4. Intellectual self-assertion

5. Intellectual self-effacement

In a related study but with dissimilar results, Chen (1994) found three factors underlying Chinese conceptualizations of intelligence: nonverbal reasoning ability, verbal reasoning ability, and rote memory. The difference may be due to subpopulations of Chinese, differing methodology, or when the studies were done.

The factors uncovered in both studies differ substantially from those identified in U.S. people's conceptions of intelligence by Sternberg, Conway, Ketron, and Bernstein (1981): practical problem solving, verbal ability, and social competence. In both cases, though, people's implicit theories of intelligence seem to go quite far beyond what conventional psychometric intelligence tests measure. Of course, comparing the Chen (1994) and Sternberg, Conway, Ketron, and Bernstein (1981) studies simultaneously varies both language and culture.

Chen and Chen (1988) varied only language. They explicitly compared the concepts of intelligence of Chinese graduates from Chinese-language and English-language schools in Hong Kong. They found that both groups considered nonverbal reasoning skills as the most relevant skills for measuring intelligence. Verbal reasoning and social skills came next, and then numerical skill. Memory was seen as least important. The group schooled in the Chinese language, however, tended to rate verbal skills as less important than did the group schooled in English. Moreover, in an earlier study, Chen, Braithwaite, and Huang (1982) found that Chinese students viewed memory of facts as important for intelligence, whereas Australian students viewed this skill as of only trivial importance.

Das (1994), also reviewing Eastern notions of intelligence, has suggested that in Buddhist and Hindu philosophies intelligence involves waking up, noticing, recognizing, understanding, and comprehending, but also includes such things as determination, mental effort, and even feelings and opinions in addition to more intellectual elements.

Cultural differences in conception of intelligence have been recognized for some time. Gill and Keats (1980) noted that Australian university students value academic skills and the ability to adapt to new events as critical to intelligence, whereas Malay students value practical skills, as well as speed and creativity. Dasen (1984) found Malay students to emphasize both social and cognitive attributes in their conception of intelligence.

The differences between East and West may be due to the kinds of skills valued by the two cultures (Srivastava and Misra, 1996). Western cultures and their schools emphasize what might be called "technological intelligence" (Mundy-Castle, 1974), and so such things as artificial intelligence and so-called smart bombs are viewed, in some sense, as intelligent, or smart.

Western schooling also emphasizes other things (Srivastava and Misra, 1996), such as generalization, or going beyond the information given (Connolly and Bruner, 1974; Goodnow, 1976), speed (Sternberg, 1985), minimal moves to a solution (Newell and Simon, 1972), and creative thinking (Goodnow, 1976). Moreover, silence is interpreted as a lack of knowledge (Irvine, 1978). In contrast, the Wolof tribe in Africa views people of higher social class and distinction as speaking less (Irvine, 1978). This difference between the Wolof and Western notions suggests the usefulness of looking at African notions of intelligence as a possible contrast to U.S. notions.

Studies in Africa in fact constitute yet another window on the substantial differences. Ruzgis and Grigorenko (1994) have argued that in Africa conceptions of intelligence revolve largely around skills that help to facilitate and maintain harmonious and stable intergroup relations; intragroup relations are probably equally important, and at times more so. For example, Serpell (1974, 1982, 1993) found that Chewa adults in Zambia emphasize social responsibilities, cooperativeness, and obedience as important to intelligence; intelligent children are expected to be respectful of adults. Kenyan parents also emphasize responsible participation in family and social life as important aspects of intelligence (Super and Harkness, 1982; Super, 1983). In Zimbabwe, the word for intelligence, *ngware*, actually means to be prudent and cautious, particularly in social relationships. Among the Baoule, service to the family and community and politeness toward and respect for elders are seen as key to intelligence (Dasen, 1984).

Similar emphasis on social aspects of intelligence has been found among two other African groups, the Songhay of Mali and the Samia of Kenya (Putnam and Kilbride, 1980). Regarding intelligence, the Yoruba, another African tribe, emphasize the importance of depth—of listening rather than just talking—and of being able to see all aspects of an issue and place it in proper overall context (Durojaiye, 1993).

Emphasis on the social aspects of intelligence is not limited to African cultures. Notions of intelligence in many Asian cultures also emphasize the social aspect of intelligence more than does the conventional Western or IQ-based notion (Azuma and Kashiwagi, 1987; Lutz, 1985; Poole, 1985; White, 1985).

In our own collaborative work, we have found that conceptions of intelligence in Kenya are quite different from those in the West (Grigorenko and others, in press). The rural Kenyan conception seems to have four parts. First, the concept of *rieko* can be translated as intelligence, smartness, knowledge, ability, skill, competence, and power. Along with the general concept of *rieko*, the Luo people distinguish among various specialized representations of this concept, some characterized by the source of *rieko* (such as school or home).

Luoro is the second main quality of children and people in general. It encompasses a whole field of concepts roughly corresponding to social qualities such as respect and care for others, obedience, diligence, consideration, and readiness to share. *Luoro* has an unequivocal positive meaning and was always mentioned as a necessity in response to questions such as "What is most important for a good child to have?" and "What should people have to lead a happy life?" When people were asked to compare the relative importance for an individual's life of *rieko* and *luoro*, respondents generally gave preference to *luoro*. Interestingly, the only two respondents ranking *rieko* higher, when compared with *luoro*, were outsiders to the local community who had a tertiary education and considerable wealth by village standards.

Rieko and *luoro* are complementary. *Rieko* is a positive attribute only if *luoro* is also present. Ideally, the power of pure individual abilities should be kept under control by social rules. A child lacking *luoro* has the potential to use his or her *rieko* for selfish interests and even against others. On the other hand, the child lacking *rieko* but possessing *luoro* is likely to develop *rieko* because, as a primary school teacher put it in an interview, "her humbleness (*luoro*) would lead her to asking people and learning by accepting their advice."

Third, *paro* overlaps with both *luoro* and *rieko* and, roughly translated, means thinking. Specifically, *paro* refers to the thought processes required to identify a problem and its solution, and to the thought processes involved in caring for other people. A child with good thinking (*paro maber*) could thus, for example, be a child who is able to react rationally in the event of another person's accident, or one who is able to collect wood, burn charcoal, and sell it at a favorable price to help his old grandmother.

The concept of *paro* stresses the procedural nature of intelligence. In essence, *paro* occupies an intermediate position between the potentiality of *rieko* (its ability aspects) and the partially moral connotation of an outcome (the deed) done with or without *luoro*. *Paro* also reflects the idea of initiative and innovation, for example, in designing a new technical device. *Paro* encompasses the process of thinking, the ability to think, and the specific kind of thinking that an individual demonstrates.

Like *rieko*, *paro* is morally ambiguous and can lead to good or bad outcomes. Also, a person can have too much *paro*. For example, too much thinking prevents the person from actually doing something; the person just thinks (*oparo kende*) but does not act.

Fourth, *winjo*, like *paro*, is linked to both *rieko* and *luoro*. *Winjo* means comprehending and understanding. It points to the child's ability to comprehend, that is, to process what is said or what is going on (here it is linked to *rieko*) and to grasp what is appropriate and inappropriate in a situation, that is, to understand and do what one is told by adults or to derive from the situation what is appropriate to do (here it is linked to *luoro*). It shares with the other key terms the feature that its meaning is a function of context. For a teacher in school, it means that a child runs an errand as told. In contrast, a grandmother teaching a child about healing might emphasize the aspect of procedural learning combined with attention to another person.

These four conceptions of intelligence emphasize social skills much more than do conventional U.S. conceptions of intelligence, at the same time that they recognize the importance of cognitive aspects of intelligence. But it is important to realize, again, that there is no one overall U.S. conception of intelligence. Indeed, Okagaki and Sternberg (1993) found that ethnic groups in San Jose, California, differed in their conceptions of what it means to be intelligent. For example, Latino parents of schoolchildren tended to emphasize the importance of social-competence skills in their conception of intelligence, whereas Asian parents tended rather heavily to emphasize the importance of cognitive skills. Anglo parents also placed more emphasis on cognitive skills.

Teachers, representing the dominant culture, tended to emphasize cognitive more than social-competence skills. The rank order of performance of children from various groups (including subgroups within the Latino and Asian groups) could be perfectly predicted by the extent to which their parents shared the teacher's conception of intelligence. In other words, teachers tended to reward those children who were socialized into a view of intelligence that happened to correspond to the teacher's own. Yet, as we shall argue later, social aspects of intelligence, broadly defined, may be as important as (or even more important than) cognitive aspects of intelligence in later life. Sometimes accepted social skills may interfere with the Western paradigm for taking ability tests.

Taking Ability Tests

Patricia Greenfield (1997) has done a number of studies in a variety of cultures and found that the kinds of test-taking expertise assumed to be universal in the United States and other Western countries are by no means universal. She found, for example, that children in Mayan cultures (and probably in other highly collectivist cultures as well) were puzzled when they were not allowed to collaborate with parents or others on test questions. In the United States, of course, such collaboration would be viewed as cheating. But in a collectivist culture, someone who had not developed this kind of collaborative expertise—and moreover, someone who did not use it—would be perceived as lacking important adaptive skills (see also Laboratory of Comparative Human Cognition, 1982).

Cognitive categories also may interfere with Western paradigms for test taking. In another famous example, Cole, Gay, Glick, and Sharp (1971) asked adult members of the Kpelle tribe to sort names of various kinds of objects, such as fruits, vegetables, or vehicles of conveyance. They found that the adults sorted functionally rather than taxonomically. For example, they might sort "apple" with "eat," or "car" with "gas," rather than sorting various kinds of apples together under the word "apple," and then "fruits," and perhaps then "foods." The Kpelle way of doing this task would be considered, in the West, cognitively immature. It is how young children would complete the task.

Indeed, virtually any theorist of cognitive development (for example, Piaget, 1972) would view functional sorting as inferior; on the vocabulary section of an intelligence test such as the Wechsler or the Stanford-Binet, a functional definition of, say, an automobile as using gas would receive less credit than a taxonomic definition, say, of an automobile as a vehicle of conveyance. The researchers tried without success to get the Kpelle to sort in an alternative way.

Finally, they gave up, and started packing. As an afterthought, a researcher asked a member of the tribe how a stupid person would sort. The man had no trouble sorting the terms—taxonomically. In other words, he considered stupid what a Western psychologist would consider smart. Why? Because in everyday life, for the most part, our thinking really is functional. For example, we think about eating an apple; we do not think about the apple as a fruit, which is a food, which is an organic substance.

Luria (1976) ran into similar issues in studies of peasants in one of the Asian republics of the former USSR. In one study, peasants were shown a hammer, a saw, a log, and a hatchet, and were asked which three items were similar. An illiterate central Asian peasant insisted that all four fit together, even when the interviewer suggested that the concept of "tool" could be used for the hammer, saw, and hatchet, but not for the log. The participant in this instance combined the features of the four items that were relevant in terms of his culture and arrived at a functional or situational concept (perhaps of "things you need to build a hut").

In many of Luria's studies, the unschooled peasants have great difficulty in solving the problems given them. Often, they appear to be thrown off by an apparent discrepancy between the terms of the problem and what they know to be true. For example, take one of the math problems: "From Shakhimardan to Vuadil it is three hours on foot, while to Fergana it is six hours. How much time does it take to go on foot from Vuadil to Fergana?" The participant's response to this problem was, "No, it's six hours from Vuadil to Shakhimardan. You're wrong. . . . It's far and you wouldn't get there in three hours" (Luria, 1976, p. 129). Clearly, the peasant did not accept the task.

Conclusion

Ability testing is often conceived of in a culturally limited way. It is understandable that people in any culture view the abilities that are important to them as the ones that are important to test anywhere. The problem is that these abilities may not have the value elsewhere that they have in the culture that creates the test, at the same time that others may be fundamentally important that are not in the culture that creates the test. Ability testing needs to take into account the context in which it is done, and to take into account exactly what kinds of developing expertise are important in a given locale.

References

Anastasi, A. & Urbina, S. (1997). *Psychological testing* (7th ed.). Upper Saddle River, NJ: Prentice Hall. (Original work published in 1957)

Azuma, H., & Kashiwagi, K. (1987). Descriptions for an intelligent person: A Japanese study. *Japanese Psychological Research, 29*, 17–26.

Berry, J. W. (1974). Radical cultural relativism and the concept of intelligence. In J. W. Berry & P. R. Dasen (Eds.), *Culture and cognition: Readings in cross-cultural psychology* (pp. 225–229). London: Methuen.

Berry, J. W. (1984). Towards a universal psychology of cognitive competence. In P. S. Fry (Ed.), *Changing conceptions of intelligence and intellectual functioning* (pp. 35–61). Amsterdam: North-Holland.

Berry, J. W., & Bennett, J. A. (1992). Cree conceptions of cognitive competence. *International Journal of Psychology, 27*, 73, 88.

Berry, J. W., Poortinga, Y. H., Segall, M. H., & Dasen, P. R. (1992). *Cross-cultural psychology: Research and applications*. New York: Cambridge University Press.

Biesheuvel, S. (1943). *African intelligence*. Johannesburg: South African Institute of Race Relations.

Biesheuvel, S., & Milcenzon, S. (1953). The effect of diet on the test performance of African mine labourers. *Journal of the National Institute of Personnel Research, South African Council of Scientific and Industrial Research, 5*, 173–175.

Boring, E. G. (1923, June 6). Intelligence as the tests test it. *New Republic*, 35–37.

Brown, A. L., & Ferrara, R. A. (1985). Diagnosing zones of proximal development. In J. V. Wertsch (Ed.), *Culture, communication, and cognition: Vygotskian perspectives* (pp. 273–305). New York: Cambridge University Press.

Budoff, M. (1987a). Measures for assessing learning potential. In C. S. Lidz (Ed.), *Dynamic assessment* (pp. 173–195). New York: Guilford Press.

Budoff, M. (1987b). The validity of learning potential. In C. S. Lidz (Ed.), *Dynamic assessment* (pp. 52–81). New York: Guilford Press.

Campione, J. C. (1989). Assisted assessment: A taxonomy of approaches and an outline of strengths and weaknesses. *Journal of Learning Disabilities, 22,* 151–165.

Carlson, J. S., & Wiedl, K. H. (1980). Applications of a dynamic testing approach in intelligence assessment: Empirical results and theoretical formulations. *Zeitschrift für Differentielle und Diagnostische Psychologie, 1*(4), 303–318.

Ceci, S. J., & Roazzi, A. (1994). The effects of context on cognition: postcards from Brazil. In R. J. Sternberg & R. K. Wagner (Eds.), *Mind in context: Interactionist perspectives on human intelligence* (pp. 74–101). New York: Cambridge University Press.

Chen, M. J. (1994). Chinese and Australian concepts of intelligence. *Psychology and Developing Societies, 6,* 101–117.

Chen, M. J., Braithwaite, V., & Huang, J. T. (1982). Attributes of intelligent behaviour: Perceived relevance and difficulty by Australian and Chinese students. *Journal of Cross-Cultural Psychology, 13,* 139–156.

Chen, M. J., & Chen, H. C. (1988). Concepts of intelligence: A comparison of Chinese graduates from Chinese and English schools in Hong Kong. *International Journal of Psychology, 223,* 471–487.

Colby, A., Jessor, R., & Shweder, R. (Eds.). (1996). *Ethnography and human development.* Chicago: University of Chicago Press.

Cole, M. (1996). *Cultural psychology: A once and future discipline.* Cambridge, MA: Harvard University Press.

Cole, M., Gay, J., Glick, J., & Sharp, D. W. (1971). *The cultural context of learning and thinking.* New York: Basic Books.

Connolly, H., & Bruner, J. (1974). Competence: Its nature and nurture. In K. Connolly & J. Bruner (Eds.), *The growth of competence.* New York: Academic Press.

Craik, F.I.M., & Lockhart, R. S. (1972). Levels of processing: A framework for memory research. *Journal of Verbal Learning and Verbal Behavior, 11,* 671–684.

Das, J. P. (1994). Eastern views of intelligence. In R. J. Sternberg (Ed.), *Encyclopedia of human intelligence* (Vol. 1, pp. 387–391). New York: Macmillan.

Dasen, P. (1984). The cross-cultural study of intelligence: Piaget and the Baoule. *International Journal of Psychology, 19,* 407–434.

Durojaiye, M.O.A. (1993). Indigenous psychology in Africa. In U. Kim & J. W. Berry (Eds.), *Indigenous psychologies: Research and experience in cultural context.* Thousand Oaks, CA: Sage.

Feuerstein, R., Rand, Y., & Hoffman, M. B. (1979). *The dynamic assessment of retarded performers: The learning potential assessment device, theory, instruments, and techniques.* Baltimore: University Park Press.

Fortes, M. (1938). Social and psychological aspects of education in Taleland. *Africa, 11(4)*, 1–64.

Gick, M., & Holyoak, K. (1980). Analogical problem solving. *Cognitive Psychology, 12*, 306–355.

Gill, R., & Keats, D. M. (1980). Elements of intellectual competence: Judgments by Australian and Malay university students. *Journal of Cross-Cultural Psychology, 11*, 233–243.

Gladwin, T. (1970). *East is a big bird.* Cambridge, MA: Harvard University Press.

Goodnow, J. J. (1976). The nature of intelligent behavior: Questions raised by cross-cultural studies. In L. Resnick (Ed.), *The nature of intelligence,* (pp. 169–188). Hillsdale, NJ: Erlbaum.

Greenfield, P. M. (1966). On culture and conservation. In J. S. Bruner, R. R. Oliver, & P. M. Greenfield (Eds.), *Studies in cognitive growth* (pp. 225–256). New York: Wiley.

Greenfield, P. M. (1997). You can't take it with you: Why abilities assessments don't cross cultures. *American Psychologist, 52(10)*, 1115–1124.

Grigorenko, E. L., Geissler, P. W., Prince, R., Okatcha, F., Nokes, C., Kenny, D. A., Bundy, D. A., & Sternberg, R. J. (in press). The organization of Luo conceptions of intelligence: A study of implicit theories in a Kenyan village. *International Journal of Behavioral Development.*

Grigorenko, E. L., & Sternberg, R. J. (in press). Analytical, creative, and practical intelligence as predictors of self-reported adaptive functioning: A case study in Russia. *Intelligence.*

Grigorenko, E. L., & Sternberg, R. J. (1998). Dynamic testing. *Psychological Bulletin, 124*, 75–111.

Guthke, J. (1992). Learning tests: The concept, main research findings, problems and trends. *Learning and Individual Differences, 4*, 137–151.

Herrnstein, R. J, & Murray, C. (1994). *The bell curve.* New York: Free Press.

Intelligence and its measurement: A symposium. 1921. *Journal of Educational Psychology, 12*, 123–147, 195–216, 271–275.

Irvine, J. T. (1978). "Wolof magical thinking": Culture and conservation revisited. *Journal of Cross-Cultural Psychology, 9*, 300–310.

Kagame, A. (1976). *La philosophie bantu comparée* [The Bantu philosophy compared]. Paris: Présence Africaine/UNESCO.

Kearins, J. M. (1981). Visual spatial memory in Australian aboriginal children of the desert regions. *Cognitive Psychology, 13*, 434–460.

Laboratory of Comparative Human Cognition (1982). Culture and intelligence. In R. J. Sternberg (Ed.), *Handbook of human intelligence* (pp. 642–719). New York: Cambridge University Press.

Lidz, C. S. (Ed.). (1987). *Dynamic assessment.* New York: Guilford Press.

Lidz, C. S. (1995). Dynamic assessment and the legacy of L. S. Vygotsky. *School Psychology International, 16*, 143–153.

Lonner, W. J., & Adamopoulos, J. (1997). Culture as antecedent to behavior. In J. W. Berry, Y. Poortinga, & J. Pandey (Eds.), *Handbook of cross-cultural psychology: Theoretical and methodological perspectives* (Vol. 1, pp. 43–83). Needham Heights, MA: Allyn & Bacon.

Luria, A. R. (1976). *Basic problems of neurolinguistics.* The Hague, Netherlands: Mouton.

Lutz, C. (1985). Ethnopsychology compared to what? Explaining behaviour and consciousness among the Ifaluk. In G. M. White & J. Kirkpatrick (Eds.), *Person, self, and experience: Exploring Pacific ethnopsychologies* (pp. 35–79). Berkeley: University of California Press.

Mukamurama, D. (1985). *La notion d'intelligence ubwenge dans la culture rwandaise: essai d'une définition émique de l'intelligence dans sa conception intra-culturelle* [The notion of intelligence: Ubwenge in the Rwandan culture: Essay on an emic definition of intelligence in their intra-cultural conception]. Fribourg: Mémoire de licence.

Mundy-Castle, A. C. (1974). Social and technological intelligence in Western or non-Western cultures. *Universitas, 4*, 46–52.

Newell, A., & Simon, H. A. (1972). *Human problem solving.* Upper Saddle River, NJ: Prentice Hall.

Nuñes, T. (1994). Street intelligence. In R. J. Sternberg (Ed.), *Encyclopedia of human intelligence* (Vol. 2, pp. 1045–1049). New York: Macmillan.

Okagaki, L., & Sternberg, R. J. (1993). Parental beliefs and children's school performance. *Child Development, 64*(1), 36–56.

Piaget, J. (1972). *The psychology of intelligence.* Totowa, NJ: Littlefield Adams.

Poole, F.J.P. (1985). Coming into social being: Cultural images of infants in Bimin-Kuskusmin folk psychology. In G. M. White & J. Kirkpatrick (Eds.), *Person, self, and experience: Exploring Pacific ethnopsychologies* (pp. 183–244). Berkeley: University of California Press.

Poortinga, Y. H. (1989). Equivalence of cross-cultural data: An overview of basic issues. *International Journal of Psychology, 24*, 737–756.

Putnam, D. B., & Kilbride, P. L. (1980). *A relativistic understanding of social intelligence among the Songhay of Mali and Samia of Kenya.* Paper presented at the meeting of the Society for Cross-Cultural Research, Philadelphia.

Ruzgis, P. M., & Grigorenko, E. L. (1994). Cultural meaning systems, intelligence and personality. In R. J. Sternberg & P. Ruzgis (Eds.), *Personality and intelligence* (pp. 248–270). New York: Cambridge University Press.

Serpell, R. (1974). Aspects of intelligence in a developing country. *African Social Research, 17,* 576–596.

Serpell, R. (1982). Measures of perception, skills, and intelligence. In W. W. Hartup (Ed.), *Review of child development research* (Vol. 6, pp. 392–440). Chicago: University of Chicago Press.

Serpell, R. (1993). *The significance of schooling: Life journeys in an African society.* New York: Cambridge University Press.

Srivastava, A. K., & Misra, G. (1996). Changing perspectives on understanding intelligence: An appraisal. *Indian Psychological Abstracts and Review, 3,* 1–34.

Sternberg, R. J. (1985). *Beyond IQ: A triarchic theory of human intelligence.* New York: Cambridge University Press.

Sternberg, R. J. (1996a). Matching abilities, instruction, and assessment: Reawakening the sleeping giant of ATI. In I. Dennis & P. Tapsfield (Eds.), *Human abilities: Their nature and measurement* (pp. 167–181). Hillsdale, NJ: Erlbaum.

Sternberg, R. J. (1996b). What should we ask about intelligence? *American Scholar, 65,* 205–217.

Sternberg, R. J. (1997). *Successful intelligence.* New York: Plume.

Sternberg, R. J. (1998). A balance theory of wisdom. *Review of General Psychology, 2*(4), 347–365.

Sternberg, R. J. (1999). Intelligence as developing expertise. *Contemporary Educational Psychology, 24,* 359–375.

Sternberg, R. J., Conway, B. E., Ketron, J. L., & Bernstein, M. (1981). People's conceptions of intelligence. *Journal of Personality and Social Psychology, 41,* 37–55.

Sternberg, R. J., & Detterman, D. K. (1986). *What is intelligence?* Norwood, NJ: Ablex.

Sternberg, R. J., Forsythe, G. B., Hedlund, J., Horvath, J., Snook, S. Williams, W. M. Wagner, R. K., & Grigorenko, E. L. (2000). *Practical intelligence in everyday life.* New York: Cambridge University Press.

Sternberg, R. J., & Grigorenko, E. L. (1997, Fall). The cognitive costs of physical and mental ill health: Applying the psychology of the developed world to the problems of the developing world. *Eye on Psi Chi, 2*(1), 20–27.

Sternberg, R. J., Grigorenko, E. L., Ngorosho, D., Tantufuye, E., Mbise, A., Nokes, K., & Bundy, D. A. (1999). Hidden intellectual potential in rural Tanzanian school children. Manuscript submitted for publication.

Sternberg, R. J., & Kaufman J. C. (1998). Human abilities. *Annual Review of Psychology, 49*, 479–502.

Sternberg, R. J., Nokes, K., Geissler, P. W., Prince, R., Okatcha, F., Bundy, D. A., & Grigorenko, E. L. (in press). The relationship between academic and practical intelligence: A case study in Kenya. *Intelligence*.

Stigler, J. W., Shweder, R. A., & Herdt, G. (Eds.). (1990). *Cultural psychology: Essays on comparative human development*. Cambridge, UK: Cambridge University Press.

Super, C. M. (1983). Cultural variation in the meaning and uses of children's "intelligence." In J. B. Detregowski, S. Dziurawiec, & R. C. Annis (Eds.), *Expiscations in cross-cultural psychology* (pp. 199–212). Lisse, Netherlands: Swets and Zeitlinger.

Super, C. M., & Harkness, S. (1982). The infant's niche in rural Kenya and metropolitan America. In L. L. Adler (ed.), *Cross-cultural research at issue* (pp. 47–56). New York: Academic Press.

van de Vijver, F. J., & Leung, K. (1997). Methods and data analysis of cross-cultural research. In J. W. Berry, Y. Poortinga, & J. Pandley (Eds.), *Handbook of cross-cultural psychology: Theoretical and methodological perspectives* (Vol. 1, pp. 257–300). Needham Heights, MA: Allyn & Bacon.

Vygotsky, L. S. (1978). *Mind in society: The development of higher psychological processes*. Cambridge, MA: Harvard University Press.

White, G. M. (1985). Premises and purposes in a Solomon Islands ethnopsychology. In G. M. White & J. Kirkpatrick (Eds.), *Person, self, and experience: Exploring Pacific ethnopsychologies* (pp. 328–366). Berkeley: University of California Press.

Wober, M. (1974). Towards an understanding of the Kiganda concept of intelligence. In J. W. Berry & P. R. Dasen (Eds.), *Culture and cognition: Readings in cross-cultural psychology* (pp. 261–280). London: Methuen.

Yang, S., & Sternberg, R. J. (1997a). Conceptions of intelligence in ancient Chinese philosophy. *Journal of Theoretical and Philosophical Psychology, 17*(2), 101–119.

Yang, S., & Sternberg, R. J. (1997b). Taiwanese Chinese people's conceptions of intelligence. *Intelligence, 25*(1), 21–36.

. . . .

15

Multicultural Issues and the Assessment of Aptitude

Lisa A. Suzuki, Ellen L. Short, Alex Pieterse, and John Kugler

One of the most controversial areas in the field of assessment is use of aptitude measures with racial or ethnic minorities. Concerns have focused on the consistent finding of significant group differences despite acknowledgement that within-group discrepancies (that is, between individual members of a racial or ethnic group) exceed between-group discrepancies (between racial or ethnic group averages). For example, numerous court cases in the 1970s and 1980s attest to the impact of intelligence tests in determining school placement and educational opportunity, and involvement of the legal system in attempts to alleviate perceived problems with their use.

The purpose of this chapter is to provide readers with updated information relevant to current assessment practices in the areas of intelligence and aptitude. Specific attention is given to:

1. Group differences on intelligence and aptitude tests (that is, overall group discrepancies and profile differences)

2. Variables having an impact on racial and ethnic group variability in performance on intelligence and aptitude measures

3. Test bias and equivalence issues

4. Alternative testing practices (translated measures, biocultural model, Gf-Gc cross battery)

5. A case example

6. Steps in the assessment process

Because of space constraints, we focus on only the most popular instruments in the area of educational aptitude, namely, the Scholastic Aptitude Test, the Graduate Record Examination, and Wechsler scales). Despite this focus on a few instruments, our discussion has implications for other measures not specifically highlighted.

Although numerous theories have evolved over the years to explain the construct of intelligence, it can be described as "a very general mental capability that among other things, involves the ability to reason, plan, solve problems, think abstractly, comprehend complex ideas, learn quickly and learn from experience" ("Mainstream Science on Intelligence," 1994, p. A18). Aptitude represents a related construct that focuses on "the capacity to learn" (Walsh and Betz, 1995). Examples include scholastic aptitude (that is, the potential to learn a particular educational curriculum) and occupational aptitude (the potential of succeeding at a particular job or career). For the purposes of this chapter, we focus primarily on intelligence tests and scholastic aptitude tests used in educational decision making.

Racial and Ethnic Group Difference on Intelligence and Aptitude Tests

One of the most consistent findings of social science research in this century is the difference in cognitive ability test (CAT) scores between racial or ethnic groups. In the area of intelligence testing, the test-score hierarchy places East Asian and Jewish group members at the top, with scores ranging from a few to ten points greater than Caucasians. African Americans are often noted to be one standard deviation below Caucasians, and Hispanics score on a range between African Americans and Caucasians (Herrnstein and Murray, 1994; "Mainstream Science on Intelligence," 1994; O'Connor, 1989).

Along with the enduring nature of these findings has been accompanying controversy as to the exact meaning of these differences.

Generally, explanation of the obtained difference has followed three arguments: hereditary, test bias, and environment. It is beyond the scope of this chapter to delve into the complexities of each perspective. However, briefly stated, the hereditary explanation includes belief in an innate inferiority in the intelligence of certain groups (for example, Herrnstein and Murray, 1994). In contrast, test bias arguments proliferate by focusing on the nature of CATs as favoring the dominant cultural orientation (for example, Helms, 1997). Finally, environmental and sociodemographic variables are also noted as influencing the lack of familiarity with educational information that in turn is reflected in differential scores on intelligence and aptitude measures (for example, Armour-Thomas and Gopaul-McNicol, 1998; O'Connor, 1989).

Of further interest are studies that attempt to examine the profile of ability for racial and ethnic group. Reviews indicate that overall aptitude scores mask the racial and ethnic group profiles that are frequently found on various measures in this domain. For example, a review of studies reveals that American Indian and Hispanic groups tend to score higher on tasks requiring visual and nonverbal reasoning ability in comparison to verbal ability (for example, Suzuki and Valencia, 1997). Asians tend to score higher on visual and numerical reasoning tests in comparison to verbal reasoning (for example, Suzuki and Gutkin, 1993). The profile for African Americans has been inconsistent, although there are indications of relative strengths in verbal areas in comparison to visual reasoning domains (Taylor and Richards, 1991). The next sections of this chapter offer specific information with regard to educational aptitude and intelligence measures.

Educational Aptitude Testing

Aptitude tests such as the Scholastic Aptitude Test (SAT; Educational Testing Service, 1948 to present), now referred to as the Scholastic Assessment Test, are often identified as gatekeepers to

higher educational opportunity. It should be noted that a significant concern has been raised because monitoring the performance
of minorities on this measure is limited by examinees who do not
self-identify their race or ethnicity (Wainer, 1988). Wainer notes
that the "no response" group can be considered a substantial
"ethnic" group on the SAT. Both scales of the SAT (Verbal and
Math) have a score range from 200 to 800 and a mean of 500 ($SD =$
100). In 1985, the SAT Verbal averages reported by racial and
ethnic group (cited by Wainer, 1988) were American Indian 392
($n = 4,000$), Asian American 404 ($n = 40,000$), Black 346 ($n =$
70,000), Mexican American 382 ($n = 17,000$), Puerto Rican 368
($n = 10,000$), White 449 ($n = 679,000$), Other 391 ($n = 19,000$),
and no response 409 ($n = 138,000$). The SAT Math averages
(n's the same as SAT Verbal) were American Indian 428, Asian
American 518, Black 376, Mexican American 426, Puerto Rican
409, White 490, Other 448, and no response 454. The figures for
n reflect the number of college-bound students in each racial or
ethnic category. Therefore, the numbers are not proportional to
census figures.

Average SAT-I (revised SAT 1995) scores obtained ten years
later appear commensurate with those reported by Wainer (1988):
for SAT-I Verbal, African/Pacific American 356 ($n = 103,872$),
American Indian 403 ($n = 8,936$), Asian American 418 ($n =$
81,514), Mexican American 376 ($n = 36,323$), Puerto Rican 372
($n = 13,056$), White 448 ($n = 674,343$), and Other 432 ($n =$
25,113). SAT-I Math (n's are the same) scores were African American 388, American Indian 447, Asian/Pacific American 538, Mexican American 426, Puerto Rican 411, White 498, and Other 486
(cited in Hsia and Peng, 1998). Examinees who did not identify
their race or ethnicity (no response) totaled 94,123. However, no
scores were provided for the no-response group in this study.

Despite the limitation of the large number of examinees who do
not indicate their race or ethnicity on the SAT, a number of studies
have been conducted to examine racial and ethnic group differences

on these measures since the test publishers released minority group data. Numerous concerns were raised about the discrepancies between groups, and they continue to this day. For example, Lay and Wakstein (1985) reported that a year and a half after the SAT data were released, "the published racial profiles precipitated a flurry of commentary—most warning against reaching hasty conclusions, many calling for a reexamination of the American educational system that perpetuates observed racial differences, and some asking for a comprehensive research effort that seeks a complete explanation of the causes and an elaboration of the consequences" (Lay and Wakstein, 1985, pp. 43–44).

The Lay and Wakstein article further noted that "it has been widely reported that Blacks score an average of more than 200 points lower than Whites on combined verbal and math SAT scores. Yet even this disturbing statistic obscures the magnitude of the educational deficit that exists between the races" (p. 48). Clearly, given the consistency of findings nearly a decade later, this concern continues today.

Much of the research examining racial and ethnic group differences on the SAT has focused on the importance of noncognitive variables affecting the scores obtained for minority students. For example, Lay and Wakstein highlight the potential impact of self-esteem with regard to self-rated ability as mediating the relationship between environmental factors and SAT performance. They note that "blacks at the same level of test performance exhibit greater self-esteem than whites on a series of self-rated abilities" (p. 43).

Fuertes, Sedlacek, and Liu (1994) cite reports that in 1991 Asian Americans had the highest average SAT Math (M = 530) and combined total (M = 941) of all racial and ethnic groups in the United States. They also note that other noncognitive variables (positive self-concept, confidence in negotiating social demands, ability to identify and cope with racism, realistic appraisal of academic and nonacademic strengths) contribute to the success and retention of Asian American college students.

Gandara and Lopez (1998) examined the impact of SAT scores for Latino students with high grade point averages. Their major findings indicated that SAT scores were not predictive of time taken for degree completion, college grades, or application to graduate school. However, "Students with low SAT scores were more likely to judge themselves as having lower ability than those who received high scores, independent of GPA, and almost half of the students were aware of missed opportunities as a result of their scores" (p. 17).

Thus, limitations in using SAT scores for college admission are noted given the impact of noncognitive variables. This discussion has only briefly highlighted some of the issues related to using these scores for college admission with minority students. Similar concerns have been raised for other aptitude measures, notably the Graduate Record Examination (GRE; Hughey, 1995). The Educational Testing Service (1994) reports in its test materials that scores on the GRE are reflective of educational and cultural experiences. Therefore, the scores of students who have significantly different backgrounds should be interpreted with caution.

Intelligence Testing

Similar discrepancies between racial and ethnic groups have been found on intelligence tests. For example, from the literature the average scores noted across intelligence tests (with a mean of 100 and standard deviation of 15) are Whites, 100; African Americans, 85; Hispanics, ranging between Whites and African Americans; Asians, somewhere above 100 (results vary depending on the study); and Native Americans, approximately 90 ("Mainstream Science on Intelligence," 1994; McShane, 1980).

Specifically, on one of the most popular intelligence instruments, the Wechsler Intelligence Scale for Children III (Wechsler, 1991), scores on the standardization sample were, for African Americans, Full Scale IQ (FSIQ) 88.6, Verbal IQ (VIQ) 90.8, Performance IQ (PIQ) 88.5; for Hispanics, FSIQ 94.1, VIQ 92.1, PIQ 97.7; and for

Whites, FSIQ 103.5, VIQ 103.6, PIQ 102.9 (Prifitera, Weiss, and Saklofske, 1998).

Unlike the data provided on the SAT, many intelligence scales are standardized on far smaller numbers. For example, the WISC-III was standardized based upon the 1988 census. The total numbers in each racial and ethnic group were Hispanic 242, Black 339, other 77, and White 1,542 (Wechsler, 1991).

Often, data on only the largest racial or ethnic groups are reported (that is, White, Black, Hispanic). For example, the WISC-III provides data by racial and ethnic group for only the three largest groups in the standardization sample (White, African American, and Hispanic).

Most state-of-the-art measures in the area incorporate test development strategies to address potential issues of bias with regard to racial and ethnic minorities. The strategies include examination of item content by expert review panels, proportional representation of racial and ethnic minorities in the standardization sample based upon current census data, racial and ethnic oversampling (number of minority group members in excess of proportional representation based on census figures), statistical procedures to evaluate test performance by racial and ethnic group (for example, Rasch modeling), specific reliability and validity studies conducted with diverse populations, and development of sociocultural norms (Valencia and Suzuki, 2000).

Information regarding racial and ethnic group performance on the most popular tests is readily available, given the importance of this area for examiners working in diverse communities. For example, research studies using the WISC-III standardization sample provide specific information on how groups perform based upon matched samples. These studies take into consideration some of the performance factors noted in the preceding discussion.

In one study, White and Black samples (matched on socioeconomic status, parental education, gender, age, region of the country, and number of parents living at home) from the standardization sample were compared on the WISC-III (Prifitera, Weiss, and Saklofske, 1998). Data indicated that the discrepancies between Whites and African Americans decreased from 14.9 to 11.0 Full Scale IQ points for matched samples. In addition, the authors noted that the discrepancy between groups changes with the age of the sample selected. The differences in Full Scale IQ are lower for younger groups than for older groups. These differences were approximately 4–5 points higher for the older children.

In addition, Prifitera and colleagues examined profile differences on WISC-III Index scores (Processing Speed Index, PSI; Freedom from Distractibility, FDI; Perceptual Organization Index, POI; and Verbal Comprehension Index, VCI). It appears that Hispanics demonstrate relatively higher PIQ and POI scores in relation to their VIQ and VCI scores. The discrepancies between African Americans and Whites on the PSI and FDI are much smaller than on the other index scores.

Thus these findings support the idea that examination of overall scores on intelligence tests (that is, FSIQ) obscures differences across ability area for racial and ethnic groups. Prifitera, Weiss, and Saklofske (1998) conclude: "The view that minorities have lower abilities is clearly wrong. IQ score differences between younger African-American and White children and Hispanic and White samples with only gross matches on SES are much less than a standard deviation, and the index scores are even smaller. What would the difference be if even more refined variables had been controlled for, such as household income, home environment (for example, parental time spent with children), per-pupil school spending, medical and nutritional history and exposure to toxins[?]" (p. 15).

These findings highlight the fact that racial and ethnic group differences on the WISC-III is clearly affected by various mediating factors. Thus, it is critical to understand the implications of such research when testing members of diverse populations.

Despite the extensive research on the most popular intelligence tests, their use in the process of educational placement (gifted and talented, special education) generated a great deal of scrutiny of particular tests (for example, WISC-III and Stanford-Binet Fourth Edition). This has led to concern regarding aspects of validity for these measures. For example, these instruments have been criticized for focusing too narrowly on particular ability areas. The majority of test developers continue to focus on two main areas (verbal and nonverbal) to the exclusion of other "intelligences" (Gardner, 1983).

In a related vein, Valencia and Suzuki (2000) note that most cognitive measures are validated according to a select group of instruments. In their review of fifty-nine measures cited in Buro's *Mental Measurement Yearbook* database (WinSPIRS), thirty-nine (66 percent) of the scales were validated on one of the Wechsler scales. This practice contributes to the level of overlap (correlation) among measures in the area to the exclusion of more innovative models of cognitive abilities (for example, multiple intelligences).

Recognizing some of the limitations of more traditional IQ tests, several intelligence tests have been developed for limited-English-proficient students. For example, the Universal Nonverbal Intelligence Test (UNIT; see Chapter Seventeen) is one of the newest scales in the intelligence domain. Scores on these measures yield a smaller discrepancy between racial and ethnic groups. In addition, scales that have been standardized for various language groups are now available. This includes the Bilingual Verbal Abilities Test (BVAT; Munoz-Sandoval, Cummins, Alvarado, and Ruef, 1998), which includes sixteen linguistic versions of the test in addition to English: Arabic, Chinese, French, German, Haitian-Creole, Hindi, Italian, Japanese, Korean, Polish, Portuguese, Russian, Spanish, Turkish, and Vietnamese. The test development process was extensive and involved back-translation procedures, field testing with native-speaking examiners and children, and age-level reviews by expert panels. Further study with instruments such as the BVAT may yield greater insight into the impact of language factors in assessing cognitive abilities.

Influences on Racial and Ethnic Group Variability

Decades of research have focused on determining the effects of sociodemographic variables on development of cognitive ability. In the first edition of this text, our chapter highlighted the issues of socioeconomic status (SES), health factors, education, residential and regional issues, language, and acculturation. All of these variables may continue to affect test performance:

- Higher SES has been related to higher intelligence test scores.

- Certain populations at higher risk for sensory loss and other health impairment tend to score lower on measures of aptitude.

- Children living in isolated communities may score lower because of lack of familiarity with test stimuli.

- The level of knowledge of English affects verbal test scores.

- The degree of familiarity with the dominant culture upon which the test is based has an impact on test performance.

In addition, factors such as family background and parenting style (Phillips and others, 1998) and parental educational level (Strickner and Rock, 1995) have been noted as variables potentially influencing performance on aptitude tests.

The impact of particular variables is dynamic and may become less salient over time. For example, although test score differences were noted between children living in rural areas and those in urban areas (Vernon, 1979), they have become smaller over time and clinically nonsignificant (Kaufman, 1990). This may be due to advances in computer technology and mass communication and improvements in education. However, because some communities may remain isolated from these influences, examiners should not automatically rule out these potential mediating variables without further exploration.

Test Bias and Equivalence Issues

Issues of test bias and equivalence are noteworthy in understanding the test score discrepancies for racial and ethnic groups. These concepts affect the validity and reliability of measures. Therefore, understanding the relationship between these concepts is imperative in using aptitude measures appropriately.

Test Bias

Thorndike (1997) describes issues of test bias in this way:

> One of the most prevalent themes in popular discussions of testing is that tests are unfair to certain groups. The term used is *bias*. It is often asserted that standardized tests are used to deprive certain groups of access to educational and employment opportunities. To the extent that tests are used mechanically as selection and placement devices, and to the extent that some groups in our society have historically performed less well on tests, tests *do* become instruments through which access to education and employment is disproportionately barred to members of these groups. The question that must be addressed is whether individuals are unjustly barred and, more generally, what constitutes fair and equitable use of tests for the selection, placement, and classification of individuals [p. 427].

Specifically, test bias refers to measures that overestimate or underestimate the true scores of a particular group. Test bias is often linked to issues of predictive validity. As noted earlier, most test makers attempt to employ some strategy to detect potential test bias in developing their instrument, such as expert panels or statistical procedures.

Issues of Equivalence

With regard to the predictive validity of cognitive ability tests, Helms (1997) focuses on cultural equivalence and the importance of obtaining a consistent measurement of constructs across cultural groups in the same manner as CATs of normative groups. Culture is defined by Helms (1997) to mean "racial, ethnic, cultural and socioeconomic conditions of socialization" (p. 518).

Multicultural assessment with aptitude measures may be affected by four types of equivalence:

1. Functional, referring to procedures designed to investigate content validity

2. Conceptual, which refers to differences in conceptual phenomena

3. Linguistic, related to problems in translation of written and verbal material

4. Metric, equivalence that involves test score differences (Moreland, 1996). Information regarding the various forms of equivalence is provided elsewhere in this *Handbook* (Chapters Eight and Eleven).

Helms (1997) contends that race, culture, and social class have a "differential" influence upon the cultural equivalence of CATs and notes the importance of considering psychological processes such as "learning styles, information-processing strategies, perceptual processes, [and] relevant attitudes . . ." when assessing individuals: "Thus, psychological processes potentially define a person's range and variety of possible responses to stimuli. However, measurement of (as opposed to speculation about) psychological processes proposedly accrued through sociogroup socialization appears to be virtually nonexistent in the psychometric literature" (p. 519).

Helms also critiques "modern-day psychometricians" for their reliance on "preexisting demographic categories" in test construction and validation procedures. Further, Helms (1997) cites culture fairness in test construction as attempts to "reduce the effects of race, culture, [or] SES on CAT performance" that infer but do not necessarily produce cultural equivalence (p. 526). Inferences of cultural equivalence by way of using culturally fair test construction focus, for example, on only the structural components of the test itself (such as between-group structural similarity): "Therefore, to develop tests that are culturally equivalent, one needs a model or models of how culture functions as well as a model of how culture interacts with manifested cognitive abilities. Culturally equivalent CATs would deliberately incorporate the properties intrinsic to the interactions between intended test takers' cultural socialization and the content of the tests by which they are assessed" (p. 526).

It is important for clinicians to consider the potentially significant limitations in the field of cognitive assessment that are highlighted by Helms. Her work indicates there is no simple solution to the complexity inherent in the relationship between cultural context and measured ability.

Alternative Testing Practice

Given the diversity of the populations being tested in school, clinics, and other settings throughout the United States, a number of strategies have been developed to enable examiners to use traditional ability measures with diverse populations. These practices include use of translators, interpreters, and translated measures; the biocultural model; and cross-battery assessment.

Using Translators, Interpreters, and Translated Measures

Most popular ability tests are normed on and recommended for administration to English-speaking participants. Although a common practice, using translated measures may adversely affect validity and reliability. For example, cultural-linguistic variations may prevent direct translations of tests, and use of translators and interpreters will be difficult given problems with accurate translation (Suzuki, Vraniak, and Kugler, 1996). In addition, examiners must attend to differences in dialect that may also affect the translation process.

There is very little research concerning the validity and reliability of translated measures. Because of the lack of available instruments normed and standardized on different language speaking populations, using interpreters and translators during the assessment process will continue. However, it is important that examiners be aware of the potential pitfalls of using such practices with limited-English speakers given issues of equivalence. Tests such as the BVAT, described earlier, represent a viable alternative to this common practice.

Specific instruments are available to assess issues of language proficiency. These may be used to determine whether an individual must be tested in his or her native language and if the results need to be interpreted with caution owing to lack of familiarity with particular concepts reflected in the test items (for example, cultural loading). For more information regarding language instruments, the reader is referred to Yansen and Shulman (1996).

Biocultural Model

Armour-Thomas and Gopaul-McNicol (1998) advocate using the Biocultural Model of Assessment. This model integrates quantitative test data with qualitative information about the examinee to obtain accurate understanding of abilities. Armour-Thomas and Gopaul-McNicol include examination of preassessment activities in the areas of health, language, prior experiences (educational and psychosocial), and family. The model incorporates biological and cognitive processes along with biological and culturally based instruments and contexts.

Four tiers are encompassed in the biocultural model. The first, psychometric assessment, refers to standardized test administration and derivation of quantitative scores. The second, psychometric potential assessment, is represented by strategies used to obtain the potential and estimated intellectual functioning of the examinee, including suspending time requirements for completion of tasks, contextualizing vocabulary words, allowing use of paper and pencil, and incorporating test-teach-retest procedures. This is sometimes referred to as "testing the limits."

The third tier, ecological assessment, comprises evaluation of family and community support with observation of the examinee's performance in school, at home, and in the community, as well as evaluation of the stage of acculturation. Finally, the fourth tier involves assessing other "intelligences," including testing for musical, bodily kinesthetic, interpersonal and intrapersonal abilities, and so on. From these four tiers, the evaluator obtains information from actual test scores and potential test scores. The actual scores are those from standardized administration of the particular cognitive measure; the potential test score indicators are obtained from modification of standard administration practices as noted.

Gf-Gc Cross-Battery Approach

The Gf-Gc cross-battery approach is a means of examining the breadth of cognitive ability areas being examined by a particular measure or battery of tests (McGrew and Flanagan, 1998). It is based upon current psychometric theory and research on the structure of intelligence and theories of crystallized and fluid abilities. McGrew and Flanagan describe a number of broad abilities (fluid intelligence, quantitative knowledge, crystallized intelligence, reading and writing, short-term memory, visual processing, auditory processing, long-term storage and retrieval, processing speed, and decision or reaction time or speed). The broad abilities can be broken down into narrower ability areas (for example, fluid intelligence is made up of general sequential reasoning, induction, and speed of reasoning).

McGrew and Flanagan assert that understanding these strata can help an examiner ensure a valid examination of a range of ability areas. They applied these broad and narrow ability concepts to a number of measures to assist examiners in selecting tests and batteries to answer particular questions. They examined the most popular instruments used for cognitive assessment in relation to the Gf-Gc (Fluid-Crystallized) ability areas.

In addition, McGrew and Flanagan provide information on cultural content and linguistic demands for particular measures. Their ratings assist examiners in determining the best available measure to use in testing individuals from diverse cultural backgrounds. Those identified as having low cultural content and low linguistic demands included many nonverbal tests.

Case Example: "Juan"

"Juan" was a nine-year-old student in a third-grade class. During the school day, he was in an English-speaking class but attended an English-as-a-second-language class for one period a day. His teacher reported that he was experiencing problems in reading and spelling, but his math skills were on grade level. She noted that in class he seemed to have difficulty following directions. His behavior was viewed as age-appropriate, and in general he attempted to finish his classwork.

At this point, however, he had barely passed the last marking quarter and was in danger of being retained in the third grade. His teacher attempted several prereferral interventions: moving his seat closer to the front of the room, pairing him with a buddy, and having a classroom assistant work with him in a small group during reading. These efforts met with some success, but he continued to struggle.

In a pretesting interview, his parents reported that their family came from Puerto Rico to the United States approximately four and a half years ago. He was five years old at the time, his older sister was eight, and his younger brother was one and a half. Neither of his siblings demonstrated difficulty with language acquisition and both attained proficiency in English at an age-appropriate level.

Juan's early developmental history indicated delays in acquiring language skills. His parents reported that he was first exposed to Spanish as the main language of the home. However, in contrast to the normal language development of his siblings, he did not speak individual words until he was almost three years old and did not speak in full sentences until after he was four.

The class he attended was in a large urban school system. In conducting bilingual assessments, psychologists are asked to provide ranges rather than actual test scores. This is done when tests are translated by the examiner or assistant and no appropriate bilingual norms are available. A caution is also included in the report, noting the potentially limited validity of translating the test without adequate research to support such practices. A bilingual Spanish psychologist who was fluent in the Puerto Rican dialect conducted the assessment. On the WISC-III, Juan obtained a Verbal score in the Borderline range, a Performance score in the Low-Average range, and Full Scale IQ in the Low-Average range. He obtained the subtest profile seen in Table 15.1.

A number of significant clinical observations were made during the evaluation that helped place the obtained results in the proper context. For example, although Juan was allowed to answer in either Spanish or English, he demonstrated significant word-finding problems in both languages. This was seen, for example, on both the Information and Picture-Completion subtests. Although he was not always able to find the precise word, he seemed to have an understanding of the concept being assessed. This was noted on several verbal subtests on which he tended to expand on his answers, imparting increasing

Table 15.1. "Juan's" subtest profile.

Verbal Scale	Range	Performance Scale	Range
Information	Deficient	Picture Completion	Low average
Similarities	Low average	Coding	Borderline
Arithmetic	Deficient	Picture Arrangement	Borderline
Vocabulary	Low average	Block Design	Average
Comprehension	Low average	Object Assembly	Average
(Digit Span)	Borderline	(Symbol Search)	Low average

information so that he eventually earned a minimally passing score on a given item. He also had a weakness on measures of short-term auditory memory. This was particularly true on tasks that tapped semantically involved material such as the word problems on the Arithmetic section. On this subtest, he often needed to have a question repeated before he attempted to answer it.

In contrast to the significant difficulties on language measures, Juan did much better with tests of spatial skills. The examiner noted that he earned age-appropriate scores on several tasks that tapped nonverbal reasoning and visual-perceptual skills. At the same time, his difficulties with Picture Arrangement were felt to reflect his verbal processing problems, as this test is often mediated by language in trying to construct a story sequence that is logical.

The evaluation suggested that a combination of gaps in his knowledge of American culture and a general language-processing problem were involved in the pattern of scores he obtained on the intelligence test. These also appeared to be affecting his performance in the classroom. Admittedly, it was very difficult to determine first the extent to which Juan's learning problems are based in cognitive processing deficits and which may be due to environmental factors. However, it is recognized that the two influence each other to a large extent. It was recommended that additional assessments be done to further elucidate his learning strengths and needs. These evaluations included more detailed evaluation of his language functioning in both Spanish and English, and more detailed educational evaluation. Inclusion of possible neuropsychological measures was also noted as a possible option. In addition, educational interventions should attempt to capitalize on Juan's nonverbal strengths as noted in the evaluation.

This scenario was developed from experience with actual cases. We believe that it reflects some of the dilemmas faced by examiners when assessing the ability of individuals from diverse backgrounds as well as the complexity in understanding the role of language in the evaluation. As illustrated, the qualitative information obtained regarding background history plays a vital role in shaping the procedures of the assessment process, in addition to affecting the interpretation of the quantitative information obtained from the tests. The next section further highlights the process of assessment.

Steps in the Assessment Process

It is important to consider various decision points in the cognitive assessment process when testing individuals from diverse backgrounds. Generally, the process begins as an individual is identified by external sources (for example, teachers) as having potential cognitive processing delays or deficits.

Obtaining Background Information

It is imperative that a comprehensive examination of the individual's background information be done prior to making a decision regarding testing. This includes information on the individual's medical, educational, developmental, and socioemotional history. At this stage it is not uncommon to reframe the child's learning difficulties in light of information obtained in these areas (medication taken, significant life events experienced, and so on). This information is used to decide what preevaluation interventions can be attempted, whether testing is needed, and if so which instruments are administered.

Determining Appropriateness for Cognitive Testing

After receiving a referral for an evaluation, it must be determined whether cognitive assessment is needed. If there are a number of emotional concerns, a cognitive evaluation may not be recommended until the affective issues have been sufficiently addressed. If the individual has recently arrived in the United States, then a period of adjustment may be allowed prior to testing. Any issues pertaining to language proficiency should be noted early on. This includes determining the level of the individual's language skills, namely, informal language in terms of interpersonal conversational skills as well as formal academic language skills (see Yansen and Shulman, 1996).

Examiners at times judge a student based upon observation taken in social situations. It should be noted that an individual may be proficient in interpersonal conversational skills but not in terms of academic language skills. More information may be needed regarding the student's understanding (both receptive and expressive) of formal academic language necessary in the educational context.

At this juncture the examiner can gather information regarding specific problems being experienced by the individual. Understanding specifics enables an appropriate decision about interventions that can be attempted prior to testing (such as educational intervention, modification of classroom materials, environmental modification in the workplace).

Selecting Appropriate Cognitive Instruments and Test Procedures

If testing is warranted, the examiner must determine the best available method to obtain accurate estimates of the individual's abilities. If English is not the first language and there are concerns about

English proficiency, the examiner may decide to use an interpreter or translator. These individuals should have training in understanding the purpose of the testing and the skills needed to facilitate the process of assessment. The examiner should meet with the interpreter or translator prior to testing to establish a collaborative relationship and pass on information about the particular case. If there are any special concerns, the interpreter or translator may be able to offer specific insight from observations during the testing. In addition to administering English-based tests, the examiner may use nonverbal measures or those developed within the particular language context of the individual examinee (for example, the BVAT).

If the examinee is English-speaking and there are no concerns regarding English proficiency, then the examiner can move forward with the assessment in the standardized fashion. However, attention should still be paid to the examinee's cultural context, which may differ from the standardization sample enough to warrant modification in administration (as with a recent immigrant from an English-speaking country).

Integrating Alternative Methods of Assessment

The examiner may also choose to incorporate an alternative method of assessment using the biocultural model or the Gf-Gc cross-battery approach as described earlier. In both cases many of the previous steps described would fit in well with these procedures. The biocultural model and the Gf-Gc cross-battery approach emphasize the need for examination of broader areas of cognitive processes.

Conclusions

Assessing the aptitude of diverse populations has been problematic because of limitations in test development and research. In addition, the lack of sensitivity to cultural context in test selection, test administration, and test interpretation is noted. It is critical that test developers, clinicians, educators, and researchers continue to reexamine current instruments and develop new practices in assessing cognitive abilities. Aptitude measures play a major role in determining future educational and occupational opportunity. It is imperative that these tests be used in ways that truly tap the intelligence and aptitude of all members of racial and ethnic groups.

References

Armour-Thomas, E., & Gopaul-McNicol, S. (1998). *Assessing intelligence: Applying a Bio-Cultural model.* Thousand Oaks, CA: Sage.

Educational Testing Service. (1994). *GRE: 1994–1995 guide to the use of the Graduate Record Examination program.* Princeton, NJ: Author.

Fuertes, J. N., Sedlacek, W. E., & Liu, W. M. (1994). Using SAT and noncognitive variables to predict the grades and retention of Asian American university students. *Measurement and Evaluation in Counseling and Development, 27,* 74–84.

Gandara, P., & Lopez, E. (1998). Latino students and college entrance exams: How much do they *really* matter? *Hispanic Journal of Behavioral Sciences, 20,* 17–38.

Gardner, H. (1983). *Frames of mind: The theory of multiple intelligences.* New York: Basic Books.

Helms, J. E. (1997). The triple quandary of race, culture, and social class in standardized cognitive ability testing. In D. P. Flanagan, J. L., Genshaft, & P. L. Harrison (Eds.), *Contemporary intellectual assessment: Theories, tests and issues* (pp. 517–531). New York: Guilford Press.

Herrnstein, R. J., & Murray, C. (1994). *The bell curve: Intelligence and class structure in American life.* New York: Free Press.

Hsia, J., & Peng, S. S. (1998). Academic achievement and performance. In L. C. Lee & N. W. Zane (Eds.), *Handbook of Asian American psychology* (pp. 325–357). Thousand Oaks, CA: Sage.

Hughey, A. W. (1995). Observed differences in Graduate Record Examination scores and mean undergraduate grade point averages by gender and race among students admitted to a master's degree program in college student affairs. *Psychological Reports, 77,* 1315–1321.

Kaufman, A. S. (1990). *Assessing adolescent and adult intelligence.* Needham Heights, MA: Allyn & Bacon.

Lay, R., & Wakstein, J. (1985). Race, academic achievement and self-concept of ability. *Research in Higher Education, 22,* 43–64.

"Mainstream science on intelligence." (1994, December 13). *Wall Street Journal,* p. A18.

McGrew K. S., & Flanagan, D. P. (1998). *The Intelligence Test Desk Reference (ITDR): Gf-Gc cross-battery assessment.* Needham Heights, MA: Allyn & Bacon.

McShane, D. A. (1980). A review of scores of American Indian children on the Wechsler Intelligence Scales. *White Cloud Journal, 1,* 3–10.

Moreland, K. L. (1996). Persistent issues in multicultural assessment of social and emotional functioning. In L. A. Suzuki, P. J. Meller, & J. G. Ponterotto (Eds.), *Handbook of multicultural assessment: Clinical, psychological and educational applications* (pp. 141–177). San Francisco: Jossey-Bass.

Munoz-Sandoval, A. F., Cummins, J., Alvarado, C. G., & Ruef, M. L. (1998). *Bilingual Verbal Ability Tests.* Itasca, IL: Riverside.

O'Connor, M. (1989). *Standardized tests: Linguistic and sociocultural factors.* Norwell, MA: Kluwer.

Phillips, M., Brooks-Gunn, J., Duncan, G. J., Klebanov, P., & Cranse, J. (1998). Family background, parenting practices and the Black-White test score gap. In C. Jencks & M. Phillips (Eds.), *The Black-White test score gap* (pp. 103–145). Washington, DC: Brookings Institution Press.

Prifitera, A., Weiss, L. G., & Saklofske, D. H. (1998). The WISC-III in context. In A. Prifitera & D. H. Saklofske (Eds.), *WISC-III clinical use and interpretation: Scientist-practitioner perspectives* (pp. 1–38). New York: Academic Press.

Strickner, L. J., & Rock, D. (1995). Examinee background characteristics and the GRE general test performance. *Intelligence, 21,* 49–67.

Suzuki, L. A., & Gutkin, T. B. (1993, August). *Racial/ethnic ability patterns on the WISC-R and theories of intelligence.* Paper presented at the 101st annual convention, American Psychological Association, Toronto.

Suzuki, L. A., & Valencia, R. (1997). Race/ethnicity and measured intelligence: Educational implications. *American Psychologist, 52*(10), 1103–1114.

Suzuki, L. A., Vraniak, D. A., & Kugler, J. F. (1996). Intellectual assessment across cultures. In L. A. Suzuki, P. J. Meller, & J. G. Ponterotto (Eds.), *Handbook of multicultural assessment: Clinical, psychological and educational applications* (pp. 141–178). San Francisco: Jossey-Bass.

Taylor, R. L., & Richards, S. B. (1991). Patterns of intellectual differences of Black, Hispanic, and White children. *Psychology in the Schools, 28,* 5–8.

Thorndike, R. M. (1997). *Measurement and evaluation in psychology and education* (6th ed.). Upper Saddle River, NJ: Merrill.

Valencia, R. R., & Suzuki, L. A. (2000). *Intelligence testing and minority students: Foundations, performance factors, and assessment issues.* Thousand Oaks, CA: Sage.

Vernon, P. E. (1979). *Intelligence, heredity and environment.* San Francisco: Freeman.

Wainer, H. (1988). How accurately can we assess changes in minority performance on the SAT? *American Psychologist, 43,* 774–778.

Walsh, W. B., & Betz, N. E. (1995). *Tests and assessment* (3rd ed.). Englewood Cliffs, NJ: Prentice Hall.

Wechsler, D. (1991). *Manual for the Wechsler Intelligence Scale for Children—Third Edition.* San Antonio: Psychological Corporation.

Yansen, E. A., & Shulman, E. L. (1996). Language assessment: Multicultural considerations. In L. A. Suzuki, P. J. Meller, & J. G. Ponterotto (Eds.), *The handbook of multicultural assessment: Clinical, psychological, and educational applications* (pp. 353–394). San Francisco: Jossey-Bass.

16

Social and Emotional Assessment

Rita J. Casey

Respecting cultural identity and variability in evaluating social and emotional functioning is one of the most challenging tasks in assessment. There are many reasons. First, in contrast to cognitive functioning, which is by far the most common and widely accepted domain of assessment, the domain of social-emotional assessment is ill-defined, with no widely accepted definition of its meaning and scope (Waters, Wippman, and Sroufe, 1979). Any survey of assessment instruments quickly demonstrates that there are many more instruments available that tap aspects of cognitive functioning relative to the number of those in the social-emotional domain (Denham, Lydick, Mitchell-Copeland, and Sawyer, 1996; Halperin and McKay, 1998).

Second, some aspects of social-emotional functioning are considered to be of little practical importance, or controversial, or impossible to measure, or simply beyond the scope of questions typically addressed in assessments, especially in educational contexts. Third, people differ in their beliefs about how important culture is to social-emotional functioning (Pianta and McCoy, 1997). Finally, the methods typically recommended for ensuring sensitive, culturally responsive assessment may be particularly difficult to apply, given that assessment itself, in any domain, is often a social event that elicits a strong emotional response.

This chapter discusses some of the central issues that should be considered in attempting to make culturally sensitive assessments within the social and emotional domain. It discusses the scope of this domain and then presents a commentary on the use of common strategies for approaching social-emotional assessment in a culturally sensitive fashion. Case examples are given, illustrating social-emotional factors in assessment. Finally, this chapter offers practical recommendations for taking social and emotional functioning into account during assessment.

The Scope of Social and Emotional Functioning

Social and emotional functioning is often defined simply as personality, or alternatively as the quantity or seriousness of psychological problems or problem behavior. For example, the typical title of graduate assessment courses that address domains beyond the cognitive, educational, and neuropsychological is simply "personality assessment." The content of these courses most often focuses on personality measures such as the MMPI, or measures that are presumed to tap psychopathology. A simple perusal of journal articles using the term *social-emotional functioning* reveals a wide range in how this term is operationalized. The definition may consist of scores on a measure of some aspect of psychopathology, such as depression; scores on behavioral checklists designed to screen for a wide range of behavior problems, such as the Child Behavior Checklist (Achenbach, 1991); a measure of self-esteem; or even peer nominations for being popular, rejected, or controversial.

This chapter defines *social functioning* as how an individual behaves within his or her social context, including the range and fit of behavior to that social context. *Emotional functioning* overlaps with social functioning, but it includes a person's felt as well as expressed emotion, and how well that emotion is suited and responsive to his or her situation. In addition, social-emotional functioning includes an individual's skills in regulating social and emotional behavior in response to the environment, consistent with the individual's level of development, so that the goals of the person and his or her society can be accomplished.

This means that questions of social and emotional functioning are almost always set in a particular context, and they are often related to other domains of functioning. For example, how well does an adolescent control her anxiety when she takes her final exams? Her general level of anxiousness, perhaps grounded in her personality, may not reveal how her fearfulness influences her performance in the special context of academic performance.

Does a college student have the social and emotional skills to delay gratification, to conform to the classroom or work routines necessary for him to meet his desired goals?

Can performance within the structure of a familiar high school routine predict how a student will perform in the absence of adult structure and accountability?

Can a first grader read the social and emotional demands of her environment well enough to carry out her expected activities and to learn as a result?

Might students who perform well in one-on-one or very small group situations that are typical of home care and preschool have significantly different skills in managing their impulses and emotions in a demanding classroom or a free-flowing playground situation?

These questions illustrate the types of information that are often sought in assessing social-emotional functioning. By their nature, they suggest that assessment within the social and emotional domain is integrally tied to assessment in other domains. Furthermore, assessment in domains such as cognition or language is necessarily linked to the social-emotional domain. Consideration of the social-emotional domain in concert with other areas of functioning is most likely to present a picture of individuals as whole, unique persons with their own pattern of strengths and weaknesses, in contrast to a listing of status and strength within a single domain.

It is not simple, however, to undertake social-emotional assessment. The array of instruments is very limited in contrast to the numerous and growing set of materials and procedures available in the cognitive domain. There are also serious limitations on tapping social-emotional processes across the many years of human development. It may be fairly simple to assess a person's anxiety, for example, as an adult or adolescent; it is significantly more difficult to do so for a child in preschool or primary grades. Some measures of social-emotional functioning, although adequate in their psychometric characteristics, tap a narrow range of the domain, or are appropriate only for a limited age range (Denham, Lydick, Mitchell-Copeland, and Sawyer, 1996).

Instruments tapping the social-emotional domain are sometimes controversial; for example, it is not unusual to hear objections to asking children about their suicidal feelings. Likewise, inquiring about children's friendships or other close relations may be a touchy area for some parents (and children). In one of the first assessments that I performed during my graduate training, the parent insisted on witnessing the entire testing session; we were fortunately able to arrange it using a one-way mirror. She informed me afterward that she had been afraid I would ask her son if he had been abused or given drugs, or that I would say something negative to her son about his family. Her expectation about the behavior of assessors was clearly different from what I expected, but her courage and honesty in voicing these issues laid the foundation for a parent-psychologist relationship that became very close and positive over time. This parent also taught me not to fear raising the questions of possible disagreements, misunderstandings, or misgivings.

In some school situations, assessment is explicitly limited to education outcomes and their cognitive underpinnings, in an effort to avoid any inappropriate investigation into things not considered to be strictly in the domain of education. Most important for purposes of this book, the relatively few measures of social-emotional functioning that are available are lacking in good validation for multicultural application.

Therefore, it is impossible to provide, as would be desirable, a listing and discussion of a range of good, well-validated assessment instruments in the social-emotional domain for use with people of multiple cultural backgrounds, because no such set of instruments exists. For a review of instruments within the social-emotional domain without consideration of cultural sensitivity, the reader is referred to excellent work by Denham, Lydick, Mitchell-Copeland, and Sawyer, 1996, and Bracken, Keith, and Walker (1998).

Approaches to Ensuring Cultural Sensitivity in Social and Emotional Assessment

There are several traditional strategies used to foster cultural sensitivity in assessment. These include examination of relative similarity and difference between majority and minority cultures, and assessing the degree of acculturation of the minority group into the dominant culture. Instruments created for the majority culture are deemed acceptable for use if other cultural groups appear to have few differences from the larger group, or if the minority group seems to be highly acculturated into the majority. Other techniques involve restriction of items or content to elements that are similar among cultures making up the population. These and other methods have their strength in aiming to eliminate aspects of assessment that contribute to group differences. However, these strategies may also create unexpected weaknesses in assessment, especially in the social emotional domain, as discussed below. Choosing any of these techniques for use must be done by considering not only what problems are avoided but also what aspects of social emotional functioning may be overlooked or inadequately measured.

Consideration of Cultural Similarities and Differences

There are some areas of social-emotional functioning presumed to be the same across cultures, such as emotional expression, and the basic nature of mood and emotion (Wallbott and Scherer, 1986;

Ellgring and Rime, 1989; Joiner, Sandin, Chorot, and Lourdes, 1997; Habel and others, 2000). If what is needed in assessment is simply knowledge of a person's range of emotional expressivity, such an assessment need not consider culture as an important factor. However, contexts in which emotions and social behavior emerge can produce varied responses from people of different cultures (McLoyd, 1990; Nuttall and others, 1996; Church and Lonner, 1998; Matsumoto, Takeuchi, Andayani, Kouznetsova, and Krupp, 1998; Cohen and Kasen, 1999).

Two first graders in my class one year were popular with their peers and had few behavior problems. However, Hani, whose parents emigrated to the United States from Vietnam, consistently smiled and looked downward whenever she found a test question difficult. Once this happened, she rarely attempted further work. In contrast, her deskmate, Rosa, produced silent tears in response to any unfamiliar word or difficult problem. She looked at me for reassurance, and if she saw a smile, she continued working.

The reactions of these two children may well have been products of their culture as well as their individual personalities and previous educational experience. Accurate evaluation of their academic achievement in the absence of consideration of social emotional factors would have been difficult if not impossible. Hani was likely to shut down during formal assessment, with further testing being strained and unproductive. Rosa, however, was very responsive to friendly examiners but needed much encouragement to persevere. Considering only their peer relations as a sole index of social-emotional functioning would have shed little light on their strikingly different responses to academic challenges.

It is important, therefore, to consider what aspects of social-emotional functioning are indicated in an assessment, and whether they are likely to be influenced by the culture of the person being assessed. If culture is a probable factor, as in someone's response to a fearful situation, it is important to account for the person's culture in selecting, using, and interpreting any assessment instruments.

Using Acculturation as a Guideline in Selecting Instruments

If an instrument was designed and validated on the dominant, white, middle-class population of the United States, assessments based on that instrument may actually reflect deviation of the assessed person's degree of difference from the dominant white cultural norm, rather than reflecting objective information about the person's social skills, adjustment, or behavior (Patterson, Kupersmidt, and Vaden, 1990).

A common recommendation in such cases is for the assessor to evaluate the target person's degree of acculturation to the majority culture early in the process of assessment (Dana, 1990). However, this is not an easy task, especially in the social-emotional domain. Instruments for assessing acculturation are limited, and generally weak in validity (for example, Utsey, 1998). Frequently, assessors rely on their own judgments, based on their impressions from talking with and observing the intended target of the assessment (Abel, 1973). Unfortunately, what is being evaluated in such cases may be the target person's similarity or dissimilarity in socioeconomic status, rather than acculturation.

Assessor's perceptions are likely to be influenced by surface characteristics such as dress, conformity to social expectations, use of standard English, and so on. Judgments may reflect how similar in appearance, behavior, education, and economic status the target person is to the assessor, rather than the cultural similarity of the target person to the majority culture (Barona and de Barona, 2000; Bernal and Castro, 1994; Abel, 1973).

Eliminating Items or Measures That Produce Differences Between Ethnic Groups

A commonly recommended solution in test design is to avoid or eliminate cultural differences by dropping items that vary among ethnic groups (Dana, 1990). However, this approach may result in a limited set of items that do not tap a domain adequately for one or more of the groups for whom the instrument is designed. It is almost always the case that items are created with the majority culture in mind. Elimination of items that differ by ethnicity may obscure important information. For example, in a longitudinal study of first-grade children, my students and I discovered that African American parents were more accurate at assessing their children's emotional response than white parents were. Should the questions leading to these data have been eliminated from consideration? Or did they indicate an area of strength that would not have been revealed had we consistently eliminated questions that produced answers varying with the group?

The Empirical Approach

One method of assessment that has been widely endorsed and used is to sample a wide range of behavior and see what patterns emerge, keeping the items that are most frequently endorsed across multiple groups of subjects (Dedrick, Greenbaum, Friedman, and Wetherington, 1997; McConaughy, 1992, 1993; McConaughy, Mattison, and Peterson, 1994). In this case, using items that are as behavioral as possible seems on the surface to be free of cultural bias. This is how the Child Behavior Checklist (Achenbach, 1991) was developed and validated. It is the most widely used instrument for assessing children's behavior problems and is frequently selected as a measure of social-emotional functioning. Responses tend to group into major clusters of acting-out, negative, or hostile behavior in one pattern and withdrawn, internalizing, ruminative behavior in the other pattern.

The Child Behavior Checklist (CBCL) and its versions for teachers and for self-report by youths have been widely used and given to children and adolescents of many cultures, including Chinese (Su and others, 1998), Japanese (Friedlmeier and Trommsdorff, 1999), Danish (Bilenberg, 1999), Dutch (Koot, Van Den Oord, Verhulst, and Boomsma, 1997; De Groot, Koot, and Verhulst, 1994), German (Friedlmeier and Trommsdorff, 1999), Hispanic

(Rubio-Stipec, Bird, Canino, and Gould, 1990), Jamaican (Lambert and Lyubansky, 1999), Native American (Powless and Elliott, 1999), Norwegian (Novik, 1999), and Russian children (Carter, Grigorenko, and Pauls, 1995), among others. In general, results indicate that the same broad bands of internalizing and externalizing behavior are found in every cultural group tested. Back-translations of items have been performed, with judgments that the content communicated is similar among different national groupings.

These explorations of the CBCL are certainly noteworthy. However, they do not necessarily mean that the instrument is valid cross-culturally, or that it is unbiased and culturally sensitive. There is no information as to whether the items constitute an adequate sampling of problem behavior within and across each of the groups to whom the instrument has been given. In addition, comparison between children of differing nationalities may be more common than adequate comparison of minorities within the multiple cultures of the United States. The children used for developing and norming the CBCL are overwhelmingly white, and the central criterion for inclusion or exclusion of items has typically been the contrast between children who are clinically referred and those who are not.

Given the admirable qualities and extensive use of the CBCL, it is in some danger of being reified as the best instrument to fit all circumstances. It is frequently the instrument to which others are compared for their own validation (Birmaher and others, 1999; Epstein, 1999; Harniss, Epstein, Ryser, and Pearson, 1999; West and Verhaagen, 1999; Jensen and others, 1996; Emerson, Crowley, and Merrell, 1994; Rey and Morris-Yates, 1992; Boggs, Eyberg, and Reynolds, 1990). Also, data from the instrument are being "mined" to see if they provide information beyond their original, intended use (for example, see Crick, Casas, and Mosher, 1997, on use to differentiate relational and overt aggression; Biederman and others, 1995, on assessing mania versus ADHD; and Beidel, Turner, and Morris, 1999, on identifying phobic children). With these extended uses, it is particularly important to give attention to the cultural sensitivity of the CBCL.

Sampling the Social-Emotional Domain with Adequate Representation of Cultures

Does the instrument adequately sample social functioning within the culture that the person being assessed comes from? Or does it simply touch on those areas of social culture that are similar between the majority and the person's particular minority culture? Simply having representativeness of multiple cultures within a norming group that matches the overall U.S. population does not mean that the multiple cultures are fairly assessed by the instruments. These norming groups rely on the match between very small samples of minorities and their larger population. Without further examination, it is unlikely that the minority cultures are well represented.

In addition, it is important to consider that minority cultures are not monolithic. Just as the majority white culture in the United States has many, often overlapping, subgroups (Irish, Southern, Jewish, and so on), minority cultures are quite diverse. People of Asian heritage in this country come from varied backgrounds and differ extensively in length of time in the country, geographic distribution, and degree of absorption into the larger culture (Kitano and Daniels, 1988; Kao, Nagata, and Peterson, 1997; Yu, 1999). Likewise, there is considerable cultural variability among African Americans (Cross, 1991) and Hispanic citizens (Velasquez and Callahan, 1992). Unfortunately, in contrast to extensive cross-cultural uses of some instruments, such as the CBCL, there has been virtually no systematic large-scale consideration of subcultural differences within the social-emotional domain.

Measuring Multiple Perspectives

One of the best methods of capturing the social-emotional domain is to employ a range of instruments that take different perspectives. Use of multiple instruments is more likely to have predictive validity

(Keith and Campbell, 2000; Carter, Little, Briggs-Gowan, and Kogan, 1999; Casat, Norton, and Boyle-Whitsel, 1999; Greenberg and others, 1999; Fox and Calkins, 1993). Furthermore, multiple measures are likely to indicate which indices demonstrate cultural differences and which do not (Cluett and others, 1998, Pianta and McCoy, 1997).

The Social and Emotional Context of Assessment

The context of assessment, people's emotional reaction to assessment, and the purpose of the assessment are strong elicitors of social and emotional reactions that may differ in important ways according to the culture of the person involved. This suggests that assessment within any domain may benefit from careful consideration of social-emotional factors. If, in addition, the social-emotional domain is included as a focus of an assessment, a dual consideration of social-emotional factors must be taken into account.

The Decision to Assess as a Social Emotional Transaction

Any assessment takes place within a social context that gives authority to particular standards, particular knowledge, and particular routines of behavior. The decision to carry out an assessment is based on an understanding, rooted in the dominant culture of the United States, that there is a socially mandated need to determine the range, characteristics, or standards of some aspects of human behavior and thought.

It is common for the assumptions underlying the decision to do an assessment to be little discussed with the person who is the target of the assessment. Too often, assessment is conducted as if everyone tacitly understands and is positively disposed toward the purpose and activity of assessment. Unfortunately, failure to discuss these issues can generate hostility, suspicion, doubt, and fear among those who do not share this understanding. In such a situation, the discussion of the need for assessment may quickly become an awkward social interaction in which the person targeted for assessment or the parents and guardians feel that they are not being told all of the important information about the proposed assessment. They may feel they lack the status necessary to have a voice in the process, and they may have erroneous ideas about the purposes and outcomes of the assessment.

Decisions to assess need to involve social transactions that begin with relationship building and discussion of the roles, rights, and responsibilities of all parties to the assessment (Dana, 1990). The decision-making process should end with joint involvement of all parties in making a decision to do an assessment, including the purpose, scope, process, and outcomes (Li, Walton, and Nuttall, 1999).

Assessors as Social and Emotional Beings

The individuals who carry out assessments are imbued with privilege and purpose that are familiar to some people but unknown and little valued by others (Dana, 1990; Abel, 1973). Explanation of why a particular person is performing an assessment often relies on an appeal to education or occupational status. These characteristics may have the unintended purpose of making the person faced with an assessment less confident, rather than reassured, about the assessment. The assessor is seen as an "other," not as a member or affiliate of the same group as the person being assessed. References to authority may generate awareness of distance and "differentness" between the assessor and the person being assessed, rather than confidence in the process of assessment.

As a new teacher, I became concerned when one of my students began to have severe crying spells in class, although her mother indicated no such behavior had happened at home. The guidance counselor called the girl's mother to suggest that her daughter be tested by the school psychologist. The mother talked to me later, saying, "Why are you asking a doctor who doesn't know my child to test her? Shouldn't you get someone who is really good with kids, someone who knows her, like the teacher she had last year?"

The typical pattern for assessors is to adopt a tone of neutrality and expertise, with careful attempts made to avoid biasing the assessment through excessive familiarity with the person being evaluated. This may be quite contrary to the cultural expectations for a person not of the majority, white, middle-class culture, who may see the assessor as being aloof, condescending, or uncaring (Cargile and Giles, 1997).

The same parent came back to school after testing to register a further concern: the school psychologist had only seen her daughter twice, and he had never spoken with the parent until the assessment was virtually finished. "I expected him to at least talk to me before he made up his mind about her," she complained. "My daughter was scared of him, and so was I."

Those who are familiar with psychologists, psychometrists, and diagnosticians must never forget what it means to be unfamiliar with such people and their work. Assessors must become familiar enough that they are seen as approachable, as persons with expertise who nonetheless respect and welcome collaboration with the individuals they assess and with other involved parties such as parents and teachers (Bernal and Castro, 1994).

Assessment as a Social-Emotional Event

People differ significantly in how well they are acculturated to the traditional environments of assessment. Some are socialized to feel comfortable in assessment environments such as academic or intellectual testing. For these people, not only the content but also the context of assessment is familiar. If anxiety is provoked, it is only to a degree that heightens perception and sharpens attention and focus in ways that help optimize performance.

In other cases, as the mother-and-child situation just described illustrates, the activities of assessment arouse a range of emotions that may extend from excitement and enthusiasm to dread and fear, to anger and contempt, or even boredom and inattention. Some people become anxious at the mere mention of being tested, so fearful that their performance suffers greatly. Others, especially some children, have been tested so much that they may not take the assessment process seriously. Discussion of assessment should include exploration of the client's feelings and attitudes about assessment, including history with assessment, and his or her worst fears and best hopes for the outcome. Unless anticipatory emotional responses and actual emotions during an assessment are explored, it can be difficult to produce an accurate evaluation of the domains being assessed.

It is often easy, therefore, to be unaware of the social and emotional context of assessment, or if such issues are brought to mind, to attempt to avoid or minimize their importance. This can lead to serious problems that damage the validity of the assessment, either by using the performance of the dominant culture as the unquestioned standard for assessment or by confining assessment to a narrow range of behavior, attitudes, and skills that do not appear to vary across multiple cultural backgrounds of people in the United States.

Practical Recommendations for Social-Emotional Assessment

Perhaps the best thing to remember in performing culturally sensitive assessment within the social and emotional domain is to take the time to involve the person being assessed (and the parents or guardians, if the client is a child) as early as possible in the process. Carefully explain what you see that indicates an assessment is advisable, and inquire about everyone's perceptions. Do not be afraid to discuss how different your perspectives are. Explore how your cultural differences may influence your reaction, and their reaction to what you are observing. Ask and discuss what the person being assessed or the parent thinks about assessment—what it consists of, how it is done, what information it will produce, and how this information is used to provide help or make further decisions about the person being assessed.

Describe the selected instruments, explaining their content, purpose, and typical use, sharing as much information as you can without compromising the integrity of the measures. If possible, double check the meaning of the wording of every instrument for the ethnic group (or groups) of the person you intend to assess. When you can, choose instruments that have been used successfully with the ethnic group of your client.

Even so, try to be aware of subcultural influences that may alter the applicability of the instrument to your client. Do not assume, for example, that a client of a particular minority is just like others from this group that you have assessed in the past. Ask the person or the parents to self-identify, and describe how his or her individual perspective makes him or her approach assessment. Avoid characterizing instruments and their results by particular ethnic or cultural group outcomes—as if any single index would ever demonstrate the characteristics of all members of a group.

If you wish to consider how much the person has absorbed the values and attitudes of the majority culture, in order to use an instrument not well validated for multicultural or cross-cultural use, do so with great caution. Take great care to become knowledgeable of your own biases and prejudices. For example, do you think that those of Asian heritage are reserved and unemotional? Do you think that Hispanics are more sociable than other ethnic groups? Is it your assumption that African Americans are more emotional than people from other cultures in the United States?

If you have such beliefs, consider that you probably haven't arrived at these beliefs through a perusal of the research literature. You may inadvertently bias your assessment activities with such beliefs. Be aware also that assessment is likely to be influenced by similarity of appearance, expression of emotion, language, and conformity to the social rules of traditional assessment. If you see a great deal of similarity when you conduct an assessment, do not be misled. This similarity should not be confused with safely assuming that instruments you select work well with the individuals to whom you administer them.

Make normative comparisons with great caution, and be clear in communicating your caveats to the person or parents involved. Remember that even if minorities are included in a norming group, this alone does not make the results valid for members of that minority group. Always consider whether representation of a minority group is as satisfactory to you as representation of the majority group in the development of the instrument.

Carefully assess potential biases of the questions that you ask, by clarifying with your client how you both understand the purpose of the assessment. Be sure that they have as good an understanding as you can make possible, given the constraints of your situation. During the assessment itself, check understanding often, particularly if the person being tested becomes uneasy, hostile, or bored, or appears unmotivated to continue. Take the time to ask how the person being tested is feeling at the moment, and what he or she is thinking about the assessment thus far. If serious difficulties arise that make the assessment problematic, call in consultants who may be more expert than you in the culture of your client, or more familiar to him or her. They can help with mediation and guidance before you force assessment onward.

Once you have finished, be cautious in interpreting the data that you obtain. Check out the results with informants, including the client, who can help you interpret the results in a fashion that reflects the social context of the client. Ask your client to process reactions to the assessment with you.

Finally, note carefully the good points and the challenging aspects of the assessment, to help you build a store of knowledge for future assessments. If you see a pattern, test it empirically and share your observations. In this fashion, cross-cultural and multicultural experiences can begin to influence each other in a transactional fashion that benefits the future of assessment (Clark, 1987).

References

Abel, T. M. (1973). *Psychological testing in cultural contexts*. New Haven, CT: College and University Press.

Achenbach, T. M. (1991). *Child Behavior Checklist*. Burlington: University of Vermont.

Barona, A., & de Barona, M. S. (2000). Assessing multicultural preschool children. In B. A. Bracken (Ed.), *The psychoeducational assessment of preschool children* (3rd ed., pp. 282–297). Needham Heights, MA: Allyn & Bacon.

Beidel, D. C., Turner, S. M., & Morris, T. L. (1999). Psychopathology of childhood social phobia. *Journal of the American Academy of Child and Adolescent Psychiatry, 38*, 643–650.

Bernal, M. E., & Castro F. G. (1994). Are clinical psychologists prepared for service and research with ethnic minorities? Report of a decade of progress. *American Psychologist, 49*, 797–805.

Biederman, J., Wozniak, J., Kiely, K., Ablon, S., Farone, S., Mick, E., Mundy, E., & Kraus, I. (1995). CBCL clinical scales discriminate prepubertal children with structured interview-derived diagnosis of mania from those with ADHD. *Journal of the American Academy of Child and Adolescent Psychiatry, 34*, 464–471.

Bilenberg, N. (1999). The Child Behavior Checklist (CBCL) and related material: Standardization and validation in Danish population based and clinically based samples. *Acta Psychiatrica Scandinavica Supplementum, 100* (Suppl. 398), 2–52.

Birmaher, B., Brent, D. A., Chiappetta, L. I., Bridge, J., Monga, S., & Baugher, M. (1999). Psychometric properties of the Screen for Child Anxiety Related Emotional Disorders (SCARED): A replication study. *Journal of the American Academy of Child and Adolescent Psychiatry, 38*, 1230–1236.

Boggs, S. R., Eyberg, S., & Reynolds, L. A. (1990). Concurrent validity of the Eyberg Child Behavior Inventory. *Journal of Clinical Child Psychology, 19*, 75–78.

Bracken, B. A., Keith, L. K., & Walker, K. C. (1998). Assessment of preschool behavior and social-emotional functioning: A review of thirteen third-party instruments. *Journal of Psychoeducational Assessment, 16*, 153–169.

Cargile, A. C., & Giles, H. (1997).Understanding language attitudes: Exploring listener affect and identity. *Language and Communication, 17*, 195–217.

Carter, A. S., Little, C., Briggs-Gowan, M. J., & Kogan, N. (1999). The Infant-Toddler Social and Emotional Assessment (ITSEA): Comparing parent ratings to laboratory observations of task mastery, emotion regulation, coping behaviors and attachment status. *Infant Mental Health Journal, 20,* 375–392.

Carter, A. S., Grigorenko, E. L., & Pauls, D. L. (1995). A Russian adaptation of the Child Behavior Checklist: Psychometric properties and associations with child and maternal affective symptomatology and family functioning. *Journal of Abnormal Child Psychology, 23,* 661–684.

Casat, C. D., Norton, H. J., & Boyle-Whitsel, M. (1999). Identification of elementary school children at risk for disruptive behavioral disturbance: Validation of a combined screening method. *Journal of the American Academy of Child and Adolescent Psychiatry, 38,* 1246–1253.

Church, A. T., & Lonner, W. J. (1998). The cross-cultural perspective in the study of personality: Rationale and current research. *Journal of Cross-Cultural Psychology, 29,* 32–62.

Clark, L. A. (1987). Mutual relevance of mainstream and cross-cultural psychology. *Journal of Consulting and Clinical Psychology, 55,* 461–470.

Cluett, S. E., Forness, S. R., Ramey, S. L., Ramey, C. T., Hsu, C., Kavale, K. A., & Gresham, F. M. (1998). Consequences of differential diagnostic criteria on identification rates of children with emotional or behavior disorders. *Journal of Emotional and Behavioral Disorders, 6,* 130–140.

Cohen, P., & Kasen, S. (1999). The context of assessment: Culture, race, and socioeconomic status as influences on the assessment of children. In D. Shaffer & C. P. Lucas (Eds.), *Diagnostic assessment in child and adolescent psychopathology* (pp. 299–318). New York: Guilford Press.

Crick, N. R., Casas, J. F., & Mosher, M. (1997). Relational and overt aggression in preschool. *Developmental Psychology, 33,* 579–588.

Cross, W. E., Jr. (1991). *Shades of black: Diversity in African-American identity.* Philadelphia: Temple University Press.

Dana, R. H. (1990). Cross-cultural and multi-ethnic assessment. In J. N. Butcher & C. Spielberger (Eds.), *Advances in personality assessment* (Vol. 8, pp. 1–26). Hillsdale, NJ: Erlbaum.

De Groot, A., Koot, H. M., & Verhulst, F. C. (1994). Cross-cultural generalizability of the Child Behavior Checklist cross-informant syndromes. *Psychological Assessment, 6,* 225–230.

Dedrick, R. F., Greenbaum, P. E., Friedman, R. M., & Wetherington, C. M. (1997). Testing the structure of the Child Behavior Checklist/4–18 using confirmatory factor analysis. *Educational and Psychological Measurement, 57,* 306–313.

Denham, S. A., Lydick, S., Mitchell-Copeland, J., & Sawyer, K. (1996). Socioemotional assessment for atypical infants and preschoolers. In M. Lewis & M. W. Sullivan (Eds.), *Emotional development in atypical children* (pp. 227–271). Hillsdale, NJ: Erlbaum.

Ellgring, H., & Rime, B. (1989). Individual differences in emotional reactions. In K. R. Scherer & H. G. Wallbott (Eds.), *Experiencing emotion: A cross-cultural study* (pp. 142–153). Cambridge, England: Cambridge University Press.

Emerson, E. N., Crowley, S. L., & Merrell, K. W. (1994). Convergent validity of the School Social Behavior scales with the Child Behavior Checklist and Teacher's Report Form. *Journal of Psychoeducational Assessment, 12,* 372–380.

Epstein, M. H. (1999). The development and validation of a scale to assess the emotional and behavioral strengths of children and adolescents. *Remedial and Special Education, 20,* 258–263.

Fox, N. A., & Calkins, S. D. (1993). Multiple-measure approaches to the study of infant emotion. In M. Lewis & J. M. Haviland (Eds.), *Handbook of emotions* (pp. 167–184). New York: Guilford Press.

Friedlmeier, W., & Trommsdorff, G. (1999). Emotion regulation in early childhood: A cross-cultural comparison between German and Japanese toddlers. *Journal of Cross-Cultural Psychology, 30,* 684–711.

Greenberg, M. T., Lengua, L. J., Coie, J. D., Pinderhughes, E. E., Bierman, K., Dodge, K. A., Lochman, J. E., & McMahon, R. (1999). Predicting developmental outcomes at school entry using a multiple-risk model: Four American communities. *Developmental Psychology, 35,* 403–417.

Habel, U., Gur, R. C., Mandal, M. K., Salloum, J. B., Gur, R. E., & Schneider, F. (2000). Emotional processing in schizophrenia across cultures: Standardized measures of discrimination and experience. *Schizophrenia Research, 42*(1), 57–66.

Halperin, J. M., & McKay, K. E. (1998). Psychological testing for child and adolescent psychiatrists: A review of the past 10 years. *Journal of the American Academy of Child and Adolescent Psychiatry, 37,* 575–584.

Harniss, M. K., Epstein, M. H., Ryser, G., & Pearson, N. (1999). The Behavioral and Emotional Rating Scale: Convergent validity. *Journal of Psychoeducational Assessment, 17*(1), 4–14.

Jensen, P. S., Watanabe, H. K., Richters, J. E., Roper, M., Hibbs, E. D., Salzberg, A. D., & Liu, S. (1996). Scales, diagnoses, and child psychopathology: II. Comparing the CBCL and the DISC against external validators. *Journal of Abnormal Child Psychology, 24,* 151–168.

Joiner, T. E., Jr., Sandin, B., Chorot, P. L., & Lourdes, M. G. (1997).
Development and factor analytic validation of the SPANAS among
women in Spain: (More) cross-cultural convergence in the structure of
mood. *Journal of Personality Assessment, 68*, 600–615.

Kao, E. M., Nagata, D. K., & Peterson, D. (1997). Explanatory style, family
expressiveness, and self-esteem among Asian American and European
American college students. *Journal of Social Psychology, 137*, 435–444.

Keith, L. K., & Campbell, J. M. (2000). Assessment of social and emotional
development in preschool children. In B. A. Bracken (Ed.), *The
psychoeducational assessment of preschool children* (3rd ed., pp. 364–382).
Needham Heights, MA: Allyn & Bacon.

Kitano, H.H.L., & Daniels, R. (1988). *Asian Americans: Emerging minorities.*
Upper Saddle River, NJ: Prentice Hall.

Koot, H. M., Van Den Oord, E.J.C.G., Verhulst, F. C., & Boomsma, D. I. (1997).
Behavioral and emotional problems in young preschoolers: Cross-cultural
testing of the validity of the Child Behavior Checklist/2–3. *Journal of
Abnormal Child Psychology, 25*, 183–196.

Lambert, M. C., & Lyubansky, M. L. (1999). Behavior and emotional problems
among Jamaican children and adolescents: An epidemiological survey of
parent, teacher, and self-reports for ages 6–18 years. *International Journal of
Intercultural Relation, 23*, 727–751.

Li, C., Walton, J. R., & Nuttall, E. V. (1999). Preschool evaluation of culturally
and linguistically diverse children. In E. V. Nuttall, I. Romero, &
J. Kalesnik (Eds.), *Assessing and screening preschoolers: Psychological and
educational dimensions* (2nd ed., pp. 296–317). Needham Heights, MA:
Allyn & Bacon.

Matsumoto, D., Takeuchi, S., Andayani, S., Kouznetsova, N., & Krupp, D.
(1998). The contribution of individualism vs. collectivism to cross-
national differences in display rules. *Asian Journal of Social Psychology, 1*,
147–165.

McConaughy, S. H., (1992). Objective assessment of children's behavioral
and emotional problems. In C. E. Walker & M. C. Roberts (Eds.),
Handbook of clinical child psychology (2nd ed., pp. 163–180).
New York: Wiley.

McConaughy, S. H. (1993). Advances in empirically based assessment of
children's behavioral and emotional problems. *School Psychology Review,
22*, 285–307.

McConaughy, S. H., Mattison, R. E., & Peterson, R. L. (1994). Behavioral/
emotional problems of children with serious emotional disturbances and
learning disabilities. *School Psychology Review, 23*, 81–98.

McLoyd, V. C. (1990). The impact of economic hardship on black families and children: Psychological distress, parenting, and socioemotional development. *Child Development, 61*, 311–346.

Novik, T. S. (1999). Validity of the Child Behaviour Checklist in a Norwegian sample. *European Child and Adolescent Psychiatry, 8*(4), 247–254.

Nuttall, E. V., Sanchez, W., Borras, L., Nuttall, R., and Varvogli, L. (1996). Assessing the culturally and linguistically different child with emotional and behavioral problems. In M. J. Breen & J. D. Fiedler-Craig (Eds.), *Behavioral approach to assessment of youth with emotional/behavioral disorders: A handbook for school-based practitioners* (pp. 451–501). Austin, TX: Pro-Ed.

Patterson, C. J., Kupersmidt, J. B., & Vaden, N. A. (1990). Income level, gender, ethnicity, and household composition as predictors of children's school-based competence. *Child Development, 61*, 485–494.

Pianta, R. C., & McCoy, S. J. (1997). The first day of school: The predictive validity of early school screening. *Journal of Applied Developmental Psychology, 18*, 1–22.

Ponterotto, J. G., & Casas, J. M. (1991). *Handbook of racial/ethnic minority counseling research*. Springfield, IL: Thomas.

Powless, D. L., & Elliott, S. N. (1999). Assessment of social skills of Native American preschoolers: Teachers' and parents' ratings. *Journal of School Psychology, 31*, 293–307.

Rey, J. M., & Morris-Yates, A. (1992). Diagnostic accuracy in adolescents of several depression rating scales extracted from a general purpose behavior checklist. *Journal of Affective Disorders, 26*, 7–16.

Rubio-Stipec, M., Bird, H., Canino, G., & Gould, M. (1990). The internal consistency and concurrent validity of a Spanish translation of the Child Behavior Checklist. *Journal of Abnormal Child Psychology, 18*, 393–406.

Su, L., Li, X., Luo, X., Wan, G., & Yang, Z. (1998). Standardization of newly revised Child Behavior Checklist (CBCL) and validity test. *Chinese Mental Health Journal, 12*(2), 67–69.

Utsey, S. O. (1998). Assessing the stressful effects of racism: A review of instrumentation. *Journal of Black Psychology, 24*, 269–288.

Velasquez, R. J., & Callahan, W. J. (1992). Psychological testing of Hispanic Americans in clinical settings: Overview and issues. In K. F. Geisinger (Ed.), *Psychological testing of Hispanics* (pp. 253–265). Washington, DC: American Psychological Association.

Wallbott, H. G., & Scherer, K. R. (1986). The antecedents of emotional experiences. In K. R. Scherer & H. G. Wallbott (Eds.), *Experiencing *emotion: A cross-cultural study* (pp. 69–83). Cambridge, England: Cambridge University Press.

Waters, E., Wippman, J., & Sroufe, A. (1979). Attachment, positive affect and competence in the peer group: Two studies of construct validation. *Child Development, 50,* 821–829.

West, H. A., & Verhaagen, D. A. (1999). The Differential Test of Conduct and Emotional Problems as an evaluative tool for the Willie M. program. *Adolescence, 34,* 437–441.

Yu, M. M. (1999). Multimodel assessment of Asian families. In K. S. Ng (Ed.), *Counseling Asian families from a systems perspective* (pp. 15–26). Alexandria, VA: American Counseling Association.

17

Assessing Intelligence in a
Population That Speaks More Than
Two Hundred Languages

A Nonverbal Solution

Bruce A. Bracken and R. Steve McCallum

Psychologists have long been interested in determining effective procedures for assessing the cognitive functioning of individuals who lack the manifest language to demonstrate their latent cognitive abilities. The French clinician Jean Itard was among the first to address this problem; he was presented with the challenge of assessing and modifying the cognitive abilities of Victor, a feral youth who has since acquired the moniker "The Wild Boy of Aveyron" (Carrey, 1995; Itard, 1932). In addition to Itard's well-publicized efforts, other clinicians are noteworthy for similar efforts. Seguin (1907), for example, is acknowledged to have developed one of the first nonverbal tests of cognitive ability, the Seguin Form Board. The Seguin Form Board (and the many modifications of the original instrument) requires examinees to place geometric pieces into cutouts of the same size and shape. The form board approach to intellectual assessment can still be seen on such current instruments as the Stanford-Binet Intelligence Scale, Fourth Edition (Thorndike, Hagen, and Sattler, 1986).

During the First World War, the Committee on the Psychological Examination of Recruits was created and charged with the responsibility of developing procedures to assess the cognitive functioning of new recruits into this country's military (Thorndike and Lohman, 1990). As a result of their efforts, one form of the examination (Army Beta) was developed as a nonverbal measure to assess the abilities of recruits who were illiterate and couldn't respond reliably to a written test or whose English-language mastery was insufficient for a valid assessment on the standard Army Alpha examination.

The Army Beta included several performance-type tasks, which were to be most prominently associated in later years with the various forms of the Wechsler Scales of intelligence. The Army Beta, and later the Wechsler Performance subtests, employed novel puzzle-completion tasks, cube constructions, speeded copying of digit symbol pairs, maze completions, picture completions, and picture arrangements. Experimental work devoted to assessing limited English proficient and illiterate individuals during this era resulted in a host of pioneer instruments, including the Kohs Cubes (Kohs, 1919), Porteus Mazes (Porteus, 1915), the Seguin Form Board (Seguin, 1907), and the Arthur Point Scale (Arthur and Woodrow, 1919). The Point Scale is especially noteworthy because it was a civilian effort that combined a variety of extant performance tests, including a revision of the Knox Cube Test (Knox, 1914), Seguin Form Board, Porteus Mazes, and an adaptation of the Healy Picture Completion Test (Healy, 1914, 1918, and 1921) into a single nonverbal battery.

Arthur's professed goal for the Point Scale was to create a nonverbal battery of cognitive tests that collectively would "furnish an IQ comparable to that obtained with the Binet scales" (Arthur, 1947, p. 1). A variety of nonverbal and "culture-fair" tests were developed in subsequent decades, but most of these tests have either met with only limited success or were coopted into standard intelligence batteries as performance subtests with verbal directions. In the past ten years, however, there has been a resurgence of interest in nonverbal test development. The reasons for the renewed interest lie primarily in the nation's rapidly changing demographic characteristics.

Linguistic and Cultural Diversity

According to the U.S. Bureau of the Census (1998), there are approximately 270 million Americans, of which about 82 percent are white. Given this overwhelming percentage, one might infer that the country is predominantly English speaking and white and thus has a homogeneous population. However, examination of the actual numbers of ethnic and racial minorities shows a different picture of the U.S. population. Table 17.1 shows that approximately forty-eight million Americans are of African, Asian or Pacific Islander, or Native American descent (that is, 18 percent of the population). Additionally, the U.S. Hispanic population cuts across these various government-classified "racial" groups because a person can be Hispanic *and* white, as well as African American, Native American, or Asian or Pacific Islander and Hispanic. When one considers the racial composition of the U.S. population and takes into account further that 11 percent of the current population is Hispanic and an estimated 10 percent of the total population is foreign-born, it becomes apparent that the U.S. population is considerably more diverse than it would appear at first glance.

U.S. demographics continue to change at a rapid pace, resulting in an increasingly diverse population and an ever more bilingual population. The U.S. Census Bureau has estimated that by the middle of the twenty-first century 25 percent of the U.S. population will be Hispanic, and through the year 2020 the Asian and Pacific

Table 17.1. Race and ethnicity in the United States.

Race or Ethnicity	Number	Percentage of Total Population
White	222,104,000	82.6
African American	34,143,000	12.7
Native American	2,338,000	0.9
Asian or Pacific Islander	10,181,000	3.8
Hispanic (any race)	28,802,000	11.1

Islander population is expected to grow at a faster rate than any other racial or ethnic group, including Hispanics (U.S. Bureau of the Census, 1996). Population diversity means not only that educators and psychologists must accommodate clients from different cultural backgrounds and nations of origin but also that with increasing frequency they will find themselves working with students who either speak English as a second language or not at all.

Second, newspaper articles recently reported the number of languages spoken by students in public schools across the country to be surprisingly high, regardless of the region of the United States. As an extreme example, the Chicago public school students collectively appear to speak more languages than any other school system—two hundred in all (Pasko, 1994). Table 17.2 shows a cross-section of schools throughout the United States and the numbers of languages spoken in each of the cited school districts. What is especially salient about the data reported in the table is the fact that linguistic diversity is not restricted to a single dominant "second" language (for example, Spanish in the Southwestern United States)

Table 17.2. Languages spoken in U.S. public schools.

Location	Number	Reference
Chicago	200	Pasko (1994)
California	140	Unz (1997)
Palm Beach, Fla.	80	Fast Fact (1996)
Tempe, Ariz.	67	Ulik (1997)
Plano, Tex.	60	Power (1996)
Des Plaines, Ill.	57	Van Duch (1997)
Broward County, Fla.	54	Donzelli (1996)
Scottsdale, Ariz.	50	Steele (1998)
Prince William County, Va.	48	O'Hanlon (1997)
Cobb County, Ga.	45	Stepp (1997)
Tukwila, Wash.	30	Searcey (1998)
Schenectady, N.Y.	22	Lipman (1997)

or to major megalopolises such as Chicago, Los Angeles, or New York City. Virtually all towns, cities, states, and regions of the country face increasingly diverse local student populations—populations that require new approaches to delivering educational and psychological services.

In addition to the linguistic diversity that has been brought about by historic and current immigration to the United States, it should be recognized that considerable linguistic diversity exists among aboriginal North Americans and many long-term residents of the United States. For example, some Native Americans, especially those who live in the Western United States (for example, the Navaho) and Alaska, as well as long-standing residents (some African Americans), either speak English as a second language or speak nonstandard forms of English. Other, smaller segments of the population also speak nonstandard forms of English to a greater or lesser degree (Cajun, Gullah). In all of these instances, it has been assumed that using verbally oriented intelligence tests to assess cognitive functioning is both fair and reasonable—an assumption that warrants renewed examination.

Language-Related Disabilities

Adding to the country's diversity is the sizeable number of individuals in the United States who are deaf or have significant hearing loss. Hearing impairment represents a unique situation in which communication between people becomes difficult, especially between those who are deaf and members of the hearing population. The U.S. Department of Health and Human Services (1997) reported that across all income levels, 23,266,000 Americans are deaf or have other significant hearing impairments. Of this subset of the population, 1.5 million people are "deaf in both ears," while the remaining individuals reportedly experience a less severe degree of hearing impairment. The Health and Human Services report also indicated that nearly three million U.S. citizens have speech impairment; again, this limits their ability to communicate effectively. There are other noteworthy lower-incidence, language-related neurological and psychiatric conditions and disabilities (among them autism, aspergers, elective or selective mutism, and traumatic brain injury) that also significantly limit many individuals' ability to communicate effectively.

What is the common denominator among all of these otherwise disparate groups? These individuals, for various reasons, may be seriously disadvantaged if their cognitive functioning is assessed by any of the available traditional, language-loaded intelligence batteries (Stanford-Binet, Wechsler Scales, Woodcock-Johnson). The examinee's disadvantage in cases of this sort lies in the linguistic or cultural demands that are placed on the person by the traditional language-loaded intelligence tests—language and cultural demands that are not essential to the process of assessing intelligence.

Not only are the ubiquitous linguistic and cultural demands of traditional intelligence tests often unnecessary but sometimes they are blatantly unfair to examinees. It is important to recall that the measurement of any construct (say, general intelligence) results in two sources of score variability: reliable variance and error variance. Any extraneous variable (for example, the linguistic or cultural demands of an intelligence test) that contributes to error variance by definition is "construct irrelevant." If the client's personal language, culture, or other noncognitive attributes cause him or her to perform less optimally on a measure of general intelligence test, such interference produces construct-irrelevant variance.

Although verbally and socially relevant intellectual factors can be an important part of a standard intellectual assessment (as in assessing verbal development or social awareness), the underlying assumption has been that all examinees have been similarly exposed to the culture and language of the test. This assumption is invalid for many people within the U.S. population.

Many millions of individuals throughout the United States are seriously and unfairly disadvantaged when they are assessed with language-loaded intelligence tests simply because they speak a language other than English; or because they have not fully integrated into U.S. or Western culture; or because they have hearing, speech, or language-related conditions or disabilities that limit effective communication with others. These are all noncognitive factors that are irrelevant to the assessment of their intellectual functioning.

Previous "Solutions"

A number of approaches have been employed to render the assessment process fairer for the many individuals for whom a language-loaded intelligence test is not appropriate. The previous "solutions" have included using performance tests or translated tests, and using unidimensional "nonverbal" tests. These approaches met with various levels of success.

Performance Tests

In a variety of test use surveys, the Wechsler Scales continue to be the dominant tests used to assess children's and adults' intelligence. Psychologists are so comfortable with and have relied so heavily on the Wechsler instruments that they resort to these tests even when they may be inappropriate. For example, the Wechsler Performance Scales have been used as nonverbal measures in instances where examinees speak English as a second language, are deaf or hard of hearing, or when children have language-related disabilities that detrimentally influence their intelligence test performance.

In such instances, psychologists have correctly reasoned that the language-reduced Performance Scale is a better choice than the Verbal Scale; however, they have incorrectly reasoned that a better choice is the *most appropriate* action to take. Psychologists often assume that examinees understand the verbal directions spoken by the examiner and therefore understand the task demands for performance subtests. This assumption is not valid in many cases.

How would a monolingual Spanish-speaking examinee possibly understand the lengthy and convoluted directions for Block Design, or the subtle corrections and admonishments vocalized by the examiner as the examinee rotates a block design during construction? Each Wechsler performance subtest has test directions that are heavily laden with wordy verbal instructions, including language concepts that are beyond the developmental levels of many examinees (Bracken, 1986; Kaufman, 1990, 1994).

Not only do the performance subtests such as Picture Arrangement have verbal directions; the item content is based in Western culture and requires an understanding of specific cultural events. In both Block Design and Picture Arrangement, nonessential verbal and cultural item content presents an unnecessary hurdle for *many* examinees. Although the Wechsler Performance Scale may be fairer for many individuals than the Verbal Scale, it is still grossly unfair to many examinees.

Translated Tests

Historically, popular and useful tests have been translated for use with individuals who speak languages other than English. Although the effort to assess an individual's intelligence in the native language is commendable, there are many problems associated with the practice. Even though quality test translations are both possible and available (for example, Bracken, 1998; Bracken and others, 1990; Bracken and Fouad, 1987; Munoz-Sandoval, Cummins, Alvarado, and Ruef, 1998), state-of-the-art test translations are rare thanks to the inordinate expense and difficulty associated with the translation and validation process. Unfortunately, most translated tests, regardless of the quality of their translation, are not normed or properly validated.

It is just as expensive to translate and norm a second-language test as it is to develop and norm a dominant-language test; however, the potential market for second-language tests is a fraction of the market for the dominant-language version—even for the most frequently spoken second language in the United States, Spanish. As a result of these basic economic conditions, publishers have little hope of recouping the sizable investment necessary to produce second-language tests, especially for populations that speak low-incidence languages (say, Vietnamese).

The shortage of second-language tests is not just the fault of test publishers. Even in an ideal world in which publishers produce a translated test for every language spoken in the United States, there would still be an irreconcilable shortage of bilingual psychologists who are available to administer the two hundred or more translated tests required. Given the relative unavailability of quality translated tests and the very limited number of bilingual psychologists, the most reasonable alternative to testing children in their native language is to remove language as a confounding variable and use nonverbal tests in the assessment process (Frisby, 1999).

Unidimensional Nonverbal Tests

Of the various nonverbal tests available, there are two basic types. One type assesses a narrow aspect of intelligence primarily through use of progressive matrices; the other is the comprehensive test of intelligence that assesses multiple facets of children's intelligence.

A plethora of the former, the progressive matrix tests, are available, but there are only two comprehensive nonverbal tests of intelligence: the Leiter International Performance Scale—Revised (Roid and Miller, 1997) and the Universal Nonverbal Intelligence Test (Bracken and McCallum, 1998a).

Unidimensional tests of the matrix-solution type include the Comprehensive Test of Nonverbal Intelligence (C-TONI, Hammill, Pearson, and Wiederholt, 1996); the Test of Nonverbal Intelligence—Third Edition (TONI-3, Brown, Sherbenou, and Johnsen, 1997); the Matrix Analogies Test (MAT; Naglieri, 1985); the Naglieri Nonverbal Ability Test (N-NAT; Naglieri, 1996); the General Ability Measure for Adults (GAMA; Naglieri and Bardos,

1997); and Raven's Progressive Matrices (Raven, Raven, and Court, 1998). Each of these measures is useful for individual, and in some instances group (for example, NNAT, GAMA), screening purposes.

Unidimensional nonverbal tests offer efficient assessment as a trade-off for comprehensive assessment. In general, unidimensional tests have some advantages over comprehensive measures of intelligence (for example, cost-effectiveness, ease of administration, testing efficiency); however, currently available comprehensive nonverbal scales also provide screening batteries, comprising a limited number of subtests.

The benefits of unidimensional nonverbal tests are offset in many cases by limitations. Several of the unidimensional nonverbal tests rely on brief verbal directions. Collectively, these tests assess a narrow and limited aspect of intelligence (that is, spatial and figural relations) through a matrix-completion testing format. Typically, these measures also do not employ adaptive testing procedures, which permit items to be administered within an examinee's ability level. Also, unidimensional tests do not sample important cognitive dimensions such as memory that are elements of most major theories of intelligence.

Given the narrow focus of the unidimensional matrix analogy type tests and the fact that many of these tests employ verbal directions, these instruments are best suited for low-stakes applications. When psychoeducational assessments are conducted for reasons of high-stakes placement, eligibility, or diagnostic decision making, then broader, more comprehensive measures of intelligence would be most appropriate.

Comprehensive Nonverbal Intelligence Tests

There exist only two comprehensive nonverbal intelligence tests: the Leiter International Performance Scale-Revised and the Universal Nonverbal Intelligence Test. The two represent the tests of choice when high-stakes decisions are being made.

Leiter International Performance Scale-Revised

The Leiter International Performance Scale–Revised (Leiter-R;
Roid and Miller, 1997) is a current version of a test with a long and
rich history. The new test, like the original, contains myriad colorful stimulus materials. Rather than the wooden blocks found in the
original test, the Leiter-R employs a variety of colorful chips, cards,
pictures, stimulus easels, and a variety of assessment activities. The
entire twenty-subtest battery can be administered in a little more
than one and one-half to two hours to individuals between the ages
of two and twenty years. An abbreviated battery is also available for
screening purposes.

The Leiter-R is divided into two cognitive batteries, each with
ten subtests:

Visual and Reasoning Subtests

1. Figure Ground (FG)
2. Design Analogies (DA)
3. Form Completion (FC)
4. Matching (M)
5. Sequential Order (SO)
6. Repeated Patterns (RP)
7. Picture Context (PC)
8. Classification (C)
9. Paper Folding (PF)
10. Figure Rotation (FR)

Attention and Memory Subtests

11. Associate Pairs (AP)
12. Immediate Recognition (IR)
13. Reverse Memory (RM)
14. Visual Coding (VC)
15. Spatial Memory (SM)
16. Forward Memory (FM)
17. Attention Sustained (AS)
18. Delayed Pairs (DP)
19. Delayed Recognition (DR)
20. Attention Divided (AD)

The first battery, Visualization and Reasoning (VR), was
designed to assess fluid reasoning and visual-spatial abilities. The
second battery, Attention and Memory (AM), assesses attention,
memory, and learning processes.

The VR Battery produces five composites, which include a Brief IQ Screener (ages two to twenty), a Full Scale IQ (ages two to twenty), Fundamental Visualization (ages two to five), Fluid Reasoning (ages two to twenty), and Spatial Visualization (ages eleven to twenty). The AM Battery produces six composites, including a Memory Screener (ages two to twenty), Recognition Memory (ages two to ten), Associative Memory (ages six to twenty), Memory Span (ages six to twenty), Attention (ages six to twenty), and Memory Process (ages six to twenty). The two batteries and their respective composites produce standard scores with means of 100 and standard deviations set at 15. Leiter-R subtests produce scaled scores with traditional subtest metrics (that is, means = 10, SD = 3).

Administration

Administration of a comprehensive nonverbal test presents some unique challenges, such as directions that are very difficult to present without verbiage. The authors of the Leiter-R chose to make administration less than totally nonverbal. For example, three subtests require the examiner to verbally indicate how much time remains during the timing of the subtests, and another subtest suggests that it "*may* require brief verbal supplementation" (Roid and Miller, 1997; p. 60). The Leiter-R does not use a standardized set of common gestures throughout the scale, and the directions sometimes can be vague and confusing. In addition, the Examiners Manual sometimes provides general directions without specific accompanying gestures. For example, the directions suggest that the examiner should "encourage the child to imitate you"; "indicate nonverbally that each pair goes together"; "indicate that the child should point to red apples only"—without specifying exactly what the examiner should do to communicate these messages.

Specific administration gestures also may be less than clear for the examiner and examinee. For example, one Leiter-R subtest direction states that the examiner should "Indicate that card is 'mentally rotated' by touching your head and eyes and nodding

'Yes.' To demonstrate that cards should not be turned, begin to physically rotate card with your hand. Lightly tap that hand, with the
other. Shake your finger back and forth to indicated (sic) 'No' to
turning the card" (Roid and Miller, 1997; p. 44).

The Examiners Manual allows some adaptation of the administration directions for exceptional populations; for example, the
directions suggest that "It may be necessary to create unusual methods by which the child can communicate their (sic) 'answers to test
items'" (p. 76). It is uncertain, however, how these modifications
affect the Leiter-R norms.

Normative Sample

The total Leiter-R sample size is impressive and appears to represent a strength; however, a molecular evaluation indicates some limitations as well. The VR Battery was normed on 1,719 children,
adolescents, and adults across the two-to-twenty-year age range.
The AM Battery normative sample included a smaller sample of
763 children, adolescents, and adults. All 763 examinees who were
administered the AM Battery during the instrument's norming also
were administered the entire VR Battery. Overall, the VR norms were
based on an average sample size of slightly fewer than 100 individuals per age level (that is, nineteen age levels, 1,719 examinees). The
AM Battery included fewer than one hundred examinees at *every*
age level across the entire age span, with samples that ranged from
forty-two examinees at four age levels (that is, seven, eight, eleven,
and eighteen to twenty years) to a maximum of eighty-six children
sampled at the two-year age level.

The Leiter-R normative sample was selected to represent the
U.S. population on the basis of gender, race, socioeconomic status,
community size, and geographic region (although the number and
location of specific standardization sites were not reported). The AM
sample, given its overall smaller size, has proportionally larger deviations from the U.S. population than does the larger VR sample.
Gender representation in the AM sample ranges from 39.6 percent

male (ages fourteen and fifteen years) to 64.6 percent male at age three, resulting in deviations from the population parameters by as much as 11 to 15 percent. Overrepresentation and underrepresentation of the population on the remaining AM stratification variables also varies more than one would anticipate. For example, the socioeconomic selection variable "parent educational level" varied considerably across the age range. Although 19.8 percent of the U.S. adult population has less than a high school education, the Leiter-R sample ranges from 2.3 percent at age six to 26.7 percent at age two on this variable.

Technical Properties

Leiter-R coefficient alphas for the VR subtests range from .75 to .90 across the age levels. The average internal consistency for the AM subtests is generally lower and ranges from .67 to .87. Reliabilities for the Leiter-R VR Battery composites range from .88 to .93 (Full Scale IQ .91 to .93) and from .75 to .93 for the AM composites.

Leiter-R VR Battery score stability was investigated across three broad age levels for a sample of 163 children and adolescents (ages two to twenty years; median age eight years, eleven months). VR subtest stability coefficients range between .61 and .81 (ages two to five), .70 and .83 (ages six to ten), and .65 and .90 (ages eleven to twenty). VR composite stability coefficients range from .83 to .90 (ages two to five), .83 to .91 (ages six to ten), and .86 to .96 (ages eleven to twenty).

These stability coefficients appear to be significantly inflated because of excessive variability among examinees' test scores. As compared to the normative standard deviation of 15, the VR Full Scale IQ produced a posttest standard deviation that was twice the normal variability (that is, 30.00); the VR pretest Full Scale IQ also demonstrated excessive variability ($SD = 29.5$). These correlation coefficients would have been more informative had they been corrected for expansion in range; both obtained and corrected correlations should have been reported in the Examiners Manual (see guidelines in AERA, APA, and NCME, 1985, 1999).

An investigation of the stability of the AM Battery was also presented in the Examiners Manual, with a sample of forty-five children and adolescents (ages six to seventeen years; median age ten years, eleven months). The AM Battery is generally less stable than the VR Battery, with corrected subtest coefficients that range from .55 to .85 (median = .615). AM composite stability coefficients range from .61 to 85 (median = .745). It is difficult to evaluate the stability of the VR and AM subtests and composites because the time intervals between initial testing and posttesting are not reported.

The Leiter-R Examiners Manual reports several validity studies that investigate the instrument's ability to discriminate among special groups. Presentation of these validity studies is admirable; however, the meaningfulness of the studies appears limited because the mean Full Scale IQs for the various samples are generally lower than one would anticipate. Every sample except the gifted students earned a mean FSIQ that was less than the test's normative mean of 100); the gifted mean Full Scale IQ was 114.6. There is no explanation in the Examiners Manual why the disparate groups of children identified as motor delayed, hearing disordered, speech delayed, or learning disabled produced mean IQs in the middle seventies and eighties.

A variety of concurrent validity studies also are reported in the Leiter-R Examiners Manual, with contrasts between the Leiter-R and other intelligence tests, such as the original Leiter, WISC-III, and select subtests from the Stanford-Binet Intelligence Scale Fourth Edition (Thorndike, Hagen, and Sattler, 1986). Although the correlation between the Leiter-R Full Scale IQ and WISC-III FSIQ for a sample of normative, cognitively delayed, gifted, and ESL-Spanish cases is reported in the Examiners Manual as .86, the standard deviations on both instruments employed in this study are between 23 and 26 IQ points. As with the Leiter-R stability studies, expanded range of variability likely produced significantly inflated validity coefficients.

Roid and Miller (1997) suggest that the Leiter-R subtests fit the proposed underlying hierarchical g model proposed for the instrument (p. 184); however, when Kaufman's criteria (1979, 1994) for "good" (> .70), "fair" (.50 to .69), and "poor" (< .50) loadings on the g factor are considered, most of the Leiter-R's subtests do not appear to be strong measures of g. All Leiter-R subtests are classified as either "fair" or "poor" measures of g, except two, according to Kaufman's criteria.

At ages two to five years, the Leiter-R g loadings range from .26 to .66 (poor to fair), with a median of .595 (fair); g loadings range from .26 to .65 (poor to fair) at ages six to ten years (median = .45, poor); and, at ages eleven to twenty years the g loadings range from .24 to .70 (poor to good), with a (fair) median of .56 (Roid and Miller, 1997, p. 192). The two Leiter-R subtests that qualify as "good" g loaders (Sequential Order and Paper Folding) meet Kaufman's criterion at only one of the three broad age levels studied (ages eleven to twenty years); these two subtests are classified as "fair" or "poor" measures of g at the remaining age levels.

As part of a cross-battery approach to test interpretation, McGrew and Flanagan (1998) examined the extent to which cultural content is embedded in various intelligence tests. Eight of the twenty Leiter-R subtests were identified by McGrew and Flanagan as containing a "high" level of cultural content (for example, pictures of culture-specific objects); three additional subtests were identified as "moderate" in their level of cultural content.

Universal Nonverbal Intelligence Test

The Universal Nonverbal Intelligence Test (UNIT; Bracken and McCallum, 1998a) was developed as a nonverbal test to assess diverse populations of children and adolescents in a 100 percent language-free fashion. It is also intended for children with conditions or disabilities that would negatively affect their performance on traditional language-loaded intelligence tests. Such conditions include language-related learning disabilities (for example, expressive language LD, nonverbal LD), psychiatric conditions (elective mutism, autism, social phobia, and so on), sensory limitations (deaf, hard of hearing, and the like), and language-impairing neurological disorders (such as traumatic brain injury).

As a comprehensive intelligence test, the UNIT was designed to assess both general intelligence and foundational cognitive abilities (memory and reasoning) through symbolic and nonsymbolic modalities. Of the six UNIT subtests, three assess short-term, working memory (Memory Scale) and three assess aspects of reasoning (Reasoning Scale); three subtests also are assigned to each of the two secondary scales, Symbolic and Nonsymbolic. Reasoning and memory are considered "primary abilities" because they represent foundational intellectual abilities identified by historical and current theorists, such as Thurstone (1938) and Carroll (1993). The Symbolic and Nonsymbolic Scales are considered as "secondary" measures because they represent the inferred processes that underlie and facilitate task solution.

The first two subtests (Symbolic Memory and Cube Design) together form the two-subtest fifteen-minute Abbreviated Battery intended for intellectual screening (see Table 17.3). The first four subtests (Symbolic Memory, Cube Design, Spatial Memory, and Analogic Reasoning) constitute a thirty-minute Standard Battery intended for placement and eligibility decision making. When all six subtests are combined, they form the Extended Battery. The

Table 17.3. UNIT scale and subtest composition.

Subtest Name	Primary Scale	Secondary Scale	Battery*
1. Symbolic Memory	Memory	Symbolic	A/S/E
2. Cube Design	Reasoning	Nonsymbolic	A/S/E
3. Spatial Memory	Memory	Nonsymbolic	S/E
4. Analogic Reasoning	Reasoning	Symbolic	S/E
5. Object Memory	Memory	Symbolic	E
6. Mazes	Reasoning	Nonsymbolic	E

Note: *A = Abbreviated, S = Standard, E = Extended.

Extended Battery requires about forty-five minutes to administer and is intended for eligibility testing and providing additional diagnostic information.

Administration

UNIT materials include bicolored (green and white) plastic blocks, stimulus chips and cards, laminated response mats, and stand-alone stimulus easels. These materials are used in a 100 percent language-free manner, along with eight standardized gestures and four distinct item types, to ensure that the examinee understands the task demands of each subtest. The four item types include traditional scored items, demonstration items, sample items, and follow-up "check point items." Check point items are scored for credit, but they allow the examiner to correct an examinee's incorrect response.

A twenty-two-minute training video (Bracken and McCallum, 1998b) was also developed to facilitate mastery of UNIT administration, scoring, and interpretation. The training video presents the theoretical orientation of the test, shows how each subtest is administered, and describes scoring criteria and interpretation procedures. In addition to detailed test directions in the Examiner's Manual, succinct abbreviated directions are printed on a laminated "Administration at a Glance" card. Once examiners feel comfortable with UNIT administration procedure, they may use this 8.5 × 11-inch laminated card to guide subsequent administration.

Normative Sample

The UNIT was normed on children and adolescents across the ages of five years through seventeen years, eleven months. A total of 175 students were tested per age level, with the exception of the age level from sixteen years to seventeen years, eleven months, which included 175 subjects for the two-year age span. An additional 1,765 students participated in UNIT reliability, validity, and fairness studies. The UNIT normative sample was drawn from 108 sites in thirty-eight states representing the four regions of the United

States. The norming sample was stratified on the basis of sex, race, Hispanic origin, region of the country, classroom placement, special-education services, and parental education attainment. The match between the UNIT normative sample and the U.S. population parameters was generally within one percentage point for the total sample on all stratifying variables (within 3–4 percentage points at individual age levels).

Special populations were included in the UNIT normative sample to ensure representation of individuals from the populations for whom the test was intended. Authorities in cross-cultural or non-biased assessment agree that test fairness is enhanced if the test's normative sample includes proportionate representation of students with various disabilities or cultural or linguistic backgrounds (for example, Barona and Santos de Barona, 1987; Caterino, 1990; Gonzales, 1982).

Technical Properties

Alpha coefficients were calculated for the entire UNIT standardization sample, a separate clinical or exceptional sample, and subsets of the standardization sample that include African American and Hispanic examinees. The average reliabilities of the Abbreviated, Standard, and Extended Battery Full Scale IQs are .91, .93, and .93 respectively for the entire standardization sample; .95, .97, and .96 for African American students; .94, .96, and .96 for Hispanic examinees; and .96, .98, and .98 for the clinical or exceptional sample. Internal consistency coefficients for the four UNIT scales ranged from .86 to .91 across the Standard and Extended Batteries, and scale reliabilities ranged from .92 to .97 for the African American, Hispanic, and clinical samples. Subtest reliability coefficients ranged from .81 to .96 for the African American, clinical, and Hispanic samples, and .64 to .91 for the standardization sample across the five year to seventeen year, eleven month age levels.

The UNIT Examiner's Manual reports coefficients of interest, known as "local reliability" coefficients, for score levels at which psychologists must make important diagnostic decisions (mental retardation: FSIQ = 70 plus or minus 10 points; gifted identification: FSIQ = 130 plus or minus 10 points). Full Scale IQ reliability for students functioning at the mental-retardation and gifted-intellectual levels were an identical .97, .98, and .98 for the Abbreviated, Standard, and Extended Batteries, respectively.

UNIT stability was examined in a test-retest study that included 197 participants, with approximately fifteen examinees in each age group between five and seventeen years. The mean test-retest interval was 20.3 days, and the sample consisted of 76.1 percent white students, 19.8 percent African American, 3 percent Asian, and 1 percent Hispanic origin students; 1 percent of the sample was designated as members of "other" racial or ethnic groups. The sample also included 49.2 percent male students and was proportionately represented in terms of students' parental educational attainment. Across the entire sample, average subtest stability coefficients, corrected for restriction in range of variability, ranged from .58 to .85 (uncorrected coefficients are also presented in the Examiner's Manual); average scale reliabilities ranged from .78 to .84, and average Full Scale reliabilities for the Abbreviated, Standard, and Extended Batteries were .83, .88, .85, respectively. Stability coefficients varied slightly across the age groups, with the older age levels evidencing greater reliability than the younger ones.

The UNIT Examiner's Manual reports strong floors and ceilings at the Full Scale, Scale, and individual subtest levels for all ages on the Standard and Extended Batteries. The floor of the Abbreviated Battery is not as strong as the other batteries at the five-year age level. Across the age levels, UNIT subtests evidence item gradients that are sufficiently sensitive such that a change in raw score by passing or failing one item does not alter the subtest scaled score by more than one-third standard deviation.

The UNIT Examiner's Manual presents concurrent validity studies with traditional comprehensive and brief intelligence tests (for example, the WISC-III; Woodcock-Johnson Psycho-Educational Battery–Revised, WJ-R; Kaufman Brief Intelligence Test), as well as several unidimensional nonverbal intelligence tests (among them the Matrix Analogies Test; Raven's Standard Progressive Matrices; and Test of Nonverbal Intelligence, Second Edition). Correlations between the UNIT and the comprehensive measures of intelligence (WISC-III, WJ-R) were conducted with a variety of samples (learning disabled, mentally retarded, gifted, Native American) and produced full scale correlations in the .65 to .88 range, with nonsignificant mean score differences between the UNIT and the criterion tests. Correlations with the unidimensional nonverbal tests produced generally lower correlations, presumably because of the limited scope of intelligence assessed by these unidimensional instruments.

The UNIT was designed to be a strong measure of general intelligence, and exploratory factor analysis of the UNIT Standard Battery provides evidence for a strong g factor. In addition to g, the exploratory factor analyses provided evidence for the two primary factors, reasoning and memory. Analysis of the Extended Battery gave evidence for a strong g factor and three additional factors. All Extended Battery subtests, except Mazes, loaded highly on either a reasoning or memory factor, as predicted. Mazes alone showed a "mixed" loading on the second (reasoning) factor *and* a relatively strong loading on the third. The unique factor created by Mazes appears to be related to *planning*, given the subtest's unique scoring system, which rewards reflective, planful responding.

Using Kaufman's classification (1979, 1994) for g loadings, five of the six UNIT subtests are rated as "good" measures of general intelligence, with loadings of .71 to .79 on the first unrotated factor. Mazes (on the Extended Battery) was the only subtest that was rated less favorably, with a g loading of .44 (poor). Although Mazes had a poor g rating, improvements made to this UNIT subtest appear to have enhanced its g loadings over the mazes subtest on the WISC-III, which had a substantially lower g loading of .30.

Fairness

The UNIT was designed for fair assessment of intelligence in minority children and children of poverty, who historically have been overrepresented and underrepresented in programs for the mentally retarded and gifted, respectively (Rycraft, 1990). In their effort to address the issue of fair assessment for children, regardless of the examinee's gender, race, nation of origin, or exceptional condition, the UNIT authors included a chapter dedicated to "fairness in testing" in the Examiner's Manual. It addresses the manner in which fairness was a consideration throughout UNIT development. In an attempt to achieve fair assessment for multilingual, multicultural, and multiracial peoples, the UNIT subtests are 100 percent nonverbal; they demonstrate sound psychometric qualities and in general are low in cultural content. Such subtest characteristics lead to fairer assessment of children for whom traditional language-loaded and culture-loaded intelligence tests would be inappropriate (Frisby, 1999).

Additionally, every UNIT item was reviewed by a comprehensive and inclusive "sensitivity panel" and subjected to extensive Differential Item Function (DIF) analysis as part of the test development process. Items identified as problematic by either the DIF analysis or the sensitivity panel were eliminated. An independent DIF investigation (Maller, in press) was also conducted on a sample of deaf students, with compelling and favorable results (that is, no UNIT items evidenced significant DIF for deaf students).

Differences in mean scores between groups (males and females, white and blacks), although not an a priori indication of test bias (Jensen, 1980), have important social implications. To address the issue of equitable test use, matched samples of whites and Hispanics, African Americans, Native Americans, Asian and Pacific Islanders, bilingual children, and children residing in Ecuador were compared and reported in the UNIT Examiner's Manual. Also, a mean score comparison between a matched sample of deaf and nondeaf children is reported in the Examiner's Manual. Sizeable reductions in the "typical" mean score discrepancies reported in the literature were found between the various matched samples on the UNIT.

Finally, in a study designed to determine population characteristics associated with certain core profile patterns, Wilhoit (2000) reports 4 percent of African Americans were found in the "highest" UNIT core profile. This value can be compared to .1 percent in the highest core profile on the WISC-III. Similarly, fewer African Americans are included in the lowest UNIT core profile relative to the lowest core profile on the WISC-III (see also Glutting, McDermott, and Konold, 1997, for WISC-III figures). Thus, the UNIT appears to identify *more* higher-ability and *fewer* lower-ability African Americans than the WISC-III using this core profiling strategy.

Summary

The United States continues to serve the world as a social melting pot, with immigrants continuously settling farther and farther from their U.S. port of entry. Rural and middle America is becoming as ethnically and linguistically diverse as the historically diverse urban coastal areas. It is impossible to translate and validate intelligence tests for a population that collectively speaks two hundred or more languages, and intelligence tests continue to carry significant weight in determining the opportunities and outcomes that are part of people's lives.

It is apparent that the traditional, language-loaded intelligence tests used at the turn of the twenty-first century are just as unfair to many individuals as the English-language tests administered to immigrants who were processed through Ellis Island during the turn of the twentieth century. Attempts to produce language-free tests have been renewed, with better success and greater acceptance in recent years. There are now many unidimensional and short forms of comprehensive nonverbal tests available for intellectual screening, and there are two comprehensive nonverbal intelligence tests that psychologists can use whenever a traditional language-loaded intelligence test is inappropriate for either screening or eligibility decision making. What is most important now is that psychologists broaden their assessment repertoire and begin to use nonverbal tests of intelligence when a client's manifest language skills inhibit the assessment of his or her latent cognitive ability.

References

AERA, APA, & NCME (1985). *Standards for educational and psychological testing.* Washington, DC: American Psychological Association.

AERA, APA, & NCME (1999). *Standards for educational and psychological testing.* Washington, DC: American Educational Research Association.

Arthur, G. (1947). *A Point Scale of Performance Tests: Clinical manual.* New York: Commonwealth Fund.

Arthur, G., & Woodrow, H. (1919). An absolute intelligence scale: A study in method. *Journal of Applied Psychology, III,* 118–137.

Barona, A., & Santos de Barona, M. (1987). A model for the assessment for limited English proficient students referred for special education services. In S. H. Fradd & W. J. Tikunoff (Eds.), *Bilingual education and bilingual special education* (pp. 183–209). Austin, TX: Pro-Ed.

Bracken, B. A. (1986). Incidence of basic concepts in the directions of five commonly used American tests of intelligence. *School Psychology International, 7,* 1–10.

Bracken, B. A. (1998). *Bracken Basic Concept Scale-Revised.* San Antonio, TX: The Psychological Corporation.

Bracken, B. A., Barona, A., Bauermeister, J. J., Howell, K. K., Poggioli, L., & Puente, A. (1990). Multinational validation of the Spanish Bracken Basic Concept Scale for cross-cultural assessment. *Journal of School Psychology, 28,* 325–341.

Bracken, B. A., & Fouad, N. (1987). Spanish translation and validation of the Bracken Basic Concept Scale. *School Psychology Review, 16,* 94–102.

Bracken, B. A., & McCallum, R. S. (1998a). *Universal Nonverbal Intelligence Test.* Itasca, IL: Riverside.

Bracken, B. A., & McCallum, R. S. (1998b). *Universal Nonverbal Intelligence Test: Training Video.* Itasca, IL: Riverside.

Brown, L., Sherbenou, R. J., & Johnsen, S. K. (1997). *Test of Nonverbal Intelligence—3rd Edition.* Austin, TX: Pro-Ed.

Carrey, N. J. (1995). Itard's 1828 memoire on "mutism caused by a lesion of the intellectual functions": A historical analysis. *Journal of the American Academy of Child and Adolescent Psychiatry, 341*, 655–661.

Carroll, J. B. (1993). *Human cognitive abilities: A survey of factor-analytic studies.* Cambridge, England: Cambridge University Press.

Caterino, L. C. (1990). Step-by-step procedure for the assessment of language-minority children. In A. Barona & E. E. Garcia (Eds.), *Children at risk: Poverty, minority status, and other issues of educational equity* (pp. 269–282). Washington, DC: National Association of School Psychologists.

Donzelli, J. (1996, September 11). How do you say "milk" in 54 different ways? *Sun Sentinel* (Fort Lauderdale), East Broward edition, community closeup section, p. 11.

Fast Fact. (1996, December 5). *Sun Sentinel* (Fort Lauderdale), Palm Beach edition, local section, p. 1B.

Frisby, C. L. (1999). Straight talk about cognitive assessment and diversity. *School Psychology Quarterly, 14*, 195–207.

Glutting, J. J., McDermott, P. A., & Konold, T. R. (1997). Ontology, structure, and diagnostic benefits of a normative subtest taxonomy from the WISC-III standardization sample. In D. P. Flanagan, J. L. Gunshaft, & P. L. Harrison (Eds.), *Contemporary intellectual assessment: Theories, tests, and issues* (pp. 349–372). New York: Guilford Press.

Gonzales, E. (1982). Issues in assessment of minorities. In H. L. Swanson & B. L. Watson (Eds.), *Educational and psychological assessment of exceptional children* (pp. 375–389). St. Louis: Mosby.

Hammill, D. D., Pearson, N. A., & Wiederholt, J. L. (1996). *Comprehensive Test of Nonverbal Intelligence.* Austin, TX: Pro-Ed.

Healy, W. L. (1914). A pictorial completion test. *Psychological Review, xx,* 189–203.

Healy, W. L. (1918). *Pictorial Completion Test II.* Chicago: C. H. Stoelting.

Healy, W. L. (1921). Pictorial Completion Test II. *Journal of Applied Psychology, 5,* 232–233.

Itard, J.M.G. (1932). *The wild boy of Aveyron.* New York: Appleton-Century-Crofts.

Jensen, A. R. (1980). *Bias in mental testing.* New York: Free Press.

Kaufman, A. S. (1979). *Intelligent testing with the WISC-R.* New York: Wiley.

Kaufman, A. S. (1990). *Assessing adolescent and adult intelligence.* Needham Heights, MA: Allyn & Bacon.

Kaufman, A. S. (1994). *Intelligent testing with the WISC-III.* New York: Wiley.

Kaufman, A. S., & Kaufman, N. L. (1990). *Kaufman Brief Intelligence Test*. Circle Pines, MN: American Guidance Service.

Knox, H. A. (1914). A scale based on the work at Ellis Island for estimating mental defect. *Journal of the American Medical Association, 62*, 741–747.

Kohs, S. C. (1919). *Intelligence measurement*. New York: Macmillan.

Lipman, H. (1997, August 3). A change in ethnic demographics presents new challenges, opportunities. *Albany Times Union*, p. A1.

Maller, S. (in press). Item invariance in four subtests of the Universal Nonverbal Intelligence Test across groups of deaf and hearing children. In J. Braden (Ed.), *Nonverbal Assessment of Intelligence: A Special Issue of the Journal of Psychoeducational Assessment*.

McGrew, K. S., & Flanagan, D. P. (1998). *The intelligence test desk reference (ITDR): Gf—Gc cross-battery assessment*. Needham Heights, MA: Allyn & Bacon.

Munoz-Sandoval, A. E., Cummins, J., Alvarado, C. G., & Ruef, M. L. (1998). *Bilingual Verbal Ability Tests*. Itasca, IL: Riverside.

Naglieri, J. A. (1985). *Matrix Analogies Test—Expanded Form*. San Antonio, TX: The Psychological Corporation.

Naglieri, J. A. (1996). *Naglieri Nonverbal Ability Test*. San Antonio: The Psychological Corporation.

Naglieri, J. A., & Bardos, A. N. (1997). *General Ability Measure for Adults*. Minneapolis, MN: NCS Assessments.

O'Hanlon, A. (1997, May 11). Non-English speakers are testing schools. *Washington Post*, Prince William extra section, p. V01.

Pasko, J. R. (1994). Chicago—don't miss it. *Communiqué, 23*(4), 2.

Porteus, S. D. (1915). Mental tests for the feebleminded: A new series. *Journal of Psycho-Asthenics, 19*, 200–213.

Power, S. (1996, May 9). Panel suggests school clerks learn Spanish: Board takes no action on report. *Dallas Morning News*, Plano section, p. 1F.

Raven, J., Raven, J. C., & Court, J. H. (1998). *Manual for Raven's Progressive Matrices and Vocabulary Scales*. Oxford, UK: Oxford University Press.

Roid, G. H., & Miller, L. J. (1997). *Leiter International Performance Scale—Revised*. Wood Dale, IL: Stoelting.

Rycraft, J. R. (1990). Behind the walls of poverty: Economically disadvantaged gifted and talented children. *Early Child Development and Care, 63*, 139–147.

Searcey, D. (1998, February 9). Tukwila high school is true cultural melting pot. *Seattle Times*, south section, p. B1.

Seguin, E. (1907). *Idiocy and its treatment by the physiological method*. New York: Teachers College, Columbia University.

Steele, M. (1998, January 23). Bilingual education program an expensive failure. *Arizona Republic,* northeast Phoenix community section, p. 2.

Stepp, D. (1997, November 20). School watch: as demographics change, language programs grow; transition help: the International Welcome Center helps non-English-speaking students adjust. *Atlanta Journal and Constitution,* extra section, p. 02g.

Thorndike, R. L., Hagen, E. P., & Sattler, J. M. (1986). *Stanford-Binet Intelligence Scale: Fourth Edition.* Itasca, IL: Riverside.

Thorndike, R. M., & Lohman, D. F. (1990). *A century of ability testing.* Chicago: Riverside.

Thurstone, L. L. (1938). Primary mental abilities. *Psychometric Monographs,* no. 1.

Ulik, C. (1997, January 6). Civil rights officials check Tempe schools; limited-English programs studied. *Arizona Republic/Phoenix Gazette,* Tempe community section, p. 1.

Unz, R. (1997, October 19). Perspective on education: bilingual is a damaging myth; a system that ensures failure is kept alive by the flow of federal dollars. A 1998 initiative would bring change. *Los Angeles Times,* opinion section, part M, p. 5.

U.S. Bureau of the Census. (1996). *Statistical abstract of the United States: 1996.* Washington, DC: Author.

U.S. Bureau of the Census. (1998). *Statistical abstract of the United States: 1998.* Washington, DC: Author.

U.S. Department of Health and Human Services (1997). *Vital and health statistics: Prevalence of selected chronic conditions: United States, 1990–1992.* Washington, DC: Author.

Van Duch, M. (1997, January 19). Learning that other language—English—can be fun. *Chicago Tribune,* tempo northwest section, zone NW, p. 2.

Wilhoit, B. (2000). Normative subtest taxonomy of the Universal Nonverbal Intelligence Test (UNIT): Applications and implications. Unpublished doctoral dissertation, University of Tennessee, Knoxville.

18

Neuropsychological Assessment in a
Multicultural Context

Arthur MacNeill Horton Jr., Christine H. Carrington,
and Ometha Lewis-Jack

In the last half century, interest in brain-behavioral relationships or neuropsychology has increased at a tremendous rate. On the one hand, there are multiple examples of the cross-cultural validity of neuropsychological research findings as well as successful application of neuropsychological assessment methods (Horton, 1994; Horton and Wedding, 1984; Reitan and Davidson, 1974; Reitan and Wolfson, 1992; Reynolds and Fletcher-Janzen, 1989). On the other hand, it would be naïve to assume that assessment of neuropsychological behavior has escaped the cultural and racial biases that are pervasive in psychological assessment (Helms, 1992; Ivey, 1991; Padilla and Medina, 1996; Sue and Sue, 1990; Chavez and Gonzalez-Singh, 1980). Culturally sensitive neuropsychological methods are likely to give us the best evidence supporting the relevance of this body of knowledge to the practice of psychological assessment in rehabilitation and other settings.

This chapter describes major neuropsychological assessment measures and the constructs they assess, as well as discussing the biases and limitations of some of these measures across ethnic and cultural domains.

Overview of Neuropsychological Assessment

Meier (1974) has defined neuropsychology as "the scientific study of brain-behavioral relationships." Twenty-five years after it was proposed, the definition is still relevant and appropriate. Horton and Puente (1990) have noted that neuropsychological performance is influenced by both organic and environmental variables. The organic nature of neuropsychological variables has been clearly demonstrated through the work of such neuropsychologists as Ralph M. Reitan, Arthur L. Benton, Charles J. Golden, and A. R. Luria, among others, over several decades. Environmental variables, of course, include the cultural aspects that are addressed in this chapter.

As is well known, the human brain is divided into two cerebral hemispheres (Luria, 1966). Each cerebral hemisphere is similar but not identical in structure and function to the other. The term *cerebral asymmetry* refers to the differences between the two cerebral hemispheres. As would be expected, given that human beings are dominant on one side of the body versus the other side, one cerebral hemisphere is usually larger than the other. In the vast majority of right-hand individuals, the left cerebral hemisphere is slightly larger than the right. It is often suggested that the reason for the left cerebral hemisphere being slightly larger is that the left subserves language functions in the human (Horton and Wedding, 1984). Essentially, the need to support spoken language and various symbolic methods of communication has resulted in areas of the brain being further developed as human beings evolve to an information intensive society.

Major Neuropsychology Assessment Approaches

The neuropsychological test batteries to be discussed are the Halstead-Reitan Neuropsychological Test Battery and the Luria-Nebraska Neuropsychological Battery. It should be noted that these neuropsychological test batteries are often supplemented by additional tests, according to the specific needs of the assessment situation; the patient's reported problem or chief complaint; and particular educational, medical neurological, and social characteristics. Indeed, it highly is recommended that standardized batteries be supplemented in special circumstances when assessing individuals from diverse cultural and ethnic groups.

Note also that the term *standard* may be a misnomer when assessing diverse cultural and ethnic groups. *Standard* implies that the test battery has been standardized on a sample that includes a representative number of persons from which the results of this group can be generalized to the population group in question. As in most cases, neuropsychological batteries (and single tests) have included too few members of diverse cultural and ethnic groups in the standardization, such that the instruments cannot be assumed to be standard but are likely to be skewed to the values and beliefs of the groups sampled. In this context, although using multiple levels of inference may assist in mitigating ethnic differences, further research is needed to empirically validate the notion that examiner biases in interpretation are minimized. Much additional research is needed to identify appropriate strategies for correcting the inherent problems of standardization noted here.

Halstead-Reitan Neuropsychological Test Battery

The Halstead-Reitan Neuropsychological Test Battery is the result of the work of Ward Halstead, an experimental psychologist who worked at the University of Chicago in the years prior to, during, and following the second World War (Horton and Wedding, 1984). Ralph M. Reitan worked with Halstead and later adapted, augmented, and modified Halstead's tests to devise a neuropsychological assessment battery for use with brain-injured patients. The Halstead-Reitan Neuropsychological Test Battery (and age-appropriate variations) used today is an adaptation of the original Halstead-Reitan Neuropsychological Test Battery for Adults (Reitan and Wolfson, 1992).

There are five major tests:

1. The Category Test consists of 208 slides organized into seven subtests with a single idea or concept running throughout it. The task is to select a number between one and four for each slide as an answer. The patient is given immediate feedback whether the answer is right or wrong; the accuracy at which the correct principle is identified is used to gauge visual abstract reasoning and concept-formation skills.

2. The Tactual Performance Test (TPT) is a psychomotor problem-solving task, involving tactile form identification, incidental memory, and special location recollection. The task is to put geometric blocks into holes in the board into which the blocks fit, while blindfolded. To assess lateralized hemispheric functioning, the task is done in three trials.

3. The Seashore Rhythm Test is a measure of nonverbal auditory perceptual skills. Essentially, the rhythm test is used to assess discrimination of rhythmic sequences. In addition to sensitivity to nonverbal patterns, the test also measures attention abilities, to a degree.

4 In the Speech Sound Perception Test, stimuli are sixty recorded nonsense words; the patient responds by underlining the response alternative that matches a tape-recorded stimulus. The test is a verbal measure of auditory perceptual skills and assesses the ability to discriminate speech-related sounds.

5. The Finger Tapping Test is a measure of fine motor skill. Essentially, a special mechanical finger-tapping device is used. The test measures motor speed and reflects the condition of the contralateral motor strip.

There are also a number of ancillary measures: the Tactile Figure Recognition Test, the Fingertip Numbering Test, and the Tactile Form Recognition Test, as well as the Aphasia Screening Test, the Strength of Grip Test, and the Trail-Making Test among others (see Horton and Wedding, 1984; or Reitan and Wolfson, 1992, for test descriptions and details of administration). In addition to the tests previously enumerated, an age-appropriate Wechsler Intelligence Scale is usually given in conjunction with the neuropsychological test battery.

Luria-Nebraska Neuropsychological Test Battery

This battery was derived from the work of A. R. Luria, the famous Russian neuropsychologist (Horton and Wedding, 1984). The Luria-Nebraska Neuropsychological Test Battery is based on an adaptation of Luria's work developed by a Scandinavian neuropsychologist, Anne-Lise Christensen, who worked with Luria in the Soviet Union some years ago. Christensen published a manual and test cards that were based on Luria's tests as described in *Higher Cortical Functions in Man* (Luria, 1966).

Charles J. Golden, a neuropsychologist in the United States, along with his graduate students, standardized the administration and scoring of Christensen's material in the late seventies and produced a version of what is now known as the Luria-Nebraska Neuropsychological Test Battery (Golden, Hammeke, and Purish, 1978). Numerous research articles have demonstrated the value of the Luria-Nebraska Neuropsychological Test Battery in neuropsychology (Horton and Wedding, 1984). The scales are Motor, Rhythm, Tactile, Visual, Receptive Speech, Expressive Speech, Writing, Reading, Arithmetic, Memory, and Intellectual Processes (Golden, Hammeke, and Purish, 1980).

To a degree, the first four scales—Motor, Rhythm, Tactile, and Visual—deal with basic perceptual motor processes. The next two scales, Receptive Speech and Expressive Language, are clearly language-related. The three scales that follow (Writing, Reading, and Arithmetic) are related to academic abilities. The last two scales, Memory and Intellectual Processes, are clearly cognitively oriented.

Regarding the perceptual-motor group of scales, the Motor scales include items assessing motor skills, coordination, drawing, and go-no-go skills. On the Rhythm scale, the patient is required to discriminate tones and rhythmetric patterns and to sing parts of songs and reproduce parts of rhythmetric speech. On the Tactile scale, specific items deal with finger localization, tactile discrimination, and the ability to identify objects placed in the hand. On the Visual scale, the patient is required to visually identify incomplete pictures and shaded figures and answer questions based on mental rotation of figures.

The first of the two language-related scales, Receptive Speech, includes comprehension of auditory sounds, such as analyzing simple phonemes and understanding verbal speech. The Expressive Speech scale requires production of oral speech, such as repeating words and phrases, naming objects, and spontaneous reactive speech. The academic scales for Writing, Reading, and Arithmetic are composed of academically related items. On the Writing scale, the patient is required to analyze words, spell, and write from visual and auditory instructions. To a degree, the Writing scale confounds the areas of writing and spelling, so an item-by-item analysis is necessary to discern which process is impaired. On the Reading scale, letter and word recognition and paragraph reading are required. On the Arithmetic scale, the patient is required to recognize numbers, compare them, and perform elementary math calculations.

Next are the cognitive scales. On the Memory scale, the patient demonstrates word list learning, visual memory, and verbal memory as well as recalling a paragraph and paired-associate learning. On the Intellectual Processes scale, the items include explaining the meaning of words, interpreting pictures and verbal stories, and comprehending text material and quickly solving arithmetic problems.

Items on the Luria-Nebraska Neuropsychological Battery are each considered separate and unique examples of behavior. Criteria for scoring may include, but are not limited to, adequacy of behavioral response, number of items produced, response latency, accuracy, and learning speed. Responses are scored in three categories or ratings. A score of zero suggest normal performance. A score of one suggests borderline or mild impairment, and a score of two clearly suggests brain damage (Golden, Hammeke, and Purish, 1980). Scale scores can be transformed into T scores with a mean of 50 and a standard deviation of 10. This allows comparison between and among the various subtests scales (Golden, Hammeke, and Purish, 1980).

Overview of Critical Issues in Neuropsychological Testing Biases and Limitations Cross-Culturally

The relevance of culture and ethnicity in formulating credible neuropsychological assessment profiles has been clearly documented across studies (Anastasi and Urbina, 1997; Bernard, 1989; Manly and others, 1998; Lichtenberg, Ross, and Christensen, 1994; Artiola i Fortuny and Mullaney, 1997). But how specific dimensions of culture and ethnicity contribute to variance in performance on neuropsychological tests is still controversial (Ford-Booker and others, 1993; Campbell and others, 1996).

Issues in this debate are wide ranging, from focusing on the lack of representativeness of standard neuropsychological instruments (because of failure to include diverse groups in the normative samples) to identifying culture-specific behaviors that all competent neuropsychologists should be aware of in the daily practice of the profession (Ford-Booker and others, 1993; Betancourt and Lopez, 1993; Lichtenberg, Ross, and Christensen, 1994).

Conceptual Domains of Culture

There is a continuing debate among social scientists about the content of culture. Although no consensus exists, there is agreement that *culture* refers to desired phenomena among people with shared beliefs, customs, folkways, traditions, and behaviors.

Ethnocentrism

The concept of ethnocentrism is not unique to any particular culture and usually operates outside of the individual's awareness within the culture (Berry, 1980). One's sense of self within a dominant cultural group in which images of "superiority" are attached to the self and to the reference group appears to be widespread, resulting in a definition of normalcy, reason, and wisdom in terms of one's own experience. The assumption that "human" is isomorphic with membership in one group only is pervasive in psychological assessment (Betancourt and Lopez, 1993). The profession of psychology has frequently either directly or indirectly ignored the existence of test biases in assessment instruments, allowing these biases to direct attitudes, perceptions, and beliefs in test construction, validation, and interpretation (Helms, 1992). Assessment practices have typically self-served the dominant American culture of Euro-Americans who have written the rules and internalized the unspoken assumptions of "superiority" (Pedersen, 1987).

The uniqueness and individual identities of a person expressed through a larger cultural identity should be recognized and respected (Pedersen, 1987). Cultural biases ill serve both the assessed and assessor, as bias obscures the true score that is the focus of all psychological assessment procedure.

In a pluralistic society that is becoming increasingly more diverse as we move into the new millennium, competencies for the clinician in the practice of neuropsychology must be compatible with the needs of the consumer served.

Acculturation

The concept of acculturation is central to understanding cultural influences on a person's behavior. *Level of acculturation* refers to the extent to which members of a host culture have adopted the beliefs, values, and practices of that culture (Westermeyer, 1993).

Measuring acculturation has been the subject of substantial historical debate in the assessment literature. There is a consensus among researchers that standard scales of measurement do not adequately capture behaviors subserved by acculturation (Cortes, Rogler, and Malgady, 1994). Factors related to acculturation include but are not limited to:

- Age (at the time of introduction to a new culture)

- Educational and occupational status

- Gender roles

- Interactions with native-born Americans

- Relationships with extended family

- Other ethnic support systems, language (Rogler, 1994; Berry, Trimble, and Olmedo, 1986; Cuellar, Harris, and Jasso, 1980; Suinn, Rickard-Figueroa, Lew, and Vigil, 1987; Paniagua, 1994).

Many researchers believe that U.S.-born African Americans who speak the same language as the dominant Euro-American culture have different levels of acculturation than do non-English-speaking cultures. Landrine and Klonoff (1994, 1995, 1996) have developed the African American Acculturation Scale, outlining the independent variables that predict who will acculturate and who will not. This scale also predicts the form that the acculturation will take: bicultural, blended or assimilated, or marginal. Living in an ethnic community buffers acculturation to the extent that some ethnic groups remain immersed in their culture of origin although residing in a foreign country.

Transculturation is a novel process in which a new *hybrid* culture develops out of the original and new cultures (de Granda, 1968). Assimilation is a process in which a member of an ethnic group loses his or her original cultural identification as he or she acquires a new identity in the second culture (LaFromboise, Coleman, and Gerton, 1993).

Failure to understand the critical role of acculturation in the assessment process is likely to render any assessment procedure questionable as a valid sample of behavior.

Specific Ethnocultural Variables Critical to the Assessment Process

Undoubtedly, differences of culture and ethnicity and other areas are critical to accurately assessing individuals, no clear formulas exist explaining how these variables should be factored into the assessment equation.

Linguistic

Language

In evaluating whether a patient's needs are being sufficiently addressed by a neuropsychologist who speaks a language different from that of the patient being assessed, one must question critically whether the evaluator's training and skills in the patient's language are proficient. Another important consideration is the appropriateness of the instrument used. For example, does it reflect the guided wisdom of culturally sensitive researchers who have identified the necessary and sufficient conditions of language translation to meet the criteria of language adequacy (Artiola i Fortuny and Mullaney, 1997; Figueroa, 1990; Sandoval and Duran, 1998)? There are no adequate statistics relating to the prevalence of nonfluent clinicians assessing linguistic minorities, but some anecdotal evidence is available.

Verbal Fluency

Fluent use of one language by the clinician when the patient speaks another language is critical to adequate assessment. Since language is the primary tool of assessment, then, if linguistic competencies are less than adequate, that is, if the clinician has difficulty communicating directly with the patient, the validity of test administration and interpretation becomes problematic. Moreover, cognitive assessment poses a unique problem whenever linguistic competence is in question. Common mistakes may be made in wording, form and content, modulations of phrasing, and accent (Sandoval and Duran, 1998).

These complexities of language bring into question the clinician's ability to accurately assess a number of variables that are critical to a comprehensive neuropsychological evaluation: gradations in affect, mood, perceptions, attitudes, and beliefs about the tasks to be performed.

Communicative Competence

Researchers in language have proposed that communicative competence requires specific capacities:

- Using grammar properly; for example, syntax, word structure, pronunciation (Canale and Swain, 1980).
- Engaging in proper discourse; for example, using word and phrase connections and boundaries to convey meaning with knowledge of "nuances" of written and spoken language. African American rap music is an explicit example of how nuances of language within the African American culture are well understood by other African Americans but may be completely foreign to other ethnic cultural groups. For example, "word up" as a literal translation does not make grammatical sense, but when understood as a phrase with connections and boundaries to other African Americans, it may be translated as "I understand you and everything is OK."
- Being able to speak, write and comprehend speaking and writing with a knowledge of the social purpose of the communication (Sandoval and Duran, 1998).

- Being able to integrate social and linguistic meanings appropriately to deal with immediate and unpredictable circumstances (Bachman and Palmer, 1982).

Culture-Specific Folkways and Mores

One of the most difficult clinician competencies to evaluate is his or her knowledge of eccentricities of specific ethnic and cultural groups. Contributory to this lack of information is the systematic exclusion of ethnically and culturally diverse courses in the curriculum in graduate programs in psychology. Many programs have seminars and workshops dealing with diversity issues, but the issues have not been integrated into the full curriculum.

Intracultural Similarities and Differences

In an important study, Manly and others (1998) examined the relationship of acculturation to neuropsychological test performance among 170 medically healthy, neurologically normal twenty-to-sixty-four-year-old African Americans and HIV positive subgroups of twenty African Americans and twenty European Americans matched on age, education, sex, and stage of HIV disease. Acculturation was measured through self-report for all participants, and linguistic behavior (use of Black English) was assessed in a subset of twenty-five medically healthy individuals.

Medically healthy African Americans reporting less acculturation obtained lower scores on the Wechsler Adult Intelligence Scale Revised (WAIS-R) information subtest and the Boston Naming Test than did more acculturated individuals. Use of Black English was associated with poor performance on the Trail-Making Test (Trails B) and the WAIS-R information subtest. HIV-African Americans scored significantly lower than their HIV-White counterparts on the Category Test, Trails B WAIS-Block Design and Vocabulary subtests, and the learning components of the Story and Figure Memory Tests.

Results suggest that there may be cultural differences within ethnic groups that relate to neuropsychological test performance, and that accounting for acculturation may improve the diagnosing accuracy of certain neuropsychological tests (Manly and others, 1998).

Blind Spots in Assessors

Although criticism of the pervasive cultural and racial bias present in neuropsychological testing is widespread, the profession of psychology is often targeted as the culprit for ignoring the existence of these biases and allowing them to direct attitudes and beliefs in test interpretation (Helms, 1992; Ivey, 1991). Psychological assessors need to increase their sensitivity to potential sources of cultural bias.

Socioeconomic Status

Socioeconomic status (SES) as a dimension of diversity has stirred controversy across many disciplines, including neuropsychology. It remains a critical variable in assessing bias in test interpretation. The most consistent variable in determining one's position in a society—prestige, power, and access to the goods and services of a specific community or cultural group—is occupational status (Dohrenwend and Dohrenhend, 1974; Gray-Little, 1995). A preponderance of research has supported the relationship between social distance of the diagnostician and patient and the diagnostic biases that are inherent in this relationship (Bernard, 1989; Betancourt and Lopez, 1993).

Personality and Identity

There is some debate in the social science literature regarding the formation of ethnic group personalities. Ethnic groups have been found to differ on such characteristics as self-disclosure, assertiveness, cooperativeness, shyness, individualism, interpersonal styles, and introversion. The context in which these groups live, that is, their hierarchical status in the society, also influences their personalities. Middle-class African American women who are clinically depressed often express feelings of guilt and remorse over their successes when they progress faster and further than mates or friends in their social groups (Carrington, 1980). Carrington (1981) also found that many of these women experienced "severe blows to the psyche" during their developmental years. The most pervasive experience of these women was racism and sexism—double jeopardy, namely, being African American and female in a society predicated on racism and sexism.

Even though numerous studies in the past focused on negative effects of racism on status as a member of an ethnic minority group, current studies are focusing on individual differences in identification, development, acculturation, and assimilation; positive aspects of ethnicity and culture; and specific measures to use in investigating the self-identification process (Cross, 1978; Parham and Helms, 1981). Some researchers are focusing more on intracultural variability and less on external cultural and societal influence. This may be seen as a positive trend promoting cultural uniqueness rather than cultural competition.

Another issue is related to possible subpopulation cultural differences. For example, in the United States the three largest Hispanic American groups are Puerto Ricans (most in the New York City area), Cubans (most in South Florida) and Mexican Americans (in the Southwestern United States). Possible differences among these subpopulations of Hispanic Americans have been suggested; actually, dozens of culturally distinct Hispanic American subgroups have been postulated. To assume intracultural homogeneity of cognitive processes may be a crucial error in neuropsychological assessment, but a vexing question is what level of cultural identification is the appropriate basis of analysis.

Multicultural Research on Neuropsychological Assessment

Clinical neuropsychology is the proverbial new kid on the block as a formal specialty area in psychology. There is considerable controversy among clinicians and researchers over the role, if any, played by ethnic-cultural differences on the process of organization and reorganization of brain functions. Proponents of the position that culture and ethnicity have significant influence on brain process (Campbell and others, 1997; Strickland, D'Elia, James, and Stein, 1997; Ramirez and Price-Williams, 1974; Stodolsky and Lesser, 1967; Adams, Boake, and Crain, 1982; Ardila, Rosselli, and Rosas, 1989; Parsons and Prigatano, 1978; Penk and others, 1981; Seidenberg and others, 1984; Thompson and Heaton, 1990), posit that the most widely used neuropsychological instruments were standardized on European Americans and designed to reflect their traditions, values, and ideals. Ethnic and culturally diverse groups were not included in the normative groups or were too few in number to reflect the breadth and depth of the cultural experience of other minority groups (African American, Hispanic American, and so on).

Human cognitive functioning, as reflected in brain-behavior interaction, cannot be separated from the cultural and immediate social context in which the behavior develops (Cole and Bruner, 1971; Cole and Scribner, 1974; Helms, 1992; and Miller-Jones, 1989). Boykin (1991) and Miller-Jones (1989) have noted that standard psychological test situations are context-specific environments that are culturally defined. These contexts exert influence on both the accessibility and deployment of cognitive processes in the specific test situation (Miller-Jones, 1989). Cognitive processes occur in culturally organized activities and indeed are usually learned within a sociocultural context; it is critical that these processes be measured in similar contexts or else distortion occurs that results in misinterpretation of neuropsychological test data. The implications of invalid test data are far-reaching. Needless to say, bias is likely to occur at the diagnostic, treatment-planning, and placement levels, as well as in agency compensation for disability.

The next sections discuss specific examples of neuropsychological test bias across ethnic and cultural groups.

African Americans

Several studies illustrate the pitfalls of a race-comparative paradigm in neuropsychology. One such study (Knuckle and Campbell, 1984) noted that when published norms were used to judge the performance of normal seventh- and eight-grade African Americans ($n = 100$) on several neuropsychological tests, an unusually large number of subjects were incorrectly classified as neuropsychologically impaired on two of these measures (Purdue Pegboard, 66 percent; Benton Visual Retention, 40 percent). In contrast, the incorrect classification rate for two other tests (Symbol Digit Modalities Test and Benton Design Copy Test) was in an acceptable range. Heverly, Isaac, and Hynd (1986) used the performance of five-to-nine-year-old Euro-American subjects as the standard for comparison for African American children of like age and implied that the generally lower scores of the African American children were due to neurodevelopmental delay of the left tertiary region in the parietal lobes. In addition to the questionable validity of the test used to measure the functioning of the left tertiary region of the brain, the practice of using a single test to judge the functional status of a cortical region is outmoded (Reitan and Wolfson, 1992).

Studies that claim to show greater neuropsychological impairment in normal African American children reflect an inherent weakness in the failure of the race-comparative paradigm to control for ethnicity and culture. Cultural realities of the specific groups tested must be taken into account during the conceptual development and validation of existing neuropsychological measures; therefore, the diagnostic validity of these instruments with African Americans remains problematic. Campbell and others (1996) and Lewis-Jack and others (1997) at Howard University designed several studies to examine the predictive accuracy of several tests of the Michigan Neuropsychological Battery (MNB) group of normal

African American adults. The level-of-performance approach (that is, cutoff scores) was used for objective test interpretation.

In one of the studies, the effects of lateralized lesions on performance on the MNB were examined. Subjects were seventy-one right-handed African Americans who served as normal controls. They were selected from a population of inpatients and outpatients in the Physical Medicine and Rehabilitation Service at Howard University Hospital who were being treated for injuries that did not involve the brain. These patients had no history of psychiatric illness or alcohol or any other drug abuse; their mean age was 53 years, with 10.7 mean years of education.

The tests selected for examination from the MNB included Russell's revision of the Wechsler Memory Scale (R-RWMS, Russell, 1975), the Symbol Digit Modalities Test (SDMT, Smith, 1982), the Benton Visual Retention Test (BVRT), Administration A and C (Sivan, 1992), the Visual Form Discrimination Test (VFD), the multiple choice variant of the BVRT (Benton, Hamsher, Varney, and Spreen, 1983), the Purdue Pegboard Test (Costa, Vaughan, Levita, and Farber, 1963), and the Hooper Visual Organization Test (VOT, Hooper, 1953). Conventional neuropsychological cutoff scores were selected from published manuals or published validation studies of these neuropsychological instruments.

Results indicated that overall the percentage of diagnostic errors was unacceptable considering a normal population was used. On the R-RWMS, Russell's new set of norms (1988) was used. Campbell and others (1997) found that applying the 1988 norms resulted in a substantial number of normal controls being incorrectly diagnosed on the Logical Memory task. On the other hand, the percentage of false positive errors on the Visual Reproduction subtest was within expectations. The number of controls incorrectly classified as impaired on the SDMT, the BVRT (administration A) and the Purdue Pegboard, however, was unacceptably high. The percentage of normal controls with VFD test scores in the impaired range was tolerable. On the VOT test, using the most liberal criterion level (fewer than twenty correct; Boyd, 1981) still allowed the number of normal controls misidentified as impaired to exceed the number of false positives reported in the test manual's normative sample by a large margin. The study results argue for separate sets of norms based on cultural and racial populations.

That information-processing styles vary cross-culturally has been shown by a number of neuropsychological studies. African American patients with right hemisphere strokes often earn a lower mean PIQ than VIQ score. Still, in contrast to the majority of studies in this area of research, the VIQ and PIQ scores of African Americans with left hemisphere strokes were virtually identical. This finding has been replicated in two subsequent studies that comprised adult African Americans with diverse types of lateralized lesion (Ford-Booker and others, 1993). Campbell and others (1996) noted that it is unclear what these findings mean in terms of the cerebral organization of the cognitive processes tapped by the WAIS-R IQ test. The disparate patterns of IQ scores observed in this sample of patients with left and right hemisphere damage, however, suggest that relative to Euro-Americans, the sample of brain-injured African Americans may have brought a different information-processing style to bear on the stimulus information processing required by WAIS-R subtests than did brain-injured Euro-Americans.

Other studies have reported more cognitive impairment in ethnic and culturally different populations than in Euro-Americans. Roberts and Hamsher (1984) found that neurologically normal Euro-Americans obtained significantly higher scores on a measure of visual naming ability than did neurologically normal African Americans, even after correcting for educational level. Using the standard cutoff score, 22 percent of normal African American would be classified as impaired on the basis of their naming performance, which was significantly more than the Euro-American group. Bernard (1989) reported that young African American males scored lower on the Category Test and higher on the Seashore Rhythm Test than did Whites and Hispanics matched on age and education.

These studies show systematically that substantial discrepancies between scores of ethnic minorities and Euro-Americans may persist, despite equating groups on demographic variables such as age, education, sex, and socioeconomic status. In assessing African Americans, the examiner should be competent in identifying bias found in specific instruments and not perpetuate the ethnocentric blind spots resulting in diagnosing impairment when none exists (Myers and others, 1997; Adams, Boake, and Crain, 1982). The data strongly argue for developing African American normative data sets for neuropsychological tests to prevent incorrect classification errors. At this point, only a single recent study can be identified (Strickland, D'Flia, James, and Stein, 1997) that has attempted to address the need for more normative data on neuropsychological tests in the African American population.

Hispanic Americans

A significant problem in the practice of neuropsychological assessment with Hispanics is that of language inadequacy in test translation and adaptation (Artiola i Fortuny and Mullaney, 1997). In evaluating the performance of Hispanic American and non-Hispanic patients with Alzheimer's disease on the Trail-Making Test parts A and B and the Fuld Object Memory Test, English-speaking patients scored higher on both. In Bernard's study (1989) of African American, Euro-Americans and Hispanic American male youths from low SES backgrounds, no racial or ethnic differences in rate of impairment on the Halstead-Reitan Neuropsychological Test Battery were found when the entire neuropsychological battery was administered. Mean individual scores however, differed significantly on selected subtest scores across ethnic and cultural lines (Category, Seashore Rhythm, and Finger Tapping tests). In addition, isolated consideration of mean scores on the Finger

Tapping test would have resulted in African American and Euro-American youths being classified as impaired.

In a study designed to assess the functional capabilities of patients with neurological damage through a process of back-translation and translation by committee, Loewenstein, Rubert, Arguelles, and Duara (1995) found that scores on both versions of the battery were highly correlated with a standard battery of neuropsychological tests. In addition, Loewenstein and coworkers (1995) found that neuropsychological tests predicted different patterns of functional ability in English-speaking and Spanish-speaking patients. Biases can significantly influence performance variance in neuropsychological tests even when linguistic factors are taken into consideration.

Asian Americans

In a large-scale Honolulu-Asia aging study (1997) of 191 noninstitutionalized Japanese American men (aged seventy-one to ninety-three years) with dementia, each had a family informant able to provide a reliable history. Each subject was assessed on performance in multiple cognitive domains, using the Consortium to Establish a Registry for Alzheimer's Disease (CERAD) Neuropsychological Assessment Battery. A remarkably high number of subjects were identified as having dementia (60 percent). Bias that related aging and its processes appears to be cross-cultural, and the failure to include follow-up medical evaluation and more extensive neuropsychological testing renders the results of this study moot. Often the elderly are diagnosed within the paradigm of "aging" and important differential diagnoses in mental health and physical health are missed or ignored.

Native Americans

Ferraro, Bercier, and Chelminski (1997) investigated the performance level of twenty-two Native American elderly adults (mean age 66.3) years on the Geriatric Depression Scale-Short Form (GDS-

SF) and neuropsychological tests. Results reveal that the only two correlation coefficients that were significant with GDS-SF performance were age and number of medications currently being taken. As GDS-SF scores increased, scores on a number of neuropsychological tests (WAIS-R Vocabulary test and the Boston Naming Test, among others) tended to decrease and the correlation coefficients were all in the negative range. Cognitive performance and depression are negatively correlated, according to findings of this study.

Comments Regarding Neuropsychological Test Interpretation

It should be noted that although the most common way to interpret tests scores is the level-of-performance model, neuropsychological test interpretation with a standardized battery has focused on using multiple levels of inference. Briefly put, a level-of-performance model is concerned with how high or low a specific test score is. By contrast, using multiple levels of inference includes the issues of pathognomonic signs, pattern of performance, and right-left comparison, as well as level of performance (see Horton and Wedding, 1984; Reitan and Wolfson, 1992 for descriptions of the multiple-level-of-inference model). The advantage of a standardized neuropsychological test battery is that it is designed to use multiple methods of inference.

It is likely that the level-of-performance methods may be the method of inference most likely to be influenced by cultural bias. Therefore, it is possible that the use of multiple levels of inference could help reduce the influence of cultural bias in the clinical situation. This notion suggests that the preferred strategy is to use a standardized neuropsychological test battery, such as the Halstead-Reitan Neuropsychological Test Battery or Luria-Nebraska Neuropsychological Test Battery, provided tests with known cultural bias are removed or eliminated from the battery.

Summary and Conclusions

That specific cross-cultural competencies need to be developed in the practice of neuropsychology is substantiated in the literature. Additionally, institutional agendas must be scrutinized if empirical evidence continues to support the need for differential diagnosis when using standard neuropsychological assessment with diverse populations to account for test bias and this evidence is ignored. Any formal scientific discipline is only as good as its content and constructs, and the instruments it develops to measure these constructs.

In summary, the extant scientific literature varies from weak to virtually nonexistent. Only a few studies have compared African Americans and Hispanic Americans with Euro-Americans, and almost nothing exists for Asian Americans and Native Americans. Indeed, even the few existing studies are problematic with respect to characterization of intracultural subpopulations. The clear need is for culturally specific normative databases to assist in neuropsychological assessment.

This need, however, raises the question of the relevance of subpopulations. For example, considering the group of Asian Americans, should separate normative databases be constructed for Korean Americans, Chinese Americans, and Vietnamese Americans (to cite but a very few of the possible Asian American subpopulations)?

Until separate normative databases are available, what is a neuropsychologist to do?

First, be sensitive to the cultural aspects of the assessment process, and become knowledgeable regarding non-Euro-American cultures. Second, administer a "standardized" neuropsychological test battery that was designed and constructed to allow use of multiple levels of inference. As seen by the brief literature review, virtually every study demonstrating cultural differences used a level-of-performance model rather than multiple levels of inference. The use of multiple levels of inference could serve to reduce the influence of cultural factors. Therefore, it is possible that the use of multiple levels of inference could help reduce the influence of cultural bias in the clinical situation.

Third, be very careful in drawing conclusions regarding brain injury in non-Euro-Americans when using tests standardized on Euro-American populations. In closing, our hope and expectation is that this chapter serves to highlight for the reader the important problems related to neuropsychological assessment in a multicultural context.

References

Adams, R., Boake, C., & Crain, C. (1982). Bias in a neuropsychological test classification related to education, age, and ethnicity. *Journal of Consulting and Clinical Psychology, 50,* 143–145.

Anastasi, A., & Urbina, S. (1997). *Psychological testing* (7th ed.). Upper Saddle River, NJ: Prentice Hall.

Ardila, A., Rosselli, M., & Rosas, P. (1989). Neuropsychological assessment in illiterates: Visuospatial and memory abilities. *Brain and Cognition, 11,* 147–166.

Artiola i Fortuny, L., & Mullaney, H. A. (1997). Neuropsychology with Spanish-speakers: Language proficiency issues for test developer. *Journal of Clinical and Experimental Neuropsychology, 19,* 615–622.

Bachman, L. F., and Palmer, A. S. (1982). The construct validation of some components of communicative proficiency. *TESOL Quarterly, 16,* 449–465.

Benton, A., Hamsher, K., Varney, N., & Spreen, O. (1983). *Contributions to neuropsychological assessment.* New York: Oxford University Press.

Bernard, L. C. (1989). Halstead-Reitan Neuropsychological Test performance of Black, Hispanic, and White young adult males from poor academic backgrounds. *Archives of Clinical Neuropsychology, 4,* 267–274.

Berry, J. W. (1980). Acculturation as varieties of adaptation. In A. Padilla (Ed.), *Acculturation: Theory, models and some new findings* (pp. 9–26). Boulder, CO: Westview Press.

Berry, J. W., Trimble, J. E., & Olmedo, E. L. (1986). Assessment of acculturation. In W. J. Lonner & J. W. Berry (Eds.), *Field methods in cross-cultural research* (pp. 291–324). Thousand Oaks, CA: Sage.

Betancourt, H., & Lopez, S. R. (1993). The study of culture, ethnicity, and race in American psychology. *American Psychologist, 48,* 629–637.

Boyd, J. (1981). A validity study of the Hooper Visual Organization Test. *Journal of Consulting and Clinical Psychology, 49*, 15–19.

Boykin, A. (1991). Black psychology and experimental psychology: A functional confluence. In R. Jones (ed.), *Black psychology* (3rd ed.). Berkeley: Cobb and Henry.

Campbell, A. L., Ford-Booker, P., Ocampo, C., Dennis, G., Brown, A., & Lewis-Jack, O. (1997). Design copying skills in brain-injured African Americans. In L. R. Sloan (Ed.), *Pathways to success*. Washington, DC: Howard University Press.

Campbell, A. L., Rorie, K. D., Dennis, G., Wood, D., Combs, S., Hearn, L., Davis, H., & Brown, A. (1996). Neuropsychological assessment of African Americans: Conceptual and methodological considerations. In R. Jones (Ed.), *Handbook of tests and measurements for Black populations*. Berkeley: Cobb and Henry.

Canale, M., & Swain, M. (1980). Theoretical bases of communicative approaches to second language teaching and testing. *Applied Linguistics, 1*, 1–47.

Carrington, C. (1980). A theoretical appraisal of depression in Black women. In L. F. Rose (Ed.), *The Black woman* (pp. 265–271). Thousand Oaks, CA: Sage.

Carrington, C. (1981). Treating depression in Black women. *Urban Research Review, 7*(3), 6–10.

Chavez, F., & Gonzalez-Singh, F. (1980). Hispanic assessment: A case study. *Professional Psychology, 11*, 163–168.

Cole, M., & Bruner, J. (1971). Cultural differences and inferences about psychological processes. *American Psychologist, 26*, 867–876.

Cole, M., & Scribner, S. (1974). *Culture and thought: A psychological introduction*. New York: Wiley.

Cortes, D. E., Rogler, L. H., & Malgady, R. G. (1994). Biculturality among Puerto Rican adults in the United States. *American Journal of Community Psychology, 22*, 707–721.

Costa, L., Vaughan, H., Levita, E., & Farber, N. (1963). Purdue Pegboard as a predictor of presence and laterality of cerebral lesions. *Journal of Consulting Psychology, 27*, 133–137.

Cross, W. E. (1978). The Cross and Thomas models of psychological nigrescence. *Journal of Black Psychology, 5*, 13–19.

Cuellar, I., Harris, L. C., & Jasso, R. (1980). An acculturation scale for Mexican American normal and clinical populations. *Hispanic Journal of Behavioral Science, 2*, 199–217.

de Granda, G. (1968). *Transculturation and linguistic interference in contemporary Puerto Rico*. Bogota, Colombia: Ediciones Bogota.

Dohrenwend, B. P., & Dohrenhend, B. S. (1974). Social and cultural influences on psychotherapy. *Annual Review of Psychology, 25*, 417–452.

Figueroa, R. (1990). Best practices in the assessment of bilingual children. In A. Thomas & J. Grimes (Eds.), *Best practices in school psychology* (Vol. 2, pp. 93–106). Washington, DC: National Association of School Psychologists.

Ferraro, F. R., Bercier, B., & Chelminski, I. (1997). Geriatric Depression Scale— Short Form (GDS-SF) performance in Native American elderly adults. *Clinical Gerontologist, (18)*1, 52–55.

Ford-Booker, P., Campbell, A., Combs, S., Lewis, S., Ocampo, C., Brown, A., Lewis-Jack, O., & Rorie, K. (1993). The predictive accuracy of neuropsychological tests in a normal population of African Americans. *Journal of Clinical and Experimental Neuropsychology, 15*, 64.

Golden, C. J. (1987). *The Luria-Nebraska Neuropsychological Battery-Children's Revision manual*. Los Angeles: Western Psychological Services.

Golden, C. J., Hammeke, T., & Purish, A. D. (1978). Diagnostic validity of a standardized neuropsychological battery derived from Luria's neuropsychological tests. *Journal Consulting and Clinical Psychology, 49*, 410–417.

Golden, C. J., Hammeke, T., & Purish, A. D. (1980). *The Luria-Nebraska Neuropsychological Battery: Test manual (revised)*. Los Angeles: Western Psychological Services.

Gray-Little, B. (1995). The assessment of psychopathology in racial and ethnic minorities. In J. N. Butcher (Ed.), *Clinical personality assessment* (pp. 140–157). New York: Oxford University Press.

Helms, J. (1992). Why is there no study of cultural equivalence in standardized cognitive ability testing? *American Psychologist, 47*, 1083–1101.

Heverly, L., Isaac, W., & Hynd, G. (1986). Neurodevelopmental and racial differences in tactile-visual (cross-modal) discrimination in normal Black and White children. *Archives of Clinical Neuropsychology, 1*, 139–145.

Hooper, H. (1953). *The Hooper Visual Organization Test manual*. Los Angeles: Western Psychological Services.

Horton, A. M., Jr. (1994). *Behavioral interventions with brain injured children*. New York: Plenum.

Horton, A. M., & Puente, A. (1990). Life-span neuropsychology: An overview. In A. M. Horton, Jr. (Ed.), *Neuropsychology across the life-span* (pp. 1–15). New York: Springer-Verlag.

Horton, A. M., Jr. & Wedding, D. (1984). *Clinical and behavioral neuropsychology*. New York: Praeger.

Ivey, A. E. (Ed.) (1991). *Developmental strategies for helpers*. Pacific Grove, CA: Brooks/Cole.

Knuckle, E., & Campbell, A. (1984). *Suitability of neuropsychological tests norms with Black adolescents*. Paper presented at the International Neuropsychological Society Meeting, Houston.

LaFromboise, T., Coleman, H.L.R., & Gerton, J. (1993). Psychological impact of biculturalism. Evidence and theory. *Psychological Bulletin, 114,* 395–412.

Landrine, H., and Klonoff, E. A. (1994). The African American Acculturation Scale: Development, reliability, and validity. *Journal of Black Psychology, 20,* 104–127.

Landrine, H., and Klonoff, E. A. (1995). The African American Acculturation Scale: II. Cross-validation and short form. *Journal of Black Psychology, 21,* 124–152.

Landrine, H., and Klonoff, E. A. (1996). The African American Acculturated Scale: Origin and current status. In R. I. Jones (Ed.), *Handbook of tests and measurements for Black populations* (vol. 2, pp. 119–138). Hampton, VA: Cobb and Henry.

Lewis-Jack, O., Campbell, A. L., Ridley, S., Ocampo, C., Brown, A., Dennis, G., Wood, D., Weir, R. (1997). Unilateral brain lesions and performance on Russell's Revision of the Wechsler Memory Scale in an African American population. *International Journal of Neuroscience, 91*(3–4), 229–240.

Lichtenberg, F. A., Ross, F., & Christensen, B. (1994). Preliminary normative data on the Boston Naming Test for older urban populations. *Clinical Neuropsychologist, 8,* 100–111.

Loewenstein, D. A., Rubert, M. P., Arguelles, T., & Duara, R. (1995). Neuropsychological test performances and prediction of functional capacities among Spanish speaking and English speaking patients with dementia. *Archives of Clinical Neuropsychology, 10,* 75–88.

Luria, A. R. (1966). *Higher cortical functions in man*. New York: Basic Books.

Manly, J. J., Jacobs, D. M., Sano, M, Bell, K., Merchant, C. A., Small, S. A., & Stern, Y. (1998). Cognitive test performance among nondemented elderly African Americans and Whites. *Neurology, 50,* 1238–1245.

Mattis, S., French, J. H., & Rapin, T. (1975). Dyslexia in children and adults: Three independent neuropsychological syndromes. *Developmental Medicine and Child Neurology, 17,* 150–163.

Meier, M. J. (1974). Some challenges for clinical neuropsychology. In R. M. Reitan & L. A. Davison (Eds.), *Clinical neuropsychology: Current status and application* (pp. 289–324). New York: Wiley.

Miller-Jones, D. (1989). Culture and testing. *American Psychologist, 44,* 360–366.

Myers, H., Satz, P., Miller, B., et al. (1997). The African American Health Project: Study overview and selected findings and high risk behavioral and psychiatric disorders in African American men. *Ethnicity and Health, 203,* 183–196.

Padilla, A. M., & Medina, A. (1996). Cross-cultural sensitivity in assessment: Using tests in culturally appropriate ways. In L. A. Suzuki, F. J. Meller, and J. G. Ponterotto (Eds.), *Handbook of multicultural assessment: Clinical, psychological, and educational applications* (pp. 3–28). San Francisco: Jossey-Bass.

Paniagua, F. A. (1994). *Assessing and treating culturally diverse clients: A practical guide.* Thousand Oaks, CA: Sage.

Parham, T. A., & Helms, J. E. (1981). The influence of Black students' racial identity attitudes on preferences for counselor's race. *Journal of Counseling Psychology, 28,* 250–257.

Parsons, O., & Prigatano, G. (1978). Methodological considerations in clinical neuropsychological research. *Journal of Consulting and Clinical Psychology, 46,* 608–619.

Pedersen, P. B. (1987). Ten frequent assumptions of cultural bias in counseling. *Journal of Multicultural Counseling and Development, 5,* 7–25.

Penk, W. E., Brown, A., Roberts, W. R., Dolan, M., Atkins, H., & Robinowitz, R. (1981). Visual memory of male Hispanic-American heroin users. *Journal of Consulting and Clinical Psychology, 49,* 771–772.

Price-Williams, D. R. (1985). Cultural psychology. In G. Lindzey & Aronson (Eds.), *Handbook of social psychology* (Vol. 11, 3rd ed., pp. 993–1042). New York: Random House.

Ramirez, M., & Price-Williams, D. (1974). Cognitive styles of children of three ethnic groups in the United States. *Journal of Cross-Cultural Psychology, 5,* 212–219.

Reitan, R. M., & Davidson, L. A. (Eds.). (1974). *Clinical neuropsychology: Current status and applications.* New York: Wiley.

Reitan, R. M., & Wolfson, D. (1992). *The Halstead-Reitan Neuropsychological Test Battery: Theory and clinical interpretation* (2nd ed.). Tucson, AZ: Neuropsychology Press.

Reynolds, C. R., & Fletcher-Janzen, E. (Eds.). (1989). *Handbook of clinical child neuropsychology.* New York: Plenum.

Roberts, R. J., & Hamsher, K. D. (1984). Effects of minority status on facial recognition and naming performance. *Journal of Clinical Psychology, 40*(2), 539–545.

Rogler, L. H. (1994). International migrations: A framework for directing research. *American Psychologist, 49,* 701–708.

Russell, E. W. (1975). A multiple scoring method for the assessment of complex memory functions. *Journal of Clinical and Experimental Neuropsychology, 43,* 800–809.

Russell, E. W. (1988). Renorming Russell's version of the Wechsler Memory Scale. *Journal of Clinical and Experimental Neuropsychology, 10,* 235–249.

Sandoval, J., & Duran, R. (1998). Language. In J. Sandoval, C. Frisby, K. Gelsinger, J. Scheuneman, & J. Grenick (Eds.), *Test interpretation and diversity: Achieving equity in assessment* (pp. 181–203). Washington, DC: American Psychological Association.

Seidenberg, M., Gamache, M., Beck, N., Smith, M., Giordani, B., Berent, S., Sackellares, J., & Boll, T. (1984). Subject variables and performances on the Halstead Neuropsychological Test Battery: A multivariate analysis. *Journal of Consulting and Clinical Psychology, 52,* 658–662.

Sivan, A. (1992). *Benton Visual Retention Test manual* (5th ed.). San Antonio: Psychological Corporation.

Smith, A. (1982). *Symbol Digit Modalities Test (SDMT) manual (revised).* Los Angeles: Western Psychological Services.

Stodolsky, S., & Lesser, G. (1967). Learning patterns in the disadvantaged. *Harvard Educational Review, 37,* 546–593.

Strickland, T. L., D'Elia, L. F., James, R., & Stein, R. (1997). Stroop color-word performance of African-Americans. *Clinical Neuropsychologist, 11*(1), 87–90.

Sue, D. W., & Sue, D. (1990). *Counseling the culturally different.* New York: Wiley.

Suinn, R. M., Rickard-Figueroa, K., Lew, S., & Vigil, P. (1985). Career decisions and an Asian acculturation scale. *Journal of the Asian American Psychological Association, 10,* 20–28.

Suinn, R. M., Rickard-Figueroa, K., Lew, S., & Vigil, P. (1987). The Suinn-Lew Asian Self-Identity Acculturation Scale: An initial report. *Educational and Psychological Measurement, 47,* 401–407.

Thompson, L., & Heaton, R. (1990). Use of demographic information in neuropsychological assessment. In D. Tupper & K. Cicerone (Eds.), *The neuropsychology of everyday life: Assessment and basic competencies* (pp. 234–256). Norwell, MA: Kluwer.

Westermeyer, J. J. (1993). Cross-cultural psychiatric assessment. In A. Gaw (Ed.), *Culture, ethnicity and mental illness* (pp. 125–144). Washington, DC: American Psychiatric Press.

19

. . . .

Family-Oriented, Culturally Sensitive (FOCUS) Assessment of Young Children

Paul J. Meller, Phyllis S. Ohr, and Rebecca A. Marcus

Since the passage of Public Law 99-457 (1986), assessment of and intervention with young children has been a source of much concern and controversy. Although there were several instruments designed to assess the developmental functioning of young children prior to PL 99-457, such as the Bayley Scales of Infant Development (Bayley, 1969) and the McCarthy Scales (McCarthy, 1972), assessment of young children was treated as a downward extension of traditional psychoeducational evaluation. Specifically, the focus of the assessment was to determine static abilities in comparison to a reference group, an approach devoid of the process or context of development. This approach is in stark contrast with the mandates of PL 99-457 (and subsequently of Part C of the Individuals with Disabilities Education Act, or IDEA, 1997) to develop intervention programs (and consequently assessment approaches) in which the family is the principle facilitator of the child's development.

In the first edition of this *Handbook*, Meller and Ohr (1996) stressed the profound influence of the home environment for very young children by pointing out that stimulation for the majority of infants and toddlers is limited to that which they receive in their home, provided primarily by their family. Given that involvement with families is at the core of assessment and intervention planning for very young children, the influence of family, social, and cultural contexts on the child are critical factors to be assessed (Bagnato and

Neisworth, 1981). According to Meller and Ohr, the developmental context provided to the child depends to a large degree upon the cultural characteristics of the family. Cultural experiences represent a critical component of the very young child's home environment. Unfortunately, models of culturally sensitive assessment are not abundant in the literature. Thus, developing an efficacious model of family-oriented, culturally sensitive assessment and intervention emerged as a priority.

Current approaches to early childhood assessment and intervention are marred by such limitations as inadequate training of the evaluator, reliance on a traditional model and techniques, and legislative mandates to perform early childhood evaluations within a brief specified time frame.

Inadequate Training in Early Assessment

Training early interventionists to be family-focused and culturally competent is essential given the requirement in the IDEA amendments that an Individualized Family Service Plan (IFSP) be developed that addresses both child and family competencies and needs. Presently there is a scarcity of professionals who can work adequately with culturally diverse families (Christensen, 1992; Lowenthal, 1996). Mental health professionals and educators who work with diverse families must be both linguistically and culturally fluent.

The first phase in developing cultural fluency is to develop cultural awareness—your own and other people's. Lowenthal (1996) suggested that cultural awareness develops when professionals learn (1) to be aware of their own culture influences and how they influence their cognition, affect, and behavior; (2) how a family's culture influences child rearing and views on disability and intervention; and (3) the cultural components of communication style. Successfully proceeding through this progression of cultural awareness is essential to developing competency in family-centered assessment and intervention.

Unfortunately, investigation of graduate school training practice to prepare school psychologists for work in the field of early intervention suggests that training is grossly inadequate. In 1986 a national survey of school psychology graduate programs indicated that training in assessing very young children and their families was a low priority, with primarily one norm-referenced cognitive measure, the Bayley Scales of Infant Development, being consistently taught (Reschly, Genshaft, and Binder, 1987). A follow-up survey by Wilson and Reschly (1996) noted that university programs still did not provide adequate training on appropriate assessment approaches for implementing Part C of IDEA. However, the researchers indicated that their survey included only traditional intellectual measures, which may be less reliable with very young children, and they suggested that future surveys emphasize a variety of instruments, including criterion-based and family measures.

Ohr and Feingold (1997) responded to the suggestions by Wilson and Reschly (1996) and conducted a study that focused on university training practices in infant and toddler as well as preschool intervention. They included a variety of measures for endorsement that covered multiple domains of child and family functioning. Consistent with the Wilson and Reschly investigation, results indicated that there was little focus on training in assessment instruments other than the traditional, norm-based tests. The Bayley Scales of Infant Development were endorsed as most frequently taught by 54 percent of the schools surveyed. The Stanford-Binet and the Wechsler Preschool and Primary Scales of Intelligence (WPPSI-R) were also endorsed for this age group, although norms limit the utility of this measure to the toddler group (ages two to three). The Battelle Developmental Inventory (BDI), a measure that can be employed as both norm-referenced and criterion-referenced, was endorsed by approximately 20 percent of the respondents.

Fewer than 20 percent of the programs offered instruction in curriculum-based and criterion-based measures, with the Carolina

Curriculum and Hawaii Early Learning Profile (HELP) being the two noted. Twenty percent of the programs that responded focused on measures assessing family and environmental factors; specifically, the Home Observation and Measure of the Environment Inventory (HOME) and the Parenting Stress Index were the two measures most frequently endorsed. Research has suggested a clear need for specialized training in graduate school as well as continuing professional development.

Reliance on Traditional Assessment Methods

Given the trend in graduate school training regarding early assessment and intervention, it is not surprising that most early interventionists rely on models of assessment that overly use norm-referenced measures and neglect the assessment of family, social-ecology, and cultural factors. Greenspan and Meisels (1996) assert that using primarily traditional modes of assessment leads to underestimating young children's potential. In addition, assessment results are more likely to reflect the orientation of professionals working with children, not what is best to meet their needs.

Greenspan and Meisels point out the importance of incorporating diverse information, including evaluating the child in his or her family context. Curriculum-based and criterion-based measures are more likely to yield an accurate estimate of a child's actual skills and stress family input, but these instruments are time consuming to administer. In addition, instruments adequate to formally assessing a family's sociocultural background do not exist. In addition to formal measures, a competent assessment of sociocultural variables involves direct observation and a thorough interview, both of which are time consuming. It is widely acknowledged that early childhood evaluation needs to be multidimensional (Bagnato and Neisworth, 1981). Information from multiple sources, multiple settings, on multiple occasions, and about multiple aspects of child and family functioning must be integrated to understand the abilities of developing children.

Legislation Mandates "Quick" Assessment

The demands of federal legislation to complete early childhood assessment also limits the form and type of assessment that may be performed. This often results in evaluations that are short on process and social data, both of which are necessary to understand the child in a cultural context. Using primarily normative measures does not capture the "dynamic developmental process as it occurs in infancy and early childhood" (Greenspan and Meisels, 1996, p. 15).

Greenspan and Meisels point out that because of the demands for quick information (despite awareness that this is in opposition to "best practice"), professionals use procedures that do not reflect a model of how young children develop within the context of their home environment. As a result, typical early childhood assessments "do not reflect an understanding of the specific types of difficulties and developmental challenges that children and families face in the first three years of life" (1996, p. 15).

A Culturally Responsive Model of Early Childhood Evaluation

Barrera (1996) conceptualized a model of early childhood assessment that is sensitive to the ecology of the family. Specifically, this model assesses how children and their families "perceive, believe, evaluate, and behave" (p. 70) and takes into account the "perceptions and mindsets" (p. 69) of the evaluators. Barrera recommended that in the event the evaluator is not familiar with the family's culture and language, a "culture-language mediator" should be employed as a resource to fully understand the interplay of the personal-social, communicative-linguistic, and sensory-cognitive dimensions of the family's particular sociocultural context.

Using a culture-language mediator is one way to strive toward ensuring a culturally responsive assessment; however it is not always possible for evaluators to have such an individual at their disposal. Rather, training in the area of early childhood assessment and intervention necessitates instructing how to assess both the child and the sociocultural context in which the child lives. Barrera indicated the steps necessary for a culturally responsive assessment of very young children, stressing evaluation of the family context and including three culturally related dimensions:

1. Expression of the family's identity (personal-social domain)

2. Communication within the family (communicative-linguistic domain)

3. Modes of information processing (sensory-cognitive dimension)

Models of Family Centered Assessment

In response to the federally mandated demand for assessment of and intervention with young children, and the inadequacy of traditional psychoeducational models to meet these needs, several comprehensive, process-oriented, and family-centered assessment models have been developed, among them the Assessment, Evaluation, and Programming System for Infants and Children (AEPS; Bricker, 1993), the Early Assessment System (Meisels, Dichtelmiller, and Marsden, in press), the Infant-Toddler Developmental Assessment (Meisels and Provence, 1989), and the Syracuse Scales of Infant and Toddler Development (Ensher and others, 1997). These systems have several common features:

- Strong emphasis on assessing the family

- Comprehensive evaluation of the child's abilities across multiple domains

- Use of multiple approaches (criterion-based, norm-referenced, play-based, observational, parent reports, and so on) to assess the child's current level of functioning

A comprehensive review of these assessment systems may be found in Paget (1999). Despite the major step forward that these assessment systems have taken in assessing children in a broader social context and including the family as an essential microsystem for development, these approaches only implicitly assess the child in the cultural context of the family. There is still need for a system in which the child's cultural context is directly considered.

Family-Oriented, Culturally Sensitive (FOCUS) Infant and Toddler Assessment and Intervention

A new approach to assessing infants, toddlers, and preschool children within the cultural context of their development is Family-Oriented, Culturally Sensitive (FOCUS) Assessment. The FOCUS approach has five essential pieces in its assessment process:

1. All professionals who are involved in assessing children from diverse cultural backgrounds must be adequately trained during their graduate studies, or via continuing professional development.

2. FOCUS assessment must involve comprehensive evaluation of family characteristics, resources, competencies, and needs.

3. A FOCUS assessment must assess all areas of developmental competency. This assessment should include both formal and informal techniques, across settings and over time.

4. FOCUS is an ongoing assessment of both the child and the family during the development and implementation of the (family) intervention plan.

5. FOCUS assessment always considers program evaluation and developmental change due to intervention.

A summary of the FOCUS approach is presented in Table 19.1.

The nature of FOCUS evaluations varies as a function of the goal of the assessment, the age of the child, the referral question, and the sociocultural context in which the child lives. Evaluating young children must entail collecting and integrating information that may be used to describe a child's current functioning as well as facilitating the development of the child. To this end, information must be

Table 19.1. Family-oriented, culturally sensitive (FOCUS) assessment of young children.

Steps	Objectives	Methods
Training in family-oriented, culturally competent infant/toddler assessment and intervention	Train how to select and administer culturally sensitive measures and evaluate impact of family and cultural values on development of child; train to evaluate and change stereotypical preconceptions of assessor, which have an impact on objective assessment of and intervention with family	Provide appropriate courses in graduate school training programs
Assessing family competencies and needs	Develop a profile of the family's strengths and weaknesses by objectively evaluating the sociocultural environment; determine impact of sociocultural influences on family, assess unique	Interview; formal and informal observation; observer report surveys; parent report surveys

(Continued)

Table 19.1. (*Continued*)

Steps	Objectives	Methods
	contributions of each family member, and look at interaction of these variables; determine similarities and divergences from culture; specify multiple dimensions of the home environment that contribute to developmental status; conduct family language assessment	
Assessing developmental competencies and needs	Choose culturally appropriate modes of assessment; develop a profile of the infant/toddler's strengths and weaknesses in the areas of cognitive, language, motor, visual-motor, adaptive, and social-interactive; be sensitive to multiple dimensions of child's environment	Formal and informal observation; normative-based, curriculum-based, and criterion-based measures; parent report surveys; observer report surveys; traditional, nontraditional formats of assessment (trans-disciplinary and multidisciplinary, ARENA)

(*Continued*)

Table 19.1. Family-oriented, culturally sensitive (FOCUS) assessment of young children. (*Concluded*)

Steps	Objectives	Methods
Family intervention planning	Multidisciplinary and parental determination of appropriate interventions considering infant/toddler's developmental profile and sensitive to multiculturally competent evaluation of family strengths and needs	Planning meeting between all professionals involved in assessment and family members
Ongoing evaluation and planning	Continually update profile of infant/toddler and family competencies and needs	Interview; normative-based, curriculum-based, and criteria-based evaluations; formal and informal observation; parent report surveys; observer report surveys

gathered regarding the child's developmental history, the cultural influences on this development, and family background and support, as well as assessment of strengths and weaknesses across multiple domains. A framework integrating these data was outlined by Barona (1990). It was suggested that assessment follow a four-step process:

1. An initial interview

2. Language assessment

3. Assessment of developmental processes

4. Placing the assessment data into a natural learning context, to permit comprehensive assessment of young children

Bagnato and Neisworth (1981) suggest that assessment of young children should yield information that may be used by adults who are significant in the child's life (namely, parents and teachers) to facilitate the child's growth and development. That is, assessment must be more than diagnostic; it must also demonstrate a high level of treatment validity. FOCUS evaluations yield data with sufficient treatment and social validity to produce acceptable and efficacious intervention.

Providing Training and Continuing Professional Development in FOCUS

Objectives

The goal in this first component of a FOCUS evaluation is to train professionals to evaluate the impact of family and cultural values on child development and enable them to develop awareness of their own values and stereotypes that may impede accurate assessment of the child and family. According to the investigations of Ohr and Feingold (1997), graduate programs are limited in training students to use measures assessing family and environmental factors. Adequate measures formally assessing sociocultural factors have not been found. Even cognitive measures that depend to some degree on parental input, thus reflecting parental perception of child functioning, were not found to be a necessary part of training.

According to Able-Boone (1997), "a family's interpretation of their child's disability or special need demands understanding and respect from the professional" (p. 201). This is often not the case. Able-Boone suggested that early interventionists are typically authoritative and hold a "deficit" orientation that stresses negative rather than positive factors. She asserts that early interventionists not only fail to acknowledge parent input but react according to their own worldview, which is often influenced by stereotypical thinking. This suggests that personal biases influence the decision-making process in early intervention.

Barrera (1996) noted that every evaluator "has particular lenses (both personal and socio-cultural) through which he or she views and evaluates what is observed" (p. 70). Furthermore, Barrera believes that assessors need to understand their own perceptions, beliefs, and behaviors and how these are related to the way they react to individual children and families with whom they work.

In addition, research in cross-cultural counseling suggests that members of diverse cultural groups are differentially responsive to directive or expert approaches in treatment (as opposed to collaborative or referent approaches). These findings suggest that evaluators must assess the need for a more directive or collaborative approach with the family while gathering the assessment data.

Methods

University training programs need to include at least one course focusing solely on early intervention assessment and intervention with an emphasis on how to conduct an infant or toddler evaluation in a family-oriented, culturally sensitive manner. This includes how to select and administer culturally sensitive measures, how to administer these measures in a nontraditional format, and how to evaluate and change stereotypical preconceptions of assessors that may have an impact on objective assessment of and interaction with the child and family. To fully understand the nature of the child and family, one must first understand how they function within their greater cultural context. Trainers should provide information on identifying broad aspects of culture, such as values, beliefs, language, and rules. Courses may be offered in ethnic and cultural diversity that include, for example, information on family structures and styles of communication.

To help early interventionists recognize subjective values that may contribute to bias in how they assess and intervene with culturally diverse families, a set of training guidelines has been offered (Chan, 1990; Chen, Brekken, and Chan, 1997; Mallach, 1993). It is recommended that more university programs provide coursework to help professionals:

- Develop awareness of their own cultural influences on decision making

- Evaluate the degree of a family's convergence with and divergence from their culture

- Identify unique aspects of the family and each member

- Develop the ability to mobilize community and family resources

- Gain an understanding of how cultural factors contribute to the family's ability to address their young child's needs

Similar training must also be made available to professionals who have begun to work in midcareer with young children from diverse cultures.

Assessing Family Characteristics

Objectives

The goal behind this second component in conducting a FOCUS assessment is to understand family factors and dynamics in order to develop a profile of the family's strengths and weaknesses within a sociocultural context. Broadly speaking, determining the impact of social and cultural influences on family functioning is the focus of this stage. Given that multiple dimensions of the family and home environment contribute to the developmental status of the infant and toddler, various measures should be considered (and will be if the assessor has received training in the FOCUS model).

Identifying behavioral similarities that are due to culture is not sufficient and may actually contribute to a stereotypical classification. It is also necessary to understand divergences from the culture as well as the degree of cultural assimilation. The interactions among cultural convergence, cultural divergence, and the unique contributions of the child and each family member must be considered. Importantly, the evaluator needs to determine the degree to which these influences contribute to the family's ability to address the young child's special needs.

Finally, it is also important to note that the most common form of developmental delay in early childhood is in speech and language processes. Therefore, examiners who assess the abilities of young children must exhibit some caution, as many young children who do not have English as their dominant language may also demonstrate limited proficiency in their native language. An issue to consider when assessing language development in young children is the language history of the child. To facilitate development of language, it is important to note to what extent English is being spoken in the home, and which other sources of English the child is exposed to.

Methods

Measures of the family and home environment are critical in a FOCUS evaluation of a young child. When measures of this type are included in an evaluation, however, they are primarily a formal inventory and do not include specific reference to sociocultural factors. Informal observation and a thorough interview yield additional important information about cultural similarity and divergence as well as the unique contributions of the child and each family member. In addition, an evaluator who is successful in evaluating his or her own subjectivity feels more confident about the objective nature of informal assessment.

There are a few reliable specialized scales to assess home and family environment. The Home Observation and Measurement of the Environment (HOME; Caldwell and Bradley, 1984) yields information regarding the content, quality, and responsiveness of the infant or toddler's home environment and is done through formal observation by a trained observer. This is an effective tool for assessing the home environments of nonimpaired children, but its application for young children with disabilities is viewed as somewhat limited at this time (Bagnato, Neisworth, and Munson, 1997). Another scale, the Infant/Toddler Environment Rating Scale (Harms, Cryer, and Clifford, 1990), is a blend of norm-referenced and curriculum-based assessment and emphasizes using both observation of skills in structured and unstructured settings and parental input.

Assessment of family needs is also accomplished through informal observation and interview. Surveys are also available to identify family strengths and needs. The Family Needs Survey (Bailey and Simeonsson, 1985) is a criterion-referenced measure that clearly identifies parent perceptions of competency and weakness. It is applicable to parents of infants with various disabilities. Two other useful instruments are the Family Support Scale (Dunst, Jenkins, and Trivette, 1988) and the Family Strengths Scale (Olson,

Larsen, and McCubbin, 1983). For a more detailed discussion on the assessment of family issues and cultural identity and acculturation, see Chapter Six (family assessment) and Chapter Four (cultural identity assessment).

A critical issue in assessing both the child and the family is language dominance and proficiency. Yansen and Shulman (1996) indicated that language fluency can be categorized along a five-level continuum: nonspeaker, very limited speaker, limited speaker, functional speaker, and fluent and proficient speaker. In addition to language proficiency, language dominance in the home must also be assessed. Short and easy instruments, such as the Home Language Survey (Ortiz, 1992), may be administered to assess language learning history, language use with the child, language use by the child, and language use among adults in the household.

Assessing Young Children's Developmental Competencies

Objectives

The goal of this next step in a FOCUS assessment is to develop a profile of the infant or toddler's strengths and weaknesses in the cognition, communication, motor, visual-motor, adaptive, social-interactive, and behavioral domains. Planning the assessment battery for a culturally competent assessment requires sensitivity to the impact of the multiple dimensions of a child's environment.

The current functioning of any child must be understood in the context of the developmental path taken to reach this point. Therefore, it is essential that accurate developmental information be collected as the first stage of any diagnostic evaluation of a preschool child. The initial interview can be conceptualized as consisting of two components, a developmental and a sociocultural phase.

Assessment of young children must include accurate information regarding the developmental trajectory of the child. To understand the context of development, information must be gathered regarding prenatal care and development, the course of perinatal development, and any pregnancy or birth complications. In addition, accurate information must be gathered with regard to developmental milestones, including fine and gross motor development, language development, cognitive development and problem solving, social and emotional development, and medical history.

It is important to note that there are great individual differences in these developmental milestones, and interpretation of a developmental history must be made in light of these variations. Many factors are associated with this individual variability, among them genetics, medical history, and life experiences. Therefore it is important to interpret the developmental history in light of familial and sociocultural histories. The sociocultural portion of the preassessment phase should include gathering information on the parents' expectations of the child's development, degree of acculturation, language use and proficiency, and social support networks available to the parents.

Methods: Infants and Toddlers

Choosing culturally appropriate modes of assessment in the areas just mentioned is mandatory. Limiting assessment to only one mode is inappropriate. When possible, normative-based, curriculum-based, and criterion-based measures should be used. See Table 19.2 for an overview of instruments that may be used as part of an early childhood evaluation.

Bagnato, Neisworth, and Munson (1997), who advocate early childhood evaluation models that link assessment and early intervention, indicate that the measure eliciting perhaps the strongest family involvement is the Assessment Evaluation and Programming System for Infants and Children (Bricker, 1993). Other measures they note for strong reliance on parental input include the Battelle Developmental Inventory (BDI; Newborg, Stock, and Wnek, 1988), the Carolina Curriculum, HELP, and the Developmental Observation Checklist System (DOCS; Hresko, Miguel, Sherbenou, and

Table 19.2. Instruments for evaluating infants and toddlers.

Instrument	Purpose	Domain of Functioning	Measurement Category
Brazelton Neonatal Behavioral Assessment Scale (NBAS; Brazelton, 1984)	Assesses developmental functioning of infants in first month of life	Motor development, alertness, sensory processes, and emotional functioning	Norm-referenced
Bayley Scale of Infant Development, Second Edition (BSID-II; Bayley, 1993)	Assesses current developmental status of infants and children; early detection of developmental delay (one to forty-two months)	Mental, motor, and behavior rating scales	Norm-referenced

Screening Instruments

Instrument	Purpose	Domain of Functioning	Measurement Category
Ages and Stages Questionnaires (ASQ; Bricker, Squires, and Mounts, 1995)	Used to assess developmental status of at-risk infants four to forty-eight months	Motor, communication, personal-social, problem solving	Norm-referenced
Battelle Developmental Inventory Screening Test (Newborg, Stock, and Wnek, 1988)	Assesses developmental functioning in children birth to eight years (subset of items forms the Battelle Developmental Inventory)	Personal-social, adaptive functioning, motor development, cognition, and communication	Criterion-referenced and norm-referenced (for the full inventory)

(Continued)

Table 19.2. (Continued)

Screening Instrument	Purpose	Domain of Functioning	Measurement Category
Denver Developmental Screening Test (DDST; Frankenburg and others, 1990)	Screen infants at risk for developmental delay (birth to six years)	Personal-social, language, fine and gross motor	Norm-referenced
Developmental Activities Screening Inventory (DASI-II; Fewell and Langley, 1984)	Early detection of developmental disabilities (one to sixty months)	Cognition, academic, perceptual, and motor skills	Criterion-based
Developmental Profile-II (Alpern, Boll, and Shearer, 1980)	Assesses child's functional developmental age level (birth to twelve years)	Physical, self-help, social, academic, communication	Norm-referenced
Curriculum-Based Measures			
Assessment, Evaluation, and Programming System (AEPS) for Infants and Young Children: Vol. 1, Measurement for Birth to Three Years (Bricker, 1993)	"Designed for assessment to determine goals and objectives, intervention activities, monitor progress; also includes family forms" (birth to three years)	Fine and gross motor, self-care, social-communication, social	Curriculum-based

(Continued)

Table 19.2. Instruments for evaluating infants and toddlers. (*Continued*)

Curriculum-Based Instrument	Purpose	Domain of Functioning	Measurement Category
The Carolina Curr. For Infants and Toddlers with Special Needs (2nd ed.) 1993	Assesses children's level of development for entry into the curriculum, and evaluates progress (birth to twenty-four months)	Cognition communication social, fine and gross motor	Curriculum-based
Hawaii Early Learning Profile	Assesses children's strengths and weaknesses and evaluates progress	Cognition, language, social, emotional, gross motor, and self-help skills	Curriculum-based
Transdisciplinary Play-Based Assessment: A Functional Approach to Working with Young Children (Rev. ed. Linder, 1993)	"Designed to provide a comprehensive integrated view of the child's development, style, and interaction patterns" (six months to six years)	Cognition, social-emotional communication and language, sensorimotor	Curriculum-based

(Continued)

Table 19.2. (*Concluded*)

Curriculum-Based Instrument	Purpose	Domain of Functioning	Measurement Category
Ordinal Scales of Infant Development/Infant Psychological Development Scales (IPDS; Uzgiris and Hunt, 1975)	Based on Piaget's theory; assesses the development of cognitive schemas throughout sensory-motor stage	Six scales: • Visual pursuit and object permanence • Development of means for obtaining desired environmental events • Vocal and gestural imitation • Operational causality • Construction of object relations in space • Development of schemes related to objects	Criterion, curriculum Play-based? Dunst (1980) published scoring system that includes age-norms and an estimated developmental age

Burton, 1994). Behavioral observations may also yield invaluable information regarding children's problem solving and functioning within their natural environment.

The process of assessing young children is somewhat different from that for older children. Younger children are less likely to attend for long periods of time, may be more active, and may be more apprehensive in the company of strangers. Their level of language development may interfere with understanding what is required of them during some of the tasks. To maintain a relaxed, attentive state for young children, it is typical to ask parents to be present during the assessment, and it is important to determine the role that they will play during this time. Information obtained from step one of this FOCUS model is integral to planning the best process for assessment and setting the stage for interaction with parents.

Assessment for infants and toddlers may be done in either a home-based or a center-based setting. Regardless of setting, making the child and parents comfortable is an important goal. The appointment should be scheduled at a convenient time, preferably when the child is in a state that maximizes attention. For these reasons, the traditional assessment process, which involves multiple appointments with one professional at a time, is not recommended. Assessors who are sensitive to the needs and interaction styles of parents and children are flexible in the process of assessment that they use and likely to use a less traditional approach.

Sandall (1997) suggests that one way to provide an optimal environment for both child and parent is to use nontraditional approaches that allow flexibility; the researcher recommends a play-based, arena-style assessment. Arena assessment involves simultaneous assessment of the child across several developmental domains. Various professionals participate in the arena procedure, but typically one of them acts as facilitator and guides the child through the tasks, with other professionals recording their observations. Parents are sometimes asked to be the facilitator if the professionals need help engaging the child.

Parents are a vital part of the arena process and are asked to provide information, and sometimes to comment on and validate their
young child's responses. This flexible approach also encourages
parent-child interaction as well as interaction among the various
professionals and the parent(s). This approach not only gives the
child an environment likely to maximize performance but also creates the opportunity to learn more about the family's attitudes, values, and behaviors; how members interact; family competencies;
and family needs.

Methods: Preschool Children

Selecting assessment techniques for evaluating culturally diverse
children should depend on the referral question. Table 19.3 gives a
list of many of the formal evaluation instruments available for
preschool children. With young children, the referral question
should contain two components. The first addresses the child's current level of functioning across developmental domains. This portion of the assessment should include a detailed analysis of the
strengths and weaknesses demonstrated by the child.

This analysis drives the second portion of the referral question:
how can we help to increase the adaptiveness of this child. Hence
information about the child must be collected in such a way as to
allow application of these results to the consultation process with
the parents or guardian, as well as generation of the individualized
educational plan. To address both components of the referral question, it is often necessary to employ formal norm-referenced procedures, curriculum-based criterion referenced procedures, and other
informal processes.

Norm-referenced assessment devices are instruments administered in a standardized fashion; the child's performance is judged
relative to that of other children of similar age. Norm-referenced
instruments produce a standard and a general level of functioning,
information necessary to address the first part of the referral question. Validity is always an issue with norm-referenced standardized

Table 19.3. Instruments for assessing preschool-aged children.

Instrument	Purpose	Domain of Functioning	Measurement Category
Preschool Assessment Instruments: Cognitive Ability (Verbal and Nonverbal)			
Differential Ability Scales (DAS)	Measures intellectual ability and achievement (two to six, to seventeen years of age); achievement tests only for school-age children	Verbal and nonverbal ability (ages three to six, to six to eleven; verbal, nonverbal, and spatial ability (five years, zero months to seventeen years, eleven months)	Norm-referenced
Kaufman Assessment Battery for Children (K-ABC; Kaufman and Kaufman, 1993	Measures intelligence and achievement in children two to twelve years of age	Sequential and simultaneous processing, achievement nonverbal abilities	Norm-referenced
Stanford-Binet Intelligence Scales, fourth edition	Measures intellectual ability in ages two to twenty-four years	Verbal, abstract/visual, quantitative, and short-term memory	Norm-referenced

(*Continued*)

Table 19.3. (Continued)

Instrument	Purpose	Domain of Functioning	Measurement Category
Wechsler Preschool and Primary Scale of Intelligence-Revised (WPPSI-R; Wechsler, 1989)	Measures intellectual ability three years to seven years, three months	Verbal and performance scales	Norm-referenced
Detroit Test of Learning Aptitude-P (DTLA-P; Hammill and Bryant, 1991)	Evaluates general cognitive ability in three-to-nine-year-olds	Verbal aptitude, nonverbal aptitude, attention-enhanced aptitude, motor-enhanced aptitude, and motor-reduced aptitude	Norm-referenced
Preschool Assessment Instruments: Cogni tive Ability (Nonverbal Only)			
Leiter International Performance Scale	A nonverbal assessment instrument that does not require the ability to speak or understand English; can be administered to individuals two years old to adult	Nonverbal intelligence	Norm-referenced

(Continued)

Table 19.3. Instruments for assessing preschool-aged children.
(*Continued*)

Preschool Assessment Instruments: Cognitive Ability (Nonverbal Only)	Purpose	Domain of Functioning	Measurement Category
Raven's Progressive Matrices (Raven, Court, and Raven, 1996)	Measure of nonverbal intelligence (Coloured Progressive Matrices, CPM, is for five to eleven years)	Perceptual ability, deductive and analogical reasoning	Norm-referenced?
Goodenough-Harris Drawing Test/ "Draw-A-Man" Test (GHDT; Goodenough and Harris, 1963).	Brief test of nonverbal intelligence for individuals three to fifteen years eleven months	Nonverbal cognitive ability based on child's drawing of a man, woman, or self	Norm-referenced?

Preschool Assessment Instruments: Adaptive Behavior			
AAMD Adaptive Behavior Scale; School Edition (ABS-SE; Lambert, Nihara, and Leland, 1993).	Measure of adaptive behavior, for children three years, three months to seventeen years, two months	Personal self-sufficiency, community self-sufficiency personal-social responsibility social adjustment, personal adjustment	Criterion-referenced and norm-referenced
Adaptive Behavior Inventory for Children (ABIC; Mercer and Lewis, 1982)	Measure of adaptive behavior in children five to eleven years, eleven months	Measures six areas of adaptive behavior:	

(*Continued*)

Table 19.3. (*Continued*)

Preschool Assessment Instruments: Adaptive Behavior	Purpose	Domain of Functioning	Measurement Category
		family, peers, community, school, earner/ consumer, and self-maintenance	
Vineland Adaptive Behavior Scales (VABS; Sparrow, Balla, and Cicchetti, 1984)	Measure of adaptive behavior, newborn to adult	Four areas (communication, daily living skills, socialization, and motor skills) and one general area of maladaptive behavior	Norm-referenced

Preschoolers: Developmental Functioning			
Battelle Developmental Inventory (BDI; Newborg, Stock, and Wnek, 1984)	Assesses developmental functioning in children, birth to eight years of age	Personal-social, adaptive functioning, motor development, cognition, and communication	Criterion-referenced and norm-referenced (can be linked to curriculum)

(*Continued*)

Table 19.3. Instruments for assessing preschool-aged children.
(Concluded)

Preschoolers: Developmental Functioning	Purpose	Domain of Functioning	Measurement Category
Brigance Diagnostic Inventory of Early Development (Brigance, 1978)	"Designed to be used with children below the developmental age of seven years. It contains ninety-eight skill sequences and lists objectives for the skills"; a prescriptive instrument		Criterion-referenced and norm-referenced (can be linked to curriculum)
Developmental Activities Screening Inventory-II (DASI-II; Fewell and Langley, 1984)	Nonverbal screening instrument designed for infants and pre-schoolers (newborn to sixty months) who are severely handicapped; can be use as a prescriptive tool for classroom planning		Criterion-referenced and norm-referenced (can be linked to curriculum)
Developmental Indicators for the Assessment of Learning-Revised (DIAL-R; Mardell-Czudnaiski, and Goldenberg, 1983)	Screening test used to identify children (two to six) with learning problems	Motor, conceptual, and language skills	Criterion-referenced and norm-referenced (can be linked to curriculum)

tests. Before any instrument is employed, a thorough review of the manual and subsequent literature must be undertaken to ensure that there is no bias or sampling problem.

Unlike the infant assessment instrument, there is fairly good predictive validity among the many of the norm-referenced preschool instruments. Good psychometric properties still should not give license to develop a prognosis based upon the test results. If prognostication is undertaken, the validity of the instrument may become a self-fulfilling prophecy. That is, if a child is thought to be moderately mentally retarded, and a program and parental expectations are developed based upon this information, the child's development may be hindered by inappropriate distancing and presentation of new material to be learned. Rather than engage in prognosis, it is far more beneficial to the child to use the predictive nature of the instruments to determine the level of risk the child is at and develop an appropriate intervention to address the risk factors.

Criterion-referenced instruments address the prescriptive portion of the referral question (Neisworth and Bagnato, 1986). Oftentimes criterion-referenced assessment devices are directly linked to the curriculum, as with informal curriculum-based assessment or systems such as the Carolina Curriculum and the Hawaii Early Learning Profile. Other forms of criterion-based assessment include theoretically based devices such as the Ordinal Scales of Infant Development, the Developmental Activities Screening Inventory—II (Fewell and Langley, 1984), the Development Indicators for the Assessment of Learning—Revised (DIAL-R; Mardell-Czudnaiski and Goldenberg, 1983), the Battelle Developmental Inventory (BDI; Newborg, Stock, and Wnek, 1988), and the Brigance Diagnostic Inventory of Early Development (Brigance, 1978). The advantage of a formal, norm-referenced procedural approach is the direct linkage of assessment to curriculum. In addition, the assessment is conducted in a naturalistic environment, which can be used for both formative and summative purposes.

There are also a number of informal procedures to obtain a great deal of information regarding the development of culturally diverse preschool children. These procedures may be conceptualized as active or passive techniques.

Passive techniques are those assessment approaches in which the examiner does not actively engage the child during the assessment process. Rather, the examiner relies on observation of the children in a variety of situations (for example, structured versus unstructured) and with various people. Passive techniques may be structured to some degree; an examiner may ask a parent to teach a child to put together a puzzle, in order to assess the dynamics of the parent-child interaction. Observations that help us understand the preschool child within multiple systems include those in a classroom, during a free-play situation, in parent-child interaction, mother-child interaction, and with peers.

The quality and type of play often mirrors a child's developmental capabilities (Rubin, 1990). Observation of children's play provides a window of opportunity to determine how cognitive, linguistic, fine and gross motor, social, and emotional development are integrated in the day-to-day reality of the child.

Active informal assessment involves engaging a child in a task that sheds light on the child's current level of development and the processes the child uses to learn. One of the most common forms is dynamic assessment, which refers to a set of assessment procedures characterized by (1) a test-teach-test sequence, (2) emphasis on assessment of processes rather than outcomes, (3) assessment of generalizable skills, (4) identification of strength and weakness, and (5) differentiation of performance and potential (Haywood, Brown, and Wingenfeld, 1986). For a detailed review of dynamic assessment procedures, refer to Chapter Twenty-One.

Family Intervention Planning

Objectives

This component of the FOCUS assessment involves determining appropriate child and family intervention, considering the infant or toddler's developmental profile while remaining sensitive to the impact of multiple dimensions of the child's environment. This culminates in developing an individualized family service plan (IFSP).

Methods

All professionals involved in assessing the child and family meet with the parents to generate the IFSP. This involves integrating the information obtained from the infant or toddler assessment regarding developmental competencies and needs as well as evaluating the family's competencies and needs. In keeping with the aims of a FOCUS evaluation, the interaction between the professionals and the parents needs to be collaborative. Barrera (1996) suggests that "many times, the greatest bias lies not in the actual assessment but in how the data are reported" (p. 81). A professional who has adequately assessed parental competencies and has gained an understanding of how unique and sociocultural variables affect that particular family is in the best position to establish a collaborative relationship. If a collaborative relationship has been established that communicates respect and understanding of the family's strengths and weaknesses, then results can be discussed and interventions planned with less bias and stereotypical judgment.

Ongoing Evaluation and Planning

Objectives

The assessment process does not end with intervention planning. In fact, the IFSP features periodic reviews—every six months at a minimum. Young children mature and change rapidly. Families are in a constant state of flux. As intervention is successful, the profile of the young child and family competencies and needs must be continually updated. Since subsequent interventions may prove to be unsuccessful, review is essential.

Methods: Infants and Toddlers

Review meetings, similar to planning meetings, are a collaboration among professionals and the family. Interview and observation yield important information regarding the progress of the child and family. Many of the curriculum-based measures used in the initial evaluation, as mentioned earlier, are appropriate for ongoing evaluation. For example, the Assessment Evaluation and Programming System for Infants and Children requires periodic evaluation of child progress along with strong family involvement. In addition, the Instrument for Measuring Progress (McAllister, 1994) and Developmental Programming for Infants and Young Children (Rogers and D'Eugenio, 1981) are good measures to check on progress; both rely on family input.

Methods: Preschool Children

Kurt Lewin, the developmental psychologist, was credited with saying if you want to learn about the development of some phenomenon, you must try to change it. In FOCUS assessment, this translates into placing a child in a diagnostic program to assess his or her capabilities, as well as the most effective means of teaching the child. Barona (1990) suggests that development placements should extend over a period of three to six months. This allows the child to acclimate to the classroom, other children, and the educational professionals. A significant period of assessment also allows educational professionals to engage in an ongoing series of classroom observations, curriculum-based assessment, and dynamic assessment.

During the course of the diagnostic placement, educational professionals may be able to gather information regarding cultural background and degree of acculturation, parental expectations, language history, and parental involvement. It is essential to consider all of these issues in developing an effective individual educational plan. In conjunction with formal assessment procedures, diagnostic placement gives educational professionals and parents the information that is essential in developing an individual educational program that helps maximally facilitate the child's development.

Summary

The need for family-focused, culturally sensitive infant or toddler assessment and intervention is increasingly apparent as the United States becomes more culturally diverse. It is estimated that more than one-third of the population of the United States is African American, Latino, Native American, Asian American, or other people of color. FOCUS is a five-component model for assessing young children that aids early intervention professionals in working with a diverse array of families, regardless of cultural similarity or disparity between the evaluator and the family.

References

Able-Boone, H. (1997). Ethics in early intervention. In A. H. Widerstrom, B. A. Mowder, & S. R. Sandall (Eds.), *Infant development and risk* (pp. 197–206). Baltimore, MD: Paul H. Brookes.

Alpern, G., Boll, T., & Shearer, A. (1980). *Developmental profile—II.* Los Angeles: Western Psychological Services.

Bagnato, S. J., & Neisworth, J. T. (1981). *Linking developmental assessment and curricula: Prescriptions for early intervention.* Rockville, MD: Aspen Systems.

Bagnato, S. J., Neisworth, J. T., & Munson, S. M. (1997). *LINKing assessment and early intervention.* Baltimore, MD: Paul H. Brookes.

Bailey, D. B., & Simeonsson, R. J. (1985). *Family needs survey.* Chapel Hill: Frank Porter Graham Child Development Center, University of North Carolina.

Barona, A. (1990). Assessment of multicultural preschool children. In B. Bracken (Ed.), *The psychoeducational assessment of preschool children* (2nd ed., pp. 374–397). Needham Heights, MA: Allyn & Bacon.

Barrera, I. (1996). Thoughts on the assessment of young children whose sociocultural background is unfamiliar to the assessor. In S. J. Meisels & E. Fenichel (Eds.), *New visions for the developmental assessment of infants and young children* (pp. 69–84). Washington, DC: Zero to Three: National Center for Infants, Toddlers, and Families.

Bayley, N. (1969). *Bayley Scales of Infant Development: Birth to Two Years.* San Antonio, TX: Psychological Corporation.

Bayley, N. (1993). *Bayley scales of infant development* (2nd ed.). San Antonio, TX: Psychological Corporation.

Brazelton, T. B. (1984). *Neonatal behavior, assessment scale* (2nd ed.). Spastics International Medical Publications: Philadelphia: Lippincott.

Bricker, D. (Ed.). (1993). *Assessment, Evaluation and Programming System for infants and children: Vol. 1. AEPS measurement for birth to three years.* Baltimore, MD: Paul H. Brookes.

Bricker, S. D., Squires, J., & Mounts, L. (1995). *Ages and stages questionnaires (ASQ).* Baltimore, MD: Paul H. Brookes.

Brigance, A. H. (1978). *Brigance Diagnostic Inventory of Early Development.* Woburn, MA: Curriculum Associates.

Caldwell, B., & Bradley, R. (1984). *Home Observation for Measurement of the Environment (HOME)*. Little Rock: Center for Research on Teaching and Learning, University of Arkansas at Little Rock.

Chan, S. (1990). Early intervention with culturally diverse families of infants and toddlers with disabilities. *Infants and Young Children, 3*, 78–87.

Chen, D., Brekken, L. J., & Chan, S. (1997). Project CRAFT: Culturally responsive and family-focused training. *Infants and Young Children, 10*(1), 61–73.

Christensen, C. M. (1992). Multicultural competencies in early intervention: Training professionals for a pluralistic society. *Infants and Young Children, 4*, 49–63.

Dunst, C. J. (1980). *The clinical and educational manual for use with the Uzgiris and Hunt scales of infant psychological development*. Baltimore: University Park Press.

Dunst, C. J., Jenkins, V., & Trivette, C. M. (1988). Family Support Scale. In C. J. Dunst, C. M. Trivette, & A. G. Deal (Eds.), *Enabling and empowering families: Principles and guidelines for practice* (pp. 155–157). Cambridge, MA: Brookline Books.

Ensher, G. L. Bobish, T., Gardner, E. F., Michaels, C., Butler, K., Foertsch, D., & Cooper, C. (1997). *Syracuse assessments for birth to three (SDA)*. Chicago: Symbolix.

Fewell, R. A., & Langley, M. B. (1984). *Developmental Screening Inventory-II*. Austin, TX: Pro-Ed.

Frankenburg, W. K., Dodds, J., Archer, P., Shapiro, H., & Bresnick, B. (1990). *Denver-II screening manual*. Denver: Denver Developmental Materials, Inc.

Goodenough, F. L., & Harris, D. (1963). *Goodenough-Harris drawing test*. San Antonio, TX: Psychological Corporation.

Greenspan, S. I., & Meisels, S. J. (1996). Toward a new vision for the developmental assessment of infants and young children. In S. J. Meisels & E. Fenichel (Eds.), *New visions for the developmental assessment of infants and young children* (pp. 11–26). Washington, DC: Zero to Three: National Center for Infants, Toddlers, and Families.

Hammill, D., & Bryant, B. (1991). *Detroit tests of learning aptitude—primary* (2nd ed.). Austin, TX: Pro-Ed.

Harms, T., Cryer, D., & Clifford, R. M. (1990). *Infant/Toddler Environment Rating Scale (ITERS)*. New York: Teachers College Press.

Haywood, H. C., Brown, A. L., & Wingenfeld, S. (1986). Dynamic approaches to psychoeducational assessment. *School Psychology Review, 19*(4), 411–422.

Hresko, W., Miguel, S., Sherbenou, R., & Burton, S. (1994). *Developmental Observation Checklist System (DOCS)*. Austin, TX: Pro-Ed.

Kaufman, A. S., & Kaufman, N. L. (1993). *Kaufman assessment battery for children (K-ABC)*. Circle Pines, MN: AGS.

Lambert, N., Nihara, K., & Leland, H. (1993). AAMD *Adaptive Behavior Scale— School* (2nd ed.). Austin, TX: Pro-Ed.

Linder, T. (1993). *Transdisciplinary play-based assessment: A functional approach to working with young children* (rev. ed.). Baltimore: Paul H. Brookes.

Lowenthal, B. (1996). Training early interventionists to work with culturally diverse families. *Infant Toddler Intervention*, 6, 145–152.

Mallach, R. S. (1993). *Culturally responsive services for children*. Bernalillo, NM: Southwest Communication Resources.

Mardell-Czudnaiski, C., & Goldenberg, D. (1983). *Developmental indicators for the assessment of learning revised*. Edison, NJ: Childcraft Education.

McAllister, J. (1994). *Instrument for Measuring Progress (IMP)*. Pittsburgh: Children's Hospital of Pittsburgh.

McCarthy, D. (1972). *Manual for the McCarthy Scales of Children's Abilities*. San Antonio, TX: Psychological Corporation.

Meisels, S. J., Dichtelmiller, M. L., & Marsden, D. B. (in press). *The Early Assessment System*. Ann Arbor: University of Michigan.

Meisels, S. J., & Provence, S. (1989). *Screening and assessment: Guidelines for identifying young disabled and developmentally vulnerable children*. Washington, DC: National Center for Clinical Infant Programs.

Meller, P. J., & Ohr, P. S. (1996). The assessment of culturally diverse infants and preschool children. In L. A. Suzuki, P. J. Meller, & J. G. Ponterotto (Eds.), *Handbook of multicultural assessment* (pp. 509–559). San Francisco: Jossey-Bass.

Mercer, J. R., & Lewis, J. F. (1982). *Adaptive behavior inventory for children*. San Antonio, TX: Psychological Corporation.

Neisworth, J. T., & Bagnato, S. J. (1986). Curriculum-based developmental assessment: Congruence of testing and teaching. *School Psychology Review*, 15, 180–199.

Newborg, J., Stock, J. R., & Wnek, L. (1984). *Battelle Developmental Inventory*. Dallas, TX: DLM/Teaching Resources.

Newborg, J., Stock, J. R., & Wnek, L. (1988). *Battelle Developmental Inventory*. Allen, TX: Teaching Resources.

Ohr, P. S., & Feingold, J. (1997). *School psychology training in early childhood assessment*. Poster presented at the 1997 meeting of the American Psychological Association, Chicago, Illinois.

Olson, D. H., Larsen, A. S., & McCubbin, H. I. (1983). Family strengths. In D. H. Olson, H. L. Muxen, & M. A. Wilson (Eds.), *Families: What makes them work?* (pp. 261–262). Thousand Oaks: Sage.

Ortiz, A. A. (1992). Considerations in the assessment of language minority students with communications disorders. *Teaching Exceptional Children*, 16(3), 208–212.

Paget, K. D. (1999). Ten years later: Trends in the assessment of infants, toddlers, preschoolers, and their families. In C. R. Reynold and T. R. Gutkin (Eds.), *The handbook of school psychology* (3rd ed.). New York: Wiley.

Provence, S., Erikson, J., Vater, S., & Palmeri, S. (1995). *Infant-toddler development assessment (IDA)*. Chicago: Riverside.

Raven, J., Court, R., & Raven, J. C. (1996). Raven's progressive matrices. San Antonio: Psychological Corporation.

Reschly, D. J., Genshaft, J., & Binder, M. S. (1987). *The 1986 NASP survey: Comparison of practitioners, NASP leadership, and university faculty on key issues.* Washington, DC: National Association of School Psychologists. (ED 300 733)

Rogers, S. J., & D'Eugenio, D. B. (1981). *Developmental Programming for Infants and Young Children (DPIYC): Vol. 2. Early Intervention Developmental Profile (EIDP)*. Ann Arbor: University of Michigan Press.

Rubin, K. H. (1990). *New directions for child development: Children's play*. San Francisco: Jossey-Bass.

Sandall, S. R. (1997). Developmental assessment in early intervention. In A. H. Widerstrom, B. A. Mowder, & S. R. Sandall (Eds.), *Infant development and risk* (pp. 211–235). Baltimore, MD: Paul H. Brookes.

Sparrow, S. S., Balla, D. A., & Cicchetti, D. V. (1984). *Vineland adaptive behavior scale*. Circle Press, MN: American Guidance Services.

Uzgiris, I., & Hunt, J. M. (1975). *Assessment in infancy: Ordinal scales of psychological development*. University of Illinois Press.

Wechsler, D. (1989). *Wechsler preschool and primary scale of intelligence—revised*. San Antonio: Psychological Corporation.

Wilson, M. S., & Reschly, D. J. (1996). Assessment in school psychology training and practice. *School Psychology Review*, 25, 9–23.

Yansen, E. A., & Shulman, E. L. (1996). Language assessment: Multicultural considerations. In L. A. Suzuki, P. J. Meller, & J. G. Ponterotto (Eds.), *Handbook of multicultural assessment: Clinical, psychological, and educational applications*. San Francisco: Jossey-Bass.

20

· ·

Multiculturally Sensitive Assessment with Older Adults

Recommendations and Areas for Additional Study

Grace Wong and Amanda L. Baden

The aging of the population of the United States, or the "graying of America" (Haley, Han, and Henderson, 1998), and the extension of the average life span to 75.7 years in 1994 (U.S. Bureau of the Census, 1997) have led to an increase in elderly people requiring psychiatric care and psychological assessment. Furthermore, the ever-changing ethnic diversity of older adults has necessitated that the psychologists who assess them better understand the issues inherent in giving the geriatric population accurate, appropriate, and comprehensive psychological assessments.

As a result of the increase in the ethnic diversity of the elderly in America, appropriate use of psychological assessment instruments for evaluating older adults has recently been receiving greater attention. However, despite increased consideration of factors that may affect assessments of a multiculturally diverse population of elderly, the knowledge base in this area continues to be sparse. The purpose of this chapter is to familiarize practitioners with those areas and issues deserving attention when psychological assessments are conducted on a multiculturally diverse population of elderly in America. With the information presented herein, clinicians can be better equipped to perform culturally sensitive assessments of the elderly, using psychological measures and research findings that reduce cultural bias within testing.

The literature addressing multicultural assessment with the geriatric population has enumerated many of the challenges found in assessing the elderly (Valle, 1998; Yeo and Gallagher-Thompson, 1996). To date, the research that has been conducted addresses five main themes. First, it cautions against potential cultural bias in many of the psychological instruments used in geriatric assessment (for example, Mahurin, Espino, and Holifield, 1992). Second, to determine whether cultural bias exists, elderly from various ethnic groups have been compared to elderly Whites on mental status examinations, tests of cognitive functioning, and neuropsychological instruments (for example, Kaufman, McLean, and Reynolds, 1988; Loewenstein, Arguelles, Barker, and Duara, 1993; and Manly and others, 1998). To remedy possible cultural bias, researchers have suggested adjustments be made to existing measures (for example, Bohnstedt, Fox, and Kohatsu, 1994; and Murden, McRae, Karner, and Bucknam, 1991).

Third, studies have also focused on the ability of a psychological measure to detect such disorders as dementia within an ethnic group, especially when using an instrument translated into the language of other ethnic groups (for example, Lopez and Romero, 1988; and Taussig, Mack, and Henderson, 1996). Similarly, a fourth theme in the literature is establishment of normative data for particular instruments with specific ethnic groups (for example, Rosselli, Ardila, Florez, and Castro, 1990). Finally, some researchers have sought to validate newly developed or revised instruments for use with multiculturally diverse elderly (Kaltreider, 1998; Liu, Lu, Yu, and Yang, 1998; and Mungas, 1996).

These areas of research demonstrate that multicultural assessment of the elderly has received some attention within the past decade and that a small base of information for use with this population exists. However, more work still needs to be done. Furthermore, practitioners continue to face situations in which they are expected to perform assessment on ethnically diverse elderly with few culturally appropriate tools and with a dearth of available norms for those over the age of seventy-five.

Moreover, the vast majority of the studies conducted thus far focused on African American or Spanish-speaking elderly populations. Unfortunately, psychological assessment with Asian American and Native American elderly has been less frequently subjected to empirical study. Thus, the information regarding assessment of multicultural geriatric populations is limited and skewed in its representation of the various ethnic groups.

Another issue of concern in making geriatric assessments with ethnically diverse elderly is underdiagnosis of psychiatric conditions in the elderly. In particular, psuedodementia and its relationship to depression is an area that we address in detail.

Culturally Biased Assessment

Practitioners, researchers, test developers, and the public in general all have concerns about test bias. One area in assessment that has extensively researched the issue of dementia, a phenomenon that is primarily but not exclusively geriatric, is neuropsychology as many cognitive changes in older adults can be traced to disease-related deterioration or brain insult. In their article on Alzheimer's disease, Loewenstein, Arguelles, Arguelles, and Linn-Fuentes (1994) stated that "one of the greatest challenges facing the neuropsychologist today is the assessment of persons who come from diverse cultural backgrounds" (p. 624).

The variety of psychological measures used to assess ethnically diverse elderly people in the United States have generally been developed both by and for White elderly individuals, that is, normative data obtained from White geriatric populations (Hays, 1996; and Mahurin, Espino, and Holifield, 1992). As a result, the most commonly used mental status examinations may "assume a particular education and cultural upbringing" (Hays, 1996, p. 192).

Moreover, the constructs and abilities tested through standardized measures may also be culturally biased. Intelligence testing, for example, is an area commonly found to have inherent biases (see, for example, Loewenstein, Arguelles, Arguelles, and Linn-Fuentes, 1994). With respect to the Wechsler Adult Intelligence Scale-III, crystallized intelligence—which is heavily influenced by educational attainment, language, and one's cultural body of information—is strongly emphasized because it is regarded as the aspect least susceptible to the effects of aging. Minority older adults are at a disadvantage when crystallized intelligence is assessed. Many minority elderly may not have been raised or educated in the United States. Furthermore, many older adults may not have received formal education, a phenomenon that was common over half a century ago, particularly among women.

Fluid intelligence is measured on the performance scales and is more heavily related to daily living skills and daily functional ability. However, although fluid intelligence is the most susceptible to decline in aging, it is likewise influenced by education. The relationship between measured levels of intelligence on educational attainment demonstrates the difficulty in measuring cognitive decline when using an instrument such as the Wechsler Scales with individuals from various ethnic groups having qualitatively different and lower levels of educational attainment than the groups used in obtaining normative data for the instruments (Dana, 1993). Many of these instruments underestimate cognitive functioning of non-White populations (Mahurin, Espino, and Holifield, 1992).

Cultural bias was also demonstrated on many of the other psychological instruments used to assess elderly populations, such as the Mini-Mental State Examination (Folstein, Folstein, and McHugh, 1975). Generally, this bias was also shown to be heavily influenced by educational attainment level. Other factors often related to performance on assessment instruments were occupational status, depression level, residence, sex, physical health, premorbid history, and environment (Cohen and Carlin, 1993;

Kaufman, McLean, and Reynolds, 1988; and Manly and others, 1998).

Elements of Culturally Sensitive, Comprehensive Assessment of Older Adults

When working with minority elderly, several issues deserve attention. An important part of any assessment is a thorough interview of the patient. Unlike evaluating a younger adult, testing an older adult often requires additional support of many kinds. Depending on the reason for referral, it is useful to invite family members or home health aides to the interview, as the patient may need physical assistance with ambulating and travel. In addition, memory deficit is often an integral part of the referral question and an alternate source of reference is crucial in validating or correcting information obtained from the patient.

Obtaining personal and medical history is critical. The latter is not always easy to access, especially when the patient is from another country or another part of the country. The patient may not be capable of reliable reporting for reasons such as poor memory and lack of familiarity with Western medicine or medical terms. In addition, the person may be fearful of being in an environment where he or she cannot speak the language. The accompanying family members or home health aides are invaluable as providers of medical information about the patient, especially if they accompany the patient to clinic appointments. Family history of Alzheimer's disease and medical conditions such as hypertension, diabetes, cerebral vascular accidents, and alcohol abuse can be important diagnostic information if the assessment is unclear or offers few clues about differential diagnosis.

Other related areas clinicians should ascertain include sensory loss and physical limitation. These should actually be ascertained prior to the patient's arrival if possible. The patient may not be able to see or hear well enough to get to the clinician's office unaccompanied or be tested fairly. Things which young adults take for granted, such as negotiating an unfamiliar setting, can be confusing for the elderly who have sensory loss or dementia; the clinician's awareness of these issues can prevent unnecessary stress and frustration for the patient.

Medications, if not properly monitored, can cause mental confusion and other side effects. They should be brought along to the assessment because the patient (as well as family) often struggle with the names and dosages of medication, both of which are hard to learn even if the patient speaks English fluently. Many elderly patients take multiple medications, and the effects of medication interaction can lead the clinician to conclude falsely that the patient is worse than the actual state. Certain medications, when mixed, can cause confusion and even be lethal.

It is important to assess the patient's educational history. Previous discussion has highlighted that level of education is an important factor influencing the results of cognitive tests. Education is also helpful in establishing a baseline for a patient's premorbid functioning since marked change is often a signal of something more serious (such as dementia). The significance of a former professor being unable to solve a simple mathematics problem or write a simple sentence is markedly different from that of a former farmhand who cannot do the same task, regardless of language. In addition, the test-bias research discussed earlier shows that little formal education can lead to a patient looking worse than he or she is, creating a "false positive."

Illiteracy, too, is more common than realized and must be explored early on, sensitively and supportively. Test selection is greatly affected by an individual's level of literacy; thus, a test may have to be dropped or replaced. In the event of varying levels of literacy, clinicians should be prepared to administer test instructions in alternative ways or have an alternative test ready that meets the needs of the assessment.

Employment is also an important measure of premorbid functioning. It provides clinical information about the individual's ability to persevere, maintain responsibility, attend and concentrate, and engage in social interaction. For those who have migrated or emigrated to the United States, employment history also imparts information about the patient's abilities in the homeland, when he or she could speak the original tongue as well as adaptive abilities in a new homeland. For the elderly, employment history establishes a baseline to compare current functioning. This is particularly useful for those who have not had formal education or were educated in a schooling system unlike that of the United States.

Ideally, an interview should be conducted in the patient's native languages with a clinician fluent in the patient's language(s). Unfortunately, this is not always possible. Steps should be taken to find an interpreter who has some clinical training rather than relying upon untrained staff, family members, or home health aides. Sometimes a family member may want the patient to do well during an interview (even though the patient is brought in for dementia assessment) and may cue the patient by nodding or mouthing answers. The family member may be unfamiliar with terms and concepts being addressed, or have personal issues that censor the patient's true response to the clinician's question. In addition, many dementia patients (unlike depressed patients) find ways of coping with memory loss by confabulation and have an uncanny ability to elicit the help of family members in answering questions. It is important to instruct the accompanying person to refrain from cueing or answering questions on behalf of the patient during the clinician's probe into the patient's deficits.

Translated versions of the Mini-Mental State Examination (MMSE), the Wechsler Adult Intelligence Scale-III, or other researched neuropsycholgical instruments (for example, the Neuropsychological Assessment Battery of the Consortium to Establish a Registry for Alzheimer's Disease, CERAD, discussed in Chapter Eighteen) are often not commonly available at clinics. Unless the clinician or the clinic makes an effort to "collect" translated assessment instruments or tests developed especially for the minority elderly population, they may be unavailable.

This chapter provides some references that might be helpful to further the reader's investigation into how some of these instruments can be found. Much of the current research on assessment of minority elderly is in the area of dementia and depression, given the status of these conditions as the primary areas of complaint and referral for the geriatric population in general. A recommended text is *Neuropsychological Evaluation of the Spanish Speaker*, by Ardila, Rosselli, and Puente (1994).

A number of tests from classical neuropsychological literature (for example, MMSE, the Boston Diagnostic Aphasia Examination, the Wechsler Memory Scale, and the Rey-Osterrieth Complex Figure) were studied, and ten additional tests prepared especially by Ardila, Rosselli, and Puente are also available. They include a Cancellation Test, Spanish Naming Test (adapted), Spanish Reading and Writing Test, Spanish Repetition Test, Spanish Phonemic Test (adapted), Spanish Grammar Test, Verbal Fluency Test (adapted), Calculation Abilities Test, Verbal Serial Learning Test, and Memory for Unfamiliar Faces (adapted). Norms are available for patients seventy-five years and older; level of education is also accounted for. Additional components of a complete battery of tests are also needed for the various ethnic groups. Currently, most of the validation studies are in individual journal articles, not all of which are easily accessible because of the international nature of this type of research.

Use of Mental Status Examinations with Older Minority Adults

The most commonly researched assessment instrument for ethnically diverse geriatric individuals is the MMSE (Folstein, Folstein, and McHugh, 1975). It assesses short-term memory functioning, orientation to time and place, comprehension ability, and attention and calculation skills (Valle, 1998). This instrument has been established as a screening tool that clinicians frequently use to determine the need for additional evaluation of cognitive impairment in the elderly, and currently multiple forms of the MMSE exist. However, several empirical studies using it to screen ethnically diverse elderly have found the MMSE to be culturally biased and to result in high false positive rates for dementia in African American elderly (Welsh and others, 1995). Furthermore, when used with older Asian or Latino adults, the MMSE needed to be translated for use. As a result, translated versions as well as alternative mental status examinations have been developed.

Studies on Native Americans were not found using the mental status exams, and the gap in the literature invites future researchers to fill in.

African Americans

When used with African American elderly, the MMSE was found to result in lower scores, that is, indicating cognitive impairment (Manly and others, 1998; Murden, McRae, Karner, and Bucknam, 1991; Welsh and others, 1995). In these studies, the difference found between African Americans and Whites when compared on the MMSE was often affected by other variables. Murden, McRae, Karner, and Bucknam (1991) cited the preponderance of studies showing that "people with poor educational backgrounds have low scores on the Mini-Mental State" (p. 149). They also noted some studies suggesting that African Americans, regardless of educational level, may perform more poorly on mental status examinations. The longitudinal study conducted by Murden and colleagues was intended to determine what cutoff scores on the MMSE could be used to minimize the number of false positives found when using the MMSE with African American elderly. They suggested that when using the MMSE with African Americans having an eighth-grade education or less, a cutoff of 17 or 18 should be used to diagnose dementia, rather than the traditional score of 23. However, with those having a ninth-grade education or better, the traditional cutoff score of 23 or 24 should be used.

The cutoff for diagnosing dementia when using the MMSE was also examined by Bohnstedt, Fox, and Kohatsu (1994). They found that when the MMSE was used with traditional cutoff scores to diagnose dementia, African Americans and Hispanics had a higher incidence of dementia; however, when diagnoses of dementia were made by clinicians, no difference was found among African American, Hispanic, and White elderly. The discrepancy in the rate of dementia diagnoses for African Americans and Hispanics versus Whites did not diminish when they controlled for age, education, occupation, sex, household income, and other areas of potential difference. They recommended changing the cutoff on the MMSE to 19 for African American and Hispanic elderly.

Manly and others (1998) also found that when Whites and African Americans were matched on educational attainment, no difference in the proportion of elderly having cognitive impairment was found. With respect to the MMSE, differences on the MMSE Orientation task were also no longer significant when researchers statistically corrected for level of educational attainment.

When using the CERAD version of the MMSE to compare neuropsychological test performance between African American and White elderly, a study by Welsh and others (1995) found that African American elderly performed more poorly than Whites on mental status tasks such as the Constructional Praxis test (that is, a measure of visuospatial and constructional abilities) and naming line drawings even after correction was made for difference of education and age. This finding as well as the others listed suggest the need to use caution in screening African American elderly for dementia, particularly when using one or another form of the MMSE.

Latino and Hispanic Americans

The MMSE has been studied to assess its potential for cultural bias when used with Spanish-speaking elderly. Loewenstein, Arguelles, Barker, and Duara (1993) conducted a study for which all neuropsychological tests used were translated into Spanish, including the Folstein, Folstein, and McHugh MMSE (1975). Findings indicated that when correction was not made for educational attainment, Spanish speakers scored significantly lower on the MMSE, and after correction for education this difference approached but did not attain statistical significance.

Similarly, using a Latino, elderly, nonimmigrant sample from New Mexico, Ortiz and others (1997) compared the MMSE and the Fuld Object Memory Examination, a measure found to be free from cultural bias (Loewenstein, Arguelles, Barker, and Duara, 1993; Ortiz and others, 1997), to examine cultural bias in the MMSE. They found that the MMSE was affected by lower educational attainment and lower income level. Thus, when used with Latino populations, the MMSE carries the risk of more false positives for dementia.

To remedy the cultural bias found in the traditional MMSE, Marshall and others (1997) developed an adjustment for the MMSE for item bias, education, and age across Spanish-speaking and English-speaking elderly. This measure is known as the MMSEAdj (Mini-Mental State Exam Adjusted) and was also studied for its efficacy in measuring cognitive impairment in minority and low-education elderly (Mungas and others, 1996). The MMSEAdj was found to have diagnostic accuracy for low-education and high-education groups and for Whites, Hispanics, and African Americans.

Asian Americans

Although some studies of mental status exams have been conducted with Asian older adults, no studies were found using Asian American elderly or elderly Asian immigrants in the United States. However, several translated versions of the MMSE have been developed in other countries for elderly people from the continent of Asia (for example, Jai, Li, Chen, and Zhang, 1999; Kua and Ko, 1992; Lindesay and others, 1997; Park and Kwon, 1990; Rait, Morley, Lambat, and Burns, 1997; Shah, 1998).

Teng and others (1994) conducted a pilot study on a new instrument for screening for cognitive impairment. The Cognitive Abilities Screening Instrument (CASI) was administered in Japan and the United States. It was found to be comparable to the MMSE for detecting dementia. Yano and others (2000) also conducted a study of the influence of language and the number of years raised in Japan on performance on the CASI among older Japanese American men living in Hawaii. Findings indicated a negative association between number of years raised in Japan and scores on CASI when testing was conducted in English, whereas a positive association was found when testing was conducted in Japanese.

A Chinese version of the CASI has also been developed and has been used in several studies (for example, Fuh and others, 1999; Liu and others, 1999). No validation studies were available for this version of the CASI.

Another study that may be relevant to elderly Asian populations in the United States was conducted by Lindesay and others (1997). A Gujarati version of the MMSE was developed for elderly immigrant Gujarati in the United Kingdom; the Gujarati elderly and British-born White elderly were screened using either the traditional English MMSE or the Gujarati version. Findings indicated that although mean MMSE scores were lower for the Gujarati group, the difference was due to the effects of age, education, and visual impairment.

When these effects were controlled, the MMSE was effective for screening moderate-to-severe dementia but less effective with milder or uncertain cases of dementia in the Gujarati elderly. The Gujarati version of the MMSE was deemed adequate for screening dementia, but researchers in the United Kingdom have cited the need to continue developing culturally sensitive versions of the MMSE for screening multiethnic elderly populations (Rait, Morley, Lambat, and Burns, 1997), such as elderly from Pakistan, Bangladesh, and India. However, the United States has given little if any attention to the elderly Asian population at this time.

Despite the lack of attention given to Asian elderly in the United States, researchers in other countries have developed modified or translated versions of the MMSE for use with elderly populations. For example, Park and Kwon (1990) developed a Korean version of the MMSE, referred to as the MMSE-K, for use with Korean elderly. They found that although educational levels affected total MMSE-K scores, use of the method for correcting the score resulted in an adequate measure for Korean-speaking elderly.

Summary

The MMSE has been found to have educational effects for those with less than eight years of education, regardless of the presence of memory deficit. Educational effects for specific ethnic groups have also been found. Hispanics and Latinos, African Americans, the Chinese, the Thai, and the Dutch have all been found to perform more poorly on the MMSE.

Using Intelligence Testing with Minority Older Adults

Intelligence tests have historically been plagued by problems of cultural bias and construct equivalence for all groups (see, for example, Dana, 1993). When assessing the elderly, obtaining an estimate of cognitive impairment and premorbid functioning is often the goal of the assessment. The Wechsler Adult Intelligence Scale-Revised (WAIS-R) or the WAIS-III (the most recent version) is primarily used with adults. WAIS-III currently provides norms for older adults up to eighty-nine years of age. Beyond that age, the clinician must use the norms with caution. However, when assessing ethnically diverse elderly, additional challenges must be addressed. First, the demographics of the population with which the Wechsler scales have been normed often do not reflect the age (beyond eighty-nine) and ethnic groups being assessed. As a result, the measured intellectual functioning of ethnically diverse elderly cannot be accurately assessed.

Another challenge frequently encountered is the poor availability of intelligence tests in languages other than English. Currently, an intelligence test exists for Spanish speakers, the *Escala de
Inteligencia Wechsler para Adultos* (EIWA), as does a translated WAIS
for Chinese speakers, WAIS-Revised for China (Dai, Ryan, Paolo,
and Harrington, 1991). Despite these two alternative intelligence
tests, issues such as cultural bias, educational attainment, and the
many ethnicities and languages not accounted for by existing intelligence tests continue to present challenges to accurate and appropriate assessment of the multicultural population of older adults.

Furthermore, the literature that does exist on testing intellectual functioning in older adults from different ethnic groups is quite
limited. As was the case with mental status examinations, no
research was located on testing of intellectual functioning with
Native American elderly. Appropriate and ethical assessments, as
well as research in this area, must be conducted.

African Americans

A small number of studies addressing the measurement of intellectual functioning have been conducted with African American
elderly. Kaufman, McLean, and Reynolds (1988) conducted one
such study. They sought to determine the degree to which the
WAIS-R subtests were related to race and education. In the study,
the oldest age group ranged between fifty-five and seventy-four years
of age. However, as previously noted, comprehensive assessment of
the elderly requires norms for individuals representative of their ages
(that is, frequently older than seventy-four), their educational backgrounds, and other sociodemographic factors.

Kaufman, McLean, and Reynolds (1988) found Whites scored
higher on all eleven subtests than did African Americans, and that
level of education attained accounted for 15–20 percent of the variance in WAIS-R scores on nine of the eleven subtests. Kaufman and
colleagues did not attempt to interpret these findings for use in evaluating cognitive impairment with the elderly, and the results did
not extend to those over age seventy-four. Manly and others (1998)

also found significant race and education effects for intelligence among African Americans. These studies reinforce the need for extreme caution when using intelligence tests to assess cognitive impairment in a population other than the one for which the test (in this case the WAIS-R) was developed.

Latino and Hispanic Americans

Measures of intellectual functioning with Latinos have also been found to be culturally biased. As previously noted, the EIWA is a Spanish adaptation of the WAIS developed in 1965 and standardized with residents of Puerto Rico. Lopez and Romero (1988) encouraged practitioners to use the EIWA because it has fewer culturally biased items and because Spanish speakers were used for standardization. However, Lopez and Romero found substantial differences from the WAIS (comparisons were made to the original WAIS rather than updated versions) in converting raw scores to scale scores, especially on the Object Assembly and Digit Span subtests of the EIWA (that is, the two subtests most similar in content to the WAIS). As a result, determining the equivalency of the WAIS and the EIWA with respect to level of difficulty on the subtests was difficult.

To account for this difficulty, Lopez and Romero (1988) suggested that, given the standardization sample used for the EIWA, the instrument is most appropriate for use with "Spanish-speaking individuals from predominantly rural communities, with little educational background (less than 9 years), and with lower status jobs" (p. 269). It is important to note that this study was not conducted a using a U.S. mainland population, and the issue of generalizability remains when using these norms with U.S. Latino and Hispanic populations.

Loewenstein, Arguelles, Barker, and Duara (1993) studied the neuropsychological performance of Spanish-speaking (95 percent of whom were Cuban American) and English-speaking White (non-Hispanic) elderly patients with Alzheimer's disease. In comparing the two groups on the WAIS-R, Loewenstein and colleagues chose to translate the WAIS-R into Spanish for their study rather than use the EIWA. They found lower educational attainment levels and lower scores on the Vocabulary, Digit Span, and Comprehension subtests of the WAIS-R for the Spanish-speaking elderly than for the White. However, when they controlled for the effects of educational attainment, differences were only seen on the WAIS-R Digit Span subtest. Level of impairment owing to Alzheimer's disease also affected performance.

After controlling for educational attainment, the researchers found that the mildly impaired Spanish speakers differed from the White elderly only on the WAIS-R Digit Span subtest, but the more moderately-to-severely impaired Spanish speakers had lower scores on the WAIS-R Digit Span and Comprehension subtests. These findings suggest that a number of factors be considered in assessing Spanish-speaking Latino elderly:

- The strong relationship between the vocabulary subtest and educational attainment

- The cultural bias found in the comprehension subtest

- The low susceptibility to cultural bias and educational attainment of the Digit Span subtest

Cultural and test bias in tests of cognitive intellectual functioning with Spanish-speaking elderly has been documented in using both the WAIS-R and the EIWA (Lopez and Taussig, 1991). Furthermore, Lopez and Taussig (1991) caution that the WAIS-R can underestimate Spanish-speaking older adults' intellectual functioning, and the EIWA can overestimate their functioning. When conducting intellectual assessments with Spanish-speaking elderly, use caution and address consideration of bias.

Asian Americans

Tests of intellectual functioning with Asian Americans have been translated for Chinese-speaking (WAIS-RC; Gong and others, 1983) and Japanese-speaking populations (as cited in Matsuda and Saito, 1998). However, no studies regarding intellectual assessment have been conducted on elderly Asian Americans. Most of the existing studies on Asians have specifically addressed issues for Chinese and Japanese individuals in their countries of origin, and they rarely included information on the elderly. One exception was a study of Chinese and White Americans by Geary and others (1997). In comparing the samples from China and America, they found no difference in computational or reasoning abilities in their sample of sixty-to-eighty-year-old participants and no differences on general intelligence. The lack of information on intelligence testing with Asian American elderly emphasizes the need for further research in this area.

Summary

Assessing intellectual functioning with ethnically diverse elderly requires normative samples for use with the elderly as well as information regarding those factors affecting intelligence tests. We recommend that further research be conducted with elderly from diverse ethnic groups to ensure freedom from cultural bias.

Depression and Pseudodementia

Depression must also be included in this chapter, given its status as the most common mental health problem found in those who are sixty-five or older (Epstein, 1976). Depression in the elderly is often underdiagnosed and thereby does not receive adequate treatment, if any (Angel and Angel, 1995). Society often expects older adults to make somatic complaints, talk about the loss of loved ones, and be less physically active. However, the prevalence of depression among older adults is due to many factors. First, many minority elderly persons live near the poverty level, have multiple chronic medical conditions, and lack acculturation to mainstream life. Social isolation is also common given that the family members of many older adults have little availability since they need to work long hours, supplement low incomes, and support school-age children.

Other factors leading to depression can be inability to speak English, difficulty traveling because of ambulatory problems or unsafe neighborhoods, physical limitation resulting from medical problems, and close friends who have moved away or died. Often, travel to their country of origin and maintaining telephone contact with those in that country may be beyond the family's budget. Many elderly experience loss of social status (perhaps from loss of professional identity and a sharp financial decline after retirement). They also may experience humiliation associated with being in a visible racial ethnic minority or loss of status by having immigrated to a new country. The stressors related to aging are many, and ethnic minority groups have their own stressors particular to their groups. In her book on ethnicity and aging, Padgett (1995) gives clinicians and researchers a thorough comparison of depression among ethnic groups.

Although psychotic depression is the most commonly seen variant in inpatient hospital units, less severe forms such as "pseudodementia" and "masked depression" are also commonly observed in inpatient as well as outpatient settings.

In masked depression, somatic symptoms are often overlooked as potential depressive symptoms. Clinicians must attend to the possibility of depression in older adults given that many cultures tend to express depression by somatization of symptoms. When individuals also have chronic medical conditions, differentiating masked depression is particularly difficult. In addition, merely living with a chronic medical condition can be stressful. Neurovegetative signs can also be an indicator of the presence of depression. Many older adults may not seek treatment and instead withdraw or fail to recognize the presence of depressive symptomatology. They may attribute feeling poorly to external circumstances (such as losses, poverty, and the like) rather than realizing that the physiological changes of age can also bring about depression in a way that makes coping more difficult.

Pseudodementia

A common assessment referral need is to make a differential diagnosis between depression and dementia. In pseudodementia, or the "dementia syndrome of depression" (Spar and LaRue, 1990), patients can appear demented as a result of their cognitive impairment, poor grooming, declining activities of daily living, poor eye contact, and slumped posture, to name a few symptoms. When tested, their performance is not at the low level that indicates organic impairment. Odd behavior typically observed in a patient having dementia, such as leaving pants unzipped, wearing underclothes over outer clothing, wandering, or confabulating, is not present. However, because many minority elderly patients having low education levels tend to have low scores on the MMSE, other behaviors consistent with dementia should be observed before considering the possibility of dementia. It is often necessary to observe the patient's response to treatment (such as medication and therapy) before a clearer picture can be seen.

Individuals with pseudodementia, unlike dementia patients, can show improvement in cognitive functioning when treated with antidepressants. Clinicians who normally do not work with the elderly and the syndrome of dementia should consult with geriatric specialists who are knowledgeable about issues of aging and aware of issues of testing bias. Misdiagnosis can lead to treatment that may not be appropriate for the patient. Spar and LaRue (1990) offered useful observations regarding differences between dementia and pseudodementia in their book *Concise Guide to Geriatric Psychiatry*.

Depression Screening Scales

Depression screening measures were originally designed for research. Although scoring within a specified range on any of the various depression screening scales is not sufficient to make a diagnosis of depression, the scales can yield helpful information about the presence of depressive symptoms. Although the scales were developed to assess depression based on the Western medical model, they continue to be used and translated into numerous languages because few other options are available. Some commonly used scales employed across cultures include the Beck Depression Scale or BDI (Beck, 1978), the Geriatric Depression Scale or GDS

(Yesavage and others, 1983), the Hamilton Rating Scale for Depression or HRSD (Hamilton, 1960), and the Zung Self-Rating Scale (Zung, 1965). With the exception of the Geriatric Depression Scale, many cross-cultural studies did not use a specifically elderly population.

The validity of the GDS has been studied for use with a Japanese American population (Iwamasa, Hilliard, and Kost, 1998), a Chinese American population (Lee, 1992), and a Mexican American and Spanish-speaking population (Baker and Espino, 1997). Long and short forms of the Chinese GDS were also compared (Liu, Lu, Yu, and Yang, 1998). In addition, the GDS has been translated into a variety of languages (Spanish, Hindi, Vietnamese, Korean, Russian, Romanian), and these versions of the GDS are available on the Internet (Yesavage, 2000).

The most common criticism of the depression screening scales is that they are not adapted to be culturally appropriate for individuals of diverse cultural backgrounds. Although this limitation results in restricted cultural validity (Marsella, Sartorius, Jablensky, and Fenton, 1985), the scales have been able to differentiate within-group differences between the depressed and nondepressed. Despite their limited utility in non-Western populations, they are still being used in clinical settings because no options are available and because they aid in quantifying depressive symptoms. However, scores must be interpreted with the utmost of caution and never in isolation from other clinical information.

Conclusion

The information presented in this chapter is intended to assist practitioners and researchers in conducting culturally sensitive assessments with older adults. A relatively small number of studies have been conducted with culturally sensitive assessments of multiethnic elderly as a goal. However, those researchers beginning to contribute to our understanding of minority elderly have made substantial gains. Already, some assessment instruments have been translated into a variety of languages and, of these, several are validated with older minority adults in the United States. The translated instruments tend to be those measures most commonly used. More specialized instruments, such as assessments of memory, problem solving, and visual organization, have yet to be prepared and validated for use with ethnically diverse elderly. Future researchers should begin to address these specialized areas. Nonverbal tests of cognitive ability such as the Beta III (Kellogg and Morton, 1999) should also be validated for use.

Clinicians must be aware of the limitations of many of the currently available translated versions of measures. For example, as noted above, the EIWA overestimates intelligence, whereas the WAIS-R underestimates it (Lopez and Taussig, 1991). As a result, such variables as the educational attainment of older adults and the ages used for normative data affect the validity of the instruments.

Another area for future research is in studying geriatric patients representative of the vast array of cultures present in the United States. Given that virtually no information was available for geriatric assessments with Native American elderly, this is clearly an area that deserves priority. Similarly, many racial ethnic groups with large U.S. populations continue to be represented by only a handful of studies. Finally, accurate normative samples should be obtained for instruments used with minority elderly.

Despite the important contributions of the researchers already identified in this chapter, a tremendous amount of work needs to be done to prepare clinicians for the steadily growing geriatric population. We hope that this review aids practitioners in providing culturally competent assessment of older adults and encourages additional work in this area.

References

Angel, J. L., & Angel, R. J. (1995). Age at migration, social connections, and well being among elderly Hispanics. *Journal of Aging and Health, 4,* 480–499.

Ardila, A., Rosselli, M., & Puente, A. E. (1994). *Neuropsychological evaluation of the Spanish speaker.* New York: Plenum Press.

Baker, F. M., & Espino, D. V. (1997). A Spanish version of the Geriatric Depression Scale in Mexican-American elders. *International Journal of Geriatric Psychiatry, 12,* 21–25.

Beck, A. T. (1978). *Beck Depression Inventory.* Philadelphia: Philadelphia Center for Cognitive Therapy.

Bohnstedt, M., Fox, P. J., & Kohatsu, N. D. (1994). Correlates of mini-mental status examination scores among elderly demented patients: The influence of race-ethnicity. *Journal of Clinical Epidemiology, 47,* 1381–1387.

Cohen, C. I., & Carlin, L. (1993). Racial differences in clinical and social variables among patients evaluated in a dementia assessment center. *Journal of the National Medical Association, 85*(5), 379–384.

Dai, X., Ryan, J. J., Paolo, A. M., & Harrington, R. G. (1991). Sex differences on the Wechsler Adult Intelligence Scale—Revised for China. *Psychological Assessment: A Journal of Consulting and Clinical Psychology, 3,* 282–284.

Dana, R. H. (1993). *Multicultural assessment perspectives for professional psychology.* Needham Heights, MA: Allyn & Bacon.

Epstein, L. J. (1976). Depression in the elderly. *Journal of Gerontology, 31,* 278–282.

Folstein, M. F., Folstein, S. E., & McHugh, P. R. (1975). Mini-mental state: A practical method for grading the mental state of patients for the clinician. *Journal of Psychiatry Research, 12,* 189–198.

Fuh, J. J., Liu, C. Y., Wang, S. J., Wang, H. C., Liu, H. C. (1999). Revised memory and behavior problems checklist in Taiwanese patients with Alzheimer's disease. *International Psychogeriatrics, 11,* 181–189.

Geary, D. C., Hamson, C. O., Chen, G. P., Liu, F., Hoard, M. K., & Salthouse, T. A. (1997). Computational and reasoning abilities in arithmetic: Cross-generational change in China and the United States. *Psychonomic Bulletin and Review, 4,* 425–430.

Gong, Y. X., et al. (1983). Revision of Wechsler's Adult Intelligence Scale in China. *Acta Psychologica Sinica, 15,* 362–370. (From PsycInfo, 1983, Abstract No. 1984–22187–001)

Haley, W. E., Han, B., & Henderson, J. N. (1998). Aging and ethnicity: Issues for clinical practice. Special issue: Race and ethnicity in the medical setting: Psychological Implications. *Journal of Clinical Psychology in Medical Settings, 5,* 393–409.

Hamilton, M. (1960). Rating depressive patients. *Journal of Clinical Psychiatry, 41,* 21–24.

Hays, P. (1996). Culturally responsive assessment with diverse older clients. *Professional Psychology: Research and Practice*, Apr. 27 (2), 188–193.

Iwamasa, G. Y., Hilliard, K. M., & Kost, C. R. (1998). The Geriatric Depression Scale and Japanese American older adults. *Clinical Gerontologist, 19*, 13–24.

Jai, X., Li, S., Chen, C., & Zhang, W. (1999). Preliminary test of the Psychogeriatric Assessment Scales (PAS). *Chinese Mental Health Journal, 13*, 193–196.

Kaltreider, L. B. (1998). Neurocognitive screening in linguo-cultural minorities: A pilot study of the Cross-Cultural Cognitive Examination in Latino elderly. *Dissertation Abstracts International: Section B: The Sciences and Engineering, 58* (11-B) 6237.

Kaufman, A. S., McLean, J. E., & Reynolds, C. R. (1988). Sex, race, residence, region, and education differences on the 11 WAIS-R subtests. *Journal of Clinical Psychology, 44*, 231–248.

Kellogg, C. E., & Morton, N. W. (1999). *Beta III*. San Antonio, TX: Harcourt Brace Educational Measurement.

Kua, E. H., & Ko, S. M. (1992). A questionnaire to screen for cognitive impairment among elderly people in developing countries. *Acta Psychiatrica Scandinavica, 85*, 119–122.

Lee, H.C.B. (1992). Chinese translation of Geriatric Depression Scale. *Clinical Gerontologist, 12*, 90–91.

Lindesay, J., Jagger, C., Mlynik-Szmid, A., Sinorwala, A., Peet, S., & Moledina, F. (1997). The Mini-Mental State Examination (MMSE) in an elderly immigrant Gujarati population in the United Kingdom. *International Journal of Geriatric Psychiatry, 12*, 1155–1167.

Liu, C. Y., Fuh, J. J., Teng, E. L., Wang, S. J., Wang, P. N., Yang, Y. Y., Liu, H. C. (1999). Depressive disorders in Chinese patients with Alzheimer's disease. *Acta Psychiatrica Scandinavica, 100*, 451–455.

Liu, C. H., Lu, C. H., Yu, S., & Yang, Y. Y. (1998). Correlations between scores on Chinese versions of long and short forms of the Geriatric Depression Scale among elderly Chinese. *Psychological Reports, 82*, 211–214.

Loewenstein, D. A., Arguelles, T., Arguelles, S., & Linn-Fuentes, P. (1994). Potential cultural bias in the neuropsychological assessment of the older adult. *Journal of Clinical and Experimental Psychology, 16*, 623–629.

Loewenstein, D. A., Arguelles, T., Barker, W. W., & Duara, R. (1993). A comparative analysis of neuropsychological test performance of Spanish-speaking and English-speaking patients with Alzheimer's disease. *Journal of Gerontology, 48*, 142–149.

Lopez, S., & Romero, A. (1988). Assessing the intellectual functioning of Spanish-speaking adults: Comparison of the EIWA and the WAIS. *Professional Psychology: Research and Practice, 19,* 263–270.

Lopez, S. R., & Taussig, I. M. (1991). Cognitive-intellectual functioning of Spanish-speaking impaired and nonimpaired elderly: Implications for culturally sensitive assessment. *Psychological Assessment, 3,* 448–454.

Mahurin, R. K., Espino, D. V., & Holifield, E. B. (1992). Mental status testing in elderly Hispanic populations: Special concerns. *Psychopharmacology Bulletin, 28,* 391–399.

Manly, J. J., Jacobs, D. M., Sano, M, Bell, K., Merchant, C. A., Small, S. A., & Stern, Y. (1998). Cognitive test performance among nondemented elderly African Americans and Whites. *Neurology, 50,* 1238–1245.

Marsella, A. J., Sartorius, N., Jablensky, A., & Fenton, F. R. (1985). Cross-cultural studies of depressive disorders. In A. Kleinman & B. Good, *Culture and Depression: Studies in the anthropology and cross-cultural psychiatry of affect and disorder* (pp. 299–324). Berkeley and Los Angeles: University of California Press.

Marshall, S. C., Mungas, D., Weldon, M., Reed, B., & Haan, M. (1997). Differential item functioning in the Mini-Mental State Examination in English and Spanish-speaking older adults. *Psychology and Aging, 12,* 718–725.

Matsuda, O., & Saito, M. (1998). Crystallized and fluid intelligence in elderly patients with mild dementia of the Alzheimer type. *International Psychogeriatrics, 10,* 147–154.

Mungas, D. (1996). The process of development of valid and reliable neuropsychological assessment measures for English- and Spanish-speaking elderly persons. In G. Yeo & D. Gallagher-Thompson (Eds.), *Ethnicity and the dementias* (pp. 33–46). Washington, DC: Taylor and Francis.

Mungas, D., Marshall, S. C., Weldon, M., Haan, M., & Reed, B. R. (1996). Age and education correction of Mini-Mental State Examination for English and Spanish-speaking elderly. *Neurology, 46,* 700–706.

Murden, R. A., McRae, T. D., Karner, S., & Bucknam, M. E. (1991). Mini-mental state exam scores vary with education in Blacks and Whites. *Journal of the American Geriatric Society, 39,* 149–155.

Ortiz, I. E., LaRue, A., Romero, L. J., Sassaman, M. F., & Lindeman, R. D. (1997). Comparison of cultural bias in two cognitive screening instruments in elderly Hispanic patients in New Mexico. *American Journal of Geriatric Psychiatry, 5,* 333–338.

Padgett, D. K. (Ed.). (1995). *Handbook on ethnicity, aging, and mental health.* Westport, CT: Greenwood Press.

Park, J. H., & Kwon, Y. C. (1990). Modification of the Mini-Mental State Examination for use in the elderly in a non-western society: I. Development of Korean version of Mini-Mental State Examination. *International Journal of Geriatric Psychiatry, 5*, 381–387.

Rait, G., Morley, M., Lambat, I., & Burns, A. (1997). Modification of brief cognitive assessments for use with elderly people from the South Asian sub-continent. *Aging and Mental Health, 1*, 356–363.

Rosselli, M., Ardila, A., Florez, A., & Castro, C. (1990). Normative data on the Boston Diagnostic Aphasia Examination in a Spanish-speaking population. *Journal of Clinical and Experimental Neuropsychology, 12*, 313–322.

Shah, A. (1998). The community study of psychiatric disorders in elderly from the Indian subcontinent living in Bradford. *International Journal of Geriatric Psychiatry, 13*, 129.

Spar, J. E., & LaRue, A. (1990). *Concise guide to geriatric psychiatry*. Washington, DC: American Psychiatric Press.

Taussig, I. M., Mack, W. J., & Henderson, V. W. (1996). Concurrent validity of Spanish-language versions of the Mini-Mental State Examination, Mental Status Questionnaire, Information-Memory-Concentration Test, and Orientation-Memory-Concentration Test: Alzheimer's disease patients and nondemented elderly comparison subjects. *Journal of the International Neuropsychological Society, 2*, 286–298.

Teng, E. L., Hasegawa, K., Homma, A., Imai, Y., Larson, E., Graves, A., Sugimoto, K., Yamaguchi, T., Sasaki, H., Chiu, D., et al. (1994). The Cognitive Abilities Screening Instrument (CASI): A practical test for cross-cultural epidemiological studies of dementia. *International Psychogeriatrics, 6*, 45–58. (From PsycInfo, 1994, Abstract No. 1994–43618–001)

U.S. Bureau of the Census. (1997). *Statistical abstract of the United States, 1997* (117th ed.). Washington, DC: U.S. Government Printing Office.

Valle, R. (1998). *Caregiving across cultures: Working with dementing illness and ethnically diverse populations*. Washington, DC: Taylor and Francis.

Welsh, K. A., Fillenbaum, G., Wilkenson, W., Heyman, A., Mohs, R. C., Stern, Y., Harrell, L., Edland, M. S., & Beekly, D. (1995). Neuropsychological test performance in African American and White patients with Alzheimer's disease. *Neurology, 45*, 2207–2211.

Yano, K., Grove, J. S., Masaki, K. H., White, L. R., Petrovitch, H., Chen, R., Teng, E. L., Ross, G. W., Rodriguez, B. L., & Curb, J. D. (2000). The effects of childhood residence in Japan and testing language on cognitive performance in late life among Japanese American men in Hawaii. *Journal of the American Geriatrics Society, 48*, 199–204.

Yeo, G., & Gallagher-Thompson, D. (Eds.). (1996). *Ethnicity and the dementias*. Washington, DC: Taylor and Francis.

Yesavage, J. A. (Accessed 4/7/2000). *Geriatric Depression Scale*. URL: http://www.stanford.edu/%7Eyesavage/GDS.html.

Yesavage, J. A., Brink, T. L., Rose, T. L., Lum, O., Huang, V., Adey, M. B., & Leirer, V. O. (1983). Development and validation of a geriatric depression screening scale: A preliminary report. *Journal of Psychiatric Research, 17,* 37–49.

Zung, W.W.K. (1965). A self-rating depression scale. *Archives of General Psychiatry, 12,* 53–60.

21

Multicultural Issues
and Dynamic Assessment

Carol S. Lidz

Assessors and developers of assessment procedures have been forced to pause and reflect about the consequences of their actions. The Hippocratic plea first to do no harm has become increasingly relevant. The gatekeeping function of assessment has proven to be both benign and malignant in its application to children from culturally diverse backgrounds. The benign consequences of traditional assessment practices include determination of eligibility for services that may be helpful to students, and that occasionally document a level of functioning higher than previously assumed. Alternatively, the same eligibility function of these procedures has led to misclassification and overidentification of children from culturally and linguistically diverse backgrounds as "handicapped" (Harry, 1994).

Traditional (that is, standardized, psychometric) procedures have also been criticized for their failure to generate meaningful information to guide intervention, and for lack of information that results in improved performance for children (Laosa, 1977). Such dissatisfaction has led to increased interest in approaches such as curriculum-based and performance-based measures, as well as other so-called "authentic" approaches such as portfolios. Though they increase the relevance of assessment information for classroom instruction, these newer approaches provide insufficient information for children who do not perform well. That is, the newer approaches provide helpful details regarding "what" children can do but no insight into obstruction of the current level of functioning or linkage to potentially effective intervention.

Each model and type of assessment procedure is most appropriately applied to the issues for which it was designed. Problems occur when these procedures are forced to respond to questions that are clearly inappropriate for that approach. As assessors, our repertory needs to expand, not decrease. We need a full menu so we can respond to the wide variety of assessment issues. We need to understand what information our procedures can provide, and what they can not. We need to understand for which children the procedure is appropriate and for which it is not. We need to detect when a procedure provides meaningful and accurate information about a child and when it does not, and we need to understand what a test is testing in the individual to whom it is applied, and not simply what the manual claims.

The typical response to the call for improved sources of assessment for individuals from culturally diverse backgrounds has been to attempt to remove or reduce the effect cultural variables have on the results of the assessment. This has led to frequent use of nonverbal measures and the frustrating search for culturally fair procedures. These efforts reflect a perseverative search for the "holy grail," the ultimate and true measure of mental capacity, with criterion validity continuing to be prediction of academic success in traditional educational settings. Dynamic assessment offers some divergent thinking about how best to respond to the assessment (and ultimately, the educational) needs of these students.

What Is Dynamic Assessment?

Dynamic assessment is no one "thing," but its most distinguishing feature is inclusion of active interaction within the context of the assessment. This facilitator or interventionist role for the assessor lends a unique character to the assessment process. In a standardized approach, as well as in curriculum-based and other "authentic" procedures, the assessor must remain in the role of neutral recorder of events that are presumed to exist within the child. The results of the assessment are then compared with products of other children of similar age or grade levels, or to predetermined hierarchical steps of a curriculum or task.

In the case of dynamic assessment, the assessor works with the child to create a "zone of next development" (Vygotsky, 1978) by first establishing the child's current level of functioning and then challenging the child to reach toward the next level. During the course of this interaction, the assessor works to understand the nature of the obstruction to the child's learning and the type of interaction that facilitates competence and success. Most dynamic assessment proceeds according to a test-intervene-retest format, focusing on the ability of the child to respond to the intervention and to demonstrate change in level of functioning between pretest and posttest.

The content of the dynamic assessment and the nature of the interactions vary with the particular model. Many assessors use either standardized or curriculum-based measures to establish the child's current level of functioning (the "zone of actual development," as Vygotsky called it).

Intervention tends to follow one of three general models. The most clinical, individualized, and diagnostically sensitive model for intervention is the "mediated learning experience," described by Feuerstein and his colleagues (Lidz, 1987, 1991). Feuerstein (Feuerstein, Rand, and Hoffman, 1979) compiled a battery of tests, called the Learning Potential Assessment Device (LPAD), administered either in pretest-intervention-posttest or intervention-posttest format. The nature of these tests is generic, g type content selected so as not to resemble academic tasks. This is a nonscripted approach that is highly responsive to input from the learner, but it focuses on providing general principles of and strategies for task completion. The assessor works to ensure that the child understands the demands of the task, makes hypotheses based on ongoing error analysis of the child's approach to problem solution, and guides the child toward success through promoting mastery of generalizable principles and strategies.

Alternatives to this approach include Budoff's standardized intervention and Campione and Brown's graduated prompts. Budoff (Lidz, 1987, 1991) uses materials and strategies similar to those of Feuerstein, but his interventions are prescripted and therefore not tailored to the specific needs of an individual child. Instead, he has predetermined the general principles and strategies relevant for task solution and offers them to all learners. In earlier work, Budoff and his associates used his measures to differentiate mentally retarded from pseudoretarded learners by estimating the children's ability to respond to the intervention; pseudoretarded learners made gains, while the performance of those thought to be mentally retarded remained stable at a low level.

In the Campione and Brown graduated prompting approach (Lidz, 1987, 1991), the assessor provides increasing approximations to task solution in response to each error of the child, until the assessor does the actual total solution for the child. The graduated prompting approach was initially developed as an attempt to operationalize Vygotsky's notion of a "zone of proximal development." The number of prompts or hints the child needed in order to solve the problem became the rubric for the ZPD; the child's decreasing need for prompts and ability to transfer learning to new problems served as evidence of his or her learning ability.

I have developed three approaches to dynamic assessment. The first (and the one I most frequently use) is what I call curriculum-based dynamic assessment (Lidz, 1991). In this case, I use any content that is relevant to specific diagnostic referral. The three phases of pretest-intervention-posttest are informally constructed, and the pretest and posttest activities are analyzed in terms of the process demands on the learner (for example, attention, perception, memory, conceptual, and executive), and the learner is observed and analyzed in terms of the application and intactness of the processes brought to the task. The intervention is guided by the components of Feuerstein's mediated learning experience; essentially, it involves working with the child to ensure understanding of the nature of the task and the basic principles and strategies relevant for task solution.

In collaboration with Greenberg (Lidz and Greenberg, 1997), I have designed a more structured and scripted dynamic assessment that serves as a screening measure for administration to classroom-size groups. This is based on four subtests from the Das/Naglieri Cognitive Assessment System (1997), adding an intervention phase to each subtest that is carried out with the entire class.

Finally, in collaboration with Jepsen (Lidz and Jepsen, submitted), I have developed a dynamic assessment for individual administration to preschool age children, the Application of Cognitive Functions Scale (ACFS). This is curriculum-based in the sense of incorporating six activities typical of preschool curriculum demands (classification, sequencing, visual memory, auditory memory, verbal planning, and perspective taking). The intervention portion is partially scripted to provide for the possibility of standardization and scoring, in order to make the procedure useful for monitoring the development of the children, as well as for purposes of data collection for research.

Dynamic assessment represents an attitude and belief system about the learner and the learning process as much as it implies how to proceed with the assessment. Traditional psychometric approaches rely on the assumption that learning ability is stable. The primary purpose of these procedures is to determine eligibility for a predetermined experience; therefore, the success of the procedure depends upon whether it selects individuals who are appropriate for this experience. If both the individual and the experience are assumed to be changeable, then quite different assessment procedures apply.

Most approaches to dynamic assessment rest on an assumption of a potentially modifiable learner becoming eligible for learning experiences that reflect the results of the assessment. The first instance of assessment (comparable to the pretest of the dynamic assessment) describes the current status of the learner and is not viewed as a necessarily accurate predictor of the future. The future becomes considerably more open-ended. The assessment not only describes the current status of the learner but also allows some inference about the responsiveness of the learner to attempts at intervention, the intensity of intervention necessary to induce change, and some direction for linkage with potentially effective approaches to intervention (all of these vary with the particular model employed).

Dynamic assessment can be paired with standardized and other informal approaches to produce in-depth, comprehensive information about the functioning of the learner. Determination of a student's current level of performance is best assessed by normed and standardized approaches, particularly those that also offer curriculum-relevant information. The need for interview and observation goes without saying for carrying out a full assessment. However, if the questions concern how the learner learns, what obstructs more optimal functioning, how intensive the intervention needs to be to induce change, and which approaches hold promise for teaching, then dynamic assessment offers the most relevant information.

Relevance of Dynamic Assessment for Culturally Diverse Populations

Children differ from each other in an almost infinite number of ways. Some of these differences have been associated with cultural and linguistic experiences (Lidz, 1997). Among the differences that may affect test performance are those involving issues of processing time and familiarity with the question-response format of the typical assessment situation. There are additional issues concerning degree of shared knowledge and experience base, and opportunity to develop skills that are prerequisite to success on an assessment task. Experiences that the family provides for the child reflect the perceptions and belief systems of the sociocultural environments; beliefs and expectations regarding child development may vary considerably across and within cultures.

Issues related to bilingualism have helped to clarify the many broader issues of the potential impact of cultural diversity on assessment. For example, mastery of a language system requires considerably more time than might be inferred from merely observing and listening to spoken language (estimated at about seven years); this would be expected to vary considerably in relation to the type of language experience with which the child has been involved. Indeed, formal (instructional) language may differ considerably from the child's informal or "street" language, and the level of the child's informal language would reflect the educational level of the family. Thus, what is measured (and how functioning is measured) by any procedure presents a real challenge. Because of the complexity of the issues associated with assessment of students from culturally diverse backgrounds, there has been considerable negative criticism about assessment practices that rely on standardized tests (for example, Ascher, 1990). Standardized tests typically rely on an assumption of prior experience and background that may or may not apply to learners from culturally diverse backgrounds.

Dynamic assessment creates a context with the potential to reduce the negative consequences of diversity on the outcome of the assessment process (Lidz, 1997). First, because intervention is embedded, the child has the opportunity to acquire the prerequisite knowledge and skills, and to learn the strategies, that relate to the assessment task. Second, the nature of dynamic assessment is to permit a comfortable social interaction to which learners from a variety of backgrounds can relate, reducing the more confrontational question-response format of the traditional assessment interaction. The nature of the interaction resembles an instructional conversation more than a test, and children are typically relaxed and able to reveal their capacities.

Third, the onus of determining what the learner knows or can do is on the assessor to elicit rather than on the child to show. If the child fails to perform successfully, the assessor becomes a diagnostic problem solver who tries to determine what it will take to move the child to a higher level of functioning. There is no assumption that performance is the same as capacity. Instead of a conclusion that the child "can't," there is the alternative conclusion that the assessor or assessment "didn't." Fourth, the focus of the assessment is on instructional implications rather than classification. The outcome is not a label, but ideas about how the learner learns and about interactions that may or may not facilitate this process.

Research Related to Diversity Applications of Dynamic Assessment

There is a particularly strong history of development of dynamic assessment procedures in Europe, with studies involving students from immigrant and minority backgrounds carried out most specifically in the Netherlands, Germany, and the United Kingdom. This is an area of active development in the United States and Canada as well.

Hegarty (1988) described one of the early attempts in England to devise an assessment procedure that reflected learning ability, the National Foundation for Educational Research's Test of Learning Ability. This test, derived from an earlier procedure by Haynes, responded to issues during the 1960s and 1970s concerning low academic performance of children from immigrant backgrounds. The subtest content included analogies, concept formation, number series, verbal learning of objects, and verbal learning of syllables. The sequence for administration of each subtest was teach-practice-test-teach-test.

In the same publication, Hegarty summarized the results of a predictive validity study with four hundred seven-year-old immigrant children. The learning ability test was compared to a short form of the WISC (assessed a year later) and found to be a stronger predictor of vocabulary, reading, and math. This was the first—and for a long time, the only—packaged learning ability test available to consumers, but apparently it was not a commercial success and is no longer available from the publisher.[1]

The work of Hamers and his associates (Hamers, Sijtsma, and Ruijssenaars, 1993) has focused on children from Turkish and Moroccan minority groups living in the Netherlands. The procedure is called the Learning Potential Test for Ethnic Minorities (LEM) and is appropriate for children between the ages of five and eight. The LEM has six subtests, including classification, word-object association recognition, word-object association naming, number series, syllable recall, and figurative analogies, assessing the constructs of inductive reasoning, paired-associate learning, and short-term memory.

The LEM was designed to function as an alternative test of intelligence, and it follows a train-within test format, rather than pretest-intervention-posttest. Training involves nonverbal demonstration and practice of instructions, followed by repeating items, offering feedback, and providing additional demonstration when necessary. Scoring reflects the degree to which the child requires help.

Hessels and Hamers (1993) reported results of their study comparing four hundred children from immigrant backgrounds on the LEM and a traditional measure of intelligence. Although there was a significant relationship between the two tests, it was far from perfect, with children who scored high on the LEM scoring low, medium, or high on the traditional measure. LEM scores were not a statistically significant better predictor of achievement than the traditional measure, but they tended to reach statistical significance in predicting achievement when the traditional measure did not. Further, the difference between the scores of children from immigrant and Dutch backgrounds was smaller for the LEM than for the traditional measure.

The Lidz and Greenberg (1997) study with first-grade students, all of whom lived on a reservation and half of whom were from Native American backgrounds, demonstrated the predictive validity of a group-administered dynamic assessment procedure. Using a modification of four subtests from the Das/Naglieri Cognitive Assessment System (1997), the scores following the intervention portions were the strongest predictors of the students' reading test scores, and in the case of three of the four subtests only the post-intervention scores reached statistical significance in relationship to reading. The students with initially lower pretest scores made the most improvement following the interventions, and the posttest scores of these initially lower-functioning students showed the strongest relationship (compared to students with higher pretest scores) with both reading and math.

Lidz and Macrine (in press) demonstrated a successful application of dynamic assessment for the purpose of identifying gifted children from culturally diverse backgrounds. This study involved students from a school with a population of more than 60 percent minority and immigrant backgrounds and a history of identifying fewer than 1 percent of its students as eligible for gifted programming. This occurred in a district where the norm for classification of students as gifted was 5 percent of the population. Using multiple screening procedures and a dynamic assessment modification of the Naglieri Nonverbal Abilities Test (Naglieri, 1997), these authors identified twenty-five students as gifted, that is, exactly 5 percent of the students in the school, with proportional representation for grade level, gender, and cultural background. There were no special manipulations of testing or scoring for students from culturally diverse backgrounds; all students were administered the same procedures in the same way.

Peña's research (Peña, 1993; Peña, Quinn, and Iglesias, 1992) addresses the challenge to speech pathologists of discriminating children with language differences from those with language deficiencies (Gonzalez, Brusca-Vega, and Yawkey, 1997). Working with preschool Latino children in the domain of vocabulary, Peña's dynamic assessment approach was successful in making this differentiation, with further demonstration that the children who profited from the intervention during the course of the assessment were those who showed the most response to the intervention program that followed the assessment (Peña, 1993).

Research in Israel with children from Ethiopian immigrant backgrounds (for example, Kaniel and others, 1991; Tzuriel and Kaufman, 1999) and in South Africa with Indian and "colored" citizens (for example, Skuy and Shmukler, 1987), both using Feuerstein's Learning Potential Assessment Device, offers further documentation of the narrowed gap between dominant and minority populations with dynamic assessment procedures.

Implications for Educators and Clinicians

Students from culturally diverse backgrounds typically score lower than students from the dominant culture on traditional standardized measures and are disproportionately identified as handicapped or in need of special services. Furthermore, these students tend to be underrepresented among those determined to be eligible for gifted programs. On the other hand, because of the difficulties associated with assessing students from minority and immigrant populations, the real needs of students with handicapping conditions may be overlooked. Results from available research with students from culturally diverse backgrounds show that dynamic procedures offer both the opportunity for higher-level assessment results as well as stronger predictive relationships between assessment instruments and instructional criteria.

The number of research studies has dramatically increased over the last several years, and evidence of the validity of a dynamic approach to assessment has meaningfully increased, but it continues to be difficult for practitioners to receive training that allows them to apply these procedures to their students. The most readily available training involves the Learning Potential Assessment Device, and the only procedure that is currently distributed by a major publisher is Swanson's Conceptual Processing Test (Swanson, 1995), an assessment of working memory. Some of the more traditional tests now have a "processing" component, and many of the newer tests incorporate practice items that reflect the authors' awareness of dynamic assessment literature. But a repertory of dynamic assessment procedures that are packaged and ready for consumer application remains to be developed.

Practitioners who are interested in dynamic assessment approaches are challenged to read the now-extensive literature,[2] contact the researchers and procedure developers, and search for opportunities at conferences and workshops for training. Nevertheless, the education laws and standards are changing and increasingly require inclusion of informal along with formal assessment measures, as well as those yielding information that is relevant for instructional planning. With increasing emphasis on an inclusive approach to education of children with special needs, issues of classification and eligibility determination decline, and practitioners need tools that generate the information that responds to their current questions. Both curriculum-based and dynamic assessment approaches show considerable promise for the newer trends.

Despite the difficulties with obtaining ready-made procedures, the literature and training in the area of dynamic assessment involve a paradigm shift (Hilliard, 1991) that is not tied to any specific approach and is relevant to the entire assessment endeavor. Assessors are challenged to think beyond the quantitative aspects of test data to consider seriously the qualities of a learner's performance.

Dynamic assessment stresses the need to consider the processing demands of the task, the processing propensity of the learner, and the extent and nature of the match between the two. For the diagnostician, it is not enough to list what the learner knows or the learner's current level of functioning; good teachers are well aware of this information and can generate it themselves. The diagnostician needs to dig deeply to reveal obstructions to learning and to offer information that facilitates learner competence. Ultimately, the proof of validity is in the growth of the learner.

Some Concluding Thoughts

In an earlier article (Lidz, 1997), I made the point that evidence that tests measure the same factors in individuals from different ethnic or cultural backgrounds does not necessarily support the interpretation that these measures are nonbiased or that results from using them are equivalent. I think this point is worth repeating, since claims that currently used instruments are unbiased continue to rely heavily on such evidence.

Cultures differ considerably in their values and beliefs, and therefore in what is emphasized in acculturating the next generation. If memory and oral narratives are highly valued and frequently modeled within a culture, then it is likely that the children raised within the culture will excel in these skills. Similarly, if simultaneous rather than sequential thinking and communication are stressed, this is again likely to become characteristic of the children. If learning through observation is the primary mode of instruction, then this is the background for readiness for cultural apprentices.

If these assumptions are correct, then what many of our procedures are measuring is the match between the culture of the school and the culture of the home along with the capacities of the individual. Interpretation of the results needs to recognize that this information includes the degree of acculturation as a significant aspect of the findings (for example, in van de Vijver, 1993). How does this relate to dynamic assessment?

If there is a general model underlying dynamic assessment, it certainly addresses the capacity-and-performance issue by making no assumptions that the two are equated. Dynamic assessment tries to reveal capacity within a setting and a relationship that are comfortable for the learner, but the ultimate focus is on the next steps of learning and how to get there. There is no need to call the student something in order to engage in this process. We all know that intragroup heterogeneity frequently is greater than intergroup heterogeneity, and this leads us back to looking at individuals within their contexts, while making no assumptions about the individual or the context.

Finally, dynamic assessment challenges traditional notions of reliability and validity. For example, high test-retest reliability suggests low construct validity for this model. It is "interscorer reliability" that would be more relevant. Also, reliance on traditional validity criteria such as achievement test scores, although hard to avoid because of convenience and other practical issues, is contrary to the basic assumptions of dynamic assessment, which challenge the performance stability for low performers; that is, the attempt is to contradict the prediction of low future performance. One meaningful predictor would be to demonstrate that students who show a high degree of responsiveness during the course of the assessment are those who are the most responsive to instruction within the classroom setting, but this presents only a partial picture of the information that should be derived from the assessment.

Endnotes

1. The one exception to this may be Jedrysek, Klapper, Pope, and Wortis's Psychoeducational Evaluation of the Preschool Child (1972), based on the pioneering work of Elsa Haeussermann with children with cerebral palsy. To my knowledge, this is another procedure that is no longer available. The motivation for development of this procedure was different from those discussed in this chapter. The author focused on children with severe motor handicaps that made existing procedures impossible to administer.

2. The articles are too numerous to list here (readers can tap into this literature through ERIC, *Dissertation Abstracts*, and

PsychLit/PsycInfo), but the books that survey the work currently available involving dynamic assessment include Carlson (1995); Feuerstein, Rand, and Hoffman (1979); Gupta and Coxhead (1988); Guthke and Wiedl (1996); Hamers, Sijtsma, and Ruijssenaars (1993); Haywood and Tzuriel (1992); Lidz (1987, 1991); and Lidz and Elliott (2000).

References

Ascher, C. (1990). Assessing bilingual students for placement and instruction. *ERIC Digest 65*. (ED OUD905; ISSN 0889 8049)

Carlson, J. (Ed.). (1995). *European contributions to dynamic assessment*. (Series title: *Advances in cognition and educational practice*, vol. 3.). Greenwich, CT: JAI Press.

Das, J. P., & Naglieri, J. A. (1997). *Das/Naglieri: The Cognitive Assessment System*. Chicago: Riverside.

Feuerstein, R., Rand, Y., & Hoffman, M. B. (1979). *The dynamic assessment of retarded performers: The Learning Potential Assessment Device, theory, instruments, and techniques*. Baltimore: University Park Press.

Gonzalez, V., Brusca-Vega, R., & Yawkey, T. (1997). *Assessment and instruction of culturally and linguistically diverse students with or at risk of learning problems: From research to practice*. Needham Heights, MA: Allyn & Bacon.

Gupta, R. M., & Coxhead, P. (Eds.). (1988). *Cultural diversity and learning efficiency: Recent developments in assessment*. New York: St. Martin's Press.

Guthke, J., & Wiedl, K. H. (1996). *Dynamisches testen: Zur psychodiagnostik der intraindividuellen variabilität*. [Dynamic testing: Toward the psychodiagnosis of intraindividual differences]. Göttingen: Hogrefe.

Hamers, J.H.M., Sijtsma, K., & Ruijssenaars, A.J.J.M. (Eds.). (1993). *Learning potential assessment*. Amsterdam: Swets and Zeitlinger.

Harry, B. (1994). *The disproportionate representation of minority students in special education: Theories and recommendations*. (Final report.). Project FORUM. (ED 374 637)

Haywood, H. C., & Tzuriel, D. (Eds.). (1992). *Interactive assessment*. New York: Springer-Verlag.

Hegarty, S. (1988). Learning ability and psychometric practice. In R. M. Gupta & P. Coxhead (Eds.), *Cultural diversity and learning efficiency: Recent developments in assessment* (pp. 22–38). New York: St. Martin's Press.

Hessels, M.G.P., & Hamers, J.H.M. (1993). The Learning Potential Test for Ethnic Minorities. In J.H.M. Hamers, K. Sijtsma, & A.J.J.M. Ruijssenaars

(Eds.), *Learning potential assessment. Theoretical, methodological and practical issues* (pp. 285–311). Amsterdam (and Berwyn, PA): Swets and Zeitlinger.

Hilliard, A. G., III. (Ed.). (1991). The Learning Potential Assessment Device and Instrumental Enrichment as a paradigm shift. In A. G. Hilliard III (Ed.), *Testing African American students: Special reissue of the Negro Educational Review* (pp. 200–208). Morristown, NJ: Aaron Press.

Jedrysek, E., Klapper, A., Pope, L., & Wortis, J. (1972). *Psychoeducational evaluation of the preschool child.* Philadelphia: Grune and Stratton.

Kaniel, S., Tzuriel, D., Feuerstein, R., Ben-Schachar, N., & Eitan, T. (1991). Dynamic assessment: Learning and transfer abilities of Ethiopian immigrants to Israel. In R. Feuerstein, P. S. Klein, & A. J. Tannenbaum (Eds.), *Mediated Learning Experience (MLE): Theoretical, psychosocial and learning implications* (pp. 179–209). London: Freund.

Laosa, L. M. (1977). Nonbiased assessment of children's abilities: Historical antecedents and current issues. In T. Oakland (Ed.), *Psychological and educational assessment of minority children* (pp. 120). New York: Brunner/Mazel.

Lidz, C. S. (Ed.). (1987). *Dynamic assessment: An interactional approach to evaluating learning potential.* New York: Guilford Press.

Lidz, C. S. (1991). *Practitioners guide to dynamic assessment.* New York: Guilford Press.

Lidz, C. S. (1997). Dynamic assessment: Psychoeducational assessment with cultural sensitivity. *Journal of Social Distress and the Homeless, 6,* 95–111.

Lidz, C. S., & Elliott, J. (Eds.). (2000). *Dynamic assessment: Prevailing models and applications.* Oxford, England: Elsevier Science.

Lidz, C. S., & Greenberg, K. H. (1997). Criterion validity of a group dynamic assessment procedure with rural first grade regular education students. *Journal of Cognitive Education, 6,* 89–99.

Lidz, C. S., & Jepsen, R. H. (Submitted). *The Application of Cognitive Functions Scale (ACFS) manual.* Unpublished manuscript, Touro College, New York.

Lidz, C. S., & Macrine, S. (In press). The contribution of dynamic assessment to identification of gifted minority students. *School Psychology International.*

Naglieri, J. A. (1997). *The Naglieri Nonverbal Abilities Test: Multilevel technical manual.* San Antonio, TX: Psychological Corporation.

Peña, E. (1993). *Dynamic assessment: A nonbiased approach for assessing the language of young children.* Unpublished doctoral dissertation, Temple University, Philadelphia.

Peña, E., Quinn, R., & Iglesias, A. (1992). The application of dynamic methods to language assessment: A nonbiased procedure. *Journal of Special Education, 26*, 269–280.

Skuy, M., & Shmukler, D. (1987). Effectiveness of the Learning Potential Device for Indian and "colored" South Africans. *International Journal of Special Education, 2*, 131–149.

Swanson, H. L. (1995). *Swanson Cognitive Processing Test.* Austin, TX: PRO-ED.

Tzuriel, D., & Kaufman, R. (1999). Mediated learning and cognitive modifiability: Dynamic assessment of young Ethiopian immigrant children to Israel. *Journal of Cross-Cultural Psychology, 30*, 359–380.

van de Vijver, F.J.R. (1993). Learning potential assessment from a cross-cultural perspective. In J.H.M. Hamers, K. Sijtsma, & A.J.J.M. Ruijssenaars (Eds.), *Learning potential assessment: Theoretical, methodological and practical issues* (pp. 313–340). Amsterdam: Swets and Zeitlinger.

Vygotsky, L. S. (1978). *Mind in society: The development of higher psychological processes* [M. Cole, V. John-Steiner, S. Scribner, & E. Souberman, Eds.]. Cambridge, MA: Harvard University Press.

22

· ·

Academic Achievement

Craig L. Frisby

What is academic achievement? In most contexts, the levels of academic achievement are evaluated by a universally recognized hierarchy of common indicators. Thus, a third grader who receives an A in a subject area is considered to be a higher achiever than a classmate who receives a B in the same subject area. Likewise, an adult who obtains a master's degree is considered to have achieved more academically, compared to a person whose highest educational level is a bachelor's degree in the same field. In some contexts, the degree of academic achievement is judged quantitatively, with respect to the sheer volume of an individual's accomplishment (for example, number of academic awards received, inventions or discoveries made, or scholarly books written). In its simplest form, academic achievement is often viewed as synonymous with a score on an academic achievement test.

Regardless of its definition, academic achievement can be influenced by factors that are both external and internal to individuals. The quality of learning environments and the availability of learning opportunities represent factors influencing academic achievement that are *external* to the individual (Lambert and McCombs, 1998). Academic achievement can also be thought of as being influenced by a constellation of psychological constructs that are *internal* to the individual. Cognitive ability, creativity, specific talents, achievement motivation, attitudes toward education, metacognitive strategies, academic self-concept, ability to delay immediate gratification, task persistence, self-efficacy, and goal orientation are all factors that come into play in shaping academic achievement (Ormrod, 1998; Phye, 1997).

Given the multifaceted nature of academic achievement, straightforward comparisons among individuals are deceptively complex. Consider this scenario involving two hypothetical high school students. Person X is average in cognitive ability, earns mostly B's and an occasional C in schoolwork, and obtains scores that average in the 40th percentile on standardized achievement tests. However, Person X has worked consistently in two after-school jobs, has saved a considerable amount of money, and is learning how to reinvest earnings in order to start a neighborhood lawn-service company. Whenever possible, Person X reads books on business investment and actively solicits tutoring help from fellow students in order to understand difficult math concepts. Friends describe Person X as "focused," "persistent in the face of failure," and highly motivated to achieve personal goals.

In contrast, Person Y is a bright student for whom difficult academic subjects are relatively easy to grasp and understand. Person Y also achieves B's and occasional A's in school, although teachers claim that Person Y could easily make straight A's with a little extra effort. Person Y finds most school subjects "boring" and has yet to identify a career path or area of personal interest. On a recent standardized achievement test, Person Y received scores that average in the 97th percentile. Given these facts, which student is the higher "academic achiever"?

This example is meant to illustrate that test scores alone may not accurately characterize what some feel reflects the essence of a high academic achiever. Nevertheless, the stark reality is that scores on academic achievement tests, along with grades and class rankings, are positively correlated with admittance to highly selective colleges, later job performance, wages, and overall success in intellectually demanding professions. This relationship, in turn, has different consequences for ethnic, racial, language, and social class groups (College Board, 1999a).

The purpose of this chapter is to survey the variety of ways in which academic achievement can be assessed. This is followed by a discussion of the extent of racial or ethnic group differences in academic achievement, and the factors identified by research as associated with these differences. The chapter ends with a discussion of a suggested method for reporting group differences in standardized achievement test scores, and a discussion of an alternative to standardized tests for special-education decision making in schools.

Assessment of Academic Achievement

Academic achievement can be assessed using a variety of methods. These methods are discussed below.

Informal Classroom Assessment

Informal classroom assessment of academic achievement consists of assessments constructed entirely by teachers for use in their classrooms (Kubiszyn and Borich, 1999). According to Guerin and Maier (1983), informal assessment "does not require a formal or defined reference group, often includes information that is idiosyncratic," and involves information that "is obtained in a setting that is natural to the student's daily experience and that involves ordinary classroom interactions" (p. 7). Some studies indicate that the majority of assessments used in classrooms are developed by teachers (for example, Salmon-Cox, 1981; Stiggins and Bridgeford, 1985), and that teachers' own observations of students and students' work has more influence on instructional decisions than state-mandated tests do (Madaus and Kellaghan, 1992).

Teachers construct informal tests by writing their own test items, using evaluation questions provided in curriculum materials, or using test items from item banks maintained by universities, private organizations, or state agencies (Naccarato, 1988; Rudner, 1998; Ward and Murray-Ward, 1994). These methods are called "informal" because such assessments yield scores that cannot be compared to a larger representative norming group, nor are standardized administration procedures guaranteed. Furthermore, course grades based on informal assessment can vary among teachers as a function of whether or not grades are based on relative versus absolute standards, or the extent to which grades incorporate student effort, attitude, degree of improvement, or cognitive ability (Ward and Murray-Ward, 1999). Although this permits much flexibility for teachers in adapting assessment to classroom objectives and personal teaching styles, similar grades may not have comparable meaning among teachers. In addition, teachers often report not feeling well prepared in educational measurement or test writing practices (Airasian, 1991; Carter, 1984; Impara and others, 1991). As a result, adequate levels of reliability and validity of informal assessments may be compromised.

Curriculum-Based Assessment

According to Shapiro and Elliott, curriculum-based assessment (CBA) methodology is characterized by three features:

1. Assessment is linked to the local curriculum and instruction.

2. Educational success is evaluated by students' progress across key indicators taken from the local curriculum.

3. The primary purpose is to determine students' instructional needs (1999, p. 383).

CBA is a generic label representing a family of methods that differ in their relationship to decision making, underlying assumptions regarding the link between assessment data and instruction, test format and type of student response required, focus of material for monitoring student progress, and level of technical adequacy (Shinn, Rosenfield, and Knutson, 1989).

CBA differs most vividly from informal classroom assessment in its attention to features that enhance technical adequacy. Curriculum-based measurement (CBM), which is one model of CBA, uses a standardized procedure for both administering assessment and monitoring student progress. CBM research demonstrates high correlations with standardized norm-referenced tests, discriminates between special-education students and those who are ineligible for special education, and incorporates interpretation based on data from local norms (for a review of these studies, see Shapiro and Elliott, 1999; Shinn, 1989, 1998).

CBM differs most vividly from published standardized achievement tests in the brevity and frequency of test administration (generally one to three minutes per administration, at least twice weekly), as well as in sensitivity to short-term changes in performance over time. Although performance or authentic assessments involve complex tasks that require integration and synthesis of cognitive problem-solving skills, CBA and CBM typically focus on mastery of discrete skills in core content areas of reading (for example, number of words read correctly), math (number of correct digits within math problems), spelling (number of correct letters or words), and writing (number of correct words written in response to "story starters") (Shapiro and Elliott, 1999).

Individual Standardized Achievement Testing

Standardized achievement tests, whether designed for individual or group administration, are characterized by certain features (adapted from Linn and Gronlund, 1995):

- They are available from large test companies or publishers that have sufficient resources to employ professional psychometricians, statisticians, curriculum consultants, and test developers.

- They include a fixed set of test items designed to measure a clearly defined subject area domain across a wide span of grade levels.

- They include specific directions for administering and scoring the test.

- They include norms based on nationally representative groups, which enable comparisons between the individual's test score and a larger group of similar individuals who have also taken the test.

- Most standardized tests include psychometrically equivalent forms, which enable students to take a different form of the test with alternate items drawn from the same subject area.

- They are often co-normed and standardized on a general aptitude or ability measure.

- A test manual and other accessory materials are included to guide administering and scoring the test, evaluating its technical qualities, and interpreting and using results.

Individually administered standardized achievement tests are used primarily for evaluating individual students who are identified as having difficulty in school, as well as students for whom there is a suspicion that special-educational services are needed. These tests are administered to an individual student by a trained examiner (resource teacher, guidance counselor or school psychologist). Selected-response or constructed-response items are typically presented in a booklet on an upright easel, from which the examiner can turn pages and control the presentation of items. Items usually assess skills in vocabulary knowledge; reading recognition and decoding; reading comprehension; math calculation and understanding or applying math concepts; spelling; oral and written language; and general informational knowledge in science, humanities, or social studies.

Group Standardized Achievement Testing

In addition to the first seven characteristics discussed in the previous section, group standardized achievement tests (GSATs) have these characteristics(adapted from Ward and Murray-Ward, 1999; Worthen, White, Fan, and Sudweeks, 1999):

- In public schools, GSATs are administered at least once yearly to a large group of test takers (that is, entire classrooms) over the course of a day or longer.

- Students mark their responses to items by writing directly in test booklets or completing separate answer sheets.

- In addition to being available from large national test publishers, many GSATs are developed through state-level testing programs.

- Publishers of GSATs provide teacher guides that relate sample test items to specific objectives gleaned from analyses of textbooks and other curriculum materials.

- Most publishers of GSATs offer brief practice tests (to give students experience in test taking) and "locator" tests (to determine the level at which children should be tested with the main GSAT).

- Test results can be scored by hand or computer.

- Publishers of GSATs offer an extensive array of computer-generated report forms that organize and summarize individual or classwide test data for parents, teachers, classrooms, and school districts.

- Most GSATs include scoring guides and analytical materials.

Regarding this last point, the GSATs typically furnish raw scores, scale scores, grade and age equivalents, normal curve equivalent scores, national and local percentiles, national and local stanines, anticipated achievement scores (based on a given aptitude score), and criterion-referenced scores indicating an individual student's level of mastery in relation to objectives measured.

Performance and Authentic Assessment

Assessments of academic achievement within this category share a common requirement that students *construct* responses, rather than *select* responses from among a specified number of options (as would be found in a multiple-choice testing format). According to Braden (1999), performance assessment "uses complex tasks that require students to understand problems, accurately apply their knowledge and skills to develop a solution to the task, and communicate their problem-solving process and solution" (p. 305). An assessment is called "authentic" when problems or test questions resemble closely the kind of complex tasks undertaken by professionals in the world outside of schools (Mabry, 1999).

Performance or authentic (P/A) tasks are heterogeneous in content, design, and scoring. They can be observed and scored as they occur, or the end results of a skill (that is, a tangible product) can be evaluated and/or scored. *On-demand tasks* require students to construct responses to teacher- or examiner-supplied prompts or problems within a relatively short period of time. *Extended tasks* have students think about an assigned topic over an extended period of time, conduct research on the topic, and then demonstrate mastery of the topic. *Demonstrations* or *exhibitions* ask students to display oral or written presentations of individual work before an audience. In *simulation tasks*, students demonstrate problem-solving skills on tasks that mirror real-life situations encountered in practical or professional contexts (Mabry, 1999). *Portfolios* require students to assemble a collection of work, finished projects, or responses to tasks (Khattri, Reeve, and Kane, 1998). *Profiles* represent a collection of ratings, checklists, or summary judgments about students' work but differ from portfolios in not including actual samples of the work (Mabry, 1999).

Performance and authentic testing projects are initiated, developed, and promoted at all levels of the educational system, which include the state departments of education; district offices; and individual schools, colleges, and universities (Khattri, Reeve, and Kane, 1998). P/A tests are also developed by national organizations such as the College Board (College Board, 1999b), the Coalition of Essential Schools (Coalition of Essential Schools, 1999), and regional educational laboratories supported by the U.S. Education Department (Mid-Continent Research for Education and Learning, 1999).

Ethnic and Racial Group Differences in Academic Achievement

In this next section, issues related to ethnic and racial differences in various measures of academic achievement are discussed.

Group Standardized Achievement Tests

Ethnic, racial, language, and social-class group differences are evident across all varieties of academic achievement testing. The National Assessment of Educational Progress (NAEP) is a testing program that monitors trends in group achievement test data among school-age students in a variety of subjects. For the reading portion of the NAEP tests, three qualitative designations are used to report student mastery levels. The "basic" level denotes partial mastery of the knowledge and skills that are fundamental for proficient work at any given grade. The "proficient" level represents solid mastery or competency in challenging subject matter. The "advanced" level represents superior reading performance at a given grade (Donahue, Voelkl, Campbell, and Mazzeo, 1999).

According to a 1998 NAEP reading assessment, about 64 percent of African American fourth graders had scores below the basic level, compared to 60 percent for Hispanics, 53 percent for Native Americans, 31 percent for Asian and Pacific Islanders, and 27 percent for Whites. Although absolute percentages decrease with age, the rank ordering of these results by ethnic or racial group remained similar across eighth-grade and twelfth-grade students in 1998, as well as across grades 4, 8, and 12 in years 1992 and 1994.

The NAEP uses scale score values of 150, 200, 250, 300, and 350 as benchmarks to distinguish between qualitative levels of math knowledge and skills. A score of 250, for instance, reflects an initial understanding of the four basic mathematical operations, the ability to apply whole-number addition and subtraction skills to one-step word and money problems, the ability to find the product of two-digit times one-digit numbers, the ability to compare information from graphs and charts, and beginning abilities in analyzing simple logical relations (Campbell, Voelkl, and Donahue, 1997, p. 56). Among a national sample of nine-year-olds (that is, fourth graders), only 10 percent of African American students obtained scaled scores at or above 250, compared to 13 percent for Hispanics and 35 percent for Whites. Among thirteen-year-olds (that is, eighth graders), these figures were 53 percent for African Americans, 58 percent for Hispanics, and 86 percent for Whites.

Curriculum-Based Assessment

Knoff and Dean (1994) administered curriculum-based measures of oral reading fluency to 243 regular-education students in grades 1 through 4, most of whom received federally subsidized free lunches and were equally divided with respect to gender and race (Caucasian and African American). They found no significant differences in mean scores and concluded that curriculum-based measurement reading probes were not "racially biased" (bias being defined as the absence of group differences).

Using a more acceptable psychometric definition of test bias, Kranzler, Miller, and Jordan (1999) analyzed results from curriculum-based measures of reading fluency and California Achievement Test (CAT) reading comprehension scores for 326 regular-education students in grades 2 through 5 (24 percent of whom were African American). They found that mean scores of African American students were significantly lower (by approximately one standard deviation) than those of Caucasians on seven out of eight group comparisons. When CAT scores were regressed on CBM scores and a common prediction line was used, the authors found that CBM performance *overestimated* reading comprehension for African Americans but *underestimated* reading comprehension for Caucasians (Kranzler, Miller, and Jordan, 1999).

Performance and Authentic Assessment

Unlike research findings from group-administered standardized tests, research dealing with group differences on P/A tasks is more limited and inadequate for drawing any strong conclusions (Braden, 1999). Several reasons account for these limitations. First, performance tasks tend to be less reliable than selection-response (that is, multiple-choice) tasks (Bond, 1995; Guion, 1995). As a result, real group differences revealed on a highly reliable instrument will be *smaller* on a less reliable instrument (Jensen, 1980). Second, responses from a particular performance assessment task often do not generalize well to other performance tasks, even those that purport to measure the same subject matter (Brennan and Johnson, 1995). Consequently, results from a study using one set of tasks cannot be assumed to generalize with any reasonable degree of certainty to any other set of tasks that are characterized as "performance assessment" (Braden, 1999).

The typical research paradigm for investigating group differences on performance tasks is to compare the effect sizes of minority versus majority group performance on traditional assessment compared to a performance assessment. Effect sizes are computed by subtracting the mean for the minority group from the mean for the majority comparison group and then dividing this figure by the standard deviation of the majority comparison group. If performance assessments reduce the achievement gap between majority and minority groups, then the result is smaller effect sizes than what is revealed with traditional assessments (Bond, Moss, and Carr, 1996).

Available research studies that use this paradigm reveal mixed results (for a comprehensive review, see Braden, 1999). For example, Linn, Baker, and Dunbar (1991) found no difference in the Black-White achievement gap between open-ended essay-writing assessment items and multiple-choice reading assessment items. In contrast, smaller differences were found in open-ended items relative to multiple-choice items when comparing students of low and high socioeconomic status (SES) and comparing Black-Hispanic versus White-Asian students on a statewide testing program (Badger, 1995).

Baxter and others (1993) analyzed the performance of English-speaking Hispanic students on selected response items from the Comprehensive Tests of Basic Skills (CTBS) mathematics section and performance assessment items designed to assess mathematical reasoning and problem solving. The authors found that Latino-Anglo performance differences were larger on the performance measure than on the multiple-choice achievement test (Baxter and others, 1993).

Based on these conflicting findings, Bond, Moss, and Carr (1996) conclude: "Given the existing evidence, there is no reason to believe that differences observed with traditional assessments between underserved minority groups and the majority comparison group will necessarily diminish with performance-based assessment. To offer any other generalization based on the existing evidence would be inappropriate" (p. 125). Braden (1999) reports similar conclusions from researchers who have reviewed the performance assessment literature.

Factors Associated with Group Differences in Academic Achievement

Conceptually, general aptitude tests (sometimes called IQ tests) are typically used to predict success or failure *before* a course of study, and usually consist of items that tap novel problem solving and sampled from a broad domain. Achievement tests consist of items that more narrowly sample-specific subject-matter areas and are generally used to reflect levels of attainment in a subject area *after* a course of study (Aiken, 2000). In a practical sense, however, there is no clear and unambiguous distinction between the kinds of mental skills measured by aptitude tests and those measured by achievement tests. When both kinds of tests are added to a large battery of measures subjected to a factor analysis, they share variance in *g*, which is the general mental ability factor found (in varying degrees) in all cognitive tests regardless of differences in item content (Jensen, 1993).

When general aptitude (IQ) tests and achievement tests share variance in common factors (including *g*), they will also be highly correlated with each other. In the discipline of applied psychometrics, there is massive evidence documenting high predictive validity of IQ tests for a variety of educational criteria, which include scholastic achievement test scores, school and college grades, retention in a school grade, school dropout rates, number of years of schooling, probability of entering college, and probability of receiving a bachelor's degree after entering college (Jensen, 1991, 1993, 1998; Matarazzo, 1972; Snow and Yalow, 1982). The correlation of IQ with grades and achievement test scores ranges from .6 to .7 in elementary school (a period of time in which the fullest range of mental ability is represented). At successively higher levels of educational attainment, correlations between IQ and grade or achievement test scores decrease because of the restriction of range produced by attrition of individuals from the lower end of the IQ distribution (Jensen, 1998).

Individual and group differences in achievement test scores can be largely attributed to individual and group differences in g. Given the same instruction (and assuming equal motivational and attentional levels), learners who differ in g will differ in their rate of consolidating new material, and hence in the amount learned per unit of instruction (Christal, 1991; Jensen, 1993). In representative samples drawn from various ethnic and racial groups, the larger the g loading of a test, the greater the size of mean group differences on the test (see Jensen, 1998, for a thorough literature review).

Group Differences and Academic Context Variables

Steinberg (1996) reports results from a large study of factors associated with the academic achievement of students attending nine high schools in Wisconsin and Northern California. The nine schools were selected to yield a diverse sample of students reflecting a variety of socioeconomic brackets and ethnic backgrounds (for example, African American, Asian American, European American, and Hispanic American).

More than 40 percent of the sample were from an ethnic minority group. The sample reflected differences in family structure (for example, intact, divorced, and remarried) and type of community (for example, urban, suburban, and rural). Nearly one-third of the sample were from single-parent households or stepfamilies, and nearly one-third came from homes in which the parents have not attended school beyond the twelfth grade. The sample was evenly divided among males and females, and among ninth through twelfth graders.

The study was conducted over a three-year period in the late 1980s, with approximately twelve thousand students participating in each year. Students were administered group questionnaires; smaller groups of students in each school participated in focused interviews; a sample of six hundred students of high, medium, and low achievement from six of the nine schools consented to one-on-one interviews; and five hundred students' parents were interviewed.

The researchers found a consistent pattern of achievement differences *within ethnic groups* along the lines of social class and parental education (Steinberg, Dornbusch, and Brown, 1992). Even when income, parental-education, and school-quality indicators were controlled, however, a consistent pattern emerged *across ethnic groups*, where Asians consistently outperformed Whites, and Whites consistently outperformed Black and Latino students in school grades and standardized measures of academic achievement.

In every school included in the sample, Asian students earned a disproportionately higher number of A's in courses relative to their numerical representation in the student bodies. In contrast, Blacks and Latinos were consistently overrepresented among students with grades of C- or lower in courses. These differences had nothing to do with perceived negative discrimination from teachers.

When separate analyses were conducted on all students who reported high levels of perceived negative teacher discrimination versus students who reported no perceived negative teacher discrimination, ethnic differences in achievement remained (Steinberg, 1996). Asian students outscored all other ethnic groups in time spent on homework, with Black and Latino students spending considerably less time on homework. The gap between Asian versus Black and Latino students was nearly twice as large as the achievement gap between students from the poorest families and the most affluent families (when all ethnic groups were combined).

No significant ethnic differences were found in students' belief that obtaining a good education leads to future rewards. However, ethnic differences were found in students' beliefs concerning the consequences of failing in school. Asian students were more likely than other students to believe that not doing well in school has negative consequences for their future. In contrast, Black and Latino students were more likely to report that doing poorly in school does *not* hurt their chances for future success. Asian students were significantly more likely than Black, Latino, or White students to believe that academic success or failure is directly linked to how hard they work (Steinberg, 1996).

Within ethnic groups, authoritative (loving but firm and supportive) parenting is associated with better outcomes, and disengaged (absent and uninvolved) parenting is associated with worse outcomes. This gap in academic achievement among parental styles within ethnic groups is most pronounced for White students. However, parenting style did not explain group differences in academic achievement. Asian students from disengaged homes earned higher grades than Black students from authoritative homes (Dornbusch and others, 1987; Lamborn, Mounts, Steinberg, and Dornbusch, 1991; Steinberg, 1996).

In the sample studied, the friends with whom Asian students socialize place relatively greater emphasis on academics than other students do. Asian students' friends have higher performance standards (that is, hold higher standards for what grades are acceptable), spend more time on homework, are more committed to education, and earn considerably higher grades in school. Black and Hispanic students' friends earn lower grades, spend less time on their studies, and have significantly lower performance standards. White students' friends fall somewhere between these two extremes. These patterns hold even among students whose best friends are from another ethnic background (Mounts and Steinberg, 1995; Steinberg, 1996).

The researchers studied Asian and Latino students whose immediate families have lived for only a short time in America (recent immigrants) versus those whose families have been living in America for some time (see also Kao and Tienda, 1995). The researchers found that immigrants generally outperform nonimmigrants on measures of school achievement. In addition, immigrants generally spent more time on homework, are more attentive in class, are more oriented to doing well in school, and are more likely to have friends who think academic achievement is important. The authors interpret the declining achievement of immigrants with each successive generation as "not the product of disenchantment in the face of limited opportunities, but a result of the *normative* socialization of ethnic minority youth into the mainstream's indifferent (or at least, ambivalent) stance toward school success. Because part of what it means to be an American teenager in contemporary society is adopting a cavalier attitude toward school, the process of Americanization leads toward more and more educational indifference" (Steinberg, 1996, p. 99).

Diagnostic Considerations with Multicultural Populations

Given the significant life and educational decisions that are made based upon achievement tests, several factors must be considered prior to these applications. Principal among them are incorporating social context in reporting group differences and a focus on data-based approaches to classification and placement of children into special education.

Incorporating Social Context in Reporting Group Differences in Achievement Scores

According to Berends and Koretz (1996), important student-reported social context data can be obtained from national assessments of academic achievement.[1] Social context data can be organized in six categories:

1. *Family background* variables include parents' highest educational attainment, family income, and parental occupation.
2. *Family composition* variables include measures of household type (that is, single- or two-parent household) and the number of siblings in the household.

3. *Language use* variables involve measures that ask students to indicate the frequency of speaking a certain language either in the home or outside of the home.

4. *Community characteristics* include region of the country in which the student resides, as well as community type (suburban, urban, rural).

5. *School characteristics* include school attendance rate, the percentage of students within the school receiving free or reduced-price lunches, school sector (private versus public), demographic composition (percentage that is Black or Hispanic), and a school's mean achievement level.

6. *Curricular differentiation* variables include the type of school program in which the student was enrolled (academic, general, or vocational curriculum), and the percentage of students in gifted/talented, or remedial reading and math, classes.

Reports of average score differences between groups can be *unadjusted*, meaning score differences are reported that do not control for significant imbalances in groups' standing on social context variables, many of which have demonstrated positive correlations with academic achievement (for example, Bogenschneider and Steinberg, 1994; Coleman and Hoffer, 1987; Lareau, 1989). When achievement score differences between groups are *adjusted*, groups are first equated on relevant social context variables. As an illustration of this technique, Berends and Koretz (1996) standardized reading and math group achievement test scores from the NAEP, NELS, and HSB databases (see endnote). Regression analyses of all three databases were used to estimate the change in the mean test score differences between White, African American, and Hispanic groups when controlling for various sets of social context measures. The unadjusted African American and White differences (expressed in standard deviation units) and effects of adjusting for different context variables in eighth-grade NELS and NAEP mathematics performance are shown in Figure 22.1.

As shown in the figure, adjusting group differences for student-reported social context variables ultimately reduced the difference from .93 to .52 SD (NAEP database) and from .77 to .34 SD (NELS database).

Berends and Koretz (1996) debate the advantages and disadvantages associated with three methods of reporting achievement score group differences. The simplest approach is to report unadjusted group differences along with corresponding information about group differences in social context variables. Although this approach avoids the statistical complexities associated with adjusting scores, it "leaves the consumer . . . with the impracticable task of disentangling the variables and interpreting what impact social context differences might have" (p. 281).

A second approach is to report groups' achievement score differences nested within the same level of a social context variable. This method incorporates the impact of social context variables, but it can be used only for one or two variables at a time. Furthermore, if the group imbalances in social context variables result in only a few cases at one level of a social context variable (for example, number of minority families earning more than $200,000 a year), then score estimates could be unreliable.

A third approach is to report adjusted scores as shown in Figure 22.1. However, this approach assumes (perhaps incorrectly) a consensus within the educational research community as to which social context variables are most important to use in an adjustment (Berends and Koretz, 1996).

Special-Education Decision Making and Data-Based Problem Solving

Limited English-speaking (LEP) students present a variety of challenges for contemporary educators (Baker, Plasencia-Peinado, and Lezcano-Lytle, 1998). Some critics fault standardized

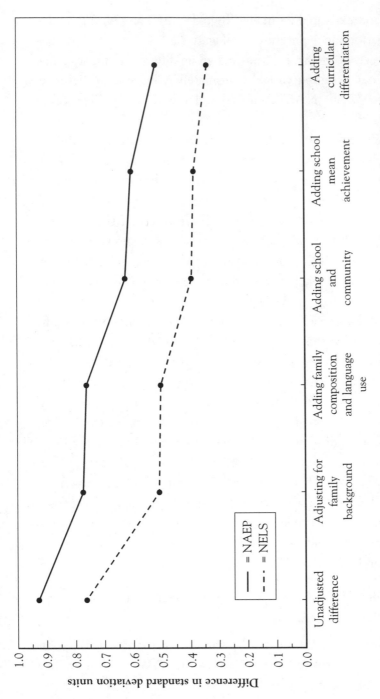

Figure 22.1. African American/White differences in standard deviation units as a function of adjustments for social-context variables for eighth-grade NELS and NAEP mathematics scores.

Source: "Reporting minority students' test scores: How well can the National Assessment of Education Progress account for differences in social context?" by M. Berends and D. M. Koretz, 1996, *Educational Assessment, 3*(3), p. 263. Copyright ©1996 by Lawrence Erlbaum Associates. Reprinted with permission.

English-language achievement tests for being largely inadequate in helping clinicians to distinguish between LEP students' learning difficulties that stem from insufficient exposure to English and those learning difficulties that are rooted in a genuine learning disability (Langdon, 1989; Rueda, 1989). For special-education decision making with individual students for whom language may be a confounding factor, there is a general consensus that the first task is for the clinician to conduct an assessment of language proficiency in both the primary and secondary languages (see Sandoval and Duran, 1998).

The practice of informally translating English-language tests is typically discouraged in the local setting (see, for example, Chavez, 1982), because of various language and psychometric problems inherent in translating words or concepts that cannot be directly translated from one language to another (Lopez, 1995). With enough time, funds, expertise, and resources, however, large test companies can take the necessary steps to adapt well-validated English achievement tests for use in another language or culture, or both (see Bracken and others, 1990; Bracken and Fouad, 1987; Geisinger, 1998; Preddy, 1984; Sandoval and Duran, 1998).

African American children are disproportionately identified and labeled as mildly mentally handicapped and consequently over-represented in special-education classes (Artiles and Trent, 1994; Oswald, Coutinho, Best, and Singh, 1999). Although the Individuals with Disabilities Education Act (IDEA) requires that psychoeducational assessment for special-education decision making be based on a variety of types of information from numerous sources, critics lay blame primarily on the use of standardized intelligence (IQ) tests (for example, Hilliard, 1989, 1994), charging that such tests do not lead to better educational, instructional, or remedial treatment for children experiencing academic problems (Gresham and Witt, 1997; Reschly, 1997).

Although research has largely failed to demonstrate that IQ tests are biased when used with African Americans (see Reynolds, Lowe, and Saenz, 1999), such criticisms shift the focus of concern to ineffective programs. Since both Hispanic and African American children are more vulnerable to being considered for special-education programs because of the "refer-test-place" decision-making model, advocates of a different philosophical approach envision an overhaul of this model as primarily benefiting these minority groups.

Shinn, Collins, and Gallagher (1998) argue for an alternative assessment system with demonstrated treatment validity, using formative assessment of curriculum-referenced tasks as the cornerstone of educational decision making. This system involves five steps:

1. *Problem Identification Stage,* collecting curriculum-based production data to determine if a discrepancy exists between the performance of typical peers (called expected performance) and the referred student's actual performance

2. *Problem Certification Stage,* where curriculum-based data are collected to determine the extent to which the gap between expected and actual performance is so severe as to warrant intervention within the context of the regular-education or special-education classroom

3. *Exploring Solutions Stage,* where intervention goals are established that include the behavior to be measured, the conditions for evaluating goal attainment, and the criterion or criteria for determining intervention success

4. *Evaluating Solutions Stage,* where data are collected to determine if instructional intervention has been effective

5. *Problem Solution Stage,* which involves deciding if a problem still exists from the evaluation of the student's rate of progress, as well as old or new peer-referenced data

Shinn, Collins, and Gallagher (1998) and Baker, Plasencia-Peinado, and Lezcano-Lytle (1998) present case studies illustrating the use of curriculum-centered data-based problem solving with students from minority and limited-English-speaking backgrounds.

Summary

The construct of academic achievement is characterized by a constellation of attitudes and beliefs in addition to scores on standardized academic achievement tests. Academic achievement is measured by a variety of methods. They include, but are not limited to, informal assessment, curriculum-based assessment, individual and group standardized achievement testing, and performance and authentic assessment.

Ethnic or racial group differences in academic achievement are pervasive and tend to show consistent patterns regardless of the methodology used. In addition, differing levels of academic achievement *within* ethnic and racial groups are related to social context variables such as parental education and family income. The size of racial or ethnic group differences in academic achievement (at least on group standardized achievement tests) can be reduced considerably if social context variables are taken into account. Special-education professionals seeking an alternative to the limitations inherent in using standardized achievement tests with ethnic or racial minority groups may discover more instructional relevance in using a curriculum-based, data-oriented problem-solving model.

Endnote

1. Three databases were used to organize social context variables: the 1990 National Assessment of Educational Progress (NAEP); the 1988 National Education Longitudinal Study (NELS), and the 1980 High School and Beyond (HSB) Survey.

References

Aiken, L. R. (2000). *Psychological testing and assessment* (10th ed.). Needham Heights, MA: Allyn & Bacon.

Airasian, P. W. (1991). Perspectives on measurement instruction. *Educational Measurement: Issues and Practice, 10*(1), 13–16.

Artiles, A. J., & Trent, S. C. (1994). Overrepresentation of minority students in special education: A continuing debate. *Journal of Special Education, 27*(4), 410–437.

Badger, E. (1995). The effect of expectations on achieving equity in state-wide testing: Lessons from Massachusetts. In M. T. Nettles & A. L. Nettles (Eds.), *Equity and excellence in educational testing and assessment* (pp. 289–308). Boston: Kluwer.

Baker, S. K., Plasencia-Peinado, J., & Lezcano-Lytle, V. (1998). The use of curriculum-based measurement with language-minority students. In M. R. Shinn (Ed.), *Advanced applications of curriculum-based measurement* (pp. 175–213). New York: Guilford Press.

Baxter, G. P., Shavelson, R. J., Herman, S. J., Brown, K. A., & Valadez, J. R. (1993). Mathematics performance assessment: Technical quality and diverse student impact. *Journal for Mathematics Education, 24*, 190–216.

Berends, M., & Koretz, D. M. (1996). Reporting minority students' test scores: How well can the National Assessment of Educational Progress account for differences in social context? *Educational Assessment, 3*(3), 249–285.

Bogenschneider, K., & Steinberg, L. (1994). Maternal employment and adolescent academic achievement: A developmental analysis. *Sociology of Education, 67*, 60–77.

Bond, L. (1995). Unintended consequences of performance assessment: Issues of bias and fairness. *Educational measurement: Issues and practice, 14*(4), 21–24.

Bond, L., Moss, P., & Carr, P. (1996). Fairness in large-scale performance assessment. In G. W. Phillips (Ed.), *Technical issues in large-scale performance assessment* (pp. 117–140). Washington, DC: National Center for Educational Statistics.

Bracken, B., Barona, A., Bauermeister, J. J., Howell K. K., Poggioli, L., & Puente, A. (1990). Multinational validation of the Spanish Bracken Basic Concept Scale for cross-cultural assessments. *Journal of School Psychology, 28*, 325–341.

Bracken, B., & Fouad, N. (1987). Spanish translation and validation of the Bracken Basic Concept Scale. *School Psychology Review, 16*(1), 94–102.

Braden, J. (1999). Performance assessment and diversity. *School Psychology Quarterly, 14*(3), 304–326.

Brennan, R. L., & Johnson, E. G. (1995). Generalizability of performance assessment. *Education measurement: Issues and practice, 14*(4), 9–12, 27.

Campbell, J. R., Voelkl, K. E., & Donahue, P. L. (1997). *NAEP 1996 trends in academic progress*. Washington, DC: U.S. Department of Education.

Carter, K. (1984). Do teachers understand principles for writing tests? *Journal of Teacher Education, 35,* 57–60.

Chavez, E. L. (1982). Analysis of a Spanish translation of the Peabody Picture Vocabulary Test. *Perceptual and Motor Skills, 54*(3), 1335–1338.

Christal, R. E. (1991). *Comparative validities of ASVAB and LAMP tests for logic gates learning* (AL-TP-1991–0031). Brooks AFB, TX: Manpower and Personnel Division, Air Force Human Resources Laboratory.

Coalition of Essential Schools. (1999). *Coalition of essential schools* [on-line]. http://www.essentialschools.org/.

Coleman, J. S., & Hoffer, T. B. (1987). *Public and private schools: The impact of communities*. New York: Basic Books.

College Board. (1999a). *Reaching the top: A report of the national task force on minority high achievement*. New York: College Board Publications.

College Board. (1999b). *The College Board* [on-line]. http://www.collegeboard.org/.

Donahue, P. L., Voelkl, K. E., Campbell, J. R., & Mazzeo, J. (1999). *NAEP 1998 reading report card for the nation and the states*. Washington, DC: U.S. Department of Education.

Dornbusch, S. M., Ritter, P. L., Leiderman, P. H., Roberts, D. F., & Fraleigh, M. J. (1987). The relation of parenting style to adolescent school performance. *Child Development, 58,* 1244–1257.

Geisinger, K. F. (1998). Psychometric issues in test interpretation. In J. Sandoval, C. L. Frisby, K. F. Geisinger, J. D. Scheuneman, & J. R. Grenier (Eds.), *Test interpretation and diversity* (pp. 17–30). Washington, DC: American Psychological Association.

Gresham, F. M., & Witt, J. C. (1997). Utility of intelligence tests for treatment planning, classification, and placement decisions: Recent empirical findings and future directions. *School Psychology Quarterly, 12,* 249–267.

Guerin, G. R., & Maier, A. S. (1983). *Informal assessment in education*. Palo Alto, CA: Mayfield.

Guion, R. M. (1995). Commentary on values and standards in performance assessment. *Educational measurement: Issues and practice, 14*(4), 25–27.

Hilliard, A. (1989). Back to Binet: The case against the use of IQ tests in the schools. *Diagnostique, 14*(2), 125–135.

Hilliard, A. (1994). What good is this thing called intelligence and why bother to measure it? *Journal of Black Psychology, 20*(4), 430–444.

Impara, J. C., Divine, K. P., Bruce, F. A., Liverman, M. R., & Gay, A. (1991). Does interpretive test score information help teachers? *Educational Measurement: Issues and Practice, 10*(4), 16–18.

Jensen, A. R. (1980). *Bias in mental testing.* New York: Free Press.

Jensen, A. R. (1991). Spearman's *g* and the problem of educational equality. *Oxford Review of Education, 17,* 169–187.

Jensen, A. R. (1993). Psychometric *g* and achievement. In B. R. Gifford (Ed.), *Policy perspectives on educational testing* (pp. 117–227). Boston: Kluwer.

Jensen, A. R. (1998). *The g factor: The science of mental ability.* Westport, CT: Praeger.

Kao, G., & Tienda, M. (1995). Optimism and achievement: The educational performance of immigrant youth. *Social Science Quarterly, 76*(1), 1–19.

Khattri, N., Reeve, A. L., & Kane, M. B. (1998). *Principles and practices of performance assessment.* Hillsdale, NJ: Erlbaum.

Knoff, H. M., & Dean, K. R. (1994). Curriculum-based measurement of at-risk students' reading skills: A preliminary investigation of bias. *Psychological Reports, 75,* 1355–1360.

Kranzler, J., Miller, D., & Jordan, L. (1999). An examination of racial/ethnic and gender bias on curriculum-based measurement of reading. *School Psychology Quarterly, 14*(3), 327–342.

Kubiszyn, T., & Borich, G. (1999). *Educational testing and measurement: Classroom application and practice* (6th ed.). New York: Wiley.

Lambert, N. M., & McCombs, B. L. (1998). *How students learn: Reforming schools through learner-centered education.* Washington, DC: American Psychological Association.

Lamborn, S., Mounts, N. S., Steinberg, L., & Dornbusch, S. M. (1991). Patterns of competence and adjustment among adolescents from authoritative, authoritarian, indulgent, and neglectful homes. *Child Development, 62,* 1049–1065.

Langdon, W. H. (1989). Language disorder or difference? Assessing the language skills of Hispanic students. *Exceptional Children, 56*(2), 160–167.

Lareau, A. (1989). *Home advantage: Social class and parental intervention in elementary education.* New York: Falmer Press.

Linn, R. L., Baker, E. L., & Dunbar, S. B. (1991). Complex, performance-based assessment: Expectations and validation criteria. *Educational Researcher, 20*(8), 15–21.

Linn, R. L., & Gronlund, N. E. (1995). *Measurement and assessment in teaching* (7th ed.). Upper Saddle River, NJ: Prentice Hall.

Lopez, E. C. (1995). Best practices in working with bilingual children. In A. Thomas & J. Grimes (Eds.), *Best practices in school psychology III* (pp. 1111–1121). Washington, DC: National Association of School Psychologists.

Mabry, L. (1999). *Portfolio plus: A critical guide to alternative assessment.* Thousand Oaks, CA: Corwin Press.

Madaus, G. F., & Kellaghan, T. (1992). In P. W. Jackson (Ed.), *Handbook of research on curriculum* (pp. 134–147). Washington, DC: American Educational Research Association.

Matarazzo, J. D. (1972). *Wechsler's measurement and appraisal of adult intelligence* (5th ed.). Baltimore, MD: Williams and Wilkins.

Mid-Continent Research for Education and Learning (McREL). (1999). *The regional laboratory network* [on-line]. http://www.mcrel.org/about/network.asp.

Mounts, N., & Steinberg, L. (1995). Peer influences on adolescent achievement and deviance: An ecological approach. *Developmental Psychology, 31,* 915–922.

Naccarato, R. W. (1988). *A guide to item banking in education.* Portland, OR: Northwest Regional Educational Laboratory.

Ormrod, J. E. (1998). *Educational psychology: Developing learners* (2nd ed.). Upper Saddle River, NJ: Prentice Hall.

Oswald, D. P., Coutinho, M. J., Best, A. M., & Singh, N. N. (1999). Ethnic representation in special education: The influence of school-related economic and demographic variables. *Journal of Special Education, 32*(4), 194–206.

Phye, G. D. (1997). *Handbook of academic learning: Construction of knowledge.* San Diego: Academic Press.

Preddy, D. (1984). PBCB: A norming of the Spanish translation of the Boehm Test of Basic Concepts. *Journal of School Psychology, 22*(4), 407–413.

Reschly, D. J. (1997). Diagnostic and treatment utility of intelligence tests. In D. P. Flanagan, J. L. Genshaft, & P. L. Harrison (Eds.), *Contemporary intellectual assessment: Theories, tests, and issues* (pp. 437–456). New York: Guilford Press.

Reynolds, C. R., Lowe, P. A., & Saenz, A. L. (1999). The problem of bias in psychological assessment. In C. R. Reynolds & T. B. Gutkin (Eds.), *Handbook of school psychology* (3rd. ed., pp. 549–595). New York: Wiley.

Rudner, L. (1998). *Item banking.* Washington, DC: Office of Educational Research and Improvement. (ERIC document Reproduction Service No. ED 423 310)

Rueda, R. (1989). Defining mild disabilities with language-minority students. *Exceptional Children, 56*(2), 121–128.

Salmon-Cox, L. (1981). Teachers and standardized achievement tests: What's really happening? *Phi Delta Kappan, 62*, 631–634.

Sandoval, J., & Duran, R. P. (1998). Language. In J. Sandoval, C. L. Frisby, K. F. Geisinger, J. D. Scheuneman, & J. R. Grenier (Eds.), *Test interpretation and diversity* (pp. 181–212). Washington, DC: American Psychological Association.

Shapiro, E. S., & Elliott, S. N. (1999). Curriculum-based assessment and other performance-based assessment strategies. In C. R. Reynolds & T. B. Gutkin (Eds.), *The handbook of school psychology* (3rd ed., pp. 383–408). New York: Wiley.

Shinn, M. (Ed.). (1989). *Curriculum-based measurement: Assessing special children.* New York: Guilford Press.

Shinn, M. (Ed.). (1998). *Advanced applications of curriculum-based measurement.* New York: Guilford Press.

Shinn, M., Collins, V. L., & Gallagher, S. (1998). Curriculum-based measurement and its use in a problem-solving model with students from minority backgrounds. In M. R. Shinn (Ed.), *Advanced applications of curriculum-based measurement* (pp. 143–174). New York: Guilford Press.

Shinn, M., Rosenfield, S., & Knutson, N. (1989). Curriculum-based assessment: A comparison of models. *School Psychology Review, 18*(3), 299–316.

Snow, R. E., & Yalow, E. (1982). Education and intelligence. In R. J. Sternberg (Ed.), *Handbook of human intelligence* (pp. 493–585). Cambridge: Cambridge University Press.

Steinberg, L. (1996). *Beyond the classroom: Why school reform has failed and what parents need to do.* New York: Simon & Schuster.

Steinberg, L., Dornbusch, S., & Brown, B. (1992). Ethnic differences in adolescent achievement: An ecological perspective. *American Psychologist, 47*, 723–729.

Stiggins, R. J., & Bridgeford, N. J. (1985). The ecology of classroom assessment. *Journal of Educational Measurement, 22*, 271–286.

Ward, A. W., & Murray-Ward, M. (1994). Guidelines for the development of item banks: An instructional module. *Educational Measurement: Issues and Practice, 13*(1), 3–39.

Ward, A. W., & Murray-Ward, M. (1999). *Assessment in the classroom.* Belmont, CA: Wadsworth.

Worthen, B. R., White, K. R., Fan, X., & Sudweeks, R. R. (1999). *Measurement and assessment in schools* (2nd ed.). White Plains, NY: Longman.

23

Multicultural Assessment

Trends and Directions Revisited

Lisa A. Suzuki, Joseph G. Ponterotto, and Paul J. Meller

As we began writing this chapter, the editors decided to first review what we had written more than five years ago in the first edition of the *Handbook of Multicultural Assessment*, in our chapter titled "Multicultural Assessment: Current Trends and Future Directions."

We concluded that issues related to multicultural assessment have changed very little since the publication of the first edition. The concerns we raised hold true today. In the political and economic arena, assessment practices are in large part still dictated by test development companies, and educational and institutional systems. What is permissible in terms of appropriate practice is still narrowly defined. Test instruments look similar to the earlier versions, and little has been done to shake up the assessment community despite the development of alternative practices. Clinicians and educators must continue to balance the various perspectives presented by testing companies, researchers, and other clinical experts, as well as integrate the growing literature focused on relevant topics in the area.

Current Multicultural Assessment Practices: A Mixed Review

Current test practices are scrutinized by consumers and the general public with regard to racial and ethnic issues in assessment of personality and ability. The chapters in this new text highlight the many limitations of popular test practice with racial or ethnic minority groups. In addition, there is an increasing sense that all evaluation procedures are multicultural in nature given the complexity of understanding cultural context. Racial and ethnic categories have been challenged as within-group differences are increasingly acknowledged.

The current state of multicultural assessment presents a mixed picture. Despite the discussion in the first edition of what might be considered the status quo in the testing field (that is, few changes), a number of relatively new assessment procedures and modifications of traditional testing practice are noted.

Educational and Clinical Settings

In education, on the one hand, procedures such as curriculum-based assessment, dynamic assessment, and portfolio assessment are finding more frequent use in educational settings. On the other hand, high-stakes assessment is advocated in school reform measures to increase accountability for educational achievement. Standardized tests are now in place in many parts of the United States that determine whether students will graduate from high school. In addition, with the weakening of affirmative action in particular states (notably California), test scores continue to be a major determining factor in access to higher educational opportunity.

These examples come from educational settings, but similar issues are evident in the mental health arena. Numerous colleagues have cited the impact of managed care on the evaluation process in mental health practices. In particular, many have noted cutbacks in reimbursement for assessment services. The need for brief, problem-focused, and targeted evaluation procedures appears paramount. Unfortunately, given the complexity of the assessment process with racial and ethnic minority group members, vital information may be overlooked in the effort to be brief and time-efficient.

The chapters in Part One of this text highlight the complexities of the assessment process beyond instrumentation (such as identity, ethics, and diagnosis). Taking time to understand the cultural context of an examinee is imperative in gaining an understanding of the individual's personality and level of cognitive ability.

Test Development Settings

Test companies continue to update, renorm, and restandardize the most popular instruments. As noted throughout this book, attention is often given to issues of test bias and equivalence in the test development process. However, concerns continue to arise as limitations are often noted with these development strategies. For example, many tests in the cognitive area employ expert panels to review items in the instrument development phase. Unfortunately, as one of us has experienced directly, panel members are often given no guidance in terms of how to conduct their cursory examination—a concern noted by Helms as well (1997). Sophisticated statistical procedures are also employed to detect item bias (for example, Rasch modeling), and this has become more commonplace with current instrument development practices.

General Assessment Practice

In addition, there appears to be greater understanding of the importance of merging qualitative and quantitative measures and procedures in many areas of assessment. Similarly, the complexity of the multicultural assessment process (for example, the need to incorporate multifaceted identity, including cultural and spiritual) is increasingly acknowledged. Since the publication of the first *Handbook*, nearly all general measurement texts have contained chapters focusing on assessing minority groups, and a number of books have been published devoted to issues related to multicultural testing practices (for example, Dana, 2000; Samuda and others, 1998; Sandoval and others, 1998).

Multicultural Assessment Competency

Maintaining competency in a particular area of assessment requires continuous attention. One must update the information database with regard to new developments and state-of-the-art practice. In conceptualizing the second edition of the *Handbook*, we attempted to identify experts in each area to be covered. Although some are clearly senior scholars, a number of up-and-coming experts were also contacted. In addition, test authors readily agreed to contribute to this volume in an effort to help you the reader understand the cultural applicability of their measures. Clearly, appropriate multicultural assessment practices are advocated at all levels of the testing enterprise.

Recommendations for appropriate assessment procedures continue to focus on understanding the purpose of the assessment (that is, in light of background information), the level of cultural loading on particular tests considered for use, and potentially useful alternative methods and procedures. In addition, the examiner must always be aware of the role of an evaluator and monitor his or her own ethical stance throughout the assessment process.

Future Directions in Multicultural Assessment

Future directions in the assessment area continue to include:

- Infusing multicultural issues into all assessment courses in education and psychology training programs

- Continuing development of alternative measures and procedures

- Increasing sensitivity to issues of equivalence as well as cultural divergence in understanding psychological and educational constructs (as noted by Sternberg and Grigorenko in this volume, tests reflect what is valued in a particular society)

- Increasing collaboration with members of racial and ethnic communities (such as bilingual and bicultural professionals, and cultural informants)

- Increasing attention in the literature to use of particular instruments with diverse populations (for example, reliability and validity studies)

In addition to these general recommendations, one must also be aware of growing areas of knowledge that may have an impact on future assessment practices. For example, Sandoval and others (1998) report future developments in psychometric theory; training in measurement theory; neurosciences (as in increased understanding of the brain-behavior relationship); and social, political, and legal issues (among them race norming and regulation of testing practices).

All of these recommendations point to the increasing need for well-educated and clinically trained professionals in all fields related to assessment. The needs of our growing global population require that we attend to the complex issues confronting our current practice. As we struggle with the various agendas of testing companies and racial and ethnic communities, and maintain balance with knowledge in the area, we hope to come into closer proximity to ideal multicultural assessment practices.

References

Dana, R. H. (Ed.). (2000). *Handbook of cross-cultural and multicultural personality assessment*. Hillsdale, NJ: Erlbaum.

Helms, J. E. (1997). The triple quandary of race, culture, and social class in standardized cognitive ability testing. In D. P. Flanagan, J. L., Genshaft, &

P. L. Harrison (Eds.), *Contemporary intellectual assessment: Theories, tests and issues* (pp. 517–531). New York: Guilford Press.

Samuda, R. J., Feuerstein, R., Kaufman, A. S., Lewis, J. E., Sternberg, R. J., & Associates. (1998). *Advances in cross-cultural assessment.* Thousand Oaks, CA: Sage.

Sandoval, J., Frisby, C. L., Geisinger, K. F., Scheuneman, J. D., & Grenier, J. R. (1998). *Test interpretation and diversity: Achieving equity in assessment.* Washington, DC: American Psychological Association.

Name Index

Subject Index